HOLT McDOUGAL

Mathematics
Grade 7

Jennie M. Bennett

Edward B. Burger

David J. Chard

Earlene J. Hall

Paul A. Kennedy

Freddie L. Renfro

Tom W. Roby

Janet K. Scheer

Bert K. Waits

HOLT McDOUGAL

 HOUGHTON MIFFLIN HARCOURT

COMMON CORE

EDITION

Cover Photo: Colorful soap bubbles in wand
HMH/Sam Dudgeon

Printed in the U.S.A.

ISBN 978-0-547-64717-3

2 3 4 5 6 7 8 9 10 0868 20 19 18 17 16 15 14 13 12 11

4500302890   B C D E F G

Jennie M. Bennett, Ed.D., is a recently retired mathematics teacher at Hartman Middle School in Houston, Texas. She is past president of the Benjamin Banneker Association, the former First Vice-President of NCSM, and a former board member of NCTM.

Edward B. Burger, Ph.D., is Professor of Mathematics and Chair at Williams College and is the author of numerous articles, books, and videos. He has won many prestigious writing and teaching awards offered by the Mathematical Association of America. In 2006, Dr. Burger was named Reader's Digest's "Best Math Teacher" in its "100 Best of America" issue. He has made numerous television and radio appearances and has given countless mathematical presentations around the world.

David J. Chard, Ph.D., is the Leon Simmons Dean of the School of Education and Human Development at Southern Methodist University. He is a Past President of the Division for Research at the Council for Exceptional Children, a member of the International Academy for Research on Learning Disabilities, and has been the Principal Investigator on numerous research projects for the U.S. Department of Education. He is the author of several research articles and books on instructional strategies for students struggling in school.

Earlene J. Hall, Ed.D., is the Middle School Mathematics Supervisor for the Detroit Public Schools district. She teaches graduate courses in Mathematics Leadership at University of Michigan Dearborn. Dr. Hall has traveled extensively throughout Africa and China and has made numerous presentations including topics such as Developing Standards Based Professional Development and Culture Centered Education. She was a member of the NCTM 2009 Yearbook Panel.

Paul A. Kennedy, Ph.D., is a professor in the Department of Mathematics at Colorado State University. Dr. Kennedy is a leader in mathematics education. His research focuses on developing algebraic thinking by using multiple representations and technology. He is the author of numerous publications.

Freddie L. Renfro, MA, has 35 years of experience in Texas education as a classroom teacher and director/coordinator of Mathematics PreK-12 for school districts in the Houston area. She has served as a reviewer and TXTEAM trainer for Texas Math Institutes and has presented at numerous math workshops.

Tom W. Roby, Ph.D., is Associate Professor of Mathematics and Director of the Quantitative Learning Center at the University of Connecticut. He founded and co-directed the Bay Area-based ACCLAIM professional development program. He also chaired the advisory board of the California Mathematics Project and reviewed content for the California Standards Tests.

Janet K. Scheer, Ph.D., Executive Director of Create A Vision™, is a motivational speaker and provides customized K-12 math staff development. She has taught and supervised internationally and nationally at all grade levels.

Bert K. Waits, Ph.D., is a Professor Emeritus of Mathematics at The Ohio State University and cofounder of T^3 (Teachers Teaching with Technology), a national professional development program. Dr. Waits is also a former board member of NCTM and an author of the original NCTM Standards.

PROGRAM REVIEWERS

FIELD TEST PARTICIPANTS

Wendy Black
Southmont Jr. High
Crawfordsville, IN

Barbara Broeckelman
Oakley Middle School
Oakley, KS

Cindy Bush
Riverside Middle School
Greer, SC

Cadian Collman
Cutler Ridge Middle School
Miami, FL

Dora Corcini
Eisenhower Middle School
Oregon, OH

Deborah Drinkwalter
Sedgefield Middle School
Goose Creek, SC

Susan Gomez
Glades Middle School
Miami, FL

LaChandra Hogan
Apollo Middle School
Hollywood, FL

Ty Inlow
Oakley Middle School
Oakley, KS

Leighton Jenkins
Glades Middle School
Miami, FL

Heather King
Clever Middle School
Clever, MO

Dianne Marrett
Pines Middle School
Pembroke Pines, FL

Angela J. McNeal
Audubon Middle School
Los Angeles, CA

Wendy Misner
Lakeland Middle School
LaGrange, IN

Vanessa Nance
Pines Middle School
Pembroke Pines, FL

Teresa Patterson
Damonte Ranch High School
Reno, NV

Traci Peters
Cario Middle School
Mount Pleasant, SC

Ashley Piatt
East Forsyth Middle School
Kernersville, NC

Jeannine Quigley
Wilbur Wright Middle School
Dayton, OH

Shioban Smith-Haye
Apollo Middle School
Hollywood, FL

Jill Snipes
Bunn Middle School
Bunn, NC

Cathy Spencer
Oakridge Junior High
Oakridge, OR

Connie Vaught
K.D. Waldo School
Aurora, IL

Shelley Weeks
Lewis Middle School
Valparaiso, FL

Jennie Woo
Gaithersburg Middle School
Gaithersburg, MD

Reggie Wright
West Hopkins School
Nebo, KY

Online Resources **go.hrw.com**

Algebraic Reasoning

Integers and Rational Numbers

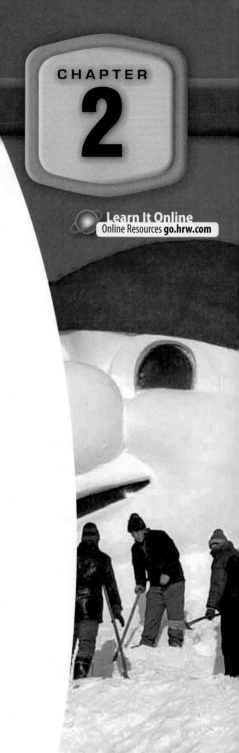

Learn It Online
Online Resources **go.hrw.com**

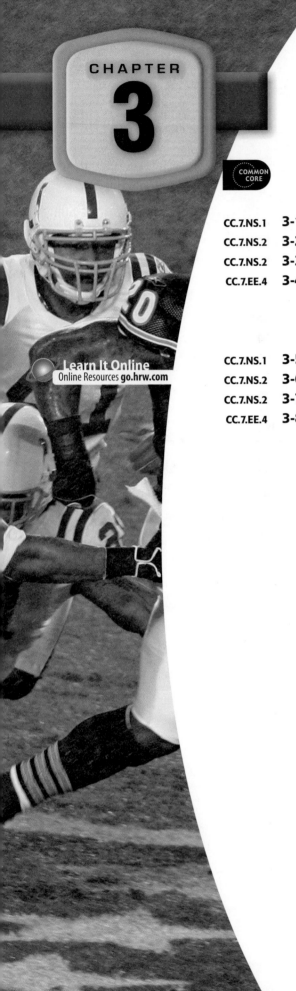

Applying Rational Numbers

COMMON CORE

Learn It Online
Online Resources **go.hrw.com**

Kevin Reece/Icon SMI/CORBIS

Proportional Relationships

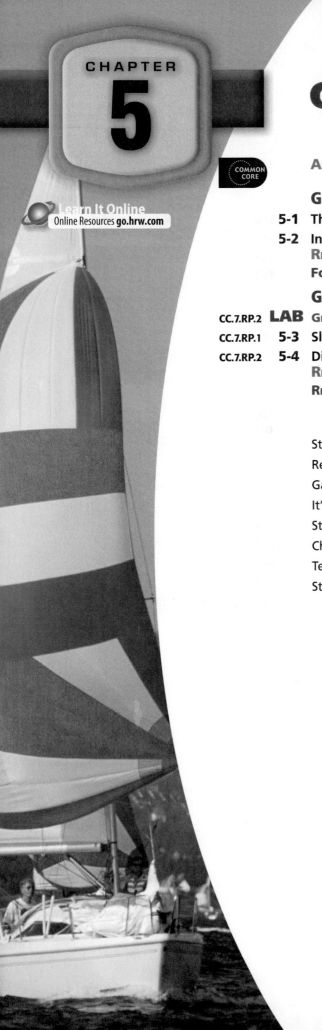

Graphs

Learn It Online
Online Resources **go.hrw.com**

Terje Rakke/Getty Images

Percents

Learn It Online
Online Resources **go.hrw.com**

Detlev van Ravenswaay/Photo Researchers, Inc.

Collecting, Displaying, and Analyzing Data

COMMON CORE

Geometric Figures

CHAPTER
8

Learn It Online
Online Resources **go.hrw.com**

COMMON CORE

Richard Cummins/Corbis

Learn It Online
Online Resources **go.hrw.com**

Measurement and Geometry

COMMON CORE

Probability

Learn It Online
Online Resources **go.hrw.com**

Icon Sports Media Inc./NewsCom

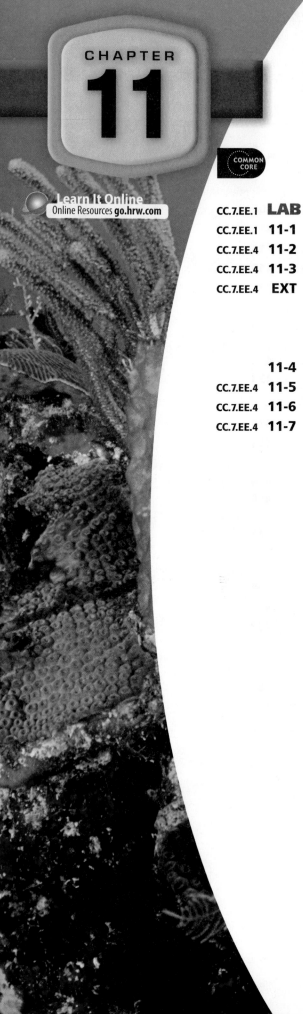

11

Learn It Online
Online Resources **go.hrw.com**

Multi-Step Equations and Inequalities

ARE YOU READY? **463**

Multi-Step Equations

CC.7.EE.1	**LAB**	Model Two-Step Equations. **466**
CC.7.EE.1	**11-1**	Solving Two-Step Equations **468**
CC.7.EE.4	**11-2**	Solving Multi-Step Equations **472**
CC.7.EE.4	**11-3**	Solving Equations with Variables on Both Sides **476**
CC.7.EE.4	**EXT**	Examine Solution Methods **480**
		READY TO GO ON? QUIZ **482**
		Focus on Problem Solving: Solve. **483**

Inequalities

	11-4	Inequalities. **484**
CC.7.EE.4	**11-5**	Solving Inequalities by Adding or Subtracting. **488**
CC.7.EE.4	**11-6**	Solving Inequalities by Multiplying or Dividing. **492**
CC.7.EE.4	**11-7**	Solving Multi-Step Inequalities. **496**
		READY TO GO ON? QUIZ **500**
		REAL-WORLD CONNECTIONS: ROCK CLIMBING **501**

Study Guide: Preview **464**
Reading and Writing Math **465**
Game Time: Flapjacks. **502**
It's in the Bag! Wired for Multi-Step Equations **503**
Study Guide: Review **504**
Chapter Test **507**
Standardized Test Prep **508**

Prisma/SuperStock

COMMON CORE

Standards for Mathematical Content
Correlation for Holt McDougal Mathematics Grade 7

Standard	Descriptor	Page Citations
CC.7.RP	**RATIOS AND PROPORTIONAL RELATIONSHIPS**	
Analyze proportional relationships and use them to solve real-world and mathematical problems		
CC.7.RP.1	Compute unit rates associated with ratios of fractions, including ratios of lengths, areas and other quantities measured in like or different units	**SE:** 150–153, 161, 184, 187, 204–208, 210
CC.7.RP.2	Recognize and represent proportional relationships between quantities	**SE:** 154–157, 204–205, 211–215
CC.7.RP.2a	Decide whether two quantities are in a proportional relationship, e.g., by testing for equivalent ratios in a table or graphing on a coordinate plane and observing whether the graph is a straight line through the origin	**SE:** 155–157, 162, 204–205, 211–215
CC.7.RP.2b	Identify the constant of proportionality (unit rate) in tables, graphs, equations, diagrams, and verbal descriptions of proportional relationships	**SE:** 151–153, 162, 204–205
CC.7.RP.2c	Represent proportional relationships by equations	**SE:** 158–161, 163–170, 180, 204–205, 212–216, 222, 333
CC.7.RP.2d	Explain what a point (x, y) on the graph of a proportional relationship means in terms of the situation, with special attention to the points $(0, 0)$ and $(1, r)$ where r is the unit rate	**SE:** 208–209
CC.7.RP.3	Use proportional relationships to solve multistep ratio and percent problems	**SE:** 244, 247–260, 265–266, 307, 313, 363, 409

SE = Student Edition

Standard	Descriptor	Page Citations
CC.7.NS	**THE NUMBER SYSTEM**	
Apply and extend previous understandings of operations with fractions to add, subtract, multiply, and divide rational numbers		
CC.7.NS.1	Apply and extend previous understandings of addition and subtraction to add and subtract rational numbers; represent addition and subtraction on a horizontal or vertical number line diagram	**SE:** 52, 54, 55, 60, 62, 100–103, 107, 118–121, 125, 138, 140–141, 197, 215, 325, 463
CC.7.NS.1a	Describe situations in which opposite quantities combine to make 0	**SE:** 46, 48, 56–57
CC.7.NS.1b	Understand $p + q$ as the number located a distance $|q|$ from p, in the positive or negative direction depending on whether q is positive or negative. Show that a number and its opposite have a sum of 0 (are additive inverses). Interpret sums of rational numbers by describing real-world contexts	**SE:** 46, 48, 52–57, 73–76, 90, 100–103, 120–121, 437
CC.7.NS.1c	Understand subtraction of rational numbers as adding the additive inverse, $p - q = p + (-q)$. Show that the distance between two rational numbers on the number line is the absolute value of their difference, and apply this principle in real-world contexts	**SE:** 60–63, 69, 101–103, 119–121, 153
CC.7.NS.1d	Apply properties of operations as strategies to add and subtract rational numbers	**SE:** 12–16, 35, 37, 40, 240–243
CC.7.NS.2	Apply and extend previous understandings of multiplication and division and of fractions to multiply and divide rational numbers	**SE:** 66–69, 93, 104–107, 112–116, 122–129, 134, 139–141, 153, 201, 313
CC.7.NS.2a	Understand that multiplication is extended from fractions to rational numbers by requiring that operations continue to satisfy the properties of operations, particularly the distributive property, leading to products such as $(-1)(-1) = 1$ and the rules for multiplying signed numbers. Interpret products of rational numbers by describing real-world contexts	**SE:** 66–67, 69, 104–105, 122, 124–125, 134, 138, 141, 240–243
CC.7.NS.2b	Understand that integers can be divided, provided that the divisor is not zero, and every quotient of integers (with non-zero divisor) is a rational number. If p and q are integers, then $-(p/q) = (-p)/q = p/(-q)$. Interpret quotients of rational numbers by describing real world contexts	**SE:** 67–69, 76, 108–111, 116, 128, 139, 201, 240–243
CC.7.NS.2c	Apply properties of operations as strategies to multiply and divide rational numbers	**SE:** 66–69, 82, 84, 86, 92–93, 240–243, 313, 403
CC.7.NS.2d	Convert a rational number to a decimal using long division; know that the decimal form of a rational number terminates in 0s or eventually repeats	**SE:** 78, 80–81, 86, 92–93, 403
CC.7.NS.3	Solve real-world and mathematical problems involving the four operations with rational numbers.[1]

[1]Computations with rational numbers extend the rules for manipulating fractions to complex fractions | **SE:** 50–55, 58–69, 76, 85, 90–91, 93, 97, 100–111, 116–129, 134–135, 138–139, 141, 153, 157, 167, 175, 197, 201, 215, 313, 325, 355, 403, 463 |

SE = Student Edition

Standard	Descriptor	Page Citations
CC.7.EE	**EXPRESSIONS AND EQUATIONS**	
Use properties of operations to generate equivalent expressions		
CC.7.EE.1	Apply properties of operations as strategies to add, subtract, factor, and expand linear expressions with rational coefficients	**SE:** 27–30, 37, 472, 474, 476–479
CC.7.EE.2	Understand that rewriting an expression in different forms in a problem context can shed light on the problem and how the quantities in it are related	**SE:** 22–25, 30, 36–37, 69, 171, 240–243, 246–247, 359
Solve real-life and mathematical problems using numerical and algebraic expressions and equations		
CC.7.EE.3	Solve multi-step real-life and mathematical problems posed with positive and negative rational numbers in any form (whole numbers, fractions, and decimals), using tools strategically. Apply properties of operations to calculate with numbers in any form; convert between forms as appropriate; and assess the reasonableness of answers using mental computation and estimation strategies	**SE:** 7–17, 35, 43, 49, 55, 111, 235–239, 240–244, 246–249, 265, 267
CC.7.EE.4	Use variables to represent quantities in a real-world or mathematical problem, and construct simple equations and inequalities to solve problems by reasoning about the quantities	**SE:** 22–25, 27–31, 36–37, 41, 69, 73, 75, 91, 113, 115–116, 131–134, 140–141, 469–471, 473–475, 477–479, 482–483, 489–491, 493–495, 497–499, 500–501, 505–507
CC.7.EE.4a	Solve word problems leading to equations of the form $px + q = r$ and $p(x + q) = r$, where p, q, and r are specific rational numbers. Solve equations of these forms fluently. Compare an algebraic solution to an arithmetic solution, identifying the sequence of the operations used in each approach	**SE:** 469–471, 473–475, 477–479, 480–483, 504–505
CC.7.EE .4b	Solve word problems leading to inequalities of the form $px + q > r$ or $px + q < r$, where p, q, and r are specific rational numbers. Graph the solution set of the inequality and interpret it in the context of the problem	**SE:** 497–501, 506–507

Standard	Descriptor	Page Citations
CC.7.G	**GEOMETRY**	
Draw, construct, and describe geometrical figures and describe the relationships between them		
CC.7.G.1	Solve problems involving scale drawings of geometric figures, including computing actual lengths and areas from a scale drawing and reproducing a scale drawing at a different scale	**SE:** 168–178, 180, 186–187
CC.7.G.2	Draw (freehand, with ruler and protractor, and with technology) geometric shapes with given conditions. Focus on constructing triangles from three measures of angles or sides, noticing when the conditions determine a unique triangle, more than one triangle, or no triangle	**SE:** 179, 323–324, 331, 334–335, 337, 342–343
CC.7.G.3	Describe the two-dimensional figures that result from slicing three-dimensional figures, as in plane sections of right rectangular prisms and right rectangular pyramids	**SE:** 378–379
Solve real-life and mathematical problems involving angle measure, area, surface area, and volume		
CC.7.G.4	Know the formulas for the area and circumference of a circle and use them to solve problems; give an informal derivation of the relationship between the circumference and area of a circle	**SE:** 361–367, 372
CC.7.G.5	Use facts about supplementary, complementary, vertical, and adjacent angles in a multi-step problem to write and solve simple equations for an unknown angle in a figure	**SE:** 314–315, 317–319, 323–325
CC.7.G.6	Solve real-world and mathematical problems involving area, volume and surface area of two- and three-dimensional objects composed of triangles, quadrilaterals, polygons, cubes, and right prisms.	**SE:** 369–372, 383–385, 387, 390–391
CC.7.SP	**STATISTICS AND PROBABILITY**	
Use random sampling to draw inferences about a population		
CC.7.SP.1	Understand that statistics can be used to gain information about a population by examining a sample of the population; generalizations about a population from a sample are valid only if the sample is representative of that population. Understand that random sampling tends to produce representative samples and support valid inferences	**SE:** 286–290, 292–293
CC.7.SP.2	Use data from a random sample to draw inferences about a population with an unknown characteristic of interest. Generate multiple samples (or simulated samples) of the same size to gauge the variation in estimates or predictions	**SE:** 290, 292–293
Draw informal comparative inferences about two populations		
CC.7.SP.3	Informally assess the degree of visual overlap of two numerical data distributions with similar variabilities, measuring the difference between the centers by expressing it as a multiple of a measure of variability	**SE:** 277–278, 292–293
CC.7.SP.4	Use measures of center and measures of variability for numerical data from random samples to draw informal comparative inferences about two populations	**SE:** 277–279, 281–283

SE = Student Edition

Standard	Descriptor	Page Citations
Investigate chance processes and develop, use, and evaluate probability models		
CC.7.SP.5	Understand that the probability of a chance event is a number between 0 and 1 that expresses the likelihood of the event occurring. Larger numbers indicate greater likelihood. A probability near 0 indicates an unlikely event, a probability around 1/2 indicates an event that is neither unlikely nor likely, and a probability near 1 indicates a likely event	**SE:** 406, 408
CC.7.SP.6	Approximate the probability of a chance event by collecting data on the chance process that produces it and observing its long-run relative frequency, and predict the approximate relative frequency given the probability	**SE:** 408–409, 411–412, 419–421, 426–429, 430–431
CC.7.SP.7	Develop a probability model and use it to find probabilities of events. Compare probabilities from a model to observed frequencies; if the agreement is not good, explain possible sources of the discrepancy	**SE:** 427–431
CC.7.SP.7a	Develop a uniform probability model by assigning equal probability to all outcomes, and use the model to determine probabilities of events	**SE:** 427–431
CC.7.SP.7b	Develop a probability model (which may not be uniform) by observing frequencies in data generated from a chance process	**SE:** 410–413, 422–423, 426–431
CC.7.SP.8	Find probabilities of compound events using organized lists, tables, tree diagrams, and simulation	**SE:** 437, 446–449
CC.7.SP.8a	Understand that, just as with simple events, the probability of a compound event is the fraction of outcomes in the sample space for which the compound event occurs	**SE:** 406, 435–437, 446–449
CC.7.SP.8b	Represent sample spaces for compound events using methods such as organized lists, tables and tree diagrams. For an event described in everyday language (e.g., "rolling double sixes"), identify the outcomes in the sample space which compose the event	**SE:** 414–417, 434–449
CC.7.SP.8c	Design and use a simulation to generate frequencies for compound events	**SE:** 424–425

MATHEMATICAL PRACTICES

Mastering the Standards
for Mathematical Practice

The topics described in the Standards for Mathematical Content will vary from year to year. However, the *way* in which you learn, study, and think about mathematics will not. The Standards for Mathematical Practice describe skills that you will use in all of your math courses. These pages show some features of your book that will help you gain these skills and use them to master this year's topics.

---

1 **Make sense of problems and persevere in solving them.**

Mathematically proficient students start by explaining to themselves the meaning of a problem... They analyze givens, constraints, relationships, and goals. They make conjectures about the form... of the solution and plan a solution pathway...

In your book

Focus on Problem Solving describes a four-step plan for problem solving. The plan is introduced at the beginning of your book, and practice appears throughout.

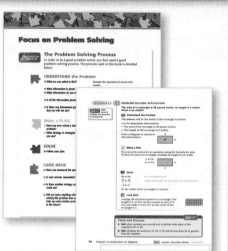

---

2 **Reason abstractly and quantitatively.**

3 **Construct viable arguments and critique the reasoning of others.**

Mathematically proficient students... justify their conclusions, [and]... distinguish correct... reasoning from that which is flawed.

In your book

Think and Discuss asks you to evaluate statements, explain relationships, apply mathematical principles, and justify your reasoning.

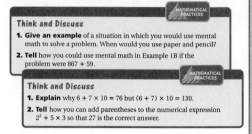

Think and Discuss

1. **Give an example** of a situation in which you would use mental math to solve a problem. When would you use paper and pencil?

2. **Tell** how you could use mental math in Example 1B if the problem were 867 + 59.

Think and Discuss

1. **Explain** why $6 + 7 \times 10 = 76$ but $(6 + 7) \times 10 = 130$.

2. **Tell** how you can add parentheses to the numerical expression $2^2 + 5 \times 3$ so that 27 is the correct answer.

④ Model with mathematics.

Mathematically proficient students can apply... mathematics... to... problems... in everyday life, society, and the workplace...

In your book

Application exercises and **Real-World Connections** apply mathematics to other disciplines and in real-world scenarios.

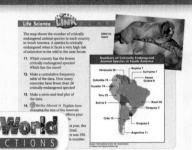

⑤ Use appropriate tools strategically.

Mathematically proficient students consider the available tools when solving a... problem... [and] are... able to use technological tools to explore and deepen their understanding...

In your book

Hands-on Labs and **Technology Labs** use concrete and technological tools to explore mathematical concepts.

⑥ Attend to precision.

Mathematically proficient students... communicate precisely... with others and in their own reasoning... [They] give carefully formulated explanations...

In your book

Reading and Writing Math and **Write About It** help you learn and use the language of math to communicate mathematics precisely.

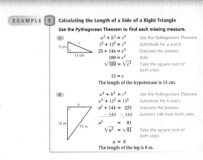

⑦ Look for and express regularity in repeated reasoning.
⑧ Look for and make use of structure.

Mathematically proficient students... look both for general methods and for shortcuts...

In your book

Lesson examples group similar types of problems together, and the solutions are carefully stepped out. This allows you to make generalizations about—and notice variations in—the underlying structures.

EXAMPLE 1 **Calculating the Length of a Side of a Right Triangle**

Use the Pythagorean Theorem to find each missing measure.

A
$a^2 + b^2 = c^2$ Use the Pythagorean Theorem.
$5^2 + 12^2 = c^2$ Substitute for a and b.
$25 + 144 = c^2$ Evaluate the powers.
$169 = c^2$ Add.
$\sqrt{169} = \sqrt{c^2}$ Take the square root of both sides.
$13 = c$
The length of the hypotenuse is 13 cm.

B
$a^2 + b^2 = c^2$ Use the Pythagorean Theorem.
$a^2 + 12^2 = 15^2$ Substitute for b and c.
$a^2 + 144 = 225$ Evaluate the powers.
$-144 \quad -144$ Subtract 144 from both sides.
$a^2 = 81$
$\sqrt{a^2} = \sqrt{81}$ Take the square root of both sides.
$a = 9$
The length of the leg is 9 m.

Countdown to Mastery

DAY 1

A marching band has 8 musicians in the first row, 11 musicians in the second row, and 14 musicians in the third row. Assuming the pattern continues, how many musicians are in the seventh row?

(A) 17   (C) 26

(B) 23   (D) 56

DAY 2

At SaveMart, notebooks cost $4, pens cost $2, and staplers cost $7. Roberto buys 3 notebooks, 4 pens, and a stapler. He has a coupon for $10 off the total cost. What is the final cost of the items before tax?

(F) $13   (H) $19

(G) $17   (J) $27

DAY 3

The table shows the approximate heights of four waterfalls in Arkansas. How much higher is Sunset Falls than Eden Falls?

(A) 1 m   (C) 3 m

(B) 2 m   (D) 4 m

Arkansas Waterfalls	
Name	Height
Boen Gulf Falls	19 m
Eden Falls	16 m
Slate Falls	16 m
Sunset Falls	20 m

DAY 4

Tom got on an elevator on floor 7. He then went up 8 floors, and down 11 floors. What floor did he end on?

(F) floor 2

(G) floor 3

(H) floor 4

(J) floor 19

DAY 5

To the nearest percent, how much more is shaded of Stage 2 than of Stage 3?

Stage 1   Stage 2   Stage 3

(A) 11%   (C) 18%

(B) 14%   (D) 25%

DAY 1

The table shows what Kayla earns each hour doing various jobs. Last week, she earned a total of $121. She baby-sat for 4 hours and did yard work for 3 hours. How many hours did she do house cleaning?

Job	Hourly Pay
Babysitting	$9
Yard Work	$7
House Cleaning	$8

Ⓐ 5 hours   Ⓒ 8 hours

Ⓑ 7 hours   Ⓓ 15 hours

DAY 2

Each week, Yoshio adds some baseball cards to his collection. The table shows the number of cards in his collection. Assuming the pattern continues, in which week will he have 150 cards in his collection?

Week	1	2	3	4
Number of Cards	15	30	45	60

Ⓕ 10

Ⓖ 15

Ⓗ 20

Ⓙ 75

DAY 3

Justine has a piece of string that is 400 centimeters long. She cuts it into pieces that are each 20 centimeters long. How many pieces does she have?

Ⓐ 5   Ⓒ 20

Ⓑ 10   Ⓓ 80

DAY 4

It costs $15 to rent a carpet cleaner for 3 hours. What is the total cost of renting the carpet cleaner for 6 hours on Monday, 9 hours on Tuesday, and 6 hours on Wednesday?

Ⓕ $45   Ⓗ $135

Ⓖ $105   Ⓙ $315

DAY 5

A display case can hold 48 rock samples. What equation can be used to determine how many display cases are needed to hold 144 rock samples?

Ⓐ $48x = 144$

Ⓑ $48 + x = 144$

Ⓒ $48 \div x = 144$

Ⓓ $144x = 48$

DAY 1

The town of Warren, Vermont, currently has a population of 1950 residents. The population is projected to grow by 23 residents per year. What expression can you use to find the population in n years?

(A) $1950n + 23$ (C) $1950 + 23 + n$

(B) $1950(23 + n)$ (D) $1950 + 23n$

DAY 2

A flat contains 30 eggs. A baker bought 18 flats of eggs. This is 7 more flats than he bought last week. How many eggs did he buy last week?

(F) 210

(G) 330

(H) 540

(J) 750

DAY 3

A water park has a special price of $15 per student when students visit the park with their class. There is also a service charge of $12 per class. A group of students pays a total of $477 to visit the park. How many students are in the class?

(A) 15   (C) 30

(B) 27   (D) 31

DAY 4

Scott has n friends. Tanya has twice as many friends as Scott. Pablo has one more friend than Tanya. How many friends does Pablo have?

(F) $n + 2$ (H) $2n + 1$

(G) $n + 3$ (J) $2(n + 1)$

DAY 5

Carolyn visits one of the Arizona state parks shown in the table. How many times as great is the area of Oracle State Park than the area of Fool Hollow Lake?

Arizona State Parks	
Park	**Area (acres)**
Catalina State Park	5,500
Dead Horse Ranch	420
Fool Hollow Lake	800
Oracle State Park	4,000

(A) 2 times   (C) 5 times

(B) 4 times   (D) 50 times

Countdown to Mastery

DAY 1

On a winter day, the temperature at noon is –3 °F. The temperature drops 2 °F every hour. What is the temperature at 5 PM?

(A) –5 °F

(B) –8 °F

(C) –10 °F

(D) –13 °F

DAY 2

An explorer descends to the deepest part of a cave. Then she ascends 25 feet per minute. After 3 minutes, she is at –195 feet. What is the depth of the cave?

(F) –100 feet

(G) –170 feet

(H) –220 feet

(J) –270 feet

DAY 3

Ann buys 3 black candles, 2 white candles, and 4 striped candles. She gives the cashier a $50 bill. About how much change should she get back?

$4.99 $5.50 $3.75

(A) $8

(B) $12

(C) $15

(D) $18

DAY 4

Miguel recorded the distances he ran each month. What is the total number of miles he ran?

Month	May	June	July
Miles	22.5	20.8	25.2

(F) 43.3 miles

(G) 46 miles

(H) 68.5 miles

(J) 69 miles

DAY 5

A contestant on a game show started with 200 points. He answered 3 questions correctly for 50 points each. He answered 4 questions incorrectly and lost 100 points for each. What was his final score?

(A) –150

(B) –50

(C) 50

(D) 150

DAY 1

The distance from Los Angeles to Moscow is 6,000 miles. A jet flies at an average speed of 500 miles per hour. How long does it take to fly from Los Angeles to Moscow?

(A) 1.2 hours

(B) 6 hours

(C) 10.5 hours

(D) 12 hours

DAY 2

The point (3, 5) lies on the graph of a direct variation. What could be the equation for the graph?

(F) $y = \frac{5}{3}x$

(G) $y = x + 2$

(H) $3x = 5y$

(J) $y = 3x + 5$

DAY 3

The figure shows the dimensions of an Olympic-size swimming pool. A lifeguard closes an Olympic-size pool for repairs by placing orange cones at the corners of the pool. She also places cones every 5 meters along the edges. How many cones does she need?

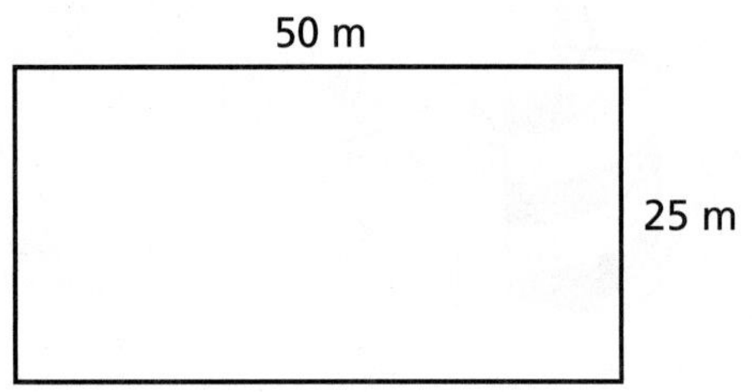

50 m

25 m

(A) 15   (C) 30

(B) 25   (D) 50

DAY 4

A canal boat went through a series of locks with the following rises and drops. A positive number shows a rise. A negative number shows a drop. At which lock was there the greatest rise?

Lock	1	2	3	4
Rise or Fall (ft)	−17	11	−8	6

(F) 1   (H) 3

(G) 2   (J) 4

DAY 5

A circle has an area of 16π square meters. What is the circumference of the circle?

(A) 8 meters   (C) 8π meters

(B) 4 meters   (D) 4π meters

DAY 1

There are 12 boys and 16 girls in Mr. Waller's class. Ms. Grey's class has the same ratio of boys to girls, but there are 4 more girls. How many boys are in Ms. Grey's class?

(A) 15 (C) 18

(B) 16 (D) 20

DAY 2

The weights of 5 watermelons in pounds are 7, 10, 8, 12, and 8. What is the mode of these data?

(F) 7 pounds (H) 9 pounds

(G) 8 pounds (J) no mode

DAY 3

The table shows the results of the first run of the bobsled competition at the 2006 Winter Olympics. The team with the fastest time won the gold medal in the event. Which team won the gold medal?

(A) Russia (C) Germany

(B) Canada (D) Switzerland

2006 Olympics: Four-Man Bobsled	
Team	Time (s)
Russia	$55\frac{11}{50}$
Canada	55.34
Germany	$55\frac{1}{5}$
Switzerland	55.26

DAY 4

The shaded regions represent left over portions of three pizzas. How much pizza is left over?

(F) $\frac{7}{8}$ (H) $2\frac{1}{16}$

(G) $1\frac{11}{12}$ (J) $2\frac{1}{8}$

DAY 5

On a platter of sandwiches, $\frac{1}{3}$ of the sandwiches are ham sandwiches. Of the ham sandwiches, $\frac{1}{4}$ are on whole-wheat bread. The platter contains 3 ham sandwiches on whole-wheat bread. How many sandwiches are there altogether?

(A) 12 (C) 36

(B) 18 (D) 48

DAY 1

Brad had $530.45 in his checking account. He wrote checks for $16.50 and $95.68. He also made a deposit of $19.13. What is the approximate final balance in his account?

(A) $400

(C) $480

(B) $440

(D) $500

DAY 2

If it takes 5 buses to carry 225 passengers, how many passengers will 3 buses carry?

(F) 45

(H) 170

(G) 135

(J) 222

DAY 3

Ira earns $81.25 per week at a part-time job. He wants to earn enough money to buy a laptop computer that costs $719.95. About how many weeks does Ira need to work in order to buy the computer?

(A) 6 weeks

(C) 9 weeks

(B) 7 weeks

(D) 11 weeks

DAY 4

Peter and a friend share a pizza. Peter eats 2 slices and his friend eats 3 slices. What fraction represents the amount of pizza both boys ate?

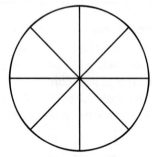

(F) $\frac{1}{8}$

(H) $\frac{3}{8}$

(G) $\frac{1}{4}$

(J) $\frac{5}{8}$

DAY 5

The table shows the weights of four famous diamonds. The Koh-I-Noor diamond weighs 60.08 carats more than the lightest diamond in the table. What is the weight of the Koh-I-Noor diamond?

Famous Diamonds	
Name	Weight (carats)
The Regent	140.5
The Blue Hope	45.52
The Idol's Eye	79.2
The Jubilee	245.33

(A) 19.12 carats

(B) 105.6 carats

(C) 139.28 carats

(D) 200.6 carats

DAY 1

The table shows the number of students in four different classes at Park Street Middle School who take the bus to school. Which class has the greatest fraction of students who take the bus to school?

Class	A	B	C	D
Students Who Take Bus	$\frac{15}{20}$	$\frac{20}{25}$	$\frac{12}{18}$	$\frac{12}{24}$

(A) Class A

(B) Class B

(C) Class C

(D) Class D

DAY 2

Tim and Sue are setting up a tent at a campground. What is the volume of the tent?

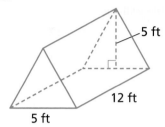

5 ft

12 ft

5 ft

(F) 135 cubic feet

(G) 150 cubic feet

(H) 250 cubic feet

(J) 300 cubic feet

DAY 3

Mrs. Robbins is knitting a scarf for her niece. She knitted $1\frac{7}{8}$ feet yesterday and $1\frac{2}{3}$ feet today. How many feet did Mrs. Robbins knit in both days?

(A) $\frac{5}{24}$ foot

(C) $2\frac{9}{11}$ feet

(B) $1\frac{3}{4}$ feet

(D) $3\frac{13}{24}$ feet

DAY 4

An orange contains $2\frac{1}{2}$ grams of fiber. Each day, Ricardo eats an orange at breakfast and another orange as an afternoon snack. How many grams of fiber does Ricardo get from eating oranges each week?

(F) $2\frac{1}{2}$ grams

(H) $17\frac{1}{2}$ grams

(G) $7\frac{1}{2}$ grams

(J) 35 grams

DAY 5

Mr. Reyes wants to fence in the area behind his house. How many meters of fencing does he need to buy?

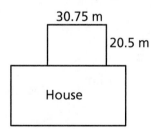

30.75 m

20.5 m

House

(A) 51.25 meters

(B) 71.75 meters

(C) 102.5 meters

(D) 630.38 meters

Countdown to Mastery

DAY 1

Ryan is making $7\frac{1}{2}$ cups of rice to serve at dinner with his friends. If he wants to give $\frac{3}{4}$ cups of rice to each guest, how many people will the rice serve?

(A) 8

(B) 10

(C) 12

(D) 14

DAY 2

A CD earns $125 simple interest. The annual simple interest rate is 2.5% and the initial value of the CD was $1000. For how many years was the CD invested?

(F) 3

(G) 5

(H) 7

(J) 9

DAY 3

Marc needs $\frac{5}{8}$ pound of blueberries to make a batch of muffins and another $\frac{1}{3}$ pound to make blueberry pancakes. How many pounds of blueberries does Marc need?

(A) $\frac{2}{9}$ pound

(B) $\frac{10}{13}$ pound

(C) $\frac{7}{12}$ pound

(D) $\frac{23}{24}$ pound

DAY 4

In the morning, Steve drives to his job at the bookstore. After work, he drives to the college where he takes classes. Then he drives back home. Which is the best estimate of the distance Steve travels each day?

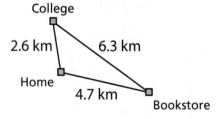

College

2.6 km

6.3 km

Home

4.7 km

Bookstore

(F) 8 kilometers

(G) 10 kilometers

(H) 12 kilometers

(J) 14 kilometers

DAY 5

You are multiplying this recipe for pesto so that you use $2\frac{1}{2}$ cups of basil leaves. How much olive oil do you need?

Pesto

1 cup basil leaves
$\frac{1}{4}$ cup parmesan cheese
$\frac{1}{2}$ cup olive oil
5 tbsp pine nuts

Blend ingredients until they form a smooth paste.

(A) $\frac{5}{8}$ cup

(B) $1\frac{1}{4}$ cups

(C) $2\frac{1}{8}$ cups

(D) $2\frac{3}{4}$ cups

DAY 1

Graciela has a piece of clay that weighs $12\frac{1}{2}$ pounds. She divides the clay into 5 equal pieces. What is the weight of 3 of the pieces?

Ⓐ $2\frac{1}{5}$ pounds   Ⓒ $7\frac{1}{2}$ pounds

Ⓑ $4\frac{1}{6}$ pounds   Ⓓ $8\frac{3}{5}$ pounds

DAY 2

Which description allows you to find the cost of renting n DVDs?

Number of DVDs, n	1	2	3	4
Cost ($)	3	5	7	9

Ⓕ Multiply n by 3.   Ⓗ Multiply n by 2, then add 1.

Ⓖ Add 2 to n.   Ⓙ Add 1 to n, then multiply by 2.

DAY 3

A map of Elmville is drawn on a coordinate plane. City hall lies at (3, −2). The library lies at (−3, −2). What is the distance between city hall and the library, assuming each unit of the coordinate plane represents one mile?

Ⓐ 2 miles   Ⓒ 5 miles

Ⓑ 4 miles   Ⓓ 6 miles

DAY 4

Mrs. Reese is taking a trip to visit her sister. If she drives 162 miles in 3 hours, what is her average rate of speed?

Ⓕ 30 miles per hour

Ⓖ 54 miles per hour

Ⓗ 62 miles per hour

Ⓙ 70 miles per hour

DAY 5

The graph shows the cost of eggs in 1928. What was the cost of 12 dozen eggs in 1928?

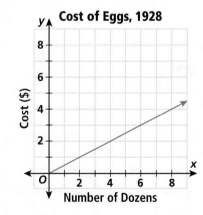

Cost of Eggs, 1928

Ⓐ $6   Ⓒ $12

Ⓑ $8   Ⓓ $24

Countdown to Mastery

DAY 1

Zinovy opens a saving account with $400. Five months later, he has $900 in the account. What is the percent change of the value of his savings account?

(A) 100%

(B) 200%

(C) 225%

(D) 500%

DAY 2

A bill for dinner at a restaurant is $91.42. Lucy wants to leave a 15% tip. Which is a good estimate for the tip?

(F) $4.50

(G) $9.10

(H) $13.50

(J) $18.20

DAY 3

The Taipei 101 skyscraper has some of the world's fastest elevators. The table shows the distance the building's elevators can travel in various amount of time. How long does it take an elevator to travel 660 feet?

(A) 10 seconds   (C) 15 seconds

(B) 12 seconds   (D) 20 seconds

Taipei 101 Elevators	
Time (s)	Distance (ft)
3	165
5	275
8	440

DAY 4

Dante recorded the following information about a seedling's growth for science class. How many inches did the seedling grow in three weeks?

Week	1	2	3
Inches Grown	$\frac{7}{8}$	$\frac{5}{6}$	$\frac{7}{24}$

(F) $1\frac{1}{6}$ inches   (H) 2 inches

(G) $1\frac{17}{24}$ inches   (J) 48 inches

DAY 5

Olivia read 125 pages of her medical textbook in 4 hours. What is her average rate of reading in pages per hour?

(A) 1.25 pages per hour

(B) 13 pages per hour

(C) 31.25 pages per hour

(D) 62.5 pages per hour

Countdown to Mastery

DAY 1

Jennifer is putting fences around some triangular garden plots. The sides of each plot measure $11\frac{1}{3}$ feet, $10\frac{2}{3}$ feet, and $12\frac{2}{3}$ feet. What is the total length of the fencing needed for 3 plots?

(A) $100\frac{1}{3}$ feet   (C) $102\frac{2}{3}$ feet

(B) 101 feet   (D) 104 feet

DAY 2

The state of Washington has an area of 43,000,000 acres. Of this area, $\frac{1}{10}$ is considered wilderness. How many acres of wilderness are in Washington state?

(F) 43,300 acres

(G) 430,000 acres

(H) 4,300,000 acres

(J) 43,000,000 acres

DAY 3

Omar enlarged a photograph, as shown in the figure. What is the perimeter of the enlarged photograph?

6.4 in.

4.4 in.

11 in.

(A) 21.6 inches   (C) 54 inches

(B) 28.2 inches   (D) 176 inches

DAY 4

A discount store is selling a case of 24 bottles of water for $12.99. What is the unit price of a bottle of water to the nearest cent?

(F) $0.27   (H) $1.85

(G) $0.54   (J) $11.01

DAY 5

The shadow of a 4-foot-tall mailbox is 2 feet long. If the shadow of a tree is 16 feet long, what is the height of the tree?

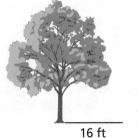

4 ft

16 ft   2 ft

(A) 18 feet   (C) 32 feet

(B) 24 feet   (D) 64 feet

DAY 1

A model car and a real car have the given dimensions. What is the length of the real car?

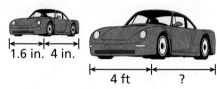

1.6 in.   4 in.

4 ft   ?

(A) 8 feet

(B) 9 feet

(C) 10 feet

(D) 12 feet

DAY 2

Waldorf and Summerville are 5 inches apart on a map. The scale of the map is 1 in:40 mi. Janelle drives from Waldorf to Summerville at an average speed of 50 miles per hour. How long does the trip take?

(F) 2 hours

(G) 4 hours

(H) 6 hours

(J) 8 hours

DAY 3

The graph shows the number of grams of protein in various amounts of cooked rice. How much rice would you need to eat in order to consume 12 grams of protein?

(A) 3 cups

(B) 6 cups

(C) 12 cups

(D) 36 cups

Nutrition Facts: Cooked Rice

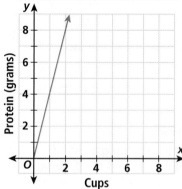

DAY 4

Randy wants to buy an MP3 player for $98.99, and it is on sale for 37% off. About how much money will Randy pay for the MP3 player before tax?

(F) $40

(G) $60

(H) $70

(J) $80

DAY 5

At a frozen yogurt shop, 50% of all the yogurts sold on Monday were chocolate yogurts and 10% were peach yogurts. If 20 peach yogurts were sold on Monday, how many chocolate yogurts were sold?

(A) 50

(B) 100

(C) 200

(D) 400

DAY 1

Kendra shades additional squares in the figure so that 30% of the figure is shadded. How many additional squares does she shade?

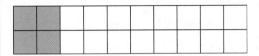

- (A) 1
- (C) 4
- (B) 2
- (D) 6

DAY 2

Which ordered pair has a graph in quadrant II?

- (F) (2, −7)
- (G) (3, 8)
- (H) (−3, 11)
- (J) (−2, −1)

DAY 3

The table shows data from the 2006-2007 season for four players on the Charlotte Bobcats basketball team. Which player made the greatest percentage of free throws?

- (A) Brevin Knight
- (B) Adam Morrison
- (C) Emeka Okafor
- (D) Gerald Wallace

Charlotte Bobcats 2006–07		
Player	Free Throws Made	Free Throws Attempted
Brevin Knight	103	128
Adam Morrison	120	169
Emeka Okafor	175	295
Gerald Wallace	309	447

DAY 4

April is standing next to a tree. The length of April's shadow is 4 feet, and the length of the tree's shadow is 32 feet. If April is 5 feet tall, how tall is the tree?

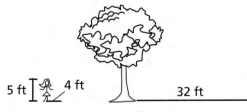

- (F) 18 feet
- (H) 32 feet
- (G) 24 feet
- (J) 40 feet

DAY 5

Susan buys leather purses from the manufacturer for $11.90 each and sells them to the public at 425% the price she paid. About how much do Susan's customers pay for a purse?

- (A) $15.50
- (C) $51.00
- (B) $42.00
- (D) $437.00

DAY 1

Ray bought the seven books shown below as well as an eighth book. The median price of all eight books was $21.90. What was the price of the eighth book?

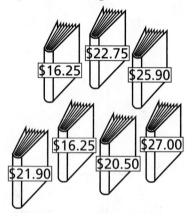

$16.25
$22.75
$25.90
$21.90
$16.25
$20.50
$27.00

(A) $10.75   (C) $21.90

(B) $16.25   (D) $27.00

DAY 2

Louis received the following scores on his English quizzes this semester: 95, 95, 80, 70, 60. Which description of this data set would make Louis' results look best?

(F) the mean of his scores

(G) the median of his scores

(H) the mode of his scores

(J) the range of his scores

DAY 3

A movie theater has regular tickets and discount tickets. At one showing of the movie, 24 discount tickets are sold. This represents 15% of all the tickets. How many regular tickets are sold?

(A) 136

(B) 160

(C) 224

(D) 360

DAY 4

The price of a meal came to $11.82 without tax or tip. Which is the best estimate of the total cost of the meal including a tip of 15% and tax of 8%?

(F) $10   (H) $15

(G) $12   (J) $20

DAY 5

Which is greatest for this set of data—the mean, median, mode, or range?

(A) mean   (C) mode

(B) median   (D) range

DAY 1

The distance *m* in miles that Brett runs this week is given by $m = 18 + 3d$, where *d* is the number of days left in the week. What might 3 represent in this function?

(A) The number of days remaining in the week

(B) The distance Brett has already run this week

(C) The distance Brett runs each day

(D) The number of miles remaining to run this week

DAY 2

What is the slope of the linear function $y = -2x + 3$?

(F) −2

(G) 1.5

(H) 2

(J) 3

DAY 3

The graph shows the number of species at the Paignton Zoo in England. Which category accounts for about 10% of the species?

(A) Invertebrates (C) Birds

(B) Fish (D) Mammals

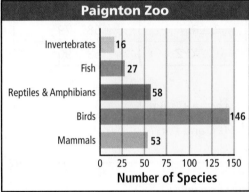

Paignton Zoo

Invertebrates	16
Fish	27
Reptiles & Amphibians	58
Birds	146
Mammals	53

0 25 50 75 100 125 150
Number of Species

DAY 4

A bookshelf contains science books and math books. The ratio of science books to math books is 2:3. There are 20 books altogether. How many science books are there?

(F) 2

(G) 4

(H) 8

(J) 10

DAY 5

According to a 2007 survey, 17% of people with an email account check their email just once per day. If 680 of the people surveyed said they checked their email just once per day, how many people were surveyed?

(A) 116 (C) 2400

(B) 796 (D) 4000

Countdown to Mastery

WEEK 17

DAY 1

Suppose $\angle J$ is supplementary to $\angle K$ and $\angle K$ is complementary to $\angle L$. The measure of $\angle L$ is 9°. What the measure of $\angle J$?

(A) 9°
(B) 19°
(C) 81°
(D) 99°

DAY 2

The manager of a store increases the price of a pair of shoes by 10%. The new price is $38.50. What was the original price of the shoes?

(F) $28.50
(G) $34.65
(H) $35.00
(J) $42.35

DAY 3

The table shows the measures of two angles in several triangles. Given that two of the triangles in the table are congruent, which two triangles must it be?

Triangle	Angle Measures
$\triangle ABC$	43°, 47°
$\triangle JKL$	43°, 58°
$\triangle RST$	58°, 79°
$\triangle XYZ$	58°, 90°

(A) $\triangle ABC$ and $\triangle JKL$
(B) $\triangle ABC$ and $\triangle RST$
(C) $\triangle JKL$ and $\triangle RST$
(D) $\triangle RST$ and $\triangle XYZ$

DAY 4

Jason recorded the number of cardinals he saw during his nature hikes below. What is the mean number of cardinals Jason saw? Round your answer to the nearest whole number.

6, 6, 8, 9, 12, 14, 15, 18, 18, 18, 19, 21

(F) 6
(G) 14
(H) 15
(J) 18

DAY 5

Jamal drew a circle and a square so that the two figures intersect each other. What is the maximum number of points in which the figures can intersect?

(A) 1
(B) 2
(C) 4
(D) 8

DAY 1

A student added a point P to the figure. Then she connected the four points and formed a rectangle. What are the coordinates of point P?

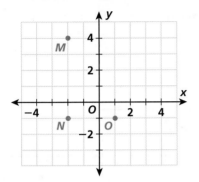

(A) (−1, 4)   (C) (2, 4)

(B) (1, 4)   (D) (4, 4)

DAY 2

Alex kept track of the number of telemarketing calls he received each month for 6 months.

14, 10, 17, 12, 11, 15

Which of the following would not change if Alex decided to add the data value 11 for a seventh month?

(F) median   (H) mode

(G) range   (J) mean

DAY 3

In Manhattan, 29th Street and 30th Street are parallel. Broadway intersects 30th Street at a 110° angle. What is the value of x?

(A) 70   (C) 90

(B) 80   (D) 110

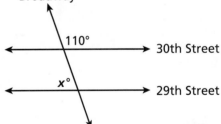

DAY 4

What is the mean of the given angle measures?

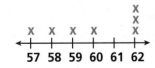

(F) 58°   (H) 60°

(G) 59°   (J) 62°

DAY 5

If a car is traveling at a speed of 48 miles per hour, how far can it travel in $1\frac{7}{8}$ hours?

(A) 50 miles   (C) 90 miles

(B) 80 miles   (D) 100 miles

DAY 1

What equation describes the relationship shown in the table?

x	5	6	7	8
y	8	10	12	14

(A) $y = x + 3$

(C) $y = -x + 13$

(B) $y = 3x - 7$

(D) $y = 2x - 2$

DAY 2

A rectangle is 4 meters wide. It is twice as long as it is wide. What is the perimeter of the rectangle?

(F) 12 meters

(H) 28 meters

(G) 24 meters

(J) 32 meters

DAY 3

What is the slope of the line?

(A) −2

(C) 2

(B) 1

(D) 3

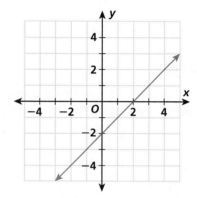

DAY 4

The measure of ∠DEF is 50% that of ∠ABC. Given that ∠JKL is complementary to ∠DEF, what is the measure of ∠JKL?

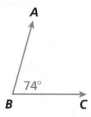

(F) 37°

(H) 106°

(G) 53°

(J) 143°

DAY 5

What is the area of the irregular figure?

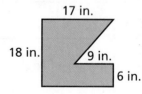

(A) 198 square in.

(B) 252 square in.

(C) 289 square in.

(D) 306 square in.

DAY 1

What is the slope of segment *JF*?

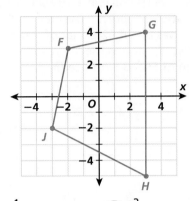

- (A) $-\frac{1}{5}$
- (B) $\frac{1}{5}$
- (C) $\frac{3}{2}$
- (D) 5

DAY 2

Each of the four triangles has the same area. If one bag of stones will cover an area of 25 square feet, how many bags will it take to cover the large triangle?

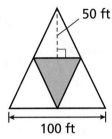

50 ft

100 ft

- (F) 25
- (H) 100
- (G) 75
- (J) 200

DAY 3

Martin is filling a trough with water. If the pail he is using can hold 9 cubic feet of water, how many times will he need to empty his pail into the trough in order to fill the trough completely?

- (A) 6
- (C) 8
- (B) 7
- (D) 9

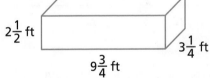

$2\frac{1}{2}$ ft

$3\frac{1}{4}$ ft

$9\frac{3}{4}$ ft

DAY 4

Kenisha flips a coin and spins a spinner at the same time. There are 16 outcomes in the sample space. How many different outcomes does the spinner have?

- (F) 2
- (H) 8
- (G) 4
- (J) 14

DAY 5

Four shovels of sand are mixed with 5 shovels of gravel to make cement. About how many shovels of gravel are needed for 45 shovels of sand?

- (A) 20
- (C) 55
- (B) 45
- (D) 75

DAY 1

Which equation has a graph that would contain segment *CD*?

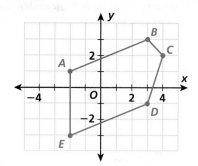

- **A** $y = 3x - 10$
- **C** $y = -3x - 10$
- **B** $y = x - 2$
- **D** $y = 3x + 3.5$

DAY 2

In 2007, the circulation of *National Geographic* magazine was 5,100,000. The circulation of *Sports Illustrated* magazine was about 62% that of *National Geographic*. What was the approximate circulation of *Sports Illustrated*?

- **F** 320,000
- **H** 3,200,000
- **G** 820,000
- **J** 8,200,000

DAY 3

A bag contains 20 red marbles, 16 blue marbles, and 14 yellow marbles. Jacob chooses a marble from the bag without looking. What is the probability that he chooses a red marble?

- **A** 20%
- **C** 40%
- **B** 28%
- **D** 60%

DAY 4

Tom is creating a model of a building. What is the height of the real building?

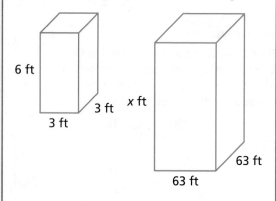

- **F** 54 feet
- **H** 126 feet
- **G** 63 feet
- **J** 3,969 feet

DAY 5

Carrie is designing a mosaic wall for her school's library. The wall measures 4 meters by 8 meters. The tiles she is using are 10 centimeters by 10 centimeters. If the tiles come 600 to a package, how many packages will Carrie need to cover the wall?

- **A** 4
- **C** 6
- **B** 5
- **D** 7

DAY 1

What is the missing angle measure of the quadrilateral?

79°
87°   85°

Ⓐ 86°   Ⓒ 109°

Ⓑ 99°   Ⓓ 149°

DAY 2

William received the following blueprint for a building. What is the area of the base of this building?

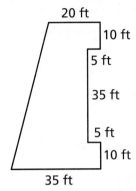

20 ft
10 ft
5 ft
35 ft
5 ft
10 ft
35 ft

Ⓕ 1,258.5 square feet

Ⓖ 1,337.5 square feet

Ⓗ 1,425.5 square feet

Ⓙ 1,512.5 square feet

DAY 3

Sonia and Zachary are renting ice skates. The price of the rental for each of them is $5 plus $2 per hour. They rent skates for the same amount of time and together they spend a total of $26. Which equation can you solve to find the number of hours for which they rented the skates?

Ⓐ $5x + 2 = 26$ Ⓑ $2x + 5 = 26$ Ⓒ $10x + 4 = 26$ Ⓓ $4x + 10 = 26$

DAY 4

Kenny is building a compost bin. What is the best estimate of the volume of the bin?

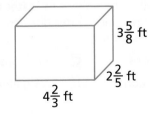

$3\frac{5}{8}$ ft

$2\frac{2}{5}$ ft

$4\frac{2}{3}$ ft

Ⓕ 11 cubic feet

Ⓖ 24 cubic feet

Ⓗ 40 cubic feet

Ⓙ 60 cubic feet

DAY 5

Trevor has a piece of yarn that is $6\frac{2}{3}$ feet long. He cuts off pieces that are $1\frac{3}{4}$ feet long. What is the maximum number of such pieces he can cut from the yarn?

Ⓐ 3   Ⓒ 5

Ⓑ 4   Ⓓ 6

DAY 1

What is the rule for the pattern in the table below?

x	1	2	3	4
y	1	4	7	10

Ⓐ $y = 2x + 2$

Ⓑ $y = 3x - 2$

Ⓒ $y = \frac{x}{2} \cdot 5$

Ⓓ $y = 2x + 1$

DAY 2

A standard IMAX® movie screen is 22 meters wide and 16 meters tall. What is the perimeter of the rectangular screen?

Ⓕ 27 meters

Ⓖ 38 meters

Ⓗ 76 meters

Ⓙ 88 meters

DAY 3

Marc has $6 to spend on snacks for the film club. He can buy any of the snacks shown in the table. Which snack should he buy if he wants to pay the least amount per ounce?

Ⓐ Raisins

Ⓑ Peanuts

Ⓒ Banana Chips

Ⓓ Cashews

Film Club Snacks		
Item	**Amount**	**Price**
Raisins	16 oz	$2.40
Peanuts	14 oz	$1.68
Banana Chips	8 oz	$1.12
Cashews	12 oz	$4.92

DAY 4

A patio has the shape of a right triangle and a trapezoid, as shown. The area of the patio is 80 square feet. What is the value of x?

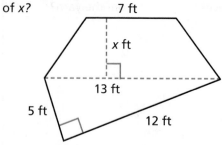

7 ft

x ft

13 ft

5 ft

12 ft

Ⓕ 5

Ⓖ 6

Ⓗ 8

Ⓙ 10

DAY 5

A typical shower uses 7.5 gallons of water in 3 minutes, 12.5 gallons of water in 5 minutes, and 17.5 gallons of water in 7 minutes. How much water does an 11-minute shower use?

Ⓐ 20 gallons

Ⓒ 25 gallons

Ⓑ 22.5 gallons

Ⓓ 27.5 gallons

Countdown to Mastery

DAY 1

The figure shows the dimensions of a circular fountain. A bug crawls around the circumference of the fountain at a rate of 2 feet per minute. About how long does it take the bug to go once around the fountain?

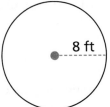

8 ft

A 13 minutes   C 50 minutes

B 25 minutes   D 100 minutes

DAY 2

What object is represented by this net?

F cone   H cylinder

G sphere   J prism

DAY 3

A spinner has red, blue, and green sections. Andrea spun the spinner 60 times and she determined that the experimental probability of the spinner landing on red is 15%. How many times did the spinner land on either a blue or green section?

A 9

B 15

C 25

D 51

DAY 4

A box has dimensions of 1.5 feet, 2 feet, and 3 feet. What is the surface area of the box?

F 9 square fee   H 27 square feet

G 13.5 square feet   J 39 square feet

DAY 5

A beach volleyball team has 8 players. In how many ways can the coach choose two players for the first match?

A 16 ways   C 64 ways

B 56 ways   D 112 ways

Focus on Problem Solving

The Problem Solving Process

In order to be a good problem solver, you first need a good problem-solving process. The process used in this book is detailed below.

UNDERSTAND the Problem

- **What are you asked to find?**

  Restate the question in your own words.

- **What information is given?**

  Identify the facts in the problem.

- **What information do you need?**

  Determine which facts are needed to answer the question.

- **Is all the information given?**

  Determine whether all the facts are given.

- **Is there any information given that you will not use?**

  Determine which facts, if any, are unnecessary to solve the problem.

Make a PLAN

- **Have you ever solved a similar problem?**

  Think about other problems like this that you successfully solved.

- **What strategy or strategies can you use?**

  Determine a strategy that you can use and how you will use it.

SOLVE

- **Follow your plan.**

  Show the steps in your solution. Write your answer as a complete sentence.

LOOK BACK

- **Have you answered the question?**

  Be sure that you answered the question that is being asked.

- **Is your answer reasonable?**

  Your answer should make sense in the context of the problem.

- **Is there another strategy you could use?**

  Solving the problem using another strategy is a good way to check your work.

- **Did you learn anything while solving this problem that could help you solve similar problems in the future?**

  Try to remember the problems you have solved and the strategies you used to solve them.

Using the Problem Solving Process

During summer vacation, Nicholas will visit first his cousin and then his grandmother. He will be gone for 5 weeks and 2 days, and he will spend 9 more days with his cousin than with his grandmother. How long will he stay with each family member?

UNDERSTAND the Problem

Identify the important information.

- Nicholas's visits will total 5 weeks and 2 days.
- He will spend 9 more days with his cousin than with his grandmother.

The answer will be how long he will stay with each family member.

Make a PLAN

You can draw a diagram to show how long Nicholas will stay. Use boxes for the length of each stay. The length of each box will represent the length of each stay.

SOLVE

Think: There are 7 days in a week, so 5 weeks and 2 days is 37 days in all. Your diagram might look like this:

Cousin | ? days | 9 days | = 37 days

Grandmother | ? days |

Cousin | 14 days | 9 days | $37 - 9 = 28$

Grandmother | 14 days | $28 \div 2 = 14$

So Nicholas will stay with his cousin for 23 days and with his grandmother for 14 days.

LOOK BACK

Twenty-three days is 9 days longer than 14 days. The total of the two stays is $23 + 14$, or 37 days, which is the same as 5 weeks and 2 days. This solution fits the description of Nicholas's trip given in the problem.

Using Your Book for Success

This book has many features designed to help you learn and study math. Becoming familiar with these features will prepare you for greater success on your exams.

Learn

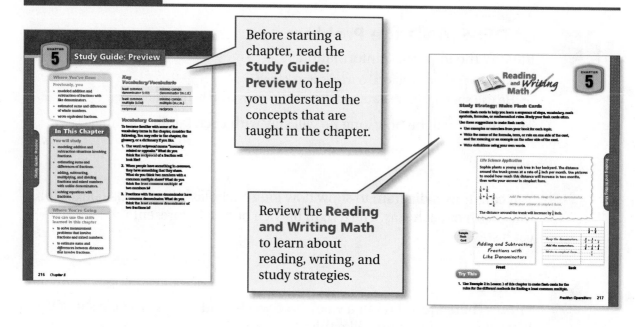

Before starting a chapter, read the **Study Guide: Preview** to help you understand the concepts that are taught in the chapter.

Review the **Reading and Writing Math** to learn about reading, writing, and study strategies.

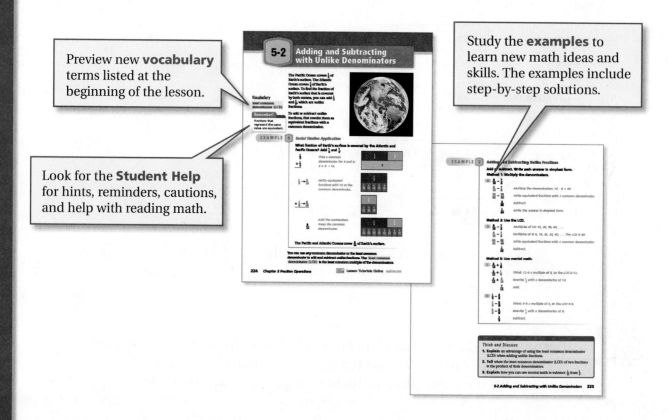

Preview new **vocabulary** terms listed at the beginning of the lesson.

Look for the **Student Help** for hints, reminders, cautions, and help with reading math.

Study the **examples** to learn new math ideas and skills. The examples include step-by-step solutions.

Practice

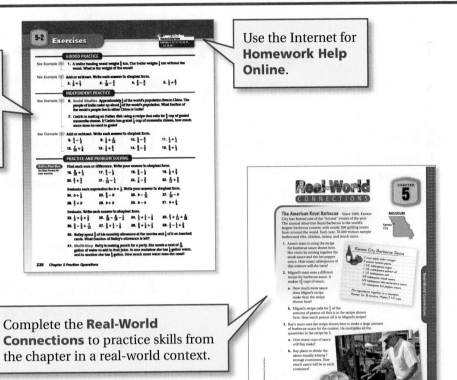

Look back at examples from the lesson to help with the **Guided Practice** and **Independent Practice** exercises.

Use the Internet for **Homework Help Online**.

Complete the **Real-World Connections** to practice skills from the chapter in a real-world context.

Review

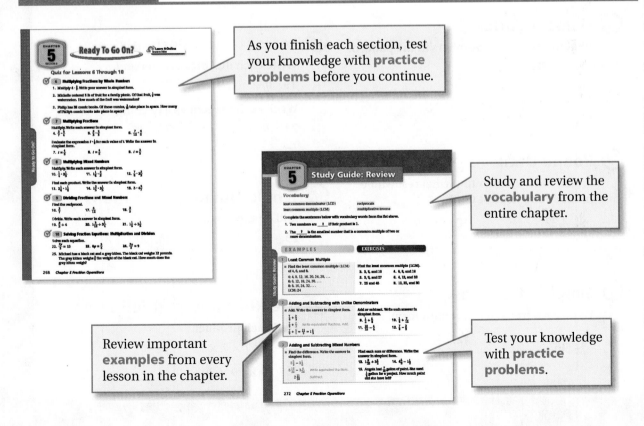

As you finish each section, test your knowledge with **practice problems** before you continue.

Study and review the **vocabulary** from the entire chapter.

Review important **examples** from every lesson in the chapter.

Test your knowledge with **practice problems**.

ARE YOU READY?
Pre-Course Test

Round Whole Numbers

Round each number to the nearest ten and nearest hundred.

1. 6,752

2. 31,817

Order Whole Numbers

Order the numbers from least to greatest.

3. 35, 53, 49, 41, 11, 20

4. 60, 331, 600, 532, 218, 311

Factors

List all the factors of each number.

5. 18

6. 125

Number Patterns

Find the next three numbers in the pattern.

7. 85, 78, 71, 64, . . .

8. $-12, 24, -48, 96, . . .$

Round Decimals

Round each number to the nearest whole number and nearest tenth.

9. 4.82

10. 26.19

Simplify Fractions

Write each fraction in simplest form.

11. $\frac{4}{16}$

12. $\frac{6}{27}$

Write an Improper Fraction as a Mixed Number

Write each improper fraction as a mixed number.

13. $\frac{17}{6}$

14. $\frac{27}{8}$

Write Equivalent Fractions

Find two fractions that are equivalent to each fraction.

15. $\frac{5}{7}$

16. $\frac{14}{19}$

Write Fractions as Decimals

Write each fraction as a decimal.

17. $\frac{28}{100}$

18. $\frac{9}{20}$

Percents and Decimals

Write each decimal as a percent.

19. 0.7

20. 1.15

Write each percent as a decimal.

21. 20%

22. 8%

Whole Number Operations

Add or subtract.

23. $58 + 39$

24. $217 - 81$

Use Repeated Multiplication

Find each product.

25. $7 \times 7 \times 7 \times 7$

26. $20 \times 20 \times 20 \times 20$

Multiply Fractions

Multiply. Write each answer in simplest form.

27. $\frac{7}{9} \times \frac{3}{5}$

28. $\frac{25}{40} \times \frac{18}{100}$

Find the Percent of a Number

Solve.

29. What is 50% of 44?

30. What is 20% of 85?

31. What is 72% of 75?

Order of Operations

Simplify.

32. $7 + 6 \times 3 - 1$

33. $4^3 \div (21 - 19)$

34. $\frac{(9-3)^2}{4} \cdot 7$

Evaluate Expressions

Evaluate each expression.

35. $\frac{2g}{h} \cdot 3$ for $g = -16$ and $h = 24$

36. $5(a + b) + 21$ for $a = 15$ and $b = -27$

Inverse Operations

Solve.

37. $w + 28 = 41$

38. $x - 21 = 56$

39. $12y = 72$

40. $\frac{z}{52} = 4$

Solve Proportions

Solve each proportion.

41. $\frac{t}{4} = \frac{39}{52}$

42. $\frac{3}{q} = \frac{24}{56}$

Graph Ordered Pairs

Use the coordinate plane below. Write the ordered pair for each point.

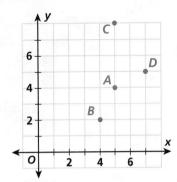

43. point A

44. point B

45. point C

46. point D

Areas of Squares, Rectangles, Triangles

Find the area of each figure.

47.

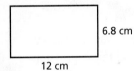

6.8 cm

12 cm

48.

5 ft

11 ft

Area of Circles

Find the area of each circle to the nearest tenth. Use 3.14 for π.

49.

6.2 ft

50.

11 yd

CHAPTER 1

Algebraic Reasoning

COMMON CORE

Chapter Focus

- Use properties of arithmetic and properties of equality.
- Write and simplify expressions to solve problems.

Why Learn This?

Yellowstone National Park was created by Congress in 1872. An algebraic expression can model the current age of the park.

Learn It Online
Chapter Project Online

(all) Oliver Grunewald/Photolibrary.com

 **Learn It Online**
Resources Online

✓ Vocabulary

Choose the best term from the list to complete each sentence.

1. The operation that gives the quotient of two numbers is __?__.

2. The __?__ of the digit 3 in 4,903,672 is thousands.

3. The operation that gives the product of two numbers is __?__.

4. In the equation $15 \div 3 = 5$, the __?__ is 5.

division

multiplication

place value

product

quotient

Complete these exercises to review skills you will need for this chapter.

✓ Find Place Value

Give the place value of the digit 4 in each number.

5. 4,092　　　**6.** 608,241　　　**7.** 7,040,000　　　**8.** 4,556,890,100

9. 3,408,289　　　**10.** 34,506,123　　　**11.** 500,986,402　　　**12.** 3,540,277,009

✓ Use Repeated Multiplication

Find each product.

13. $2 \cdot 2 \cdot 2$　　　**14.** $9 \cdot 9 \cdot 9 \cdot 9$　　　**15.** $14 \cdot 14 \cdot 14$　　　**16.** $10 \cdot 10 \cdot 10 \cdot 10$

17. $3 \cdot 3 \cdot 5 \cdot 5$　　　**18.** $2 \cdot 2 \cdot 5 \cdot 7$　　　**19.** $3 \cdot 3 \cdot 11 \cdot 11$　　　**20.** $5 \cdot 10 \cdot 10 \cdot 10$

✓ Division Facts

Find each quotient.

21. $49 \div 7$　　　**22.** $54 \div 9$　　　**23.** $96 \div 12$　　　**24.** $88 \div 8$

25. $42 \div 6$　　　**26.** $65 \div 5$　　　**27.** $39 \div 3$　　　**28.** $121 \div 11$

✓ Whole Number Operations

Add, subtract, multiply, or divide.

29.　$\begin{array}{r} 425 \\ + 12 \\ \hline \end{array}$　　　**30.**　$\begin{array}{r} 619 \\ + 254 \\ \hline \end{array}$　　　**31.**　$\begin{array}{r} 62 \\ - 47 \\ \hline \end{array}$　　　**32.**　$\begin{array}{r} 373 \\ + 86 \\ \hline \end{array}$

33.　$\begin{array}{r} 62 \\ \times 42 \\ \hline \end{array}$　　　**34.**　$\begin{array}{r} 122 \\ \times 15 \\ \hline \end{array}$　　　**35.** $7\overline{)623}$　　　**36.** $24\overline{)149}$

Study Guide: Preview

Where You've Been

Previously, you

- used order of operations to simplify whole number expressions without exponents.

- used multiplication and division to solve problems involving whole numbers.

In This Chapter

You will study

- simplifying numerical expressions involving order of operations and exponents.

- using variables and symbols to translate words into math.

- simplifying algebraic expressions using properties of addition and multiplication.

Where You're Going

You can use the skills learned in this chapter

- to evaluate expressions.

- to solve problems in math and science classes such as Algebra and Physics.

Key Vocabulary/Vocabulario

algebraic expression	expresión algebraica
Associative Property	propiedad asociativa
Commutative Property	propiedad conmutativa
Distributive Property	propiedad distributiva
numerical expression	expresión numérica
order of operations	orden de las operaciones
term	término
variable	variable

Vocabulary Connections

To become familiar with some of the vocabulary terms in the chapter, consider the following. You may refer to the chapter, the glossary, or a dictionary if you like.

1. The word *numerical* means "of numbers." How might a **numerical expression** differ from an expression such as "the sum of two and five"?

2. When something is *variable,* it has the ability to change. In mathematics, a **variable** is an algebraic symbol. What special property do you think this type of symbol has?

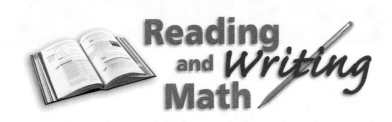 

Reading Strategy: Use Your Book for Success

Understanding how your textbook is organized will help you locate and use helpful information.

As you read through an example problem, pay attention to the **margin notes**, such as Helpful Hints, Reading Math notes, and Caution notes. These notes will help you understand concepts and avoid common mistakes.

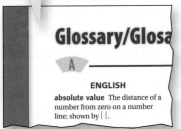

Reading Math

Read -4^3 as "-4 to the 3rd power or -4 cubed".

Writing Math

A repeating decimal can be written with a bar over the digits that repeat. So

Helpful Hint

In Example 1A, parentheses are not needed because multiplication is

Caution!

An open circle means that the corresponding value not a solution. A sol

The **glossary** is found in the back of your textbook. Use it to find definitions and examples of unfamiliar words or properties.

The **index** is located at the end of your textbook. Use it to find the page where a particular concept is taught.

The **Skills Bank** is found in the back of your textbook. These pages review concepts from previous math courses.

Glossary/Glosa

A

ENGLISH

absolute value The distance of a number from zero on a number line; shown by | |.

Index . . .

A

Absolute value, 73
Accuracy, 524
Acute angles, 454

Skills Bank . . .

Read and Write D

When reading and writing a dec to know the place value of the d

Try This

Use your textbook for the following problems.

1. Use the index to find the page where *variable* is defined.

2. Use the glossary to find the definition of the term *numerical expression*.

3. Where can you review how to read and write decimals?

Reading and Writing Math

Mastering *the* Standards

for Mathematical Practice

The topics described in the Standards for Mathematical Content will vary from year to year. However, the *way* in which you learn, study, and think about mathematics will not. The Standards for Mathematical Practice describe skills that you will use in all of your math courses.

Mathematical Practices

1. *Make sense of problems and persevere in solving them.*
2. *Reason abstractly and quantitatively.*
3. *Construct viable arguments and critique the reasoning of others.*
4. *Model with mathematics.*
5. *Use appropriate tools strategically.*
6. *Attend to precision.*
7. *Look for and make use of structure.*
8. *Look for and express regularity in repeated reasoning.*

1 Make sense of problems and persevere in solving them.

Mathematically proficient students start by explaining to themselves the meaning of a problem... They analyze givens, constraints, relationships, and goals. They make conjectures about the form... of the solution and plan a solution pathway...

In your book

Focus on Problem Solving describes a four-step plan for problem solving. The plan is introduced at the beginning of your book, and practice with the plan appears throughout the book.

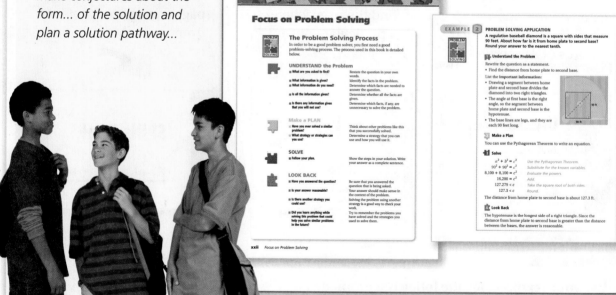

Getty Images/PhotoDisc

1-1 Order of Operations

To assemble the correct product, directions must be followed in the correct order. In mathematics, some tasks must also be done in a certain order.

A **numerical expression** is made up of numbers and operations. When simplifying a numerical expression, rules must be followed so that everyone gets the same answer. That is why mathematicians have agreed upon the **order of operations** .

Vocabulary

numerical expression

order of operations

Interactivities Online ▶

ORDER OF OPERATIONS

1. Perform operations within grouping symbols.
2. Evaluate powers.
3. Multiply and divide in order from left to right.
4. Add and subtract in order from left to right.

EXAMPLE 1 **Using the Order of Operations**

Simplify each expression. Use the order of operations to justify your answer.

A $27 - 18 \div 6$

$27 - 18 \div 6$ *Divide.*

$27 - 3$ *Subtract.*

24

B $36 - 18 \div 2 \cdot 3 + 8$

$36 - 18 \div 2 \cdot 3 + 8$ *Divide and multiply from left to right.*

$36 - 9 \cdot 3 + 8$

$36 - 27 + 8$ *Subtract and add from left to right.*

$9 + 8$

17

C $5 + 6^2 \cdot 10$

$5 + 6^2 \cdot 10$ *Evaluate the power.*

$5 + 36 \cdot 10$ *Multiply.*

$5 + 360$ *Add.*

365

EXAMPLE 2 **Using the Order of Operations with Grouping Symbols**

Simplify each expression.

A $36 - (2 \cdot 6) \div 3$

$36 - (2 \cdot 6) \div 3$	*Perform the operation in parentheses.*
$36 - 12 \div 3$	*Divide.*
$36 - 4$	*Subtract.*
32	

Helpful Hint

When an expression has a set of grouping symbols within a second set of grouping symbols, begin with the innermost set.

B $[(4 + 12 \div 4) - 2]^3$

$[(4 + 12 \div 4) - 2]^3$	*The parentheses are inside the brackets,*
$[(4 + 3) - 2]^3$	*so perform the operations inside the*
$[7 - 2]^3$	*parentheses first.*
5^3	
125	

EXAMPLE 3 *Career Application*

Maria works part-time in a law office, where she earns $20 per hour. The table shows the number of hours she worked last week. Simplify the expression $(6 + 5 \cdot 3) \cdot 20$ to find out how much money Maria earned last week.

Day	Hours
Monday	6
Tuesday	5
Wednesday	5
Thursday	5

$(6 + 5 \cdot 3) \cdot 20$	*Perform the operations in parentheses.*
$(6 + 15) \cdot 20$	*Add.*
$21 \cdot 20$	*Multiply.*
420	

Maria earned $420 last week.

MATHEMATICAL PRACTICES

Think and Discuss

1. **Apply** the order of operations to determine if the expressions $3 + 4^2$ and $(3 + 4)^2$ have the same value.

2. **Give** the correct order of operations for simplifying $(5 + 3 \cdot 20) \div 13 + 3^2$.

3. **Determine** where grouping symbols should be inserted in the expression $3 + 9 - 4 \cdot 2$ so that its value is 13.

Video Lesson Tutorials Online my.hrw.com

Learn It Online
Homework Help Online
Exercises 1–18, 21, 23, 27, 29, 33, 35, 37

GUIDED PRACTICE

See Example **1** Simplify each expression. Use the order of operations to justify your answer.

1. $43 + 16 \div 4$　　**2.** $28 - 4 \cdot 3 \div 6 + 4$　　**3.** $25 - 4^2 \div 8$

See Example **2** **4.** $26 - (7 \cdot 3) + 2$　　**5.** $(3^2 + 11) \div 5$　　**6.** $32 + 6(4 - 2^2) + 8$

See Example **3** **7. Career** Caleb earns $10 per hour. He worked 4 hours on Monday, Wednesday, and Friday. He worked 8 hours on Tuesday and Thursday. Simplify the expression $(3 \cdot 4 + 2 \cdot 8) \cdot 10$ to find out how much Caleb earned in all.

INDEPENDENT PRACTICE

See Example **1** Simplify each expression. Use the order of operations to justify your answer.

8. $3 + 7 \cdot 5 - 1$　　**9.** $5 \cdot 9 - 3$　　**10.** $3 - 2 + 6 \cdot 2^2$

See Example **2** **11.** $(3 \cdot 3 - 3)^2 \div 3 + 3$　　**12.** $2^5 - (4 \cdot 5 + 3)$　　**13.** $(3 \div 3) + 3 \cdot (3^3 - 3)$

14. $4^3 \div 8 - 2$　　**15.** $(8 - 2)^2 \cdot (8 - 1)^2 \div 3$　　**16.** $9{,}234 \div [3 \cdot 3(1 + 8^3)]$

See Example **3** **17. Consumer Math** Maki paid a $14 basic fee plus $25 a day to rent a car. Simplify the expression $14 + 5 \cdot 25$ to find out how much it cost her to rent the car for 5 days.

18. Consumer Math Enrico spent $20 per square yard for carpet and $35 for a carpet pad. Simplify the expression $35 + 20(12^2 \div 9)$ to find out how much Enrico spent to carpet a 12 ft by 12 ft room.

PRACTICE AND PROBLEM SOLVING

Extra Practice
See Extra Practice for more exercises.

Simplify each expression.

19. $90 - 36 \times 2$　　**20.** $16 + 14 \div 2 - 7$　　**21.** $64 \div 2^2 + 4$

22. $(4.5 \times 10^2) + (6 \div 3)$　　**23.** $(9 - 4)^2 - 12 \times 2$　　**24.** $[1 + (2 + 5)^2] \times 2$

Compare. Write $<$, $>$, or $=$.

25. $8 \cdot 3 - 2$ ▉ $8 \cdot (3 - 2)$　　**26.** $(6 + 10) \div 2$ ▉ $6 + 10 \div 2$

27. $12 \div 3 \cdot 4$ ▉ $12 \div (3 \cdot 4)$　　**28.** $18 + 6 - 2$ ▉ $18 + (6 - 2)$

29. $[6(8 - 3) + 2]$ ▉ $6(8 - 3) + 2$　　**30.** $(18 - 14) \div (2 + 2)$ ▉ $18 - 14 \div 2 + 2$

Critical Thinking Insert grouping symbols to make each statement true.

31. $4 \cdot 8 - 3 = 20$　　**32.** $5 + 9 - 3 \div 2 = 8$　　**33.** $12 - 2^2 \div 5 = 20$

34. $4 \cdot 2 + 6 = 32$　　**35.** $4 + 6 - 3 \div 7 = 1$　　**36.** $9 \cdot 8 - 6 \div 3 = 6$

37. Bertha earned $8.00 per hour for 4 hours babysitting and $10.00 per hour for 5 hours painting a room. Simplify the expression $8 \cdot 4 + 10 \cdot 5$ to find out how much Bertha earned in all.

38. Consumer Math Mike bought a painting for $512. He sold it at an antique auction for 4 times the amount that he paid for it, and then he purchased another painting with half of the profit that he made. Simplify the expression $(512 \cdot 4 - 512) \div 2$ to find how much Mike paid for the second painting.

39. Multi-Step Anelise bought four shirts and two pairs of jeans. She paid $6 in sales tax.

   a. Write an expression that shows how much she spent on shirts.

   b. Write an expression that shows how much she spent on jeans.

   c. Write and evaluate an expression to show how much she spent on clothes, including sales tax.

40. Choose a Strategy There are four children in a family. The sum of the squares of the ages of the three youngest children equals the square of the age of the oldest child. How old are the children?

   Ⓐ 1, 4, 8, 9   Ⓑ 1, 3, 6, 12   Ⓒ 4, 5, 8, 10   Ⓓ 2, 3, 8, 16

41. Write About It Describe the order in which you would perform the operations to find the correct value of $[(2 + 4)^2 - 2 \cdot 3] \div 6$.

42. Challenge Use the numbers 3, 5, 6, 2, 54, and 5 in that order to write an expression that has a value of 100.

Test Prep

43. Multiple Choice Which operation should be performed first to simplify the expression $18 - 1 \cdot 9 \div 3 + 8$?

   Ⓐ Addition   Ⓑ Subtraction   Ⓒ Multiplication   Ⓓ Division

44. Multiple Choice Which expression does NOT simplify to 81?

   Ⓕ $9 \cdot (4 + 5)$ Ⓖ $7 + 16 \cdot 4 + 10$ Ⓗ $3 \cdot 25 + 2$ Ⓙ $10^2 - 4 \cdot 5 + 1$

45. Multiple Choice Quinton bought 2 pairs of jeans for $30 each and 3 pairs of socks for $5 each. Which expression can be simplified to determine the total amount Quinton paid for the jeans and socks?

   Ⓐ $2 \cdot 3(30 + 5)$ Ⓑ $(2 + 3) \cdot (30 + 5)$ Ⓒ $2 \cdot (30 + 5) \cdot 3$ Ⓓ $2 \cdot 30 + 3 \cdot 5$

Explore Order of Operations

Use with Order of Operations

MATHEMATICAL PRACTICES Use appropriate tools strategically.

> **REMEMBER**
>
> The order of operations
> 1. Perform operations within grouping symbols.
> 2. Evaluate powers.
> 3. Multiply and divide in order from left to right.
> 4. Add and subtract in order from left to right.

Many calculators have an key that allows you to find the square of a number. On calculators that do not have this key, or to use exponents other than 2, you can use the caret key, ∧ .

For example, to evaluate 3^5, press 3 ∧ 5, and then press ENTER .

Activity

1 Simplify $4 \cdot 2^3$ using paper and pencil. Then check your answer with a calculator.

First simplify the expression using paper and pencil:
$4 \cdot 2^3 = 4 \cdot 8 = 32$.

Then simplify $4 \cdot 2^3$ using your calculator.

Notice that the calculator automatically evaluates the power first. If you want to perform the multiplication first, you must put that operation inside parentheses.

2 Use a calculator to simplify $\dfrac{(2 + 5 \cdot 4)^3}{4^2}$.

Think and Discuss

1. Is $2 + 5 \cdot 4^3 + 4^2$ equivalent to $(2 + 5 \cdot 4^3) + 4^2$? Explain.

Try This

Simplify each expression with pencil and paper. Check your answers with a calculator.

1. $3 \cdot 2^3 + 5$　　**2.** $3 \cdot (2^3 + 5)$　　**3.** $(3 \cdot 2)^2$　　**4.** $3 \cdot 2^2$　　**5.** $2^{(3 \cdot 2)}$

Use a calculator to simplify each expression. Round your answers to the nearest hundredth.

6. $(2.1 + 5.6 \cdot 4^3) \div 6^4$　　**7.** $[(2.1 + 5.6) \cdot 4^3] \div 6^4$　　**8.** $[(8.6 - 1.5) \div 2^3] \div 5^2$

Properties of Numbers

CC.7.NS.1 Apply and extend previous understandings of addition and subtraction to add and subtract rational numbers; represent addition and subtraction on a horizontal or vertical number line diagram. *Also CC.7.NS.1d, CC.7.EE.3*

In the previous lesson you learned how to use the order of operations to simplify numerical expressions. The following properties of numbers are also useful when you simplify expressions.

Commutative Property		
Words	**Numbers**	**Algebra**
You can add numbers in any order and multiply numbers in any order.	$3 + 8 = 8 + 3$ $5 \cdot 7 = 7 \cdot 5$	$a + b = b + a$ $ab = ba$

Associative Property		
Words	**Numbers**	**Algebra**
When you add or multiply, you can group the numbers together in any combination.	$(4 + 5) + 1 = 4 + (5 + 1)$ $(9 \cdot 2) \cdot 6 = 9 \cdot (2 \cdot 6)$	$(a + b) + c = a + (b + c)$ $(a \cdot b) \cdot c = a \cdot (b \cdot c)$

Identity Property		
Words	**Numbers**	**Algebra**
The sum of 0 and any number is the number. The product of 1 and any number is the number.	$4 + 0 = 4$ $8 \cdot 1 = 8$	$a + 0 = a$ $a \cdot 1 = a$

Vocabulary

Commutative Property

Associative Property

Identity Property

Distributive Property

EXAMPLE 1 **Identifying Properties of Addition and Multiplication**

Tell which property is represented.

A $2 + (7 + 8) = (2 + 7) + 8$

$2 + (7 + 8) = (2 + 7) + 8$ *The numbers are regrouped.*

Associative Property

B $25 \cdot 1 = 25$

$25 \cdot 1 = 25$ *One of the factors is 1.*

Identity Property

C $xy = yx$

$xy = yx$ *The order of the variables is switched.*

Commutative Property

   Video **Lesson Tutorials Online** my.hrw.com

You can use properties and mental math to rearrange or regroup numbers into combinations that are easier to work with.

EXAMPLE 2 **Using Properties to Simplify Expressions**

Simplify each expression. Justify each step.

A $12 + 19 + 18$

$12 + 19 + 18 = 19 + 12 + 18$	*Commutative Property*
$= 19 + (12 + 18)$	*Associative Property*
$= 19 + 30$	*Add.*
$= 49$	

B $25 \cdot 13 \cdot 4$

$25 \cdot 13 \cdot 4 = 25 \cdot 4 \cdot 13$	*Commutative Property*
$= (25 \cdot 4) \cdot 13$	*Associative Property*
$= 100 \cdot 13$	*Multiply.*
$= 1{,}300$	

You can use the Distributive Property to multiply numbers mentally by breaking apart one of the numbers and writing it as a sum or difference.

Remember!

Multiplication can be written as $a(b + c)$ or $a \cdot (b + c)$.

Distributive Property		
Numbers	$6(9 + 14) = 6 \cdot 9 + 6 \cdot 14$	$8(5 - 2) = 8 \cdot 5 - 8 \cdot 2$
Algebra	$a(b + c) = ab + ac$	$a(b - c) = ab - ac$

EXAMPLE 3 **Using the Distributive Property to Multiply Mentally**

Use the Distributive Property to find $7(29)$.

Method 1

$7(29) = 7(20 + 9)$	*Rewrite 29.*
$= (7 \cdot 20) + (7 \cdot 9)$	*Use the Distributive Property.*
$= 140 + 63$	*Multiply.*
$= 203$	*Simplify.*

Method 2

$7(29) = 7(30 - 1)$
$= (7 \cdot 30) - (7 \cdot 1)$
$= 210 - 7$
$= 203$

MATHEMATICAL PRACTICES

Think and Discuss

1. Describe two different ways to simplify the expression $7 \cdot (3 + 9)$.

2. Explain how the Distributive Property can help you find $6 \cdot 102$ using mental math.

Learn It Online
Homework Help Online
Exercises 1–36, 41, 47, 49, 51, 53

GUIDED PRACTICE

See Example 1 — Tell which property is represented.

1. $1 + (6 + 7) = (1 + 6) + 7$ **2.** $1 \cdot 10 = 10$ **3.** $3 \cdot 5 = 5 \cdot 3$

4. $6 + 0 = 6$ **5.** $4 \cdot (4 \cdot 2) = (4 \cdot 4) \cdot 2$ **6.** $x + y = y + x$

See Example 2 — Simplify each expression. Justify each step.

7. $8 + 23 + 2$ **8.** $2 \cdot (17 \cdot 5)$ **9.** $(25 \cdot 11) \cdot 4$

10. $17 + 29 + 3$ **11.** $16 + (17 + 14)$ **12.** $5 \cdot 19 \cdot 20$

See Example 3 — Use the Distributive Property to find each product.

13. $2(19)$ **14.** $5(31)$ **15.** $(22)2$

16. $(13)6$ **17.** $8(26)$ **18.** $(34)6$

INDEPENDENT PRACTICE

See Example 1 — Tell which property is represented.

19. $1 + 0 = 1$ **20.** $xyz = x \cdot (yz)$ **21.** $9 + (9 + 0) = (9 + 9) + 0$

22. $11 + 25 = 25 + 11$ **23.** $7 \cdot 1 = 7$ **24.** $16 \cdot 4 = 4 \cdot 16$

See Example 2 — Simplify each expression. Justify each step.

25. $50 \cdot 16 \cdot 2$ **26.** $9 + 34 + 1$ **27.** $4 \cdot (25 \cdot 9)$

28. $27 + 28 + 3$ **29.** $20 + (63 + 80)$ **30.** $25 + 17 + 75$

See Example 3 — Use the Distributive Property to find each product.

31. $9(15)$ **32.** $(14)5$ **33.** $3(58)$

34. $10(42)$ **35.** $(23)4$ **36.** $(16)5$

PRACTICE AND PROBLEM SOLVING

Extra Practice
See Extra Practice for more exercises.

Write an example of each property using whole numbers.

37. Commutative Property **38.** Identity Property

39. Associative Property **40.** Distributive Property

41. Architecture The figure shows the floor plan for a studio loft. To find the area of the loft, the architect multiplies the length and the width: $(14 + 8) \cdot 10$. Use the Distributive Property to find the area of the loft.

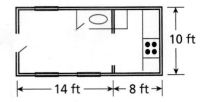

10 ft

14 ft — 8 ft

Simplify each expression. Justify each step.

42. $32 + 26 + 43$ **43.** $50 \cdot 45 \cdot 2^2$ **44.** $5 + 16 + 5^2$ **45.** $35 \cdot 25 \cdot 20$

Complete each equation. Then tell which property is represented.

46. $5 + 16 = 16 + \blacksquare$

47. $15 \cdot 1 = \blacksquare$

48. $\blacksquare \cdot (4 + 7) = 3 \cdot 4 + 3 \cdot 7$

49. $20 + \blacksquare = 20$

50. $2 \cdot \blacksquare \cdot 9 = (2 \cdot 13) \cdot 9$

51. $8 + (\blacksquare + 4) = (8 + 8) + 4$

52. $2 \cdot (6 + 1) = 2 \cdot \blacksquare + 2 \cdot 1$

53. $(12 - 9) \cdot \blacksquare = 12 \cdot 2 - 9 \cdot 2$

54. **Sports** Janice wants to know the total number of games won by the Denver Nuggets basketball team over the three seasons shown in the table. What expression should she simplify? Explain how she can use mental math and the properties of this lesson to simplify the expression.

Denver Nuggets		
Season	Won	Lost
2001–02	27	55
2002–03	17	65
2003–04	43	39

 55. **What's the Error?** A student simplified the expression $6 \cdot (9 + 12)$ as shown. What is the student's error?

$$6 \cdot (9 + 12) = 6 \cdot 9 + 12$$
$$= 54 + 12$$
$$= 66$$

 56. **Write About It** Do you think there is a Commutative Property of Subtraction? Give an example to justify your answer.

57. **Challenge** Use the Distributive Property to simplify $\frac{1}{6} \cdot (36 + \frac{1}{2})$.

Test Prep

58. **Multiple Choice** Which is an example of the Associative Property?

Ⓐ $4 + 0 = 4$

Ⓒ $5 + 7 = 7 + 5$

Ⓑ $9 + 8 + 2 = 9 + (8 + 2)$

Ⓓ $5 \cdot (12 + 3) = 5 \cdot 12 + 5 \cdot 3$

59. **Multiple Choice** Which property is $2 \cdot (3 + 7) = (2 \cdot 3) + (2 \cdot 7)$ an example of?

Ⓕ Associative   Ⓖ Commutative   Ⓗ Distributive   Ⓙ Identity

60. **Short Response** Show how to use the Distributive Property to simplify the expression $8(27)$.

Ready To Go On?

Learn It Online
Resources Online

Quiz for Lesson 1 and 2

 1 Order of Operations

Simplify each expression.

1. $3 + 18 \div 3$ **2.** $(3 + 18) \div 3$

3. $8 - 14 \div (9 - 2)$ **4.** $54 - 6 \cdot 3 + 4^2$

5. $4 - 24 \div 2^3$ **6.** $4(3 + 2)^2 - 9$

7. The seven members of a costume crew made 30 costumes for a school play. Two of the members had volunteered to make five costumes each. Use the expression $(30 - 2 \cdot 5) \div 5$ to find the number of costumes each of the remaining members made.

2 Properties of Numbers

Tell which property is represented.

8. $2 \cdot 3 = 3 \cdot 2$ **9.** $17 + (3 + 1) = (17 + 3) + 1$

10. $5(3 + 8) = 5 \cdot 3 + 5 \cdot 8$ **11.** $y \cdot 1 = y$

Simplify each expression. Justify each step.

12. $29 + 50 + 21$ **13.** $5 \cdot 18 \cdot 20$

14. $34 + 62 + 36$ **15.** $3 \cdot 11 \cdot 20$

16. Use the Distributive Property to find the product $14(11)$.

Focus on Problem Solving

 Solve

• **Choose an operation: multiplication or division**

To solve a word problem, you must determine which mathematical operation you can use to find the answer. One way of doing this is to determine the action the problem is asking you to take. If you are putting equal parts together, then you need to multiply. If you are separating something into equal parts, then you need to divide.

Decide what action each problem is asking you to take, and tell whether you must multiply or divide. Then explain your decision.

1 Judy plays the flute in the band. She practices for 3 hours every week. Judy practices only half as long as Angie, who plays the clarinet. How long does Angie practice playing the clarinet each week?

2 Each year, members of the band and choir are invited to join the bell ensemble for the winter performance. There are 18 bells in the bell ensemble. This year, each student has 3 bells to play. How many students are in the bell ensemble this year?

3 For every percussion instrument in the band, there are 4 wind instruments. If there are 48 wind instruments in the band, how many percussion instruments are there?

4 A group of 4 people singing together in harmony is called a quartet. At a state competition for high school choir students, 7 quartets from different schools competed. How many students competed in the quartet competition?

Variables and Algebraic Expressions

Harrison Ford was born in 1942. You can find out what year Harrison turned 18 by adding 18 to the year he was born.

$$1942 + 18$$

Vocabulary
variable

constant

algebraic expression

evaluate

In algebra, letters are often used to represent numbers. You can use a letter such as *a* to represent Harrison Ford's age. When he turns *a* years old, the year will be

$$1942 + a.$$

The letter *a* has a value that can change, or vary. When a letter represents a number that can vary, it is called a **variable**. The year 1942 is a **constant** because the number cannot change.

An **algebraic expression** consists of one or more variables. It usually contains constants and operations. For example, $1942 + a$ is an algebraic expression for the year Harrison Ford turns a certain age.

Age	Year born + age	= year at age
18	1942 + 18	1960
25	1942 + 25	1967
36	1942 + 36	1978
63	1942 + 63	2005
a	1942 + *a*	

To **evaluate** an algebraic expression, substitute a number for the variable.

EXAMPLE 1 Evaluating Algebraic Expressions

Evaluate $n + 7$ for each value of *n*.

A $n = 3$
$$n + 7$$
$$3 + 7 \qquad \textit{Substitute 3 for n.}$$
$$10 \qquad \textit{Add.}$$

Interactivities Online ▶

B $n = 5$
$$n + 7$$
$$5 + 7 \qquad \textit{Substitute 5 for n.}$$
$$12 \qquad \textit{Add.}$$

Video **Lesson Tutorials Online** my.hrw.com

Multiplication and division of variables can be written in several ways, as shown in the table.

When evaluating expressions, use the order of operations.

Multiplication		Division	
$7t$	$7 \cdot t$	$\dfrac{q}{2}$	$q/2$
$7(t)$	$7 \times t$	$q \div 2$	
ab	$a \cdot b$	$\dfrac{s}{r}$	s/r
$a(b)$	$a \times b$	$s \div r$	

EXAMPLE 2 **Evaluating Algebraic Expressions Involving Order of Operations**

Evaluate each expression for the given value of the variable.

A $3x - 2$ for $x = 5$

$3(5) - 2$	*Substitute 5 for x.*
$15 - 2$	*Multiply.*
13	*Subtract*

B $n \div 2 + n$ for $n = 4$

$4 \div 2 + 4$	*Substitute 4 for n.*
$2 + 4$	*Divide.*
6	*Add.*

C $6y^2 + 2y$ for $y = 2$

$6(2)^2 + 2(2)$	*Substitute 2 for y.*
$6(4) + 2(2)$	*Evaluate the power.*
$24 + 4$	*Multiply.*
28	*Add.*

EXAMPLE 3 **Evaluating Algebraic Expressions with Two Variables**

Evaluate $\dfrac{3}{n} + 2m$ for $n = 3$ and $m = 4$.

$\dfrac{3}{n} + 2m$	
$\dfrac{3}{3} + 2(4)$	*Substitute 3 for n and 4 for m.*
$1 + 8$	*Divide and multiply from left to right.*
9	*Add.*

Think and Discuss

1. Write each expression another way. **a.** $12x$ **b.** $\dfrac{4}{y}$ **c.** $\dfrac{3xy}{2}$

2. Explain the difference between a variable and a constant.

GUIDED PRACTICE

See Example **1** Evaluate $n + 9$ for each value of n.

1. $n = 3$ **2.** $n = 2$ **3.** $n = 11$

See Example **2** Evaluate each expression for the given value of the variable.

4. $2x - 3$ for $x = 4$ **5.** $n \div 3 + n$ for $n = 6$ **6.** $5y^2 + 3y$ for $y = 2$

See Example **3** Evaluate each expression for the given values of the variables.

7. $\frac{8}{n} + 3m$ for $n = 2$ and $m = 5$ **8.** $5a - 3b + 5$ for $a = 4$ and $b = 3$

INDEPENDENT PRACTICE

See Example **1** Evaluate $n + 5$ for each value of n.

9. $n = 17$ **10.** $n = 9$ **11.** $n = 0$

See Example **2** Evaluate each expression for the given value of the variable.

12. $5y - 1$ for $y = 3$ **13.** $10b - 9$ for $b = 2$ **14.** $p \div 7 + p$ for $p = 14$

15. $n \div 5 + n$ for $n = 20$ **16.** $3x^2 + 2x$ for $x = 10$ **17.** $3c^2 - 5c$ for $c = 3$

See Example **3** Evaluate each expression for the given values of the variables.

18. $\frac{12}{n} + 7m$ for $n = 6$ and $m = 4$ **19.** $7p - 2t + 3$ for $p = 6$ and $t = 2$

20. $9 - \frac{3x}{4} + 20y$ for $x = 4$ and $y = 5$ **21.** $r^2 + 15k$ for $r = 15$ and $k = 5$

PRACTICE AND PROBLEM SOLVING

Extra Practice
See Extra Practice for more exercises.

Evaluate each expression for the given values of the variables.

22. $20x - 10$ for $x = 4$ **23.** $4d^2 - 3d$ for $d = 2$

24. $22p \div 11 + p$ for $p = 3$ **25.** $q + q^2 + q \div 2$ for $q = 4$

26. $\frac{16}{k} + 7h$ for $k = 8$ and $h = 2$ **27.** $f \div 3 + f$ for $f = 18$

28. $3t \div 3 + t$ for $t = 13$ **29.** $9 + 3p - 5t + 3$ for $p = 2$ and $t = 1$

30. $108 - 12j + j$ for $j = 9$ **31.** $3m^3 + \frac{y}{5}$ for $m = 2$ and $y = 35$

32. The expression $60m$ gives the number of seconds in m minutes. Evaluate $60m$ for $m = 7$. How many seconds are there in 7 minutes?

33. **Money** Betsy has n quarters. You can use the expression $0.25n$ to find the total value of her coins in dollars. What is the value of 18 quarters?

34. **Physical Science** A color TV has a power rating of 200 watts. The expression $200t$ gives the power used by t color TV sets. Evaluate $200t$ for $t = 13$. How much power is used by 13 TV sets?

35. Physical Science The expression $1.8c + 32$ can be used to convert a temperature in degrees Celsius c to degrees Fahrenheit. What is the temperature in degrees Fahrenheit if the temperature is 30 °C?

36. Physical Science The graph shows the changes of state for water.

    a. What is the boiling point of water in degrees Celsius?

    b. Use the expression $1.8c + 32$ to find the boiling point of water in degrees Fahrenheit.

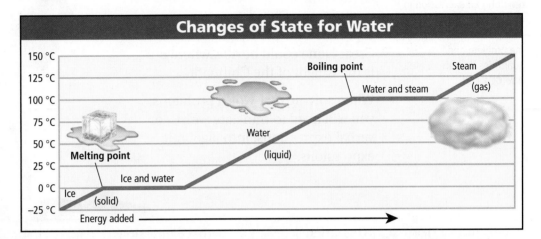

37. What's the Error? A student was asked to identify the variable in the expression $72x + 8$. The student answered $72x$. What was the student's error?

38. Write About It Explain why letters such as x, p, and n used in algebraic expressions are called variables. Use examples to illustrate your response.

39. Challenge Evaluate the expression $\frac{x + y}{y - x}$ for $x = 6$ and $y = 8$.

Test Prep

40. Multiple Choice Which expression does NOT equal 15?

   Ⓐ $3t$ for $t = 5$ Ⓑ $3 + t$ for $t = 12$ Ⓒ $t \div 3$ for $t = 60$ Ⓓ $t - 10$ for $t = 25$

41. Multiple Choice A group of 11 students go rock climbing at a local gym. It costs $12 per student plus $4 for each shoe rental. If only 8 students rent shoes, what is the total cost for the group to go climbing? Use the expression $12x + 4y$, where x represents the total number of students and y represents the number of students who rent shoes.

   Ⓕ $132   Ⓖ $140   Ⓗ $164   Ⓙ $176

1-4 Translating Words into Math

CC.7.EE.2 Understand that rewriting an expression in different forms in a problem context can shed light on the problem and how the quantities in it are related.
Also CC.7.EE.4

Although they are closely related, a Great Dane weighs about 40 times as much as a Chihuahua. An expression for the weight of the Great Dane could be 40*c*, where *c* is the weight of the Chihuahua.

When solving real-world problems, you will need to translate words, or verbal expressions, into algebraic expressions.

Interactivities Online ▶

Operation	Verbal Expressions	Algebraic Expression
➕	• add 3 to a number • a number plus 3 • the sum of a number and 3 • 3 more than a number • a number increased by 3	$n + 3$
➖	• subtract 12 from a number • a number minus 12 • the difference of a number and 12 • 12 less than a number • a number decreased by 12 • take away 12 from a number • a number less 12	$x - 12$
✖	• 2 times a number • 2 multiplied by a number • the product of 2 and a number	$2m$ or $2 \cdot m$
➗	• 6 divided into a number • a number divided by 6 • the quotient of a number and 6	$a \div 6$ or $\frac{a}{6}$

EXAMPLE 1 Translating Verbal Expressions into Algebraic Expressions

Write each phrase as an algebraic expression.

A the product of 20 and *t*

product means "multiply"

$20t$

B 24 less than a number

less than means "subtract from"

$n - 24$

Video Lesson Tutorials Online my.hrw.com

moodboard/Alamy

Write each phrase as an algebraic expression.

C 4 times the sum of a number and 2

4 times the sum of a number and 2

4 · $n + 2$

$4(n + 2)$

D the sum of 4 times a number and 2

the sum of 4 times a number and 2

4 · n $+ 2$

$4n + 2$

When solving real-world problems, you may need to determine the action to know which operation to use.

Action	Operation
Put parts together	Add
Put equal parts together	Multiply
Find how much more or less	Subtract
Separate into equal parts	Divide

 EXAMPLE 2 **Translating Real-World Problems into Algebraic Expressions**

A Jed reads *p* pages each day of a 200-page book. Write an algebraic expression for how many days it will take Jed to read the book.

You need to *separate* the total number of pages *into equal parts*. This involves division.

$$\frac{\text{total number of pages}}{\text{pages read each day}} = \frac{200}{p}$$

B To rent a certain car for a day costs \$84 plus \$0.29 for every mile the car is driven. Write an algebraic expression to show how much it costs to rent the car for a day.

The cost includes \$0.29 per mile. Use *m* for the number of miles.

Multiply to *put equal parts together:* $0.29m$

In addition to the fee per mile, the cost includes a flat fee of \$84.

Add to *put parts together:* $84 + 0.29m$

MATHEMATICAL PRACTICES

Think and Discuss

1. Write three different verbal expressions that can be represented by $2 - y$.

2. Explain how you would determine which operation to use to find the number of chairs in 6 rows of 100 chairs each.

Exercises

Learn It Online
Homework Help Online
Exercises 1–13, 15, 17, 19, 21, 23, 25, 31

GUIDED PRACTICE

See Example **1**   **Write each phrase as an algebraic expression.**

1. the product of 7 and p

2. 3 less than a number

3. 12 divided into a number

4. 3 times the sum of a number and 5

See Example **2**   **5.** Carly spends $5 for n notebooks. Write an algebraic expression to represent the cost of one notebook.

6. A company charges $46 for cable TV installation and $21 per month for basic cable service. Write an algebraic expression to represent the total cost of m months of basic cable service, including installation.

INDEPENDENT PRACTICE

See Example **1**   **Write each phrase as an algebraic expression.**

7. the sum of 5 and a number

8. 2 less than a number

9. the quotient of a number and 8

10. 9 times a number

11. 10 less than the product of a number and 3

See Example **2**   **12.** Video Express sells used tapes. Marta bought v tapes for $45. Write an algebraic expression for the average cost of each tape.

13. A 5-foot pine tree was planted and grew 2 feet each year. Write an algebraic expression for the height of the tree after t years.

PRACTICE AND PROBLEM SOLVING

Extra Practice
See Extra Practice for more exercises.

Write each phrase as an algebraic expression.

14. m plus the product of 6 and n

15. the quotient of 23 and u minus t

16. 14 less than the quantity k times 6

17. 2 times the sum of y and 5

18. the quotient of 100 and the quantity 6 plus w

19. 35 multiplied by the quantity r less 45

20. **Multi-Step** An ice machine can produce 17 pounds of ice in one hour.

    a. Write an algebraic expression to describe the number of pounds of ice produced in n hours.

    b. How many pounds of ice can the machine produce in 4 hours?

21. **Career** Karen earns $65,000 a year as an optometrist. She received a bonus of b dollars last year and expects to get double that amount as a bonus this year. Write an algebraic expression to show the total amount Karen expects to earn this year.

Reddish-brown spots appear on the leaves and fruit of plants infested by rust mites.

Write a verbal expression for each algebraic expression.

22. $h + 3$ **23.** $90 \div y$ **24.** $s - 405$ **25.** $16t$

26. $5(a - 8)$ **27.** $4p - 10$ **28.** $(r + 1) \div 14$ **29.** $\frac{m}{15} + 3$

30. Life Science Tiny and harmless, follicle mites live in our eyebrows and eyelashes. They are relatives of spiders and like spiders, they have eight legs. Write an algebraic expression for the number of legs in m mites.

Nutrition The table shows the estimated number of grams of carbohydrates commonly found in various types of foods.

Food	Carbohydrates
1 c skim milk	12 g
1 piece of fruit	15 g
1 slice of bread	15 g
1 oz lean meat	0 g

31. Write an algebraic expression for the number of grams of carbohydrates in y pieces of fruit and 1 cup of skim milk.

32. How many grams of carbohydrates are in a sandwich made from t ounces of lean meat and 2 slices of bread?

33. What's the Question? Al has twice as many baseball cards as Frank and four times as many football cards as Joe. The expression $2x + 4y$ can be used to show the total number of baseball and football cards Al has. If the answer is y, then what is the question?

34. Write About It If you are asked to compare two numbers, what two operations might you use? Why?

35. Challenge In 2006, one U.S. dollar was equivalent, on average, to $1.134 in Canadian dollars. Write an algebraic expression for the number of U.S. dollars you could get for n Canadian dollars.

Test Prep

36. Multiple Choice Which verbal expression does NOT represent $9 - x$?

Ⓐ x less than nine

Ⓒ subtract x from nine

Ⓑ x decreased by nine

Ⓓ the difference of nine and x

37. Short Response A room at the Oak Creek Inn costs $104 per night for two people. There is a $19 charge for each extra person. Write an algebraic expression that shows the cost per night for a family of four staying at the inn. Then evaluate your expression for 3 nights.

Simplifying Algebraic Expressions

COMMON CORE

CC.7.EE.1 Apply properties of operations as strategies to add, subtract, factor, and expand linear expressions with rational coefficients.
Also CC.7.EE.4

Vocabulary

term

coefficient

Individual skits at the talent show can last up to x minutes each, and group skits can last up to y minutes each. Intermission will be 15 minutes. The expression $7x + 9y + 15$ represents the maximum length of the talent show if 7 individuals and 9 groups perform.

In the expression $7x + 9y + 15$, $7x$, $9y$, and 15 are *terms*. A **term** can be a number, a variable, or a product of numbers and variables. Terms in an expression are separated by plus or minus signs.

> **Caution!**
>
> A variable by itself, such as y, has a coefficient of 1.
> So $y = 1y$.

In the term $7x$, 7 is called the *coefficient*. A **coefficient** is a number that is multiplied by a variable in an algebraic expression.

Coefficient →  ← Variable

Like terms are terms with the same variables raised to the same exponents. The coefficients do not have to be the same. Constants, like 5, $\frac{1}{2}$, and 3.2, are also like terms.

Like Terms	$3x$ and $2x$	w and $\frac{w}{7}$	5 and 1.8
Unlike Terms	$5x^2$ and $2x$ *The exponents are different.*	$6a$ and $6b$ *The variables are different.*	3.2 and n *Only one term contains a variable.*

EXAMPLE 1 **Identifying Like Terms**

Identify like terms in the list.

$$5a \quad \frac{t}{2} \quad 3y^2 \quad 7t \quad x^2 \quad 4z \quad k \quad 4.5y^2 \quad 2t \quad \frac{2}{3}a$$

Look for like variables with like powers.

> **Helpful Hint**
>
> Use different shapes or colors to indicate sets of like terms.

$$⬡5a \quad \boxed{\frac{t}{2}} \quad ⬡3y^2 \quad \boxed{7t} \quad x^2 \quad 4z \quad k \quad ⬡4.5y^2 \quad \boxed{2t} \quad ⬡\frac{2}{3}a$$

Like terms: $5a$ and $\frac{2}{3}a$ $\quad$ $\frac{t}{2}$, $7t$, and $2t$ $\quad$ $3y^2$ and $4.5y^2$

Video **Lesson Tutorials Online** my.hrw.com

To simplify an algebraic expression that contains like terms, combine the terms. Combining like terms is like grouping similar objects.

$$4x \quad + \quad 5x \quad = \quad 9x$$

To combine like terms that have variables, add or subtract the coefficients.

EXAMPLE 2 **Simplifying Algebraic Expressions**

Simplify. Justify your steps using the Commutative, Associative, and Distributive Properties when necessary.

A $7x + 2x$

$7x + 2x$	*7x and 2x are like terms.*
$9x$	*Add the coefficients.*

B $5x^3 + 3y + 7x^3 - 2y - 4x^2$

$5x^3 + 3y + 7x^3 - 2y - 4x^2$	*Identify like terms.*
$5x^3 + 7x^3 + 3y - 2y - 4x^2$	*Commutative Property*
$(5x^3 + 7x^3) + (3y - 2y) - 4x^2$	*Associative Property*
$12x^3 + y - 4x^2$	*Add or subtract the coefficients.*

C $2(a + 2a^2) + 2b$

$2(a + 2a^2) + 2b$	
$2a + 4a^2 + 2b$	*Distributive Property*

There are no like terms to combine.

EXAMPLE 3 *Geometry Application*

Remember!

To find the perimeter of a figure, add the lengths of the sides.

Write an expression for the perimeter of the rectangle. Then simplify the expression.

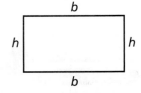

$b + h + b + h$	*Write an expression using the side lengths.*
$(b + b) + (h + h)$	*Identify and group like terms.*
$2b + 2h$	*Add the coefficients.*

MATHEMATICAL PRACTICES

Think and Discuss

1. Explain whether $5x$, $5x^2$, and $5x^3$ are like terms.

2. Explain how you know when an expression cannot be simplified.

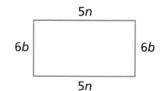
Learn It Online
Homework Help Online
Exercises 1–17, 19, 21, 23, 25, 29

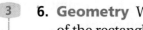
GUIDED PRACTICE

See Example **1** **Identify like terms in each list.**

1. $6b$ $5x^2$ $4x^3$ $\dfrac{b}{2}$ x^2 $2e$ **2.** $12a^2$ $4x^3$ b $4a^2$ $3.5x^3$ $\dfrac{5}{6}b$

See Example **2** **Simplify. Justify your steps using the Commutative, Associative, and Distributive Properties when necessary.**

3. $5x + 3x$ **4.** $6a^2 - a^2 + 16$ **5.** $4a^2 + 5a + 14b$

See Example **3** **6. Geometry** Write an expression for the perimeter of the rectangle. Then simplify the expression.

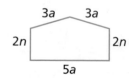

INDEPENDENT PRACTICE

See Example **1** **Identify like terms in each list.**

7. $2b$ b^6 b x^4 $3b^6$ $2x^2$ **8.** 6 $2n$ $3n^2$ $6m^2$ $\dfrac{n}{4}$ 7

9. $10k^2$ m 3^3 $\dfrac{p}{6}$ $2m$ 2 **10.** 6^3 y^3 $3y^2$ 6^2 y $5y^3$

See Example **2** **Simplify. Justify your steps using the Commutative, Associative, and Distributive Properties when necessary.**

11. $3a + 2b + 5a$ **12.** $5b + 7b + 10$ **13.** $a + 2b + 2a + b + 2c$

14. $y + 4 + 2x + 3y$ **15.** $q^2 + 2q + 2q^2$ **16.** $18 + 2d^3 + d + 3d$

See Example **3** **17. Geometry** Write an expression for the perimeter of the given figure. Then simplify the expression.

PRACTICE AND PROBLEM SOLVING

Extra Practice
See Extra Practice for more exercises.

Simplify each expression.

18. $4x + 5x$ **19.** $32y - 5y$ **20.** $4c^2 + 5c + 2c$

21. $5d^2 - 3d^2 + d$ **22.** $5f^2 + 2f + f^2$ **23.** $7x + 8x^2 - 3y$

24. $3(p + 9q - 2 + 9) + 14p$ **25.** $6b + 6b^2 + 4b^3$ **26.** $2(a^2 + 2b + 2a^2) + b + 2c$

27. Geometry Write an expression for the perimeter of the given triangle. Then evaluate the perimeter when n is 1, 2, 3, 4, and 5.

n		1	2	3	4	5
Perimeter						

Business

The winner of each year's National Best Bagger Competition gets a bag-shaped trophy and a cash prize.

28. **Critical Thinking** Determine whether the expression $9m^2 + k$ is equal to $7m^2 + 2(2k - m^2) + 5k$. Use properties to justify your answer.

29. **Multi-Step** Brad makes d dollars per hour as a cook at a deli. The table shows the number of hours he worked each week in June.

   a. Write and simplify an expression for the amount of money Brad earned in June.

   b. Evaluate your expression from part **a** for $d = \$9.50$.

   c. What does your answer to part **b** represent?

Hours Brad Worked	
Week	Hours
1	21.5
2	23
3	15.5
4	19

 30. **Business** Ashley earns $8 per hour working at a grocery store. Last week she worked h hours bagging groceries and twice as many hours stocking shelves. Write and simplify an expression for the amount Ashley earned.

31. **Critical Thinking** The terms $3x$, $23x^2$, $6y^2$, $2x$, y^2 and one other term can be written in an expression which, when simplified, equals $5x + 7y^2$. Identify the term missing from the list and write the expression.

32. **What's the Question?** At one store, a pair of jeans costs $29 and a shirt costs $25. At another store, the same kind of jeans costs $26 and the same kind of shirt costs $20. The answer is $29j - 26j + 25s - 20s = 3j + 5s$. What is the question?

33. **Write About It** Describe the steps for simplifying the expression $2x + 3 + 5x - 15$.

34. **Challenge** A rectangle has a width of $x + 2$ and a length of $3x + 1$. Write and simplify an expression for the perimeter of the rectangle.

Test Prep

35. **Multiple Choice** Translate "six times the sum of x and y" and "five less than y." Which algebraic expression represents the sum of these two verbal expressions?

   Ⓐ $6x + 5$ Ⓑ $6x + 2y - 5$ Ⓒ $6x + 5y + 5$ Ⓓ $6x + 7y - 5$

36. **Multiple Choice** The side length of a square is $2x + 3$. Which expression represents the perimeter of the square?

   Ⓕ $2x + 12$ Ⓖ $4x + 6$ Ⓗ $6x + 7$ Ⓙ $8x + 12$

Quiz for Lessons 3 Through 5

 3 **Variables and Algebraic Expressions**

Evaluate each expression for the given values of the variables.

1. $7(x + 4)$ for $x = 5$ **2.** $11 - n \div 3$ for $n = 6$

3. $p + 6t^2$ for $p = 11$ and $t = 3$ **4.** $8 - \frac{6x}{y} + 2x$ for $x = 2$ and $y = 4$

 4 **Translating Words into Math**

Write each phrase as an algebraic expression.

5. the quotient of a number and 15   **6.** a number decreased by 13

7. 10 times the difference of p and 2   **8.** 3 plus the product of a number and 8

9. A long-distance phone company charges a $2.95 monthly fee plus $0.14 for each minute. Write an algebraic expression to show the cost of calling for t minutes in one month.

 5 **Simplifying Algebraic Expressions**

Identify like terms in each list.

10. $3d \quad d^3 \quad 4d^2 \quad 5d^2 \quad 3g \quad 10d$ **11.** $12 \quad x^2 \quad \frac{x}{2} \quad 4x^2 \quad 4x^3 \quad 5x$

Simplify each expression. Justify your steps.

12. $2y + 5y^2 - 2y^2$ **13.** $x + 4 + 7x + 9$ **14.** $10 + 9b - 6a - b$

15. Write an expression for the perimeter of the given figure. Then simplify the expression.

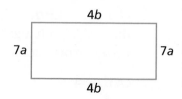

Willis Tower When it was completed in 1973, the Willis Tower in Chicago became the tallest building in the United States. The tower's Skydeck on the 103rd floor offers an incredible view that attracts 1.3 million visitors per year. The express elevators to the Skydeck are among the fastest in the world.

ILLINOIS
Chicago

For 1–4, use the table.

1. The table shows the distance the Skydeck elevators travel in seconds. Describe the pattern in the table.

2. Find the distance an elevator can travel in 7 seconds. Explain how you found the distance.

3. Write an expression that gives the distance an elevator travels in *s* seconds.

4. It takes 50 seconds for an elevator to go from the ground up to the Skydeck. What numerical expression could you use to find about how many feet the elevator travels?

Skydeck Elevators	
Time (s)	Distance (ft)
1	27
2	54
3	81
4	108

5. Show the steps you could use to find the product in Exercise 4 using the Distributive Property.

6. The Willis Tower has 3,100 more windows than two times the number of windows *n* in the Empire State Building. Write an expression for the number of windows in the Willis Tower.

Game Time

Jumping Beans

You will need a grid that is 4 squares by 6 squares. Each square must be large enough to contain a bean. Mark off a 3-square by 3-square section of the grid. Place nine beans in the nine spaces, as shown below.

You must move all nine beans to the nine marked-off squares in the fewest number of moves.

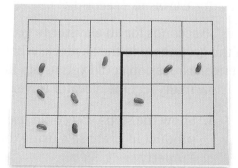

Follow the rules below to move the beans.

❶ You may move to any empty square in any direction.

❷ You may jump over another bean in any direction to an empty square.

❸ You may jump over other beans as many times as you like.

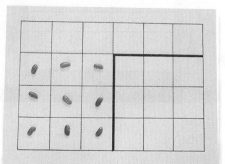

Moving all the beans in ten moves is not too difficult, but can you do it in nine moves?

Trading Spaces

The purpose of the game is to replace the red counters with the yellow counters, and the yellow counters with the red counters, in the fewest moves possible. The counters must be moved one at a time in an L-shape. No two counters may occupy the same square.

A complete copy of the rules and a game board are available online.

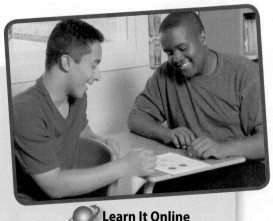

Learn It Online
Game Time Extra

(all) Jenny Thomas/HMH

Materials
- 1 full sheet of decorative paper
- 3 smaller pieces of decorative paper
- stapler
- scissors
- markers
- pencil

It's in the Bag!

PROJECT ▶ **Step-by-Step Algebra**

This "step book" is a great place to record sample algebra problems.

Directions

❶ Lay the $11\frac{1}{2}$-by-$7\frac{3}{4}$ inch sheet of paper in front of you. Fold it down $2\frac{1}{2}$ inches from the top and make a crease. **Figure A**

❷ Slide the $7\frac{1}{4}$-by-$7\frac{3}{4}$-inch sheet of paper under the flap of the first piece. Do the same with the $5\frac{1}{2}$-by-$7\frac{3}{4}$-inch and $3\frac{3}{4}$-by-$7\frac{3}{4}$-inch sheets of paper to make a step book. Staple all of the sheets together at the top. **Figure B**

❸ Use a pencil to divide the three middle sheets into thirds. Then cut up from the bottom along the lines you drew to make slits in these three sheets. **Figure C**

❹ On the top step of your booklet, write the number and title of the chapter.

Taking Note of the Math

Label each of the steps in your booklet with important concepts from the chapter: "Using the Order of Operations," "Properties of Numbers," and so on. On the bottom sheet, write "Simplifying Expressions." Write sample problems from the chapter on the appropriate steps.

33

Vocabulary

algebraic expression	constant	numerical expression
Associative Property	Distributive Property	order of operations
coefficient	evaluate	term
Commutative Property	Identity Property	variable

Complete the sentences below with vocabulary words from the list above.

1. A(n) ___?___ is a mathematical phrase made up of numbers and operations.

2. The ___?___ states that the product of 1 and any number is the number.

3. A(n) ___?___ consists of constants, variables, and operations.

4. The ___?___ is the number multiplied by a variable in an algebraic expression.

5. To ___?___ an algebraic expression, substitute a number for the variable.

EXAMPLES

1 **Order of Operations**

■ Simplify $150 - (18 + 6) \cdot 5$.

$150 - (18 + 6) \cdot 5$	*Perform the operation in parentheses.*
$150 - 24 \cdot 5$	*Multiply.*
$150 - 120$	*Subtract.*
30	

EXERCISES

Simplify each expression.

6. $2 + (9 - 6) \div 3$ 7. $12 \cdot 3^2 - 5$

8. $11 + 2 \cdot 5 - (9 + 7)$ 9. $75 \div 5^2 + 8^2$

10. Lola decides to join a 15 mile walk-a-thon. Her parents give her $3 for each mile walked and her brother gives her $10. Simplify the expression $3 \cdot 15 + 10$ to find out how much money she raised.

2 Properties of Numbers

■ **Tell which property is represented.**

$(10 \cdot 13) \cdot 28 = 10 \cdot (13 \cdot 28)$
Associative Property

Tell which property is represented.

11. $42 + 17 = 17 + 42$

12. $m + 0 = m$

13. $6 \cdot (x - 5) = 6 \cdot x - 6 \cdot 5$

Simplify each expression. Justify each step.

14. $28 + 15 + 22$ **15.** $20 \cdot 23 \cdot 5$

Use the Distributive Property to find each product.

16. $8(35)$ **17.** $(28)6$

Complete each statement. Then tell which property is represented.

18. $4 \cdot 6 = 6 \cdot \blacksquare$ **19.** $32 + 0 = \blacksquare$

20. $15 + (3 + 8) = (\blacksquare + 3) + 8$

3 Variables and Algebraic Expressions

■ **Evaluate $5a - 6b + 7$ for $a = 4$ and $b = 3$.**

$5a - 6b + 7$
$5(4) - 6(3) + 7$
$20 - 18 + 7$
9

Evaluate each expression for the given values of the variables.

21. $4x - 5$ for $x = 6$

22. $8y^3 + 3y$ for $y = 4$

23. $\frac{n}{5} + 6m - 3$ for $n = 5$ and $m = 2$

24. The expression $55t$ can be used to find the number of miles traveled in t hours by a car traveling at a rate of 55 miles per hour. Evaluate $55t$ for $t = 4$. How far did the car travel in 4 hours?

4 **Translating Words into Math**

■ Write as an algebraic expression.

5 times the sum of a number and 6

$5(n + 6)$

Write as an algebraic expression.

25. the quotient of a number and 9

26. 6 less than two times a number

27. 4 divided by the sum of a number and 12

28. 2 times the difference of t and 11

29. Missy spent \$32 on s shirts. Write an algebraic expression to represent the cost of one shirt.

5 **Simplifying Algebraic Expressions**

■ Simplify the expression.

$4x^3 + 5y + 8x^3 - 4y - 5x^2$

$4x^3 + 5y + 8x^3 - 4y - 5x^2$

$\quad 12x^3 + y - 5x^2$

Identify like terms in each list.

30. 18 $\quad p^5 \quad p^3 \quad 2p^3 \quad 5 \quad \dfrac{p}{5}$

31. $3a^3 \quad 3a^4 \quad 2b^4 \quad 2a^4 \quad 6b \quad \dfrac{1}{3}b$

Simplify each expression.

32. $7b^2 + 8 + 3b^2$

33. $12a^2 + 4 + 3a^2 - 2$

34. $x^2 + x^3 + x^4 + 5x^2$

35. Write an expression for the perimeter of the given figure. Then simplify the expression.

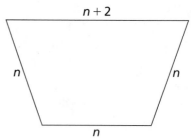

Study Guide: Review

CHAPTER
1

Chapter Test

Simplify each expression.

1. $18 \cdot 3 \div 3^3$ 2. $36 + 16 - 50$ 3. $149 - (2^8 - 200)$ 4. $(4 \div 2) \cdot 9 + 11$

5. Chris bought 6 shirts for $12 each and 4 pairs of pants for $25 each. The store also gave a discount of $8 off the entire purchase. Use the expression $6 \cdot 12 + 4 \cdot 25 - 8$ to find the total amount Chris paid for the shirts and pants.

Tell which property is represented.

6. $0 + 45 = 45$ 7. $(r + s) + t = r + (s + t)$ 8. $84 \cdot 3 = 3 \cdot 84$

Use the Distributive Property to find each product.

9. $8(22)$ 10. $6(72)$ 11. $(39)5$ 12. $(14)12$

Evaluate each expression for the given values of the variables.

13. $4a + 6b + 7$ for $a = 2$ and $b = 3$ 14. $7y^2 + 7y$ for $y = 3$

Write each phrase as an algebraic expression.

15. a number increased by 12   16. the quotient of a number and 7

17. 5 less than the product of 7 and s 18. the difference between 3 times x and 4

Simplify each expression. Justify your steps.

19. $b + 2 + 5b$ 20. $16 + 5b + 3b + 9$ 21. $5a + 6t + 9 + 2a$

22. To join the gym Halle must pay a $75 enrollment fee and $32 per month. Write an algebraic expression to represent the total cost of m months at the gym, including the enrollment fee.

Test Tackler
STANDARDIZED TEST STRATEGIES

Multiple Choice: Eliminate Answer Choices

With some multiple-choice test items, you can use mental math or number sense to quickly eliminate some of the answer choices before you begin solving the problem.

EXAMPLE 1

Which expression best represents the group of figures shown?

Ⓐ 22x **Ⓑ** 1 + 7 + 15 **Ⓒ** x + 7 + 15 **Ⓓ** 7x + 15

LOOK at the figures drawn. Then try to **eliminate** some of the answer choices.

Use number sense:
The figures show one x-bucket and two groups of apples. There is only one x-bucket, so choices A and D, 22x and 7x + 15, do not make sense. Also, the bucket represents the variable x, not necessarily the number 1, so you can eliminate choice B.

The correct answer choice is C.

EXAMPLE 2

What is the value of the expression 18x + 6 for x = 5?

Ⓕ 90 **Ⓖ** 96 **Ⓗ** 191 **Ⓙ** 198

LOOK at the choices. Then try to **eliminate** some of the answer choices.

Use mental math:
Estimate the value of the expression. Round 18 to 20 to make the multiplication easier.

20x + 6
20(5) + 6   *Substitute 5 for x.*
106   *Multiply. Then add.*

Because you rounded up, the value of the expression should be less than 106. You can eliminate choices H and J because they are too large.

The correct answer choice is G.

Read each test item and answer the questions that follow.

Item A
During the August back-to-school sale, 2 pairs of shoes cost $34, a shirt costs $15, and a pair of pants costs $27. Janet bought 2 pairs of shoes, 4 shirts, and 4 pairs of pants and then paid an additional $7 for tax. Which expression shows the total that Janet spent?

(A) $34 + 4(15 + 27)$

(B) $34 + 4(15 + 27) + 7$

(C) $4(34 + 15 + 27) + 7$

(D) $34 + 15 + 4 \cdot 27$

1. Can any of the answer choices be eliminated immediately? If so, which choices and why?

2. Describe how you can determine the correct answer from the remaining choices.

Item B
Anthony saved $1 from his first paycheck, $2 from his second paycheck, then $4, $8, and so on. How much money did Anthony save from his tenth paycheck?

(F) $10   (H) $512

(G) $16   (J) $1,023

3. Are there any answer choices you can eliminate immediately? If so, which choices and why?

4. What common error was made in finding answer choice F?

Item C
Craig has three weeks to read an 850-page book. Which expression can be used to find the number of pages Craig has to read each day?

(A) $850 \cdot 3$ (C) $850 \div 3$

(B) $850 \div 21$ (D) $850 \cdot 21$

5. Describe how to use number sense to eliminate at least one answer choice.

6. What common error was made in finding answer choice D?

Item D
For what value of t is the expression $22t$ equal to 132?

(F) 6   (H) 154

(G) 110   (J) 2,904

7. Which choices can be eliminated by using number sense? Explain.

8. What common error was made in finding answer choice J?

9. Describe how you could check your answer to this problem.

Item E
What is the value of the expression $(1 + 2)^2 + 14 \div 2 + 5$?

(A) 0   (C) 17

(B) 11   (D) 21

10. Use mental math to quickly eliminate one answer choice. Explain your choice.

11. What common error was made in finding answer choice B?

12. What common error was made in finding answer choice C?

Cumulative Assessment

Multiple Choice

1. Which expression has a value of 74 when $x = 10$, $y = 8$, and $z = 12$?

- Ⓐ $4xyz$
- Ⓒ $2xz - 3y$
- Ⓑ $x + 5y + 2z$
- Ⓓ $6xyz + 8$

2. Tell which property is represented.

$$3 \cdot (6 \cdot 12) = (3 \cdot 6) \cdot 12$$

- Ⓕ Associative
- Ⓗ Distributive
- Ⓖ Commutative
- Ⓙ Identity

3. A contractor charges $22 to install one miniblind. How much does the contractor charge to install m miniblinds?

- Ⓐ $22m$
- Ⓒ $22 + m$
- Ⓑ $\frac{m}{22}$
- Ⓓ $\frac{22}{m}$

4. Which of the following is an example of the Commutative Property?

- Ⓕ $20 + 10 = 2(10 + 5)$
- Ⓖ $20 + 10 = 10 + 20$
- Ⓗ $5 + (20 + 10) = (5 + 20) + 10$
- Ⓙ $20 + 0 = 20$

5. Which expression simplifies to $9x + 3$ when you combine like terms?

- Ⓐ $10x^2 - x^2 - 3$
- Ⓑ $3x + 7 - 4 + 3x$
- Ⓒ $18 + 4x - 15 + 5x$
- Ⓓ $7x^2 + 2x + 6 - 3$

6. Which pair shows like terms?

- Ⓕ 8 and $8x$
- Ⓗ $6y^4$ and $6z^4$
- Ⓖ $2x^4$ and $3x^7$
- Ⓙ $5y^3$ and $7y^3$

7. Tia maps out her jogging route as shown in the table.

Tia's Jogging Route	
Street	Meters
1st to Park	428
Park to Windsor	112
Windsor to East	506
East to Manor	814
Manor to Vane	660
Vane to 1st	480

When Tia has reached East Street, how much further must she jog to reach 1st Street?

- Ⓐ 480 m
- Ⓒ 1,954 m
- Ⓑ 660 m
- Ⓓ 3,000 m

8. To make a beaded necklace, Kris needs 88 beads. If Kris has 1,056 beads, how many necklaces can she make?

- Ⓕ 968
- Ⓗ 264
- Ⓖ 12
- Ⓙ 8

9. What are the next two numbers in the pattern?

$$75, 70, 60, 55, 45, 40, \ldots$$

- Ⓐ 35, 30
- Ⓒ 30, 25
- Ⓑ 30, 20
- Ⓓ 35, 25

10. Marc spends $78 for n shirts. Which expression can be used to represent the cost of one shirt?

- Ⓕ $\frac{n}{78}$
- Ⓗ $\frac{78}{n}$
- Ⓖ $78n$
- Ⓙ $78 + n$

11. Which situation best matches the expression $0.29x + 2$?

Ⓐ A taxi company charges a $2.00 flat fee plus $0.29 for every mile.

Ⓑ Jimmy ran 0.29 miles, stopped to rest, and then ran 2 more miles.

Ⓒ There are 0.29 grams of calcium in 2 servings of Hearty Health Cereal.

Ⓓ Amy bought 2 pieces of gum for $0.29 each.

12. Which of the following should be performed first to simplify this expression?

$$16 \cdot 2 + (20 \div 5) - 3^2 \div 3 + 1$$

Ⓕ $3^2 \div 3$

Ⓖ $20 \div 5$

Ⓗ $16 \cdot 2$

Ⓙ $3 + 1$

 HOT TIP! When you read a word problem, cross out any information that is not needed to solve the problem.

Gridded Response

13. If $x = 15$ and $y = 5$, what is the value of $\frac{2x}{y} + 3y$?

14. If $m = 4$ and $p = 2$, what is the value of $3m^2 - 5p$?

15. An airplane has seats for 198 passengers. If each row seats 6 people, how many rows are on the plane?

16. What is the value of the expression $3^2 \times (2 + 3 \times 4) - 5$?

17. What is the product of 5 and the sum of 6 and 2?

18. What is the sum of 4 and the product of 9 and 5?

Short Response

S1. Luke can swim 25 laps in one hour. Write an algebraic expression to show how many laps Luke can swim in h hours. How many hours will it take Luke to swim 100 laps?

S2. An aerobics instructor teaches a 45-minute class at 9:30 A.M., three times a week. She dedicates 12 minutes during each class to stretching. The rest of the class consists of aerobic dance. How many minutes of each class does the instructor spend teaching aerobic dance? Write and solve an equation to explain how you found your answer.

S3. Ike and Joe ran the same distance but took different routes. Ike ran 3 blocks east and 7 blocks south. Joe ran 4 blocks west and then turned north. How far north did Joe run? Show your work.

Extended Response

E1. The Raiders and the Hornets are buying new uniforms for their baseball teams. Each team member will receive a new cap, a jersey, and a pair of pants.

Uniform Costs		
	Raiders	**Hornets**
Cap	$15	$15
Jersey	$75	$70
Pants	$60	$70

a. Let r represent the number of Raiders team members, and let h represent the number of Hornets team members. For each team, write an expression that gives the total cost of the team's uniforms.

b. If the Raiders and the Hornets both have 12 team members, how much will each team spend on uniforms? Which team will spend the most, and by how much? Show your work.

Integers and Rational Numbers

COMMON CORE

Chapter Focus
- Add, subtract, multiply and divide intergers.
- Express fractions as decimals.

Why Learn This?

Integers are commonly used to describe temperatures. In many parts of the world, winter temperatures are often negative integers, meaning it is colder than 0°.

Learn It Online
Chapter Project Online

(all) Gao Ming/HLJRB/ChinaFotoPress/Kyodo News/NewsCom

✓ Vocabulary

Choose the best term from the list to complete each sentence.

1. To __?__ a number on a number line, mark and label the point that corresponds to that number.

2. The expression $1 < 3 < 5$ tells the __?__ of these three numbers on a number line.

3. A(n)__?__ is a mathematical statement showing two things are equal.

4. Each number in the set 0, 1, 2, 3, 4, 5, 6, 7, . . . is a(n) __?__.

5. To __?__ an equation, find a value that makes it true.

whole number

expression

graph

solve

equation

order

Complete these exercises to review skills you will need for this chapter.

✓ Order of Operations

Simplify.

6. $7 + 9 - 5 \cdot 2$

7. $12 \cdot 3 - 4 \cdot 5$

8. $115 - 15 \cdot 3 + 9(8 - 2)$

9. $20 \cdot 5 \cdot 2 (7 + 1) \div 4$

10. $300 + 6(5 - 3) - 11$

11. $14 - 13 + 9 \cdot 2$

✓ Write and Read Decimals

Write the decimal in standard form and word form.

12. Think: $40 + 1 + 0.2 + 0.04$
    Standard Form: ____?____
    Word Form: ____?____ and
    ____?____ hundredths

13. Think: $5,000 + 300 + 10 + 4 + 0.8$
    Standard Form: ____?____
    Word Form: ____?____ and
    ____?____ tenths

14. $800 + 50 + 2 + 0.03 + 0.005$
    Standard Form: ____?____
    Word Form: ____?____
    _____?_____

15. $100,000 + 30,000 + 600 + 3 + 0.05$
    Standard Form: ____?____
    Word Form: ____?____
    _____?_____

✓ Use Inverse Operations to Solve Equations

Solve.

16. $n + 3 = 10$

17. $x - 4 = 16$

18. $9p = 63$

19. $\dfrac{t}{5} = 80$

20. $x - 3 = 14$

21. $\dfrac{q}{3} = 21$

22. $9 + r = 91$

23. $15p = 45$

Study Guide: Preview

Where You've Been

Previously, you

- compared and ordered non-negative rational numbers.
- generated equivalent forms of rational numbers including whole numbers, fractions, and decimals.
- used integers to represent real-life situations.

In This Chapter

You will study

- comparing and ordering integers and rational numbers.
- converting between fractions and decimals mentally, on paper, and with a calculator.
- using models to add, subtract, multiply, and divide integers.

Where You're Going

You can use the skills learned in this chapter

- to express negative numbers related to scientific fields such as marine biology or meteorology.
- to find equivalent measures.

Key Vocabulary/Vocabulario

absolute value	valor absoluto
additive inverse	inverso aditivo
integer	entero
opposites	opuestos
rational number	número racional
repeating decimal	decimal periódico
terminating decimal	decimal finito

Vocabulary Connections

To become familiar with some of the vocabulary terms in the chapter, consider the following. You may refer to the chapter, the glossary, or a dictionary if you like.

1. Another word for *inverse* is *reverse*. The word *additive* relates to the operation of addition. What do you think an **additive inverse** is?

2. The word *absolute* means "not limited by restrictions." How can you use this definition to explain what the **absolute value** of a number is?

3. A decimal is a number that has digits to the right of the decimal point. What might you predict about those digits in a **repeating decimal**?

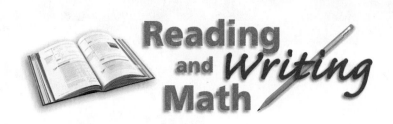

Reading and Writing Math

Writing Strategy: Translate Between Words and Math

As you read a real-world math problem, look for key words to help you translate between the words and the math.

Example

At FunZone the cost to play laser tag is $8 per game. The cost to play miniature golf is $5 per game. The one-time admission fee to the park is $3. Jonna wants to play both laser tag and miniature golf. Write an algebraic expression to find the total amount Jonna would pay to play ℓ laser tag games and m golf games at FunZone.

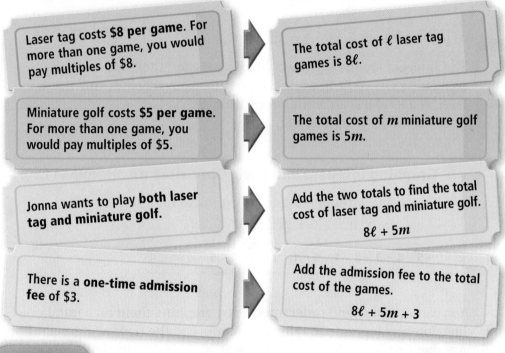

Laser tag costs **$8 per game.** For more than one game, you would pay multiples of $8.

⮕ The total cost of ℓ laser tag games is 8ℓ.

Miniature golf costs **$5 per game.** For more than one game, you would pay multiples of $5.

⮕ The total cost of m miniature golf games is $5m$.

Jonna wants to play **both laser tag and miniature golf.**

⮕ Add the two totals to find the total cost of laser tag and miniature golf.
$8\ell + 5m$

There is a **one-time admission fee of $3.**

⮕ Add the admission fee to the total cost of the games.
$8\ell + 5m + 3$

Try This

Write an algebraic expression that describes the situation. Explain why you chose each operation in the expression.

1. School supplies are half-price at Bargain Mart this week. The original prices were $2 per package of pens and $4 per notebook. Cally buys 1 package of pens and n notebooks. How much does Cally spend?

2. Fred has f cookies, and Gary has g cookies. Fred and Gary each eat 3 cookies. How many total cookies are left?

Integers

The **opposite**, or **additive inverse**, of a number is the same distance from 0 on a number line as the original number, but on the other side of 0. Zero is its own opposite.

Vocabulary

opposite

additive inverse

integer

absolute value

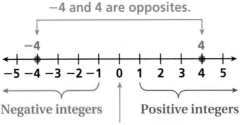

−4 and 4 are opposites.

Negative integers   Positive integers

0 is neither positive nor negative.

Dr. Sylvia Earle holds the world record for the deepest solo dive.

> **Remember!**
>
> The whole numbers are the natural numbers and zero: 0, 1, 2, 3, ...

The **integers** are the set of whole numbers and their opposites. By using integers, you can express elevations above, below, and at sea level. Sea level has an elevation of 0 feet. Sylvia Earle's record dive was to an elevation of −1,250 feet.

EXAMPLE 1 **Graphing Integers and Their Opposites on a Number Line**

Graph the integer −3 and its opposite on a number line.

3 units   3 units

The opposite of −3 is 3.

You can compare and order integers by graphing them on a number line. Integers increase in value as you move to the right along a number line. They decrease in value as you move to the left.

EXAMPLE 2 **Comparing Integers Using a Number Line**

Compare the integers. Use < or >.

> **Remember!**
>
> The symbol < means "is less than," and the symbol > means "is greater than."

A 2 ▮ −2

2 is farther to the right than −2, so 2 > −2.

Video **Lesson Tutorials Online** my.hrw.com

Compare the integers. Use < or >.

B −10 ▨ −7

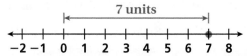

−10 is farther to the left than −7, so −10 < −7.

EXAMPLE 3 **Ordering Integers Using a Number Line**

Use a number line to order the integers −2, 5, −4, 1, −1, and 0 from least to greatest.

Graph the integers on a number line. Then read them from left to right.

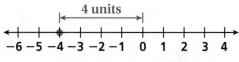

The numbers in order from least to greatest are −4, −2, −1, 0, 1, and 5.

A number's **absolute value** is its distance from 0 on a number line. Since distance can never be negative, absolute values are never negative. They are always positive or zero.

EXAMPLE 4 **Finding Absolute Value**

Use a number line to find each absolute value.

A |7|

7 units

−2 −1 0 1 2 3 4 5 6 7 8

7 is 7 units from 0, so |7| = 7.

B |−4|

4 units

−6 −5 −4 −3 −2 −1 0 1 2 3 4

−4 is 4 units from 0, so |−4| = 4.

MATHEMATICAL PRACTICES

Think and Discuss

1. Tell which number is greater: −4,500 or −10,000.

2. Name the greatest negative integer and the least nonnegative integer. Then compare the absolute values of these integers.

GUIDED PRACTICE

See Example 1   Graph each integer and its opposite on a number line.

1. 2   **2.** −9   **3.** −1   **4.** 6

See Example 2   Compare the integers. Use < or >.

5. 5 ☐ −5   **6.** −9 ☐ −18   **7.** −21 ☐ −17   **8.** −12 ☐ 12

See Example 3   Use a number line to order the integers from least to greatest.

9. 6, −3, −1, −5, 4   **10.** 8, −2, 7, 1, −8   **11.** −6, −4, 3, 0, 1

See Example 4   Use a number line to find each absolute value.

12. |−2| **13.** |8| **14.** |−7| **15.** |−10|

INDEPENDENT PRACTICE

See Example 1   Graph each integer and its opposite on a number line.

16. −4   **17.** 10   **18.** −12   **19.** 7

See Example 2   Compare the integers. Use < or >.

20. −14 ☐ −7   **21.** 9 ☐ −9   **22.** −12 ☐ 12   **23.** −31 ☐ −27

See Example 3   Use a number line to order the integers from least to greatest.

24. −3, 2, −5, −6, 5   **25.** −7, −9, −2, 0, −5   **26.** 3, −6, 9, −1, −2

See Example 4   Use a number line to find each absolute value.

27. |−16| **28.** |12| **29.** |−20| **30.** |15|

PRACTICE AND PROBLEM SOLVING

Extra Practice
See Extra Practice for more exercises.

Compare. Write <, >, or =.

31. −25 ☐ 25   **32.** 18 ☐ −55   **33.** |−21| ☐ 21   **34.** −9 ☐ −27

35. 34 ☐ |34| **36.** 64 ☐ |−75| **37.** |−3| ☐ |3| **38.** −100 ☐ −82

39. Earth Science The table shows the average temperatures in Vostok, Antarctica from March to October. List the months in order from coldest to warmest.

Month	Mar	Apr	May	Jun	Jul	Aug	Sep	Oct
Temperature (°F)	−72	−84	−86	−85	−88	−90	−87	−71

40. What is the opposite of |32|?   **41.** What is the opposite of |−29|?

42. Business A company reported a net loss of $2,000,000 during its first year. In its second year it reported a profit of $5,000,000. Write each amount as an integer.

43. Critical Thinking Give an example in which a negative number has a greater absolute value than a positive number.

44. Social Studies Lines of latitude are imaginary lines that circle the globe in an east-west direction. They measure distances north and south of the equator. The equator represents 0° latitude.

    a. What latitude is opposite of 30° north latitude?

    b. How do these latitudes' distances from the equator compare?

Sports The graph shows how participation in several sports changed between 1999 and 2000 in the United States.

45. By about what percent did participation in racquetball increase or decrease?

46. By about what percent did participation in wall climbing increase or decrease?

 47. What's the Error? At 9 A.M. the outside temperature was −3 °F. By noon, the temperature was −12 °F. A newscaster said that it was getting warmer outside. Why is this incorrect?

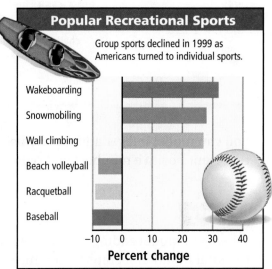

Source: USA Today, July 6, 2001

 48. Write About It Explain how to compare two integers.

49. Challenge What values can x have if $|x| = 11$?

Test Prep

50. Multiple Choice Which list shows the integers in order from least to greatest?

    Ⓐ −5, −6, −7, 2, 3   Ⓑ 2, 3, −5, −6, −7   Ⓒ −7, −6, −5, 2, 3   Ⓓ 3, 2, −7, −6, −5

51. Multiple Choice The table shows the average temperatures in Barrow, Alaska, for several months. In which month is the average temperature lowest?

    Ⓕ January   Ⓗ May

    Ⓖ March   Ⓙ July

Monthly Temperatures	
January	−12 °F
March	−13 °F
May	20 °F
July	40 °F

Hands-on LAB

Model Integer Addition

Use with Adding Integers

KEY

 = 1

= −1

+ = 0

REMEMBER

• Adding or subtracting zero does not change the value of an expression.

Use appropriate tools strategically.
CC.7.NS.1 Apply and extend previous understandings of addition and subtraction to add and subtract rational numbers; represent addition and subtraction on a horizontal or vertical number line diagram. *Also CC.7.NS.3*

You can model integer addition by using integer chips. Yellow chips represent positive numbers and red chips represent negative numbers.

Activity

When you model adding numbers with the same sign, you can count the total number of chips to find the sum.

The total number of positive chips is 7.

$3 + 4 = 7$

The total number of negative chips is 7.

$-3 + (-4) = -7$

1 Use integer chips to find each sum.

   a. $2 + 4$ **b.** $-2 + (-4)$ **c.** $6 + 3$ **d.** $-5 + (-4)$

When you model adding numbers with different signs, you cannot count the chips to find their sum.

 + = 2 and + = −2

but + = 0   *A red chip and a yellow chip make a neutral pair.*

When you model adding a positive and a negative number, you need to remove all of the neutral pairs that you can find—that is, all pairs of 1 red chip and 1 yellow chip. These pairs have a value of zero, so they do not affect the sum.

You cannot just count the colored chips to find their sum.

$3 + (-4) = \blacksquare$

Before you count the chips, you need to remove all of the zero pairs.

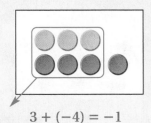

When you remove the zero pairs, there is one red chip left. So the sum of the chips is −1.

$3 + (-4) = -1$

2 Use integer chips to find each sum.

   a. $4 + (-6)$ **b.** $-5 + 2$ **c.** $7 + (-3)$ **d.** $-6 + 3$

Think and Discuss

1. Will $8 + (-3)$ and $-3 + 8$ give the same answer? Why or why not?

2. If you have more red chips than yellow chips in a group, is the sum of the chips positive or negative?

3. If you have more yellow chips than red chips in a group, is the sum of the chips positive or negative?

4. **Make a Conjecture** Make a conjecture for the sign of the answer when negative and positive integers are added. Give examples.

Try This

Use integer chips to find each sum.

1. $4 + (-7)$ **2.** $-5 + (-4)$ **3.** $-5 + 1$ **4.** $6 + (-4)$

Write the addition problems modeled below.

5.

6.

7.

8.

CC.7.NS.1 Apply and extend previous understandings of addition and subtraction to add and subtract rational numbers; represent addition and subtraction on a horizontal or vertical number line diagram. **Also** *CC.7.NS.1b, CC.7.NS.3, CC.7.EE.3*

2-2 Adding Integers

The math team wanted to raise money for a trip to Washington, D.C. They began by estimating their income and expenses.

Income items are positive, and expenses are negative. By adding all your income and expenses, you can find your total earnings or losses.

One way to add integers is by using a number line.

Club Ledger

Estimated Income and Expenses

Description	Amount
Car wash supplies	–$25.00
Car wash earnings	$300.00
Bake sale supplies	–$50.00
Bake sale earnings	$250.00

EXAMPLE 1 Modeling Integer Addition

Interactivities Online ▶

Use a number line to find each sum.

A $-3 + (-6)$

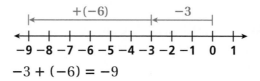

$-3 + (-6) = -9$

Start at 0. Move left 3 units. Then move left 6 more units.

B $4 + (-7)$

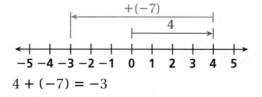

$4 + (-7) = -3$

Start at 0. Move right 4 units. Then move left 7 units.

You can also use absolute value to add integers.

Adding Integers

To add two integers with the same sign, find the sum of their absolute values. Use the sign of the two integers.

To add two integers with different signs, find the difference of their absolute values. Use the sign of the integer with the greater absolute value.

MATHCOUNTS Foundation

EXAMPLE **Adding Integers Using Absolute Values**

Find each sum.

A $-7 + (-4)$

The signs are the **same**. Find the **sum** of the absolute values.

$-7 + (-4)$ *Think: 7 + 4 = 11.*
-11 *Use the sign of the two integers.*

> **Helpful Hint**
>
> When adding integers, think: If the signs are the *same,* find the *sum.*
> If the signs are *different,* find the *difference.*

B $-8 + 6$

The signs are **different**. Find the **difference** of the absolute values.

$-8 + 6$ *Think: 8 − 6 = 2.*
-2 *Use the sign of the integer with the greater absolute value.*

EXAMPLE **Evaluating Expressions with Integers**

Evaluate $a + b$ **for** $a = 6$ **and** $b = -10$.

$a + b$
$6 + (-10)$ *Substitute 6 for a and −10 for b. The signs are **different**. Think: 10 − 6 = 4.*
-4 *Use the sign of the integer with the greater absolute value (negative).*

EXAMPLE 4 *Banking Application*

The math team's income from a car wash was $300, including tips. Supply expenses were $25. Use integer addition to find the team's total profit or loss.

$300 + (-25)$ *Use negative for the expenses.*
$300 - 25$ *Find the difference of the absolute values.*
275 *The answer is positive.*
The team earned $275.

Think and Discuss

1. Explain whether $-7 + 2$ is the same as $7 + (-2)$.

2. Use the Commutative Property to write an expression that is equivalent to $3 + (-5)$.

Video **Lesson Tutorials Online** my.hrw.com

2-2 Adding Integers **53**

Learn It Online
Homework Help Online
Exercises 1–32, 33, 37, 39, 43, 47, 49, 51

GUIDED PRACTICE

See Example 1 **Use a number line to find each sum.**

1. $9 + 3$ **2.** $-4 + (-2)$ **3.** $7 + (-9)$ **4.** $-3 + 6$

See Example 2 **Find each sum.**

5. $7 + 8$ **6.** $-1 + (-12)$ **7.** $-25 + 10$ **8.** $31 + (-20)$

See Example 3 **Evaluate $a + b$ for the given values.**

9. $a = 5, b = -17$ **10.** $a = 8, b = -8$ **11.** $a = -4, b = -16$

See Example 4 **12. Sports** A football team gains 8 yards on one play and then loses 13 yards on the next. Use integer addition to find the team's total yardage.

INDEPENDENT PRACTICE

See Example 1 **Use a number line to find each sum.**

13. $-16 + 7$ **14.** $-5 + (-1)$ **15.** $4 + 9$ **16.** $-7 + 8$

17. $10 + (-3)$ **18.** $-20 + 2$ **19.** $-12 + (-5)$ **20.** $-9 + 6$

See Example 2 **Find each sum.**

21. $-13 + (-6)$ **22.** $14 + 25$ **23.** $-22 + 6$ **24.** $35 + (-50)$

25. $-81 + (-7)$ **26.** $28 + (-3)$ **27.** $-70 + 15$ **28.** $-18 + (-62)$

See Example 3 **Evaluate $c + d$ for the given values.**

29. $c = 6, d = -20$ **30.** $c = -8, d = -21$ **31.** $c = -45, d = 32$

See Example 4 **32.** The temperature dropped 17 °F in 6 hours. The final temperature was −3 °F. Use integer addition to find the starting temperature.

PRACTICE AND PROBLEM SOLVING

Extra Practice
See Extra Practice for more exercises.

Find each sum.

33. $-8 + (-5)$ **34.** $14 + (-7)$ **35.** $-41 + 15$

36. $-22 + (-18) + 22$ **37.** $27 + (-29) + 16$ **38.** $-30 + 71 + (-70)$

Compare. Write <, >, or =.

39. $-23 + 18$ ▧ -41 **40.** $59 + (-59)$ ▧ 0 **41.** $31 + (-20)$ ▧ 9

42. $-24 + (-24)$ ▧ 48 **43.** $25 + (-70)$ ▧ -95 **44.** $16 + (-40)$ ▧ -24

45. Personal Finance Cody made deposits of $45, $18, and $27 into his checking account. He then wrote checks for $21 and $93. Write an expression to show the change in Cody's account. Then simplify the expression.

Evaluate each expression for $w = -12$, $x = 10$, and $y = -7$.

46. $7 + y$ **47.** $-4 + w$ **48.** $w + y$ **49.** $x + y$ **50.** $w + x$

51. Recreation Hikers along the Appalachian Trail camped overnight at Horns Pond, at an elevation of 3,100 ft. Then they hiked along the ridge of the Bigelow Mountains to West Peak, which is one of Maine's highest peaks. Use the diagram to determine the elevation of West Peak.

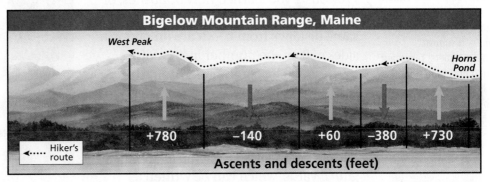

Bigelow Mountain Range, Maine
West Peak
Horns Pond
+780   −140   +60   −380   +730
Hiker's route
Ascents and descents (feet)

The Appalachian Trail extends about 2,160 miles from Maine to Georgia. It takes about 5 to 7 months to hike the entire trail.

52. Multi-Step Hector and Luis are playing a game. In the game, each player starts with 0 points, and the player with the most points at the end wins. Hector gains 5 points, loses 3, loses 2, and then gains 3. Luis loses 5 points, gains 1, gains 5, and then loses 3. Determine the final scores by modeling the problem on a number line. Then tell who wins the game and by how much.

53. What's the Question? The temperature was $-8\,°F$ at 6 A.M. and rose $15\,°F$ by 9 A.M. The answer is $7\,°F$. What is the question?

54. Write About It Compare the method used to add integers with the same sign and the method used to add integers with different signs.

55. Challenge A business had losses of $225 million, $75 million, and $375 million and profits of $15 million and $125 million. How much was its overall profit or loss?

Test Prep

56. Multiple Choice Which expression is represented by the model?

   Ⓐ $-4 + (-1)$ Ⓒ $-4 + 3$

   Ⓑ $-4 + 0$ Ⓓ $-4 + 4$

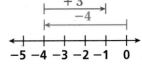

57. Multiple Choice Which expression has the greatest value?

   Ⓕ $-4 + 8$ Ⓖ $-2 + (-3)$ Ⓗ $1 + 2$ Ⓙ $4 + (-6)$

Additive Inverse and Absolute Value

CC.7.NS.1 Apply and extend previous understandings of addition and subtraction to add and subtract rational numbers; represent addition and subtraction on a horizontal or vertical number line diagram. **Also CC.7.NS.1a, CC.7.NS.1b**

Previously you learned how opposites, or additive inverses, are numbers that are the same distance from 0, but are on opposite sides of 0 on the number line. Additive inverses can be combined to equal 0.

A football player gets tackled for a *loss* of 5 yards, which can be written as −5. To get back to the line of scrimmage, or where the players originally started, the team must *gain* 5 yards, which can be written as +5 or 5.

The sum of the additive inverses −5 and 5 is 0.

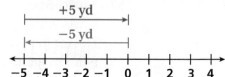

-5 -4 -3 -2 -1 $\ 0\ $ 1 $\ 2$ $\ 3$ $\ 4$

EXAMPLE **1** **Finding the Additive Inverse**

Write an integer to represent each situation. Then find the additive inverse of the integer, and describe what it represents.

Reading Math

Words such as *gain, loss, up,* and *down* indicate the positive or negative sign of an integer.

A The State Capitol building in Denver, Colorado is approximately 5,280 feet above sea level.

Integer: +5,280   *"Above" indicates a positive integer.*
Additive inverse: −5,280   *−5,280 and 5,280 are opposites.*

Check $5{,}208 + (-5{,}280) = 0$ ✓
The additive inverse represents the number of feet downward back to sea level.

B A corporation had a total loss of $400 in profits last year.

Integer: −400   *"Loss" indicates a negative integer.*
Additive inverse: 400   *400 and −400 are opposites.*

Check $-400 + 400 = 0$ ✓
The additive inverse represents the amount of profit, in dollars, needed for the corporation to make exactly $0 and break even.

Recall that absolute value is a number's distance from zero. In real-world situations, absolute value is used to indicate a distance, amount, or size of change, but not a direction such as up or down .

EXAMPLE 2 **Finding the Amount of Change**

Write an integer to represent each situation. Then find the absolute value of that integer, and describe what it represents in the situation.

A Adam delivers 25 newpapers in a day.

Integer: −25   *"Delivers" indicates a negative integer.*
|−25| = 25   *Find the absolute value of −25.*

The amount of change in newspapers is 25.

B The temperature in Miami increased 7° F from sunrise to noon.

Integer: +7   *"Increased" indicates a positive integer.*
|+7| = 7   *Find the absolute value of 7.*

The amount of change in temperature is 7° F.

EXTENSION

Exercises

Anna and Bob get on two different elevators at the 50th floor of a building. Anna rides up to the 82nd floor. Bob rides his elevator down to the 15th floor.

1. What integer value represents Anna's change in floors during her ride?

2. What integer value represents Bob's change in floors during his ride?

3. Find the distance, in floors, that Anna traveled.

4. Find the distance, in floors, that Bob traveled.

5. What is the additive inverse of their starting point? What does this represent?

The table shows the approximate elevation records for several different types of aircraft and boats. Use the table for Exercises 6–10.

6. What integer value represents the record elevation of a glider?

7. What integer value represents the record elevation of a submarine?

8. Find the absolute value of the record elevation of the helicopter.

Type of Transportation	Elevation Record
Glider	15 km above sea level
Helicopter	9 km above sea level
Hot Air Balloon	21 km above sea level
Submarine	11 km below sea level

9. What is the difference in elevations between the submarine and the hot air balloon?

? 10. **What's the Error?** Isaac determines that the intger value of the elevation of the submarine is −11. He determines that the additive inverse is −11. Explain Isaac's error and give the correct additive inverse.

Model Integer Subtraction

Use with Subtracting Integers

 Learn It Online
Lab Resources Online

KEY

○ = 1
● = −1
○ + ● = 0

REMEMBER
- Adding or subtracting zero does not change the value of an expression.

 **Use appropriate tools strategically.**
CC.7.NS.1 Apply and extend previous understandings of addition and subtraction to add and subtract rational numbers; represent addition and subtraction on a horizontal or vertical number line diagram. **Also CC.7.NS.3**

You can model integer subtraction by using integer chips.

Activity

These groups of chips show three different ways of modeling 2.

1️⃣ Show two other ways of modeling 2.

These groups of chips show two different ways of modeling −2.

2️⃣ Show two other ways of modeling −2.

You can model subtraction problems involving two integers with the same sign by taking away chips.

   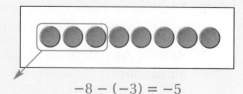

$$8 - 3 = 5$$ $$-8 - (-3) = -5$$

3️⃣ Use integer chips to find each difference.

a. $6 - 5$ **b.** $-6 - (-5)$ **c.** $10 - 7$ **d.** $-7 - (-4)$

To model subtraction problems involving two integers with different signs, such as −6 − 3, you will need to add zero pairs before you can take chips away.

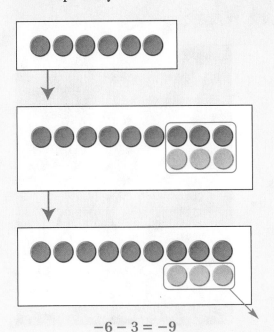

Use 6 red chips to represent −6.

Since you cannot take away 3 yellow chips, add 3 yellow chips paired with 3 red chips.

Now you can take away 3 yellow chips.

$$-6 - 3 = -9$$

4 Use integer chips to find each difference.

a. −6 − 5   **b.** 5 − (−6)   **c.** 4 − 7   **d.** −2 − (−3)

Think and Discuss

1. How could you model the expression 0 − 5?

2. When you add zero pairs to model subtraction using chips, does it matter how many zero pairs you add?

3. Would 2 − 3 have the same answer as 3 − 2? Why or why not?

4. **Make a Conjecture** Make a conjecture for the sign of the answer when a positive integer is subtracted from a negative integer. Give examples.

Try This

Use integer chips to find each difference.

1. 4 − 2   **2.** −4 − (−2)   **3.** −2 − (−3)

4. 3 − 4   **5.** 2 − 3   **6.** 0 − 3

7. 5 − 3   **8.** −3 − (−5)   **9.** 6 − (−4)

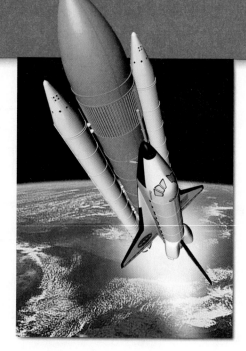

2-3 Subtracting Integers

COMMON CORE

CC.7.NS.1 Apply and extend previous understandings of addition and subtraction to add and subtract rational numbers; represent addition and subtraction on a horizontal or vertical number line diagram. *Also CC.7.NS.1c*

During flight, the space shuttle may be exposed to temperatures as low as −250 °F and as high as 3,000 °F.

To find the difference in these temperatures, you need to know how to subtract integers with different signs.

You can model the difference between two integers using a number line. When you subtract a positive number, the difference is *less* than the original number, so you move to the *left*. To subtract a negative number, move to the *right*.

EXAMPLE 1 **Modeling Integer Subtraction**

Use a number line to find each difference.

A 3 − 8

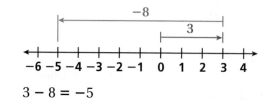

Start at 0.
Move right 3 units.
To subtract 8,
move to the left.

3 − 8 = −5

> **Helpful Hint**
>
> If the number being subtracted is less than the number it is subtracted from, the answer will be positive. If the number being subtracted is greater, the answer will be negative.

B −4 − 2

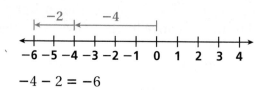

Start at 0.
Move left 4 units.
To subtract 2,
move to the left.

−4 − 2 = −6

C 2 − (−3)

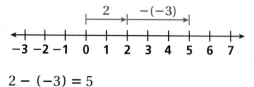

Start at 0.
Move right 2 units.
To subtract −3,
move to the right.

2 − (−3) = 5

Addition and subtraction are inverse operations—they "undo" each other. Instead of subtracting a number, you can *add its opposite.*

Video **Lesson Tutorials Online**   my.hrw.com

EXAMPLE 2

Subtracting Integers by Adding the Opposite

Interactivities Online ▶

Find each difference.

A $5 - 9$

$5 - 9 = 5 + (-9)$ *Add the opposite of 9.*

$\quad\quad\; = -4$

B $-9 - (-2)$

$-9 - (-2) = -9 + 2$ *Add the opposite of −2.*

$\quad\quad\quad\;\; = -7$

C $-4 - 3$

$-4 - 3 = -4 + (-3)$ *Add the opposite of 3.*

$\quad\quad\quad = -7$

EXAMPLE 3

Evaluating Expressions with Integers

Evaluate $a - b$ **for each set of values.**

A $a = -6, b = 7$

$a - b$

$-6 - 7 = -6 + (-7)$ *Substitute for a and b. Add the opposite*

$\quad\quad\;\; = -13$ *of 7.*

B $a = 14, b = -9$

$a - b$

$14 - (-9) = 14 + 9$ *Substitute for a and b. Add the opposite*

$\quad\quad\quad = 23$ *of −9.*

EXAMPLE 4

Temperature Application

Find the difference between 3,000 °F and −250 °F, the temperatures the space shuttle must endure.

$3,000 - (-250)$

$3,000 + 250 = 3,250$ *Add the opposite of −250.*

The difference in temperatures the shuttle must endure is 3,250 °F.

MATHEMATICAL PRACTICES

Think and Discuss

1. Suppose you subtract one negative integer from another. Will your answer be greater than or less than the number you started with?

2. Tell whether you can reverse the order of integers when subtracting and still get the same answer. Why or why not?

Learn It Online
Homework Help Online
Exercises 1–35, 39 41, 43, 45, 47, 51, 53

GUIDED PRACTICE

See Example **1** Use a number line to find each difference.

1. $4 - 7$ **2.** $-6 - 5$ **3.** $2 - (-4)$ **4.** $-8 - (-2)$

See Example **2** Find each difference.

5. $6 - 10$ **6.** $-3 - (-8)$ **7.** $-1 - 9$ **8.** $-12 - (-2)$

See Example **3** Evaluate $a - b$ for each set of values.

9. $a = 5, b = -2$ **10.** $a = -8, b = 6$ **11.** $a = 4, b = 18$

See Example **4** **12.** In 1980, in Great Falls, Montana, the temperature rose from -32 °F to 15 °F in seven minutes. How much did the temperature increase?

INDEPENDENT PRACTICE

See Example **1** Use a number line to find each difference.

13. $7 - 12$ **14.** $-5 - (-9)$ **15.** $2 - (-6)$ **16.** $7 - (-8)$

17. $9 - (-3)$ **18.** $-4 - 10$ **19.** $8 - (-8)$ **20.** $-3 - (-3)$

See Example **2** Find each difference.

21. $-22 - (-5)$ **22.** $-4 - 21$ **23.** $27 - 19$ **24.** $-10 - (-7)$

25. $30 - (-20)$ **26.** $-15 - 15$ **27.** $12 - (-6)$ **28.** $-31 - 15$

See Example **3** Evaluate $a - b$ for each set of values.

29. $a = 9, b = -7$ **30.** $a = -11, b = 2$ **31.** $a = -2, b = 3$

32. $a = 8, b = 19$ **33.** $a = -10, b = 10$ **34.** $a = -4, b = -15$

See Example **4** **35.** In 1918, in Granville, North Dakota, the temperature rose from -33 °F to 50 °F in 12 hours. How much did the temperature increase?

PRACTICE AND PROBLEM SOLVING

Extra Practice
See Extra Practice for more exercises.

Simplify.

36. $2 - 8$ **37.** $-5 - 9$ **38.** $15 - 12 - 8$

39. $6 + (-5) - 3$ **40.** $1 - 8 + (-6)$ **41.** $4 - (-7) - 9$

42. $(2 - 3) - (5 - 6)$ **43.** $5 - (-8) - (-3)$ **44.** $10 - 12 + 2$

Evaluate each expression for $m = -5$, $n = 8$, and $p = -14$.

45. $m - n + p$ **46.** $n - m - p$ **47.** $p - m - n$ **48.** $m + n - p$

49. Patterns Find the next three numbers in the pattern $7, 3, -1, -5, -9, \ldots$ Then describe the pattern.

50. The temperature of Mercury can be as high as 873 °F. The temperature of Pluto is about −393 °F. What is the difference between these temperatures?

51. One side of Mercury always faces the Sun. The temperature on this side can reach 873 °F. The temperature on the other side can be as low as −361 °F. What is the difference between the two temperatures?

52. Earth's moon rotates relative to the Sun about once a month. The side facing the Sun at a given time can be as hot as 224 °F. The side away from the Sun can be as cold as −307 °F. What is the difference between these temperatures?

53. The highest recorded temperature on Earth is 136 °F. The lowest is −129 °F. What is the difference between these temperatures?

Use the graph for Exercises 54 and 55.

54. How much deeper is the deepest canyon on Mars than the deepest canyon on Venus?

55. ⭐ **Challenge** What is the difference between Earth's highest mountain and its deepest ocean canyon? What is the difference between Mars' highest mountain and its deepest canyon? Which difference is greater? How much greater is it?

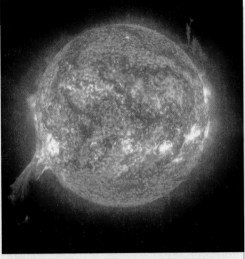

Temperatures in the Sun range from about 5,500 °C at its surface to more than 15 million °C at its core.

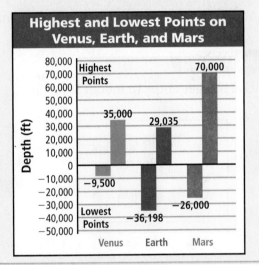

Highest and Lowest Points on Venus, Earth, and Mars

Highest Points: Venus 35,000; Earth 29,035; Mars 70,000

Lowest Points: Venus −9,500; Earth −36,198; Mars −26,000

Depth (ft)

Test Prep

56. Multiple Choice Which expression does NOT have a value of −3?

ⓐ −2 − 1   ⓑ 10 − 13   ⓒ 5 − (−8)   ⓓ −4 − (−1)

57. Extended Response If $m = -2$ and $n = 4$, which expression has the least absolute value: $m + n$, $n - m$, or $m - n$? Explain your answer.

Model Integer Multiplication and Division

Learn It Online
Lab Resources Online

KEY

● = 1

● = −1

● + ● = 0

REMEMBER

- The Commutative Property states that two numbers can be multiplied in any order without changing the product.
- Multiplication is repeated addition.
- Multiplication and division are inverse operations.

Use appropriate tools strategically.
CC.7.NS.2 Apply and extend previous understandings of multiplication and division and of fractions to multiply and divide rational numbers. *Also CC.7.NS.3*

You can model integer multiplication and division by using integer chips.

Activity 1

Use integer chips to model $3 \cdot (-5)$.

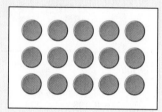

Think: $3 \cdot (-5)$ means 3 groups of −5.

Arrange 3 groups of 5 red chips.
There are a total of 15 red chips.

$3 \cdot (-5) = -15$

1 Use integer chips to find each product.

a. $2 \cdot (-2)$ **b.** $3 \cdot (-6)$ **c.** $5 \cdot (-4)$ **d.** $6 \cdot (-3)$

Use integer chips to model $-4 \cdot 2$.

Using the Commutative Property, you can write $-4 \cdot 2$ as $2 \cdot (-4)$.

Think: $2 \cdot (-4)$ means 2 groups of −4.

Arrange 2 groups of 4 red chips.
There are a total of 8 red chips.

$-4 \cdot 2 = -8$

2 Use integer chips to find each product.

a. $-6 \cdot 5$ **b.** $-4 \cdot 6$ **c.** $-3 \cdot 4$ **d.** $-2 \cdot 3$

1. What is the sign of the product when you multiply two positive numbers? a negative and a positive number? two negative numbers?

2. If 12 were the answer to a multiplication problem, list all of the possible factors that are integers.

Try This

Use integer chips to find each product.

1. $4 \cdot (-5)$ 2. $-3 \cdot 2$ 3. $1 \cdot (-6)$ 4. $-5 \cdot 2$

5. On days that Kathy has swimming lessons, she spends $2.00 of her allowance on snacks. Last week, Kathy had swimming lessons on Monday, Wednesday, and Friday. How much of her allowance did Kathy spend on snacks last week? Use integer chips to model the situation and solve the problem.

Activity 2

Use integer chips to model $-15 \div 3$.

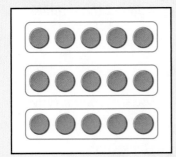

Think: −15 is separated into 3 equal groups.

Arrange 15 red chips into 3 equal groups.

There are 5 red chips in each group.

$-15 \div 3 = -5$

1 Use integer chips to find each quotient.

    a. $-20 \div 5$ b. $-18 \div 6$ c. $-12 \div 4$ d. $-24 \div 8$

Think and Discuss

1. What is the sign of the answer when you divide two negative integers? a negative integer by a positive integer? a positive integer by a negative integer?

2. How are multiplication and division of integers related?

Try This

Use integer chips to find each quotient.

1. $-21 \div 7$ 2. $-12 \div 4$ 3. $-8 \div 2$ 4. $-10 \div 5$

5. Ty spent $18 of his allowance at the arcade. He hit baseballs, played pinball, and played video games. Each of these activities cost the same amount at the arcade. How much did each activity cost? Use integer chips to model the situation and solve the problem.

Multiplying and Dividing Integers

COMMON CORE

CC.7.NS.2 Apply and extend previous understandings of multiplication and division and of fractions to multiply and divide rational numbers. *Also CC.7.EE.2*

You can think of multiplication as repeated addition.

$$3 \cdot 2 = 2 + 2 + 2 = 6$$
$$3 \cdot (-2) = (-2) + (-2) + (-2) = -6$$

E X A M P L E 1   Multiplying Integers Using Repeated Addition

Interactivities Online ▶

Use a number line to find each product.

A $3 \cdot (-3)$

$+(-3)$ $+(-3)$ $+(-3)$

$-10\ -9\ -8\ -7\ -6\ -5\ -4\ -3\ -2\ -1\ \ 0\ \ 1$

Think: Start at 0. Add −3 three times.

$3 \cdot (-3) = -9$

B $-4 \cdot 2$

$-4 \cdot 2 = 2 \cdot (-4)$

Use the Commutative Property.

$+(-4)$ $+(-4)$

$-10\ -9\ -8\ -7\ -6\ -5\ -4\ -3\ -2\ -1\ \ 0\ \ 1$

Think: Start at 0. Add −4 two times.

$-4 \cdot 2 = -8$

Remember!

Multiplication and division are inverse operations. They "undo" each other. Notice how these operations undo each other in the patterns shown.

The patterns below suggest that when the signs of two integers are different, their product or quotient is negative. The patterns also suggest that the product or quotient of two negative integers is positive.

$-3 \cdot\ \ \ \ 2 = -6$	$-6 \div (-3) =\ \ \ 2$
$-3 \cdot\ \ \ \ 1 = -3$	$-3 \div (-3) =\ \ \ 1$
$-3 \cdot\ \ \ \ 0 =\ \ \ 0$	$0 \div (-3) =\ \ \ 0$
$-3 \cdot (-1) =\ \ \ 3$	$3 \div (-3) = -1$
$-3 \cdot (-2) =\ \ \ 6$	$6 \div (-3) = -2$

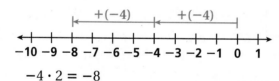

Multiplying and Dividing Two Integers	
If the signs are:	**Your answer will be:**
the same ⟶	positive
different ⟶	negative

Video **Lesson Tutorials Online**   my.hrw.com

EXAMPLE **2** Multiplying Integers

Find each product.

A −4 · (−2)

−4 · (−2)   *Both signs are*
              negative, so the
    8   *product is positive.*

B −3 · 6

−3 · 6   *The signs are*
           different, so the
  −18   *product is negative.*

EXAMPLE **3** Dividing Integers

Find each quotient.

A 72 ÷ (−9)   *The signs are*
  72 ÷ (−9)   *different, so the*
     −8   *quotient is negative.*

B −100 ÷ (−5)   *The signs are the*
  −100 ÷ (−5)   *same, so the*
      20   *quotient is positive.*

Zero divided by any number is zero, but you cannot find an answer for division by zero. For example, −6 ÷ 0 ≠ 0, because 0 · 0 ≠ −6. We say that division by zero is undefined.

EXAMPLE **4** *Sports Application*

A football team must move the ball forward at least 10 yards from its starting point to make a first down. If the team has 2 losses of 3 yards each and a gain of 14 yards, does the team make a first down?

Add the total loss to the gain to find how far the ball moved forward.

2 · (−3) + 14   *Multiply −3 by 2 to find the total loss;*
                  then add the gain of 14.

  −6 + 14   *Use the order of operations. Multiply first.*

    8   *Then add.*

The team moved the ball forward 8 yards, so it did not make a first down.

Think and Discuss

1. List at least four different multiplication examples that have 24 as their product. Use both positive and negative integers.

2. Explain why the rules for multiplying integers make sense.

Exercises

Learn It Online
Homework Help Online
Exercises 1–34, 35, 37, 39, 41, 43, 45, 47

GUIDED PRACTICE

See Example **1**   **Use a number line to find each product.**

     1. $5 \cdot (-3)$ **2.** $5 \cdot (-2)$ **3.** $-3 \cdot 5$ **4.** $-4 \cdot 6$

See Example **2**   **Find each product.**

     5. $-5 \cdot (-3)$ **6.** $-2 \cdot 5$ **7.** $3 \cdot (-5)$ **8.** $-7 \cdot (-4)$

See Example **3**   **Find each quotient.**

     9. $32 \div (-4)$ **10.** $-18 \div 3$ **11.** $-20 \div (-5)$ **12.** $49 \div (-7)$

     13. $-63 \div (-9)$ **14.** $-50 \div 10$ **15.** $63 \div 0$ **16.** $-45 \div (-5)$

See Example **4**   **17.** Angelina hiked along a 2,250-foot mountain trail. She stopped 5 times along the way to rest, walking the same distance between each stop. How far did Angelina hike before the first stop?

INDEPENDENT PRACTICE

See Example **1**   **Use a number line to find each product.**

     18. $2 \cdot (-1)$ **19.** $-5 \cdot 2$ **20.** $-4 \cdot 2$ **21.** $3 \cdot (-4)$

See Example **2**   **Find each product.**

     22. $4 \cdot (-6)$ **23.** $-6 \cdot (-8)$ **24.** $-8 \cdot 4$ **25.** $-5 \cdot (-7)$

See Example **3**   **Find each quotient.**

     26. $48 \div (-6)$ **27.** $-35 \div (-5)$ **28.** $-16 \div 4$ **29.** $-64 \div 8$

     30. $-42 \div 0$ **31.** $81 \div (-9)$ **32.** $-77 \div 11$ **33.** $27 \div (-3)$

See Example **4**   **34.** A scuba diver descended below the ocean's surface in 35-foot intervals as he examined a coral reef. He dove to a total depth of 140 feet. In how many intervals did the diver make his descent?

PRACTICE AND PROBLEM SOLVING

Extra Practice
See Extra Practice for more exercises.

Find each product or quotient.

     35. $-4 \cdot 10$ **36.** $-3 \div 0$ **37.** $-45 \div 15$ **38.** $-3 \cdot 4 \cdot (-1)$

     39. $-500 \div (-10)$ **40.** $5 \cdot (-4) \cdot (-2)$ **41.** $225 \div (-75)$ **42.** $0 \div (-3)$

Evaluate each expression for $a = -5$, $b = 6$, and $c = -12$.

     43. $-2c + b$ **44.** $4a - b$ **45.** $ab + c$ **46.** $ac \div b$

     47. **Earth Science** A scuba diver is swimming at a depth of -12 feet in the Flower Garden Banks National Marine Sanctuary. She dives down to a coral reef that is at five times this depth. What is the depth of the coral reef?

Simplify each expression. Justify your steps using the Commutative, Associative, and Distributive Properties when necessary.

48. $(-3)^2$ **49.** $-(-2+1)$ **50.** $8 + (-5)^3 + 7$ **51.** $(-1)^5 \cdot (9 + 3)$

52. $29 - (-7) - 3$ **53.** $-4 \cdot 14 \cdot (-25)$ **54.** $25 - (-2) \cdot 4^2$ **55.** $8 - (6 \div (-2))$

56. Earth Science The table shows the depths of major caves in the United States. Approximately how many times deeper is Jewel Cave than Kartchner Caverns?

Depths of Major U.S. Caves	
Cave	**Depth (ft)**
Carlsbad Caverns	−1,022
Caverns of Sonora	−150
Ellison's Cave	−1,000
Jewel Cave	−696
Kartchner Caverns	−137
Mammoth Cave	−379

Source: NSS U.S.A. Long Cave List

Personal Finance Does each person end up with more or less money than he started with? By how much?

57. Kevin spends $24 a day for 3 days.

58. Devin earns $15 a day for 5 days.

59. Evan spends $20 a day for 3 days. Then he earns $18 a day for 4 days.

60. What's the Error? A student writes, "The quotient of an integer divided by an integer of the opposite sign has the sign of the integer with the greater absolute value." What is the student's error?

61. Write About It Explain how to find the product and the quotient of two integers.

62. Challenge Use > or < to compare $-2 \cdot (-1) \cdot 4 \cdot 2 \cdot (-3)$ and $-1 + (-2) + 4 + (-25) + (-10)$.

Test Prep

63. Multiple Choice Which of the expressions are equal to −20?

I $-2 \cdot 10$ **II** $-40 \div (-2)$ **III** $-5 \cdot (-2)^2$ **IV** $-4 \cdot 2 - 12$

  A I only   **B** I and II   **C** I, III, and IV   **D** I, II, III, IV

64. Multiple Choice Which expression has a value that is greater than the value of $-25 \div (-5)$?

  F $36 \div (-6)$ **G** $-100 \div 10$ **H** $-50 \div (-10)$ **J** $-45 \div (-5)$

Hands-On LAB

Model Integer Equations

Use with Solving Equations Containing Integers

Learn It Online
Lab Resources Online

KEY

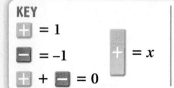

REMEMBER
* Adding or subtracting zero does not change the value of an expression.

Use appropriate tools strategically.

CC.7.EE.4 Use variables to represent quantities in a real-world or mathematical problem, and construct simple equations and inequalities to solve problems by reasoning about the quantities.

You can use algebra tiles to model and solve equations.

Activity

To solve the equation $x + 2 = 3$, you need to get x alone on one side of the equal sign. You can add or remove tiles as long as you add the same amount or remove the same amount on both sides.

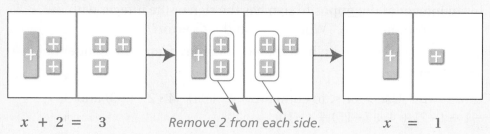

$x + 2 = 3$ *Remove 2 from each side.* $x = 1$

1 Use algebra tiles to model and solve each equation.

a. $x + 3 = 5$ **b.** $x + 4 = 9$ **c.** $x + 5 = 8$ **d.** $x + 6 = 6$

The equation $x + 6 = 4$ is more difficult to model because there are not enough tiles on the right side of the mat to remove 6 from each side.

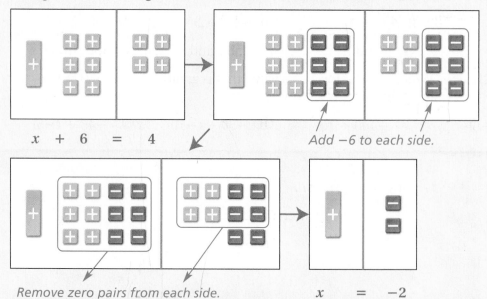

$x + 6 = 4$ *Add −6 to each side.*

Remove zero pairs from each side. $x = -2$

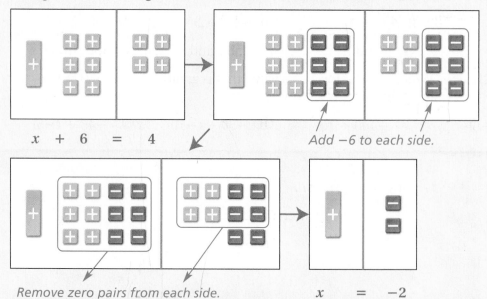

2 Use algebra tiles to model and solve each equation.

a. $x\ 5\ 3$ **b.** $x\ 4\ 2$ **c.** $x\ 7\ 3$ **d.** $x\ 6\ 2$

When modeling an equation that involves subtraction, such as $x\ 62$, you must first rewrite the equation as an addition equation. For example, the equation $x\ 62$ can be rewritten as $x(6)2$.

Modeling equations that involve addition of negative numbers is similar to modeling equations that involve addition of positive numbers.

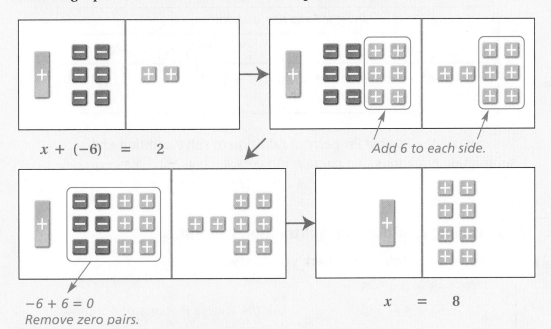

$x + (-6) = 2$

Add 6 to each side.

$-6 + 6 = 0$
Remove zero pairs.

$x = 8$

3 Use algebra tiles to model and solve each equation.

a. $x\ 4\ 3$ **b.** $x\ 2\ 8$ **c.** $x\ 5\ 5$ **d.** $x\ 7\ 0$

Think and Discuss

1. When you remove tiles, what operation are you modeling? When you add tiles, what operation are you modeling?

2. How can you use the original model to check your solution?

3. To model $x62$, you must rewrite the equation as $x(6)2$. Why are you allowed to do this?

Try This

Use algebra tiles to model and solve each equation.

1. $x\ 7\ 10$ **2.** $x\ 5\ 8$ **3.** $x\ (5)\ 4$ **4.** $x\ 2\ 1$

5. $x\ 4\ 8$ **6.** $x\ 3\ 2$ **7.** $x\ (1)\ 9$ **8.** $x\ 7\ 6$

Solving Equations Containing Integers

COMMON CORE

CC.7.EE.4 Use variables to represent quantities in a real-world or mathematical problem, and construct simple equations and inequalities to solve problems by reasoning about the quantities. *Also CC.7.NS.1b*

Recall that the sum of a number and its opposite is 0. This is called the Inverse Property of Addition.

Inverse Property of Addition		
Words	**Numbers**	**Algebra**
The sum of a number and its opposite, or additive inverse, is 0.	$3 + (-3) = 0$	$a + (-a) = 0$

You can use the Inverse Property of Addition to solve addition and subtraction equations that contain integers, such as $-3 + y = -5$.

EXAMPLE **1**

Interactivities Online ▶

Solving Addition and Subtraction Equations

Solve each equation. Check your answer.

A $-3 + y = -5$

$$-3 + y = -5$$
$$\underline{+\,3 \qquad +\,3}$$ *Use the Inverse Property of Addition.*
                 Add 3 to both sides.
$$y = -2$$

Check $-3 + y = -5$
$$-3 + (-2) \overset{?}{=} -5 \qquad \textit{Substitute –2 for y.}$$
$$-5 \overset{?}{=} -5 \checkmark \qquad \textit{True.}$$

B $n + 3 = -10$

$$n + 3 = -10$$
$$\underline{+\,(-3) \quad +\,(-3)} \qquad \textit{Use the Inverse Property of Addition.}$$
                 Add −3 to both sides.
$$n = -13$$

Check $n + 3 = -10$
$$-13 + 3 \overset{?}{=} -10 \qquad \textit{Substitute −13 for n.}$$
$$-10 \overset{?}{=} -10 \checkmark \qquad \textit{True.}$$

C $x - 8 = -32$

$$x - 8 = -32$$
$$\underline{+\,8 \quad +\,8} \qquad \textit{Use the Inverse Property of Addition.}$$
                Add 8 to both sides.
$$x = -24$$

Check $x - 8 = -32$
$$-24 - 8 \overset{?}{=} -32 \qquad \textit{Substitute −24 for x.}$$
$$-32 \overset{?}{=} -32 \checkmark \qquad \textit{True.}$$

   Video **Lesson Tutorials Online** my.hrw.com

You can also use inverse operations to solve multiplication and division equations that contain integers.

EXAMPLE **2**

Solving Multiplication and Division Equations

Solve each equation. Check your answer.

A $\frac{a}{-3} = 9$

$(-3)\left(\frac{a}{-3}\right) = (-3)9$ *Multiply both sides by −3.*

$a = -27$

Check $\frac{a}{-3} = 9$

$\frac{-27}{-3} \overset{?}{=} 9$ *Substitute −27 for a.*

$9 \overset{?}{=} 9 ✔$ *True.*

B $-120 = 6x$

$\frac{-120}{6} = \frac{6x}{6}$ *Divide both sides by 6.*

$-20 = x$

Check $-120 = 6x$

$-120 \overset{?}{=} 6(-20)$ *Substitute −20 for x.*

$-120 \overset{?}{=} -120 ✔$ *True.*

EXAMPLE **3**

Business Application

A shoe manufacturer made a profit of $800 million. This amount is $200 million more than last year's profit. What was last year's profit?

Let p represent last year's profit (in millions of dollars).

This year's profit	is	$200 million	more than	last year's profit.
800	=	200	+	p

$800 = 200 + p$

$\underline{-200 \quad -200}$

$600 = \quad p$ Last year's profit was $600 million.

Think and Discuss

1. Tell what value of n makes $-n + 32$ equal to zero.

2. Explain why you would or would not multiply both sides of an equation by 0 to solve it.

Exercises

GUIDED PRACTICE

Solve each equation. Check your answer.

See Example **1**

1. $w - 6 = -2$

2. $x + 5 = -7$

3. $k = -18 + 11$

See Example **2**

4. $\frac{n}{-4} = 2$

5. $-240 = 8y$

6. $-5a = 300$

See Example **3**

7. Business Last year, a chain of electronics stores had a loss of $45 million. This year the loss is $12 million more than last year's loss. What is this year's loss?

INDEPENDENT PRACTICE

Solve each equation. Check your answer.

See Example **1**

8. $b - 7 = -16$

9. $k + 6 = 3$

10. $s + 2 = -4$

11. $v + 14 = 10$

12. $c + 8 = -20$

13. $a - 25 = -5$

See Example **2**

14. $9c = -99$

15. $\frac{t}{8} = -4$

16. $-16 = 2z$

17. $\frac{n}{-5} = -30$

18. $200 = -25p$

19. $\frac{\ell}{12} = 12$

See Example **3**

20. The temperature in Nome, Alaska, was $-50\ °F$. This was $18\ °F$ less than the temperature in Anchorage, Alaska, on the same day. What was the temperature in Anchorage?

PRACTICE AND PROBLEM SOLVING

Extra Practice
See Extra Practice for more exercises.

Solve each equation. Check your answer.

21. $9y = 900$

22. $d - 15 = 45$

23. $j + 56 = -7$

24. $\frac{s}{-20} = 7$

25. $-85 = -5c$

26. $v - 39 = -16$

27. $11y = -121$

28. $\frac{n}{36} = 9$

29. $w + 41 = 0$

30. $\frac{r}{238} = 8$

31. $-23 = x + 35$

32. $0 = -15m$

33. $4x = 2 + 14$

34. $c + c + c = 6$

35. $t - 3 = 4 + 2$

36. Geometry The three angles of a triangle have equal measures. The sum of their measures is 180°. What is the measure of each angle?

37. Sports Herb has 42 days to prepare for a cross-country race. During his training, he will run a total of 126 miles. If Herb runs the same distance every day, how many miles will he run each day?

38. Multi-Step Jared bought one share of stock for $225.
   a. He sold the stock for a profit of $55. What was the selling price of the stock?
   b. The price of the stock dropped $40 the day after Jared sold it. At what price would Jared have sold it if he had waited until then?

Translate each sentence into an equation. Then solve the equation.

39. The sum of −13 and a number *p* is 8.

40. A number *x* divided by 4 is −7.

41. 9 less than a number *t* is −22.

42. Physical Science On the Kelvin temperature scale, pure water boils at 373 K. The difference between the boiling point and the freezing point of water on this scale is 100 K. What is the freezing point of water?

Recreation The graph shows the most popular travel destinations over Labor Day weekend. Use the graph for Exercises 43 and 44.

43. Which destination was 5 times more popular than theme or amusement parks?

44. According to the graph, the mountains were as popular as state or national parks and what other destination combined?

Top Labor Day Destinations

Destination	Percent
Cities	23%
Oceans or beaches	20%
Towns or rural areas	19%
Mountains	14%
Lakes	8%
State or national parks	6%
Theme or amusement parks	4%
Other	6%

0

Source: AAA

45. Choose a Strategy Matthew (*M*) earns $23 less a week than his sister Allie (*A*). Their combined salaries are $93. How much does each of them earn per week?

 **A** *A: $35; M: $12*   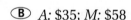 **B** *A: $35; M: $58*    **C** *A: $58; M: $35*

46. Write About It Explain how to isolate a variable in an equation.

47. Challenge Write an equation that includes the variable *p* and the numbers 5, 3, and 31 so that the solution is *p* = 16.

Test Prep

48. Multiple Choice Solve −15*m* = 60.

  A *m* = −4   **B** *m* = 5   **C** *m* = 45   **D** *m* = 75

49. Multiple Choice For which equation does *x* = 2?

  F −3*x* = 6   **G** *x* + 3 = −5   **H** *x* + *x* = 4   **J** $\frac{x}{4}$ = −8

Ready To Go On?

Quiz for Lessons 1 Through 5

1 Integers

Compare the integers. Use < or > .

1. $5 \ \blacksquare \ -8$

2. $-2 \ \blacksquare \ -6$

3. $-4 \ \blacksquare \ 3$

4. Use a number line to order the integers $-7, 3, 6, -1, 0, 5, -4,$ and 7 from least to greatest.

Use a number line to find each absolute value.

5. $|-23|$

6. $|17|$

7. $|-10|$

2 Adding Integers

Find each sum.

8. $-6 + 3$

9. $5 + (-9)$

10. $-7 + (-11)$

Evaluate $p + t$ for the given values.

11. $p = 5, t = -18$

12. $p = -4, t = -13$

13. $p = -37, t = 39$

3 Subtracting Integers

Find each difference.

14. $-21 - (-7)$

15. $9 - (-11)$

16. $6 - 17$

17. When Cai traveled from New Orleans, Louisiana, to the Ozark Mountains in Arkansas, the elevation changed from 7 ft below sea level to 2,314 ft above sea level. How much did the elevation increase?

4 Multiplying and Dividing Integers

Find each product or quotient.

18. $-7 \cdot 3$

19. $30 \div (-15)$

20. $-5 \cdot (-9)$

21. After reaching the top of a cliff, a rock climber descended the rock face using a 65 ft rope. The distance to the base of the cliff was 585 ft. How many rope lengths did it take the climber to complete her descent?

5 Solving Equations Containing Integers

Solve each equation. Check your answer.

22. $3x = 30$

23. $k - 25 = 50$

24. $y + 16 = -8$

25. This year, 72 students completed projects for the science fair. This was 23 more students than last year. How many students completed projects for the science fair last year?

Focus on Problem Solving

Make a Plan

• Choose a method of computation

When you know the operation you must use and you know exactly which numbers to use, a calculator might be the easiest way to solve a problem. Sometimes, such as when the numbers are small or are multiples of 10, it may be quicker to use mental math.

Sometimes, you have to write the numbers to see how they relate in an equation. When you are working an equation, using a pencil and paper is the simplest method to use because you can see each step as you go.

For each problem, tell whether you would use a calculator, mental math, or pencil and paper to solve it. Explain your answer. Then solve the problem.

1 A scouting troop is collecting aluminum cans to raise money for charity. Their goal is to collect 3,000 cans in 6 months. If they set a goal to collect an equal number of cans each month, how many cans can they expect to collect each month?

2 The Grand Canyon is 29,000 meters wide at its widest point. The Empire State Building, located in New York City, is 381 meters tall. Laid end to end, about how many Empire State Buildings would fit across the Grand Canyon at its widest point?

3 On a piano keyboard, all but one of the black keys are arranged in groups so that there are 7 groups with 2 black keys each and 7 groups with 3 black keys each. How many black keys are there on a piano?

4 Some wind chimes are made of rods. The rods are usually of different lengths, producing different sounds. The frequency (which determines the pitch) of the sound is measured in hertz (Hz). If one rod on a chime has a frequency of 55 Hz and another rod has a frequency that is twice that of the first rod's, what is the frequency of the second rod?

Equivalent Fractions and Decimals

CC.7.NS.3 Solve real-world and mathematical problems involving the four operations with rational numbers. *Also CC.7.NS.2c*

COMMON CORE

In baseball, a player's batting average compares the number of hits with the number of times the player has been at bat. The statistics below are for the 2006 Major League Baseball season.

Vocabulary

terminating decimal

repeating decimal

Player	Hits	At Bats	Hits / At Bats	Batting Average (thousandths)
Miguel Cabrera	195	576	$\frac{195}{576}$	$195 \div 576 \approx 0.339$
Ichiro Suzuki	224	695	$\frac{224}{695}$	$224 \div 695 \approx 0.322$

To convert a fraction to a decimal, divide the numerator by the denominator.

EXAMPLE 1 Writing Fractions as Decimals

Write each fraction as a decimal. Round to the nearest hundredth, if necessary.

A $\frac{3}{4}$

$$\begin{array}{r} 0.75 \\ 4\overline{)3.00} \\ -28 \\ \hline 20 \\ -20 \\ \hline 0 \end{array}$$

$\frac{3}{4} = 0.75$

B $\frac{6}{5}$

$$\begin{array}{r} 1.2 \\ 5\overline{)6.0} \\ -5 \\ \hline 10 \\ -10 \\ \hline 0 \end{array}$$

$\frac{6}{5} = 1.2$

C $\frac{1}{3}$

$$\begin{array}{r} 0.333\ldots \\ 3\overline{)1.000} \\ -9 \\ \hline 10 \\ -9 \\ \hline 10 \\ -9 \\ \hline 1 \end{array}$$

$\frac{1}{3} = 0.333\ldots$
≈ 0.33

Helpful Hint

You can use a calculator to check your division:

3 ÷ 4 = 0.75

6 ÷ 5 = 1.2

1 ÷ 3 = 0.333...

The decimals 0.75 and 1.2 in Example 1 are **terminating decimals** because the decimals come to an end. The decimal 0.333… is a **repeating decimal** because the decimal repeats a pattern forever. You can also write a repeating decimal with a bar over the repeating part.

$$0.333\ldots = 0.\overline{3} \qquad 0.8333\ldots = 0.8\overline{3} \qquad 0.727272\ldots = 0.\overline{72}$$

Video **Lesson Tutorials Online** my.hrw.com

Otto Greule Jr/Getty Images

You can use place value to write some fractions as decimals.

EXAMPLE 2 **Using Mental Math to Write Fractions as Decimals**

Write each fraction as a decimal.

A $\frac{2}{5}$

$\frac{2}{5} \times \frac{2}{2} = \frac{4}{10}$ *Multiply to get a power of ten in the denominator.*

$= 0.4$

B $\frac{7}{25}$

$\frac{7}{25} \times \frac{4}{4} = \frac{28}{100}$ *Multiply to get a power of ten in the denominator.*

$= 0.28$

You can also use place value to write a terminating decimal as a fraction. Use the place value of the last digit to the right of the decimal point as the denominator of the fraction.

EXAMPLE 3 **Writing Decimals as Fractions**

Write each decimal as a fraction in simplest form.

Reading Math

You read the decimal 0.036 as "thirty-six thousandths."

A 0.036

$0.036 = \frac{36}{1,000}$ *6 is in the thousandths place.*

$= \frac{36 \div 4}{1,000 \div 4}$

$= \frac{9}{250}$

B 1.28

$1.28 = \frac{128}{100}$ *8 is in the hundredths place.*

$= \frac{128 \div 4}{100 \div 4}$

$= \frac{32}{25}$, or $1\frac{7}{25}$

EXAMPLE 4 *Sports Application*

During a football game, Albert completed 23 of the 27 passes he attempted. Find his completion rate to the nearest thousandth.

Fraction	What the Calculator Shows	Completion Rate
$\frac{23}{27}$	23 [÷] 27 [ENTER] .8518518519	0.852

His completion rate is 0.852.

MATHEMATICAL PRACTICES

Think and Discuss

1. Tell how to write a fraction as a decimal.

2. Explain how to use place value to convert 0.2048 to a fraction.

GUIDED PRACTICE

See Example 1 | Write each fraction as a decimal. Round to the nearest hundredth, if necessary.

1. $\frac{4}{7}$ **2.** $\frac{21}{8}$ **3.** $\frac{11}{6}$ **4.** $\frac{7}{9}$

See Example 2 | Write each fraction as a decimal.

5. $\frac{3}{25}$ **6.** $\frac{7}{10}$ **7.** $\frac{1}{20}$ **8.** $\frac{3}{5}$

See Example 3 | Write each decimal as a fraction in simplest form.

9. 0.008   **10.** −0.6   **11.** −2.05   **12.** 3.75

See Example 4 | **13. Sports** After sweeping the Baltimore Orioles at home in 2001, the Seattle Mariners had a record of 103 wins out of 143 games played. Find the Mariners' winning rate. Write your answer as a decimal rounded to the nearest thousandth.

INDEPENDENT PRACTICE

See Example 1 | Write each fraction as a decimal. Round to the nearest hundredth, if necessary.

14. $\frac{9}{10}$ **15.** $\frac{32}{5}$ **16.** $\frac{18}{25}$ **17.** $\frac{7}{8}$

18. $\frac{16}{11}$ **19.** $\frac{500}{500}$ **20.** $\frac{17}{3}$ **21.** $\frac{23}{12}$

See Example 2 | Write each fraction as a decimal.

22. $\frac{5}{4}$ **23.** $\frac{4}{5}$ **24.** $\frac{15}{25}$ **25.** $\frac{11}{20}$

See Example 3 | Write each decimal as a fraction in simplest form.

26. 0.45   **27.** 0.01   **28.** −0.25   **29.** −0.08

30. 1.8   **31.** 15.25   **32.** 5.09   **33.** 8.375

See Example 4 | **34. School** On a test, Caleb answered 73 out of 86 questions correctly. What portion of his answers was correct? Write your answer as a decimal rounded to the nearest thousandth.

PRACTICE AND PROBLEM SOLVING

Extra Practice
See Extra Practice for more exercises.

Give two numbers equivalent to each fraction or decimal.

35. $8\frac{3}{4}$ **36.** 0.66   **37.** 5.05   **38.** $\frac{8}{25}$

39. 15.35   **40.** $8\frac{3}{8}$ **41.** $4\frac{3}{1,000}$ **42.** $3\frac{1}{3}$

Determine whether the numbers in each pair are equivalent.

43. $\frac{3}{4}$ and 0.75   **44.** $\frac{7}{20}$ and 0.45   **45.** $\frac{11}{21}$ and 0.55   **46.** 0.8 and $\frac{4}{5}$

47. 0.275 and $\frac{11}{40}$ **48.** $1\frac{21}{25}$ and 1.72   **49.** 0.74 and $\frac{16}{25}$ **50.** 0.35 and $\frac{7}{20}$

Use the table for Exercises 51 and 52.

XYZ Stock Values (October 2006)				
Date	Open	High	Low	Close
Oct 16	17.89	18.05	17.5	17.8
Oct 17	18.01	18.04	17.15	17.95
Oct 18	17.84	18.55	17.81	18.20

Traders watch the stock prices change from the floor of a stock exchange.

51. Write the highest value of stock XYZ for each day as a mixed number in simplest form.

52. On which date did the price of stock XYZ change by $\frac{9}{25}$ of a dollar between the open and close of the day?

53. ✐ **Write About It** Until recently, prices of stocks were expressed as mixed numbers, such as $24\frac{15}{32}$ dollars. The denominators of such fractions were multiples of 2, such as 2, 4, 6, 8, and so forth. Today, the prices are expressed as decimals to the nearest hundredth, such as 32.35 dollars.

   a. What are some advantages of using decimals instead of fractions?

   b. The old ticker-tape machine punched stock prices onto a tape. Perhaps because fractions could not be shown using the machine, the prices were punched as decimals. Write some decimal equivalents of fractions that the machine might print.

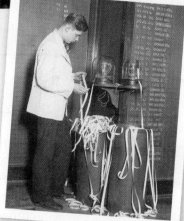

Before the days of computer technology, ticker-tape machines were used to punch the stock prices onto paper strands.

54. ★ **Challenge** Write $\frac{1}{9}$ and $\frac{2}{9}$ as decimals. Use the results to predict the decimal equivalent of $\frac{8}{9}$.

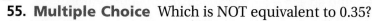

Test Prep

55. Multiple Choice Which is NOT equivalent to 0.35?

   Ⓐ $\frac{35}{100}$ Ⓑ $\frac{7}{20}$ Ⓒ $\frac{14}{40}$ Ⓓ $\frac{25}{80}$

56. Gridded Response Write $\frac{6}{17}$ as a decimal rounded to the nearest hundredth.

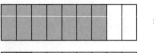

2-7 Comparing and Ordering Rational Numbers

COMMON CORE

CC.7.NS.3 Solve real-world and mathematical problems involving the four operations with rational numbers. **Also CC.7.NS.2c**

Vocabulary

rational number

Which is greater, $\frac{7}{9}$ or $\frac{2}{9}$?

To compare fractions with the same denominator, just compare the numerators.

$\frac{7}{9} > \frac{2}{9}$ because $7 > 2$.

$\boxed{} = \frac{7}{9}$

$\boxed{} = \frac{2}{9}$

To compare fractions with unlike denominators, first write equivalent fractions with common denominators. Then compare the numerators.

"I would like an extra-large pizza with $\frac{1}{2}$ pepperoni, $\frac{4}{5}$ sausuage, $\frac{3}{8}$ anchovies on the pepperoni side, $\frac{5}{11}$ pineapple, $\frac{2}{13}$ doggie treats, $\frac{1}{16}$ catnip . . . and extra cheese."

EXAMPLE 1 **Comparing Fractions**

Compare the fractions. Write < or >.

A $\frac{5}{6} \ \blacksquare \ \frac{7}{10}$

The LCM of the denominators 6 and 10 is 30.

$\frac{5}{6} = \frac{5 \cdot 5}{6 \cdot 5} = \frac{25}{30}$ *Write equivalent fractions with 30 as the denominator.*

$\frac{7}{10} = \frac{7 \cdot 3}{10 \cdot 3} = \frac{21}{30}$

$\frac{25}{30} > \frac{21}{30}$, and so $\frac{5}{6} > \frac{7}{10}$.   *Compare the numerators.*

B $-\frac{3}{5} \ \blacksquare \ -\frac{5}{9}$

Both fractions can be written with a denominator of 45.

$-\frac{3}{5} = \frac{-3 \cdot 9}{5 \cdot 9} = \frac{-27}{45}$ *Write equivalent fractions with 45 as the denominator. Put the negative signs in the numerators.*

$-\frac{5}{9} = \frac{-5 \cdot 5}{9 \cdot 5} = \frac{-25}{45}$

$\frac{-27}{45} < \frac{-25}{45}$, and so $-\frac{3}{5} < -\frac{5}{9}$.

Helpful Hint

A fraction less than 0 can be written as $-\frac{3}{5}$, $\frac{-3}{5}$, or $\frac{3}{-5}$.

Video **Lesson Tutorials Online** my.hrw.com

To compare decimals, line up the decimal points and compare digits from left to right until you find the place where the digits are different.

EXAMPLE 2 **Comparing Decimals**

Compare the decimals. Write < or >.

A 0.81 ▨ 0.84

0.81
↕
0.84

Line up the decimal points.
The tenths are the same.
Compare the hundredths: 1 < 4.

Since 0.01 < 0.04, 0.81 < 0.84.

B $0.\overline{34}$ ▨ 0.342

$0.\overline{34} = 0.3434\ldots$
↕
0.342

$0.\overline{34}$ is a repeating decimal.
Line up the decimal points.
The tenths and hundredths are the same.
Compare the thousandths: 3 > 2.

Since 0.003 > 0.002, $0.\overline{34} > 0.342$.

A **rational number** is a number that can be written as a fraction with an integer for its numerator and a nonzero integer for its denominator. When rational numbers are written in a variety of forms, you can compare the numbers by writing them all in the same form.

EXAMPLE 3 **Ordering Fractions and Decimals**

Order $\frac{3}{5}$, $0.\overline{77}$, −0.1, and $1\frac{1}{5}$ from least to greatest.

$\frac{3}{5} = 0.60$	$0.\overline{77} \approx 0.78$
0.1 0.10	$1\frac{1}{5}$ 1.20

Write as decimals with the same number of places.

Graph the numbers on a number line.

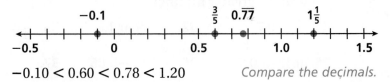

$-0.10 < 0.60 < 0.78 < 1.20$ *Compare the decimals.*

From least to greatest, the numbers are −0.1, $\frac{3}{5}$, $0.\overline{77}$, and $1\frac{1}{5}$.

> **Remember!**
>
> The values on a number line increase as you move from left to right.

MATHEMATICAL PRACTICES

Think and Discuss

1. Tell how to compare two fractions with different denominators.

2. Explain why −0.31 is greater than −0.325 even though 2 > 1.

GUIDED PRACTICE

See Example **1** Compare the fractions. Write < or >.

1. $\frac{3}{5}$ ■ $\frac{4}{5}$

2. $-\frac{5}{8}$ ■ $-\frac{7}{8}$

3. $-\frac{2}{3}$ ■ $-\frac{4}{7}$

4. $3\frac{4}{5}$ ■ $3\frac{2}{3}$

See Example **2** Compare the decimals. Write < or >.

5. 0.622 ■ 0.625

6. 0.405 ■ $0.\overline{45}$

7. -3.822 ■ -3.819

See Example **3** Order the numbers from least to greatest.

8. $0.\overline{55}, \frac{3}{4}, 0.505$

9. $2.5, 2.05, -\frac{13}{5}$

10. $\frac{5}{8}, -0.875, 0.877$

INDEPENDENT PRACTICE

See Example **1** Compare the fractions. Write < or >.

11. $\frac{6}{11}$ ■ $\frac{7}{11}$

12. $-\frac{5}{9}$ ■ $-\frac{6}{9}$

13. $-\frac{5}{6}$ ■ $-\frac{8}{9}$

14. $10\frac{3}{4}$ ■ $10\frac{3}{5}$

15. $\frac{5}{7}$ ■ $\frac{2}{7}$

16. $-\frac{3}{4}$ ■ $\frac{1}{4}$

17. $\frac{7}{4}$ ■ $-\frac{1}{4}$

18. $-\frac{2}{3}$ ■ $\frac{4}{3}$

See Example **2** Compare the decimals. Write < or >.

19. 3.8 ■ 3.6

20. 0.088 ■ 0.109

21. $4.\overline{26}$ ■ 4.266

22. -1.902 ■ 0.920

23. -0.7 ■ -0.07

24. $3.\overline{08}$ ■ 3.808

See Example **3** Order the numbers from least to greatest.

25. $0.7, 0.755, \frac{5}{8}$

26. $1.82, 1.6, 1\frac{4}{5}$

27. $-2.25, 2.05, \frac{21}{10}$

28. $-3.\overline{02}, -3.02, 1\frac{1}{2}$

29. $2.88, -2.98, -2\frac{9}{10}$

30. $\frac{5}{6}, \frac{4}{5}, 0.82$

PRACTICE AND PROBLEM SOLVING

Extra Practice
See Extra Practice for
more exercises.

Choose the greater number.

31. $\frac{3}{4}$ or 0.7

32. 0.999 or 1.0

33. $\frac{7}{8}$ or $\frac{13}{20}$

34. -0.93 or 0.2

35. 0.32 or 0.088

36. $-\frac{1}{2}$ or -0.05

37. $-\frac{9}{10}$ or $-\frac{7}{8}$

38. 23.44 or 23

39. Earth Science Density is a measure of mass in a specific unit of space. The mean densities (in g/cm³) of the planets of our solar system are given in the table below. Rearrange the planets from least to most dense.

Planet	Density	Planet	Density	Planet	Density
Mercury	5.43	Mars	3.93	Uranus	1.32
Venus	5.20	Jupiter	1.32	Neptune	1.64
Earth	5.52	Saturn	0.69	Pluto*	2.05

*designated a dwarf planet in 2006

40. Multi-Step Twenty-four karat gold is considered pure.

    a. Angie's necklace is 22-karat gold. What is its purity as a fraction?

    b. Luke's ring is 0.75 gold. If Angie's necklace and Luke's ring weigh the same amount, which contains more gold?

41. Life Science Sloths are tree-dwelling animals that live in South and Central America. They generally sleep about $\frac{3}{4}$ of a 24-hour day. Humans sleep an average of 8 hours each day. Which sleep the most each day, sloths or humans?

42. Ecology Of Beatrice's total household water use, $\frac{5}{9}$ is for bathing, toilet flushing, and laundry. How does her water use for these purposes compare with that shown in the graph?

43. What's the Error? A recipe for a large cake called for $4\frac{1}{2}$ cups of flour. The chef added 10 one-half cupfuls of flour to the mixture. What was the chef's error?

44. Write About It Explain how to compare a mixed number with a decimal.

45. Challenge Scientists estimate that Earth is approximately 4.6 billion years old. We are currently in what is called the Phanerozoic eon, which has made up about $\frac{7}{60}$ of the time that Earth has existed. The first eon, called the Hadean, made up approximately 0.175 of the time Earth has existed. Which eon represents the most time?

Average Daily Household Use of Water

$\frac{3}{5}$ Bathing, toilet flushing, laundry

$\frac{8}{25}$ Lawn watering, car washing, pool maintenance

$\frac{2}{25}$ Drinking, cooking, washing dishes, running garbage disposal

Test Prep

46. Multiple Choice Which number is the greatest?

   Ⓐ 0.71   Ⓑ $\frac{5}{8}$ Ⓒ 0.65   Ⓓ $\frac{5}{7}$

47. Multiple Choice Which shows the order of the animals from fastest to slowest?

   Ⓕ Spider, tortoise, snail, sloth

   Ⓖ Snail, sloth, tortoise, spider

   Ⓗ Tortoise, spider, snail, sloth

   Ⓙ Spider, tortoise, sloth, snail

Maximum Speed (mi/h)				
Animal	Snail	Tortoise	Spider	Sloth
Speed	0.03	0.17	1.17	0.15

Quiz for Lessons 6 Through 7

 6 **Equivalent Fractions and Decimals**

Write each fraction as a decimal. Round to the nearest hundredth, if necessary.

1. $\frac{7}{10}$ **2.** $\frac{5}{8}$ **3.** $\frac{2}{3}$ **4.** $\frac{14}{15}$

Write each decimal as a fraction in simplest form.

5. 0.22   **6.** −0.135   **7.** −4.06   **8.** 0.07

9. In one 30-gram serving of snack crackers, there are 24 grams of carbohydrates. What fraction of a serving is made up of carbohydrates? Write your answer as a fraction and as a decimal.

10. During a softball game, Sara threw 70 pitches. Of those pitches, 29 were strikes. What portion of the pitches that Sara threw were strikes? Write your answer as a decimal rounded to the nearest thousandth.

 7 **Comparing and Ordering Rational Numbers**

Compare the fractions. Write < or >.

11. $\frac{3}{7}$ ▉ $\frac{2}{4}$ **12.** $-\frac{1}{8}$ ▉ $-\frac{2}{11}$ **13.** $\frac{5}{4}$ ▉ $\frac{4}{5}$ **14.** $-1\frac{2}{3}$ ▉ $\frac{1}{2}$

Compare the decimals. Write < or >.

15. 0.521 ▉ 0.524   **16.** 2.05 ▉ −2.50   **17.** 3.001 ▉ 3.010   **18.** −0.26 ▉ −0.626

Order the numbers from least to greatest.

19. $\frac{3}{7}$, −0.372, $-\frac{2}{3}$, 0.5   **20.** $2\frac{9}{11}$, $\frac{4}{5}$, 2.91, 0.9

21. −5.36, 2.36, $-5\frac{1}{3}$, $-2\frac{3}{6}$ **22.** 8.75, $\frac{7}{8}$, 0.8, $\frac{8}{7}$

23. Rafael measured the rainfall at his house for 3 days. On Sunday, it rained $\frac{2}{5}$ in. On Monday, it rained $\frac{5}{8}$ in. On Wednesday, it rained 0.57 in. List the days in order from the least to the greatest amount of rainfall.

CONNECTIONS

Reason abstractly and quantitatively.

CHAPTER 2

Amphibians and Reptiles of Arizona The desert climate of Arizona makes the state an ideal habitat for amphibians and reptiles. In fact, the state has more than 140 different species of lizards, turtles, snakes, frogs, and toads. Visitors to the state may even see one of the 11 species of rattlesnakes found in Arizona.

ARIZONA

1. Most reptiles can survive only in temperatures between –4 °C and 36 °C. What is the difference between these temperatures?

2. In Arizona, there are 28 species of amphibians and 52 species of snakes. An employee at a museum is arranging photos of these species on a wall. The photos will be placed in rows. Each row will have the same number of species of amphibians and the same number of species of snakes.

Gila monster

   a. The employee wants to make as many rows of photos as possible. How many rows can the employee make?

   b. How many photos of amphibians will be in each row? How many photos of snakes will be in each row?

For 3–5, use the table.

3. Write the length of the Gila monster as a decimal.

4. Write the length of the desert iguana as a mixed number in simplest form.

5. List the five species of lizards in order from shortest to longest. Explain how you put the species in order.

Lizards of Arizona	
Species	**Length (cm)**
Gila Monster	$35\frac{3}{5}$
Desert Iguana	14.6
Great Plains Skink	$\frac{133}{10}$
Common Chuckwalla	22.9
Zebra-Tailed Lizard	$\frac{51}{5}$

(c) Tim Flach/Getty Images; (b) Joseph T. Collins/Photo Researchers, Inc.

Real-World Connection **87**

Game Time

Magic Squares

A magic square is a grid with numbers, such that the numbers in each row, column, and diagonal have the same "magic" sum. Test the square at right to see an example of this.

You can use a magic square to do some amazing calculations. Cover a block of four squares (2 × 2) with a piece of paper. There is a way you can find the sum of these squares without looking at them. Try to find it. (*Hint:* What number in the magic square can you subtract from the magic sum to give you the sum of the numbers in the block? Where is that number located?)

Here's the answer: To find the sum of any block of four numbers, take 65 (the magic sum) and subtract from it the number that is diagonally two squares away from a corner of the block.

18	10	22	14	1
12	4	16	8	25
6	23	15	2	19
5	17	9	21	13
24	11	3	20	7

65 − 21 = 44

18	10	22	14	1
12	4	16	8	25
6	23	15	2	19
5	17	9	21	13
24	11	3	20	7

65 − 1 = 64

The number you subtract must fall on an extension of a diagonal of the block. For each block that you choose, there will be only one direction you can go.

Try to create a 3 × 3 magic square with the numbers 1–9.

Modified Tic-Tac-Toe

The board has a row of nine squares numbered 1 through 9. Players take turns selecting squares. The goal of the game is for a player to select squares such that any three of the player's squares add up to 15. The game can also be played with a board numbered 1 through 16 and a sum goal of 34.

Learn It Online
Game Time Extra

A complete copy of the rules and a game board are available online.

Jenny Thomas/HMH

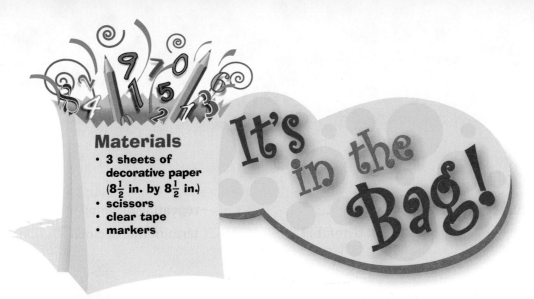

Materials

- 3 sheets of decorative paper ($8\frac{1}{2}$ in. by $8\frac{1}{2}$ in.)
- scissors
- clear tape
- markers

It's in the Bag!

PROJECT | ## Flipping Over Integers and Rational Numbers

Create your own flip-flop-fold book and use it to write definitions, sample problems, and practice exercises.

Directions

❶ Stack the sheets of decorative paper. Fold the stack into quarters and then unfold it. Use scissors to make a slit from the edge of the stack to the center of the stack along the left-hand crease. **Figure A**

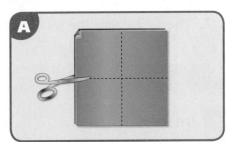

❷ Place the stack in front of you with the slit on the left side. Fold the top left square over to the right side of the stack. **Figure B**

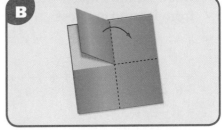

❸ Now fold down the top two squares from the top right corner. Along the slit, tape the bottom left square to the top left square. **Figure C**

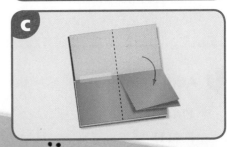

❹ Continue folding around the stack, always in a clockwise direction. When you get to the second layer, tape the slit in the same place as before.

Taking Note of the Math

Unfold your completed booklet. This time, as you flip the pages, add definitions, sample problems, practice exercises, or any other notes you need to help you study the material in the chapter.

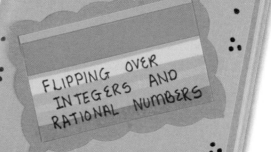

FLIPPING OVER INTEGERS AND RATIONAL NUMBERS

Study Guide: Review

Vocabulary

absolute value   opposite   repeating decimal

additive inverse   rational number   terminating decimal

integer

Complete the sentences below with vocabulary words from the list above.

1. A(n) ___?___ can be written as the ratio of one ___?___ to another and can be represented by a repeating or ___?___.

2. The ___?___ are the set of whole numbers and their ___?___(s).

EXAMPLES

EXERCISES

1 Integers

- Use a number line to order the integers from least to greatest.

3, 4, −2, 1, −3

−3, −2, 1, 3, 4

Compare the integers. Use < or >.

3. −8 ▯ −15   **4.** −7 ▯ 7

Use a number line to order the integers from least to greatest.

5. −6, 4, 0, −2, 5   **6.** 8, −3, 2, −8, 1

Use a number line to find each absolute value.

7. |0| **8.** |−17| **9.** |6|

2 Adding Integers

- Find the sum.

7 (11)

7 (11)   *The signs are the same.*

  18

Find each sum.

10. 85   **11.** 7(6)

12. 16(40)   **13.** 9 18

14. 2 16 (4)   **15.** 12 (18) 1

16. The temperature was 9 °F at 5 A.M. and rose 20° by 10 A.M. What was the temperature at 10 A.M.?

3 Subtracting Integers

■ **Find the difference.**

5 (3)

5 32 *Add the opposite of 3.*

Find each difference.

17. 82 **18.** 1019

19. 6(5) **20.** 54 **21.** 6 (5) 8

22. 10 (3) (1)

23. Evaluate *a* *b* for the values *a* 2 and *b* 8. Find each product or quotient.

4 Multiplying and Dividing Integers

■ 12 (3)   *The signs are different, so*
  36   *the product is negative.*

■ 16 (4)   *The signs are the same, so*
   4   *the quotient is positive.*

Find each product or quotient.

24. 5 (10) **25.** 27(9)

26. 2 (8) **27.** 4020

28. 3 4 **29.** 45(15)

30. John took $15 out of the bank each week for 8 weeks. How much money did he take out of his account?

5 Solving Equations Containing Integers

Solve.

■ *x* 12 4

  12   12   *Add 12 to each side.*

  x   16

■   10 2*f*

   $\frac{10}{2}$ $\frac{2f}{2}$ *Divide each side by 2.*

    5 *f*

Solve.

31. 7*y* 70 **32.** *d* 86

33. *j* 233 **34.** $\frac{n}{36}$ 2

35. 26 2*c* **36.** 28 7*m*

37. A scuba diver is at the 30 foot level. How many feet will she have to rise to be at the 12 foot level?

Study Guide: Review

6 **Equivalent Fractions and Decimals**

■ Write 0.75 as a fraction in simplest form.

$$0.75 = \frac{75}{100} = \frac{75 \div 25}{100 \div 25} = \frac{3}{4}$$

■ Write $\frac{5}{4}$ as a decimal.

$$\frac{5}{4} = 5 \div 4 = 1.25$$

Write each decimal as a fraction in simplest form.

38. 0.25   **39.** −0.004   **40.** 0.05

Write each fraction as a decimal.

41. $\frac{7}{2}$ **42.** $\frac{3}{5}$ **43.** $\frac{2}{3}$

44. Sam spent $\frac{1}{3}$ of his time this past weekend studying, $\frac{2}{5}$ of his time sleeping, and 0.25 of his time eating. Write his time eating as a fraction in simplest form.

7 **Comparing and Ordering Rational Numbers**

■ Compare. Write < or >.

$$-\frac{3}{4} \; \blacksquare \; -\frac{2}{3}$$

$$-\frac{3}{4} \cdot \frac{3}{3} \; \blacksquare \; -\frac{2}{3} \cdot \frac{4}{4}$$

Write as fractions with common denominators.

$$-\frac{9}{12} < -\frac{8}{12}$$

Compare. Write < or > .

45. $\frac{4}{5}$ ▨ 0.81   **46.** 0.22 ▨ $\frac{3}{20}$

47. $-\frac{3}{5}$ ▨ −1.5   **48.** $1\frac{1}{8}$ ▨ $1\frac{2}{9}$

49. Order $\frac{6}{13}$, 0.58, −0.55, and $\frac{1}{2}$ from least to greatest.

Chapter Test

Use a number line to order the integers from least to greatest.

1. $-4, 3, -2, 0, 1$

2. $7, -6, 5, -8, -3$

Use a number line to find each absolute value.

3. $|11|$

4. $|-5|$

5. $|-74|$

6. $|-1|$

Find each sum, difference, product, or quotient.

7. $-7 + (-3)$

8. $-6 - 3$

9. $17 - (-9) - 8$

10. $102 + (-97) + 3$

11. $-3 \cdot 20$

12. $-36 \div 12$

13. $-400 \div (-10)$

14. $-5 \cdot (-2) \cdot 9$

Evaluate each expression for the values $a = -3$ and $b = -7$.

15. $a + b$

16. $b - a$

17. $a + 2b$

18. ab

Solve.

19. $w - 4 = -6$

20. $x + 5 = -5$

21. $-6a = 60$

22. $\frac{n}{-4} = 12$

23. Kathryn's tennis team has won 52 matches. Her team has won 9 more matches than Rebecca's team. How many matches has Rebecca's team won this season?

Write each fraction as a decimal. Write each decimal as a fraction in simplest form.

24. $\frac{3}{50}$

25. $\frac{25}{10}$

26. 3.15

27. 0.004

28. The Drama Club has 52 members. Of these members, 18 are in the seventh grade. What fraction of the Drama Club is made up of seventh-graders? Write your answer as a fraction and a decimal. Round the decimal to the nearest thousandth.

Compare. Write < or >.

29. $\frac{2}{3} \ \blacksquare \ 0.62$

30. $1.5 \ \blacksquare \ 1\frac{6}{20}$

31. $-\frac{9}{7} \ \blacksquare \ -1$

32. $\frac{11}{5} \ \blacksquare \ 1\frac{2}{3}$

Order the numbers from least to greatest.

33. $0.5, \frac{1}{4}, -0.4$

34. $0.66, \frac{2}{3}, 0.67$

35. $-4.2, -4.3, 4.1, -4\frac{3}{4}$

36. $\frac{45}{6}, 7\frac{1}{3}, 7.4$

Cumulative Assessment

Multiple Choice

1. During a week in January in Cleveland, Ohio, the daily high temperatures were −4 °F, −2 °F, −12 °F, 5 °F, 12 °F, 16 °F, and 20 °F. Which expression can be used to find the difference between the highest temperature of the week and the lowest temperature of the week?

   (A) 20 − 2

   (B) 20 − (−2)

   (C) 20 − 12

   (D) 20 − (−12)

2. Use the Distributive Property for find 16(12).

   (F) 32

   (G) 42

   (H) 162

   (J) 192

3. The fraction $\frac{3}{5}$ is found between which pair of fractions on a number line?

   (A) $\frac{1}{2}$ and $\frac{2}{10}$

   (B) $\frac{1}{2}$ and $\frac{7}{10}$

   (C) $\frac{3}{10}$ and $\frac{5}{15}$

   (D) $\frac{3}{10}$ and $\frac{8}{15}$

4. Maxie earns $210 a week working as a lifeguard. After she gets paid, she gives each of her three sisters $20, and her mom $120 for her car payment. Which equation can be used to find p, the amount of money Maxie has left after she pays her mom and sisters?

   (F) $p = 210 - (3 \times 20) - 120$

   (G) $p = 210 - 20 - 120$

   (H) $p = 120 - (3 \times 20) - 120$

   (J) $p = 3 \times (210 - 20 - 120)$

5. Which expression can be used to represent a pattern in the table?

x	?
−3	4
−5	2
−7	0
−9	−2

   (A) $x + 2$

   (B) $-2x$

   (C) $x - (-7)$

   (D) $x - 7$

6. Which of the following shows a list of numbers in order from least to greatest?

   (F) −1.05, −2.55, −3.05

   (G) −2.75, $2\frac{5}{6}$, 2.50

   (H) −0.05, −0.01, $3\frac{1}{4}$

   (J) $-1\frac{2}{8}$, $-1\frac{4}{8}$, 1.05

7. Which of the following is an example of the Associative Property?

   (A) $5 + (4 + 1) = (5 + 4) + 1$

   (B) $32 + (2 + 11) = 32 + (11 + 2)$

   (C) $(2 \times 10) + (2 \times 4) = 2 \times 14$

   (D) $4(2 \times 7) = (4 \times 2) + (4 \times 7)$

8. There are 100 centimeters in 1 meter. Which decimal represents 625 centimeters in meters?

   (F) 6.25 meters

   (G) 6.50 meters

   (H) 6.40 meters

   (J) 6.60 meters

9. An artist is creating a design with 6 stripes. The first stripe is 2 meters long. The second stripe is 4 meters long, the third stripe is 8 meters long, and the fourth stripe is 16 meters long. If the pattern continues, how long is the sixth stripe?

Ⓐ 24 meters   Ⓒ 64 meters

Ⓑ 32 meters   Ⓓ 128 meters

10. Simplify the expression $(-5)^2 - 3 \cdot 4$.

Ⓕ −112   Ⓗ 13

Ⓖ −37   Ⓙ 88

11. Evaluate $a - b$ for $a = -5$ and $b = 3$.

Ⓐ −8   Ⓒ 2

Ⓑ −2   Ⓓ 8

 HOT TIP! Gridded responses cannot be negative numbers. If you get a negative value, you likely made an error. Check your work!

Gridded Response

12. Find the missing value in the table.

t	$-t + 3 \cdot 5$
5	10
10	?

13. Solve for x and y in each equation. Grid the sum of x and y.

$x + 6 = -4$ $-3y = -39$

14. What is the absolute value of the least number in the group $-\frac{1}{5}$, $-\frac{1}{3}$, and -0.5?

15. What is the value of the expression $18 - 3t + 4w$ for $t = -3$ and $w = 2$?

16. What is the value of 8^3 ?

Short Response

S1. The sponsors of the marching band provided 128 sandwiches for a picnic. After the picnic, s sandwiches were left.

a. Write an expression that shows how many sandwiches were handed out.

b. Evaluate your expression for $s = 15$. What does your answer represent?

S2. Casey said the solution to the equation $x + 42 = 65$ is 107. Identify the error that Casey made. Explain why this answer is unreasonable. Show how to solve this equation correctly. Explain your work.

Extended Response

E1. Mary's allowance is based on the amount of time that she spends practicing different activities each week. This week Mary spent 12 hours practicing and earned $12.00.

a. Mary spent the following amounts of time on each activity: $\frac{1}{5}$ practicing flute, $\frac{1}{6}$ studying Spanish, $\frac{1}{3}$ playing soccer, and $\frac{3}{10}$ studying math. Write an equivalent decimal for the amount of time that she spent on each activity. Round to the nearest hundredth, if necessary.

b. For each activity, Mary earned the same fraction of her allowance as the time spent on a particular activity. This week, she was paid $2.00 for studying Spanish. Was this the correct amount? Explain how you know.

c. Order the amount of time that Mary spent practicing each activity from least to greatest.

d. Next week Mary plans to spend 0.45 of her time studying math. Write this amount as a fraction in simplest form.

Applying Rational Numbers

Chapter Focus

- Add, subtract, multiply and divide rational numbers.
- Solve equations containing fractions.

Why Learn This?

By using operations with decimals, you can determine statistics for football players and teams.

Learn It Online
Chapter Project Online

(al) Kevin Reece/Icon SMI/Corbis

 **Are You Ready?**

✓ Vocabulary

Choose the best term from the list to complete each sentence.

1. A(n) __?__ is a number that is written using the base-ten place value system.

2. An example of a(n) __?__ is $\frac{14}{5}$.

3. A(n) __?__ is a number that represents a part of a whole.

decimal

fraction

improper fraction

mixed number

simplest form

Complete these exercises to review the skills you will need for this chapter.

✓ Simplify Fractions

Write each fraction in simplest form.

4. $\frac{24}{40}$ 5. $\frac{64}{84}$ 6. $\frac{66}{78}$ 7. $\frac{64}{192}$

8. $\frac{21}{35}$ 9. $\frac{11}{99}$ 10. $\frac{16}{36}$ 11. $\frac{20}{30}$

✓ Write Mixed Numbers as Fractions

Write each mixed number as an improper fraction.

12. $7\frac{1}{2}$ 13. $2\frac{5}{6}$ 14. $1\frac{14}{15}$ 15. $3\frac{2}{11}$

16. $3\frac{7}{8}$ 17. $8\frac{4}{9}$ 18. $4\frac{1}{7}$ 19. $5\frac{9}{10}$

✓ Write Fractions as Mixed Numbers

Write each improper fraction as a mixed number.

20. $\frac{23}{6}$ 21. $\frac{17}{3}$ 22. $\frac{29}{7}$ 23. $\frac{39}{4}$

24. $\frac{48}{5}$ 25. $\frac{82}{9}$ 26. $\frac{69}{4}$ 27. $\frac{35}{8}$

✓ Add, Subtract, Multiply, or Divide Integers

Find each sum, difference, product, or quotient.

28. $-11 + (-24)$ 29. $-11 - 7$ 30. $-4 \cdot (-10)$

31. $-22 \div (-11)$ 32. $23 + (-30)$ 33. $-33 - 74$

34. $-62 \cdot (-34)$ 35. $84 \div (-12)$ 36. $-26 - 18$

Where You've Been

Previously, you

- added, subtracted, multiplied, and divided whole numbers.

- used models to solve equations with whole numbers.

In This Chapter

You will study

- using addition, subtraction, multiplication, and division to solve problems involving fractions and decimals.

- solving equations with rational numbers.

Where You're Going

You can use the skills learned in this chapter

- to find the total cost when purchasing several items at the grocery store.

- to find measurements in fields such as carpentry.

Key Vocabulary/Vocabulario

multiplicative inverse	inverso multiplicativo
reciprocal	recíproco

Vocabulary Connections

To become familiar with some of the vocabulary terms in the chapter, consider the following. You may refer to the chapter, the glossary, or a dictionary if you like.

1. When fractions are **reciprocals** of each other, they have a special relationship. The fractions $\frac{3}{5}$ and $\frac{5}{3}$ are reciprocals of each other. What do you think the relationship between reciprocals is?

2. Inverse operations "undo" each other. For example, if you add 5 to any number, then add the opposite of 5, -5, the result is the number you started with. Why do you think **multiplicative inverse** is another name for the reciprocal of a nonzero number?

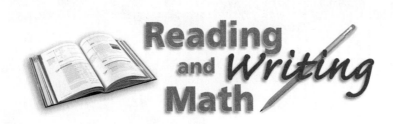 **Reading** and **Writing Math**

Study Strategy: Use Your Notes Effectively

Taking notes helps you understand and remember information from your textbook and lessons in class. Listed below are some steps for effectively using your notes before and after class.

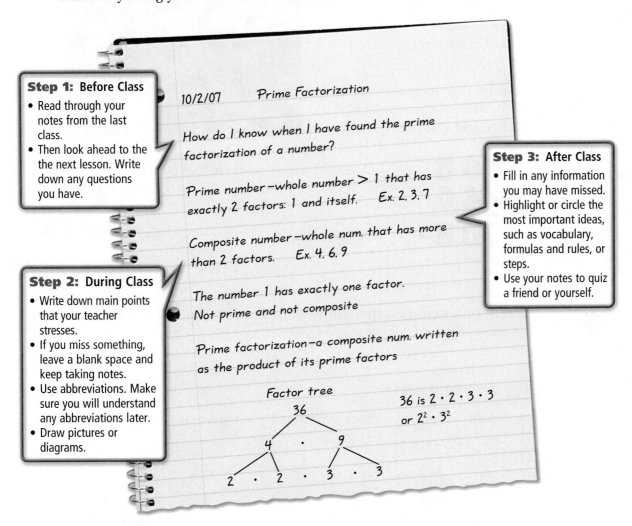

Step 1: Before Class
- Read through your notes from the last class.
- Then look ahead to the the next lesson. Write down any questions you have.

Step 2: During Class
- Write down main points that your teacher stresses.
- If you miss something, leave a blank space and keep taking notes.
- Use abbreviations. Make sure you will understand any abbreviations later.
- Draw pictures or diagrams.

Step 3: After Class
- Fill in any information you may have missed.
- Highlight or circle the most important ideas, such as vocabulary, formulas and rules, or steps.
- Use your notes to quiz a friend or yourself.

10/2/07   Prime Factorization

How do I know when I have found the prime factorization of a number?

Prime number—whole number > 1 that has exactly 2 factors: 1 and itself.   Ex. 2, 3, 7

Composite number—whole num. that has more than 2 factors.   Ex. 4, 6, 9

The number 1 has exactly one factor. Not prime and not composite

Prime factorization—a composite num. written as the product of its prime factors

Factor tree
36
4 · 9
2 · 2 · 3 · 3

36 is $2 · 2 · 3 · 3$
or $2^2 · 3^2$

Reading and Writing Math

Try This

1. Look at the next lesson in your textbook. Think about how the new vocabulary terms relate to previous lessons. Write down any questions you have.

2. With a classmate, compare the notes you took during the last class. Are there differences in the main points that you each recorded? Then brainstorm two ways you can improve your note-taking skills.

Adding and Subtracting Decimals

COMMON CORE

CC.7.NS.1 Apply and extend previous understandings of addition and subtraction to add and subtract rational numbers; represent addition and subtraction on a horizontal or vertical number line diagram. *Also CC.7.NS.1b, CC.7.NS.1c, CC.7.NS.3*

One of the coolest summers on record in the Midwest was in 1992. The average summertime temperature that year was 66.8 °F. Normally, the average temperature is 4 °F higher than it was in 1992.

To find the normal average summertime temperature in the Midwest, you can add 66.8 °F and 4 °F.

Interactivities Online ▶

$$\begin{array}{r} 66.8 \\ + \ 4.0 \\ \hline 70.8 \end{array}$$

Use zero as a placeholder so that both numbers have the same number of digits after their decimal points.

Add each column just as you would add integers.

Line up the decimal points.

The normal average summertime temperature in the Midwest is 70.8 °F.

E X A M P L E **1** **Adding Decimals**

Add. Estimate to check whether each answer is reasonable.

A 3.62 + 18.57

$$\begin{array}{r} 3.62 \\ + \ 18.57 \\ \hline 22.19 \end{array}$$

Line up the decimal points.

Add.

Estimate

4 + 19 = 23   *22.19 is a reasonable answer.*

B 9 + 3.245

$$\begin{array}{r} 9.000 \\ + \ 3.245 \\ \hline 12.245 \end{array}$$

Use zeros as placeholders.
Line up the decimal points.
Add.

Estimate

9 + 3 = 12   *12.245 is a reasonable answer.*

Video **Lesson Tutorials Online**   my.hrw.com

Add. Estimate to check whether each answer is reasonable.

C $-5.78 + (-18.3)$

$-5.78 + (-18.3)$	*Think: 5.78 + 18.3.*
5.78	*Line up the decimal points.*
$+\ 18.30$	*Use zero as a placeholder.*
24.08	*Add.*
$-5.78 + (-18.3) = -24.08$	*Use the sign of the two numbers.*

Estimate

$-6 + (-18) = -24$ *—24.08 is a reasonable answer.*

EXAMPLE 2 **Subtracting Decimals**

Subtract.

A $12.49 - 7.25$

12.49	*Line up the decimal points.*
$-\ 7.25$	
5.24	*Subtract.*

B $14 - 7.32$

$\overset{13\quad\ 9\ 10}{\cancel{14.00}}$	*Use zeros as placeholders.*
$-\ 7.32$	*Line up the decimal points.*
6.68	*Subtract.*

EXAMPLE 3 *Transportation Application*

During one month in the United States, 492.23 million commuter trips were taken on buses, and 26.331 million commuter trips were taken on light rail. How many more trips were taken on buses than on light rail? Estimate to check whether your answer is reasonable.

492.230	*Use zero as a placeholder.*
$-\ 26.331$	*Line up the decimal points.*
465.899	*Subtract.*

Estimate

$490 - 30 = 460$ *465.899 is a reasonable answer.*

465.899 million more trips were taken on buses than on light rail.

MATHEMATICAL PRACTICES

Think and Discuss

1. **Tell** whether the addition is correct. If it is not, explain why not.

$$\begin{array}{r} 12.3 \\ +\ 4.68 \\ \hline 5.91 \end{array}$$

2. **Describe** how you can check an answer when adding and subtracting decimals.

Exercises

Learn It Online
Homework Help Online
Exercises 1–27, 29, 31, 33, 35, 37, 39, 43

GUIDED PRACTICE

See Example **1** Add. Estimate to check whether each answer is reasonable.

1. $5.37 + 16.45$ **2.** $2.46 + 11.99$ **3.** $7 + 5.826$ **4.** $-5.62 + (-12.9)$

See Example **2** Subtract.

5. $7.89 - 5.91$ **6.** $17 - 4.12$ **7.** $4.97 - 3.2$ **8.** $9 - 1.03$

See Example **3** **9.** In 1990, international visitors to the United States spent $58.3 billion. In 1999, international visitors spent $95.5 billion. By how much did spending by international visitors increase from 1990 to 1999?

INDEPENDENT PRACTICE

See Example **1** Add. Estimate to check whether each answer is reasonable.

10. $7.82 + 31.23$ **11.** $5.98 + 12.99$ **12.** $4.917 + 12$ **13.** $-9.82 + (-15.7)$

14. $6 + 9.33$ **15.** $10.022 + 0.11$ **16.** $8 + 1.071$ **17.** $-3.29 + (-12.6)$

See Example **2** Subtract.

18. $5.45 - 3.21$ **19.** $12.87 - 3.86$ **20.** $15.39 - 2.6$ **21.** $21.04 - 4.99$

22. $5 - 0.53$ **23.** $14 - 8.9$ **24.** $41 - 9.85$ **25.** $33 - 10.23$

See Example **3** **26.** Angela runs her first lap around the track in 4.35 minutes and her second lap in 3.9 minutes. What is her total time for the two laps?

27. A jeweler has 122.83 grams of silver. He uses 45.7 grams of the silver to make a necklace and earrings. How much silver does he have left?

PRACTICE AND PROBLEM SOLVING

Extra Practice
See Extra Practice for more exercises.

Add or subtract. Estimate to check whether each answer is reasonable.

28. $-7.238 + 6.9$ **29.** $4.16 - 9.043$ **30.** $-2.09 - 15.271$

31. $5.23 - (-9.1)$ **32.** $-123 - 2.55$ **33.** $5.29 - 3.37$

34. $32.6 - (-15.86)$ **35.** $-32.7 + 62.82$ **36.** $-51 + 81.623$

37. $5.9 - 10 + 2.84$ **38.** $-4.2 + 2.3 - 0.7$ **39.** $-8.3 + 5.38 - 0.537$

40. **Multi-Step** Students at Hill Middle School plan to run a total of 2,462 mi, which is the distance from Los Angeles to New York City. So far, the sixth grade has run 273.5 mi, the seventh grade has run 275.8 mi, and the eighth grade has run 270.2 mi. How many more miles must the students run to reach their goal?

41. **Critical Thinking** Why must you line up the decimal points when adding and subtracting decimals?

Egg-drop competitions challenge students to build devices that will protect eggs when they are dropped from as high as 100 ft.

Weather The graph shows the five coolest summers recorded in the Midwest. The average summertime temperature in the Midwest is 70.8 °F.

42. How much warmer was the average summertime temperature in 1950 than in 1915?

43. In what year was the temperature 4.4 °F cooler than the average summertime temperature in the Midwest?

44. **Physical Science** To float in water, an object must have a density of less than 1 gram per milliliter. The density of a fresh egg is about 1.2 grams per milliliter. If the density of a spoiled egg is about 0.3 grams per milliliter less than that of a fresh egg, what is the density of a spoiled egg? How can you use water to tell whether an egg is spoiled?

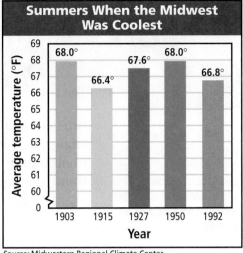

Summers When the Midwest Was Coolest

68.0° 66.4° 67.6° 68.0° 66.8°
1903 1915 1927 1950 1992

Year

Average temperature (°F)

Source: Midwestern Regional Climate Center

45. **Choose a Strategy** How much larger in area is Agua Fria than Pompeys Pillar?

 (A) 6.6 thousand acres

 (B) 20.1 thousand acres

 (C) 70.59 thousand acres

 (D) 71.049 thousand acres

National Monument	Area (thousand acres)
Agua Fria	71.1
Pompeys Pillar	0.051

46. **Write About It** Explain how to find the sum or difference of two decimals.

47. **Challenge** Find the missing number. $5.11 + 6.9 - 15.3 + \blacksquare = 20$

Test Prep

48. Multiple Choice In the 1900 Olympic Games, the 200-meter dash was won in 22.20 seconds. In 2000, the 200-meter dash was won in 20.09 seconds. How many seconds faster was the winning time in the 2000 Olympics?

 (A) 1.10 seconds   (B) 2.11 seconds   (C) 2.29 seconds   (D) 4.83 seconds

49. Multiple Choice John left school with $2.38. He found a quarter on his way home and then stopped to buy a banana for $0.89. How much money did he have when he got home?

 (F) $1.24   (G) $1.74   (H) $3.02   (J) $3.52

3-2 Multiplying Decimals

COMMON CORE

CC.7.NS.2 Apply and extend previous understandings of multiplication and division and of fractions to multiply and divide rational numbers. *Also CC.7.NS.1, CC.7.NS.2a, CC.7.NS.3*

You can use decimal grids to model multiplication of decimals. Each large square represents 1. Each row and column represents 0.1. Each small square represents 0.01. The area where the shading overlaps shows the product of the two decimals.

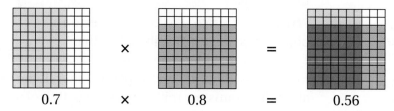

$$0.7 \times 0.8 = 0.56$$

Interactivities Online ▶

To multiply decimals, multiply as you would with integers. To place the decimal point in the product, count the number of decimal places in each factor. The product should have the same number of decimal places as the sum of the decimal places in the factors.

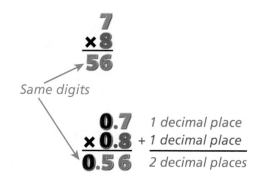

$$\begin{array}{r} 7 \\ \times\, 8 \\ \hline 56 \end{array}$$

Same digits

$$\begin{array}{r} 0.7 \\ \times\, 0.8 \\ \hline 0.56 \end{array}$$

1 decimal place
+ 1 decimal place
2 decimal places

EXAMPLE 1 Multiplying Integers by Decimals

Multiply.

A 6 · 0.1

$$\begin{array}{r} 6 \\ \times\, 0.1 \\ \hline 0.6 \end{array}$$

0 decimal places
1 decimal place
0 + 1 = 1 decimal place

B −2 · 0.04

$$\begin{array}{r} -2 \\ \times\, 0.04 \\ \hline -0.08 \end{array}$$

0 decimal places
2 decimal places
0 + 2 = 2 decimal places. Use zero as a placeholder.

C 1.25 · 23

$$\begin{array}{r} 1.25 \\ \times\, 23 \\ \hline 3\,75 \\ +\, 25\,00 \\ \hline 28.75 \end{array}$$

2 decimal places
0 decimal places

2 + 0 = 2 decimal places

Video **Lesson Tutorials Online** my.hrw.com

EXAMPLE **2** **Multiplying Decimals by Decimals**

Multiply. Estimate to check whether each answer is reasonable.

A $1.2 \cdot 1.6$

$$
\begin{array}{r}
1.2 \\
\times\ 1.6 \\
\hline
72 \\
120 \\
\hline
1.92
\end{array}
$$

1 decimal place
1 decimal place

1 + 1 = 2 decimal places

Estimate

$1 \cdot 2 = 2$ *1.92 is a reasonable answer.*

B $-2.78 \cdot 0.8$

$$
\begin{array}{r}
-2.78 \\
\times\ 0.8 \\
\hline
-2.224
\end{array}
$$

2 decimal places
1 decimal place
2 + 1 = 3 decimal places

Estimate

$-3 \cdot 1 = -3$ *−2.224 is a reasonable answer.*

EXAMPLE **3** *Nutrition Application*

On average, Americans eat 0.25 lb of peanut butter per month. How many pounds of peanut butter are eaten by the approximately 302 million Americans living in the United States per month?

$$
\begin{array}{r}
302 \\
\times\ 0.25 \\
\hline
1510 \\
6040 \\
\hline
75.50
\end{array}
$$

0 decimal places
2 decimal places

0 + 2 = 2 decimal places

Estimate

$300 \cdot 0.3 = 90$ *75.50 is a reasonable answer.*

Approximately 75.50 million (75,500,000) pounds of peanut butter are eaten by Americans each month.

Think and Discuss

1. Explain whether the multiplication $2.1 \cdot 3.3 = 69.3$ is correct.

2. Compare multiplying integers with multiplying decimals.

Exercises

Learn It Online
Homework Help Online
Exercises 1–27, 31, 33, 37, 39, 41, 43, 47

GUIDED PRACTICE

See Example **1** **Multiply.**

1. $-9 \cdot 0.4$ **2.** $3 \cdot 0.2$ **3.** $0.06 \cdot 3$ **4.** $-0.5 \cdot 2$

See Example **2** **Multiply. Estimate to check whether each answer is reasonable.**

5. $1.7 \cdot 1.2$ **6.** $2.6 \cdot 0.4$ **7.** $1.5 \cdot (-0.21)$ **8.** $-0.4 \cdot 1.17$

See Example **3** **9.** If Carla is able to drive her car 24.03 miles on one gallon of gas, how far could she drive on 13.93 gallons of gas?

INDEPENDENT PRACTICE

See Example **1** **Multiply.**

10. $8 \cdot 0.6$ **11.** $5 \cdot 0.07$ **12.** $-3 \cdot 2.7$ **13.** $0.8 \cdot 4$

14. $6 \cdot 4.9$ **15.** $1.7 \cdot (-12)$ **16.** $43 \cdot 2.11$ **17.** $-7 \cdot (-1.3)$

See Example **2** **Multiply. Estimate to check whether each answer is reasonable.**

18. $2.4 \cdot 3.2$ **19.** $2.8 \cdot 1.6$ **20.** $5.3 \cdot 4.6$ **21.** $4.02 \cdot 0.7$

22. $-5.14 \cdot 0.03$ **23.** $1.04 \cdot (-8.9)$ **24.** $4.31 \cdot (-9.5)$ **25.** $-6.1 \cdot (-1.01)$

See Example **3** **26.** Nicholas bicycled 15.8 kilometers each day for 18 days last month. How many kilometers did he bicycle last month?

27. While walking, Lara averaged 3.63 miles per hour. How far did she walk in 1.5 hours?

PRACTICE AND PROBLEM SOLVING

Extra Practice
See Extra Practice for more exercises.

Multiply. Estimate to check whether each answer is reasonable.

28. $-9.6 \cdot 2.05$ **29.** $0.07 \cdot 0.03$ **30.** $4 \cdot 4.15$

31. $-1.08 \cdot (-0.4)$ **32.** $1.46 \cdot (-0.06)$ **33.** $-3.2 \cdot 0.9$

34. $-325.9 \cdot 1.5$ **35.** $14.7 \cdot 0.13$ **36.** $-28.5 \cdot (-1.07)$

37. $-7.02 \cdot (-0.05)$ **38.** $1.104 \cdot (-0.7)$ **39.** $0.072 \cdot 0.12$

40. **Multi-Step** Bo earns $8.95 per hour plus commission. Last week, he worked 32.5 hours and earned $28.75 in commission. How much money did Bo earn last week?

41. **Weather** As a hurricane increases in intensity, the air pressure within its eye decreases. In a Category 5 hurricane, which is the most intense, the air pressure measures approximately 27.16 inches of mercury. In a Category 1 hurricane, which is the least intense, the air pressure is about 1.066 times that of a Category 5 hurricane. What is the air pressure within the eye of a Category 1 hurricane? Round your answer to the nearest hundredth.

42. Estimation The graph shows the results of a survey about river recreation activities.

a. A report claimed that about 3 times as many people enjoyed canoeing in 1999–2000 than in 1994–1995. According to the graph, is this claim reasonable?

b. Suppose a future survey shows that 6 times as many people enjoyed kayaking in 2016–2017 than in 1999–2000. About how many people reported that they enjoyed kayaking in 2016–2017?

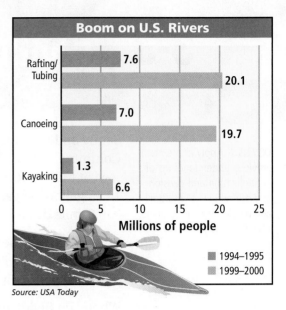

Boom on U.S. Rivers

Rafting/Tubing 7.6, 20.1
Canoeing 7.0, 19.7
Kayaking 1.3, 6.6

Millions of people

■ 1994–1995
■ 1999–2000

Source: USA Today

Multiply. Estimate to check whether each answer is reasonable.

43. $0.3 \cdot 2.8 \cdot (-10.6)$

44. $1.3 \cdot (-4.2) \cdot (-3.94)$

45. $0.6 \cdot (-0.9) \cdot 0.05$

46. $-6.5 \cdot (-1.02) \cdot (-12.6)$

47. $-22.08 \cdot (-5.6) \cdot 9.9$

48. $-63.75 \cdot 13.46 \cdot 7.8$

49. What's the Question? In a collection, each rock sample has a mass of 4.35 kilograms. There are a dozen rocks in the collection. If the answer is 52.2 kilograms, what is the question?

50. Write About It How do the products $4.3 \cdot 0.56$ and $0.43 \cdot 5.6$ compare? Explain.

51. Challenge Evaluate $(0.2)^5$.

Test Prep

52. Multiple Choice Which expression is equal to -4.3?

Ⓐ $0.8 \cdot (-5.375)$ Ⓑ $-1.2 \cdot (-3.6)$ Ⓒ $-0.75 \cdot 5.6$ Ⓓ $2.2 \cdot (-1.9)$

53. Gridded Response Julia walked 1.8 mi each day from Monday through Friday. On Saturday, she walked 2.3 mi. How many miles did she walk in all?

Dividing Decimals

COMMON CORE

CC.7.NS.2 Apply and extend previous understandings of multiplication and division and of fractions to multiply and divide rational numbers. *Also CC.7.NS.2b*

Sandy and her family traveled from Columbus, Ohio, to Chicago, Illinois, to visit Millennium Park. They used 14.95 gallons of gas for their 358.8-mile drive.

To find the number of miles per gallon the car got, you will need to divide a decimal by a decimal.

When you divide two numbers, you can multiply *both numbers* by the same power of ten without changing the final answer.

Multiply both 0.6 and 0.3 by 10: $0.6 \cdot 10 = 6$ and $0.3 \cdot 10 = 3$

$$0.6 \div 0.3 = 2 \quad \text{and} \quad 6 \div 3 = 2$$

By multiplying both numbers by the same power of ten, you can make the divisor an integer. Dividing by an integer is much easier than dividing by a decimal.

EXAMPLE **1**

Dividing Decimals by Decimals

Divide.

Helpful Hint

Multiply both numbers by the least power of ten that will make the divisor an integer.

A $4.32 \div 3.6$

$4.32 \div 3.6 = 43.2 \div 36$

$$\begin{array}{r} 1.2 \\ 36\overline{)43.2} \\ -36 \\ \hline 7\,2 \\ -7\,2 \\ \hline 0 \end{array}$$

Multiply both numbers by 10 to make the divisor an integer. Divide as with whole numbers.

B $12.95 \div (-1.25)$

$12.95 \div (-1.25) = 1295 \div (-125)$

$$\begin{array}{r} 10.36 \\ 125\overline{)1,295.00} \\ -1\,25 \\ \hline 45\,0 \\ -37\,5 \\ \hline 7\,50 \\ -7\,50 \\ \hline 0 \end{array}$$

$12.95 \div (-1.25) = -10.36$

Multiply both numbers by 100 to make the divisor an integer.

Use zeros as placeholders. Divide as with whole numbers.

The signs are different.

Video **Lesson Tutorials Online** my.hrw.com

EXAMPLE 2   **Dividing Integers by Decimals**

Divide. Estimate to check whether each answer is reasonable.

A $9 \div 1.25$

$9.00 \div 1.25 = 900 \div 125$ *Multiply both numbers by 100 to make the divisor an integer.*

$$
\begin{array}{r}
7.2 \\
125\overline{)900.0} \\
-875 \\
\hline
25\,0 \\
-25\,0 \\
\hline
0
\end{array}
$$

Use zero as a placeholder. Divide as with whole numbers.

Estimate $9 \div 1 = 9$ *7.2 is a reasonable answer.*

B $-12 \div (-1.6)$

$-12.0 \div (-1.6) = -120 \div (-16)$ *Multiply both numbers by 10 to make the divisor an integer.*

$$
\begin{array}{r}
7.5 \\
16\overline{)120.0} \\
-112 \\
\hline
8\,0 \\
-8\,0 \\
\hline
0
\end{array}
$$

Divide as with whole numbers.

$-12 \div (-1.6) = 7.5$ *The signs are the same.*

Estimate $-12 \div (-2) = 6$ *7.5 is a reasonable answer.*

EXAMPLE 3   *Transportation Application*

If Sandy and her family used 14.95 gallons of gas to drive 358.8 miles, how many miles per gallon did the car get?

$358.80 \div 14.95 = 35{,}880 \div 1{,}495$ *Multiply both numbers by 100 to make the divisor an integer.*

$$
\begin{array}{r}
24 \\
1{,}495\overline{)35{,}880} \\
-29\,90 \\
\hline
5\,980 \\
-5\,980 \\
\hline
0
\end{array}
$$

Divide as with whole numbers.

Helpful Hint

To calculate miles per gallon, divide the number of miles driven by the number of gallons of gas used.

The car got 24 miles per gallon.

Think and Discuss

1. **Explain** whether $4.27 \div 0.7$ is the same as $427 \div 7$.

2. **Explain** how to divide an integer by a decimal.

GUIDED PRACTICE

See Example **1** **Divide.**

1. $3.78 \div 4.2$
2. $13.3 \div (-0.38)$
3. $14.49 \div 3.15$

4. $1.06 \div 0.2$
5. $-9.76 \div 3.05$
6. $263.16 \div (-21.5)$

See Example **2** **Divide. Estimate to check whether each answer is reasonable.**

7. $3 \div 1.2$
8. $84 \div 2.4$
9. $36 \div (-2.25)$

10. $24 \div (-1.2)$
11. $-18 \div 3.75$
12. $189 \div 8.4$

See Example **3** **13. Transportation** Samuel used 14.35 gallons of gas to drive his car 401.8 miles. How many miles per gallon did he get?

INDEPENDENT PRACTICE

See Example **1** **Divide.**

14. $81.27 \div 0.03$
15. $-0.408 \div 3.4$
16. $38.5 \div (-5.5)$

17. $-1.12 \div 0.08$
18. $27.82 \div 2.6$
19. $14.7 \div 3.5$

See Example **2** **Divide. Estimate to check whether each answer is reasonable.**

20. $35 \div (-2.5)$
21. $361 \div 7.6$
22. $63 \div (-4.2)$

23. $5 \div 1.25$
24. $14 \div 2.5$
25. $-78 \div 1.6$

See Example **3** **26. Transportation** Lonnie used 26.75 gallons of gas to drive his truck 508.25 miles. How many miles per gallon did he get?

27. Mitchell walked 8.5 laps in 20.4 minutes. If he walked each lap at the same pace, how long did it take him to walk one full lap?

PRACTICE AND PROBLEM SOLVING

Extra Practice

See Extra Practice for more exercises.

Divide. Estimate to check whether each answer is reasonable.

28. $-24 \div 0.32$
29. $153 \div 6.8$
30. $-2.58 \div (-4.3)$

31. $4.12 \div (-10.3)$
32. $-17.85 \div 17$
33. $64 \div 2.56$

Simplify each expression. Justify your steps using the Commutative, Associative, and Distributive Properties when neccessary.

34. $2^2 \cdot (6.8 \div 3.4) \cdot 5$
35. $11.7 \div (0.7 + 0.6) \cdot 2$

36. $4 \cdot 5(0.6 + 0.)2 \cdot 0.25$
37. $(1.6 \div 3.2) \cdot (4.2 + 8.6)$

38. Critical Thinking A car loan totaling $13,456.44 is to be paid off in 36 equal monthly payments. Lin Yao can afford no more than $350 per month. Can she afford the loan? Explain.

39. Earth Science Glaciers form when snow accumulates faster than it melts and thus becomes compacted into ice under the weight of more snow. Once the ice reaches a thickness of about 18 m, it begins to flow. If ice were to accumulate at a rate of 0.0072 m per year, how long would it take to start flowing?

40. Critical Thinking Explain why using estimation to check the answer to $56.21457 \div 7$ is useful.

41. Recreation The graph shows the approximate number of total visits to the three most visited U.S. national parks in 2006. What was the average number of visits to these three parks? Round your answer to the nearest hundredth.

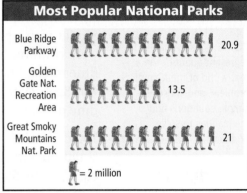

Most Popular National Parks

Blue Ridge Parkway — 20.9

Golden Gate Nat. Recreation Area — 13.5

Great Smoky Mountains Nat. Park — 21

= 2 million

Source: National Park Service

42. Write a Problem Find some supermarket advertisements. Use the ads to write a problem that can be solved by dividing a decimal by a whole number.

43. Write About It Can you use the Commutative Property when dividing decimals? Explain.

44. Challenge Use a calculator to simplify the expression $(2^3 \cdot 7.5 + 3.69) \div 48.25 \div [1.04 - (0.08 \cdot 2)]$.

Test Prep

45. Multiple Choice Which expression is NOT equal to -1.34?

Ⓐ $-6.7 \div 5$ Ⓑ $16.08 \div (-12)$ Ⓒ $-12.06 \div (-9)$ Ⓓ $-22.78 \div 17$

46. Multiple Choice A deli is selling 5 sandwiches for $5.55, including tax. A school spent $83.25 on roast beef sandwiches for its 25 football players. How many sandwiches did each player get?

Ⓕ 1   Ⓖ 2   Ⓗ 3   Ⓙ 5

47. Gridded Response Rujuta spent a total of $49.65 on 5 CDs. What was the average cost in dollars for each CD?

3-4 Solving Equations Containing Decimals

COMMON CORE

CC.7.EE.4 Use variables to represent quantities in a real-world or mathematical problem, and construct simple equations and inequalities to solve problems… *Also CC.7.NS.2*

Interactivities Online ▶

Students in a physical education class were running 40-yard dashes as part of a fitness test. The slowest time in the class was 3.84 seconds slower than the fastest time of 7.2 seconds.

You can write an equation to represent this situation. The slowest time s minus 3.84 is equal to the fastest time of 7.2 seconds.

$$s - 3.84 = 7.2$$

EXAMPLE 1 Solving Equations by Adding or Subtracting

Solve. Justify your steps.

A $s - 3.84 = 7.2$

$$
\begin{array}{rl}
s - 3.84 = & 7.20 \\
+\ 3.84 & +\ 3.84 \\
\hline
s \quad = & 11.04
\end{array}
$$

Use the Addition Property of Equality. Add 3.84 to both sides.

B $y + 20.51 = 26$

$$
\begin{array}{rl}
y + 20.51 = & 2\overset{5\ \ 9\ 10}{6.00} \\
-\ 20.51 & -\ 20.51 \\
\hline
y \quad = & 5.49
\end{array}
$$

Use the Subtraction Property of Equality. Subtract 20.51 from both sides.

> **Remember!**
>
> You can solve an equation by performing the same operation on both sides of the equation to isolate the variable.

EXAMPLE 2 Solving Equations by Multiplying or Dividing

Solve. Justify your steps.

A $\dfrac{w}{3.9} = 1.2$

$$\frac{w}{3.9} = 1.2$$

$$\frac{w}{3.9} \cdot 3.9 = 1.2 \cdot 3.9$$

$$w = 4.68$$

Use the Multiplication Property of Equality. Multiply by 3.9 on both sides.

B $4 = 1.6c$

$$4 = 1.6c$$

$$\frac{4}{1.6} = \frac{1.6c}{1.6}$$

$$\frac{4}{1.6} = c$$

$$2.5 = c$$

Use the Division Property of Equality. Divide by 1.6 on both sides.

Think: $4 \div 1.6 = 40 \div 16$.

Sam Dudgeon/HMH

Video **Lesson Tutorials Online** my.hrw.com

EXAMPLE 3

PROBLEM SOLVING APPLICATION

Yancey wants to buy a new snowboard that costs $396.00. If she earns $8.25 per hour at work, how many hours must she work to earn enough money to buy the snowboard?

 Understand the Problem

Rewrite the question as a statement.

• Find the number of hours Yancey must work to earn $396.00.

List the **important information**:
• Yancey earns $8.25 per hour.
• Yancey needs $396.00 to buy a snowboard.

2 Make a Plan

Yancey's pay is equal to her hourly pay times the number of hours she works. Since you know how much money she needs to earn, you can write an equation with h being the number of hours.

$$8.25h = 396$$

3 Solve

$$8.25h = 396$$

$$\frac{8.25h}{8.25} = \frac{396}{8.25} \qquad \text{Use the Division Property of Equality.}$$

$$h = 48$$

Yancey must work 48 hours.

4 Look Back

You can round 8.25 to 8 and 396 to 400 to estimate how many hours Yancey needs to work.

$$400 \div 8 = 50$$

So 48 hours is a reasonable answer.

Think and Discuss

1. Describe how to solve the equation $-1.25 + x = 1.25$. Then solve.

2. Explain how you can tell if 1.01 is a solution of $10s = -10.1$ without solving the equation.

Make sense of problems and persevere in solving them.

Exercises

GUIDED PRACTICE

See Example 1 Solve. Justify your steps.

1. $w - 5.8 = 1.2$

2. $x + 9.15 = 17$

3. $k + 3.91 = 28$

4. $n - 1.35 = 19.9$

See Example 2 **5.** $\frac{b}{1.4} = 3.6$

6. $\frac{x}{0.8} = 7.2$

7. $3.1t = 27.9$

8. $7.5 = 5y$

See Example 3 **9. Consumer Math** Jeff bought a sandwich and a salad for lunch. His total bill was $7.10. The salad cost $2.85. How much did the sandwich cost?

INDEPENDENT PRACTICE

See Example 1 Solve. Justify your steps.

10. $v + 0.84 = 6$

11. $c - 32.56 = 12$

12. $d - 14.25 = -23.9$

13. $3.52 + a = 8.6$

14. $w - 9.01 = 12.6$

15. $p + 30.34 = -22.87$

See Example 2 **16.** $3.2c = 8$

17. $72 = 4.5z$

18. $21.8x = -124.26$

19. $\frac{w}{2.8} = 4.2$

20. $\frac{m}{0.19} = 12$

21. $\frac{a}{21.23} = -3.5$

See Example 3 **22.** At the fair, 25 food tickets cost $31.25. What is the cost of each ticket?

23. To climb the rock wall at the fair, you must have 5 ride tickets. If each ticket costs $1.50, how much does it cost to climb the rock wall?

PRACTICE AND PROBLEM SOLVING

Extra Practice

See Extra Practice for more exercises.

Solve. Justify your steps.

24. $1.2y = -1.44$

25. $\frac{n}{8.2} = -0.6$

26. $w - 4.1 = -5$

27. $r + 0.48 = 1.2$

28. $x - 5.2 = -7.3$

29. $1.05 = -7m$

30. $a + 0.81 = -6.3$

31. $60k = 54$

32. $\frac{h}{-7.1} = 0.62$

33. $\frac{t}{-0.18} = -5.2$

34. $7.9 = d + 12.7$

35. $-1.8 + v = -3.8$

36. $-k = 287.658$

37. $-n = -12.254$

38. $0.64f = 12.8$

39. $15.217 - j = 4.11$

40. $-2.1 = p + (-9.3)$

41. $\frac{27.3}{g} = 54.6$

42. The Drama Club at Smith Valley Middle School is selling cookie dough in order to raise money for costumes. If each tub of cookie dough costs $4.75, how many tubs must members sell to make $570.00?

43. Consumer Math Gregory bought a computer desk at a thrift store for $38. The regular price of a similar desk at a furniture store is 4.5 times as much. What is the regular price of the desk at the furniture store?

44. Physical Science Pennies minted, or created, before 1982 are made mostly of copper and have a density of 8.85 g/cm^3. Because of an increase in the cost of copper, the density of pennies made after 1982 is 1.71 g/cm^3 less. What is the density of pennies minted today?

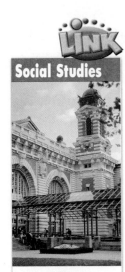
45. Social Studies The table shows the most common European ancestral origins of Americans (in millions), according to a Census 2000 supplementary survey. In addition, 19.6 million people stated that their ancestry was "American."

Ancestral Origins of Americans	
European Ancestry	**Number (millions)**
English	28.3
French	9.8
German	46.5
Irish	33.1
Italian	15.9
Polish	9.1
Scottish	5.4

  a. How many people claimed ancestry from the countries listed, according to the survey?

  b. If the data were placed in order from greatest to least, between which two nationalities would "American" ancestry be placed?

46. What's the Error? A student's solution to the equation $m + 0.63 = 5$ was $m = 5.63$. What is the error? What is the correct solution?

47. Write About It Compare the process of solving equations containing integers with the process of solving equations containing decimals.

48. Challenge Solve the equation $-2.8 + (b - 1.7) = -0.6 \cdot 9.4$

Test Prep

49. Multiple Choice What is the solution to the equation $-4.55 + x = 6.32$?

  Ⓐ $x = -1.39$ Ⓑ $x = 1.77$ Ⓒ $x = 10.87$ Ⓓ $x = 28.76$

50. Multiple Choice The pep squad is selling tickets for a raffle. The tickets are $0.25 each or 5 for $1.00. Julie bought a pack of 5 tickets. Which equation can be used to find how much Julie paid per ticket?

  Ⓕ $5x = 0.25$ Ⓖ $0.25x = 1.00$ Ⓗ $5x = 1.00$ Ⓙ $1.00x = 0.25$

51. Extended Response Write a word problem that the equation $6.25x = 125$ can be used to solve. Solve the problem and explain what the solution means.

Quiz for Lessons 1 Through 4

1 **Adding and Subtracting Decimals**

Add or subtract.

1. $4.73 + 29.68$ **2.** $-6.89 - (-29.4)$ **3.** $23.58 - 8.36$ **4.** $-15 + (-9.44)$

2 **Multiplying Decimals**

Multiply.

5. $3.4 \cdot 9.6$ **6.** $-2.66 \cdot 0.9$ **7.** $-7 \cdot (-0.06)$ **8.** $6.94 \cdot (-24)$

9. Cami can run 7.02 miles per hour. How many miles can she run in 1.75 hours? Round your answer to the nearest hundredth.

3 **Dividing Decimals**

Divide.

10. $55 \div 12.5$ **11.** $-126.45 \div (-4.5)$ **12.** $-3.3 \div 0.11$ **13.** $-36 \div (-0.9)$

14. $10.4 \div (-0.8)$ **15.** $18 \div 2.4$ **16.** $-45.6 \div 12$ **17.** $-99.36 \div (-4)$

18. Cynthia ran 17.5 laps in 38.5 minutes. If she ran each lap at the same pace, how long did it take her to run one full lap?

19. A jewelry store sold a 7.4-gram gold necklace for $162.18. How much was the necklace worth per gram? Round your answer to the nearest tenth.

4 **Solving Equations Containing Decimals**

Solve.

20. $3.4 + n = 8$ **21.** $x - 1.75 = -19$ **22.** $-3.5 = -5x$ **23.** $10.1 = \frac{s}{8}$

24. Pablo earns $5.50 per hour. His friend Raymond earns 1.2 times as much. How much does Raymond earn per hour?

Focus on Problem Solving

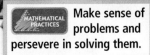
 Look Back

• **Does your solution answer the question in the problem?**

Sometimes, before you solve a problem, you first need to use the given data to find additional information. Any time you find a solution for a problem, you should ask yourself if your solution answers the question being asked, or if it just gives you the information you need to find the final answer.

Read each problem, and determine whether the given solution answers the question in the problem. Explain your answer.

1 At one store, a new CD costs $15.99. At a second store, the same CD costs 0.75 as much. About how much does the second store charge?

Solution: The second store charges about $12.00.

2 Bobbie is 1.4 feet shorter than her older sister. If Bobbie's sister is 5.5 feet tall, how tall is Bobbie?

Solution:
Bobbie is 4.1 feet tall.

3 Juanita ran the 100-yard dash 1.12 seconds faster than Kellie. Kellie's time was 0.8 seconds faster than Rachel's. If Rachel's time was 15.3 seconds, what was Juanita's time?

Solution: Kellie's time was 14.5 seconds.

4 The playscape at a local park is located in a triangular sandpit. Side A of the sandpit is 2 meters longer than side B. Side B is twice as long as side C. If side C is 6 meters long, how long is side A?

Solution: Side B is 12 meters long.

5 Both Tyrone and Albert walk to and from school every day. Albert has to walk 1.25 miles farther than Tyrone does each way. If Tyrone's house is 0.6 mi from school, how far do the two boys walk altogether?

Solution: Albert lives 1.85 mi from school.

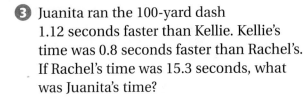

Adding and Subtracting Fractions

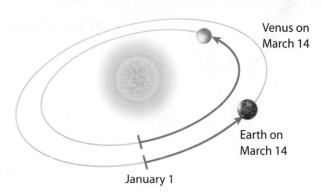

CC.7.NS.1 Apply and extend previous understandings of addition and subtraction to add and subtract rational numbers; represent addition and subtraction on a horizontal or vertical number line diagram. *Also CC.7.NS.1b, CC.7.NS.1c, CC.7.NS.3*

From January 1 to March 14 of any given year, Earth completes approximately $\frac{1}{5}$ of its circular orbit around the Sun, while Venus completes approximately $\frac{1}{3}$ of its orbit. To find out how much more of its orbit Venus completes than Earth, you need to subtract fractions.

Venus on March 14

Earth on March 14

January 1

EXAMPLE **1** **Adding and Subtracting Fractions with Like Denominators**

Add or subtract. Write each answer in simplest form.

A $\frac{3}{10} + \frac{1}{10}$

$$\frac{3}{10} + \frac{1}{10} = \frac{3 + 1}{10}$$ *Add the numerators and keep the common denominator.*

$$= \frac{4}{10} = \frac{2}{5}$$ *Simplify.*

B $\frac{7}{9} - \frac{4}{9}$

$$\frac{7}{9} - \frac{4}{9} = \frac{7 - 4}{9}$$ *Subtract the numerators and keep the common denominator.*

$$= \frac{3}{9} = \frac{1}{3}$$ *Simplify.*

To add or subtract fractions with different denominators, you must rewrite the fractions with a common denominator.

Two Ways to Find a Common Denominator	
Method 1: Find the LCM (least common multiple) of the denominators.	**Method 2:** Multiply the denominators.
$\frac{1}{2} + \frac{1}{4} = \frac{1 \cdot 2}{2 \cdot 2} + \frac{1}{4}$ *The LCM of the denominators is 4.*	$\frac{1}{2} + \frac{1}{4} = \frac{1 \cdot 4}{2 \cdot 4} + \frac{1 \cdot 2}{4 \cdot 2}$ *Multiply the denominators.*
$\frac{2}{4} + \frac{1}{4} = \frac{3}{4}$	$\frac{4}{8} + \frac{2}{8} = \frac{6}{8} = \frac{3}{4}$

Helpful Hint

The LCM of two denominators is the lowest common denominator (LCD) of the fractions.

Video **Lesson Tutorials Online** my.hrw.com

EXAMPLE **2** **Adding and Subtracting Fractions with Unlike Denominators**

Add or subtract. Write each answer in simplest form.

A $\frac{3}{8} + \frac{5}{12}$

$$\frac{3}{8} + \frac{5}{12} = \frac{3 \cdot 3}{8 \cdot 3} + \frac{5 \cdot 2}{12 \cdot 2}$$ *The LCM of the denominators is 24.*

$$= \frac{9}{24} + \frac{10}{24} = \frac{19}{24}$$ *Write equivalent fractions. Add.*

Estimate $\frac{1}{2} + \frac{1}{2} = 1$ *$\frac{19}{24}$ is a reasonable answer.*

B $\frac{1}{10} - \frac{5}{8}$

$$\frac{1}{10} - \frac{5}{8} = \frac{1 \cdot 4}{10 \cdot 4} - \frac{5 \cdot 5}{8 \cdot 5}$$ *The LCM of the denominators is 40.*

$$= \frac{4}{40} - \frac{25}{40} = -\frac{21}{40}$$ *Write equivalent fractions. Subtract.*

Estimate $0 - \frac{1}{2} = -\frac{1}{2}$ *$-\frac{21}{40}$ is a reasonable answer.*

C $-\frac{2}{3} + \frac{7}{8}$

$$-\frac{2}{3} + \frac{7}{8} = -\frac{2 \cdot 8}{3 \cdot 8} + \frac{7 \cdot 3}{8 \cdot 3}$$ *Multiply the denominators.*

$$= -\frac{16}{24} + \frac{21}{24} = \frac{5}{24}$$ *Write equivalent fractions. Add.*

Estimate $-1 + 1 = 0$ *$\frac{5}{24}$ is a reasonable answer.*

EXAMPLE **3** *Astronomy Application*

From January 1 to March 14, Earth completes about $\frac{1}{5}$ of its orbit, while Venus completes about $\frac{1}{3}$ of its orbit. How much more of its orbit does Venus complete than Earth?

$$\frac{1}{3} - \frac{1}{5} = \frac{1 \cdot 5}{3 \cdot 5} - \frac{1 \cdot 3}{5 \cdot 3}$$ *The LCM of the denominators is 15.*

$$= \frac{5}{15} - \frac{3}{15}$$ *Write equivalent fractions.*

$$= \frac{2}{15}$$ *Subtract.*

Venus completes $\frac{2}{15}$ more of its orbit than Earth does.

Think and Discuss

1. Describe the process for subtracting fractions with different denominators.

2. Explain whether $\frac{3}{4} + \frac{2}{3} = \frac{5}{7}$ is correct.

Exercises

Learn It Online
Homework Help Online
Exercises 1–27, 29, 31, 37, 47, 49, 51, 55

GUIDED PRACTICE

See Example **1** Add or subtract. Write each answer in simplest form.

1. $\frac{2}{3} - \frac{1}{3}$ **2.** $\frac{1}{12} + \frac{1}{12}$ **3.** $\frac{16}{21} - \frac{7}{21}$ **4.** $\frac{4}{17} + \frac{11}{17}$

See Example **2** **5.** $\frac{1}{6} + \frac{1}{3}$ **6.** $\frac{9}{10} - \frac{3}{4}$ **7.** $\frac{2}{3} + \frac{1}{8}$ **8.** $\frac{5}{8} - \frac{3}{10}$

See Example **3** **9.** Parker spends $\frac{1}{4}$ of his earnings on rent and $\frac{1}{6}$ on entertainment. How much more of his earnings does Parker spend on rent than on entertainment?

INDEPENDENT PRACTICE

See Example **1** Add or subtract. Write each answer in simplest form.

10. $\frac{2}{3} + \frac{1}{3}$ **11.** $\frac{3}{20} + \frac{7}{20}$ **12.** $\frac{5}{8} + \frac{7}{8}$ **13.** $\frac{6}{15} + \frac{3}{15}$

14. $\frac{7}{12} - \frac{5}{12}$ **15.** $\frac{5}{6} - \frac{1}{6}$ **16.** $\frac{8}{9} - \frac{5}{9}$ **17.** $\frac{9}{25} - \frac{4}{25}$

See Example **2** **18.** $\frac{1}{5} + \frac{2}{3}$ **19.** $\frac{1}{6} + \frac{1}{12}$ **20.** $\frac{5}{6} + \frac{3}{4}$ **21.** $\frac{1}{2} + \frac{2}{8}$

22. $\frac{21}{24} - \frac{1}{2}$ **23.** $\frac{3}{4} - \frac{11}{12}$ **24.** $\frac{1}{2} - \frac{2}{7}$ **25.** $\frac{7}{10} - \frac{1}{6}$

See Example **3** **26.** Seana picked $\frac{3}{4}$ quart of blackberries. She ate $\frac{1}{12}$ quart. How much was left?

27. Armando lives $\frac{2}{3}$ mi from his school. If he has walked $\frac{1}{2}$ mi already this morning, how much farther must he walk to get to his school?

PRACTICE AND PROBLEM SOLVING

Extra Practice
See Extra Practice for more exercises.

Find each sum or difference. Write your answer in simplest form.

28. $\frac{4}{5} + \frac{6}{7}$ **29.** $\frac{5}{6} - \frac{1}{9}$ **30.** $\frac{1}{2} - \frac{3}{4}$ **31.** $\frac{2}{3} + \frac{2}{15}$

32. $\frac{5}{7} + \frac{1}{3}$ **33.** $\frac{1}{2} - \frac{7}{12}$ **34.** $\frac{3}{4} + \frac{2}{5}$ **35.** $\frac{9}{14} - \frac{1}{7}$

36. $\frac{7}{8} + \frac{2}{3} + \frac{5}{6}$ **37.** $\frac{3}{5} + \frac{1}{10} - \frac{3}{4}$ **38.** $\frac{3}{10} + \frac{5}{8} + \frac{1}{5}$ **39.** $\frac{2}{5} - \frac{1}{6} + \frac{7}{10}$

40. $-\frac{1}{2} + \frac{3}{8} + \frac{2}{7}$ **41.** $\frac{1}{3} + \frac{3}{7} - \frac{1}{9}$ **42.** $\frac{2}{9} - \frac{7}{18} + \frac{1}{6}$ **43.** $\frac{2}{15} + \frac{4}{9} + \frac{1}{3}$

44. $\frac{9}{35} - \frac{4}{7} - \frac{5}{14}$ **45.** $\frac{1}{3} - \frac{5}{7} + \frac{8}{21}$ **46.** $-\frac{2}{9} - \frac{1}{12} - \frac{7}{18}$ **47.** $-\frac{2}{3} + \frac{4}{5} + \frac{5}{8}$

48. **Cooking** One fruit salad recipe calls for $\frac{1}{2}$ cup of sugar. Another recipe calls for 2 tablespoons of sugar. Since 1 tablespoon is $\frac{1}{16}$ cup, how much more sugar does the first recipe require?

49. It took Earl $\frac{1}{2}$ hour to do his science homework and $\frac{1}{3}$ hour to do his math homework. How long did Earl work on homework?

50. **Music** In music written in 4/4 time, a half note lasts for $\frac{1}{2}$ measure and an eighth note lasts for $\frac{1}{8}$ measure. In terms of a musical measure, what is the difference in the duration of the two notes?

Fitness Four friends had a competition to see how far they could walk while spinning a hoop around their waists. The table shows how far each friend walked. Use the table for Exercises 51–53.

Person	Distance (mi)
Rosalyn	$\frac{1}{8}$
Cai	$\frac{3}{4}$
Lauren	$\frac{2}{3}$
Janna	$\frac{7}{10}$

51. How much farther did Lauren walk than Rosalyn?

52. What is the combined distance that Cai and Rosalyn walked?

53. Who walked farther, Janna or Cai?

54. **Measurement** A shrew weighs $\frac{3}{16}$ lb. A hamster weighs $\frac{1}{4}$ lb.

   a. How many more pounds does a hamster weigh than a shrew?

   b. There are 16 oz in 1 lb. How many more ounces does the hamster weigh than the shrew?

55. **Multi-Step** To make $\frac{3}{4}$ lb of mixed nuts, how many pounds of cashews would you add to $\frac{1}{8}$ lb of almonds and $\frac{1}{4}$ lb of peanuts?

56. **Make a Conjecture** Suppose the pattern $1, \frac{7}{8}, \frac{3}{4}, \frac{5}{8}, \frac{1}{2} \ldots$ is continued forever. Make a conjecture about the rest of the numbers in the pattern.

57. **Write a Problem** Use facts you find in a newspaper or magazine to write a problem that can be solved using addition or subtraction of fractions.

58. **Write About It** Explain the steps you use to add or subtract fractions that have different denominators.

59. **Challenge** The sum of two fractions is 1. If one fraction is $\frac{3}{8}$ greater than the other, what are the two fractions?

Test Prep

60. **Multiple Choice** What is the value of the expression $\frac{3}{7} + \frac{1}{5}$?

   Ⓐ $\frac{1}{3}$ Ⓑ $\frac{22}{35}$ Ⓒ $\frac{2}{3}$ Ⓓ $\frac{26}{35}$

61. **Gridded Response** Grace has $\frac{1}{2}$ pound of apples. Julie has $\frac{2}{5}$ pound of apples. They want to combine their apples to use in a recipe that calls for 1 pound of apples. How many more pounds of apples do they need?

Multiplying Fractions and Mixed Numbers

COMMON CORE

CC.7.NS.2 Apply and extend previous understandings of multiplication and division and of fractions to multiply and divide rational numbers. *Also CC.7.NS.1, CC.7.NS.2a, CC.7.NS.3*

The original Sunshine Skyway Bridge connecting St. Petersburg and Palmetto, Florida, opened in 1954 and had a toll of $1.75. The current Sunshine Skyway Bridge opened in 1987, replacing the original. In 2007, the toll for a car crossing the bridge was $\frac{4}{7}$ of the toll in 1954. To find the toll in 2007, you will need to multiply the toll in 1954 by a fraction.

To multiply fractions, multiply the numerators to find the product's numerator. Then multiply the denominators to find the product's denominator.

EXAMPLE 1 **Multiplying Fractions**

Multiply. Write each answer in simplest form.

A $-15 \cdot \frac{2}{3}$

$$-15 \cdot \frac{2}{3} = -\frac{15}{1} \cdot \frac{2}{3}$$ *Write –15 as a fraction.*

$$= -\frac{\overset{5}{\cancel{15}} \cdot 2}{1 \cdot \cancel{3}_1}$$ *Simplify.*

$$= -\frac{10}{1}$$ *Multiply numerators. Multiply denominators.*

$$= -10$$

> **Helpful Hint**
>
> The product of two positive proper fractions is less than either fraction.

B $\frac{1}{4} \cdot \frac{4}{5}$

$$\frac{1}{4} \cdot \frac{4}{5} = \frac{1 \cdot \cancel{4}^{1}}{_{1}\cancel{4} \cdot 5}$$ *Simplify.*

$$= \frac{1}{5}$$ *Multiply numerators. Multiply denominators.*

C $\frac{3}{4} \cdot \left(-\frac{1}{2}\right)$

$$\frac{3}{4} \cdot \left(-\frac{1}{2}\right) = -\frac{3 \cdot 1}{4 \cdot 2}$$ *The signs are different, so the answer will be negative.*

$$= -\frac{3}{8}$$ *Multiply numerators. Multiply denominators.*

Video **Lesson Tutorials Online** my.hrw.com

EXAMPLE 2 Multiplying Mixed Numbers

Multiply. Write each answer in simplest form.

A $8 \cdot 2\frac{3}{4}$

$8 \cdot 2\frac{3}{4} = \frac{8}{1} \cdot \frac{11}{4}$ *Write mixed numbers as improper fractions.*

$= \frac{\overset{2}{\cancel{8}} \cdot 11}{1 \cdot \cancel{4}_1}$ *Simplify.*

$= \frac{22}{1} = 22$ *Multiply numerators. Multiply denominators.*

B $\frac{1}{3} \cdot 4\frac{1}{2}$

$\frac{1}{3} \cdot 4\frac{1}{2} = \frac{1}{3} \cdot \frac{9}{2}$ *Write the mixed number as an improper fraction.*

$= \frac{1 \cdot \overset{3}{\cancel{9}}}{_1\cancel{3} \cdot 2}$ *Simplify.*

$= \frac{3}{2}$ or $1\frac{1}{2}$ *Multiply numerators. Multiply denominators.*

C $3\frac{3}{5} \cdot 1\frac{1}{12}$

$3\frac{3}{5} \cdot 1\frac{1}{12} = \frac{18}{5} \cdot \frac{13}{12}$ *Write mixed numbers as improper fractions.*

$= \frac{\overset{3}{\cancel{18}} \cdot 13}{5 \cdot \cancel{12}_2}$ *Simplify.*

$= \frac{39}{10}$ or $3\frac{9}{10}$ *Multiply numerators. Multiply denominators.*

EXAMPLE 3 *Transportation Application*

In 1954, the Sunshine Skyway Bridge toll for a car was $1.75. In 2007, the toll was $\frac{4}{7}$ of the toll in 1954. What was the toll in 2007?

$1.75 \cdot \frac{4}{7} = 1\frac{75}{100} = 1\frac{3}{4} \cdot \frac{4}{7}$ *Write the decimal as a fraction.*

$= \frac{7}{4} \cdot \frac{4}{7}$ *Write the mixed number as an improper fraction.*

$= \frac{\overset{1}{\cancel{7}} \cdot \overset{1}{\cancel{4}}}{_1\cancel{4} \cdot \cancel{7}_1}$ *Simplify.*

$= \frac{1}{1} = 1$ *Multiply numerators. Multiply denominators.*

The Sunshine Skyway Bridge toll for a car was $1.00 in 2007.

Think and Discuss

1. Describe how to multiply a mixed number and a fraction.

2. Explain why $\frac{1}{2} \cdot \frac{1}{3} \cdot \frac{1}{4} = \frac{1}{24}$ is or is not correct.

3. Explain why you may want to simplify before multiplying $\frac{2}{3} \cdot \frac{3}{4}$ What answer will you get if you don't simplify first?

Exercises

Learn It Online
Homework Help Online
Exercises 1–27, 33, 39, 43, 45, 49, 53, 55

GUIDED PRACTICE

See Example 1 **Multiply. Write each answer in simplest form.**

1. $-8 \cdot \frac{3}{4}$
2. $\frac{2}{3} \cdot \frac{3}{5}$
3. $\frac{1}{4} \cdot \left(-\frac{2}{3}\right)$
4. $\frac{3}{5} \cdot (-15)$

See Example 2
5. $4 \cdot 3\frac{1}{2}$
6. $\frac{4}{9} \cdot 5\frac{2}{5}$
7. $1\frac{1}{2} \cdot 1\frac{5}{9}$
8. $2\frac{6}{7} \cdot (-7)$

See Example 3
9. On average, people spend $\frac{1}{4}$ of the time they sleep in a dream state. If Maxwell slept 10 hours last night, how much time did he spend dreaming? Write your answer in simplest form.

INDEPENDENT PRACTICE

See Example 1 **Multiply. Write each answer in simplest form.**

10. $5 \cdot \frac{1}{8}$
11. $4 \cdot \frac{1}{8}$
12. $3 \cdot \frac{5}{8}$
13. $6 \cdot \frac{2}{3}$

14. $\frac{2}{5} \cdot \frac{5}{7}$
15. $\frac{3}{8} \cdot \frac{2}{3}$
16. $\frac{1}{2} \cdot \left(-\frac{4}{6}\right)$
17. $-\frac{5}{6} \cdot \frac{2}{3}$

See Example 2
18. $7\frac{1}{2} \cdot 2\frac{2}{5}$
19. $6 \cdot 7\frac{2}{5}$
20. $2\frac{4}{7} \cdot \frac{1}{6}$
21. $2\frac{5}{8} \cdot 6\frac{2}{3}$

22. $\frac{2}{3} \cdot 2\frac{91}{4}$
23. $1\frac{1}{2} \cdot 1\frac{5}{9}$
24. $7 \cdot 5\frac{1}{8}$
25. $3\frac{3}{4} \cdot 2\frac{1}{5}$

See Example 3
26. Sherry spent 4 hours exercising last week. If $\frac{5}{6}$ of the time was spent jogging, how much time did she spend jogging? Write your answer in simplest form.

27. **Measurement** A cookie recipe calls for $\frac{1}{3}$ tsp of salt for 1 batch. Doreen is making cookies for a school bake sale and wants to bake 5 batches. How much salt does she need? Write your answer in simplest form.

PRACTICE AND PROBLEM SOLVING

Extra Practice

See Extra Practice for more exercises.

Multiply. Write each answer in simplest form.

28. $\frac{5}{8} \cdot \frac{4}{5}$
29. $4\frac{3}{7} \cdot \frac{5}{6}$
30. $-\frac{2}{3} \cdot 6$
31. $2 \cdot \frac{1}{6}$

32. $\frac{1}{8} \cdot 5$
33. $-\frac{3}{4} \cdot \frac{2}{9}$
34. $4\frac{2}{3} \cdot 2\frac{4}{7}$
35. $-\frac{4}{9} \cdot \left(-\frac{3}{16}\right)$

36. $3\frac{1}{2} \cdot 5$
37. $\frac{1}{2} \cdot \frac{2}{3} \cdot \frac{3}{5}$
38. $\frac{6}{7} \cdot 5$
39. $1\frac{1}{2} \cdot \frac{3}{5} \cdot \frac{7}{9}$

40. $-\frac{2}{3} \cdot 1\frac{1}{2} \cdot \frac{2}{3}$
41. $\frac{8}{9} \cdot \frac{3}{11} \cdot \frac{33}{40}$
42. $\frac{1}{6} \cdot 6 \cdot 8\frac{2}{3}$
43. $-\frac{8}{9} \cdot \left(-1\frac{1}{8}\right)$

Complete each multiplication sentence.

44. $\frac{1}{2} \cdot \frac{\blacksquare}{8} = \frac{3}{16}$
45. $\frac{2}{3} \cdot \frac{\blacksquare}{4} = \frac{1}{2}$
46. $\frac{\blacksquare}{3} \cdot \frac{5}{8} = \frac{5}{12}$
47. $\frac{3}{5} \cdot \frac{\blacksquare}{7} = \frac{3}{7}$

48. $\frac{5}{6} \cdot \frac{3}{\blacksquare} = \frac{1}{4}$
49. $\frac{4}{\blacksquare} \cdot \frac{4}{5} = \frac{8}{15}$
50. $\frac{2}{3} \cdot \frac{9}{\blacksquare} = \frac{3}{11}$
51. $\frac{\blacksquare}{15} \cdot \frac{3}{5} = \frac{1}{25}$

52. **Measurement** A standard paper clip is $1\frac{1}{4}$ in. long. If you laid 75 paper clips end to end, how long would the line of paper clips be?

53. Physical Science The weight of an object on the moon is $\frac{1}{6}$ its weight on Earth. If a bowling ball weighs $12\frac{1}{2}$ pounds on Earth, how much would it weigh on the moon?

54. In a survey, 200 students were asked what most influenced them to download songs. The results are shown in the circle graph.

a. How many students said radio most influenced them?

b. How many more students were influenced by radio than by a music video channel?

c. How many said a friend or relative influenced them or they heard the song in a store?

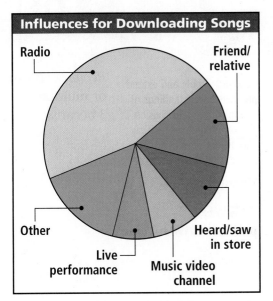

Influences for Downloading Songs

55. The Mississippi River flows at a rate of 2 miles per hour. If Eduardo floats down the river in a boat for $5\frac{2}{3}$ hours, how far will he travel?

56. Choose a Strategy What is the product of $\frac{1}{2} \cdot \frac{2}{3} \cdot \frac{3}{4} \cdot \frac{4}{5}$?

(A) $\frac{1}{5}$ (B) 5 (C) $\frac{1}{20}$ (D) $\frac{3}{5}$

57. Write About It Two positive proper fractions are multiplied. Is the product less than or greater than one? Explain.

58. Challenge Write three multiplication problems to show that the product of two fractions can be less than, equal to, or greater than 1.

Test Prep

59. Multiple Choice Which expression is greater than $5\frac{5}{8}$?

(A) $8 \cdot \frac{9}{16}$ (B) $-\frac{7}{9} \cdot \left(-8\frac{2}{7}\right)$ (C) $3\frac{1}{2} \cdot \frac{5}{7}$ (D) $-\frac{3}{7} \cdot \frac{14}{27}$

60. Multiple Choice The weight of an object on Mars is about $\frac{3}{8}$ its weight on Earth. If Sam weighs 85 pounds on Earth, how much would he weigh on Mars?

(F) 11 pounds (G) $31\frac{7}{8}$ pounds (H) $120\frac{4}{5}$ pounds (J) $226\frac{2}{3}$ pounds

Dividing Fractions and Mixed Numbers

CC.7.NS.2 Apply and extend previous understandings of multiplication and division and of fractions to multiply and divide rational numbers. *Also CC.7.NS.2b, CC.7.NS.3*

Vocabulary

reciprocal

multiplicative inverse

Reciprocals can help you divide by fractions. Two numbers are **reciprocals** or **multiplicative inverses** if their product is 1. The reciprocal of $\frac{1}{3}$ is 3 because

$$\frac{1}{3} \cdot 3 = \frac{1}{3} \cdot \frac{3}{1} = \frac{3}{3} = 1.$$

Dividing by a number is the same as multiplying by its reciprocal.

Reciprocals

$$6 \div 3 = 2 \qquad 6 \cdot \frac{1}{3} = 2$$

Same answer

Interactivities Online ▶ You can use this rule to divide by fractions.

EXAMPLE 1 Dividing Fractions

Divide. Write each answer in simplest form.

A $\frac{2}{3} \div \frac{1}{5}$

$$\frac{2}{3} \div \frac{1}{5} = \frac{2}{3} \cdot \frac{5}{1}$$ *Multiply by the reciprocal of $\frac{1}{5}$.*

$$= \frac{2 \cdot 5}{3 \cdot 1}$$

$$= \frac{10}{3} \text{ or } 3\frac{1}{3}$$

B $\frac{3}{5} \div 6$

$$\frac{3}{5} \div 6 = \frac{3}{5} \cdot \frac{1}{6}$$ *Multiply by the reciprocal of 6.*

$$= \frac{{}^{1}3 \cdot 1}{5 \cdot 6_{2}}$$ *Simplify.*

$$= \frac{1}{10}$$

EXAMPLE 2 Dividing Mixed Numbers

Divide. Write each answer in simplest form.

A $4\frac{1}{3} \div 2\frac{1}{2}$

$$4\frac{1}{3} \div 2\frac{1}{2} = \frac{13}{3} \div \frac{5}{2}$$ *Write mixed numbers as improper fractions.*

$$= \frac{13}{3} \cdot \frac{2}{5}$$ *Multiply by the reciprocal of $\frac{5}{2}$.*

$$= \frac{26}{15} \text{ or } 1\frac{11}{15}$$

Divide. Write each answer in simplest form.

B $\dfrac{5}{6} \div 7\dfrac{1}{7}$

$$\dfrac{5}{6} \div 7\dfrac{1}{7} = \dfrac{5}{6} \div \dfrac{50}{7} \qquad \textit{Write } 7\tfrac{1}{7} \textit{ as an improper fraction.}$$

$$= \dfrac{5}{6} \cdot \dfrac{7}{50} \qquad \textit{Multiply by the reciprocal of } \tfrac{50}{7}.$$

$$= \dfrac{\overset{1}{\cancel{5}} \cdot 7}{6 \cdot \cancel{50}_{10}} \qquad \textit{Simplify.}$$

$$= \dfrac{7}{60}$$

C $4\dfrac{4}{5} \div \dfrac{6}{7}$

$$4\dfrac{4}{5} \div \dfrac{6}{7} = \dfrac{24}{5} \div \dfrac{6}{7} \qquad \textit{Write } 4\tfrac{4}{5} \textit{ as an improper fraction.}$$

$$= \dfrac{24}{5} \cdot \dfrac{7}{6} \qquad \textit{Multiply by the reciprocal of } \tfrac{6}{7}.$$

$$= \dfrac{\overset{4}{\cancel{24}} \cdot 7}{5 \cdot \cancel{6}_{1}} \qquad \textit{Simplify.}$$

$$= \dfrac{28}{5} \text{ or } 5\dfrac{3}{5}$$

EXAMPLE 3 *Social Studies Application*

Use the bar graph to determine how many times longer a $100 bill is expected to stay in circulation than a $1 bill.

The life span of a $1 bill is $1\dfrac{1}{2}$ years. The life span of a $100 bill is 9 years.

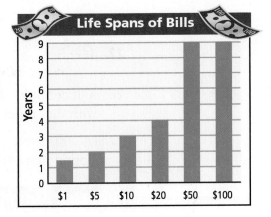
Life Spans of Bills

Think: How many $1\tfrac{1}{2}$'s are there in 9?

$$9 \div 1\dfrac{1}{2} = \dfrac{9}{1} \div \dfrac{3}{2} \qquad \textit{Write both numbers as improper fractions.}$$

$$= \dfrac{9}{1} \cdot \dfrac{2}{3} \qquad \textit{Multiply by the reciprocal of } \tfrac{3}{2}.$$

$$= \dfrac{\overset{3}{\cancel{9}} \cdot 2}{1 \cdot \cancel{3}_{1}} \qquad \textit{Simplify.}$$

$$= \dfrac{6}{1} \text{ or } 6$$

A $100 bill is expected to stay in circulation 6 times longer than a $1 bill.

MATHEMATICAL PRACTICES

Think and Discuss

1. **Explain** whether $\dfrac{1}{2} \div \dfrac{2}{3}$ is the same as $2 \cdot \dfrac{2}{3}$.

2. **Compare** the steps used in multiplying mixed numbers with those used in dividing mixed numbers.

Learn It Online
Homework Help Online
Exercises 1–27, 29, 31, 33, 35, 37, 43, 47

GUIDED PRACTICE

See Example **1** Divide. Write each answer in simplest form.

1. $6 \div \frac{1}{3}$ **2.** $\frac{3}{5} \div \frac{3}{4}$ **3.** $\frac{3}{4} \div 8$ **4.** $-\frac{5}{9} \div \frac{2}{5}$

See Example **2** **5.** $\frac{5}{6} \div 3\frac{1}{3}$ **6.** $5\frac{5}{8} \div 4\frac{1}{2}$ **7.** $10\frac{4}{5} \div 5\frac{2}{5}$ **8.** $2\frac{1}{10} \div \frac{3}{5}$

See Example **3** **9.** Kareem has $12\frac{1}{2}$ yards of material. A cape for a play takes $3\frac{5}{6}$ yards. How many capes can Kareem make with the material?

INDEPENDENT PRACTICE

See Example **1** Divide. Write each answer in simplest form.

10. $2 \div \frac{7}{8}$ **11.** $10 \div \frac{5}{9}$ **12.** $\frac{3}{4} \div \frac{6}{7}$ **13.** $\frac{7}{8} \div \frac{1}{5}$

14. $\frac{8}{9} \div \frac{1}{4}$ **15.** $\frac{4}{9} \div 12$ **16.** $\frac{9}{10} \div 6$ **17.** $-16 \div \frac{2}{5}$

See Example **2** **18.** $\frac{7}{11} \div 4\frac{1}{5}$ **19.** $\frac{3}{4} \div 2\frac{1}{10}$ **20.** $22\frac{1}{2} \div 4\frac{2}{7}$ **21.** $-10\frac{1}{2} \div \frac{3}{4}$

22. $3\frac{5}{7} \div 9\frac{1}{7}$ **23.** $14\frac{2}{3} \div 1\frac{1}{6}$ **24.** $7\frac{7}{10} \div 2\frac{2}{5}$ **25.** $8\frac{2}{5} \div \frac{7}{8}$

See Example **3** **26.** A juicer holds $43\frac{3}{4}$ pints of juice. How many $2\frac{1}{2}$-pint bottles can be filled with that much juice?

27. **Measurement** How many $24\frac{1}{2}$ in. pieces of ribbon can be cut from a roll of ribbon that is 147 in. long?

PRACTICE AND PROBLEM SOLVING

Extra Practice
See Extra Practice for more exercises.

Evaluate. Write each answer in simplest form.

28. $6\frac{2}{3} \div \frac{7}{9}$ **29.** $-1\frac{7}{11} \div \left(\frac{9}{11}\right)$ **30.** $\frac{2}{3} \div \frac{8}{9}$ **31.** $-1\frac{3}{5} \div 2\frac{1}{2}$

32. $\frac{1}{2} \div 4\frac{3}{4}$ **33.** $\left(2\frac{3}{4} + 3\frac{2}{3}\right) \div \frac{11}{18}$ **34.** $\left(\frac{1}{2} + \frac{2}{3}\right) \div 1\frac{1}{2}$ **35.** $\frac{4}{5} \cdot \frac{3}{8} \div \frac{9}{10}$

36. $\frac{1}{2}\left(\frac{3}{5} - \frac{2}{15}\right) + \frac{2}{9} \div \frac{1}{3}$ **37.** $\frac{3}{7} \div \frac{15}{28} \div \left(-\frac{4}{5}\right)$ **38.** $\frac{7}{8} \div 2\frac{1}{10}$

39. $\frac{2}{3} \div \left(\frac{5}{6} + \frac{1}{12}\right) - 2 \cdot \frac{1}{2}$ **40.** $\frac{3}{4} + \frac{3}{20} \div \frac{2}{5} \cdot \frac{7}{8} - 1$ **41.** $\left(\frac{1}{2}\right)^2 + \frac{1}{3} \div \frac{1}{6} - \frac{1}{4}$

42. Three friends will be driving to an amusement park that is $226\frac{4}{5}$ mi from their town. If each friend drives the same distance, how far will each drive? Explain how you decided which operation to use to solve this problem.

43. **Multi-Step** How many $\frac{1}{4}$ lb hamburger patties can be made from a $10\frac{1}{4}$ lb package and an $11\frac{1}{2}$ lb package of ground meat?

 44. **Write About It** Explain what it means to divide $\frac{2}{3}$ by $\frac{1}{3}$. Use a model in your explanation.

45. Multi-Step The students in Mr. Park's woodworking class are making birdhouses. The plans call for the side pieces of the birdhouses to be $7\frac{1}{4}$ inches long. If Mr. Park has 6 boards that are $50\frac{3}{4}$ inches long, how many side pieces can be cut?

46. Critical Thinking Brandy is stamping circles from a strip of aluminum. If each circle is $1\frac{1}{4}$ inches tall, how many circles can she get from an $8\frac{3}{4}$-inch by $1\frac{1}{4}$-inch strip of aluminum?

47. For his drafting class, Manuel is drawing plans for a bookcase. Because he wants his drawing to be $\frac{1}{4}$ the actual size of the bookcase, Manuel must divide each measurement of the bookcase by 4. If the bookcase will be $3\frac{2}{3}$ feet wide, how wide will Manuel's drawing be?

48. The table shows the total number of hours that the students in each of Mrs. Anwar's 5 industrial arts classes took to complete their final projects. If the third-period class has 17 students, how many hours did each student in that class work on average?

Period	Hours
1st	$200\frac{1}{2}$
2nd	$179\frac{2}{5}$
3rd	$199\frac{3}{4}$
5th	$190\frac{3}{4}$
6th	$180\frac{1}{4}$

49. ⭐ **Challenge** Alexandra is cutting wood stencils to spell her first name with capital letters. Her first step is to cut a square of wood that is $3\frac{1}{2}$ in. long on a side for each letter in her name. Will Alexandra be able to make all of the letters of her name from a single piece of wood that is $7\frac{1}{2}$ in. wide and 18 in. long? Explain your answer.

Test Prep

50. Multiple Choice Which expression is NOT equivalent to $2\frac{2}{3} \div 1\frac{5}{8}$?

(A) $\frac{8}{3} \cdot \frac{8}{13}$ (B) $2\frac{2}{3} \div \frac{13}{8}$ (C) $\frac{8}{3} \div \frac{13}{8}$ (D) $\frac{8}{3} \cdot 1\frac{5}{8}$

51. Multiple Choice What is the value of the expression $\frac{3}{5} \cdot \frac{1}{6} \div \frac{2}{5}$?

(F) $\frac{1}{25}$ (G) $\frac{1}{4}$ (H) $\frac{15}{22}$ (J) 25

52. Gridded Response Each cat at the animal shelter gets $\frac{3}{4}$ c of food every day. If Alysse has $16\frac{1}{2}$ c of cat food, how many cats can she feed?

Solving Equations Containing Fractions

COMMON CORE

CC.7.EE.4 Use variables to represent quantities in a real-world or mathematical problem, and construct simple equations and inequalities to solve problems by reasoning about the quantities.

Gold classified as 24 karat is pure gold, while gold classified as 18 karat is only $\frac{3}{4}$ pure. The remaining $\frac{1}{4}$ of 18-karat gold is made up of one or more different metals, such as silver, copper, or zinc.

Equations can help you determine the amounts of metals in different kinds of gold. The goal when solving equations that contain fractions is the same as when working with other kinds of numbers—*to isolate the variable* on one side of the equation.

EXAMPLE **1** **Solving Equations by Adding or Subtracting**

Solve. Write each answer in simplest form.

A $x - \frac{1}{5} = \frac{3}{5}$

$$x - \frac{1}{5} = \frac{3}{5}$$

$$x - \frac{1}{5} + \frac{1}{5} = \frac{3}{5} + \frac{1}{5}$$ *Use the Addition Property of Equality.*

$$x = \frac{4}{5}$$ *Add.*

B $\frac{7}{18} + u = -\frac{14}{27}$

$$\frac{7}{18} + u = -\frac{14}{27}$$

$$\frac{7}{18} + u - \frac{7}{18} = -\frac{14}{27} - \frac{7}{18}$$ *Use the Subtraction Property of Equality.*

$$u = -\frac{28}{54} - \frac{21}{54}$$ *Find a common denominator.*

$$u = -\frac{49}{54}$$ *Subtract.*

Helpful Hint

You can also isolate the variable *y* by adding the opposite of $\frac{7}{18}$, $-\frac{7}{18}$, to both sides.

Recall that the product of a nonzero number and its reciprocal is 1. This is called the Multiplicative Inverse Property.

Multiplicative Inverse Property		
Words	**Numbers**	**Algebra**
The product of a nonzero number and its reciprocal, or multiplicative inverse, is one.	$\frac{4}{5} \cdot \frac{5}{4} = 1$	$\frac{a}{b} \cdot \frac{b}{a} = 1$

You can use the Multiplicative Inverse Property to solve multiplication equations that contain fractions and whole numbers.

Video **Lesson Tutorials Online**   my.hrw.com

vario images GmbH & Co.KG/Alamy

EXAMPLE 2 Solving Equations by Multiplying

Solve. Write each answer in simplest form.

A $\frac{2}{3}x = \frac{4}{5}$

$$\frac{2}{3}x = \frac{4}{5}$$ *Use the Multiplicative Inverse Property.*

$$\frac{2}{3}x \cdot \frac{3}{2} = \frac{2\cancel{4}}{5} \cdot \frac{3}{\cancel{2}_1}$$ *Multiply by the reciprocal of $\frac{2}{3}$. Then simplify.*

$$x = \frac{6}{5} \text{ or } 1\frac{1}{5}$$

B $3y = \frac{6}{7}$

$$3y = \frac{6}{7}$$ *Use the Multiplicative Inverse Property.*

$$3y \cdot \frac{1}{3} = \frac{2\cancel{6}}{7} \cdot \frac{1}{\cancel{3}_1}$$ *Multiply by the reciprocal of 3. Then simplify.*

$$y = \frac{2}{7}$$

Caution!

To undo multiplying by $\frac{2}{3}$, you must divide by $\frac{2}{3}$ or multiply by its reciprocal, $\frac{3}{2}$.

EXAMPLE 3 *Physical Science Application*

Pink gold is made of pure gold, silver, and copper. There is $\frac{11}{20}$ more pure gold than copper in pink gold. If pink gold is $\frac{3}{4}$ pure gold, what portion of pink gold is copper?

Let *c* represent the amount of copper in pink gold.

$$c + \frac{11}{20} = \frac{3}{4}$$ *Write an equation.*

$$c + \frac{11}{20} - \frac{11}{20} = \frac{3}{4} - \frac{11}{20}$$ *Subtract to isolate c.*

$$c = \frac{15}{20} - \frac{11}{20}$$ *Find a common denominator.*

$$c = \frac{4}{20}$$ *Subtract.*

$$c = \frac{1}{5}$$ *Simplify.*

Pink gold is $\frac{1}{5}$ copper.

MATHEMATICAL PRACTICES

Think and Discuss

1. **Show** the first step you would use to solve $m + 3\frac{5}{8} = 12\frac{1}{2}$.

2. **Describe** how to decide whether $\frac{2}{3}$ is a solution of $\frac{7}{8}y = \frac{3}{5}$.

3. **Explain** why solving $\frac{2}{5}c = \frac{8}{9}$ by multiplying both sides by $\frac{5}{2}$ is the same as solving it by dividing both sides by $\frac{2}{5}$.

GUIDED PRACTICE

See Example 1   Solve. Write each answer in simplest form.

1. $a - \frac{1}{2} = \frac{1}{4}$

2. $m + \frac{1}{6} = \frac{5}{6}$

3. $p - \frac{2}{3} = \frac{5}{6}$

See Example 2   4. $\frac{1}{5}x = 8$

5. $\frac{2}{3}r = \frac{3}{5}$

6. $3w = \frac{3}{7}$

See Example 3   7. Kara has $\frac{3}{8}$ cup less oatmeal than she needs for a cookie recipe. If she has $\frac{3}{4}$ cup of oatmeal, how much oatmeal does she need?

INDEPENDENT PRACTICE

See Example 1   Solve. Write each answer in simplest form.

8. $n - \frac{1}{5} = \frac{3}{5}$

9. $t - \frac{3}{8} = \frac{1}{4}$

10. $s - \frac{7}{24} = \frac{1}{3}$

11. $x + \frac{2}{3} = 2\frac{7}{8}$

12. $h + \frac{7}{10} = \frac{7}{10}$

13. $y + \frac{5}{6} = \frac{19}{20}$

See Example 2   14. $\frac{1}{5}x = 4$

15. $\frac{1}{4}w = \frac{1}{8}$

16. $5y = \frac{3}{10}$

17. $6z = \frac{1}{2}$

18. $\frac{5}{8}x = \frac{2}{5}$

19. $\frac{5}{8}n = 1\frac{1}{5}$

See Example 3   20. **Earth Science** Carbon-14 has a half-life of 5,730 years. After 17,190 years, $\frac{1}{8}$ of the carbon-14 in a sample will be left. If 5 grams of carbon-14 are left after 17,190 years, how much was in the original sample?

PRACTICE AND PROBLEM SOLVING

Extra Practice
See Extra Practice for more exercises.

Solve. Write each answer in simplest form.

21. $\frac{4}{5}t = \frac{1}{5}$

22. $m - \frac{1}{2} = \frac{2}{3}$

23. $\frac{1}{8}w = \frac{3}{4}$

24. $\frac{8}{9} + t = \frac{17}{18}$

25. $\frac{5}{3}x = 1$

26. $j + \frac{5}{8} = \frac{11}{16}$

27. $\frac{4}{3}n = 3\frac{1}{5}$

28. $z + \frac{1}{6} = 3\frac{9}{15}$

29. $\frac{3}{4}y = \frac{3}{8}$

30. $-\frac{5}{26} + m = -\frac{7}{13}$

31. $-\frac{8}{77} + r = -\frac{1}{11}$

32. $y - \frac{3}{4} = -\frac{9}{20}$

33. $h - \frac{3}{8} = -\frac{11}{24}$

34. $-\frac{5}{36}t = -\frac{5}{16}$

35. $-\frac{8}{13}v = -\frac{6}{13}$

36. $4\frac{6}{7} + p = 5\frac{1}{4}$

37. $d - 5\frac{1}{8} = 9\frac{3}{10}$

38. $6\frac{8}{21}k = 13\frac{1}{3}$

39. **Food** Each person in Finland drinks an average of $24\frac{1}{4}$ lb of coffee per year. This is $13\frac{1}{16}$ lb more than the average person in Italy consumes. On average, how much coffee does an Italian drink each year?

40. **Weather** Yuma, Arizona, receives $102\frac{1}{100}$ fewer inches of rain each year than Quillayute, Washington, which receives $105\frac{9}{50}$ inches per year. (*Source:* National Weather Service). How much rain does Yuma get in one year?

41. Life Science Scientists have discovered $1\frac{1}{2}$ million species of animals. This is estimated to be $\frac{1}{10}$ the total number of species thought to exist. About how many species do scientists think exist?

42. History The circle graph shows the birthplaces of the United States' presidents who were in office between 1789 and 1845.

    a. If six of the presidents represented in the graph were born in Virginia, how many presidents are represented in the graph?

    b. Based on your answer to **a**, how many of the presidents were born in Massachusetts?

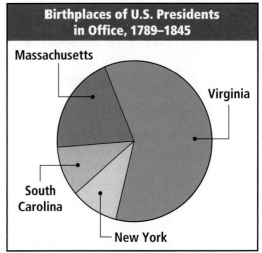

Birthplaces of U.S. Presidents in Office, 1789–1845

Massachusetts
Virginia
South Carolina
New York

43. Architecture In Indianapolis, the Market Tower has $\frac{2}{3}$ as many stories as the Chase Tower. If the Market Tower has 32 stories, how many stories does the Chase Tower have?

44. Multi-Step Each week, Jennifer saves $\frac{1}{5}$ of her allowance and spends some of the rest on lunches. This week, she had $\frac{2}{15}$ of her allowance left after buying her lunch each day. What fraction of her allowance did she spend on lunches?

45. What's the Error? A student solved $\frac{3}{5}x = \frac{2}{3}$ and got $x = \frac{2}{5}$. Find the error.

46. Write About It Solve $3\frac{1}{3}z = 1\frac{1}{2}$. Explain why you need to write mixed numbers as improper fractions when multiplying and dividing.

47. Challenge Solve $\frac{3}{5}w = 0.9$. Write your answer as a fraction and as a decimal.

Test Prep

48. Multiple Choice Which value of y is the solution to the equation $y - \frac{7}{8} = \frac{3}{5}$?

  Ⓐ $y = -\frac{11}{40}$ Ⓑ $y = \frac{10}{13}$ Ⓒ $y = 1\frac{19}{40}$ Ⓓ $y = 2$

49. Multiple Choice Which equation has the solution $x = -\frac{2}{5}$?

  Ⓕ $\frac{2}{5}x = -1$ Ⓖ $-\frac{3}{4}x = \frac{6}{20}$ Ⓗ $-\frac{4}{7} + x = \frac{2}{3}$ Ⓙ $x - 3\frac{5}{7} = 3\frac{1}{2}$

Ready To Go On?

Quiz for Lessons 5 Through 8

5 Adding and Subtracting Fractions

Add or subtract. Write each answer in simplest form.

1. $\frac{5}{8} + \frac{1}{8}$

2. $\frac{14}{15} - \frac{11}{15}$

3. $-\frac{1}{3} + \frac{6}{9}$

4. $\frac{5}{8} - \frac{2}{3}$

5. Sridhar and Tom are painting a room. On Saturday, Sridhar paints $\frac{1}{5}$ of the room, and on Sunday, Tom paints $\frac{1}{3}$ of the room. Was at least half of the room painted over the weekend? Explain.

6 Multiplying Fractions and Mixed Numbers

Multiply. Write each answer in simplest form.

6. $-12 \cdot \frac{5}{6}$

7. $\frac{5}{14} \cdot \frac{7}{10}$

8. $8\frac{4}{5} \cdot \frac{10}{11}$

9. $10\frac{5}{12} \cdot 1\frac{3}{5}$

10. A recipe calls for $1\frac{1}{3}$ cups flour. Tom is making $2\frac{1}{2}$ times the recipe for his family reunion. How much flour does he need? Write your answer in simplest form.

7 Dividing Fractions and Mixed Numbers

Divide. Write each answer in simplest form.

11. $\frac{1}{6} \div \frac{5}{6}$

12. $\frac{2}{3} \div 4$

13. $5\frac{3}{5} \div \frac{4}{5}$

14. $4\frac{2}{7} \div 1\frac{1}{5}$

15. Nina has $9\frac{3}{7}$ yards of material. She needs $1\frac{4}{7}$ yards to make a pillow case. How many pillow cases can Nina make with the material?

8 Solving Equations Containing Fractions

Solve. Write each answer in simplest form.

16. $x - \frac{2}{3} = \frac{2}{15}$

17. $\frac{4}{9} = -2q$

18. $\frac{1}{6}m = \frac{1}{9}$

19. $\frac{3}{8} + p = -\frac{1}{6}$

20. A recipe for Uncle Frank's homemade hush puppies calls for $\frac{1}{8}$ teaspoon of cayenne pepper. The recipe calls for 6 times as much salt as it does cayenne pepper. How much salt does Uncle Frank's recipe require?

Real-World CONNECTIONS

Reason abstractly and quantitatively.

Civil Rights in Education Heritage Trail The roots of free public education in the United States can be traced to southern Virginia. A self-guided driving tour of the area takes visitors to more than 40 schools, libraries, and other sites that played a key role in the story of civil rights in education.

VIRGINIA

The Wilson family is driving the Civil Rights in Education Heritage Trail. Use the map to solve these problems about their trip.

1. The Wilsons drive from Appomattox to Petersburg on the first day of their trip. How many miles do they drive?

2. On the second day of the trip, they drive from Petersburg to South Hill. How much farther do they drive on the first day than on the second day?

3. The distance from South Boston to Halifax is $\frac{1}{6}$ of the distance from Farmville to Nottoway. What is the distance from South Boston to Halifax?

4. The entire trip from Appomattox to Halifax is 202.1 miles. The Wilsons' car gets 21.5 miles to the gallon. How many gallons of gas will they use for the trip?

5. Gas costs $3.65 per gallon. How much will gas cost for the entire trip?

Appomattox $29\frac{1}{10}$ mi Farmville $24\frac{4}{5}$ mi Petersburg $49\frac{4}{5}$ mi

Virginia State University

Carver-Price School

R.R. Moton High School **460** Nottoway

V I R G I N I A

85

Mary M. Bethune High School

$49\frac{9}{10}$ mi

Southside Virginia Community College Christanna Campus

N

501 Halifax South Hill **58** **95**

South Boston

0		25 miles
0		25 kilometers

Courtesy of Civil Rights in Education Heritage Trail

Real-World Connections

Game Time

Number Patterns

The numbers one through ten form the pattern below. Each arrow indicates some kind of relationship between the two numbers. Four relates to itself. Can you figure out what the pattern is?

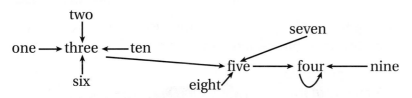

The Spanish numbers *uno* through *diez* form a similar pattern. In this case, *cinco* relates to itself.

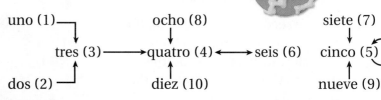

Other interesting number patterns involve cyclic numbers. Cyclic numbers sometimes occur when a fraction converts to a repeating nonterminating decimal. One of the most interesting cyclic numbers is produced by converting the fraction $\frac{1}{7}$ to a decimal.

$$\frac{1}{7} = 0.142857142857142\ldots$$

Multiplying 142857 by the numbers 1–6 produces the same digits in a different order.

$1 \cdot 142857 = 142857$ $3 \cdot 142857 = 428571$ $5 \cdot 142857 = 714285$

$2 \cdot 142857 = 285714$ $4 \cdot 142857 = 571428$ $6 \cdot 142857 = 857142$

Fraction Action

Roll four number cubes and use the numbers to form two fractions. Add the fractions and try to get a sum as close to 1 as possible. To determine your score on each turn, find the difference between the sum of your fractions and 1. Keep a running total of your score as you play. The winner is the player with the lowest score at the end of the game.

A complete copy of the rules are available online.

Learn It Online
Game Time Extra

Jenny Thomas/HMH

Materials
- file folder
- ruler
- pencil
- scissors
- markers

It's in the Bag!

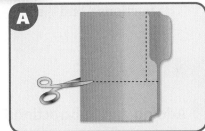

A

PROJECT Operation Slide Through

Slide notes through the frame to review key concepts about operations with rational numbers.

Directions

1 Keep the file folder closed throughout the project. Cut off a $3\frac{1}{2}$-inch strip from the bottom of the folder. Trim the remaining folder so that is has no tabs and measures 8 inches by 8 inches. **Figure A**

2 Cut out a thin notch about 4 inches long along the middle of the folded edge. **Figure B**

3 Cut a $3\frac{3}{4}$-inch slit about 2 inches to the right of the notch. Make another slit, also $3\frac{3}{4}$ inches long, about 3 inches to the right of the first slit. **Figure C**

4 Weave the $3\frac{1}{2}$-inch strip of the folder into the notch, through the first slit, and into the second slit. **Figure D**

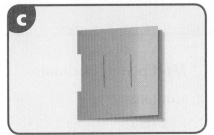

B

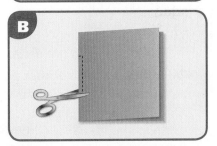

C

D

Taking Note of the Math

As you pull the strip through the frame, divide the strip into several sections. Use each section to record vocabulary and practice problems from the chapter.

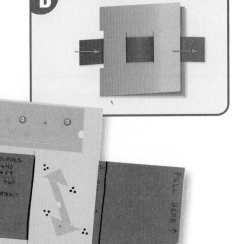

Study Guide: Review

Vocabulary

multiplicative inverse   reciprocal

Complete the sentence below with a vocabulary word from the list above.

1. The fractions $\frac{3}{8}$ and $\frac{8}{3}$ are ___?___ because they multiply to give 1.

EXAMPLES

EXERCISES

1 | Adding and Subtracting Decimals

■ **Add.**

5.67 + 22.44

$$
\begin{array}{r}
5.67 \\
+\ 22.44 \\
\hline
28.11
\end{array}
$$ *Line up the decimal points.*

Add.

Add or subtract.

2. 4.99 + 22.89   **3.** −6.7 + (−44.5)

4. 18.09 − 11.87   **5.** 47 + 5.902

6. 23 − 8.905   **7.** 4.68 + 31.2

8. The water level in a rain barrel is at 24.4 cm. After a storm, the water level rose 4.8 cm. What is the new water level of the rain barrel?

2 | Multiplying Decimals

■ **Multiply.**

1.44 · 0.6

$$
\begin{array}{r}
1.44 \\
\times\ 0.6 \\
\hline
0.864
\end{array}
$$

2 decimal places
1 decimal place
2 + 1 = 3 decimal places

Multiply.

9. 7 · 0.5   **10.** −4.3 · 9

11. 4.55 · 8.9   **12.** 7.88 · 7.65

13. 63.4 · 1.22   **14.** −9.9 · 1.9

15. Fred buys 4 shirts at $9.52 per shirt. How much did Fred spend?

3 Dividing Decimals

■ Divide.

7 ÷ 2.8

$$
\begin{array}{r}
2.5 \\
28\overline{)70.0} \\
\underline{56} \\
140 \\
\underline{140} \\
0
\end{array}
$$

Multiply both numbers by 10 to make the divisior an integer.

■ Divide.

0.96 ÷ 1.6

$$
\begin{array}{r}
0.6 \\
16\overline{)9.6} \\
\underline{-9\,6} \\
0
\end{array}
$$

Multiply both numbers by 10 to make the divisor an integer.

Divide.

16. $16 \div 3.2$ **17.** $50 \div (-1.25)$

18. $48 \div 0.06$ **19.** $31 \div (-6.2)$

20. $78 \div (-12.5)$ **21.** $816 \div 2.4$

22. $7.65 \div 1.7$ **23.** $9.483 \div (-8.7)$

24. $126.28 \div (-8.2)$ **25.** $2.5 \div (-0.005)$

26. $9 \div 4.5$ **27.** $13 \div 3.25$

28. In qualifying for an auto race, one driver had lap speeds of 195.3 mi/h, 190.456 mi/h, 193.557 mi/h, and 192.757 mi/h. What was the driver's average speed for these four laps?

4 Solving Equations Containing Decimals

■ Solve.

$$
\begin{array}{l}
n - 4.77 = 8.60 \\
\underline{+\,4.77 \quad +\,4.77} \\
n \quad\quad = 13.37
\end{array}
$$

Add to isolate n.

Solve.

29. $x + 40.44 = 30$ **30.** $\frac{s}{1.07} = 100$

31. $0.8n = 0.0056$ **32.** $k - 8 = 0.64$

33. $3.65 + e = -1.4$ **34.** $\frac{w}{-0.2} = 15.4$

35. Sam wants to buy a new wakeboard that costs $434. If he makes $7.75 per hour, how many hours must he work to earn enough money for the wakeboard?

5 Adding and Subtracting Fractions

■ Add.

$$
\frac{1}{3} + \frac{2}{5} = \frac{5}{15} + \frac{6}{15}
$$
$$
= \frac{11}{15}
$$

Write equivalent fractions using a common denominator.

Add or subtract. Write each answer in simplest form.

36. $\frac{3}{4} - \frac{1}{3}$ **37.** $\frac{1}{4} + \frac{3}{5}$

38. $\frac{4}{11} + \frac{4}{44}$ **39.** $\frac{4}{9} - \frac{1}{3}$

6 Multiplying Fractions and Mixed Numbers

■ Multiply. Write the answer in simplest form.

$$4\frac{1}{2} \cdot 5\frac{3}{4} = \frac{9}{2} \cdot \frac{23}{4}$$
$$= \frac{207}{8} \text{ or } 25\frac{7}{8}$$

Multiply. Write each answer in simplest form.

40. $1\frac{2}{3} \cdot 4\frac{1}{2}$ **41.** $\frac{4}{5} \cdot 2\frac{3}{10}$

42. $4\frac{6}{7} \cdot 3\frac{5}{9}$ **43.** $3\frac{4}{7} \cdot 1\frac{3}{4}$

7 Dividing Fractions and Mixed Numbers

■ Divide.

$$\frac{3}{4} \div \frac{2}{5} = \frac{3}{4} \cdot \frac{5}{2} \qquad \textit{Multiply by the}$$
$$= \frac{15}{8} \text{ or } 1\frac{7}{8} \qquad \textit{reciprocal of } \frac{2}{5}.$$

Divide. Write each answer in simplest form.

44. $\frac{1}{3} \div 6\frac{1}{4}$ **45.** $\frac{1}{2} \div 3\frac{3}{4}$

46. $\frac{11}{13} \div \frac{11}{13}$ **47.** $2\frac{7}{8} \div 1\frac{1}{2}$

48. A 21-inch long loaf of bread is cut into $\frac{3}{4}$-inch slices. How many slices will there be?

8 Solving Equations Containing Fractions

■ Solve. Write the answer in simplest form.

$$\frac{1}{4}x = \frac{1}{6}$$
$$\frac{4}{1} \cdot \frac{1}{4}x = \frac{1}{6} \cdot \frac{4}{1} \qquad \textit{Multiply by the}$$
$$x = \frac{4}{6} = \frac{2}{3} \qquad \textit{reciprocal of } \frac{1}{4}.$$

Solve. Write each answer in simplest form.

49. $\frac{1}{5}x = \frac{1}{3}$ **50.** $\frac{1}{3} + y = \frac{2}{5}$

51. $\frac{1}{6}x = \frac{2}{7}$ **52.** $\frac{2}{7} + x = \frac{3}{4}$

53. Ty had $2\frac{1}{2}$ cups of oil and used $\frac{3}{4}$ cup for a recipe. How many cups of oil are left?

Chapter Test

Add or subtract.

1. $3.086 + 6.152$ **2.** $5.91 + 12.8$ **3.** $3.1 - 2.076$ **4.** $14.75 - 6.926$

Multiply or divide.

5. $3.25 \cdot 24$ **6.** $-3.79 \cdot 0.9$ **7.** $32 \div 1.6$ **8.** $3.57 \div (-0.7)$

Solve.

9. $w - 5.3 = 7.6$ **10.** $4.9 = c + 3.7$ **11.** $b \div 1.8 = 2.1$ **12.** $4.3h = 81.7$

Add or subtract. Write each answer in simplest form.

13. $\frac{3}{10} + \frac{2}{5}$ **14.** $\frac{11}{16} - \frac{7}{8}$ **15.** $\frac{5}{12} + \frac{1}{12}$ **16.** $-\frac{3}{5} + \frac{1}{2}$

Multiply or divide. Write each answer in simplest form.

17. $5 \cdot 4\frac{1}{3}$ **18.** $2\frac{7}{10} \cdot 2\frac{2}{3}$ **19.** $\frac{3}{10} \div \frac{4}{5}$ **20.** $2\frac{1}{5} \div 1\frac{5}{6}$

21. A recipe calls for $4\frac{4}{5}$ tbsp of butter. Nasim is making $3\frac{1}{3}$ times the recipe for his soccer team. How much butter does he need? Write your answer in simplest form.

22. Brianna has $11\frac{2}{3}$ cups of milk. She needs $1\frac{1}{6}$ cups of milk to make a pot of hot cocoa. How many pots of hot cocoa can Brianna make?

Solve. Write each answer in simplest form.

23. $\frac{1}{5}a = \frac{1}{8}$ **24.** $\frac{1}{4}c = 980$ **25.** $-\frac{7}{9} + w = \frac{2}{3}$ **26.** $z - \frac{5}{13} = \frac{6}{7}$

27. Alan finished his homework in $1\frac{1}{2}$ hours. It took Jimmy $\frac{3}{4}$ of an hour longer than Alan to finish his homework. How long did it take Jimmy to finish his homework?

28. Mya played in two softball games one afternoon. The first game lasted 42 min. The second game lasted $1\frac{2}{3}$ times longer than the first game. How long did Mya's second game last?

Test Tackler
STANDARDIZED TEST STRATEGIES

Gridded Response: Write Gridded Responses

When responding to a test item that requires you to place your answer in a grid, you must fill in the grid on your answer sheet correctly, or the item will be marked as incorrect.

EXAMPLE 1

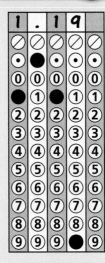

Gridded Response: Solve the equation $0.23 + r = 1.42$.

$$0.23 + r = 1.42$$
$$\underline{-\ 0.23 \qquad\quad -\ 0.23}$$
$$r = 1.19$$

• Using a pencil, write your answer in the answer boxes at the top of the grid. Put the first digit of your answer in the leftmost box, or put the last digit of your answer in the rightmost box. On some grids, the fraction bar and the decimal point have a designated box.

• Put only one digit or symbol in each box. Do not leave a blank box in the middle of an answer.

• Shade the bubble for each digit or symbol in the same column as in the answer box.

EXAMPLE 2

Gridded Response: Divide. $3 \div 1\frac{4}{5}$

$$3 \div 1\frac{4}{5} = \frac{3}{1} \div \frac{9}{5}$$

$$= \frac{3}{1} \cdot \frac{5}{9}$$

$$= \frac{15}{9} = \frac{5}{3} = 1\frac{2}{3} = 1.\overline{6}$$

The answer simplifies to $\frac{5}{3}$, $1\frac{2}{3}$, or $1.\overline{6}$.

• Mixed numbers and repeating decimals cannot be gridded, so you must grid the answer as $\frac{5}{3}$.

• Write your answer in the answer boxes at the top of the grid.

• Put only one digit or symbol in each box. Do not leave a blank box in the middle of an answer.

• Shade the bubble for each digit or symbol in the same column as in the answer box.

Read each statement, and then answer the questions that follow.

Sample A
A student correctly solved an equation for *x* and got 42 as a result. Then the student filled in the grid as shown.

1. What error did the student make when filling in the grid?

2. Explain a second method of filling in the answer correctly.

Sample B
A student correctly multiplied 0.16 and 0.07. Then the student filled in the grid as shown.

3. What error did the student make when filling in the grid?

4. Explain how to fill in the answer correctly.

Sample C
A student subtracted −12 from 5 and got an answer of −17. Then the student filled in the grid as shown.

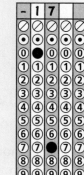

5. What error did the student make when finding the answer?

6. Explain why you cannot fill in a negative number on a grid.

7. Explain how to fill in the answer to 5 − (−12) correctly.

Sample D
A student correctly simplified $\frac{5}{6} + \frac{11}{12}$ and got $1\frac{9}{12}$ as a result. Then the student filled in the grid as shown.

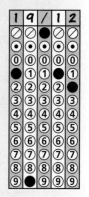

8. What answer is shown in the grid?

9. Explain why you cannot show a mixed number in a grid.

10. Write two equivalent forms of the answer $1\frac{9}{12}$ that could be filled in the grid correctly.

Standardized Test Prep

Cumulative Assessment

Multiple Choice

1. A cell phone company charges $0.05 per text message. Which expression represents the cost of t text messages?

   Ⓐ $0.05t$ Ⓒ $0.05 - t$

   Ⓑ $0.05 + t$ Ⓓ $0.05 \div t$

2. Ahmed had $7.50 in his bank account on Sunday. The table shows his account activity for each day last week. What was the balance in Ahmed's account on Friday?

Monday	$25.25	none
Tuesday	none	−$108.13
Wednesday	$65.25	none
Thursday	$32.17	none
Friday	none	−$101.50

   Ⓕ −$86.96   Ⓗ $0

   Ⓖ −$79.46   Ⓙ $96.46

3. Natasha is designing a doghouse. She wants the front of the doghouse to be $3\frac{1}{2}$ feet wide, and she wants the side of the doghouse to be $2\frac{3}{4}$ feet wider than the front. Which equation can be used to find x, the length of the side of the doghouse?

   Ⓐ $3\frac{1}{2} + 2\frac{3}{4} = x$ Ⓒ $3\frac{1}{2} \cdot 2\frac{3}{4} = x$

   Ⓑ $3\frac{1}{2} - 2\frac{3}{4} = x$ Ⓓ $3\frac{1}{2} \div 2\frac{3}{4} = x$

4. What is the value of $5\frac{2}{3} \div \frac{3}{9}$?

   Ⓕ 17   Ⓗ 10

   Ⓖ $\frac{17}{9}$ Ⓙ $5\frac{1}{3}$

5. Mrs. Herold has $5\frac{1}{4}$ yards of material to make two dresses. The larger dress requires $3\frac{3}{4}$ yards of material. Which equation can be used to find t, the number of yards of material remaining to make the smaller dress?

   Ⓐ $3\frac{3}{4} - t = 5\frac{1}{4}$ Ⓒ $3\frac{3}{4} \div t = 5\frac{1}{4}$

   Ⓑ $3\frac{3}{4} \cdot t = 5\frac{1}{4}$ Ⓓ $3\frac{3}{4} + t = 5\frac{1}{4}$

6. Carl buys 1.5 pounds of grapes. The grapes cost $2.39 per pound. To the nearest cent, how much does Carl pay for the grapes?

   Ⓕ $1.59   Ⓗ $3.59

   Ⓖ $3.45   Ⓙ $3.79

7. A used car is on sale for $4,800. Amy makes an offer equal to $\frac{3}{4}$ of this price. How much does Amy offer for the car?

   Ⓐ $1,200   Ⓒ $4,000

   Ⓑ $3,600   Ⓓ $6,400

8. What is the prime factorization of 110?

   Ⓕ $55 \cdot 2$ Ⓗ $11 \cdot 5 \cdot 2$

   Ⓖ $22 \cdot 5 \cdot 2$ Ⓙ $110 \cdot 1$

9. Solve: $x - 3.4 = 3.4$

   Ⓐ $x = -3.4$ Ⓒ $x = 6.8$

   Ⓑ $x = 0$ Ⓓ no solution

HOT TIP! When possible, use logic to eliminate at least two answer choices.

10. Samuel is ordering pizzas for a party. For every guest, he'd like to have $\frac{1}{3}$ of a pizza. If he expects 23 guests, how many pizzas should he buy?

Ⓕ 7 pizzas

Ⓖ 8 pizzas

Ⓗ 9 pizzas

Ⓙ 12 pizzas

11. The table shows the different types of pets owned by the 15 students in Mrs. Sizer's Spanish class. What fraction of the students listed own a dog?

Cat	5
Dog	9
Hamster	1

Ⓐ $\frac{3}{5}$

Ⓒ $\frac{1}{15}$

Ⓑ $\frac{1}{5}$

Ⓓ $\frac{1}{9}$

Gridded Response

12. Frieda earns $5.85 per hour. To find the amount of money Frieda earns working x hours, use the equation $y = 5.85x$. How many dollars does Frieda earn if she works 2.4 hours?

13. Solve the equation $\frac{5}{12}x = \frac{1}{4}$ for x.

14. What is the value of the expression $2(3.1) + 1.02(-4) - 8 + 3^2$?

Short Response

S1. Louise is staying on the 22nd floor of a hotel. Her mother is staying on the 43rd floor. Louise wants to visit her mother, but the elevator is temporarily out of service. Write and solve an equation to find the number of floors that Louise must climb if she takes the stairs.

S2. Mari bought 3 packages of colored paper. She used $\frac{3}{4}$ of a package to make greeting cards and used $1\frac{1}{6}$ packages for an art project. She gave $\frac{2}{3}$ of a package to her brother. How much colored paper does Mari have left? Show the steps you used to find the answer.

S3. A building proposal calls for 6 acres of land to be divided into $\frac{3}{4}$-acre lots. How many lots can be made? Explain your answer.

Extended Response

E1. A high school is hosting a triple-jump competition. In this event, athletes make three leaps in a row to try to cover the greatest distance.

a. Tony's first two jumps were $11\frac{2}{3}$ ft and $11\frac{1}{2}$ ft. His total distance was 44 ft. Write and solve an equation to find the length of his final jump.

b. Candice's three jumps were all the same length. Her total distance was 38 ft. What was the length of each of her jumps?

c. The lengths of Davis's jumps were 11.6 ft, $11\frac{1}{4}$ ft, and $11\frac{2}{3}$ ft. Plot these lengths on a number line. What was the farthest distance he jumped? How much farther was this distance than the shortest distance Davis jumped?

Proportional Relationships

Why Learn This?

Proportions can be used to find the heights of objects that are too tall to measure directly, such as a lighthouse.

Learn It Online
Chapter Project Online

Chapter Focus

- Use proportionality to solve problems, including problems involving similar objects, units of measurement, and rates.

(cl) Steve Winter/National Geographic/Getty Images

Are You Ready?

✓ Vocabulary

Choose the best term from the list to complete each sentence.

1. A(n) __?__ states that two expressions are equivalent.

2. To __?__ an expression is to substitute a number for the variable and simplify.

3. A value of the variable in an equation that makes the statement true is a(n) __?__ of the equation.

4. A(n) __?__ is a number that can be written as a ratio of two integers.

equation

evaluate

irrational number

rational number

solution

Complete these exercises to review skills you will need for this chapter.

✓ Evaluate Expressions

Evaluate each expression.

5. $x + 5$ for $x = -18$

6. $-9y$ for $y = 13$

7. $\frac{z}{-6}$ for $z = 96$

8. $w - 9$ for $w = -13$

9. $-3z + 1$ for $z = 4$

10. $3w + 9$ for $w = 7$

11. $5 - \frac{y}{3}$ for $y = -3$

12. $x^2 + 1$ for $x = -2$

✓ Solve Equations

Solve each equation.

13. $y + 14 = -3$

14. $-4y = -72$

15. $y - 6 = 39$

16. $\frac{y}{3} = -9$

17. $56 = 8y$

18. $26 = y + 2$

19. $25 - y = 7$

20. $\frac{121}{y} = 11$

21. $-72 = 3y$

22. $25 = \frac{150}{y}$

23. $15 + y = 4$

24. $-120 = -2y$

✓ Number Patterns

Find the next three numbers in the pattern.

25. 95, 112, 129, 146, . . .

26. 85, 65, 60, 40, 35, . . .

27. 20, 20, 100, 100, 500, . . .

28. 12, 14, 17, 21, 26, . . .

29. 1, 3, 5, 7, . . .

30. −19, −12, −5, 2, . . .

31. 5, −10, 20, −40, 80, . . .

32. 0, −10, −5, −15, −10, . . .

Study Guide: Preview

Where You've Been

Previously, you

- wrote fractions in simplest form.

- used ratios to describe proportional situations.

- used ratios to make predictions in proportional situations.

In This Chapter

You will study

- using division to find unit rates and ratios in proportional relationships.

- estimating and finding solutions to application problems involving proportional relationships.

- using critical attributes to define similarity.

- using ratios and proportions in scale drawings and scale models.

Where You're Going

You can use the skills learned in this chapter

- to read and interpret maps.

- to find heights of objects that are too tall to measure.

Key Vocabulary/Vocabulario

corresponding angles	ángulos correspondientes
corresponding sides	lados correspondientes
equivalent ratios	razones equivalentes
indirect measurement	medición indirecta
proportion	proporción
rate	tasa
scale	escala
scale drawing	dibujo a escala
scale model	modelo a escala
similar	semejante

Vocabulary Connections

To become familiar with some of the vocabulary terms in the chapter, consider the following. You may refer to the chapter, the glossary, or a dictionary if you like.

1. "Miles per hour," "students per class," and "Calories per serving" are all examples of *rates*. What other rates can you think of? How would you describe a **rate** to someone if you couldn't use examples in your explanation?

2. The word *indirect* means "not direct." What do you think it means to find the length of something using **indirect measurement**?

3. *Similar* means "having characteristics in common." If two triangles are **similar**, what might they have in common?

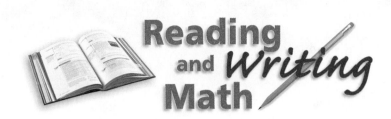 Reading and Writing Math

Writing Strategy: Use Your Own Words

Using your own words to explain a concept can help you understand the concept. For example, learning how to solve equations might seem difficult if the textbook does not explain solving equations in the same way that you would.

As you work through each lesson:

- Identify the important ideas from the explanation in the book.

- Use your own words to explain these ideas.

What Sara Reads

An **equation** is a mathematical statement that two expressions are equal in value.

When an equation contains a variable, a value of the variable that makes the statement true is called a **solution** of the equation.

If a variable is multiplied by a number, you can often use division to isolate the variable. Divide both sides of the equation by the number.

What Sara Writes

An equation has an equal sign to show that two expressions are equal to each other.

The solution of an equation that has a variable in it is the number that the variable is equal to.

When the variable is multiplied by a number, you can undo the multiplication and get the variable alone by dividing both sides of the equation by the number.

Try This

Rewrite each sentence in your own words.

1. When solving addition equations involving integers, isolate the variable by adding opposites.

2. When you solve equations that have one operation, you use an inverse operation to isolate the variable.

CC.7.RP.2 Recognize and represent proportional relationships between quantities. *Also CC.7.RP.1, CC.7.RP.2b*

Vocabulary

rate

unit rate

The Lawsons are going camping at Rainbow Falls, which is 288 miles from their home. They would like to reach the campground in 6 hours. What should their average speed be in miles per hour?

In order to answer the question above, you need to find the family's *rate* of travel. A **rate** is a ratio that compares two quantities measured in different units.

The Lawson family's rate is $\frac{288 \text{ miles}}{6 \text{ hours}}$.

A **unit rate** is a rate whose denominator is 1 when it is written as a fraction. To change a rate to a unit rate, first write the rate as a fraction and then divide both the numerator and denominator by the denominator.

E X A M P L E **1** **Finding Unit Rates**

Interactivities Online ▶

A **During exercise, Sonia's heart beats 675 times in 5 minutes. How many times does it beat per minute?**

$\dfrac{675 \text{ beats}}{5 \text{ minutes}}$ *Write a rate that compares heart beats and time.*

$\dfrac{675 \text{ beats} \div 5}{5 \text{ minutes} \div 5}$ *Divide the numerator and denominator by 5.*

$\dfrac{135 \text{ beats}}{1 \text{ minute}}$ *Simplify.*

Sonia's heart beats 135 times per minute.

B **To make 4 large pizza pockets, Paul needs 14 cups of broccoli. How much broccoli does he need for 1 large pizza pocket?**

$\dfrac{14 \text{ cups broccoli}}{4 \text{ pizza pockets}}$ *Write a rate that compares cups to pockets.*

$\dfrac{14 \text{ cups broccoli} \div 4}{4 \text{ pizza pockets} \div 4}$ *Divide the numerator and denominator by 4.*

$\dfrac{3.5 \text{ cups broccoli}}{1 \text{ pizza pocket}}$ *Simplify.*

Paul needs 3.5 cups of broccoli to make 1 large pizza pocket.

Video **Lesson Tutorials Online** my.hrw.com

An average rate of speed is the ratio of distance traveled to time. The ratio is a rate because the units being compared are different.

EXAMPLE **2** **Finding Average Speed**

The Lawsons want to drive 288 miles to Rainbow Falls in 6 hours. What should their average speed be in miles per hour?

$\dfrac{288 \text{ miles}}{6 \text{ hours}}$ *Write the rate as a fraction.*

$\dfrac{288 \text{ miles} \div 6}{6 \text{ hours} \div 6} = \dfrac{48 \text{ miles}}{1 \text{ hour}}$ *Divide the numerator and denominator by the denominator.*

Their average speed should be 48 miles per hour.

A unit price is the price of one unit of an item. The unit used depends on how the item is sold. The table shows some examples.

Type of Item	Examples of Units
Liquid	Fluid ounces, quarts, gallons, liters
Solid	Ounces, pounds, grams, kilograms
Any item	Bottle, container, carton

EXAMPLE **3** *Consumer Math Application*

The Lawsons stop at a roadside farmers' market. The market offers lemonade in three sizes. Which size lemonade has the lowest price per fluid ounce?

Size	Price
12 fl oz	$0.89
18 fl oz	$1.69
24 fl oz	$2.09

Divide the price by the number of fluid ounces (fl oz) to find the unit price of each size.

$\dfrac{\$0.89}{12 \text{ fl oz}} \approx \dfrac{\$0.07}{\text{fl oz}}$ $\dfrac{\$1.69}{18 \text{ fl oz}} \approx \dfrac{\$0.09}{\text{fl oz}}$ $\dfrac{\$2.09}{24 \text{ fl oz}} \approx \dfrac{\$0.09}{\text{fl oz}}$

Since $\$0.07 < \$0.09$, the 12 fl oz lemonade has the lowest price per fluid ounce.

Think and Discuss

1. Explain how you can tell whether a rate represents a unit rate.

2. Suppose a store offers cereal with a unit price of $0.15 per ounce. Another store offers cereal with a unit price of $0.18 per ounce. Before determining which is the better buy, what variables must you consider?

GUIDED PRACTICE

See Example **1**

1. A faucet leaks 668 milliliters of water in 8 minutes. How many milliliters of water does the faucet leak per minute?

2. A recipe for 6 muffins calls for 360 grams of oat flakes. How many grams of oat flakes are needed for each muffin?

See Example **2**

3. An airliner makes a 2,748-mile flight in 6 hours. What is the airliner's average rate of speed in miles per hour?

See Example **3**

4. **Consumer Math** During a car trip, the Webers buy gasoline at three different stations. At the first station, they pay $18.63 for 9 gallons of gas. At the second, they pay $29.54 for 14 gallons. At the third, they pay $33.44 for 16 gallons. Which station offers the lowest price per gallon?

INDEPENDENT PRACTICE

See Example **1**

5. An after-school job pays $116.25 for 15 hours of work. How much money does the job pay per hour?

6. It took Samantha 324 minutes to cook an 18 lb turkey. How many minutes per pound did it take to cook the turkey?

See Example **2**

7. **Sports** The first Indianapolis 500 auto race took place in 1911. The winning car covered the 500 miles in 6.7 hours. What was the winning car's average rate of speed in miles per hour?

See Example **3**

8. **Consumer Math** A supermarket sells orange juice in three sizes. The 32 fl oz container costs $1.99, the 64 fl oz container costs $3.69, and the 96 fl oz container costs $5.85. Which size orange juice has the lowest price per fluid ounce?

PRACTICE AND PROBLEM SOLVING

Extra Practice
See Extra Practice for more exercises.

Find each unit rate. Round to the nearest hundredth, if necessary.

9. 9 runs in 3 games

10. $207,000 for 1,800 ft²

11. $2,010 in 6 mo

12. 52 songs on 4 CDs

13. 226 mi on 12 gal

14. 324 words in 6 min

15. 12 hr for $69

16. 6 lb for $12.96

17. 488 mi in 4 trips

18. 220 m in 20 s

19. 1.5 mi in 39 min

20. 24,000 km in 1.5 hr

21. In Grant Middle School, each class has an equal number of students. There are 38 classes and a total of 1,026 students. Write a rate that describes the distribution of students in the classes at Grant. What is the unit rate?

22. **Estimation** Use estimation to determine which is the better buy: 450 minutes of phone time for $49.99 or 800 minutes for $62.99.

Find each unit price. Then decide which is the better buy.

23. $\dfrac{\$2.52}{42\ oz}$ or $\dfrac{\$3.64}{52\ oz}$

24. $\dfrac{\$28.40}{8\ yd}$ or $\dfrac{\$55.50}{15\ yd}$

25. $\dfrac{\$8.28}{0.3\ m}$ or $\dfrac{\$13.00}{0.4\ m}$

26. Sports At the track meet, Justin won the 100-meter race in 12.61 seconds. Shawn won the 200-meter race in 26.38 seconds. Which runner ran at a faster average rate?

27. Social Studies The population density of a country is the average number of people per unit of area. Write the population densities of the countries in the map at right as unit rates. Round your answers to the nearest person per square mile. Then rank the countries from least population density to greatest population density.

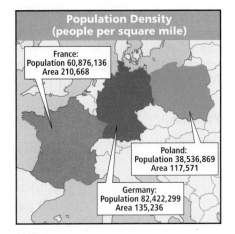

Population Density (people per square mile)

France: Population 60,876,136 Area 210,668

Poland: Population 38,536,869 Area 117,571

Germany: Population 82,422,299 Area 135,236

28. Write a Problem A store sells paper towels in packs of 6 and packs of 8. Use this information to write a problem about comparing unit rates.

29. Write About It Michael Jordan has the highest scoring average in NBA history. During his career, he played in 1,072 games and scored a total of 32,292 points. Explain how to find a unit rate to describe his scoring average. What is the unit rate?

30. Challenge Mike fills his car's gas tank with 20 gallons of regular gas at $2.01 per gallon. His car averages 25 miles per gallon. Serena fills her car's tank with 15 gallons of premium gas at $2.29 per gallon. Her car averages 30 miles per gallon. Compare the drivers' unit costs of driving one mile.

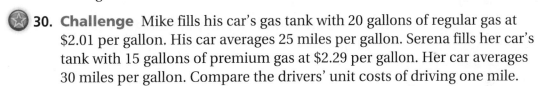

Test Prep

31. Multiple Choice What is the unit price of a 16-ounce box of cereal that sells for $2.48?

Ⓐ $0.14 Ⓑ $0.15 Ⓒ $0.0155 Ⓓ $0.155

32. Short Response A carpenter needs 3 minutes to make 5 cuts in a board. Each cut takes the same length of time. At what rate is the carpenter cutting?

Identifying and Writing Proportions

COMMON CORE

CC.7.RP.2 Recognize and represent proportional relationships between quantities. **Also CC.7.NS.3, CC.7.RP.2a**

Vocabulary

equivalent ratios

proportion

Students in Mr. Howell's math class are measuring the width w and the length ℓ of their faces. The ratio of ℓ to w is 6 inches to 4 inches for Jean and 21 centimeters to 14 centimeters for Pat.

Oval face: $\frac{\ell}{w}$ $\frac{3}{2}$

Round face: ℓ w

These ratios can be written as $\frac{6}{4}$ and $\frac{21}{14}$. Since both ratios simplify to $\frac{3}{2}$, they are equivalent. **Equivalent ratios** are ratios that name the same comparison.

An equation stating that two ratios are equivalent is called a **proportion**. The equation, or proportion, below states that the ratios $\frac{6}{4}$ and $\frac{21}{14}$ are equivalent.

$$\frac{6}{4} = \frac{21}{14}$$

If two ratios are equivalent, they are said to be *proportional*, or *in proportion*.

Reading Math

Read the proportion $\frac{6}{4} = \frac{21}{14}$ by saying "six is to four as twenty-one is to fourteen."

EXAMPLE **1** **Comparing Ratios in Simplest Form**

Determine whether the ratios are proportional.

A $\frac{2}{7}$, $\frac{6}{21}$

$\frac{2}{7}$ *$\frac{2}{7}$ is already in simplest form.*

$\frac{6}{21} = \frac{6 \div 3}{21 \div 3} = \frac{2}{7}$ *Simplify $\frac{6}{21}$.*

Since $\frac{2}{7} = \frac{2}{7}$, the ratios are proportional.

B $\frac{8}{24}$, $\frac{6}{20}$

$\frac{8}{24} = \frac{8 \div 8}{24 \div 8} = \frac{1}{3}$ *Simplify $\frac{8}{24}$.*

$\frac{6}{20} = \frac{6 \div 2}{20 \div 2} = \frac{3}{10}$ *Simplify $\frac{6}{20}$.*

Since $\frac{1}{3}$ $\frac{3}{10}$, the ratios are *not* proportional.

    Video **Lesson Tutorials Online** my.hrw.com

EXAMPLE 2

Comparing Ratios Using a Common Denominator

Use the data in the table to determine whether the ratios of oats to water are proportional for both servings of oatmeal.

Servings of Oatmeal	Cups of Oats	Cups of Water
8	2	4
12	3	6

Write the ratios of oats to water for 8 servings and for 12 servings.

Ratio of oats to water, 8 servings: $\frac{2}{4}$ *Write the ratio as a fraction.*

Ratio of oats to water, 12 servings: $\frac{3}{6}$ *Write the ratio as a fraction.*

$$\frac{2}{4} = \frac{2 \cdot 6}{4 \cdot 6} = \frac{12}{24}$$

$$\frac{3}{6} = \frac{3 \cdot 4}{6 \cdot 4} = \frac{12}{24}$$

Write the fractions with a common denominator, such as 24.

Since both ratios are equal to $\frac{12}{24}$, they are proportional.

You can find an equivalent ratio by multiplying or dividing both terms of a ratio by the same number.

EXAMPLE 3

Finding Equivalent Ratios and Writing Proportions

Find a ratio equivalent to each ratio. Then use the ratios to write a proportion.

A $\frac{8}{14}$

$$\frac{8}{14} = \frac{8 \cdot 20}{14 \cdot 20} = \frac{160}{280}$$

Multiply both terms by any number, such as 20.

$$\frac{8}{14} = \frac{160}{280}$$

Write a proportion.

B $\frac{4}{18}$

$$\frac{4}{18} = \frac{4 \div 2}{18 \div 2} = \frac{2}{9}$$

Divide both terms by a common factor, such as 2.

$$\frac{4}{18} = \frac{2}{9}$$

Write a proportion.

Life Science LINK

The ratios of the sizes of the segments of a nautilus shell are approximately equal to the *golden ratio*, 1.618.... This ratio can be found in many places in nature.

MATHEMATICAL PRACTICES

Think and Discuss

1. **Explain** why the ratios in Example 1B are not proportional.

2. **Describe** what it means for ratios to be proportional.

3. **Give an example** of a proportion. Then tell how you know it is a proportion.

James L. Amos/SuperStock

Exercises

Learn It Online
Homework Help Online
Exercises 1–28, 29, 39, 41, 43

GUIDED PRACTICE

See Example 1   **Determine whether the ratios are proportional.**

1. $\frac{2}{3}, \frac{4}{6}$ **2.** $\frac{5}{10}, \frac{8}{18}$ **3.** $\frac{9}{12}, \frac{15}{20}$ **4.** $\frac{3}{4}, \frac{8}{12}$

See Example 2   **5.** $\frac{10}{12}, \frac{15}{18}$ **6.** $\frac{6}{9}, \frac{8}{12}$ **7.** $\frac{3}{4}, \frac{5}{6}$ **8.** $\frac{4}{6}, \frac{6}{9}$

See Example 3   **Find a ratio equivalent to each ratio. Then use the ratios to write a proportion.**

9. $\frac{1}{3}$ **10.** $\frac{9}{21}$ **11.** $\frac{8}{3}$ **12.** $\frac{10}{4}$

INDEPENDENT PRACTICE

See Example 1   **Determine whether the ratios are proportional.**

13. $\frac{5}{8}, \frac{7}{14}$ **14.** $\frac{8}{24}, \frac{10}{30}$ **15.** $\frac{18}{20}, \frac{81}{180}$ **16.** $\frac{15}{20}, \frac{27}{35}$

See Example 2   **17.** $\frac{2}{3}, \frac{4}{9}$ **18.** $\frac{18}{12}, \frac{15}{10}$ **19.** $\frac{7}{8}, \frac{14}{24}$ **20.** $\frac{18}{54}, \frac{10}{30}$

See Example 3   **Find a ratio equivalent to each ratio. Then use the ratios to write a proportion.**

21. $\frac{5}{9}$ **22.** $\frac{27}{60}$ **23.** $\frac{6}{15}$ **24.** $\frac{121}{99}$

25. $\frac{11}{13}$ **26.** $\frac{5}{22}$ **27.** $\frac{78}{104}$ **28.** $\frac{27}{72}$

PRACTICE AND PROBLEM SOLVING

Extra Practice
See Extra Practice for more exercises.

Complete each table of equivalent ratios.

29.

angelfish	4	8		20
tiger fish		6	18	

30.

squares	2	4	6	8
circles		16		

Find two ratios equivalent to each given ratio.

31. 3 to 7   **32.** 6:2   **33.** $\frac{5}{12}$ **34.** 8:4

35. 6 to 9   **36.** $\frac{10}{50}$ **37.** 10:4   **38.** 1 to 10

39. Ecology If you recycle one aluminum can, you save enough energy to run a TV for four hours.

     a. Write the ratio of cans to hours.

     b. Marti's class recycled enough aluminum cans to run a TV for 2,080 hours. Did the class recycle 545 cans? Justify your answer using equivalent ratios.

40. Critical Thinking The ratio of girls to boys riding a bus is 15:12. If the driver drops off the same number of girls as boys at the next stop, does the ratio of girls to boys remain 15:12? Explain.

41. Critical Thinking Write all possible proportions using only the numbers 1, 2, and 4.

42. School Last year in Kerry's school, the ratio of students to teachers was 22:1. Write an equivalent ratio to show how many students and teachers there could have been at Kerry's school.

43. Life Science Students in a biology class visited four different ponds to determine whether salamanders and frogs were inhabiting the area.

Pond	Number of Salamanders	Number of Frogs
Cypress Pond	8	5
Mill Pond	15	10
Clear Pond	3	2
Gill Pond	2	7

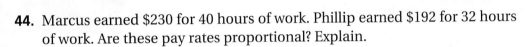

a. What was the ratio of salamanders to frogs in Cypress Pond?

b. In which two ponds was the ratio of salamanders to frogs the same?

44. Marcus earned $230 for 40 hours of work. Phillip earned $192 for 32 hours of work. Are these pay rates proportional? Explain.

45. What's the Error? A student wrote the proportion $\frac{13}{20} = \frac{26}{60}$. What did the student do wrong?

46. Write About It Explain two different ways to determine if two ratios are proportional.

47. Challenge A skydiver jumps out of an airplane. After 0.8 second, she has fallen 100 feet. After 3.1 seconds, she has fallen 500 feet. Is the rate (in feet per second) at which she falls the first 100 feet proportional to the rate at which she falls the next 400 feet? Explain.

Test Prep

48. Multiple Choice Which ratio is NOT equivalent to $\frac{32}{48}$?

Ⓐ $\frac{2}{3}$ Ⓑ $\frac{8}{12}$ Ⓒ $\frac{64}{96}$ Ⓓ $\frac{128}{144}$

49. Multiple Choice Which ratio can form a proportion with $\frac{5}{6}$?

Ⓕ $\frac{13}{18}$ Ⓖ $\frac{25}{36}$ Ⓗ $\frac{70}{84}$ Ⓙ $\frac{95}{102}$

Solving Proportions

COMMON CORE

CC.7.RP.2 Recognize and represent proportional relationships between quantities. *Also CC.7.RP.1, CC.7.RP.2c*

Vocabulary

cross product

Interactivities Online ▶

Density is a ratio that compares a substance's mass to its volume. If you are given the density of ice, you can find the mass of 3 mL of ice by solving a proportion.

For two ratios, the product of the first term in one ratio and the second term in the other is a **cross product** . If the cross products are equal, then the ratios form a proportion.

Ice floats in water because the density of ice is less than the density of water.

$$5 \cdot 6 = 30$$
$$\frac{2}{5} \times \frac{6}{15}$$
$$2 \cdot 15 = 30$$

CROSS PRODUCTS

In the proportion $\frac{a}{b} = \frac{c}{d}$, where $b \neq 0$ and $d \neq 0$,

the cross products, $a \cdot d$ and $b \cdot c$, are equal.

You can use cross products to solve proportions with variables.

EXAMPLE 1 **Solving Proportions Using Cross Products**

Use cross products to solve the proportion $\frac{p}{6} = \frac{10}{3}$.

$$\frac{p}{6} \times \frac{10}{3}$$

$10 \cdot 6 = p \cdot 3$	*The cross products are equal.*
$60 = 3p$	*Multiply.*
$\frac{60}{3} = \frac{3p}{3}$	*Divide each side by 3.*
$20 = p$	

It is important to set up proportions correctly. Each ratio must compare corresponding quantities in the same order. Suppose a boat travels 16 miles in 4 hours and 8 miles in x hours at the same speed. Either of these proportions could represent this situation.

Trip 1 ⟶ $\left(\frac{16 \text{ mi}}{4 \text{ h}}\right) = \left(\frac{8 \text{ mi}}{x \text{ h}}\right)$ ⟵ Trip 2 $\dfrac{\overline{16 \text{ mi} \quad 4 \text{ h}}}{\overline{8 \text{ mi} \quad x \text{ h}}}$ ⟵ Trip 1
⟵ Trip 2

Video **Lesson Tutorials Online** my.hrw.com

PROBLEM SOLVING APPLICATION

Density is the ratio of a substance's mass to its volume. The density of ice is 0.92 g/mL. What is the mass of 3 mL of ice?

MATHEMATICAL PRACTICES Make sense of problems and persevere in solving them.

1. Understand the Problem

Rewrite the question as a statement.

• Find the mass, in grams, of 3 mL of ice.

List the **important information:**

• density = $\dfrac{\text{mass (g)}}{\text{volume (mL)}}$

• density of ice = $\dfrac{0.92 \text{ g}}{1 \text{ mL}}$

2. Make a Plan

Set up a proportion using the given information. Let m represent the mass of 3 mL of ice.

$\dfrac{0.92 \text{ g}}{1 \text{ mL}} = \dfrac{m}{3 \text{ mL}}$ ← *mass*
← *volume*

3. Solve

Solve the proportion.

$\dfrac{0.92}{1} = \dfrac{m}{3}$ *Write the proportion.*

$m \cdot 1 = 0.92 \cdot 3$ *The cross products are equal.*

$m = 2.76$ *Multiply.*

The mass of 3 mL of ice is 2.76 g.

4. Look Back

Since the density of ice is 0.92 g/mL, each milliliter of ice has a mass of a little less than 1 g. So 3 mL of ice should have a mass of a little less than 3 g. Since 2.76 is a little less than 3, the answer is reasonable.

MATHEMATICAL PRACTICES

Think and Discuss

1. Explain how the term *cross product* can help you remember how to solve a proportion.

2. Describe the error in these steps: $\frac{2}{3} = \frac{x}{12}$; $2x = 36$; $x = 18$.

3. Show how to use cross products to decide whether the ratios 6:45 and 2:15 are proportional.

Exercises

Learn It Online
Homework Help Online
Exercises 1–15, 29, 31, 33, 35, 37, 39

GUIDED PRACTICE

See Example 1   **Use cross products to solve each proportion.**

1. $\frac{6}{10}\ \frac{36}{x}$

2. $\frac{4}{7}\ \frac{5}{p}$

3. $\frac{12.3}{m}\ \frac{75}{100}$

4. $\frac{t}{42}\ \frac{1.5}{3}$

See Example 2   **5.** A stack of 2,450 one-dollar bills weighs 5 pounds. How much does a stack of 1,470 one-dollar bills weigh?

INDEPENDENT PRACTICE

See Example 1   **Use cross products to solve each proportion.**

6. $\frac{4}{36} = \frac{x}{180}$

7. $\frac{7}{84} = \frac{12}{h}$

8. $\frac{3}{24} = \frac{r}{52}$

9. $\frac{5}{140} = \frac{12}{v}$

10. $\frac{45}{x} = \frac{15}{3}$

11. $\frac{t}{6} = \frac{96}{16}$

12. $\frac{2}{5} = \frac{s}{12}$

13. $\frac{14}{n} = \frac{5}{8}$

See Example 2   **14.** Euro coins come in eight denominations. One denomination is the one-euro coin, which is worth 100 cents. A stack of 10 one-euro coins is 21.25 millimeters tall. How tall would a stack of 45 one-euro coins be? Round your answer to the nearest hundredth of a millimeter.

15. There are 18.5 ounces of soup in a can. This is equivalent to 524 grams. Jenna has 8 ounces of soup. How many grams does she have? Round your answer to the nearest whole gram.

PRACTICE AND PROBLEM SOLVING

Extra Practice
See Extra Practice for more exercises.

Solve each proportion. Then find another equivalent ratio.

16. $\frac{4}{h}\ \frac{12}{24}$

17. $\frac{x}{15}\ \frac{12}{90}$

18. $\frac{39}{4}\ \frac{t}{12}$

19. $\frac{5.5}{6}\ \frac{16.5}{w}$

20. $\frac{1}{3}\ \frac{y}{25.5}$

21. $\frac{18}{x}\ \frac{1}{5}$

22. $\frac{m}{4}\ \frac{175}{20}$

23. $\frac{8.7}{2}\ \frac{q}{4}$

24. $\frac{r}{84}\ \frac{32.5}{182}$

25. $\frac{76}{304}\ \frac{81}{k}$

26. $\frac{9}{500}\ \frac{p}{2,500}$

27. $\frac{5}{j}\ \frac{6}{19.8}$

28. A certain shade of paint is made by mixing 5 parts blue paint with 2 parts white paint. To get the correct shade, how many quarts of white paint should be mixed with 8.5 quarts of blue paint?

29. Measurement If you put an object that has a mass of 40 grams on one side of a balance scale, you would have to put about 18 U.S. dimes on the other side to balance the weight. About how many dimes would balance the weight of a 50-gram object?

30. Sandra drove 126.2 miles in 2 hours at a constant speed. Use a proportion to find how long it would take her to drive 189.3 miles at the same speed.

31. Multi-Step In June, a camp has 325 campers and 26 counselors. In July, 265 campers leave and 215 new campers arrive. How many counselors does the camp need in July to keep an equivalent ratio of campers to counselors?

Arrange each set of numbers to form a proportion.

32. 10, 6, 30, 18

33. 4, 6, 10, 15

34. 12, 21, 7, 4

35. 75, 4, 3, 100

36. 30, 42, 5, 7

37. 5, 90, 108, 6

38. **Life Science** On Monday a marine biologist took a random sample of 50 fish from a pond and tagged them. On Tuesday she took a new sample of 100 fish. Among them were 4 fish that had been tagged on Monday.

a. What comparison does the ratio $\frac{4}{100}$ represent?

b. What ratio represents the number of fish tagged on Monday to n, the total number of fish in the pond?

c. Use a proportion to estimate the number of fish in the pond.

This catfish was 7 feet, 7 inches long and weighed 212 pounds! She was caught and re-released in the River Ebro, near Barcelona, Spain.

39. **Chemistry** The table shows the type and number of atoms in one molecule of citric acid. Use a proportion to find the number of oxygen atoms in 15 molecules of citric acid.

Composition of Citric Acid	
Type of Atom	**Number of Atoms**
Carbon	6
Hydrogen	8
Oxygen	7

40. **Earth Science** You can find your distance from a thunderstorm by counting the number of seconds between a lightning flash and the thunder. For example, if the time difference is 21 s, then the storm is about 7 km away. About how far away is a storm if the time difference is 9 s?

41. **What's the Question?** There are 20 grams of protein in 3 ounces of sautéed fish. If the answer is 9 ounces, what is the question?

42. **Write About It** Give an example from your own life that can be described using a ratio. Then tell how a proportion can give you additional information.

43. **Challenge** Use the Multiplication Property of Equality and the proportion $\frac{a}{b} = \frac{c}{d}$ to show that the cross product rule works for all proportions.

Test Prep

44. **Multiple Choice** Which proportion is correct?

Ⓐ $\frac{4}{8} = \frac{6}{10}$

Ⓑ $\frac{2}{7} = \frac{10}{15}$

Ⓒ $\frac{7}{14} = \frac{15}{30}$

Ⓓ $\frac{16}{25} = \frac{13}{18}$

45. **Gridded Response** Find a ratio to complete the proportion $\frac{2}{3} = \frac{?}{?}$ so that the cross products are equal to 12. Grid your answer in the form of a fraction.

Quiz for Lessons 1 Through 3

 **1** **Rates**

Find each unit rate. Round to the nearest hundredth, if necessary.

1. $140 for 18 ft^2

2. 346 mi on 22 gal

3. 14 lb for $2.99

4. Shaunti drove 621 miles in 11.5 hours. What was her average speed in miles per hour?

5. A grocery store sells a 7 oz bag of raisins for $1.10 and a 9 oz bag of raisins for $1.46. Which size bag has the lower price per ounce?

2 **Identifying and Writing Proportions**

Find a ratio equivalent to each ratio. Then use the ratios to write a proportion.

6. $\frac{10}{16}$

7. $\frac{21}{28}$

8. $\frac{12}{25}$

9. $\frac{40}{48}$

10. Ryan earned $272 for 40 hours of work. Jonathan earned $224 for 32 hours of work. Are these pay rates proportional? Explain.

11. On a given day, the ratio of dollars to euros was approximately 1:0.735. Is the ratio 20 to 14.70 an equivalent ratio? Explain.

3 **Solving Proportions**

Use cross products to solve each proportion.

12. $\frac{n}{8} = \frac{15}{4}$

13. $\frac{20}{t} = \frac{2.5}{6}$

14. $\frac{6}{11} = \frac{0.12}{z}$

15. $\frac{15}{24} = \frac{x}{10}$

16. One human year is said to be about 7 dog years. Cliff's dog is 5.5 years old in human years. Estimate his dog's age in dog years.

Focus on Problem Solving

Make a Plan

• **Choose a problem-solving strategy**

The following are strategies that you might choose to help you solve a problem:

- Make a table
- Find a pattern
- Make an organized list
- Work backward
- Use a Venn diagram

- Draw a diagram
- Guess and test
- Use logical reasoning
- Solve a simpler problem
- Make a model

Tell which strategy from the list above you would use to solve each problem. Explain your choice.

1 A recipe for blueberry muffins calls for 1 cup of milk and 1.5 cups of blueberries. Ashley wants to make more muffins than the recipe yields. In Ashley's muffin batter, there are 4.5 cups of blueberries. If she is using the recipe as a guide, how many cups of milk will she need?

2 There are 32 students in Samantha's math class. Of those students 18 are boys. Write the ratio in simplest form of the number of girls in Samantha's class to the number of boys.

3 Jeremy is the oldest of four brothers. Each of the four boys gets an allowance for doing chores at home each week. The amount of money each boy receives depends on his age. Jeremy is 13 years old, and he gets $12.75. His 11-year-old brother gets $11.25, and his 9-year-old brother gets $9.75. How much money does his 7-year-old brother get?

4 According to an article in a medical journal, a healthful diet should include a ratio of 2.5 servings of meat to 4 servings of vegetables. If you eat 7 servings of meat per week, how many servings of vegetables should you eat?

Similar Figures and Proportions

COMMON CORE

CC.7.RP.2 Recognize and represent proportional relationships between quantities. **Also CC.7.NS.3, CC.7.RP.2c**

Vocabulary

similar

corresponding sides

corresponding angles

Similar figures are figures that have the same shape but not necessarily the same size. The symbol ~ means "is similar to."

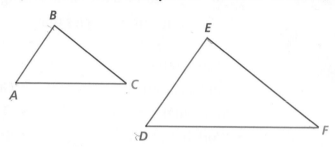

Corresponding angles of two or more similar polygons are in the same relative position. **Corresponding sides** of two or more similar polygons are in the same relative position. When naming similar figures, list the corresponding angles in the same order. For the triangles above, $\triangle ABC \sim \triangle DEF$.

SIMILAR FIGURES

Two figures are similar if

- the measures of their corresponding angles are equal.

- the ratios of the lengths of their corresponding sides are proportional.

E X A M P L E **1** **Determining Whether Two Triangles Are Similar**

Reading Math

A side of a figure can be named by its endpoints with a bar above, such as $\overline{AB}$. Without the bar, the letters indicate the *length* of the side.

Tell whether the triangles are similar.

The corresponding angles of the figures have equal measures.

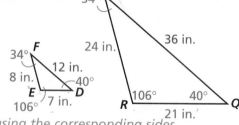

$\overline{DE}$ corresponds to $\overline{QR}$.
$\overline{EF}$ corresponds to $\overline{RS}$.
$\overline{DF}$ corresponds to $\overline{QS}$.

$\dfrac{DE}{QR} \stackrel{?}{=} \dfrac{EF}{RS} \stackrel{?}{=} \dfrac{DF}{QS}$ *Write ratios using the corresponding sides.*

$\dfrac{7}{21} \stackrel{?}{=} \dfrac{8}{24} \stackrel{?}{=} \dfrac{12}{36}$ *Substitute the lengths of the sides.*

$\dfrac{1}{3} = \dfrac{1}{3} = \dfrac{1}{3}$ *Simplify each ratio.*

Since the measures of the corresponding angles are equal and the ratios of the corresponding sides are equivalent, the triangles are similar.

Video **Lesson Tutorials Online** my.hrw.com

With triangles, if the corresponding side lengths are all proportional, then the corresponding angles *must* have equal measures. With figures that have four or more sides, if the corresponding side lengths are all proportional, then the corresponding angles *may or may not* have equal angle measures.

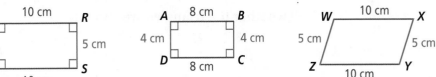

ABCD and QRST
are similar.

ABCD and WXYZ
are not similar.

EXAMPLE 2

Determining Whether Two Four-Sided Figures Are Similar

Tell whether the figures are similar.

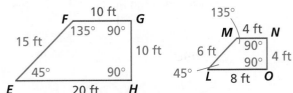

The corresponding angles of the figures have equal measures. Write each set of corresponding sides as a ratio.

$\dfrac{EF}{LM}$ $\overline{EF}$ corresponds to $\overline{LM}$. $\dfrac{FG}{MN}$ $\overline{FG}$ corresponds to $\overline{MN}$.

$\dfrac{GH}{NO}$ $\overline{GH}$ corresponds to $\overline{NO}$. $\dfrac{EH}{LO}$ $\overline{EH}$ corresponds to $\overline{LO}$.

Determine whether the ratios of the lengths of the corresponding sides are proportional.

$\dfrac{EF}{LM} \stackrel{?}{=} \dfrac{FG}{MN} \stackrel{?}{=} \dfrac{GH}{NO} \stackrel{?}{=} \dfrac{EH}{LO}$ Write ratios using the corresponding sides.

$\dfrac{15}{6} \stackrel{?}{=} \dfrac{10}{4} \stackrel{?}{=} \dfrac{10}{4} \stackrel{?}{=} \dfrac{20}{8}$ Substitute the lengths of the sides.

$\dfrac{5}{2} = \dfrac{5}{2} = \dfrac{5}{2} = \dfrac{5}{2}$ Write the ratios in simplest form.

Since the measures of the corresponding angles are equal and the ratios of the corresponding sides are equivalent, *EFGH* ~ *LMNO*.

MATHEMATICAL PRACTICES

Think and Discuss

1. Identify the corresponding angles of △*JKL* and △*UTS*.

2. Explain whether all rectangles are similar. Give specific examples to justify your answer.

Exercises

Learn It Online
Homework Help Online
Exercises 1–8, 11, 23

GUIDED PRACTICE

See Example **1** Tell whether the triangles are similar.

1.
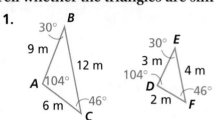

2.
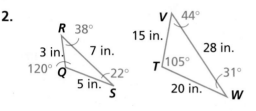

See Example **2** Tell whether the figures are similar.

3.
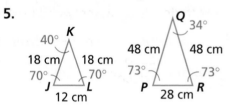

4.
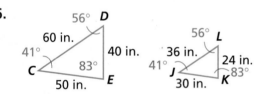

INDEPENDENT PRACTICE

See Example **1** Tell whether the triangles are similar.

5.
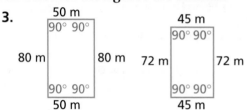

6.
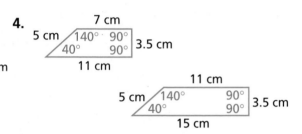

See Example **2** Tell whether the figures are similar.

7.
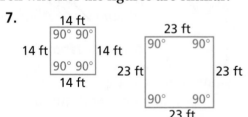

8.
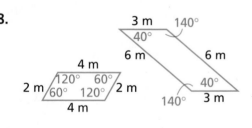

PRACTICE AND PROBLEM SOLVING

Extra Practice

See Extra Practice for more exercises.

9. Tell whether the parallelogram and trapezoid could be similar. Explain your answer.

10. Kia wants similar prints in small and large sizes of a favorite photo. The photo lab sells prints in these sizes: 3 in. × 5 in., 4 in. × 6 in., 8 in. × 18 in., 9 in. × 20 in., and 16 in. × 24 in. Which could she order to get similar prints?

Tell whether the triangles are similar.

11.

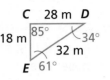

12.

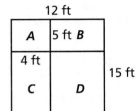

The figure shows a 12 ft by 15 ft rectangle divided into four rectangular parts. Explain whether the rectangles in each pair are similar.

13. rectangle *A* and the original rectangle

14. rectangle *C* and rectangle *B*

15. the original rectangle and rectangle *D*

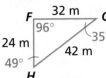

Critical Thinking For Exercises 16–19, justify your answers using words or drawings.

16. Are all squares similar?

17. Are all parallelograms similar?

18. Are all rectangles similar?

19. Are all right triangles similar?

20. Choose a Strategy What number gives the same result when multiplied by 6 as it does when 6 is added to it?

21. Write About It Tell how to decide whether two figures are similar.

22. Challenge Two triangles are similar. The ratio of the lengths of the corresponding sides is $\frac{5}{4}$. The length of one side of the larger triangle is 40 feet. What is the length of the corresponding side of the smaller triangle?

Test Prep

23. Multiple Choice Luis wants to make a deck that is similar to one that is 10 feet long and 8 feet wide. Luis's deck must be 18 feet long. What must its width be?

(A) 20 feet   (B) 16 feet   (C) 14.4 feet   (D) 22.5 feet

24. Short Response A real dollar bill measures 2.61 inches by 6.14 inches. A play dollar bill measures 3.61 inches by 7.14 inches. Is the play money similar to the real money? Explain your answer.

Using Similar Figures

COMMON CORE

CC.7.G.1 Solve problems involving scale drawings of geometric figures, including computing actual lengths and areas from a scale drawing... *Also CC.7.RP.2c, CC.7.EE.2*

Vocabulary

indirect
measurement

Native Americans of the Northwest carved totem poles out of tree trunks. These poles could stand up to 80 feet tall. Totem poles include carvings of animal figures, such as bears and eagles, which symbolize traits of the family or clan who built them.

Measuring the heights of tall objects, like some totem poles, cannot be done by using a ruler or yardstick. Instead, you can use *indirect measurement*.

<u>Interactivities Online</u> ▶ **Indirect measurement** is a method of using proportions to find an unknown length or distance in similar figures.

EXAMPLE **1** **Finding Unknown Measures in Similar Figures**

$\triangle ABC \sim \triangle JKL$. **Find the unknown measures.**

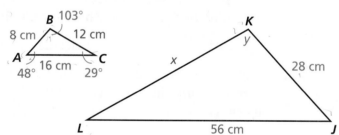

Step 1 Find x.

$\dfrac{AB}{JK} = \dfrac{BC}{KL}$	*Write a proportion using corresponding sides.*
$\dfrac{8}{28} = \dfrac{12}{x}$	*Substitute the lengths of the sides.*
$8 \cdot x = 28 \cdot 12$	*Find the cross products.*
$8x = 336$	*Multiply.*
$\dfrac{8x}{8} = \dfrac{336}{8}$	*Divide each side by 8.*
$x = 42$	

KL is 42 centimeters.

Step 2 Find y.

$\angle K$ corresponds to $\angle B$.   *Corresponding angles of similar triangles have equal angle measures.*

$y = 103°$

EXAMPLE 2 *Measurement Application*

A volleyball court is a rectangle that is similar in shape to an Olympic-sized pool. Find the width of the pool.

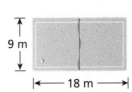

9 m

|← 18 m →|

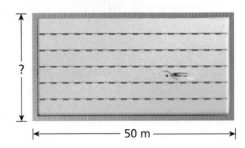

?

|← 50 m →|

Let w = the width of the pool.

$\frac{18}{50} = \frac{9}{w}$ *Write a proportion using corresponding side lengths.*

$18 \cdot w = 50 \cdot 9$ *Find the cross products.*

$18w = 450$ *Multiply.*

$\frac{18w}{18} = \frac{450}{18}$ *Divide each side by 18.*

$w = 25$

The pool is 25 meters wide.

EXAMPLE 3 **Estimating with Indirect Measurement**

Estimate the height of the totem pole shown at right.

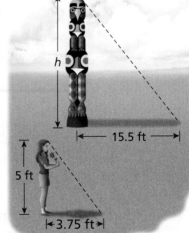

$\frac{h}{5} = \frac{15.5}{3.75}$ *Write a proportion.*

$\frac{h}{5} \approx \frac{16}{4}$ *Use compatible numbers to estimate.*

$\frac{h}{5} \approx 4$ *Simplify.*

$5 \cdot \frac{h}{5} \approx 5 \cdot 4$ *Multiply each side by 5.*

$h \approx 20$

The totem pole is about 20 feet tall.

h

|← 15.5 ft →|

5 ft

|←3.75 ft→|

MATHEMATICAL PRACTICES

Think and Discuss

1. Write another proportion that could be used to find the value of x in Example 1.

2. Name two objects that it would make sense to measure using indirect measurement.

Exercises

Learn It Online
Homework Help Online
Exercises 1–8, 9, 15

GUIDED PRACTICE

See Example **1** △XYZ ~ △PQR in each pair. Find the unknown measures.

1.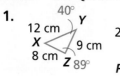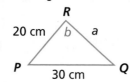

2.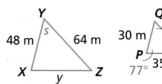

See Example **2** **3.** The rectangular gardens at right are similar in shape. How wide is the smaller garden?

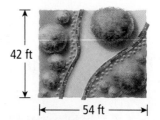 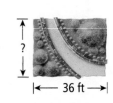

See Example **3** **4.** A water tower casts a shadow that is 21 ft long. A tree casts a shadow that is 8 ft long. Estimate the height of the water tower.

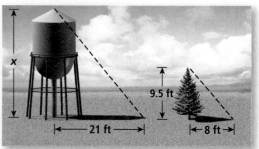

INDEPENDENT PRACTICE

See Example **1** △ABC ~ △DEF in each pair. Find the unknown measures.

5.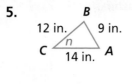

6.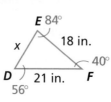

See Example **2** **7.** The movie still and its projected image at right are similar. What is the height of the projected image to the nearest hundredth of an inch?

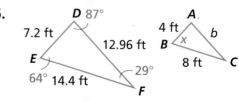

See Example **3** **8.** A cactus casts a shadow that is 14 ft 7 in. long. A gate nearby casts a shadow that is 5 ft long. Estimate the height of the cactus.

 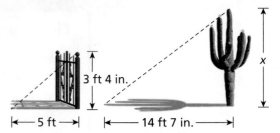

Extra Practice

See Extra Practice for more exercises.

9. A building with a height of 14 m casts a shadow that is 16 m long while a taller building casts a 24 m long shadow. What is the height of the taller building?

10. Two common envelope sizes are $3\frac{1}{2}$ in. $\times$ $6\frac{1}{2}$ in. and 4 in. $\times$ $9\frac{1}{2}$ in. Are these envelopes similar? Explain.

11. **Art** An art class has painted a mural composed of brightly colored geometric shapes. All of the right triangles in the design are similar to the red right triangle. Find the heights of the three other right triangles in the mural. Round your answers to the nearest tenth.

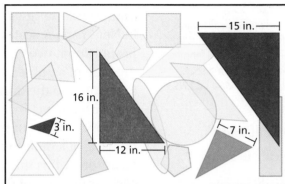

12. **Write a Problem** Write a problem that can be solved using indirect measurement.

13. **Write About It** Assume you know the side lengths of one triangle and the length of one side of a second similar triangle. Explain how to use the properties of similar figures to find the unknown lengths in the second triangle.

14. **Challenge** $\triangle ABE \sim \triangle ACD$. What is the value of y in the diagram?

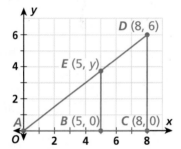

Test Prep

15. **Multiple Choice** Find the unknown length in the similar figures.

   (A) 10 cm   (C) 15 cm

   (B) 12 cm   (D) 18 cm

16. **Gridded Response** A building casts a 16-foot shadow. A 6-foot man standing next to the building casts a 2.5-foot shadow. What is the height, in feet, of the building?

Scale Drawings and Scale Models

COMMON CORE

CC.7.G.1 Solve problems involving scale drawings of geometric figures, including computing actual lengths and areas from a scale drawing… *Also CC.7.NS.3*

Vocabulary

scale drawing

scale factor

scale model

scale

Interactivities Online ▶

The drawing at right shows a *scale drawing* of the Guggenheim Museum in New York. A **scale drawing** is a proportional two-dimensional drawing of an object. Its dimensions are related to the dimensions of the actual object by a ratio called the **scale factor**. For example, if a drawing of a building has a scale factor of $\frac{1}{87}$, this means that each dimension of the drawing is $\frac{1}{87}$ of the corresponding dimension of the actual building.

A **scale model** is a proportional three-dimensional model of an object. A **scale** is the ratio between two sets of measurements. Scales can use the same units or different units. Both scale drawings and scale models can be smaller or larger than the objects they represent.

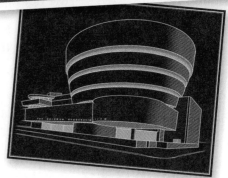

EXAMPLE 1 **Finding a Scale Factor**

Identify the scale factor.

	Race Car	Model
Length (in.)	132	11
Height (in.)	66	5.5

Caution!

A scale factor is always the ratio of the model's dimensions to the actual object's dimensions.

You can use the lengths *or* heights to find the scale factor.

$\dfrac{\text{model length}}{\text{race car length}} = \dfrac{11}{132} = \dfrac{1}{12}$ *Write a ratio. Then simplify.*

$\dfrac{\text{model height}}{\text{race car height}} = \dfrac{5.5}{66} = \dfrac{1}{12}$

The scale factor is $\frac{1}{12}$. This is reasonable because $\frac{1}{10}$ the length of the race car is 13.2 in. The length of the model is 11 in., which is less than 13.2 in., and $\frac{1}{12}$ is less than $\frac{1}{10}$.

Video **Lesson Tutorials Online** my.hrw.com

EXAMPLE 2 Using Scale Factors to Find Unknown Lengths

A photograph of Rene Magritte's painting *The Schoolmaster* has dimensions 5.4 cm and 4 cm. The scale factor is $\frac{1}{15}$. Find the size of the actual painting.

Think: $\dfrac{\text{photo}}{\text{painting}} = \dfrac{1}{15}$

$\dfrac{5.4}{\ell} = \dfrac{1}{15}$ *Write a proportion to find the length ℓ.*

$\ell = 5.4 \cdot 15$ *Find the cross products.*

$\ell = 81$ cm   *Multiply.*

$\dfrac{4}{w} = \dfrac{1}{15}$ *Write a proportion to find the width w.*

$w = 4 \cdot 15$ *Find the cross products.*

$w = 60$ cm   *Multiply.*

The painting is 81 cm long and 60 cm wide.

EXAMPLE 3 *Measurement Application*

On a map of Florida, the distance between Hialeah and Tampa is 10.5 cm. The map scale is 3 cm:128 km. What is the actual distance *d* between these two cities?

Think: $\dfrac{\text{map distance}}{\text{actual distance}} = \dfrac{3}{128}$

$\dfrac{3}{128} = \dfrac{10.5}{d}$ *Write a proportion.*

$3 \cdot d = 128 \cdot 10.5$ *Find the cross products.*

$3d = 1,344$

$\dfrac{3d}{3} = \dfrac{1,344}{3}$ *Divide both sides by 3.*

$d = 448$ km

The distance between the cities is 448 km.

MATHEMATICAL PRACTICES

Think and Discuss

1. **Explain** how you can tell whether a model with a scale factor of $\frac{5}{3}$ is larger or smaller than the original object.

2. **Describe** how to find the scale factor if an antenna is 60 feet long and a scale drawing shows the length as 1 foot long.

GUIDED PRACTICE

See Example ① Identify the scale factor.

1.

	Grizzly Bear	Model
Height (in.)	84	6

2.

	Moray Eel	Model
Length (ft)	5	$1\frac{1}{2}$

See Example ② **3.** In a photograph, a sculpture is 4.2 cm tall and 2.5 cm wide. The scale factor is $\frac{1}{16}$. Find the size of the actual sculpture.

See Example ③ **4.** Ms. Jackson is driving from South Bend to Indianapolis. She measures a distance of 4.3 cm between the cities on her Indiana road map. The map scale is 1 cm:48 km. What is the actual distance between these two cities?

INDEPENDENT PRACTICE

See Example ① Identify the scale factor.

5.

	Eagle	Model
Wingspan (in.)	90	6

6.

	Dolphin	Model
Length (cm)	260	13

See Example ② **7.** On a scale drawing, a tree is $6\frac{3}{4}$ inches tall. The scale factor is $\frac{1}{20}$. Find the height of the actual tree.

See Example ③ **8.** **Measurement** On a road map of Virginia, the distance from Alexandria to Roanoke is 7.6 cm. The map scale is 2 cm:80 km. What is the actual distance between these two cities?

PRACTICE AND PROBLEM SOLVING

Extra Practice
See Extra Practice for more exercises.

The scale factor of each model is 1:12. Find the missing dimensions.

	Item	Actual Dimensions	Model Dimensions
9.	Lamp	Height: ■	Height: $1\frac{1}{3}$ in.
10.	Couch	Height: 32 in. Length: 69 in.	Height: ■ Length: ■
11.	Table	Height: ■ Width: ■ Length: ■	Height: 6.25 cm Width: 11.75 cm Length: 20 cm

12. An artist transferred a rectangular design 13 cm long and 6 cm wide to a similar canvas 260 cm long and 120 cm wide. What is the scale factor?

13. **Critical Thinking** A countertop is 18 ft long. How long is it on a scale drawing with the scale 1 in:3 yd?

 14. **Write About It** A scale for a scale drawing is 10 cm:1 mm. Which will be larger, the actual object or the scale drawing? Explain.

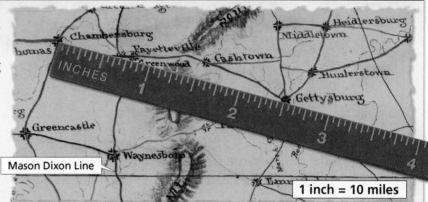

Mason Dixon Line

1 inch = 10 miles

Use the map for Exercises 15–16.

15. In 1863, Confederate troops marched from Chambersburg to Gettysburg in search of badly needed shoes. Use the ruler and the scale of the map to estimate how far the Confederate soldiers, many of whom were barefoot, marched.

16. Before the Civil War, the Mason-Dixon Line was considered the dividing line between the North and the South. Gettysburg is about 8.1 miles north of the Mason-Dixon Line. How far apart in inches are Gettysburg and the Mason-Dixon Line on the map?

17. Multi-Step Toby is making a scale model of the battlefield at Fredericksburg. The area he wants to model measures about 11 mi by 7.5 mi. He plans to put the model on a 3.25 ft by 3.25 ft square table. On each side of the model he wants to leave at least 3 in. between the model and the table edges. What is the largest scale he can use?

18. ⭐ **Challenge** A map of Vicksburg, Mississippi, has a scale of "1 mile to the inch." The map has been reduced so that 5 inches on the original map appears as 1.5 inches on the reduced map. The distance between two points on the reduced map is 1.75 inches. What is the actual distance in miles?

President Abraham Lincoln, Major Allan Pinkerton, and General John A. McCleland, October 1862.

Test Prep

19. Multiple Choice On a scale model with a scale of $\frac{1}{16}$, the height of a shed is 7 inches. What is the approximate height of the actual shed?

  Ⓐ 2 feet   Ⓑ 9 feet   Ⓒ 58 feet   Ⓓ 112 feet

20. Gridded Response On a map, the scale is 3 centimeters:120 kilometers. The distance between two cities on the map is 6.8 centimeters. What is the distance between the actual cities in kilometers?

Hands-on LAB

Make Scale Drawings and Models

Use with Scale Drawings and Scale Models

Scale drawings and scale models are used in mapmaking, construction, and other trades. You can create scale drawings and models using graph paper. If you measure carefully and convert your measurements correctly, your scale drawings and models will be similar to the actual objects they represent.

Use appropriate tools strategically.
CC.7.G.1 Solve problems involving scale drawings of geometric figures, including computing actual lengths and areas from a scale drawing and reproducing a scale drawing at a different scale.

Activity 1

Make a scale drawing of a classroom and items with the following dimensions.

Classroom	6 Student Desks	Teacher's Desk	Aquarium
12 ft × 20 ft	2 ft × 3 ft	2 ft × 6 ft	5 ft × 2 ft

1 You can use graph paper for your drawing. When making a scale drawing, you can use any scale you wish. For this activity, use a scale in which 2 squares represent 1 foot. To convert each measurement, multiply the number of feet by 2.

2 This means that the room measures 24 squares (2 · 12 ft) by 40 squares (2 · 20 ft). Convert the other measurements in the table using the same scale.

Classroom	6 Student Desks	Teacher's Desk	Aquarium
24 sq × 40 sq	4 sq × 6 sq	4 sq × 12 sq	10 sq × 4 sq

3 Now sketch the room and items on graph paper. Place the items anywhere in the room you wish.

Think and Discuss

1. Write ratios to compare the widths and lengths of the actual classroom and the drawing. Can you make a proportion with your ratios? Explain.

2. Describe how your drawing would change if you used a scale in which 1 square represents 2 feet.

Try This

1. Measure the dimensions of your classroom as well as some items in the room. Then make a scale drawing. Explain the scale you used.

Activity 2

Make a scale model of a school gym whose floor is 20 meters × 32 meters and whose walls are 12 meters tall.

1 You can use graph paper for your model. For this activity, use a scale in which 1 square represents 2 meters. To convert each measurement, divide the number of meters by 2.

2 The two longer sides of the gym floor are 16 squares (32 m ÷ 2). The other two sides are 10 squares (20 m ÷ 2). The walls are 6 squares (12 m ÷ 2) tall.

	Floor Length	Floor Width	Wall Height
Actual	20 m	32 m	12 m
Model	10 squares	16 squares	6 squares

3 Sketch the walls on graph paper as shown. Then cut them out and tape them together to make an open rectangular box to represent the gym.

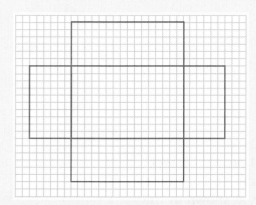

Think and Discuss

1. A different gym has a floor that is 120 feet × 75 feet and a height of 45 feet. A model of the gym has a height of 9 squares. What are the dimensions of the model's floor? What scale was used to create this model?

Try This

1. Make a scale model of the building shown. Explain the scale you used to create your model.

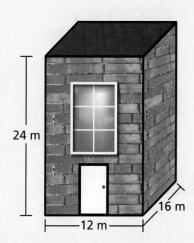

24 m

12 m

16 m

Hands-on LAB

Use Scale Drawings

Learn It Online
Lab Resources Online

Use appropriate tools strategically.

CC.7.G.1 Solve problems involving scale drawings of geometric figures, including computing actual lengths and areas from a scale drawing and reproducing a scale drawing at a different scale.

You have found lengths of actual objects when given a scale, and you have also made scale drawings to represent actual objects. In Activity 1, you will combine these skills to find lengths of actual objects given a scale drawing.

Activity 1

The design for a small café is shown in the scale drawing. Use the scale drawing to find lengths and the perimeter of the actual café.

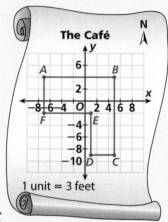

❶ Find the actual length in feet of the east side of the café, represented by $\overline{BC}$.

❷ Find the perimeter of the actual café.

❸ Find the actual area in square feet of the floor of the café.

Hint: Recall that to find the area of composite figures, you need to first find the areas of the separate figures that compose the larger figure. Then add the separate areas to get the composite area. There are two ways you can separate the composite figure, as shown by the dashed red line in the drawings below.

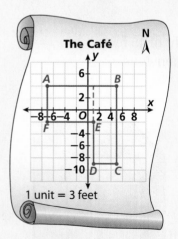

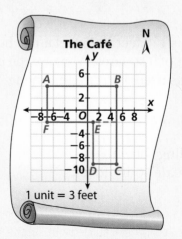

Think and Discuss

1. Discuss how to use a scale drawing to find the actual length of an object.

2. Explain how to use the scale factor to find the actual area of an object.

The design for a letter T to be placed on a company sign is shown in the scale drawing. Use the scale drawing to find lengths and the perimeter of the actual letter.

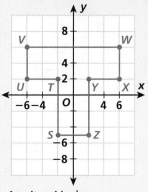

1 unit = 4 inches

1. Find the actual length in inches of the top of the letter T.

2. Find the perimeter for the actual letter T.

3. Find the actual area in square inches for the letter T.

Activity 2

Refer to the scale drawing of the café from Activity 1 at right. Complete the steps to create a new scale drawing with a scale 1 unit = 2 feet.

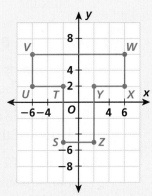

The Café

1 unit = 3 feet

① Find the actual length in feet of each side of the café.

AB =	DE =
BC = 39 ft	EF =
CD =	FA =

② Find the length that each side will be in the new scale drawing with a scale of 1 unit = 2 feet.

AB =	DE =
$BC = 39 \text{ ft} \cdot \frac{1 \text{ unit}}{2 \text{ ft}} = 19\frac{1}{2}$ units	EF =
CD =	FA =

③ Redraw the scale drawing of the café with a new scale of 1 unit = 2 feet.

Think and Discuss

1. Discuss how to redraw a scale drawing with a new scale and the different methods that could possibly be used.

Try This

1. The design for a letter T from Activity 1 Try This is shown. Redraw the scale drawing of the letter T with a new scale of 1 unit = 8 inches.

1 unit = 4 inches

Ready to Go On?

Quiz for Lessons 4 Through 6

4 | Similar Figures and Proportions

1. Tell whether the triangles are similar.

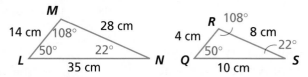

2. Tell whether the figures are similar.

5 | Using Similar Figures

$\triangle ABC \sim \triangle XYZ$ in each pair. Find the unknown measures.

3.

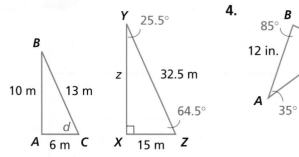

4.

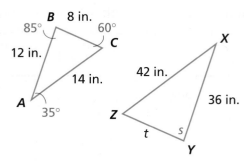

5. Reynaldo drew a rectangular design that was 6 in. wide and 8 in. long. He used a copy machine to enlarge the rectangular design so that the width was 10 in. What was the length of the enlarged design?

6. Redon is 6 ft 2 in. tall, and his shadow is 4 ft 1 in. long. At the same time, a building casts a shadow that is 19 ft 10 in. long. Estimate the height of the building.

6 | Scale Drawings and Scale Models

7. An actor is 6 ft tall. On a billboard for a new movie, the actor's picture is enlarged so that his height is 16.8 ft. What is the scale factor?

8. On a scale drawing, a driveway is 6 in. long. The scale factor is $\frac{1}{24}$. Find the length of the actual driveway.

9. A map of Texas has a scale of 1 in:65 mi. The distance from Dallas to San Antonio is 260 mi. What is the distance in inches between these two cities on the map?

Paul Bunyan Statues According to legend, Paul Bunyan was a giant lumberjack whose footsteps created Minnesota's ten thousand lakes. Statues honoring this mythical figure can be found throughout the state. One of the largest, in Brainerd, stands 26 feet tall and can greet you by name!

MINNESOTA

1. A tourist who is 1.8 m tall stands next to the statue of Paul Bunyan in Bemidji, MN. He measures the length of his shadow and the shadow cast by the statue. The measurements are shown in the figure. What is the height of the statue?

2. Show how to use dimensional analysis to convert the height of the statue to feet. Round to the nearest foot. (*Hint*: 1 m = 3.28 ft)

3. The Bemidji statue includes Paul Bunyan's companion, Babe, the Blue Ox. The statue's horns are 14 feet across. The statue was made using the dimensions of an actual ox and a scale of 3:1. What was the length of the horns of the actual ox?

4. The kneeling Paul Bunyan statue in Akeley, MN, is 25 feet tall. The ratio of the statue's height to its width is 17:11. What is the width of the statue to the nearest tenth of a foot?

5. A souvenir of the Akeley statue is made using the scale 2 in:5 ft. What is the height of the souvenir?

h

1.8 m

1.35 m   0.45 m

Game Time

Water Works

You have three glasses: a 3-ounce glass, a 5-ounce glass, and an 8-ounce glass. The 8-ounce glass is full of water, and the other two glasses are empty. By pouring water from one glass to another, how can you get exactly 6 ounces of water in one of the glasses? The step-by-step solution is described below.

1 Pour the water from the 8 oz glass into the 5 oz glass.

2 Pour the water from the 5 oz glass into the 3 oz glass.

3 Pour the water from the 3 oz glass into the 8 oz glass.

You now have 6 ounces of water in the 8-ounce glass.

Start again, but this time try to get exactly 4 ounces of water in one glass. (*Hint:* Find a way to get 1 ounce of water. Start by pouring water into the 3-ounce glass.)

Next, using 3-ounce, 8-ounce, and 11-ounce glasses, try to get exactly 9 ounces of water in one glass. Start with the 11-ounce glass full of water. (*Hint:* Start by pouring water into the 8-ounce glass.)

Look at the sizes of the glasses in each problem. The volume of the third glass is the sum of the volumes of the first two glasses: $3 + 5 = 8$ and $3 + 8 = 11$. Using any amounts for the two smaller glasses, and starting with the largest glass full, you can get any multiple of the smaller glass's volume. Try it and see.

Concentration

Each card in a deck of cards has a ratio on one side. Place each card face down. Each player or team takes a turn flipping over two cards. If the ratios on the cards are equivalent, the player or team can keep the pair. If not, the next player or team flips two cards. After every card has been turned over, the player or team with the most pairs wins.

Learn It Online
Game Time Extra

A complete copy of the rules and the game pieces are available online.

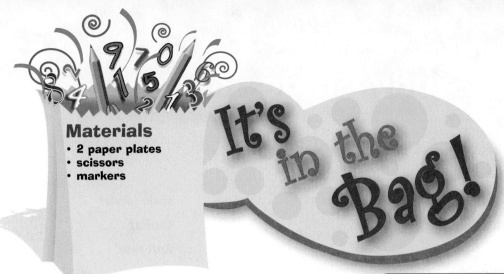

Materials
- 2 paper plates
- scissors
- markers

It's in the Bag!

PROJECT **Paper Plate Proportions**

Serve up some proportions on this book made from paper plates.

① Fold one of the paper plates in half. Cut out a narrow rectangle along the folded edge. The rectangle should be as long as the diameter of plate's inner circle. When you open the plate, you will have a narrow window in the center. **Figure A**

② Fold the second paper plate in half and then unfold it. Cut slits on both sides of the crease beginning from the edge of the plate to the inner circle. **Figure B**

③ Roll up the plate with the slits so that the two slits touch each other. Then slide this plate into the narrow window in the other plate. **Figure C**

④ When the rolled-up plate is halfway through the window, unroll it so that the slits fit on the sides of the window. **Figure D**

⑤ Close the book so that all the plates are folded in half.

Taking Note of the Math

Write the number and name of the chapter on the cover of the book. Then review the chapter, using the inside pages to take notes on ratios, rates, proportions, and similar figures.

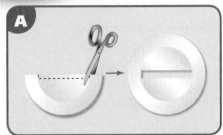

A

B

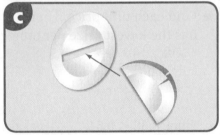

C

D

Study Guide: Review

Vocabulary

corresponding angles   proportion   scale model

corresponding sides   rate   similar

cross product   scale   unit rate

equivalent ratios   scale drawing

indirect measurement   scale factor

Complete the sentences below with vocabulary words from the list above.

1. ___?___ figures have the same shape but not necessarily the same size.

2. A(n) ___?___ is a ratio that compares two quantities measured in different units.

3. The ratio used to enlarge or reduce similar figures is a(n) ___?___.

EXAMPLES

EXERCISES

1   Rates

■ **Find each unit price. Then decide which has the lowest price per ounce.**

$\dfrac{\$2.70}{5 \text{ oz}}$ or $\dfrac{\$4.32}{12 \text{ oz}}$

$\dfrac{\$2.70}{5 \text{ oz}} = \dfrac{\$0.54}{\text{oz}}$ and $\dfrac{\$4.32}{12 \text{ oz}} = \dfrac{\$0.36}{\text{oz}}$

Since $0.36 < 0.54$, $\dfrac{\$4.32}{12 \text{ oz}}$ has the lowest price per ounce.

Find each unit rate.

4. 540 ft in 90 s   5. 436 mi in 4 hr

Find each unit price. Then decide which is the better buy.

6. $\dfrac{\$56}{25 \text{ gal}}$ or $\dfrac{\$32.05}{15 \text{ gal}}$ 7. $\dfrac{\$160}{5 \text{ g}}$ or $\dfrac{\$315}{9 \text{ g}}$

8. Beatríz earned $197.50 for 25 hours of work. How much money did she earn per hour?

Study Guide: Review

2 Identifying and Writing Proportions

■ Determine if $\frac{5}{12}$ and $\frac{3}{9}$ are proportional.

$\frac{5}{12}$ $\frac{5}{12}$ *is already in simplest form.*

$\frac{3}{9} = \frac{1}{3}$ *Simplify* $\frac{3}{9}$.

$\frac{5}{12} \neq \frac{1}{3}$ *The ratios are not proportional.*

Determine if the ratios are proportional.

9. $\frac{9}{27}, \frac{6}{20}$ **10.** $\frac{15}{25}, \frac{20}{30}$ **11.** $\frac{21}{14}, \frac{18}{12}$

Find a ratio equivalent to the given ratio. Then use the ratios to write a proportion.

12. $\frac{10}{12}$ **13.** $\frac{45}{50}$ **14.** $\frac{9}{15}$

3 Solving Proportions

■ Use cross products to solve $\frac{p}{8} = \frac{10}{21}$.

$\frac{p}{8} = \frac{10}{12}$

$p \cdot 12 = 8 \cdot 10$ *Multiply the cross*
$12p = 80$ *products.*

$\frac{12p}{12} = \frac{80}{12}$ *Divide each side by 12.*

$p = \frac{20}{3}$, or $6\frac{2}{3}$

Use cross products to solve each proportion.

15. $\frac{4}{6} = \frac{n}{3}$ **16.** $\frac{2}{a} = \frac{5}{15}$

17. $\frac{b}{1.5} = \frac{8}{3}$ **18.** $\frac{16}{11} = \frac{96}{x}$

19. $\frac{2}{y} = \frac{1}{5}$ **20.** $\frac{7}{2} = \frac{70}{w}$

4 Similar Figures and Proportions

■ Tell whether the figures are similar.

The corresponding angles of the figures have equal measures.

$\frac{5}{30} \stackrel{?}{=} \frac{3}{18} \stackrel{?}{=} \frac{5}{30} \stackrel{?}{=} \frac{3}{18}$

$\frac{1}{6} = \frac{1}{6} = \frac{1}{6} = \frac{1}{6}$

The ratios of the corresponding sides are equivalent. The figures are similar.

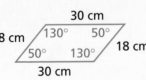

Tell whether the figures are similar.

21.

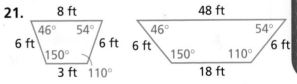

22.

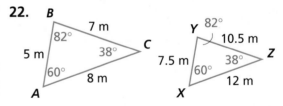

5 **Using Similar Figures**

■ △ABC ~ △LMN. Find the unknown measures.

$$\frac{AB}{LM} = \frac{AC}{LN}$$

$$\frac{8}{t} = \frac{11}{44}$$

$$8 \cdot 44 = t \cdot 11$$

$$352 = 11t$$

$$\frac{352}{11} = \frac{11t}{11}$$

$$32 \text{ in.} = t$$

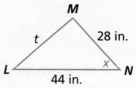

∠N corresponds to ∠C.

$$x = 46°$$

△JKL ~ △DEF. Find the unknown measures.

23.

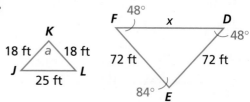

24. A rectangular photo frame is 24 cm long and 9 cm wide. A frame that is similar in shape is 3 cm wide. Find the length of the frame.

25. A tree casts a $30\frac{1}{2}$ ft shadow at the time of day when a 2 ft stake casts a $7\frac{2}{3}$ ft shadow. Estimate the height of the tree.

6 **Scale Drawings and Scale Models**

■ A model boat is 4 inches long. The scale factor is $\frac{1}{24}$. How long is the actual boat?

$$\frac{\text{model}}{\text{boat}} = \frac{1}{24}$$

$$\frac{4}{n} = \frac{1}{24} \qquad \textit{Write a proportion.}$$

$$4 \cdot 24 = n \cdot 1 \qquad \textit{Find the cross products.}$$

$$96 = n \qquad \textit{Solve.}$$

The boat is 96 inches long.

26. The Wright brothers' *Flyer* had a 48inch wingspan. Carla bought a model of the plane with a scale factor of $\frac{1}{40}$. What is the model's wingspan?

27. The distance from Austin to Houston on a map is 4.3 inches. The map scale is 1 inch:38 miles. What is the actual distance?

Study Guide: Review

Chapter Test

1. Lenny sold 576 tacos in 48 hours. What was Lenny's average rate of taco sales?

2. A store sells a 5 lb box of detergent for $5.25 and a 10 lb box of detergent for $9.75. Which size box has the lowest price per pound?

Determine whether the ratios are proportional.

3. $\frac{5}{6}$, $\frac{12}{15}$

4. $\frac{4}{10}$, $\frac{6}{15}$

5. $\frac{110}{175}$, $\frac{22}{35}$

6. $\frac{18}{22}$, $\frac{52}{66}$

Find a ratio equivalent to each ratio. Then use the ratios to write a proportion.

7. $\frac{22}{30}$

8. $\frac{7}{9}$

9. $\frac{18}{54}$

10. $\frac{10}{17}$

Use cross products to solve each proportion.

11. $\frac{9}{12} = \frac{m}{6}$

12. $\frac{x}{2} = \frac{18}{6}$

13. $\frac{3}{7} = \frac{21}{t}$

14. $\frac{5}{p} = \frac{10}{2}$

15. A certain salsa is made with 6 parts tomato and 2 parts bell pepper. To correctly make the recipe, how many cups of tomato should be combined with 1.5 cups of bell pepper?

Tell whether the figures are similar.

16.

99° C
9 ft ___ 5 ft
B ___ A   17 ft   F   102°   11 ft
27° 11 ft 54°
E   29°   49°   D
22 ft

17.

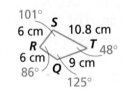

18.

37° W
6 in.   M   10 in.
27°   5 in.
3 in.
Y   4 in.   Z   O   a   n   N
116°

△WYZ ~ △MNO in each pair. Find the unknown measures.

19.

Y
c   33 m
24 m
W   x   Z

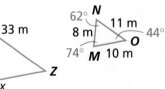

20. A scale model of a building is 8 in. by 12 in. The scale is 1 in:15 ft. What are the dimensions of the actual building?

21. The distance from Portland to Seaside is 75 mi. What is the distance in inches between the two towns on a map whose scale is $1\frac{1}{4}$ in:25 mi?

Cumulative Assessment

Multiple Choice

1. What is the unknown length *b* in similar triangles *ABC* and *DEF*?

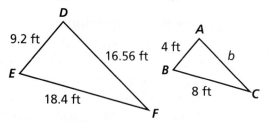

D
9.2 ft
16.56 ft
E
18.4 ft
F
A
4 ft
B
b
8 ft
C

Ⓐ 7.2 feet   Ⓒ 4 feet

Ⓑ 6 feet   Ⓓ 5.6 feet

2. The total length of the Golden Gate Bridge in San Francisco, California, is 8,981 feet. A car is traveling at a speed of 45 miles per hour. How many minutes will it take the car to cross the bridge?

Ⓕ 0.04 minute   Ⓗ 1.7 minutes

Ⓖ 1.28 minutes   Ⓙ 2.27 minutes

3. For which equation is $x = \frac{2}{5}$ the solution?

Ⓐ $5x - \frac{25}{2} = 0$

Ⓑ $-\frac{1}{5}x + \frac{2}{25} = 0$

Ⓒ $\frac{1}{5}x - 2 = 0$

Ⓓ $-5x + \frac{1}{2} = 0$

4. A hot air balloon descends 38.5 meters in 22 seconds. If the balloon continues to descend at this rate, how long will it take to descend 125 meters?

Ⓕ 25.25 seconds   Ⓗ 71.43 seconds

Ⓖ 86.5 seconds   Ⓙ 218.75 seconds

5. Which value completes the table of equivalent ratios?

Microphones	3	9	15	36
Karaoke Machines	1	3	?	12

Ⓐ 5   Ⓒ 8

Ⓑ 7   Ⓓ 9

6. On a baseball field, the distance from home plate to the pitcher's mound is $60\frac{1}{2}$ feet. The distance from home plate to second base is about $127\frac{7}{24}$ feet. What is the difference between the two distances?

Ⓕ $61\frac{1}{3}$ feet   Ⓗ $66\frac{19}{24}$ feet

Ⓖ $66\frac{5}{6}$ feet   Ⓙ $66\frac{5}{24}$ feet

7. Which word phrase best describes the expression $n - 6$?

Ⓐ 6 more than a number

Ⓑ A number less than 6

Ⓒ 6 minus a number

Ⓓ A number decreased by 6

8. A football weighs about $\frac{3}{20}$ kilogram. A coach has 15 footballs in a large bag. Which is the best description of the total weight of the footballs?

Ⓕ Not quite 3 kilograms

Ⓖ A little more than 2 kilograms

Ⓗ Almost 1 kilogram

Ⓙ Between 1 and 2 kilograms

9. The scale on a map is 1 centimeter: 70 kilometers. The distance between two cities on the map is 8.2 centimeters. Which is the best estimate of the actual distance?

Ⓐ 85 kilometers

Ⓑ 471 kilometers

Ⓒ 117 kilometers

Ⓓ 574 kilometers

10. On a scale drawing, a cell phone tower is 1.25 feet tall. The scale factor is $\frac{1}{150}$. What is the height of the actual cell phone tower?

Ⓕ 37.5 feet   Ⓗ 148 feet

Ⓖ 120 feet   Ⓙ 187.5 feet

 HOT TIP!

When a diagram or graph is not provided, quickly sketch one to clarify the information provided in the test item.

Gridded Response

11. The Liberty Bell, a symbol of freedom in the United States, weighs 2,080 pounds. How many tons does the Liberty Bell weigh?

12. Find the quotient of −51.03 and −8.1.

13. A scale drawing of a rectangular garden has a length of 4 inches and a width of 2.5 inches. The scale is 1 inch:3 feet. What is the perimeter of the actual garden in feet?

14. A florist is preparing bouquets of flowers for an exhibit. The florist has 84 tulips and 56 daisies. Each bouquet will have the same number of tulips and the same number of daisies. How many bouquets can the florist make for this exhibit?

Short Response

S1. Jana began the month with $102.50 in her checking account. During the month, she deposited $8.50 that she earned from baby-sitting, withdrew $9.75 to buy a CD, deposited $5.00 that her aunt gave her, and withdrew $6.50 for a movie ticket. Using compatible numbers, write and evaluate an expression to estimate the balance in Jana's account at the end of the month.

S2. A lamppost casts a shadow that is 18 feet long. At the same time of day, Alyce casts a shadow that is 4.2 feet long. Alyce is 5.3 feet tall. Draw a picture of the situation. Set up and solve a proportion to find the height of the lamppost to the nearest foot. Show your work.

Extended Response

E1. Riley is drawing a map of the state of Virginia. From east to west, the greatest distance across the state is about 430 miles. From north to south, the greatest distance is about 200 miles.

a. Riley is using a map scale of 1 inch: 24 miles. Find the length of the map from east to west and the length from north to south. Round your answers to the nearest tenth.

b. The length between two cities on Riley's map is 9 inches. What is the actual distance between the cities in miles?

c. About how many minutes will it take for an airplane traveling at a speed of 520 miles per hour to fly from east to west across the widest part of Virginia? Show your work.

Why Learn This?

You can use linear equations to represent how far a sailboat moving at a constant rate has traveled after a certain amount of time.

Learn It Online
Chapter Project Online

Chapter Focus

• Graph linear relationships and identify the slope of the line.

• Identify proportional relationships ($y = kx$).

Terje Rakke/Getty Images

Are You Ready?

✅ Vocabulary

Choose the best term from the list to complete each sentence.

1. A(n) __?__ is a number that represents a part of a whole.

2. A closed figure with three sides is called a(n) __?__.

3. Two fractions are __?__ if they represent the same number.

4. One way to compare two fractions is to first find a(n) __?__.

common
  denominator

equivalent

fraction

quadrilateral

triangle

Complete these exercises to review skills you will need for this Chapter.

✅ Write Equivalent Fractions

Find two fractions that are equivalent to each fraction.

5. $\frac{2}{5}$ 6. $\frac{7}{11}$ 7. $\frac{25}{100}$ 8. $\frac{4}{6}$

9. $\frac{5}{17}$ 10. $\frac{15}{23}$ 11. $\frac{24}{78}$ 12. $\frac{150}{325}$

✅ Compare Fractions

Compare. Write < or >.

13. $\frac{5}{6}$ ■ $\frac{2}{3}$ 14. $\frac{3}{8}$ ■ $\frac{2}{5}$ 15. $\frac{6}{11}$ ■ $\frac{1}{4}$ 16. $\frac{5}{8}$ ■ $\frac{11}{12}$

17. $\frac{8}{9}$ ■ $\frac{12}{13}$ 18. $\frac{5}{11}$ ■ $\frac{7}{21}$ 19. $\frac{4}{10}$ ■ $\frac{3}{7}$ 20. $\frac{3}{4}$ ■ $\frac{2}{9}$

✅ Solve Multiplication Equations

Solve each equation.

21. $3x = 12$ 22. $15t = 75$ 23. $2y = 14$ 24. $7m = 84$

25. $25c = 125$ 26. $16f = 320$ 27. $11n = 121$ 28. $53y = 318$

✅ Multiply Fractions

Solve. Write each answer in simplest form.

29. $\frac{2}{3} \cdot \frac{5}{7}$ 30. $\frac{12}{16} \cdot \frac{3}{9}$ 31. $\frac{4}{9} \cdot \frac{18}{24}$ 32. $\frac{1}{56} \cdot \frac{50}{200}$

33. $\frac{1}{5} \cdot \frac{5}{9}$ 34. $\frac{7}{8} \cdot \frac{4}{3}$ 35. $\frac{25}{100} \cdot \frac{30}{90}$ 36. $\frac{46}{91} \cdot \frac{3}{6}$

Study Guide: Preview

Where You've Been

Previously, you

- graphed ordered pairs of non-negative rational numbers on a coordinate plane.

- graphed linear equations.

- formulated equations from problem situations.

In This Chapter

You will study

- plotting and identifying ordered pairs of integers on a coordinate plane.

- graphing to demonstrate relationships between data sets.

- using rates of change to solve problems.

- writing and graphing linear equations to solve problems.

Where You're Going

You can use the skills learned in this chapter

- to sketch or interpret a graph that shows how a measurement such as distance, speed, cost, or temperature changes over time.

- to solve problems involving rates of speed or pay rates.

Key Vocabulary/Vocabulario

coordinate plane	plano cartesiano
ordered pair	par ordenado
origin	origen
quadrant	cuadrante
x-axis	eje *x*
y-axis	eje *y*

Vocabulary Connections

To become familiar with some of the vocabulary terms in the chapter, consider the following. You may refer to the chapter, the glossary, or a dictionary if you like.

1. An *origin* is the point at which something begins. Can you describe where to begin when you plot a point on a coordinate plane? Can you guess why the point where the *x*-axis and *y*-axis cross is called the **origin**?

2. *Quadrupeds* are animals with four feet, and a *quadrilateral* is a four-sided figure. A coordinate plane has sections called **quadrants**. What does this word imply about the number of sections in a coordinate plane?

Study Guide: Preview

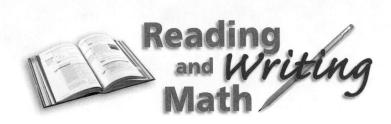

Writing Strategy:
Write a Convincing Argument

A convincing argument or explanation should include the following:

• The problem restated in your own words

• A short response

• Evidence to support the response

• A summary statement

 Write About It
Explain how to find the next three integers in the pattern -43, -40, -37, -34, ...

Step 1 **Identify the goal.**

Explain how to find the next three integers in the pattern -43, -40, -37, -34, ...

Step 2 **Provide a short response.**

As the pattern continues, the integers increase in value. Find the amount of increase from one integer to the next. Then add that amount to the last integer in the pattern. Follow this step two more times to get the next three integers in the pattern.

Step 3 **Provide evidence to support your response.**

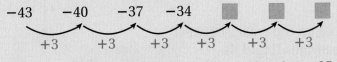

Find the amount of increase from one integer to the next.

$-34 + 3 = -31$ $-31 + 3 = -28$ $-28 + 3 = -25$

The next three integers are -31, -28, and -25.

The pattern is to add 3 to each integer to get the next integer.

Step 4 **Summarize your argument.**

To find the next three integers in the pattern -43, -40, -37, -34, . . . , find the amount that is added to each integer to get the next integer in the pattern.

Try This

Write a convincing argument using the method above.

1. Explain how to find the next three integers in the pattern 0, -2, -4, -6, ...

2. Explain how to find the seventh integer in the pattern -18, -13, -8, -3, ...

5-1 The Coordinate Plane

A **coordinate plane** is
a plane containing a
horizontal number line,
the *x*-axis, and a vertical
number line, the *y*-axis.
The intersection of these
axes is called the **origin**.

The axes divide the
coordinate plane into four
regions called **quadrants**,
which are numbered I, II,
III, and IV.

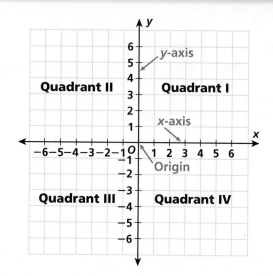

Vocabulary

coordinate plane

x-axis, *y*-axis

origin

quadrant

ordered pair

E X A M P L E 1 Identifying Quadrants on a Coordinate Plane

**Identify the quadrant that
contains each point.**

A P

P lies in Quadrant II.

B Q

Q lies in Quadrant IV.

C R

R lies on the *x*-axis, between
Quadrants II and III.

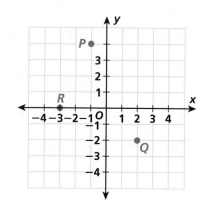

An **ordered pair** is a pair of numbers
that can be used to locate a point on
a coordinate plane. The two numbers
that form the ordered pair are called
coordinates. The origin is identified by
the ordered pair (0,0).

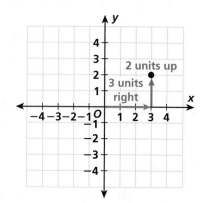

Ordered pair

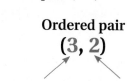

x-coordinate
Units right
or left from 0

y-coordinate
Units up
or down from 0

Video **Lesson Tutorials Online** my.hrw.com

EXAMPLE 2

Plotting Points on a Coordinate Plane

Plot each point on a coordinate plane.

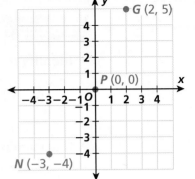

A *G* (2, 5)

Start at the origin. Move 2 units right and 5 units up.

B *N* (−3, −4)

Start at the origin. Move 3 units left and 4 units down.

C *P* (0, 0)

Point P is at the origin.

EXAMPLE 3

Identifying Points on a Coordinate Plane

Give the coordinates of each point.

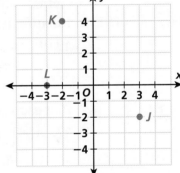

A *J*

Start at the origin. Point J is 3 units right and 2 units down.

The coordinates of *J* are (3, −2).

B *K*

Start at the origin. Point K is 2 units left and 4 units up.

The coordinates of *K* are (−2, 4).

C *L*

Start at the origin. Point L is 3 units left on the x-axis.

The coordinates of *L* are (−3, 0).

Think and Discuss

1. **Explain** whether point (4, 5) is the same as point (5, 4).

2. **Name** the *x*-coordinate of a point on the *y*-axis. Name the *y*-coordinate of a point on the *x*-axis.

3. **Suppose** the equator represents the *x*-axis on a map of Earth and a line called the *prime meridian,* which passes through England, represents the *y*-axis. Starting at the origin, which of these directions —east, west, north, and south—are positive? Which are negative?

GUIDED PRACTICE

See Example **1** Identify the quadrant that contains each point.

1. A **2.** B

3. C **4.** D

See Example **2** Plot each point on a coordinate plane.

5. $E(-1, 2)$ **6.** $N(2, -4)$

7. $H(-3, -4)$ **8.** $T(5, 0)$

See Example **3** Give the coordinates of each point.

9. J **10.** P

11. S **12.** M

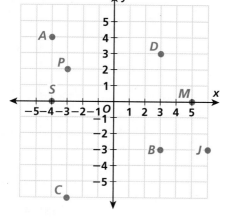

INDEPENDENT PRACTICE

See Example **1** Identify the quadrant that contains each point.

13. F **14.** J

15. K **16.** E

See Example **2** Plot each point on a coordinate plane.

17. $A(-1, 1)$ **18.** $M(2, -2)$

19. $W(-5, -5)$ **20.** $G(0, -3)$

See Example **3** Give the coordinates of each point.

21. Q **22.** V

23. R **24.** P

25. S **26.** L

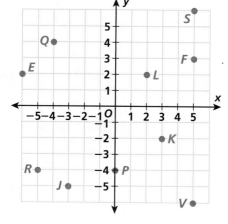

PRACTICE AND PROBLEM SOLVING

Extra Practice
See Extra Practice for more exercises.

Graph each set of ordered pairs. Then connect the points, identify the figure created, and name the quadrants in which it is located.

27. $(-8, 1)$; $(4, 3)$; $(-3, 6)$ **28.** $(-8, -2)$; $(-1, -2)$; $(-1, 3)$; $(-8, 3)$

Identify the quadrant of each point described below.

29. The x-coordinate and the y-coordinate are both negative.

30. The x-coordinate is negative and the y-coordinate is positive.

31. The x-coordinate is positive and the y-coordinate is negative.

32. What point is 5 units left and 2 units down from point $(1, 2)$?

33. What point is 9 units right and 3 units up from point (3, 4)?

34. What point is 4 units left and and 7 units up from point (−2, −4)?

35. What point is 10 units right and and 1 unit down from point (−10, 1)?

36. Critical Thinking After being moved 6 units right and 4 units down, a point is located at (6, 1). What were the original coordinates of the point?

37. Weather The map shows the path of Hurricane Rita. Estimate to the nearest integer the coordinates of the storm for each of the times below.

a. when Rita first became a hurricane

b. when Rita made landfall in the United States

c. when Rita weakened to a tropical depression

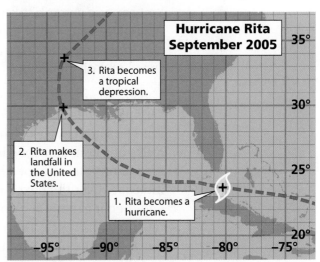

38. What's the Error? To plot (−12, 1), a student started at (0, 0) and moved 12 units right and 1 unit down. What did the student do wrong?

39. Write About It Why is order important when graphing an ordered pair on a coordinate plane?

40. Challenge Armand and Kayla started jogging from the same point. Armand jogged 4 miles south and 6 miles east. Kayla jogged west and 4 miles south. If they were 11 miles apart when they stopped, how far west did Kayla jog?

Test Prep

41. Multiple Choice Which of the following points lie within the circle graphed at right?

  Ⓐ (2, 6)   Ⓑ (−4, 4)   Ⓒ (0, −4)   Ⓓ (−6, 6)

42. Multiple Choice Which point on the *x*-axis is the same distance from the origin as (0, −3)?

  Ⓕ (0, 3)   Ⓖ (3, 0)   Ⓗ (3, −3)   Ⓙ (−3, 3)

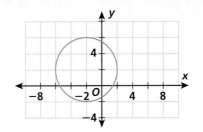

5-2 Interpreting Graphs

You can use a graph to show the relationship between speed and time, time and distance, or speed and distance.

The graph at right shows the varying speeds at which Emma exercises her horse. The horse walks at a constant speed for the first 10 minutes. Its speed increases over the next 7 minutes, and then it gallops at a constant rate for 20 minutes. Then it slows down over the next 3 minutes and then walks at a constant pace for 10 minutes.

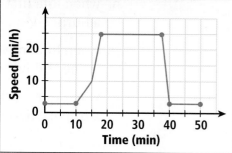

EXAMPLE 1 Relating Graphs to Situations

Jenny leaves home and drives to the beach. She stays at the beach all day before driving back home. Which graph best shows the situation?

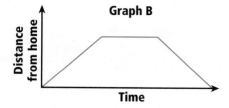

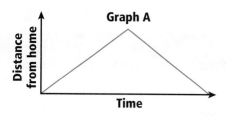

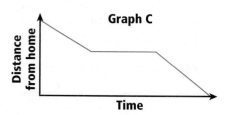

As Jenny drives to the beach, her distance from home *increases*. While she is at the beach, her distance from home is *constant*. As she drives home, her distance from home *decreases*. The answer is graph B.

Thinkstock/Corbis

Video **Lesson Tutorials Online** my.hrw.com

EXAMPLE 2

PROBLEM SOLVING APPLICATION

MATHEMATICAL PRACTICES Make sense of problems and persevere in solving them.

Maili and Katrina traveled 10 miles from Maili's house to the movie theater. They watched a movie, and then they traveled 5 miles farther to a restaurant to eat lunch. After eating they returned to Maili's house. Sketch a graph to show the distance from Maili's house compared to time. Use your graph to find the total distance traveled.

1 Understand the Problem

The answer will be the total distance that Katrina and Maili traveled.

List the **important information:**

- The friends traveled 10 miles from Maili's house to the theater.
- They traveled an additional 5 miles and then ate lunch.
- They returned to Maili's house.

2 Make a Plan

Sketch a graph that represents the situation. Then use the graph to find the total distance Katrina and Maili traveled.

3 Solve

The distance from Maili's house increases from 0 to 10 miles when the friends travel to the theater. The distance does not change while the friends watch the movie and eat lunch. The distance increases from 10 to 15 miles when they go to the restaurant. The distance decreases from 15 to 0 miles when they return home.

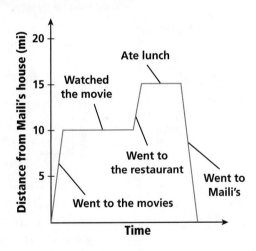

Maili and Katrina traveled a total of 30 miles.

4 Look Back

The theater is 10 miles away, so the friends must have traveled twice that distance just to go to the theater and return. The answer, 30 miles, is reasonable since it is greater than 20 miles.

MATHEMATICAL PRACTICES

Think and Discuss

1. **Explain** the meaning of a horizontal segment on a graph that compares distance to time.

2. **Describe** a real-world situation that could be represented by a graph that has connected lines or curves.

GUIDED PRACTICE

See Example **1**

1. The temperature of an ice cube increases until it starts to melt. While it melts, its temperature stays constant. Which graph best shows the situation?

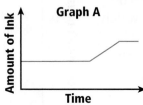

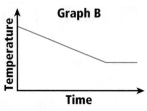

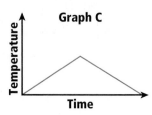

See Example **2**

2. Mike and Claudia rode a bus 15 miles from home to a wildlife park. They waited in line to ride a train, which took them on a 3-mile ride around the park. After the train ride, they ate lunch, and then they rode the bus home. Sketch a graph to show the distance from their home compared to time. Use your graph to find the total distance traveled.

INDEPENDENT PRACTICE

See Example **1**

3. The ink in a printer is used until the ink cartridge is empty. The cartridge is refilled, and the ink is used up again. Which graph best shows the situation?

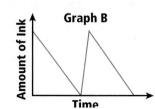

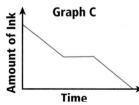

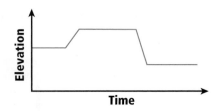

See Example **2**

4. On her way from home to the grocery store, a 6-mile trip, Veronica stopped at a gas station to buy gas. After filling her tank, she continued to the grocery store. She then returned home after shopping. Sketch a graph to show the distance from Veronica's home compared to time. Use your graph to find the total distance traveled.

PRACTICE AND PROBLEM SOLVING

Extra Practice

See Extra Practice for more exercises.

5. Describe a situation that fits the graph at right.

6. Lynn jogged for 2.5 miles. Then she walked a little while before stopping to stretch. Sketch a graph to show Lynn's speed compared to time.

7. On his way to the library, Jeff runs two blocks and then walks three more blocks. Sketch a graph to show the distance Jeff travels compared to time.

8. **Critical Thinking** The graph at right shows high school enrollment, including future projections.

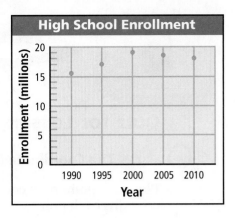

High School Enrollment

a. Describe what is happening in the graph.

b. Does it make sense to connect the points in the graph? Explain.

c. Graphs that are not connected are called *discrete*. Describe another situation where the graph that shows the situation would be discrete.

9. **Choose a Strategy** Three bananas were given to two mothers who were with their daughters. Each person had a banana to eat. How is that possible?

10. **Write About It** A driver sets his car's cruise control to 55 mi/h. Describe a graph that shows the car's speed compared to time. Then describe a second graph that shows the distance traveled compared to time.

11. **Challenge** The graph at right shows the temperature of an oven after the oven is turned on. Explain what the graph shows.

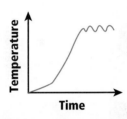

Temperature / Time

Test Prep

12. **Multiple Choice** How does speed compare to time in the graph at right?

Ⓐ It increases.

Ⓑ It decreases.

Ⓒ It stays the same.

Ⓓ It fluctuates.

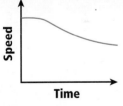

Speed / Time

13. **Short Response** Keisha takes a big drink from a bottle of water. She sets the bottle down to tie her shoe and then picks up the bottle to take a small sip of water. Sketch a graph to show the amount of water in the bottle over time.

Quiz for Lessons 1 Through 2

  1 **The Coordinate Plane**

Plot each point on a coordinate plane. Then identify the quadrant that contains each point.

1. $W(1, 5)$ **2.** $X(5, -3)$ **3.** $Y(-1, -5)$ **4.** $Z(-8, 2)$

  2 **Interpreting Graphs**

5. Raj climbs to the top of a cliff. He descends a little bit to another cliff, and then he begins to climb again. Which graph best shows the situation?

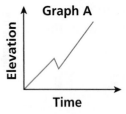
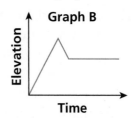
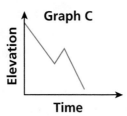

6. Ty walks 1 mile to the mall. An hour later, he walks $\frac{1}{2}$ mile farther to a park and eats lunch. Then he walks home. Sketch a graph to show the distance Ty traveled compared to time. Use your graph to find the total distance traveled.

Focus on Problem Solving

Understand the Problem

- **Sequence and prioritize information**

When you are reading a math problem, putting events in order, or in *sequence,* can help you understand the problem better. It helps to *prioritize* the information when you put it in order. To prioritize, you decide which of the information in your list is most important. The most important information has highest priority.

 Use the information in the list or table to answer each question.

1 The list at right shows all of the things that Roderick has to do on Saturday. He starts the day without any money.

a. Which two activities on Roderick's list must be done before any of the other activities? Do these two activities have higher or lower priority?

b. Is there more than one way that he can order his activities? Explain.

c. List the order in which Roderick's activities could occur on Saturday.

> **Saturday Activities**
> - Attend birthday party at 4 P.M.
> - Buy gift - either a CD for $18 or a computer game for $25.
> - Get haircut at 2 P.M.; pay $16.
> - Mow Mrs. Mayberry's lawn before 10 A.M.; earn $15.
> - Mow Mr. Boyar's lawn and trim hedge anytime after 10 A.M.; earn $25.

2 Tara and her family will visit Ocean World Park from 9:30 to 4:00. They want to see the waterskiing show at 10:00. Each show in the park is 50 minutes long. The time they choose to eat lunch will depend on the schedule they choose for seeing the shows.

a. Which of the information given in the paragraph above has the highest priority? Which has the lowest priority?

b. List the order in which they can see all of the shows, including the time they will see each.

c. At what time should they plan to have lunch?

Show Times at Ocean World Park	
9:00, 12:00	Underwater acrobats
9:00, 3:00	Whale acts
10:00, 2:00	Dolphin acts
10:00, 1:00	Waterskiing
11:00, 4:00	Aquarium tour

Graph Proportional Relationships

Learn It Online
Lab Resources Online

You can express proportional relationships with words, equations, tables, or graphs. Graphs of proportional relationships can be very useful because you can determine equivalent ratios from them.

MATHEMATICAL PRACTICES **Use appropriate tools strategically.**
CC.7.RP.2 Recognize and represent proportional relationships between quantities. *Also CC.7.RP.1, CC.7.RP.2a, CC.7.RP.2b, CC.7.RP.2c*

Activity 1

De'Nae rides her bike at a rate of about $\frac{1}{4}$ mile per minute.

1 Complete the table below for De'Nae's distance and time.

Time (min) *x*	1	2				
Distance (mi) *y*	$\frac{1}{4}$	$\frac{1}{2}$	$\frac{3}{4}$	1	$1\frac{1}{4}$	$1\frac{1}{2}$

2 Graph the points on a coordinate plane.

3 A *unit rate* is a rate that has the denominator 1 when written as a fraction. What is De'Nae's unit rate of speed (distance per time) in miles per minute?

4 Draw a line through the points on your graph. Use the graph to find two different rates of speed in miles per minute that are equivalent to the unit rate. Circle the points on the graph representing your two equivalent rates.

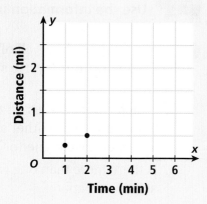

Think and Discuss

1. If you continued the line, would the point (0, 0) fall on the line? What does this point represent in this situation?

Try This

1. Write the unit rate of speed for De'Nae in miles per hour.

$$\frac{\frac{1}{4}\text{ mi}}{1\text{ min}} = \frac{}{60\text{ min}} = \frac{}{1\text{ hour}}$$

2. Graph the unit rate in miles per hour on a coordinate plane and use your graph to find two different rates of speed in miles per hour that are equivalent to the unit rate.

Activity 2

Boone rides his bike at a rate of about 1 mile every 5 minutes.

1 Complete the table for Boone's distance over time.

Time (min) x	5	10	15			30
Distance (mi) y	1					

2 Graph the points on the coordinate plane.

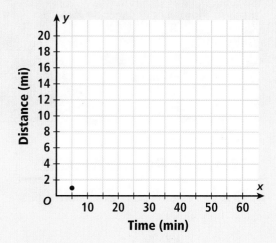

3 What is Boone's unit rate of speed in miles per minute?

$$\frac{1 \text{ mi}}{5 \text{ min}} = \frac{}{1 \text{ min}}$$

4 Draw a line through the points on your graph. Use your graph to find two different rates of speed in miles per minute that are equivalent to the unit rate. Circle the points on your graph representing your two equivalent rates.

Think and Discuss

1. Explain how a graph can show equivalent rates.

2. Describe the shape of a graph that shows equivalent rates.

3. Discuss whether the graph of a proportional relationship goes through the origin.

Try This

1. Write Boone's speed in miles per hour.

2. Graph Boone's speed in miles per hour on a coordinate plane.

3. Use your graph to find two different rates of speed in miles per hour that are equivalent to the unit rate.

4. What would the point (5, 60) represent?

Slope and Rates of Change

COMMON CORE

CC.7.RP.1 Compute unit rates associated with ratios of fractions, including ratios of lengths… **Also** **CC.7.RP.2d**

Vocabulary

slope

rate of change

Baldwin Street, located in Dunedin, New Zealand, is considered one of the world's steepest streets. The *slope* of the street is about $\frac{1}{3}$.

The **slope** of a line is a measure of its steepness and is the ratio of rise to run:

$$\text{slope} = \frac{\text{rise}}{\text{run}} = \frac{\text{vertical change}}{\text{horizontal change}}$$

If a line rises from left to right, its slope is positive. If a line falls from left to right, its slope is negative.

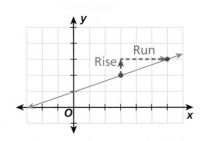

EXAMPLE 1 **Identifying the Slope of the Line**

Tell whether the slope is positive or negative. Then find the slope.

A

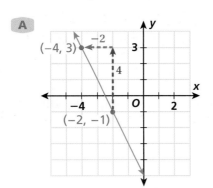

The line falls from left to right.

The slope is negative.

$$\text{slope} = \frac{\text{rise}}{\text{run}}$$

$$= \frac{4}{-2} \qquad \text{\textit{The rise is 4.}}$$
$$\qquad \qquad \text{\textit{The run is −2.}}$$

$$= -2$$

B

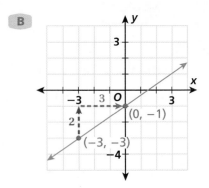

The line rises from left to right.

The slope is positive.

$$\text{slope} = \frac{\text{rise}}{\text{run}}$$

$$= \frac{2}{3} \qquad \text{\textit{The rise is 2.}}$$
$$\qquad \qquad \text{\textit{The run is 3.}}$$

Video **Lesson Tutorials Online** my.hrw.com

Jill Ferry/Photographers Direct

You can graph a line if you know its slope and one of its points.

EXAMPLE **2** **Using Slope and a Point to Graph a Line**

Use the given slope and point to graph each line.

Helpful Hint

Slope of a line can be represented as a unit rate. For example, $-\frac{3}{4}$ can be thought of as a rise of $-\frac{3}{4}$ to a run of 1.

A $-\frac{3}{4};\ (-3, 2)$

slope $= \frac{\text{rise}}{\text{run}} = \frac{-3}{4}$ or $\frac{3}{-4}$

From point $(-3, 2)$, move 3 units down and 4 units right, or move 3 units up and 4 units left. Mark the points, and draw a line through the two points.

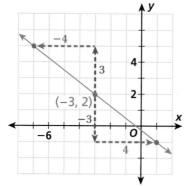

B $3;\ (-1, -2)$

$3 = \frac{3}{1}$ *Write the slope as a fraction.*

slope $= \frac{\text{rise}}{\text{run}} = \frac{3}{1}$

From point $(-1, -2)$, move 3 units up and 1 unit right. Mark the points, and draw a line through the two points.

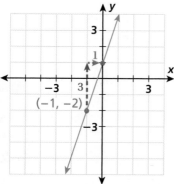

The ratio of two quantities that change, such as slope, is a **rate of change**.

A *constant rate of change* describes changes of the same amount during equal intervals. Linear functions have a constant rate of change. The graph of a constant rate of change is a line.

A *variable rate of change* describes changes of a different amount during equal intervals. The graph of a variable rate of change is not a line.

EXAMPLE **3** **Identifying Rates of Change in Graphs**

Tell whether each graph shows a constant or variable rate of change.

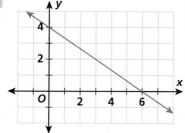

The graph is a line, so the rate of change is constant.

The graph is not a line, so the rate of change is variable.

EXAMPLE 4 Using Rate of Change to Solve Problems

The graph shows the distance a bicyclist travels over time. Does the bicyclist travel at a constant or variable speed? How fast does the bicyclist travel?

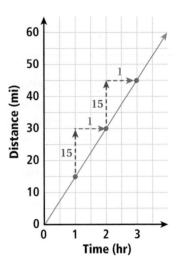

The graph is a line, so the bicyclist is traveling at a constant speed.

The amount of distance is the rise, and the amount of time is the run. You can find the speed by finding the slope.

$$\text{slope (speed)} = \frac{\text{rise (distance)}}{\text{run (time)}} = \frac{15}{1}$$

The bicyclist travels at 15 miles per hour.

MATHEMATICAL PRACTICES

Think and Discuss

1. Describe a line with a negative slope.

2. Compare constant and variable rates of change.

3. Give an example of a real-world situation involving a rate of change.

5-3 Exercises

Learn It Online
Homework Help Online
Exercises 1–20, 21, 25, 29

GUIDED PRACTICE

See Example 1 Tell whether the slope is positive or negative. Then find the slope.

1.

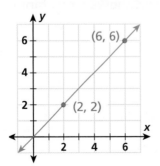

2.

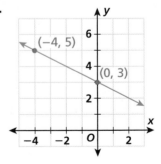

See Example 2 Use the given slope and point to graph each line.

3. 3; (4, −2) **4.** −2; (−3, −2) **5.** −$\frac{1}{4}$; (0, 5) **6.** $\frac{3}{2}$; (−1, 1)

Video Lesson Tutorials Online my.hrw.com

Tell whether each graph shows a constant or variable rate of change.

7.
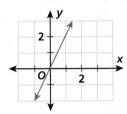

8.
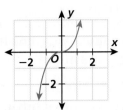

9.
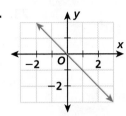

10. The graph shows the distance a trout swims over time. Does the trout swim at a constant or variable speed? How fast does the trout swim?

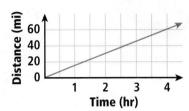

INDEPENDENT PRACTICE

Tell whether the slope is positive or negative. Then find the slope.

11.
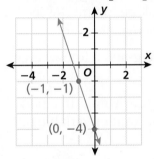

12.
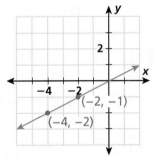

Use the given slope and point to graph each line.

13. -1; $(-1, 4)$ 14. 4; $(-1, -3)$ 15. $\frac{3}{5}$; $(3, -1)$ 16. $\frac{2}{3}$; $(0, 5)$

Tell whether each graph shows a constant or variable rate of change.

17.
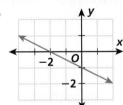

18.
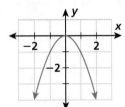

19.
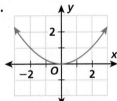

20. The graph shows the amount of rain that falls over time. Does the rain fall at a constant or variable rate? How much rain falls per hour?

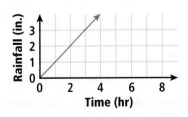

PRACTICE AND PROBLEM SOLVING

Extra Practice

See Extra Practice for more exercises.

21. **Multi-Step** A line has a slope of 5 and passes through the points $(4, 3)$ and $(2, y)$. What is the value of y?

22. A line passes through the origin and has a slope of $-\frac{3}{2}$. Through which quadrants does the line pass?

Agriculture

This water tower can be seen in Poteet, Texas, where the Poteet Strawberry Festival® is held every April. Known as the "Strawberry Capital of Texas," Poteet produces 40% of Texas' strawberries.

Graph the line containing the two points, and then find the slope.

23. $(-2, 13), (1, 4)$ **24.** $(-2, -6), (2, 2)$ **25.** $(-2, -3), (2, 3)$ **26.** $(2, -3), (3, -5)$

27. Explain whether you think it would be more difficult to run up a hill with a slope of $\frac{1}{3}$ or a hill with a slope of $\frac{3}{4}$.

28. **Agriculture** The graph at right shows the cost per pound of buying strawberries.

   a. Is the cost per pound a constant or variable rate?

   b. Find the slope of the line.

   c. Remember, a unit rate is a rate whose denominator is one. Using the slope from part **b,** find the unit rate of the line. What does it tell you?

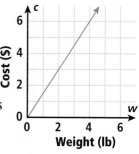

29. **Critical Thinking** A line has a negative slope. Explain how the y-values of the line change as the x-values increase.

30. **What's the Error?** Kyle graphed a line, given a slope of $-\frac{4}{3}$ and the point $(2, 3)$. When he used the slope to find the second point, he found $(5, 7)$. What error did Kyle make?

31. **Write About It** Explain how to graph a line when given the slope and one of the points on the line.

32. **Challenge** The population of prairie dogs in a park doubles every year. Does this population show a constant or variable rate of change? Explain.

Test Prep

33. **Multiple Choice** To graph a line, Caelyn plotted the point $(2, 1)$ and then used the slope $-\frac{1}{2}$ to find another point on the line. Which point could be the other point on the line that Caelyn found?

   Ⓐ $(1, 3)$ Ⓑ $(4, 0)$ Ⓒ $(1, -1)$ Ⓓ $(0, 0)$

34. **Multiple Choice** A line has a positive slope and passes through the point $(-1, 2)$. Through which quadrant can the line NOT pass?

   Ⓕ Quadrant I   Ⓖ Quadrant II   Ⓗ Quadrant III   Ⓙ Quadrant IV

35. **Short Response** Explain how you can use three points on a graph to determine whether the rate of change is constant or variable.

5-4 Direct Variation

CC.7.RP.2 Recognize and represent proportional relationships between quantities. **Also CC.7.NS.1, CC.7.RP.2a**

Vocabulary

direct variation

constant of variation

Reading Math

You can read direct variation as "*y* varies directly as *x*" or "*y* is directly proportional to *x*" or "*y* varies with *x*."

An Eastern box turtle can travel at a speed of about 18 feet per minute. The chart shows the distance an Eastern box turtle can travel when moving at a constant speed.

The distance traveled is found by multiplying time by 18. Distance and time are directly proportional.

Time (min)	1	2	3	4
Distance (ft)	18	36	54	72

Direct variation is a linear relationship between two variables that can be written in the form $y = kx$ or $k = \frac{y}{x}$, where $k \neq 0$. The fixed number k in a direct variation equation is the **constant of variation**.

$$y = kx \qquad k = \frac{y}{x}$$

To check whether an equation represents a direct variation, solve for *y*. If the equation can be written as $y = kx$, then it represents a direct variation.

EXAMPLE **1** **Identifying a Direct Variation from an Equation**

Tell whether each equation represents a direct variation. If so, identify the constant of variation.

A $2y = x$

$\frac{2y}{2} = \frac{x}{2}$ *Solve the equation for y. Divide both sides by 2.*

$y = \frac{1}{2}x$ *Write $\frac{x}{2}$ as $\frac{1}{2}x$.*

The equation is in the form $y = kx$, so the original equation $2y = x$ is a direct variation. The constant of variation is $\frac{1}{2}$.

B $y + 1 = 2x$

$y + 1 = 2x$ *Solve the equation for y. Subtract 1 from both sides.*

$\underline{-1 \qquad\quad -1}$

$y = 2x - 1$

The equation is not in the form $y = kx$, so $y + 1 = 2x$ is not a direct variation.

Sebastian Green/Alamy

The equation $y = kx$ can be solved for the constant of variation, $k = \frac{y}{x}$. If $\frac{y}{x}$ is the same for all ordered pairs in a set of data, then the data set represents a direct variation. To write a direct variation equation for a set of data, substitute the value of $\frac{y}{x}$ for k in $y = kx$.

EXAMPLE 2 **Identifying a Direct Variation from a Table**

Tell whether each set of data represents a direct variation. If so, identify the constant of variation and then write the direct variation equation.

Ⓐ

Weight (lb)	1	2	3
Price ($)	3	6	9

Find $\frac{y}{x}$ for each ordered pair.

$$\frac{y}{x} = \frac{3}{1} = 3 \qquad \frac{y}{x} = \frac{6}{2} = 3 \qquad \frac{y}{x} = \frac{9}{3} = 3$$

$k = 3$ for each ordered pair.

The data represent a direct variation where $k = 3$. The equation is $y = 3x$.

Ⓑ

Constant Speed (mi/h)	10	20	30
Time (h)	3	1.5	1

Find $\frac{y}{x}$ for each ordered pair.

$$\frac{y}{x} = \frac{3}{10} \qquad \frac{y}{x} = \frac{1.5}{20} = \frac{3}{40} \qquad \frac{y}{x} = \frac{1}{30} = \frac{1}{30}$$

k is not the same for each ordered pair.

The data do not represent a direct variation.

The graph of any direct variation is a straight line that passes through the origin, $(0, 0)$. The slope of a line of direct variation is the constant of variation, k.

EXAMPLE 3 **Identifying a Direct Variation from a Graph**

Tell whether each graph represents a direct variation. If so, identify the constant of variation and then write the direct variation equation.

Ⓐ

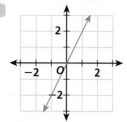

Ⓑ

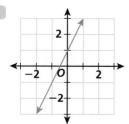

The graph is a line through $(0, 0)$. This is a direct variation. The slope of the line is 2, so $k = 2$. The equation is $y = 2x$.

The line does not pass through $(0, 0)$. This is not a direct variation.

[Video] **Lesson Tutorials Online** my.hrw.com

EXAMPLE 4 *Life Science Application*

An Eastern box turtle travels on the ground at a speed of about 18 feet per minute.

a. Write a direct variation equation for the distance y an Eastern box turtle travels in x minutes.

distance	=	18 feet per minute	times	number of minutes	*Use the*
y	=	18	$\bullet$	x	*formula $y = kx$.*

$$y = 18x$$

k = 18

b. Graph the data.

Make a table. Since time cannot be negative, use nonnegative numbers for x.

x	$y = 18x$	y	(x, y)
0	$y = 18(0)$	0	(0, 0)
1	$y = 18(1)$	18	(1, 18)
2	$y = 18(2)$	36	(2, 36)

Use the ordered pairs to plot the points on a coordinate plane. Connect the points in a straight line. Label the axes.

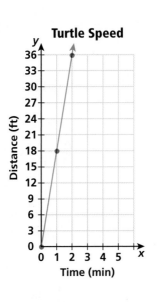

Turtle Speed

Distance (ft) / *Time (min)*

Check

$y = 18x$ is in slope-intercept form with $m = 18$ and $b = 0$. The graph shows a slope of 18 and a y-intercept of 0.

c. How long does it take an Eastern box turtle to travel 162 feet?

Find the value of x when $y = 162$.

$y = 18x$	*Write the equation for the direct variation.*
$162 = 18x$	*Substitute 162 for y.*
$\dfrac{162}{18} = \dfrac{18x}{18}$	*Divide both sides by 18.*
$9 = x$	

It will take an Eastern box turtle 9 minutes to travel 162 feet.

Helpful Hint

In this problem the variable x represents time and y represents distance, so 162 will be substituted for y.

MATHEMATICAL PRACTICES

Think and Discuss

1. Explain how to use a table of data to check whether the relationship between two variables is a direct variation.

2. Describe how to recognize a direct variation from an equation, from a table, and from a graph.

3. Discuss why every direct variation equation is a linear equation, but not every linear equation is a direct variation equation.

Exercises

Learn It Online
Homework Help Online
Exercises 1–18, 19, 25, 27

GUIDED PRACTICE

See Example 1 Tell whether each equation represents a direct variation. If so, identify the constant of variation.

1. $y = 5x + 8$ 2. $y = 3.6x$ 3. $8y = 2x$ 4. $x = 3y + 1$

See Example 2 Tell whether each set of data or graph represents a direct variation. If so, identify the constant of variation and then write the direct variation equation.

5.
Number of Boxes	2	3	4
Rolls of Tape Needed	1	2	5

6.
x	2	4	8
y	3	7	15

See Example 3

7.
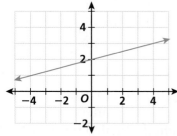

8.
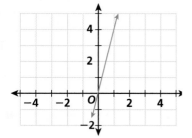

See Example 4 9. **Physical Science** Belinda's garden hose sprays about 4 gallons of water each minute.

　　a. Write a direct variation equation for the number of gallons y Belinda uses during x minutes of watering her garden.

　　b. Graph the data.

　　c. How many gallons of water does Belinda use in 20 minutes?

INDEPENDENT PRACTICE

See Example 1 Tell whether each equation represents a direct variation. If so, identify the constant of variation.

10. $y = \frac{x}{7}$ 11. $\frac{y}{x} = \frac{2}{3}$ 12. $3y = 15 - 6x$ 13. $3xy = 9x$

See Example 2 Tell whether each set of data or graph represents a direct variation. If so, identify the constant of variation and then write the direct variation equation.

14.
x	7	8	9
y	0.5	1.2	1.5

15.
Cans of Food	2	4	6
Dinners Made	4	8	12

See Example 3 16.
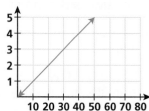

17.
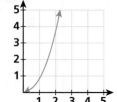

See Example 4

18. **Physical Science** Neil Armstrong's weight on the moon was about $\frac{1}{6}$ his weight on Earth.

    a. Write a direct variation equation for the number of pounds y an object on the moon weighs if the object weighs x pounds on Earth.

    b. Graph the data.

    c. Li would weigh 24 pounds on the moon. What does he weigh on Earth?

PRACTICE AND PROBLEM SOLVING

Extra Practice
See Extra Practice for more exercises.

Life Science

Sea snakes are found in warm waters ranging from the Indian Ocean to the Pacific. They do not have gills and must surface regularly to breathe.

Write an equation for the direct variation that includes each point.

19. (7, 2)   **20.** (6, 30)   **21.** (4, 8)   **22.** (17, 31)

23. If y varies directly as x, and $y = 8$ when $x = 2$, find y when $x = 10$.

24. Is a direct variation a function? Explain.

Tell whether each relationship is a direct variation. Explain.

25. pay per hour and the number of hours worked

26. pay per hour and the number of hours worked, including a $100 bonus

27. **Life Science** A sea snake can swim at a rate of 60 meters per minute. How far can a sea snake swim in half an hour?

28. **Critical Thinking** If you double an x-value in a direct variation equation, will the y-value double? Explain your answer.

29. **What's the Error?** Phil says that the graph represents a direct variation because it passes through the origin. What's the error?

30. **Write About It** Compare the graphs of a direct variation equation with a slope of 3 and an equation with the same slope and a y-intercept of 2.

31. **Challenge** Explain why the graph of a line that does not pass through the origin cannot be a direct variation.

Test Prep

32. **Multiple Choice** Which equation does NOT show direct variation?

    Ⓐ $y = 16x$ Ⓑ $y - 19 = x - 19$ Ⓒ $20y = x$ Ⓓ $y = 25$

33. **Short Response** Ron buys 5 pounds of apples for $3.25. Write a direct variation equation for the cost y of x pounds of apples. Find the cost of 21 lbs of apples.

Quiz for Lessons 3 Through 4

3 Slope and Rates of Change

Tell whether the slope is positive or negative. Then find the slope.

1.

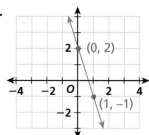

2.

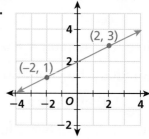

3.

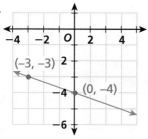

Tell whether each graph shows a constant or variable rate of change.
If constant, find the slope.

4.

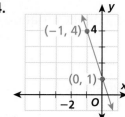

5.

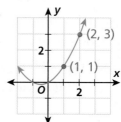

6.

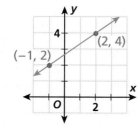

4 Direct Variation

Tell whether each set of data represents a direct variation. If so, identify the constant
of variation, and then write the direct variation equation.

7.

Weight (lb)	1	2	3
Price ($)	1.50	3.00	4.50

8.

x	1	2	3
y	4	5	7

Real-World CONNECTIONS

MATHEMATICAL PRACTICES Reason abstractly and quantitatively.

The Alabama National Fair Where can you see trapeze acts, a cheerleading competition, and racing pigs all in one place? Since the 1950s, the annual Alabama National Fair has brought all of this—and much more—to the Agricultural Center and Fairgrounds in Montgomery.

ALABAMA

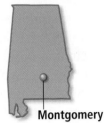

Montgomery

A teacher is planning to take some of her students to the fair.

1. The Alabama National Fair has one admission fee for adults and a different fee for students. The table can be used to determine how much it will cost for the teacher and her students to attend the fair. Complete the table.

2. What is the fair's admission fee for adults? What is the fair's admission fee for students?

3. Suppose x represents the number of students that the teacher brings to the fair and y represents the total cost. Write an equation that describes the data in the table.

4. Use the equation you wrote in Problem 3 to find the total cost of bringing 14 students to the fair.

5. Graph the equation you wrote in Exercise 4.

6. What is the slope of the line in your graph?

7. A county fair offers admission to a teacher and any number of students for $85. For what number of students would it be less expensive for the teacher to take her students to the county fair than the Alabama National Fair?

ADMIT ONE

Number of Students	Rule	Total Cost
0	▨	$9
1	9 + 7(1)	$16
2	▨	$23
3	9 + 7(3)	▨
4	▨	$37
6	9 + 7(6)	▨
8	▨	$65
12	▨	▨

Real-World Connections **217**

Game Time

Clothes Encounters

Five students from the same math class met to study for an upcoming test. They sat around a circular table with seat 1 and seat 5 next to each other. No two students were wearing the same color of shirt or the same type of shoes. From the clues provided, determine where each student sat, each student's shirt color, and what type of shoes each student was wearing.

1 The girls' shoes were sandals, flip-flops, and boots.

2 Robin, wearing a blue shirt, was sitting next to the person wearing the green shirt. She was not sitting next to the person wearing the orange shirt.

3 Lila was sitting between the person wearing sandals and the person in the yellow shirt.

4 The boy who was wearing the tennis shoes was wearing the orange shirt.

5 April had on flip-flops and was sitting between Lila and Charles.

6 Glenn was wearing loafers, but his shirt was not brown.

7 Robin sat in seat 1.

You can use a chart like the one below to organize the information given. Put X's in the spaces where the information is false and O's in the spaces where the information is true. Some of the information from the first two clues has been included on the chart already. You will need to read through the clues several times and use logic to complete the chart.

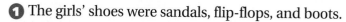

	Seat 1	Seat 2	Seat 3	Seat 4	Seat 5	Blue shirt	Green shirt	Orange shirt	Yellow shirt	Brown shirt	Sandals	Flip-flops	Boots	Tennis shoes	Loafers
Lila					X									X	X
Robin					O	X	X	X	X					X	X
April					X									X	X
Charles					X										
Glenn					X										

Materials
- **6 sheets of unlined paper**
- **scissors**
- **markers**

It's in the Bag!

PROJECT **Graphs Fold-A-Books**

A

These handy books will store your notes from each lesson of the chapter.

Directions

1 Fold a sheet of paper in half down the middle. Then open the paper and lay it flat so it forms a peak. **Figure A**

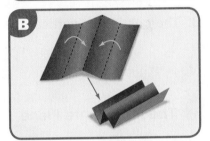
B

2 Fold the left and right edges to the crease in the middle. When you're done, the paper will be folded into four sections, accordion-style. **Figure B**

3 Pinch the middle sections together. Use scissors to cut a slit down the center of these sections, stopping when you get to the folds. **Figure C**

C

4 Hold the paper on either side of the slit. As you open the slit, the paper will form a four-page book. **Figure D**

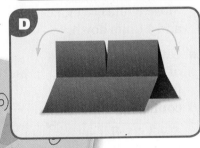
D

5 Crease the top edges and fold the book closed. Repeat all the steps to make five more books.

Taking Note of the Math

On the cover of each book, write the number and name of a lesson from the chapter. Use the remaining pages to take notes on the lesson.

Graphs

Study Guide: Review

Vocabulary

constant of variation	quadrant
coordinate plane	rate of change
direct variation	slope
ordered pair	*x*-axis
origin	*y*-axis

Complete the sentences below with vocabulary words from the list above.

1. A(n) __?__ is one of the four regions into which the axes divide a coordinate plane.

2. A(n) __?__ is the ratio of two quantities that change.

3. The __?__ is the vertical axis in a coordinate plane.

EXAMPLES

EXERCISES

1 | The Coordinate Plane

Plot each point on a coordinate plane.

- ■ **M(−3, 1)**
  Start at the origin.
  Move 3 units left
  and 1 unit up.

- ■ **R(3, −4)**
  Start at the origin.
  Move 3 units right
  and 4 units down.

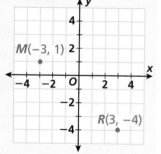

- ■ Give the coordinates
  of each point and
  tell which quadrant
  contains it.

  A(−3, 2); II
  B(2, −3); IV
  C(−2, −3); III
  D(3, 2); I

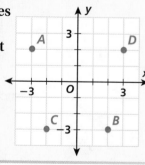

Plot each point on a coordinate plane.

4. A(4, 2)   **5.** B(−4, −2)

6. C(−2, 4)   **7.** D(2, −4)

Give the coordinates of each point and tell which quadrant contains it.

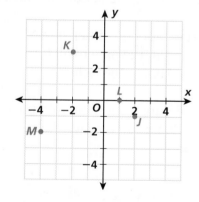

8. *J*   **9.** *K*   **10.** *L*   **11.** *M*

2 Interpreting Graphs

■ Ari visits his grandmother, who lives 45 miles away. After the visit, he returns home, stopping for gas along the way. Sketch a graph to show the distance Ari traveled compared to time. Use your graph to find the total distance traveled.

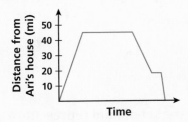

The graph increases from 0 to 45 miles and then decreases from 45 to 0 miles. The distance does not change while Ari visits his grandmother and stops for gas. Ari traveled a total of 90 miles.

12. Amanda walks 1.5 miles to school in the morning. After school, she walks 0.5 mile to the public library. After she has chosen her books, she walks 2 miles home. Sketch a graph to show the distance Amanda traveled compared to time. Use your graph to find the total distance traveled.

13. Joel rides his bike to the park, 12 miles away, to meet his friends. He then rides an additional 6 miles to the grocery store and then 18 miles back home. Sketch a graph to show the distance Joel traveled compared to time. Use your graph to find the total distance traveled.

3 **Slope and Rates of Change**

■ Tell whether the graph shows a constant or variable rate of change. If constant, find the slope.

The graph is a line, so the rate of change is constant.

slope = $\frac{\text{rise}}{\text{run}}$

$= \frac{-4}{1} = -4$

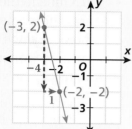

Tell whether each graph shows a constant or variable rate of change. If constant, find the slope.

14.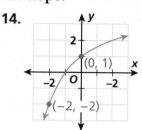

15.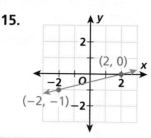

4 **Direct Variation**

■ Tell whether each equation represents a direct variation. If so, identify the constant of variation.

$3y = x$

$\frac{3y}{3} = \frac{x}{3}$ *Solve the equation for y.*

$y = \frac{1}{3}x$ *Divide by 3 on both sides.*

The constant of variation is $\frac{1}{3}$.

Tell whether the set of data represents a direct variation. If so, identify the constant of variation and then write the direct variation equation.

16.

x	1	2	3
y	18	36	54

17.

x	1	2	3
y	4	7	10

Plot each point on a coordinate plane. Then identify the quadrant that contains each point.

1. $L(4, -3)$ **2.** $M(-5, 2)$ **3.** $N(7, 1)$ **4.** $O(-7, -2)$

5. Ian jogs 4 miles to the lake and then rests for 30 min before jogging home. Sketch a graph to show the distance Ian traveled compared to time. Use your graph to find the total distance traveled.

Tell whether the slope is positive or negative. Then find the slope.

6.
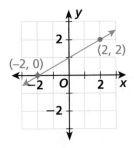

7.
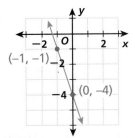

Tell whether each graph shows a constant or variable rate of change. If constant, find the slope.

8.
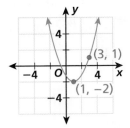

9.
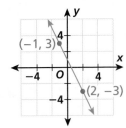

Tell whether each equation represents a direct variation. If so, identify the constant of variation.

10. $5y = 10x$ **11.** $y - 3 = x$ **12.** $x + y = 4$ **13.** $-7x = y$

Test Tackler
STANDARDIZED TEST STRATEGIES

Extended Response: Understand the Scores

Extended-response test items usually involve multiple steps and require a detailed explanation. The items are scored using a 4-point rubric. A complete and correct response is worth 4 points, a partial response is worth 2 to 3 points, an incorrect response with no work shown is worth 1 point, and no response at all is worth 0 points.

EXAMPLE 1

Extended Response A 10-pound bag of apples costs $4. Write and solve a proportion to find how much a 15-pound bag of apples would cost at the same rate. Explain how the increase in weight is related to the increase in cost.

Here are examples of how different responses were scored using the scoring rubric shown.

4-point response:

Let c = the cost of the 15 lb bag.
$$\frac{10 \text{ pounds}}{\$4} = \frac{15 \text{ pounds}}{c}$$
$$10 \cdot c = 4 \cdot 15$$
$$\frac{10c}{10} = \frac{60}{10}$$
$$c = 6$$

The 15 lb bag costs $6.

For every additional 5 pounds, the cost increases by 2 dollars.

3-point response:

Let c = the cost of the 15 lb bag.
$$\frac{10 \text{ pounds}}{\$4} = \frac{15 \text{ pounds}}{c}$$
$$10 \cdot c = 4 \cdot 15$$
$$\frac{10c}{10} = \frac{60}{10}$$
$$c = 6$$

The 15 lb bag costs $6.

For every additional 5 pounds, the cost increases by 6 dollars.

The proportion is set up and solved correctly, and all work is shown, but the explanation is incorrect.

2-point response:

Let c = the cost of the apples.
$$\frac{10 \text{ pounds}}{\$4} = \frac{c}{15 \text{ pounds}}$$
$$10 \cdot 15 = 4 \cdot c$$
$$\frac{150}{4} = \frac{4c}{4}$$
$$37.5 = c$$

The proportion is set up incorrectly, and no explanation is given.

1-point response:

$$37.5 = c$$

The answer is incorrect, no work is shown, and no explanation is given.

Read each test item and answer the questions that follow using the scoring rubric below.

Scoring Rubric

4 points: The student correctly answers all parts of the question, shows all work, and provides a complete and correct explanation.

3 points: The student answers all parts of the question, shows all work, and provides a complete explanation that demonstrates understanding, but the student makes minor errors in computation.

2 points: The student does not answer all parts of the question but shows all work and provides a complete and correct explanation for the parts answered, or the student correctly answers all parts of the question but does not show all work or does not provide an explanation.

1 point: The student gives incorrect answers and shows little or no work or explanation, or the student does not follow directions.

0 points: The student gives no response.

Item A
Extended Response Alex drew a model of a birdhouse using a scale of 1 inch to 3 inches. On the drawing, the house is 6 inches tall. Define a variable, and then write and solve a proportion to find how many inches tall the actual birdhouse is.

1. Should the response shown receive a score of 4 points? Why or why not?

$$\frac{1 \text{ inch}}{6 \text{ inches}} = \frac{3 \text{ inches}}{h}$$
$$1 \cdot h = 3 \cdot 6$$
$$h = 18$$
The actual birdhouse is 18 inches tall.

Item B
Extended Response Consider the ordered pairs (1, 2), (2, 4), (3, 9), and (4, 16). Use a table to write an equation for y in terms of x. Then find the values of y for $x = 5$, 6, and 7.

2. What should you add to the response shown, if anything, so that it receives full credit?

x	1	2	3	4
y	2	4	8	16
Rule	$y = 2^1$	$y = 2^2$	$y = 2^3$	$y = 2^4$

The rule is $y = 2^x$.

Item C
Extended Response The figures are similar. Find the value of x and the sum of the side lengths of one of the figures.

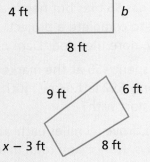

3. What needs to be included in a response that would receive 4 points?

4. Write a response that would receive full credit.

Standardized Test Prep

Learn It Online
State Test Practice

Cumulative Assessment

Multiple Choice

1. The fraction $\frac{7}{12}$ is found between which pair of numbers on a number line?

   Ⓐ $\frac{5}{12}$ and $\frac{1}{2}$ Ⓒ $\frac{1}{3}$ and $\frac{11}{24}$

   Ⓑ $\frac{13}{24}$ and $\frac{3}{4}$ Ⓓ $\frac{2}{3}$ and $\frac{5}{6}$

2. For which equation is $x = -10$ the solution?

   Ⓕ $2x - 20 = 0$

   Ⓖ $\frac{1}{5}x + 2 = 0$

   Ⓗ $\frac{1}{5}x - 2 = 0$

   Ⓙ $-2x + 20 = 0$

3. What is the least common multiple of 10, 25, and 30?

   Ⓐ 5   Ⓒ 150

   Ⓑ 50   Ⓓ 200

4. Which problem situation matches the equation below?

   $$x + 55 = 92$$

   Ⓕ Liam has 55 tiles but needs a total of 92 to complete a project. How many more tiles does Liam need?

   Ⓖ Cher spent $55 at the market and has only $92 left. How much did Cher start with?

   Ⓗ Byron drove 55 miles each day for 92 days. How many total miles did he drive?

   Ⓙ For every 55 students who buy "spirit wear," the boosters donate $92. How many students have bought spirit wear so far?

5. A recipe that makes 2 cups of guacamole dip calls for $1\frac{3}{4}$ cups of mashed avocados. How much avocado is needed to make 4 cups of dip with this recipe?

   Ⓐ 3.25 cups   Ⓒ 3.75 cups

   Ⓑ 3.5 cups   Ⓓ 4 cups

6. Which ordered pair is located on the x-axis?

   Ⓕ $(0, -5)$ Ⓗ $(-5, 0)$

   Ⓖ $(5, -5)$ Ⓙ $(1, -5)$

7. Which ordered pair is NOT a solution of $y = 5x - 4$?

   Ⓐ $(2, 6)$ Ⓒ $(1, 0)$

   Ⓑ $(0, -4)$ Ⓓ $(-1, -9)$

 HOT TIP! Work backward from the answer choices if you cannot remember how to solve a problem.

8. Carolyn makes between $5.75 and $9.50 per hour baby-sitting. Which is the best estimate of the total amount she makes for 9 hours of baby-sitting?

   Ⓕ From $30 to $55

   Ⓖ From $55 to $80

   Ⓗ From $80 to $105

   Ⓙ From $105 to $130

Gridded Response

9. Patrick plans to spend the next 28 days preparing for a weight-lifting competition. He plans to spend a total of 119 hours at the gym. If Patrick is at the gym for the same amount of time every day, how many hours will he be at the gym each day?

10. Solve the equation $-4.3x = -0.215$ for x.

11. Determine the y-coordinate of the point.

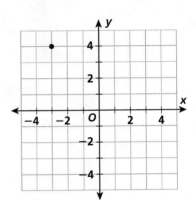

Short Response

S1. A teacher discussed 112 of the 164 pages of the textbook. What portion of the pages did the teacher discuss? Write your answer as a decimal rounded to the nearest thousandth and as a fraction in simplest form.

S2. A bag of nickels and quarters contains four times as many nickels as quarters. The total value of the coins in the bag is $1.35.

  a. How many nickels are in the bag?

  b. How many quarters are in the bag?

S3. Describe in what order you would perform the operations to find the value of $(4 \cdot 4 - 6)^2 + (5 \cdot 7)$.

S4. A recipe calls for $\frac{3}{4}$ cup flour and $\frac{2}{3}$ cup butter. Does the recipe require more flour or butter? Is this still true if the recipe is doubled? Explain how you determined your answer.

Extended Response

E1. A bus travels at an average rate of 50 miles per hour from Nashville, Tennessee, to El Paso, Texas. To find the distance y traveled in x hours, use the equation $y = 50x$.

  a. Make a table of ordered pairs using the domain $x = 1, 2, 3, 4,$ and 5.

  b. Graph the solutions from the table of ordered pairs on a coordinate plane.

  c. Brett leaves Nashville by bus at 6:00 A.M. He needs to be in El Paso by 5:00 A.M. the following day. If Nashville is 1,100 miles from El Paso, will Brett make it on time? Explain how you determined your answer.

Percents

Chapter Focus
- Work with proportions involving percents.
- Solve a wide variety of percent problems.

Why Learn This?

Percents are commonly used to express and compare ratios. For example, about 70% of the Earth's surface is covered in water.

Learn It Online
Chapter Project Online

Detlev van Ravenswaay/Photo Researchers, Inc.

Are You Ready?

✓ Vocabulary

Choose the best term from the list to complete each sentence.

1. A statement that two ratios are equivalent is called a(n) __?__.

2. To write $\frac{2}{3}$ as a(n) __?__, divide the numerator by the denominator.

3. A(n) __?__ is a comparison by division of two quantities.

4. The __?__ of $\frac{9}{24}$ is $\frac{3}{8}$.

decimal

equation

fraction

proportion

ratio

simplest form

Complete these exercises to review skills you will need for this chapter.

✓ Write Fractions as Decimals

Write each fraction as a decimal.

5. $\frac{8}{10}$ **6.** $\frac{53}{100}$ **7.** $\frac{739}{1,000}$ **8.** $\frac{7}{100}$

9. $\frac{2}{5}$ **10.** $\frac{5}{8}$ **11.** $\frac{7}{12}$ **12.** $\frac{13}{20}$

✓ Write Decimals as Fractions

Write each decimal as a fraction in simplest form.

13. 0.05   **14.** 0.92   **15.** 0.013   **16.** 0.8

17. 0.006   **18.** 0.305   **19.** 0.0007   **20.** 1.04

✓ Solve Multiplication Equations

Solve each equation.

21. $100n = 300$ **22.** $38 = 0.4x$ **23.** $16p = 1,200$

24. $9 = 72y$ **25.** $0.07m = 56$ **26.** $25 = 100t$

✓ Solve Proportions

Solve each proportion.

27. $\frac{2}{3} = \frac{x}{12}$ **28.** $\frac{x}{20} = \frac{3}{4}$ **29.** $\frac{8}{15} = \frac{x}{45}$

30. $\frac{16}{28} = \frac{4}{n}$ **31.** $\frac{p}{100} = \frac{12}{36}$ **32.** $\frac{42}{12} = \frac{14}{n}$

33. $\frac{8}{y} = \frac{10}{5}$ **34.** $\frac{6}{9} = \frac{d}{24}$ **35.** $\frac{21}{a} = \frac{7}{5}$

Where You've Been

Previously, you

- modeled percents.

- wrote equivalent fractions, decimals, and percents.

- solved percent problems involving discounts, sales tax, and tips.

In This Chapter

You will study

- modeling and estimating percents.

- writing equivalent fractions, decimals, and percents, including percents less than 1 and greater than 100.

- solving percent problems involving discounts, sales tax, tips, profit, percent of change, commissions, and simple interest.

- comparing fractions, decimals, and percents.

Where You're Going

You can use the skills learned in this chapter

- to find or estimate discounts, sales tax, and tips when shopping and eating out.

- to solve problems involving banking.

Key Vocabulary/Vocabulario

interest	interés
percent of change	porcentaje de cambio
percent of decrease	porcentaje de disminución
percent of increase	porcentaje de incremento
principal	capital
simple interest	interés simple

Vocabulary Connections

To become familiar with some of the vocabulary terms in the chapter, consider the following. You may refer to the chapter, the glossary, or a dictionary if you like.

1. The word *interest* stems from Latin (*inter- + esse*) and means "to be between" and "to make a difference." In business, interest is an amount collected or paid for the use of money. How can you relate the Latin roots and meanings to the business definition of **interest**?

2. *Principal* is the amount of money deposited or borrowed. Interest builds upon the principal. How might common definitions of *principal*, such as "leader of a school" and "a matter of primary importance," help you remember this business meaning of **principal**?

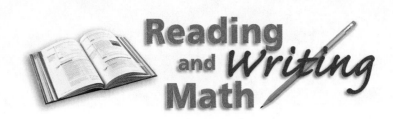 

Reading and Writing Math

Study Strategy: Use Multiple Representations

When a new math concept is introduced, the explanation given often presents the topic in more than one way. As you study, pay attention to any models, tables, lists, graphs, diagrams, symbols, and words used to describe a concept.

In this example, the concept of finding equivalent fractions is represented in model, number, and word form.

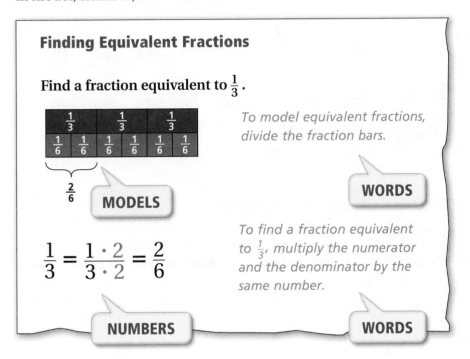

Finding Equivalent Fractions

Find a fraction equivalent to $\frac{1}{3}$.

| $\frac{1}{3}$ | $\frac{1}{3}$ | $\frac{1}{3}$ |

| $\frac{1}{6}$ | $\frac{1}{6}$ | $\frac{1}{6}$ | $\frac{1}{6}$ | $\frac{1}{6}$ | $\frac{1}{6}$ |

$\frac{2}{6}$

MODELS

To model equivalent fractions, divide the fraction bars.

WORDS

$$\frac{1}{3} = \frac{1 \cdot 2}{3 \cdot 2} = \frac{2}{6}$$

To find a fraction equivalent to $\frac{1}{3}$, multiply the numerator and the denominator by the same number.

NUMBERS

WORDS

Try This

1. Explain why it could be beneficial to represent a new idea in more than one way when taking notes.

2. Explain how you can use models and numbers to find equivalent fractions. Which method do you prefer? Explain.

6-1 Fractions, Decimals, and Percents

COMMON CORE

CC.7.EE.3 Solve multi-step real-life and mathematical problems posed with positive and negative rational numbers in any form (whole numbers, fractions, and decimals), using tools strategically. Apply properties of operations to calculate with numbers in any form; convert between forms as appropriate; and assess the reasonableness of answers using mental computation and estimation strategies.

The students at Westview Middle School are collecting cans of food for the local food bank. Their goal is to collect 2,000 cans in one month. After 10 days, they have 800 cans of food.

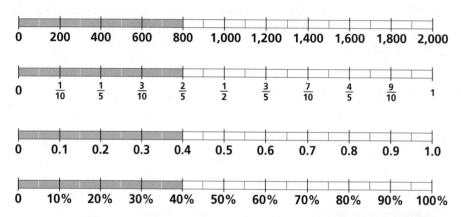

Interactivities Online ▶

The models show that 800 out of 2,000 can be written as $\frac{800}{2,000}$, $\frac{2}{5}$, 0.4, or 40%. The students have reached 40% of their goal.

EXAMPLE **Writing Decimals as Percents**

Write 0.2 as a percent.

Method 1: Use pencil and paper.

$0.2 = \frac{2}{10} = \frac{20}{100}$ *Write the decimal as a fraction with a denominator of 100.*

$= 20\%$ *Write the numerator with a percent sign.*

Method 2: Use mental math.

$0.20 = 20.0\%$

$= 20\%$ *Move the decimal point two places to the right and add a percent sign.*

EXAMPLE **Writing Fractions as Percents**

Write $\frac{4}{5}$ as a percent.

Remember!

To divide 4 by 5, use long division and place a decimal point followed by a zero after the 4.

$$\begin{array}{r} 0.8 \\ 5\overline{)4.0} \end{array}$$

Method 1: Use pencil and paper.

$\frac{4}{5} = 4 \div 5$ *Use division to write the fraction as a decimal.*

$= 0.8$

$= 0.80$

$= 80\%$ *Write the decimal as a percent.*

Method 2: Use mental math.

$\frac{4 \cdot 20}{5 \cdot 20} = \frac{80}{100}$ *Write an equivalent fraction with a denominator of 100.*

$= 80\%$ *Write the numerator with a percent sign.*

---

232   *Chapter 6 Percents*   Video **Lesson Tutorials Online**   my.hrw.com

EXAMPLE 3

Ordering Rational Numbers

Order $1\frac{4}{5}$, $0.\overline{33}$, -1.6, 3, $2\frac{1}{5}$, and 70.2% from least to greatest.

Step 1 Write the numbers as decimals with the same number of decimal places.

$$1\frac{4}{5} = 1.8 \qquad 0.\overline{33} \approx 0.3 \qquad -1.6 = -1.6$$
$$3 = 3.0 \qquad 2\frac{1}{5} = 2.2 \qquad 70.2\% \approx 0.7$$

Step 2 Graph the numbers on a number line.

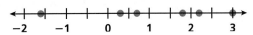

Step 3 Compare the decimals.

$$-1.6 < 0.3 < 0.7 < 1.8 < 2.2 < 3.0$$

From least to greatest, the numbers are: -1.6, $0.\overline{33}$, 70.2%, $1\frac{4}{5}$, $2\frac{1}{5}$, 3

EXAMPLE 4

Choosing a Method of Computation

Decide whether using pencil and paper, mental math, or a calculator is most useful when solving the following problem. Then solve.

In a survey, 55 people were asked whether they prefer cats or dogs. Twenty-nine people said they prefer cats. What percent of the people surveyed said they prefer cats?

29 out of $55 = \frac{29}{55}$

Think: Since 29 ÷ 55 does not divide evenly, pencil and paper is not a good choice.

Think: Since the denominator is not a factor of 100, mental math is not a good choice.

Using a calculator is the best method.

29 ÷ 55 ENTER [0.5272727273]

$0.5272727273 = 52.72727273\%$ *Write the decimal as a percent.*

$\approx 52.7\%$ *Round to the nearest tenth of a percent.*

About 52.7% of the people surveyed said they prefer cats.

MATHEMATICAL PRACTICES

Think and Discuss

1. Describe two methods you could use to write $\frac{3}{4}$ as a percent.

2. Write the ratio 25:100 as a fraction, as a decimal, and as a percent.

GUIDED PRACTICE

See Example 1 | **Write each decimal as a percent.**

1. 0.6   **2.** 0.32   **3.** 0.544   **4.** 0.06   **5.** 0.087

See Example 2 | **Write each fraction as a percent.**

6. $\frac{1}{4}$ **7.** $\frac{3}{25}$ **8.** $\frac{11}{20}$ **9.** $\frac{7}{40}$ **10.** $\frac{5}{8}$

See Example 3 | **Order the numbers from least to greatest.**

11. $0.\overline{5}$, 50%, $\frac{11}{20}$ **12.** $\frac{7}{8}$, -0.9, 90%

13. 10%, 1%, $-\frac{1}{10}$ **14.** -0.8, $\frac{4}{5}$, 8%

15. 72%, $\frac{35}{54}$, $0.\overline{6}$ **16.** $-\frac{1}{2}$, 5%, -0.05

See Example 4 | **17. Decide whether using pencil and paper, mental math, or a calculator is most useful when solving the following problem. Then solve.**

In a survey, 50 students were asked whether they prefer pepperoni pizza or cheese pizza. Twenty students said they prefer cheese pizza. What percent of the students surveyed said they prefer cheese pizza?

INDEPENDENT PRACTICE

See Example 1 | **Write each decimal as a percent.**

18. 0.15   **19.** 0.83   **20.** 0.325   **21.** 0.081   **22.** 0.42

See Example 2 | **Write each fraction as a percent.**

23. $\frac{3}{4}$ **24.** $\frac{2}{5}$ **25.** $\frac{3}{8}$ **26.** $\frac{3}{16}$ **27.** $\frac{7}{25}$

See Example 3 | **Order the numbers from least to greatest.**

28. $0.\overline{6}$, 6%, $\frac{3}{5}$ **29.** $-\frac{2}{3}$, -0.7, 7%

30. $\frac{8}{3}$, 30%, 3   **31.** -0.1, 1%, $-\frac{1}{9}$

32. 2%, $\frac{5}{4}$, $1.\overline{1}$ **33.** $-\frac{1}{6}$, -0.01, 2%

See Example 4 | **Decide whether using pencil and paper, mental math, or a calculator is most useful when solving each of the following problems. Then solve.**

34. In a theme-park survey, 75 visitors were asked whether they prefer the Ferris wheel or the roller coaster. Thirty visitors prefer the Ferris wheel. What percent of the visitors surveyed said they prefer the Ferris wheel?

35. In a survey, 65 students were asked whether they prefer television sitcoms or dramas. Thirteen students prefer dramas. What percent of the students surveyed prefer dramas?

Extra Practice
See Extra Practice for more exercises.

Compare. Write <, >, or =.

36. 9% ▮ 0.9

37. 45% ▮ $\frac{2}{5}$

38. 0.037 ▮ 37%

39. $\frac{7}{12}$ ▮ 60%

40. **Life Science** Rain forests are home to 90,000 of the 250,000 identified plant species in the world. What percent of the world's identified plant species are found in rain forests?

41. **Multi-Step** One-half of the 900 students at Jefferson Middle School are boys. One-tenth of the boys are in the band, and one-fifth of those play the trumpet. What percent of the students at Jefferson are boys who play the trumpet in the band?

Use the table for Exercises 42–45.

42. What percent of the championship appearances did Dudley win?

43. Write the schools in order from least portion of games won to greatest portion of games won.

44. Which school won 5 out of 6 games?

45. Estimate the percent of the games Wallace-Rose Hill lost.

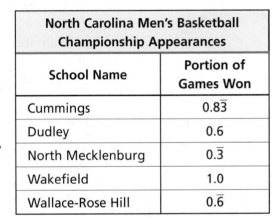

North Carolina Men's Basketball Championship Appearances	
School Name	Portion of Games Won
Cummings	$0.8\overline{3}$
Dudley	0.6
North Mecklenburg	$0.\overline{3}$
Wakefield	1.0
Wallace-Rose Hill	$0.\overline{6}$

46. **What's the Error?** A student wrote $\frac{2}{5}$ as 0.4%. What was the error?

47. **Write About It** Describe two ways to change a fraction to a percent.

48. **Challenge** A desert area's average rainfall is 12 inches a year. This year the area received 15 inches of rain. What percent of the average rainfall amount is 15 inches?

One of the world's largest flowers, the Titan arum, is native to the Sumatran rain forests. These flowers can grow to over 6 feet tall; the tallest ever recorded was over 10 feet tall.

Test Prep

49. **Multiple Choice** Which value is NOT equivalent to 45%?

Ⓐ $\frac{9}{20}$ Ⓑ 0.45   Ⓒ $\frac{45}{100}$ Ⓓ 0.045

50. **Short Response** Melanie's room measures 10 ft by 12 ft. Her rug covers 90 ft². Explain how to determine the percent of floor covered by the rug.

Estimating with Percents

CC.7.EE.3 Solve multi-step real-life and mathematical problems posed with positive and negative rational numbers in any form (whole numbers, fractions, and decimals)… using mental computation and estimation strategies.

A basketball at Hoops Haven costs $14.99. Cam's Sports is offering the same basketball at 20% off the regular price of $19.99. To find out which store is offering the better deal on the basketball, you can use estimation.

The table shows common percents and their fraction equivalents. You can estimate the percent of a number by substituting a fraction that is close to a given percent.

Percent	10%	20%	25%	$33\frac{1}{3}$%	50%	$66\frac{2}{3}$%
Fraction	$\frac{1}{10}$	$\frac{1}{5}$	$\frac{1}{4}$	$\frac{1}{3}$	$\frac{1}{2}$	$\frac{2}{3}$

EXAMPLE 1 Using Fractions to Estimate Percents

Use a fraction to estimate 48% of 79.

48% of $79 \approx \frac{1}{2} \cdot 79$ *Think: 48% is about 50% and 50% is equivalent to $\frac{1}{2}$.*

$\approx \frac{1}{2} \cdot 80$ *Change 79 to a compatible number.*

≈ 40 *Multiply.*

48% of 79 is about 40.

Remember!

Compatible numbers are close to the numbers in a problem and help you use mental math to find a solution.

EXAMPLE 2 *Consumer Math Application*

Cam's Sports is offering 20% off a basketball that costs $19.99. The same basketball costs $14.99 at Hoops Haven. Which store offers the better deal?

First find the discount on the basketball at Cam's Sports.

20% of $\$19.99 = \frac{1}{5} \cdot \$19.99$ *Think: 20% is equivalent to $\frac{1}{5}$.*

$\approx \frac{1}{5} \cdot \$20$ *Change $19.99 to a compatible number.*

$\approx \$4$ *Multiply.*

The discount is approximately $4. Since $20 − $4 = $16, the $14.99 basketball at Hoops Haven is the better deal.

Video **Lesson Tutorials Online** my.hrw.com

Another way to estimate percents is to find 1% or 10% of a number. You can do this by moving the decimal point in the number.

1% of 45: 45.0   10% of 45: 45.0

= 0.45   = 4.5

To find 1% of a number, move the decimal point two places to the left.   *To find 10% of a number, move the decimal point one place to the left.*

E X A M P L E 3 Estimating with Simple Percents

Use 1% or 10% to estimate the percent of each number.

A **3% of 59**

59 is about 60, so find 3% of 60.

1% of 60 = 60.0 = **0.60**

3% of 60 = 3 · 0.60 = 1.8   *3% equals 3 · 1%.*

3% of 59 is about 1.8.

B **18% of 45**

18% is about 20%, so find 20% of 45.

10% of 45 = 45.0 = 4.5

20% of 45 = 2 · 4.5 = 9.0   *20% equals 2 · 10%.*

18% of 45 is about 9.

E X A M P L E 4 *Consumer Math Application*

Eric and Selena spent $25.85 for their meals at a restaurant. About how much money should they leave for a 15% tip?

Since $25.85 is about $26, find 15% of $26.

15% = **10%** + **5%**   *Think: 15% is 10% plus 5%.*

10% of $26 = **$2.60**

5% of $26 = **$2.60** ÷ 2 = **$1.30**   *5% is $\frac{1}{2}$ of 10%, so divide $2.60 by 2.*

$2.60 + **$1.30** = **$3.90**   *Add the 10% and 5% estimates.*

Eric and Selena should leave about $3.90 for a 15% tip.

Think and Discuss

1. Describe two ways to estimate 51% of 88.

2. Explain why you might divide by 7 or multiply by $\frac{1}{7}$ to estimate a 15% tip.

3. Give an example of a situation in which an estimate of a percent is sufficient and a situation in which an exact percent is necessary.

GUIDED PRACTICE

See Example 1 **Use a fraction to estimate the percent of each number.**

    1. 30% of 86   **2.** 52% of 83   **3.** 10% of 48   **4.** 27% of 63

See Example 2   **5.** Darden has $35. He finds a backpack on sale for 35% off the regular price of $43.99. Does Darden have enough to buy the backpack? Explain.

See Example 3 **Use 1% or 10% to estimate the percent of each number.**

    6. 5% of 82   **7.** 39% of 19   **8.** 21% of 68   **9.** 7% of 109

See Example 4   **10.** Mrs. Coronado spent $23 on a manicure. About how much money should she leave for a 15% tip?

INDEPENDENT PRACTICE

See Example 1 **Use a fraction to estimate the percent of each number.**

    11. 8% of 261   **12.** 34% of 93   **13.** 53% of 142   **14.** 23% of 98

    15. 51% of 432   **16.** 18% of 42   **17.** 11% of 132   **18.** 54% of 39

See Example 2   **19. Consumer Math** A pair of shoes at The Value Store costs $20. Fancy Feet has the same shoes on sale for 25% off the regular price of $23.99. Which store offers the better price on the shoes?

See Example 3 **Use 1% or 10% to estimate the percent of each number.**

    20. 41% of 16   **21.** 8% of 310   **22.** 83% of 70   **23.** 2% of 634

    24. 58% of 81   **25.** 24% of 49   **26.** 11% of 99   **27.** 63% of 39

See Example 4   **28.** Marc's lunch cost $8.92. He wants to leave a 15% tip for the service. About how much should his tip be?

PRACTICE AND PROBLEM SOLVING

Extra Practice
See Extra Practice for more exercises.

Estimate.

    29. 31% of 180   **30.** 18% of 150   **31.** 3% of 96   **32.** 2% of 198

    33. 78% of 90   **34.** 52% of 234   **35.** 19% of 75   **36.** 4% of 311

37. The new package of Marti's Snacks contains 20% more snack mix than the old package. There were 22 ounces of snack mix in the old package. About how many ounces are in the new package?

38. Frameworks charges $60.85 for framing. Including the 7% sales tax, about how much will it cost to have a painting framed?

39. Multi-Step Camden's lunch cost $11.67, and he left a $2.00 tip. About how much more than 15% of the bill did Camden leave for the tip?

40. Sports Last season, Ali had a hit 19.3% of the times he came to bat. If Ali batted 82 times last season, about how many hits did he have?

41. Business The graph shows the results of a survey about the Internet. The number of people interviewed was 391.

a. Estimate the number of people willing to give out their e-mail address.

b. Estimate the number of people not willing to give out their credit card number.

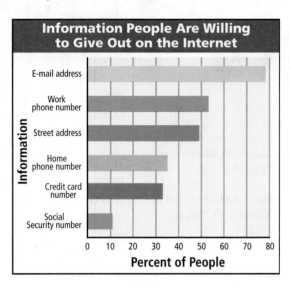

42. Estimation Sandi earns $43,000 per year. This year, she plans to spend about 27% of her income on rent.

a. About how much does Sandi plan to spend on rent this year?

b. About how much does she plan to spend on rent each month?

43. Write a Problem Use information from the graph in Exercise 41 to write a problem that can be solved by using estimation of a percent.

44. Write About It Explain why it might be important to know whether your estimate of a percent is too high or too low. Give an example.

45. Challenge Use the graph from Exercise 41 to estimate how many more people will give out their work phone number than their Social Security number. Show your work using two different methods.

Test Prep

46. Multiple Choice About 65% of the people answering a survey said that they have read a "blog," or Web log, online. Sixty-six people were surveyed. Which is the best estimate of the number of people surveyed who have read a blog?

Ⓐ 30   Ⓑ 35   Ⓒ 45   Ⓓ 50

47. Short Response Ryan's dinner bill is $35.00. He wants to leave a 15% tip. Explain how to use mental math to determine how much he should leave as a tip.

Using Properties with Rational Numbers

COMMON CORE

CC.7.EE.2 Understand that rewriting an expression in different forms in a problem context can shed light on the problem and how the quantities in it are related *Also CC.7.NS.1d, CC.7.NS.2a, CC.7.NS.2b, CC.7.NS.2c, CC.7.EE.3*

Orlando works part-time at a moving company to earn money for a car. He earns $12.75 per hour.

You can use the Distributive Property to calculate Orlando's total earnings two different ways.

The Distributive Property can be used to help you perform calculations more easily by writing equivalent expressions.

EXAMPLE 1 **Writing Equivalent Expressions**

Orlando works part-time at a moving company. He earns $12.75 per hour. He works for 4 hours on Friday and 7 hours on Saturday. Use the Distributive Property to write equivalent expressions showing two ways to calculate Orlando's total earnings.

Write an expression to show Orlando's total earnings using his pay per hour and how many hours he works. Then use the Distributive Property to write an equivalent expression.

> **Remember!**
>
> The Distributive Property states:
> $a(b + c) = ab + ac$
> $a(b - c) = ab - ac$

Pay per hour	·	Total number of hours	=	Pay per hour	·	Fri hours	+	Pay per hour	·	Sat hours
$12.75	·	(4 + 7)	=	$12.75	·	4	+	$12.75	·	7

Simplify each expression to calculate Orlando's total earnings.

Method 1	Method 2
$12.75 · (4 + 7)	$12.75 · 4 + $12.75 · 7
$12.75 · 11	$51 + $89.25
$140.25	$140.25

Both methods result in a calculation of $140.25 for Orlando's total earnings.

Properties of rational numbers can also be used to make solving equations equations easier.

EXAMPLE 2 | **Writing Equivalent Equations without Fractions**

Write an equivalent equation for $\frac{1}{3}x - 4 = \frac{2}{5}$ that does not contain fractions. Then solve the equation.

$$\frac{1}{3}x - 4 = \frac{2}{5}$$ *The LCM of the denominators is 15.*

$$15\left(\frac{1}{3}x - 4\right) = 15\left(\frac{2}{5}\right)$$ *Multiply both sides by 15.*

$$\overset{5}{15}\left(\frac{1}{\cancel{3}_1}x\right) - 15(4) = \overset{3}{15}\left(\frac{2}{\cancel{5}_1}\right)$$ *Simplify.*

$$5x - 60 = 6$$ *$5x - 60 = 6$ is an equivalent equation.*

$$\underline{+60 \quad +60}$$ *Add 60 to each side.*

$$\frac{5x}{5} = \frac{66}{5}$$ *Divide both sides by 5.*

$$x = 13\frac{1}{5}$$

An equivalent equation is $5x - 60 = 6$ and the solution is $13\frac{1}{5}$.

EXAMPLE 3 | *Construction Application*

Maxine is replacing a 14.25-meter row of wood floor. She has already placed a strip that is 0.75 meter long. How many 1.5-meter strips of wood does she need to finish the row? Write and solve an equivalent equation without decimals.

Write an equation to represent the situation.

Number of 1.5-m strips left	+	0.75-m strip placed	=	14.25 m total
1.5x	+	0.75	=	14.25

Write an equivalent equation without decimals.

Helpful Hint

0.75 can also be written as $\frac{75}{100}$.

$$1.5x + 0.75 = 14.25$$ *The equation has decimals to the hundredths, so multiply both sides by 100.*

$$100(1.5x + 0.75) = 100(14.25)$$

$$100(1.5x) + 100(0.75) = 100(14.25)$$ *Use the Distributive Property.*

$$150x + 75 = 1{,}425$$ *Simplify to get an equivalent equation without decimals.*

$$\underline{-75 \quad -75}$$

$$150x = 1{,}350$$

$$\frac{150x}{150} = \frac{1{,}350}{150}$$

$$x = 9$$

The number of 1.5-meter strips of wood that Maxine needs is 9.

MATHEMATICAL PRACTICES

Think and Discuss

1. Explain how the Multiplication Property of Equality is used to write an equivalent equation without fractions or decimals.

See Example **1** Use the Distributive Property to write equivalent expressions showing two ways to calculate each problem.

1. Kate earns $14.25 per hour and Joan earns $11.75 per hour. They each work 8 hours. How much do they earn together?

2. Kimber and Andy each can assemble 12 circuit boards in one hour. Kimber works for 6 hours and Andy works for 12 hours. How many more circuit boards does Andy assemble than Kimber?

See Example **2** Write an equivalent equation that does not contain fractions. Then solve the equation.

3. $\frac{2}{3}x - 9 = \frac{3}{4}$

4. $\frac{1}{5}x + 8 = \frac{3}{4}$

5. $\frac{3}{7}x + 3 = \frac{1}{8}$

6. $\frac{1}{6}x - 4 = \frac{2}{9}$

7. $\frac{5}{8}x - 10 = \frac{3}{4}$

8. $\frac{4}{5}x - 12 = \frac{3}{4}$

See Example **3** 9. Nancy places $7.15 in an envelope each week. She currently has $64.25 in it. In how many weeks will she have $121.45 in the envelope? Write and solve an equivalent equation without decimals.

See Example **1** Use the Distributive Property to write equivalent expressions showing two ways to calculate each problem.

10. Clare bought 11 pens at $1.39 each and 11 pencils at $0.79 each. How much did she spend altogether?

11. Mr. Cramer runs on a treadmill 4 days per week for 1.5 hours per day. He rides a bike on the other 3 days for 1.5 hours per day. How many hours per week does Mr. Cramer exercise?

See Example **2** Write an equivalent equation that does not contain fractions. Then solve the equation.

12. $\frac{1}{5}x + 6 = \frac{3}{4}$

13. $\frac{2}{3}x - 7 = \frac{1}{2}$

14. $\frac{1}{7}x + 9 = \frac{3}{5}$

15. $\frac{5}{8}x - 3 = \frac{3}{4}$

16. $\frac{4}{5}x + 12 = \frac{3}{10}$

17. $\frac{2}{3}x + 8 = \frac{5}{6}$

18. $\frac{4}{5}x - 2 = \frac{2}{3}$

19. $\frac{2}{7}x + 10 = \frac{1}{3}$

20. $\frac{5}{6}x - 7 = \frac{3}{4}$

See Example **3** 21. Tony spent $50.35 on office supplies. He bought markers for $3.80 each and an organizer for $19.95. How many markers did Tony buy? Write and solve an equivalent equation without decimals.

Health

Long hair can be cut and donated to make real-hair wigs. Various criteria apply for different organizations and most donations must be at least 8, 10, or even 12 inches in length.

22. There are 34 students in a watercolor painting class, and 21 students in a oil painting class. Each student submits 6 art pieces to be graded. How many more pieces of art did the watercolor painting class submit?

23. Jack and Karl take turns driving to and from work. This week, Karl drives 3 days, and Jack drives 2 days. The distance each day is the same, 89 miles round trip. How many more miles does Karl drive than Jack this week?

24. Health The average rate of growth for human hair is about 0.3 millimeter per day. Write and solve an equation to find about how many days it will take a hair that is 12 millimeters long to grow to be 16.5 millimeters long.

Write an equivalent equation that does not contain fractions or decimals. Then solve the equation.

25. $\frac{1}{2}x + 6 = \frac{3}{4}$

26. $\frac{5}{6}x - 7 = \frac{1}{3}$

27. $\frac{2}{3}x - 7 = \frac{2}{5}$

28. $0.25x - 4 = 0.5$

29. $0.5x - 6.8 = 12.4$

30. $0.25x - 0.25 = 0.125$

31. What's the Error? A student solved the equation $\frac{3}{4}x + 8 = \frac{1}{3}$ as shown to the right. Explain the error the student made. What is the correct answer?

$$\frac{3}{4}x + 8 = \frac{1}{3}$$
$${}^{3}\cancel{12}\left(\frac{3}{\cancel{4}_1}x + 8\right) = {}^{4}\cancel{12}\left(\frac{1}{\cancel{3}_1}\right)$$
$$9x + 8 = 4$$
$$9x = -4$$
$$x = -\frac{4}{9}$$

32. Write About It Explain how to write an equivalent equation that does not contain fractions from an equation that does contain fractions.

33. Challenge Solve the equation $\frac{3}{5}x + \frac{1}{2} = \frac{3}{4}$ by writing an equivalent equation that does not contain fractions.

Test Prep

34. Multiple Choice Which equation has a solution of $x = -18$?

   Ⓐ $\frac{1}{8}x - 3 = \frac{3}{4}$ Ⓑ $\frac{1}{8}x + 3 = \frac{3}{4}$ Ⓒ $\frac{1}{6}x + 9 = \frac{1}{3}$ Ⓓ $\frac{1}{2}x - 9 = \frac{1}{6}$

35. Gridded Response Solve the equation $2.5x + 9 = 26.5$ by writing an equivalent equation without decimals.

Ready To Go On?

Quiz for Lessons 1 Through 3

 1 **Fractions, Decimals, and Percents**

Write each decimal as a percent.

1. 0.85 **2.** 0.026 **3.** 0.1111 **4.** 0.56

Write each fraction as a percent. Round to the nearest tenth of a percent, if necessary.

5. $\frac{14}{81}$ **6.** $\frac{25}{52}$ **7.** $\frac{55}{78}$ **8.** $\frac{13}{32}$

 2 **Estimating with Percents**

Estimate.

9. 49% of 46 **10.** 9% of 25 **11.** 36% of 150 **12.** 5% of 60

13. 18% of 80 **14.** 26% of 115 **15.** 91% of 300 **16.** 42% of 197

17. Carlton spent $21.85 on lunch for himself and a friend. About how much should he leave for a 15% tip?

 3 **Using Properties with Rational Numbers**

Write an equivalent equation that does not contain fractions. Then solve the equation.

18. $\frac{3}{4}x - 7 = \frac{1}{2}$ **19.** $\frac{2}{3}x + 3 = \frac{3}{5}$ **20.** $\frac{3}{5}x - 1 = \frac{1}{2}$

21. Armando spent $9.70 at the grocery store. He spent $2.95 on a bag of baby spinach and bought tomatoes at $2.25 per pound. How many pounds of tomatoes did he buy? Write and solve an equivalent equation without decimals.

Focus on Problem Solving

Make sense of problems and persevere in solving them.

Make a Plan

• **Estimate or find an exact answer**

Sometimes an estimate is sufficient when you are solving a problem. Other times you need to find an exact answer. Before you try to solve a problem, you should decide whether an estimate will be sufficient. Usually if a problem includes the word *about*, then you can estimate the answer.

Read each problem. Decide whether you need an exact answer or whether you can solve the problem with an estimate. Explain how you know.

1 Barry has $21.50 left from his allowance. He wants to buy a book for $5.85 and a CD for $14.99. Assuming these prices include tax, does Barry have enough money left to buy both the book and the CD?

2 Last weekend Valerie practiced playing the drums for 3 hours. This is 40% of the total time she spent practicing last week. How much time did Valerie spend practicing last week?

3 Amber is shopping for a winter coat. She finds one that costs $157. The coat is on sale and is discounted 25% today only. About how much money will Amber save if she buys the coat today?

4 Marcus is planning a budget. He plans to spend less than 35% of his allowance each week on entertainment. Last week Marcus spent $7.42 on entertainment. If Marcus gets $20.00 each week, did he stay within his budget?

5 An upright piano is on sale for 20% off the original price. The original price is $9,840. What is the sale price?

6 The Mapleton Middle School band has 41 students. Six of the students in the band play percussion instruments. Do more than 15% of the students play percussion instruments?

Percent of Change

CC.7.RP.3 Use proportional relationships to solve multistep ratio and percent problems. *Also CC.7.EE.2, CC.7.EE.3*

Vocabulary

percent of change

percent of increase

percent of decrease

According to the U.S. Consumer Product Safety Commission, emergency rooms treated more than 50,000 skateboarding injuries in 2000. This was a 67% decrease from the peak of 150,000 skateboarding injuries in 1977.

A percent can be used to describe an amount of change. The **percent of change** is the amount, stated as a percent, that a number increases or decreases. If the amount goes up, it is a **percent of increase**. If the amount goes down, it is a **percent of decrease**.

You can find the percent of change by using the following formula.

$$\text{percent of change} = \frac{\text{amount of change}}{\text{original amount}}$$

EXAMPLE 1 **Finding Percent of Change**

Find each percent of change. Round answers to the nearest tenth of a percent, if necessary.

A **27 is decreased to 20.**

$27 - 20 = 7$ *Find the amount of change.*

$\text{percent of change} = \frac{7}{27}$ *Substitute values into formula.*

≈ 0.259259 *Divide.*

$\approx 25.9\%$ *Write as a percent. Round.*

The percent of decrease is about 25.9%.

B **32 is increased to 67.**

$67 - 32 = 35$ *Find the amount of change.*

$\text{percent of change} = \frac{35}{32}$ *Substitute values into formula.*

$= 1.09375$ *Divide.*

$\approx 109.4\%$ *Write as a percent. Round.*

The percent of increase is about 109.4%.

> **Helpful Hint**
>
> When a number is decreased, subtract the new amount from the original amount to find the amount of change. When a number is increased, subtract the original amount from the new amount.

Video Lesson Tutorials Online my.hrw.com

Megapress/Alamy

EXAMPLE **2** **Using Percent of Change**

The regular price of an MP3 player at TechSource is $79.99. This week the MP3 player is on sale for 25% off. What is the sale price?

Step 1 Find the amount of the discount.

$$\frac{25}{100} = \frac{d}{\$79.99}$$ *Write a proportion.*

$$25 \cdot \$79.99 = 100d$$ *Set the cross products equal.*

$$\frac{1999.75}{100} = \frac{100d}{100}$$ *Multiply. Then divide each side by 100.*

$$\$20.00 \approx d$$

The amount of the discount *d* is $20.00.

Step 2 Find the sale price.

regular price	−	amount of discount	=	sale price
$79.99	−	$20.00	=	$59.99

The sale price is $59.99.

EXAMPLE **3** *Business Application*

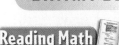
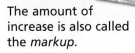

Reading Math

The amount of increase is also called the *markup.*

Winter Wonders buys snow globes from a manufacturer for $9.20 each and sells them at a 95% increase in price. What is the retail price of the snow globes?

Step 1 Find the amount *n* of increase.

95% · 9.20 = *n*   *Think: 95% of $9.20 is what number?*

0.95 · 9.20 = *n*   *Write the percent as a decimal.*

8.74 = *n*

Step 2 Find the retail price.

wholesale price	+	amount of increase	=	retail price
$9.20	+	$8.74	=	$17.94

The retail price of the snow globes is $17.94 each.

MATHEMATICAL PRACTICES

Think and Discuss

1. **Explain** what is meant by a 100% decrease.

2. **Give an example** in which the amount of increase or markup is greater than the original amount. What do you know about the percent of increase?

GUIDED PRACTICE

See Example 1 Find each percent of change. Round answers to the nearest tenth of a percent, if necessary.

1. 25 is decreased to 18.

2. 36 is increased to 84.

3. 62 is decreased to 52.

4. 28 is increased to 96.

See Example 2 **5.** The regular price of a sweater is $42.99. It is on sale for 20% off. Find the sale price.

See Example 3 **6. Business** The retail price of a pair of shoes is a 98% increase from its wholesale price. The wholesale price of the shoes is $12.50. What is the retail price?

INDEPENDENT PRACTICE

See Example 1 Find each percent of change. Round answers to the nearest tenth of a percent, if necessary.

7. 72 is decreased to 45.

8. 55 is increased to 90.

9. 180 is decreased to 140.

10. 230 is increased to 250.

See Example 2 **11.** A skateboard that sells for $65 is on sale for 15% off. Find the sale price.

See Example 3 **12. Business** A jeweler buys a ring from an artisan for $85. He sells the ring in his store at a 135% increase in price. What is the retail price of the ring?

PRACTICE AND PROBLEM SOLVING

Extra Practice
See Extra Practice for more exercises.

Find each percent of change, amount of increase, or amount of decrease. Round answers to the nearest tenth, if necessary.

13. $8.80 is increased to $17.60.

14. 6.2 is decreased to 5.9.

15. 39.2 is increased to 56.3.

16. $325 is decreased to $100.

17. 75 is decreased by 40%.

18. 28 is increased by 150%.

19. A water tank holds 45 gallons of water. A new water tank can hold 25% more water. What is the capacity of the new water tank?

20. Business Marla makes stretchy beaded purses and sells them to Bangles 'n' Beads for $7 each. Bangles 'n' Beads makes a profit of 28% on each purse. Find the retail price of the purses.

21. Multi-Step A store is discounting all of its stock. The original price of a pair of sunglasses was $44.95. The sale price is $26.97. At this discount, what was the original price of a bathing suit that has a sale price of $28.95?

22. Critical Thinking Explain why a change in price from $20 to $10 is a 50% decrease, but a change in price from $10 to $20 is a 100% markup.

23. The information at right shows the expenses for the Kramer family for one year.

    a. The Kramers spent $2,905 on auto expenses. What was their income for the year?

    b. How much money was spent on household expenses?

    c. The Kramers pay $14,400 per year on their mortgage. What percent of their household expenses is this? Round your answer to the nearest tenth.

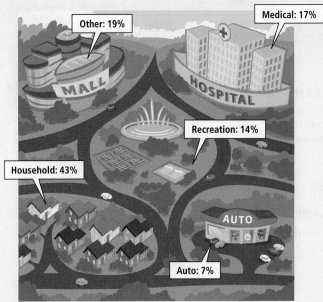

Other: 19%
Medical: 17%
Recreation: 14%
Household: 43%
Auto: 7%
MALL
HOSPITAL
AUTO

24. United States health expenses were $428.7 billion in 1985 and $991.4 billion in 1995. What was the percent of increase in health expenses during this ten-year period? Round your answer to the nearest tenth of a percent.

25. In 1990, the total amount of energy consumed for transportation in the United States was 22,540 trillion British thermal units (Btu). From 1950 to 1990, there was a 165% increase in energy consumed for transportation. About how many Btu of energy were consumed in 1950?

26. ⭐ **Challenge** In 1960, 21.5% of U.S. households did not have a telephone. This statistic decreased by 75.8% between 1960 and 1990. In 1990, what percent of U.S. households had a telephone?

Test Prep

27. **Multiple Choice** Find the percent of change if the price of a 20-ounce bottle of water increases from $0.85 to $1.25. Round to the nearest tenth.

    Ⓐ 47.1%   Ⓑ 40.0%   Ⓒ 32.0%   Ⓓ 1.7%

28. **Extended Response** A store buys jeans from the manufacturer for $30 each and sells them at a 50% markup in price. At the end of the season, the store puts the jeans on sale for 50% off. Is the sale price $30? Explain your reasoning.

Applications of Percents

CC.7.RP.3 Use proportional relationships to solve multistep ratio and percent problems.

Salespeople often work for *commission*. A **commission** is a fee paid to a person who makes a sale. It is usually a percent of the selling price. This percent is called the **commission rate**.

commission rate • sales = commission

Vocabulary
commission
commission rate

Often salespeople are paid a commission plus a regular salary. The total pay is a percent of the sales they make plus a salary.

EXAMPLE **1** **Multiplying by Percents to Find Commission Amounts**

Julie is paid a monthly salary of $2100 plus commissions. Last month she sold one car for $39,500, earning a 4% commission on the sale. How much was her commission? What was her total pay for the month?

First find her commission.

$4\% \cdot \$39{,}500 = c$	*commission rate · sales = commission*
$0.04 \cdot 39{,}500 = c$	*Change the percent to a decimal.*
$1580 = c$	*Solve for c.*

She earned a commission of $1580 on the sale.

Now find her total pay for last month.

$\$1580 + \$2100 = \$3680$ *commission + salary = total pay*

Her total pay for last month was $3680.

Sales tax is the tax on the sale of an item or service. It is a percent of the purchase price and is collected by the seller.

EXAMPLE **2** **Multiplying by Percents to Find Sales Tax Amounts**

If the sales tax rate is 7.75%, how much tax would Meka pay if she bought a portable DVD player for $145.80 and two DVDs for $15.99 each?

DVD player: 1 at $145.80	→	$145.80
DVDs: 2 at $15.99	→	$31.98
		$177.78 *Total price*

$0.0775 \cdot 177.78 = 13.77795$ *Write the tax rate as a decimal and multiply by the total price.*

Meka would pay $13.78 in sales tax.

Jorge earns $36,000 yearly. Of that, he pays $12,240 for rent. What percent of Jorge's earnings goes to rent?

Think: What percent of $36,000 is $12,240?

$$\frac{n}{100} = \frac{12,240}{36,000}$$ *Set up a proportion.*

$$n \cdot 36,000 = 100 \cdot 12,240$$ *Find the cross products.*

$$36,000n = 1,224,000$$ *Simplify.*

$$\frac{36,000n}{36,000} = \frac{1,224,000}{36,000}$$ *Divide both sides by 36,000.*

$$n = 34$$ *Simplify.*

So 34% of Jorges's earnings goes to rent.

The total amount of money brought in is *revenue*. After costs are subtracted from revenue, the amount remaining is *profit*.

EXAMPLE **4** **Dividing by Percents to Find Total Revenue**

Students wash cars to raise funds for class trips. The class made a profit of $326.60 from last Saturday's car wash, which was 92% of its revenue. How much was the revenue for the car wash?

Think: 326.60 is 92% of what number?

Let r = revenue for the car wash

$$326.6 = 0.92 \cdot r$$ *Set up an equation.*

$$\frac{326.6}{0.92} = \frac{0.92r}{0.92}$$ *Divide both sides by 0.92.*

$$355 = r$$ *Simplify.*

The revenue for the car wash was $355.

Think and Discuss

1. Tell how finding commission is similar to finding sales tax.

2. Explain whether adding 6% sales tax to a total gives the same result as finding 106% of the total.

3. Explain how to find the price of an item if you know the total cost after 5% sales tax.

4. Explain whether the sales tax on a $20 item would be double the sales tax on a $10 item. Justify your answer.

Learn It Online
Homework Help Online
Exercises 1–9, 11, 13, 17

GUIDED PRACTICE

See Example 1 **1.** Aaron earns a weekly salary of $350 plus a 7% commission on sales. Last week, his sales totaled $3200. What was his total pay?

See Example 2 **2.** In a state with a sales tax rate of 7%, Hernando buys a radio for $59.99 and a CD for $13.99. How much is the sales tax?

See Example 3 **3.** Last year, Nadia earned $31,025. Of that amount, she spent $3612.59 on food. What percent of her income went to food, to the nearest tenth of a percent?

See Example 4 **4.** Shane works at a computer store. If he earns $20.93 from a 7% commission on the sale of a printer, what is the price of the printer?

INDEPENDENT PRACTICE

See Example 1 **5.** Kayla earns a weekly salary of $290 plus a 5.5% commission on sales at a gift shop. How much would she make in a week if she sold $5700 worth of merchandise?

See Example 2 **6.** The sales tax rate in Brad's town is 4.25%. If he buys 3 lamps for $22.49 each and a sofa for $829.99, how much sales tax does he owe?

See Example 3 **7.** Jada typically earns $1545 each month, of which $47.20 is spent on electricity. What percent of Jada's earnings are spent on electricity each month, to the nearest tenth of a percent?

See Example 4 **8.** Heather works in a clothes shop, where she earns a commission of 5% and no weekly salary. What will Heather's weekly sales have to be for her to earn $375 in one week?

PRACTICE AND PROBLEM SOLVING

Extra Practice
See Extra Practice for more exercises.

Find each sales tax to the nearest cent.

9. total sales: $210.13
sales tax rate: 7.25%

10. total sales: $42.99
sales tax rate: 9%

11. total sales: $895.75
sales tax rate: 4.25%

Find the total sales to the nearest cent.

12. commission: $63.06
commission rate: 5%

13. commission: $2842
commission rate: 3.5%

14. Consumer Economics Roz takes home $1600 each month. She budgets 30% of her paycheck for rent, 20% for food, and 10% for utilities. The remainder is divided evenly among entertainment, clothes, transportation, savings, and charity. How much money does Roz budget each month for each category?

15. Critical Thinking Deborah can choose between a monthly salary of $1800 plus 6.5% of sales or $2100 plus 4% of sales. She expects sales between $5,000 and $10,000 a month. Which salary option should she choose? Explain.

Tax brackets are used to determine how much income tax people pay. Depending upon a person's taxable income, tax is given by the formula base tax + tax rate (amount over). "Amount over" refers only to the income above the amount listed. Refer to the table for Exercises 16–18.

2005 IRS Income Tax Brackets (Single)			
Taxable Income Range	**Base Tax**	**Tax Rate**	**Amount Over**
$0–$7,300	$0	10%	$0
$7,300–$29,700	$730	15%	$7,300
$29,700–$71,950	$4,090	25%	$29,700
$71,950–$150,150	$14,652.50	28%	$71,950
$150,150–$326,450	$36,548.50	33%	$150,150
$326,450 and up	$94,727.50	35%	$326,450

16. Tina's pay stub is shown at right. Find the missing numbers.

17. Anna earned $71,458 total in 2005. She was able to deduct $7250 for job-related expenses. This amount is subtracted from her total income to determine her taxable income.

   a. What was Anna's taxable income in 2005?

   b. How much income tax did she owe?

   c. What percent of Anna's total income did the tax represent?

   d. What percent of her taxable income did the tax represent?

18. ⭐ **Challenge** Charlena paid $10,050 in taxes in 2005. How much taxable income did she earn that year?

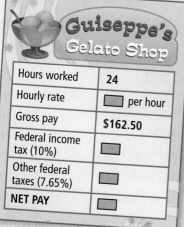

Test Prep

19. Short Answer Gabrielle earned a weekly salary of $235 plus 8% commission on sales over $500. What was her weekly pay if she had $6,250 in sales?

20. Gridded Response Rafael buys a video game for $49.95. The sales tax rate is 6.5%. What is the total cost, including tax, to the nearest dollar?

6-6 Simple Interest

CC.7.RP.3 Use proportional relationships to solve multistep ratio and percent problems.

Interest is the amount of money charged for borrowing or using money. When you deposit money into a savings account, you are paid interest. **Simple interest** is one type of fee paid for the use of money.

Simple interest is money paid only on the principal.

Rate of interest is the percent charged or earned.

$$I = P \cdot r \cdot t$$

Principal is the amount of money borrowed or invested.

Time in years that the money is borrowed or invested

EXAMPLE 1 Finding Interest and Total Payment on a Loan

Vocabulary

interest

simple interest

principal

rate of interest

Tristan borrowed $14,500 from his brother and promised to pay him back over 5 years at an annual simple interest rate of 7%. How much interest will he pay if he pays off the entire loan at the end of the fifth year? What is the total amount he will repay?

First, find the interest he will pay.

$I = P \cdot r \cdot t$	*Use the formula.*
$I = 14,500 \cdot 0.07 \cdot 5$	*Substitute. Use 0.07 for 7%.*
$I = 5075$	*Solve for I.*

Tristan will pay $5075 in interest.

You can find the total amount A to be repaid on a loan by adding the principal P to the interest I.

$P + I = A$	*principal + interest = amount*
$14,500 + 5075 = A$	*Substitute.*
$19,575 = A$	*Solve for A.*

Tristan will repay a total of $19,575 on his loan.

EXAMPLE 2 Determining the Amount of Investment Time

Isaiah invested $3500 in a mutual fund at a yearly rate of 6%. He earned $945 in interest. For how long was the money invested?

$I = P \cdot r \cdot t$	*Use the formula.*
$945 = 3500 \cdot 0.06 \cdot t$	*Substitute.*
$945 = 210t$	*Simplify.*
$4.5 = t$	*Solve for t.*

The money was invested for 4.5 years, or 4 years and 6 months.

Video **Lesson Tutorials Online** my.hrw.com

EXAMPLE **3** **Computing Total Savings**

Nadia's aunt deposited $3000 into a savings account as a college fund for Nadia. How much will be in this account after 5 years if the account earns a yearly simple interest rate of 3.5%?

$I = P \cdot r \cdot t$	*Use the formula.*
$I = 3000 \cdot 0.035 \cdot 5$	*Substitute. Use 0.035 for 3.5%.*
$I = 525$	*Solve for I.*

Now you can find the total.

$P + I = A$	*Use the formula.*
$3000 + 525 = A$	*Substitute.*
$3525 = A$	*Solve for A.*

Nadia will have $3525 in her savings account after 5 years.

EXAMPLE **4** **Finding the Rate of Interest**

To pay for her college expenses, Hannah borrows $7000. She plans to repay the loan in 5 years at simple interest. If Hannah repays a total of $9187.50, what is the interest rate?

$P + I = A$	*Use the formula.*
$7000 + I = 9187.5$	*Substitute.*
$\underline{-7000 \qquad -7000}$	*Subtract 7000 from both sides.*
$I = 2187.5$	*Simplify.*

She paid $2187.50 in interest. Use the amount of interest to find the interest rate.

$I = P \cdot r \cdot t$	*Use the formula.*
$2187.5 = 7000 \cdot r \cdot 5$	*Substitute.*
$2187.5 = 35,000r$	*Simplify.*
$\frac{2187.5}{35,000} = \frac{35,000r}{35,000}$	*Divide both sides by 35,000.*
$0.0625 = r$	*Simplify.*

The simple annual rate is 6.25%, or $6\frac{1}{4}\%$.

MATHEMATICAL PRACTICES

Think and Discuss

1. Explain the meaning of each variable in the interest formula.

2. Tell what value should be used for t when referring to 6 months.

3. Name the variables in the simple interest formula that represent dollar amounts.

4. Demonstrate that doubling the time while halving the interest rate results in the same amount of simple interest.

Exercises

GUIDED PRACTICE

See Example 1

1. Nick borrowed $7150, to be repaid after 5 years at an annual simple interest rate of 6.25%. How much interest will be due after 5 years? How much will Nick have to repay?

See Example 2

2. Mr. Williams invested $4000 in a bond with a yearly interest rate of 4%. His total interest on the investment was $800. What was the length of the investment?

See Example 3

3. Paige deposited $1277 in a savings account. How much would she have in the account after 3 years at an annual simple interest rate of 4%?

See Example 4

4. Tom borrowed $35,000 to remodel his house. At the end of the 5-year loan, he had repaid a total of $46,375. At what simple interest rate did he borrow the money?

INDEPENDENT PRACTICE

See Example 1

5. A bank offers an annual simple interest rate of 7% on home improvement loans. How much would Billy owe if he borrowed $18,500 over a period of 3.5 years?

See Example 2

6. Eliza deposits $8500 in a college fund. If the fund earns an annual simple interest rate of 6.5%, how long must the money be in the fund to earn $9392.50 in interest?

See Example 3

7. Jessika gave a security deposit of $1200 to her landlord, Mr. Allen, 8 years ago. Mr. Allen now intends to give her the deposit back with simple interest of 2.85%. How much will he return to her?

See Example 4

8. Premier Bank loaned a construction company $275,000 at an annual simple interest rate. After 5 years, the company repaid the bank $350,625. What was the interest rate on the loan?

PRACTICE AND PROBLEM SOLVING

Extra Practice

See Extra Practice for more exercises.

Find the interest and the total amount to the nearest cent.

9. $315 at 6% per year for 5 years

10. $800 at 9% per year for 1 year

11. $4250 at 7% per year for 1.5 years

12. $550 at 5.5% per year for 3 years

13. $617 at 6% per year for 3 months

14. $2975 at 6% per year for 5 years

15. $900 at 7.25% per year for 3 years

16. $200 at 7% per year for 9 months

17. Jabari borrowed $1700 for 15 months at 16% annual simple interest rate. How much interest will he have to pay? What is the total amount he will repay?

18. Selena borrowed $9500 to buy a used car. The credit union charged 7% simple interest per year. She paid $3325 in interest. For what period of time did she borrow money?

Many bank ATMs in Bangkok, Thailand, are located in sculptures to attract customers.

19. Critical Thinking Meghan and Sabrina compared the amount of interest they each earned on their savings accounts. Each had deposited $1000, but Meghan earned $140 interest and Sabrina earned $157.50. Whose savings account had a higher interest rate? Explain.

20. Money The Smiths will borrow $35,500 from a bank to start a business. They have two loan options. Option A is a 5-year loan; option B is a 4-year loan. Use the graph to answer the following questions.

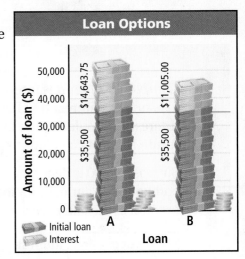

a. What is the total amount the Smiths would pay under each loan option?

b. What would be the interest rate under each loan option?

c. What would be the monthly payment under each loan option?

d. How much interest will the Smiths save by choosing loan option B?

21. What's the Question? Alice places $700 in a savings account with a simple annual interest rate of 4%. When Alice withdraws the money, she has $840. What is the question?

22. Write About It Which loan would cost a borrower less: $3000 at 6% for 4 years or $3000 at 7.5% for 3 years? How much interest would the borrower save by taking the cheaper loan?

23. Challenge How would the total payment on a 5-year loan at 3% annual simple interest compare with the total payment on a 5-year loan where one-twelfth of that simple interest, 0.25%, is calculated monthly? Give an example.

Test Prep

24. Multiple Choice Sam invested $2500 for 2 years in a savings account. The savings account paid an annual simple interest rate of 2.5% How much interest did Sam earn during the 2 years?

Ⓐ $62.50　　　Ⓑ $125　　　Ⓒ $1250　　　Ⓓ $2625

25. Multiple Choice Toni invested $250 in a savings account for 4 years. The total interest earned on the investment was $125. What was the interest rate on the account?

Ⓕ 3.125%　　　Ⓖ 12.5%　　　Ⓗ 125%　　　Ⓙ 1125%

Explore Compound Interest

Use with Simple Interest

Learn It Online
Lab Resources Online

Use appropriate tools strategically.
CC.7.RP.3 Use proportional relationships to solve multistep ratio and percent problems.

Compound interest is interest paid not only on the principal but also on any interest that has already been earned. Every time interest is calculated, the interest is added to the principal for future interest calculations.

Suppose $1000 is deposited into an account paying 5% interest compounded annually for four years. The table shows the amount A in the account at the end of each year, rounded to the nearest cent.

Year	Beginning Balance	Interest = *Prt*	Amount = *P + I*
1	$1000	*I* = 1000(0.05) = $50	*A* = 1000 + 50 = $1050
2	$1050	*I* = 1050(0.05) = $52.50	*A* = 1050 + 52.50 = $1102.50
3	$1102.50	*I* = 1102.50(0.05) = $55.13	*A* = 1102.50 + 55.13 = $1157.63
4	$1157.63	*I* = 1157.63(0.05) = $57.88	*A* = 1157.63 + 57.88 = $1215.51

Activity 1

Suppose $1000 were deposited into an account paying 10% interest compounded annually. Find the amount A in the account at the end of each year for 5 years. How much interest is added after the first year? How much interest is added after the fifth year?

1 Press 1000 `ENTER`

2 Then press `2nd` `(−)` `×` 1.1 `ENTER`.

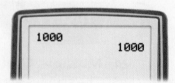

3 Then press `ENTER` 4 more times to repeat multiplication by 1.1.

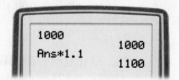

The amounts in the account after each year are $1100, $1210, $1331, $1464.10, and $1610.51.

Interest added after the first year is $1100 − $1000 = $100.

Interest added after the fifth year is $1610.51 − $1464.10 = $146.41.

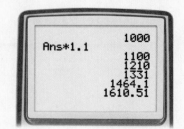

1. Suppose Activity 1 was done using simple interest. How would the interest added after the first year and the interest added after the fifth year compare? Why?

2. Suppose the interest was compounded *biannually* (2 times a year) at 5% interest each time interest compounds. Would the amount after one year be less, more, or equal to $1100? Justify your reasoning.

The formula for compound interest is $A = P(1 + r)^n$, where A is the final dollar value, P is the initial dollar investment, r is the rate for each interest period, and n is the number of interest periods.

Activity 2

Use a calculator to find the value after 9 years of $1500 invested in a savings bank that pays 3% interest compounded annually.

The initial investment P is $1500. The rate r is 3% = 0.03. The interest period is one year. The number of interest periods n is 9.

$$A = 1500(1.03)^9$$

1 On your graphing calculator, press

1500 ✕ 1.03 ⌃ 9 ENTER .

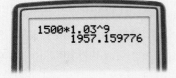

After 9 years, the initial investment of $1500 will be worth $1957.16 (rounded to the nearest cent).

Think and Discuss

1. Compare the value of an initial deposit of $1000 at 6% simple interest for 10 years with the same initial deposit at 6% annual compound interest for 10 years. Which is greater? Why?

Try This

Find the value of an initial investment of $2500 for the specified term and interest rate.

1. 8 years, 5% compounded annually
2. 20 years, 3% compounded annually
3. 6 years, 12% compounded annually
4. 12 years, 6% compounded annually

Quiz for Lessons 4 Through 6

 **4** **Percent of Change**

Find each percent of change. Round answers to the nearest tenth of a percent, if necessary.

1. 37 is decreased to 17.

2. 121 is increased to 321.

3. 89 is decreased to 84.

4. 45 is increased to 60.

5. 61 is decreased to 33.

6. 86 is increased to 95.

7. Since Frank is increasing the distance of his daily runs, he needs to carry more water. His current water bottle holds 16 ounces. Frank's new bottle holds 25% more water than his current bottle. What is the capacity of Frank's new water bottle?

 **5** **Applications of Percents**

Find each commission or sales tax to the nearest cent.

8. total sales: $12,500
commission rate: 3.25%

9. total sales: $14.23
sales tax rate: 8.25%

10. total sales: $25,000
commission rate: 2.75%

11. total sales: $251.50
sales tax rate: 7.5%

12. total sales: $10,500
commission rate: 4%

13. total sales: $75.99
sales tax rate: 6.125%

14. Josh earns a weekly salary of $300 plus a 6% commission on sales. Last week, his sales totaled $3500. What was his total pay?

6 **Simple Interest**

Find the interest and the total amount to the nearest cent.

15. $225 at 5% per year for 3 years

16. $775 at 8% per year for 1 year

17. Leroy borrowed $8250 to be repaid after 3 years at an annual simple interest rate of 7.25%. How much interest will be due after 3 years? How much will Leroy have to repay?

18. Kim deposited $1422 in a savings account. How much would she have in the account after 5 years at an annual simple interest rate of 3%?

19. Akule borrowed $1500 at an annual simple interest rate of 12%. He paid $270 in interest. For what period of time did Akule borrow the money?

Real-World CONNECTIONS

Corn Nebraska's nickname is the Cornhusker State, which seems appropriate because corn is Nebraska's top crop in terms of acres and dollar value. In 2007, nearly 1.5 billion bushels of corn were harvested in the state.

NEBRASKA

For 1–2, use the table.

1. The recommended daily allowance (RDA) of carbohydrates for a teenage girl is 130 grams.

   a. What percent of the RDA of carbohydrates does a teenage girl consume by eating an ear of corn? Round to the nearest percent.

   b. Write the percent as a decimal and as a fraction.

Nutrition Facts	
Serving Size: One medium ear of corn	
Amount per serving	
Calories	78
Carbohydrates	17 g
Protein	3 g
Fat	1.1 g
Dietary Fiber	2.5 g

2. A student's dinner included a medium ear of corn. The corn provided 12% of the Calories in the meal. How many Calories did the student consume at dinner?

3. In 2007, 9.4 million acres of corn were planted in Nebraska. In the United States, 93.6 million acres of corn were planted. Estimate the percent of all corn in the United States that was planted in Nebraska. Explain how you made the estimate.

4. The 9.4 million acres of corn planted in Nebraska in 2007 was an 11% increase from the amount of corn planted in the state in 2006.

   a. How many acres of corn were planted in Nebraska in 2006?

   b. Suppose 10 million acres of corn were planted in Nebraska in 2008. Find the percent increase from 2007 to 2008. Round to the nearest percent.

Game Time

Lighten Up

On a digital clock, up to seven light bulbs make up each digit on the display. You can label each light bulb as shown below.

If each number were lit up for the same amount of time, you could find out which light bulb is lit the greatest percent of the time. You could also find out which light bulb is lit the least percent of the time.

For each number 0–9, list the letters of the light bulbs that are used when that number is showing. The first few numbers have been done for you.

Once you have determined which bulbs are lit for each number, count how many times each bulb is lit. What percent of the time is each bulb lit? What does this tell you about which bulb will burn out first?

Percent Bingo

Use the bingo cards with numbers and percents provided online. The caller has a collection of percent problems. The caller reads a problem. Then the players solve the problem, and the solution is a number or a percent. If players have the solution on their card, they mark it off. Normal bingo rules apply. You can win with a horizontal, vertical, or diagonal row.

A complete copy of the rules and game pieces is available online.

Learn It Online
Game Time Extra

Materials

- 2 pieces of card stock ($5\frac{1}{4}$ by 12 in.)
- 21 strips of colored paper ($1\frac{1}{2}$ by $5\frac{1}{2}$ in.)
- glue
- markers

It's in the Bag!

PROJECT Percent Strips

This colorful booklet holds questions and answers about percents.

Directions

A

❶ Fold one piece of card stock in half. Cut along the crease to make two rectangles that are each $5\frac{1}{4}$ inches by 6 inches. You will use these later as covers for your booklet.

B

❷ On the other piece of card stock, make accordion folds about $\frac{3}{4}$-inch wide. When you are done, there should be 16 panels. These panels will be the pages of your booklet. **Figure A**

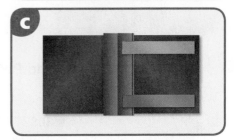

C

❸ Fold up the accordion strip. Glue the covers to the top and bottom panels of the strip. **Figure B**

❹ Open the front cover. Glue a strip of colored paper to the top and bottom of the first page. **Figure C**

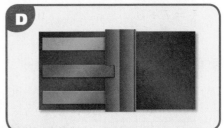

D

❺ Turn the page. Glue a strip of colored paper to the back of the first page between the other two strips. **Figure D**

❻ Glue strips to the other pages in the same way.

Putting the Math into Action

Write a question about percents on the front of each strip. Write the answer on the back. Trade books with another student and put your knowledge of percents to the test.

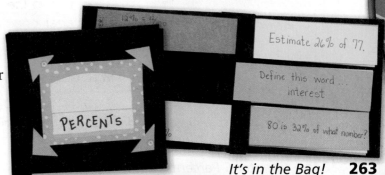

Vocabulary

commission

commission rate

interest

percent of change

percent of decrease

percent of increase

principal

rate of interest

simple interest

Complete the sentences below with vocabulary words from the list above.

1. ___?___ is an amount that is collected or paid for the use of money. The equation $I = P \cdot r \cdot t$ is used for calculating ___?___. The letter P represents the ___?___ and the letter r represents the ___?___.

2. The ratio of an amount of increase to the original amount is the ___?___.

3. The ratio of an amount of decrease to the original amount is the ___?___.

4. Percent is used to calculate a(n) ___?___, a fee paid to a person who makes a sale.

EXAMPLES

EXERCISES

1 **Fractions, Decimals, and Percents**

Write as a percent.

■ $\frac{7}{8}$

$\frac{7}{8} = 7 \div 8$

$= 0.875$

$= 87.5\%$

■ 0.82

$0.82 = \frac{82}{100}$

$= 82\%$

Write as a percent. Round to the nearest tenth of a percent, if necessary.

5. $\frac{3}{5}$ 6. $\frac{1}{6}$

7. 0.09   8. 0.8

9. $\frac{2}{3}$ 10. 0.0056

11. Order $0.\overline{33}$, -2.6, $2\frac{3}{5}$, and 30% from least to greatest.

2 Estimating with Percents

■ Estimate 26% of 77.

26% of 77 $\approx \frac{1}{4} \cdot 77$ *26% is about 25% and 25% is equivalent to $\frac{1}{4}$.*

$\approx \frac{1}{4} \cdot 80$ *Change 77 to 80.*

≈ 20 *Multiply.*

26% of 77 is about 20.

Estimate.

12. 22% of 44   **13.** 74% of 120

14 43% of 64   **15.** 31% of 97

16. 49% of 82   **17.** 6% of 53

18. Byron and Kate's dinner cost $18.23. About how much money should they leave for a 15% tip?

19. Salvador's lunch cost $9.85, and he left a $2.00 tip. About how much more than 15% of the bill did Salvador leave for the tip?

3 Using Properties with Rational Numbers

■ Write an equivalent equation for $\frac{4}{5}x - 3 = \frac{1}{3}$ that does not contain fractions. Then solve the equation.

$\frac{4}{5}x - 3 = \frac{1}{3}$ *The LCM of the denominators is 15.*

$15\left(\frac{4}{5}x - 3\right) = 15\left(\frac{1}{3}\right)$ *Multiply both sides by 15.*

$12x = 65$ *Simplify.*

$x = 4\frac{1}{6}$

An equivalent equation is $12x - 45 = 65$ and the solution is $4\frac{1}{6}$.

Write an equivalent equation that does not contain fractions. Then solve the equation.

20. $\frac{1}{6}x + 3 = \frac{3}{4}$ **21.** $\frac{3}{5}x - 2 = \frac{1}{10}$

22. $\frac{3}{10}x - 1 = \frac{3}{4}$ **23.** $\frac{3}{8}x + 2 = \frac{5}{6}$

24. $\frac{4}{9}x - 1 = \frac{1}{9}$ **25.** $\frac{5}{12}x - 4 = \frac{5}{6}$

4 Percent of Change

Find each percent of change. Round answers to the nearest tenth of a percent, if necessary.

■ 25 is decreased to 16.

$25 - 16 = 9$ *Find the amount of change.*

percent of change $= \frac{9}{25}$

$= 0.36$

$= 36\%$

The percent of decrease is 36%.

Find each percent of change. Round answers to the nearest tenth of a percent, if necessary.

26. 54 is increased to 81.

27. 14 is decreased to 12.

28. 110 is increased to 143.

29. 90 is decreased to 15.2.

30. 26 is increased to 32.

31. 84 is decreased to 21.

5 **Applications of Percents**

■ As an appliance salesman, Gavin earns a base pay of $525 per week plus a 6% commission on his weekly sales. Last week, his sales totaled $3250. How much did he earn for the week?

Find the amount of commission.

$$6\% \cdot \$3250 = c$$

$$0.06 \cdot 3250 = c \quad \textit{Write 6\% as a decimal.}$$

$$195 = c \quad \textit{Multiply.}$$

Add the commission amount to his base pay.

$$\$195 + \$525 = \$720$$

Last week Gavin earned $720.

32. As a real estate agent, Kensho earns $4\frac{1}{2}\%$ commission on the houses he sells. In the first quarter of this year, he sold two houses, one for $175,000 and the other for $199,000. How much was Kensho's commission for this quarter?

33. If the sales tax is $8\frac{1}{4}\%$, how much tax would Luisa pay for a picture frame that costs $17.99 and a desk calendar that costs $24.99?

6 **Simple Interest**

■ For home improvements, the Walters borrowed $10,000 for 3 years at simple interest. They repaid a total of $11,050. What was the interest rate of the loan?

Find the amount of interest.

$$P + I = A \quad \textit{Use the formula.}$$

$$10,000 + I = 11,050 \quad \textit{Substitute.}$$

$$\underline{-10,000 \qquad -10,000} \quad \begin{array}{l}\textit{Subtract 10,000}\\\textit{from both sides.}\end{array}$$

$$I = 1050 \quad \textit{Simplify.}$$

The amount of interest was $1050. Substitute into the simple interest formula.

$$I = P \cdot r \cdot t \quad \textit{Use the formula.}$$

$$1050 = 10,000 \cdot r \cdot 3 \quad \textit{Substitute.}$$

$$1050 = 30,000r \quad \textit{Simplify.}$$

$$\frac{1050}{30,000} = \frac{30,000r}{30,000} \quad \begin{array}{l}\textit{Divide both}\\\textit{sides by 30,000.}\end{array}$$

$$0.035 = r \quad \textit{Simplify.}$$

The interest rate of the loan was 3.5%.

Using the simple interest formula, find the missing number.

34. interest = ■; principal = $14,500; rate = $6\frac{1}{4}\%$ per year; time = $3\frac{1}{2}$ years

35. interest = $32; principal = ■; rate = 2% per year; time = 4 years

36. interest = $367.50; principal = $1500; rate per year = ■; time = $3\frac{1}{2}$ years

37. interest = $1787.50; principal = $55,000; rate = $6\frac{1}{2}\%$ per year; time = ■

38. Which simple-interest loan would cost the borrower less? How much less? $1000 at 3% for 4 years or $1000 at 3.75% for 3 years

39. Wade borrowed $12,500 from his uncle at 4.5% simple interest to use for travel and repaid the loan in 4 years. How much did he pay back?

Study Guide: Review

Chapter Test

Write as a percent. Round to the nearest tenth of a percent, if necessary.

1. 0.75 **2.** 0.12 **3.** 0.8 **4.** 0.0039

5. $\frac{3}{10}$ **6.** $\frac{9}{20}$ **7.** $\frac{5}{16}$ **8.** $\frac{7}{21}$

Estimate.

9. 48% of 8 **10.** 3% of 119 **11.** 26% of 32 **12.** 76% of 280

13. The Pattersons spent $47.89 for a meal at a restaurant. About how much should they leave for a 15% tip?

Write an equivalent equation that does not contain fractions. Then solve the equation.

14. $\frac{3}{4}x + 3 = \frac{3}{8}$ **15.** $\frac{7}{10}x + 20 = \frac{2}{5}$ **16.** $\frac{2}{3}x - 1 = \frac{3}{4}$

17. Louisa paid $12.25 for books at a yard sale. She spent $2.50 on a hardcover book, and the rest on 13 softcover books. Each of the softcover books cost the same. What was the cost of a single softcover book? Write and solve an equivalent equation

Find each percent of change. Round answers to the nearest tenth, if necessary.

18. 30 is increased to 45. **19.** 115 is decreased to 46.

20. 116 is increased to 145. **21.** 129 is decreased to 32.

22. A community theater sold 8,500 tickets to performances during its first year. By its tenth year, ticket sales had increased by 34%. How many tickets did the theater sell during its tenth year?

Find each commission or sales tax to the nearest cent.

23. total sales: $13,600
commission rate: 2.75%

24. total sales: $135.50
sales tax rate: 8.25%

25. total sales: $20,250
commission rate: 3.9%

26. Ms. Tan earns $350 per week plus an 8% commission on her shoe sales. She sold $560 last week. What was her total pay for the week?

27. George earns an annual salary of $36,000. In addition to this, he earns a 3% commission on all sales he makes. If George had $264,000 in sales last year, what was his total pay?

28. Dena borrowed $7500 to buy a used car. The credit union charged 9% simple interest per year. She paid $2025 in interest. For what period of time did she borrow the money?

29. At Thrift Bank, if you keep $675 in a savings account for 12 years, your money will earn $486 in interest. What annual simple interest rate does the bank offer?

Standardized Test Prep

Cumulative Assessment

Multiple Choice

1. Which ratio corresponds to the similar figures shown?

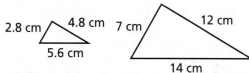

2.8 cm   4.8 cm
5.6 cm

7 cm   12 cm
14 cm

Ⓐ $\frac{4.2}{1}$ Ⓒ $\frac{1}{2}$

Ⓑ $\frac{2.5}{1}$ Ⓓ $\frac{1}{4}$

2. Which of the following is NOT equivalent to 12%?

Ⓕ 0.012   Ⓗ 0.12

Ⓖ $\frac{12}{100}$ Ⓙ $\frac{3}{25}$

3. Which situation corresponds to the graph?

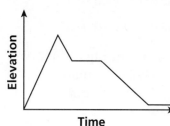

Elevation

Time

Ⓐ Ty rides his bike up a hill, immediately heads back down, stops and rests for a while, continues down the hill, and then rests.

Ⓑ Paul runs up a hill, stops a while for a water break, and then jogs back down the hill.

Ⓒ Sue rollerskates down a hill, stops for lunch, and then continues along a flat course for a while.

Ⓓ Eric swims across a pool, rests for a while when he gets to the other side, and then swims numerous laps without stopping.

4. Which point is NOT on the graph of $y = x^2 - 3$?

Ⓕ (0, −3)   Ⓗ (−2, −7)

Ⓖ (2, 1)   Ⓙ (−1, −2)

5. Which equation is an example of the Identity Property?

Ⓐ 100 + 10 = 2(50 + 5)

Ⓑ 50 + 10 = 10 + 50

Ⓒ 25 + (50 + 10) = (25 + 50) + 10

Ⓓ 50 + 0 = 50

6. A basketball goal that usually sells for $825 goes on sale for $650. What is the percent of decrease, to the nearest whole percent?

Ⓕ 12%   Ⓗ 27%

Ⓖ 21%   Ⓙ 79%

7. In Oregon, about 40 of the state's nearly 1,000 public water systems add fluoride to their water. What percent best represents this situation?

Ⓐ 0.4%   Ⓒ 40%

Ⓑ 4%   Ⓓ 400%

8. The number of whooping cranes wintering in Texas reached an all time high in 2004 at 213. The lowest number ever recorded was 15 whooping cranes in 1941. What is the percent of increase of whooping cranes wintering in Texas from 1941 to 2004?

Ⓕ 7%   Ⓗ 198%

Ⓖ 91%   Ⓙ 1,320%

9. What is the value of $8\frac{2}{5} - 2\frac{3}{4}$?

Ⓐ $5\frac{9}{20}$ Ⓒ $6\frac{1}{9}$

Ⓑ $5\frac{13}{20}$ Ⓓ $6\frac{7}{20}$

10. Which point lies outside of the circle?

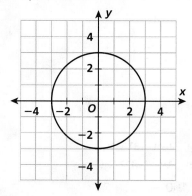

Ⓕ (−3, 0)   Ⓗ (3, 3)

Ⓖ (1, 2)   Ⓙ (−2, 1)

 HOT TIP!

Make sure that your answer makes sense before marking it as your response. Reread the question and determine whether your answer is reasonable.

Gridded Response

11. Jarvis deposits $1,200 in an account that earns 3% simple interest. How many years will it take him to earn $432 in interest?

12. Sylas finished a 100-meter freestyle swim in 80.35 seconds. The winner of the race finished in 79.22 seconds. How many seconds faster was the winning time than Sylas's time?

13. A baseball coach has a rule that for every time a player strikes out, that player has to do 12 push ups. If Cal strikes out 27 times, how many push ups will he be required to do?

14. Write a decimal equivalent to 65%.

15. What is the denominator of the value of $\frac{3}{2} + \frac{5}{6}$ when written in simplest form?

Short Response

S1. The graph shows the number of boys and the number of girls who participated in a talent show.

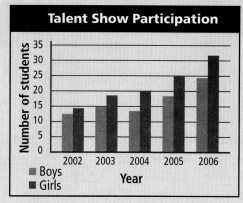

a. What is the approximate percent of increase of girls participating in the talent show from 2002 to 2005?

b. What percent of students participating in the talent show in 2006 were boys? Explain how you found your answer.

S2. A homemaker association has 134 members. If 31 of these members are experts in canning vegetables, are more or less than 25% of the members canning experts? Explain how you know.

Extended Response

E1. Riley and Louie each have $5,000 to invest. They both invest at a 2.5% simple interest rate.

a. Riley keeps her money invested for 7 years. How much interest will she earn? How much will her investment be worth?

b. What is the value of Louie's investment if he invests for 3 years, then removes and spends $1,000, and then invests what is remaining for 4 more years at a rate of 4%?

c. Using the information from parts **a** and **b**, who has more money in 7 years, Louie or Riley? Explain your reasoning.

CHAPTER 7

Collecting, Displaying, and Analyzing Data

Chapter FOCUS

- Make and interpret graphs, such as box-and-whisker plots.
- Make estimates relating to a population based on a sample.

Why Learn This?

Biologists can take random samples of a wildlife population, such as sea lions, to make estimates about population growth or infectious diseases that might affect the group.

Learn It Online
Chapter Project Online

Mark Jones/Photolibrary

Are You Ready?

Learn It Online
Resources Online

Complete these exercises to review skills you will need for this chapter.

✓ Order of Operations

Simplify the expression.

1. $\dfrac{3 + 5 + 4 + 7}{4}$ **2.** $\dfrac{83 + 88}{2}$ **3.** $\dfrac{2.2 + 1.7 + 1.8}{3}$

✓ Order Whole Numbers

Order the numbers from least to greatest.

4. 45, 23, 65, 15, 42, 18

5. 103, 105, 102, 118, 87, 104

6. 56, 65, 24, 19, 76, 33, 82

7. 8, 3, 6, 2, 5, 9, 3, 4, 2

✓ Whole Number Operations

Add or subtract.

8. $18 + 26$ **9.** $23 + 17$ **10.** $75 + 37$ **11.** $98 + 64$

12. $133 - 35$ **13.** $54 - 29$ **14.** $200 - 88$ **15.** $1,055 - 899$

✓ Read a Table

Use the data in the table for Exercises 16 and 17.

16. Which animal is the fastest?

17. Which animal is faster, a rabbit or a zebra?

| Top Speeds of Some Animals ||
Animal	Speed (mi/h)
Elephant	25
Lion	50
Rabbit	35
Zebra	40

Study Guide: Preview

Where You've Been

Previously, you

- used an appropriate representation for displaying data.

- identified mean, median, mode, and range of a set of data.

- solved problems by collecting, organizing, and displaying data.

In This Chapter

You will study

- using an appropriate representation for displaying relationships among data.

- choosing among mean, median, mode, or range to describe a set of data.

- making inferences and convincing arguments based on analysis of data.

Where You're Going

You can use the skills learned in this chapter

- to analyze trends and make business and marketing decisions.

- to strengthen a persuasive argument by presenting data and trends in visual displays.

Key Vocabulary/Vocabulario

box-and-whisker plot	gráfica de mediana y rango
mean	media
median	mediana
mode	moda
random sample	muestra escogida al azar

Vocabulary Connections

To become familiar with some of the vocabulary terms in the chapter, consider the following. You may refer to the chapter, the glossary, or a dictionary if you like.

1. The word *median* comes from the Latin word *medius*, meaning "middle." What is the **median** value in a set of data? What other words come from this Latin root?

2. The average value of a data set is its **mean**. In astronomy, the mean Earth-Sun distance is approximately 92,955,807 miles. What do you think this means?

3. The word *random* can be defined as "occurring without reason or pattern." Why do you think a **random sample** might be desired for a survey?

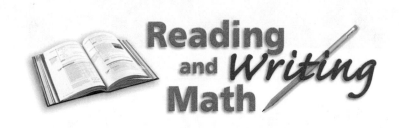

Reading and Writing Math

Reading Strategy: Read a Lesson for Understanding

Before you begin reading a lesson, find out what its main focus, or objective, is. Each lesson is centered on a specific objective, which your teacher will provide to you. Reading with the objective in mind will help guide you through the lesson material. You can use the following tips to help you follow the math as you read.

Percent of Change

> The title of a lesson can tell you the main idea, or objective, of the lesson. Skim through the lesson to get a sense of where the objective is covered.

"How do I find a percent of change?"

> As you read through the lesson, write down any questions, problems, or trouble spots you may have.

A **27 is decreased to 20.**

$27 - 20 = 7$ *Find the amount of change.*

percent of change $= \frac{7}{27}$ *Substitute values into formula.*

≈ 0.259259 *Divide.*

$\approx 25.9\%$ *Write as a percent.*

The percent of decrease is about 25.9%.

> Work through each example, as the examples help demonstrate the objectives.

Think and Discuss

1. Explain what is meant by a 100% decrease.

> Check your understanding of the lesson by answering the Think and Discuss questions.

Try This

Choose a lesson of this chapter to answer each question.

1. What is the objective of the lesson?

2. What new terms are defined in the lesson?

3. What skills are being taught in Example 2 of the lesson?

4. Which parts of the lesson can you use to answer Think and Discuss question 1?

Collecting, Displaying, and Analyzing Data **273**

Mastering *the* Standards

for Mathematical Practice

The topics described in the Standards for Mathematical Content will vary from year to year. However, the *way* in which you learn, study, and think about mathematics will not. The Standards for Mathematical Practice describe skills that you will use in all of your math courses.

Mathematical Practices

1. *Make sense of problems and persevere in solving them.*
2. *Reason abstractly and quantitatively.*
3. *Construct viable arguments and critique the reasoning of others.*
4. *Model with mathematics.*
5. *Use appropriate tools strategically.*
6. *Attend to precision.*
7. *Look for and make use of structure.*
8. *Look for and express regularity in repeated reasoning.*

4 Model with mathematics.

Mathematically proficient students can apply... mathematics... to... problems... in everyday life, society, and the workplace...

In your book

Application exercises and **Real-World Connections** apply mathematics to other disciplines and in real-world scenarios.

7-1 Mean, Median, Mode, and Range

To crack secret messages in code, you can list the number of times each symbol of the code appears in the message. The symbol that appears the most often represents the *mode*, which likely corresponds to the letter *e*.

The mode, along with the *mean* and the *median*, is a measure of *central tendency* used to represent the "middle" of a data set.

Vocabulary

mean

median

mode

range

outlier

• The **mean** is the sum of the data values divided by the number of data items.

• The **median** is the middle value of an odd number of data items arranged in order. For an even number of data items, the median is the mean of the two middle values.

• The **mode** is the value or values that occur most often. When all the data values occur the same number of times, there is no mode.

The **range** of a set of data is the difference between the greatest and least values.

EXAMPLE **1**

Interactivities Online ▶

Helpful Hint

The mean is sometimes called the *average*.

Finding the Mean, Median, Mode, and Range of a Data Set

Find the mean, median, mode, and range of the data set.

2, 1, 8, 0, 2, 4, 3, 4

mean:

$2 + 1 + 8 + 0 + 2 + 4 + 3 + 4 = 24$ *Add the values.*

$24 \div 8 = 3$ *Divide the sum by the*

The mean is 3.   *number of items.*

median:

0, 1, 2, **2**, **3**, 4, 4, 8   *Arrange the values in order.*

$\frac{2 + 3}{2} = 2.5$ *There are two middle values,*

The median is 2.5.   *so find the mean of these values.*

mode:

0, 1, **2**, **2**, 3, **4**, **4**, 8   *The values 2 and 4 occur twice.*

The modes are 2 and 4.

range: $8 - 0 = 8$ *Subtract the least value from*

The range is 8.   *the greatest value.*

Dennis Hallinan/Alamy

Often one measure of central tendency is more appropriate for describing a set of data than another measure is. Think about what each measure tells you about the data. Then choose the measure that best answers the question being asked.

EXAMPLE 2 **Choosing the Best Measure to Describe a Set of Data**

The line plot shows the number of hours 15 people exercised in one week. Which measure of central tendency best describes these data? Justify your answer.

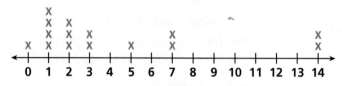

Number of hours

mean:

$$\frac{0 + 1 + 1 + 1 + 1 + 2 + 2 + 2 + 3 + 3 + 5 + 7 + 7 + 14 + 14}{15} = \frac{63}{15} = 4.2$$

The mean is 4.2.

Most of the people exercised fewer than 4 hours, so the mean does not describe the data set best.

median:

0, 1, 1, 1, 1, 2, 2, 2, 3, 3, 5, 7, 7, 14, 14
The median is 2.

The median best describes the data set because a majority of the data is clustered around the data value 2.

mode:

The greatest number of **X**'s occur above the number 1 on the line plot.
The mode is 1.

The mode represents only 4 of the 15 people. The mode does not describe the entire data set.

In the data set in Example 2, the value 14 is much greater than the other values in the set. An extreme value such as this is called an **outlier**. Outliers can greatly affect the mean of a data set.

Measure	Most Useful When
mean	the data are spread fairly evenly
median	the data set has an outlier
mode	the data involve a subject in which many data points of one value are important, such as election results

EXAMPLE **3** **Exploring the Effects of Outliers on Measures of Central Tendency**

The table shows the number of art pieces created by students in a glass-blowing workshop. Identify the outlier in the data set, and determine how the outlier affects the mean, median, and mode of the data. Then tell which measure of central tendency best describes the data with and without the outlier.

Name	Number of Pieces
Suzanne	5
Glen	1
Charissa	3
Eileen	4
Hermann	14
Tom	2

The outlier is 14.

Without the Outlier

mean:

$$\frac{5 + 1 + 3 + 4 + 2}{5} = 3$$

The mean is 3.

With the Outlier

mean:

$$\frac{5 + 1 + 3 + 4 + 14 + 2}{6} \approx 4.8$$

The mean is about 4.8.

The outlier increases the mean of the data by about 1.8.

median:

1, 2, 3, 4, 5

median:

1, 2, 3, 4, 5, 14

$$\frac{3 + 4}{2} = 3.5$$

The median is 3.

The median is 3.5.

The outlier increases the median of the data by 0.5.

mode:

There is no mode.

mode:

There is no mode.

The outlier does not change the mode of the data.

The median best describes the data with the outlier. The mean and median best describe the data without the outlier.

> **Caution!**
>
> Since all the data values occur the same number of times, the set has no mode.

Think and Discuss

1. **Describe** a situation in which the mean would best describe a data set.

2. **Tell** which measure of central tendency must be a data value.

3. **Explain** how an outlier affects the mean, median, and mode of a data set.

Learn It Online
Homework Help Online
Exercises 1–11, 13, 15

GUIDED PRACTICE

See Example **1** Find the mean, median, mode, and range of each data set.

1. 5, 30, 35, 20, 5, 25, 20

2. 44, 68, 48, 61, 59, 48, 63, 49

See Example **2** **3.** The line plot shows cooking temperatures required by different recipes. Which measure of central tendency best describes the data? Justify your answer.

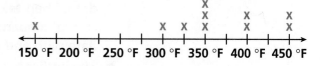

See Example **3** **4.** The table shows the number of glasses of water consumed in one day. Identify the outlier in the data set. Then determine how the outlier affects the mean, median, and mode of the data. Then tell which measure of central tendency best describes the data with and without the outlier.

Water Consumption							
Name	Randy	Lori	Anita	Jana	Sonya	Victor	Mark	Jorge
Glasses	4	12	3	1	4	7	5	4

INDEPENDENT PRACTICE

See Example **1** Find the mean, median, mode, and range of each data set.

5. 92, 88, 65, 68, 76, 90, 84, 88, 93, 89

6. 23, 43, 5, 3, 4, 14, 24, 15, 15, 13

7. 2.0, 4.4, 6.2, 3.2, 4.4, 6.2, 3.7

8. 13.1, 7.5, 3.9, 4.8, 17.1, 14.6, 8.3, 3.9

See Example **2** **9.** The line plot shows the number of letters in the spellings of the 12 months. Which measure of central tendency best describes the data set? Justify your answer.

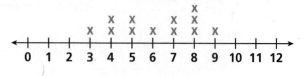

See Example **3** Identify the outlier in each data set. Then determine how the outlier affects the mean, median, and mode of the data. Then tell which measure of central tendency best describes the data with and without the outlier.

10. 13, 18, 20, 5, 15, 20, 13, 20

11. 45, 48, 63, 85, 151, 47, 88, 44, 68

PRACTICE AND PROBLEM SOLVING

Extra Practice
See Extra Practice for more exercises.

12. Health Based on the data from three annual checkups, Jon's mean height is 62 in. At the first two checkups Jon's height was 58 in. and 61 in. What was his height at the third checkup?

13. Find the mean, median, and mode of the data displayed in the line plot. Then determine how the outlier affects the mean.

```
                        X
          X   X         X
      X X X X X X   X X X               X
    +-+-+-+-+-+-+-+-+-+-+-+-+-+
    0   2   4   6   8  10  12  14  16  18  20  22
```

14. Critical Thinking The values in a data set are 95, 93, 91, 95, 100, 99, and 92. What value can be added to the set so that the mean, median, and mode remain the same?

 Sports The ages of the participants in a mountain bike race are 14, 23, 20, 24, 26, 17, 21, 31, 27, 25, 14, and 28. Make a stem-and-leaf plot of the data and find the mean, median, and mode. Which measure of central tendency best represents the ages of the participants? Explain.

The Leadville Trail 100 Mountain Bicycle Race is a 100-mile mountain-bike race held in Leadville, Colorado. Bikers climb over 12,000 ft through-out the Sawatch Range. In 2007, David Wiens won his fifth straight race.

16. Estimation The table shows the monthly rainfall in inches for six months. Estimate the mean, median, and range of the data.

Month	Rainfall (in.)
Jan	4.33
Feb	1.62
Mar	2.17
Apr	0.56
May	3.35
Jun	1.14

17. What's the Question? The values in a data set are 10, 7, 9, 5, 13, 10, 7, 14, 8, and 11. What is the question about central tendency that gives the answer 9.5 for the data set?

18. Write About It Which measure of central tendency is most often affected by including an outlier? Explain.

19. Challenge Pick a measure of central tendency that describes each situation. Explain your choice.

a. the number of siblings in a family **b.** the number of days in a month

Test Prep

20. Multiple Choice What is the mean of the winning scores shown in the table?

Ⓐ 276 Ⓒ 282.1

Ⓑ 276.8 Ⓓ 285

Masters Tournament Winning Scores					
Year	2001	2002	2003	2004	2005
Score	272	276	281	279	276

21. Multiple Choice In which data set are the mean, median, and mode all the same number?

Ⓕ 6, 2, 5, 4, 3, 4, 1 Ⓗ 2, 3, 7, 3, 8, 3, 2

Ⓖ 4, 2, 2, 1, 3, 2, 3 Ⓙ 4, 3, 4, 3, 4, 6, 4

Box-and-Whisker Plots

COMMON CORE

CC.7.SP.4 Use measures of center and measures of variability for numerical data from random samples to draw informal comparative inferences... *Also CC.7.SP.2*

Vocabulary

box-and-whisker plot

lower quartile

upper quartile

interquartile range

Carson is planning a deep-sea fishing trip. He chooses a fishing charter based on the number of fish caught on different charters.

A **box-and-whisker plot** uses a number line to show the distribution of a set of data.

To make a box-and-whisker plot, first divide the data into four parts using *quartiles*. The median, or *middle quartile*, divides the data into a lower half and an upper half. The median of the lower half is the **lower quartile**, and the median of the upper half is the **upper quartile**.

EXAMPLE 1 Making a Box-and-Whisker Plot

Use the data to make a box-and-whisker plot.

26, 17, 21, 23, 19, 28, 17, 20, 29

Step 1: Order the data from least to greatest. Then find the least and greatest values, the median, and the lower and upper quartiles.

> **Caution!**
>
> To find the median of a data set with an even number of values, find the mean of the two middle values.

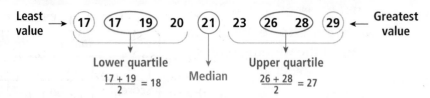

Least value → 17 (17 19) 20 (21) 23 (26 28) (29) ← Greatest value

Lower quartile $\frac{17 + 19}{2} = 18$ Median   Upper quartile $\frac{26 + 28}{2} = 27$

Step 2: Draw a number line. Above the number line, plot a point for each value in Step 1.

Step 3: Draw a box from the lower to the upper quartile. Inside the box, draw a vertical line through the median. Then draw the "whiskers" from the box to the least and greatest values.

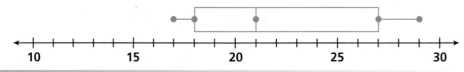

Image Bank/Getty Images

The **interquartile range** of a data set is the difference between the lower and upper quartiles. It tells how large the spread of data around the median is.

You can use a box-and-whisker plot to analyze how data in a set are distributed. You can also use box-and-whisker plots to help you compare two sets of data.

EXAMPLE 2 Comparing Box-and-Whisker Plots

The box-and-whisker plots below show the distribution of the number of fish caught per trip by two fishing charters.

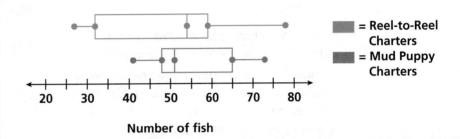

■ = Reel-to-Reel Charters

■ = Mud Puppy Charters

Number of fish

A Which fishing charter has a greater median?

The median number of fish caught on Reel-to-Reel Charters, about 54, is greater than the median number of fish caught on Mud Puppy Charters, about 51.

B Which fishing charter has a greater interquartile range?

The length of the box in a box-and-whisker plot indicates the interquartile range. Reel-to-Reel Charters has a longer box, so it has a greater interquartile range.

C Which fishing charter appears to be more predictable in the number of fish that might be caught on a fishing trip?

The range and interquartile range are smaller for Mud Puppy Charters, which means that there is less variation in the data. So the number of fish caught on Mud Puppy Charters is more predictable.

Think and Discuss

1. Describe what you can tell about a data set from a box-and-whisker plot.

2. Explain how the range and the interquartile range of a set of data are different. Which measure tells you more about central tendency?

GUIDED PRACTICE

See Example **1** **Use the data to make a box-and-whisker plot.**

1. 46   35   46   38   37   33   49   42   35   40   37

See Example **2** **Use the box-and-whisker plots of inches flown by two different paper airplanes for Exercises 2–4.**

2. Which paper airplane has a greater median flight length?

3. Which paper airplane has a greater interquartile range of flight lengths?

4. Which paper airplane appears to have a more predictable flight length?

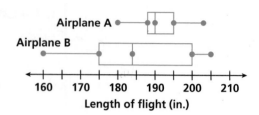

INDEPENDENT PRACTICE

See Example **1** **Use the data to make a box-and-whisker plot.**

5. 81   73   88   85   81   72   86   72   79   75   76

See Example **2** **Use the box-and-whisker plots of apartment rental costs in two different cities for Exercises 6–8.**

6. Which city has a greater median apartment rental cost?

7. Which city has a greater interquartile range of apartment rental costs?

8. Which city appears to have a more predictable apartment rental cost?

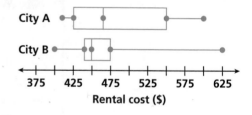

PRACTICE AND PROBLEM SOLVING

Extra Practice
See Extra Practice for more exercises.

The points scored per game by a basketball player are shown below. Use the data for Exercises 9–11.

12   7   15   23   10   18   39   15   20   8   13

9. Make two box-and-whisker plots of the data on the same number line: one plot with the outlier and one plot without the outlier.

10. How does the outlier affect the interquartile range of the data?

11. Which is affected more by the outlier: the range or the interquartile range?

12. Make a box-and-whisker plot of the data shown in the line plot.

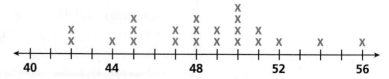

13. **Sports** The table shows the countries that were the top 15 medal winners in the 2004 Olympics.

Country	Medals	Country	Medals	Country	Medals
USA	103	Russia	92	China	63
Australia	49	Germany	48	Japan	37
France	33	Italy	32	Britain	30
Korea	30	Cuba	27	Ukraine	23
Netherlands	22	Romania	19	Spain	19

a. Make a box-and-whisker plot of the data.

b. Describe the distribution of the number of medals won.

14. **Measurement** The stem-and-leaf plot shows the heights in inches of a class of seventh graders.

a. Make a box-and-whisker plot of the data.

b. Three-fourths of the students are taller than what height?

c. Three-fourths of the students are shorter than what height?

Student Heights

Stems	Leaves
5	3 5 6 6 8 8 8 9 9
6	0 0 1 1 1 1 1 2 2 2 4

Key: 5|3 means 53

15. **What's the Error?** Using the data 2, 9, 5, 14, 8, 13, 7, 5, and 8, a student found the upper quartile to be 9. What did the student do wrong?

16. **Write About It** Two box-and-whisker plots have the same median and equally long whiskers. If the box of one plot is longer, what can you say about the difference between the two data sets?

17. **Challenge** An outlier is defined to be at least 1.5 times the interquartile range. Name the value that would be considered an outlier in the data set 1, 2, 4, 2, 1, 0, 6, 8, 1, 6, and 2.

Test Prep

Use the graph for Exercises 18 and 19.

18. **Multiple Choice** What is the difference between the interquartile ranges for the two data sets?

Ⓐ 21   Ⓒ 9

Ⓑ 18   Ⓓ 0

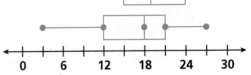

19. **Gridded Response** What is the lower quartile of the box-and-whisker plot with the greater range?

Technology LAB

Explore Box-and-Whisker Plots

Use with Box-and-Whisker Plots

Learn It Online
Lab Resources Online

You can use a graphing calculator to analyze data in box-and-whisker plots.

MATHEMATICAL PRACTICES **Use appropriate tools strategically.**
CC.7.SP.4 Use measures of center and measures of variability...to draw informal comparative inferences about two populations.

Activity 1

Ms. Garza's math class took a statewide math test. The data below are the scores of her 19 students.

79, 80, 61, 66, 74, 92, 88, 75, 93, 61, 77, 94, 25, 79, 86, 85, 48, 99, 80

Use a graphing calculator to make a box-and-whisker plot of the data.

To make a list of the scores, press **STAT** and choose **Edit**. Enter each value under List 1 (L1).

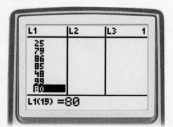

Use the **STAT PLOT** editor to set up the box-and-whisker plot.

Press **2nd** **Y=** (STAT PLOT). Press **ENTER** to select **Plot1**. Turn the plot **On** and use the arrow to select the plot type. The box-and-whisker plot is the fifth type shown.

The plot's values will come from the values listed in L1, so **Xlist: L1** should be visible. The **Freq** should also be set at 1.

Press **ZOOM** and select **9: ZoomStat** to display the plot. Press **TRACE** and use the arrows to see the values of the least value **(minX)**, greatest value **(maxX)**, median **(Med)**, and lower **(Q1)** and upper **(Q3)** quartiles.

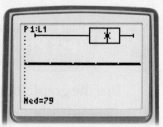

Think and Discuss

1. What five values do you need to construct a box-and-whisker plot? What values must you find before you can identify the upper and lower quartiles?

2. What does the box-and-whisker plot tell you about the data?

Try This

1. Survey your classmates to find the number of U.S. states that each student has visited. Use your calculator to make a box-and-whisker plot of the data.

2. Identify the least value, greatest value, range, median, lower quartile and upper quartile. What is the range between the upper and lower quartile?

Ray surveys 15 seventh-grade students and 15 teachers at his
school to find the number of hours they sleep at night.
The table shows the results.

	Average Number of Hours of Sleep Per Night
Students	9, 7, 10, 6, 11, 7, 9, 10, 10, 7, 9, 10, 8, 9, 11
Teachers	7, 6, 8, 9, 8, 7, 10, 6, 7, 9, 6, 7, 5, 7, 8

Use a graphing calculator to make a box-and-whisker plot for each
set of data.

Enter the first set of student data in L1.

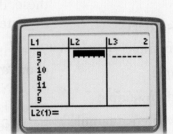

Press [>] to move right into the L2 column.
Enter the teacher data.

Set up **Plot1** as shown in Activity 1. Repeat the steps to set up **Plot2**.
Set the **Xlist** to L2 by pressing [2nd] [2].

Press [ZOOM] and select **9: ZoomStat** to display both
box-and-whisker plots. Press [TRACE] to display the statistics and
use the left and right arrows to move along the plots. Use the up
and down arrows to move between plots. The display in the left
corner tells which plot (P1 or P2) and which list (L1 or L2)
the statistics are for.

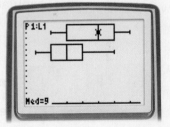

Think and Discuss

1. How can you use the box-and-whisker plots to compare the
   ranges of the data sets?

2. **Make a Conjecture** What do the graphs tell you about the
   sleeping habits of students and teachers?

Try This

1. Survey the boys and the girls in your class to find how many minutes they each
   talk on the phone. Use your calculator to make separate box-and-whisker plots
   for each set of data.

2. What are the least and greatest values and the median and lower and upper
   quartile for each box and-whisker-plot?

3. Are there any differences in the plots? What do these differences tell you about
   boys talking on the phone as compared to girls?

Populations and Samples

CC.7.SP.1 Understand that statistics can be used to gain information about a population by examining a sample of the population...

Vocabulary

population

sample

random sample

convenience sample

biased sample

Helpful Hint

A random sample is more likely to be representative of a population than a convenience sample is.

In 2002, there were claims that Chronic Wasting Disease (CWD), or Mad Elk Disease, was spreading westward across North America. In order to verify claims such as these, the elk population had to be tested.

When information is gathered about a group, such as all the elk in North America, the entire group is called the **population**. Because testing each member of a large group can be difficult or impossible, researchers often study a part of the population, called a **sample**.

For a **random sample**, members of the population are chosen at random. This gives every member of the population an equal chance of being chosen. A **convenience sample** is based on members of the population that are readily available, such as 30 elk in a wildlife preservation area.

E X A M P L E **Analyzing Sampling Methods**

Determine which sampling method will better represent the entire population. Justify your answer.

Football Game: Student Attendance	
Sampling Method	**Results of Survey**
Arnie surveys 80 students by randomly choosing names from the school directory.	62% attend football games
Vic surveys 28 students that were sitting near him during lunch.	81% attend football games

Arnie's method produces results that better represent the entire student population because he uses a random sample.

Vic's method produces results that are not as representative of the entire student population because he uses a convenience sample.

Video **LESSON Tutorials Online**

A **biased sample** does not fairly represent the population. A study of 50 elk belonging to a breeder could be biased because the breeder's elk might be less likely to have Mad Elk Disease than elk in the wild.

EXAMPLE **2** **Identifying Potentially Biased Samples**

Determine whether each sample may be biased. Explain.

A The first 50 people exiting a movie are surveyed to find out what type of movie people in the town like to see.

The sample is biased. It is likely that not everyone in the town likes to see the same type of movie that those 50 people just saw.

B A librarian randomly chooses 100 books from the library's database to calculate the average length of a library book.

The sample is not biased. It is a random sample.

Given data about a random sample, you can use proportional reasoning to make predictions or verify claims about the entire population.

EXAMPLE **3** **Verifying Claims Based on Statistical Data**

A biologist estimates that more than 700 of the 4,500 elk at a wildlife preserve are infected with a parasite. A random sample of 50 elk shows that 8 of them are infected. Determine whether the biologist's estimate is likely to be accurate.

Set up a proportion to predict the total number of infected elk.

$$\frac{\text{infected elk in sample}}{\text{size of sample}} = \frac{\text{infected elk in population}}{\text{size of population}}$$

$$\frac{8}{50} = \frac{x}{4,500}$$ *Let x represent the number of infected elk at the preserve.*

$$8 \cdot 4,500 = 50 \cdot x$$ *The cross products are equal.*

$$36,000 = 50x$$ *Multiply.*

$$\frac{36,000}{50} = \frac{50x}{50}$$ *Divide each side by 50.*

$$720 = x$$

Based on the sample, you can predict that there are 720 infected elk at the preserve. The biologist's estimate is likely to be accurate.

> **Remember!**
>
> In the proportion $\frac{a}{b} = \frac{c}{d}$, the cross products, $a \cdot d$ and $b \cdot c$ are equal.

MATHEMATICAL PRACTICES

Think and Discuss

1. Describe a situation in which you would want to use a sample rather than survey the entire population.

2. Explain why it might be difficult to obtain a truly random sample of a very large population.

GUIDED PRACTICE

See Example **1**

1. Determine which sampling method will better represent the entire population. Justify your answer.

Lone Star Cars: Customer Satisfaction	
Sampling Method	Results of Survey
Nadia surveys 200 customers on the car lot one Saturday morning.	92% are satisfied
Daria mails surveys to 100 randomly-selected customers.	68% are satisfied

See Example **2**

Determine whether each sample may be biased. Explain.

2. A company randomly selects 500 customers from its computer database and then surveys those customers to find out how they like their service.

3. A city-hall employee surveys 100 customers at a restaurant to learn about the jobs and salaries of city residents.

See Example **3**

4. A factory produces 150,000 light bulbs per day. The manager of the factory estimates that fewer than 1,000 defective bulbs are produced each day. In a random sample of 250 light bulbs, there are 2 defective bulbs. Determine whether the manager's estimate is likely to be accurate. Explain.

INDEPENDENT PRACTICE

See Example **1**

5. Determine which sampling method will better represent the entire population. Justify your answer.

Midville Morning News: Subscription Renewals	
Sampling Method	Results of Survey
Suzanne surveys 80 subscribers in her neighborhood.	61% intend to renew subscription
Vonetta telephones 150 randomly-selected subscribers.	82% intend to renew subscription

See Example **2**

Determine whether each sample may be biased. Explain.

6. A disc jockey asks the first 10 listeners who call in if they liked the last song that was played.

7. Members of a polling organization survey 700 registered voters by randomly choosing names from a list of all registered voters.

See Example **3**

8. A university has 30,600 students. In a random sample of 240 students, 20 speak three or more languages. Predict the number of students at the university who speak three or more languages.

PRACTICE AND PROBLEM SOLVING

Extra Practice
See Extra Practice for more exercises.

Life Science

North American fruit flies are known to damage cherries, apples, and blueberries. In the Mediterranean, fruit flies are a threat to citrus fruits.

Explain whether you would survey the entire population or use a sample.

9. You want to know the favorite painters of employees at a local art museum.

10. You want to know the types of calculators used by middle school students across the country.

11. You want to know how many hours per week the students in your social studies class spend on their homework.

12. **Life Science** A biologist chooses a random sample of 50 out of 750 fruit flies. She finds that 2 of them have mutated genes causing deformed wings. The biologist claims that approximately 30 of the 750 fruit flies have deformed wings. Do you agree? Explain.

13. A *biased question* is one that leads people to a certain answer. Kelly decides to use a random sampling to determine her classmates' favorite color. She asks, "Is green your favorite color?" Is this question biased? If so, give an example of an unbiased question.

14. **Critical Thinking** Explain why surveying 100 people who are listed in the phone book may not be a random sample.

15. **Write About It** Suppose you want to know whether the seventh-grade students at your school spend more time watching TV or using a computer. How might you choose a random sample from the population?

16. **Challenge** A manager at XQJ Software surveyed 200 company employees to find out how many of the employees walk to work. The results are shown in the table. Do you think the manager chose a random sample? Why or why not?

Employees at XQJ Software		
	Total Number	Number Who Walk
Population	9,200	300
Sample	200	40

Test Prep

17. **Multiple Choice** Banneker Middle School has 580 students. Wei surveys a random sample of 30 students and finds that 12 of them have pet dogs. How many students at the school are likely to have pet dogs?

Ⓐ 116   Ⓑ 232   Ⓒ 290   Ⓓ 360

18. **Short Response** Give an example of a biased sample. Explain why it is biased.

 **Hands-on LAB**

Explore Samples

Use with Populations and Samples

 **Learn It Online**
Lab Resources Online

REMEMBER
- Be sure that your sample reflects your population.

 Use appropriate tools strategically.
CC.7.SP.2 Use data from a random sample to draw inferences about a population with an unknown characteristic of interest... *Also CC.7.SP.1*

You can predict data about a population by collecting data from a representative sample.

Activity

Look through a magazine or a newspaper to find an article that includes the results of a survey. For example, you might find an article that shows a circle graph of people's favorite colors.

Conduct a similar survey at your school, and compare the results in the article to the results of your own survey. Follow the steps below to plan your survey.

1 Choose your population.
- every student in the school
- only your class
- all 8th grade students
- all girls
- all boys
- teachers

2 Choose two different sampling methods. Discuss the pros and cons of each method listed.
- random
- systematic
- convenience
- self-selected

3 Determine what question you will present to your sample. Decide whether your question will be multiple-choice or whether you will allow survey participants to give any answer they wish.

Think and Discuss

1. Describe how the population used for your survey differs from the population used for the survey in the article.

2. Explain how you can ensure that your sample will be representative of your population.

Try This

1. Create forms for your survey listing the different options. Then survey your sample. Make a table of your results.

2. Explain what your table tells you about your population. How do your results compare to the results from the survey in the article?

Focus on Problem Solving

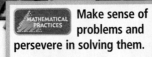

Make sense of problems and persevere in solving them.

Solve

• Choose an operation: addition or subtraction

In order to decide whether to add or subtract to solve a problem, you need to determine what action is taking place in the problem. If you are combining or putting together numbers, you need to add. If you are taking away or finding how far apart two numbers are, you need to subtract.

Determine the action in each problem. Then determine which operation could be used to solve the problem. Use the table for problems 5 and 6.

1 Betty, Raymond, and Helen ran a three-person relay race. Their individual times were 48 seconds, 55 seconds, and 51 seconds. What was their total time?

2 The Scots pine and the sessile oak are trees native to Northern Ireland. The height of a mature Scots pine is 111 feet, and the height of a mature sessile oak is 90 feet. How much taller is the Scots pine than the sessile oak?

3 Mr. Hutchins has $35.00 to buy supplies for his social studies class. He wants to buy items that cost $19.75, $8.49, and $7.10. Does Mr. Hutchins have enough money to buy all of the supplies?

4 The running time for the 1998 movie *Antz* is 83 minutes. Jordan has watched 25 minutes of the movie. How many minutes does he have left to watch?

Sizes of Marine Mammals	
Mammal	**Weight (kg)**
Killer whale	3,600
Manatee	400
Sea lion	200
Walrus	750

5 The table gives the approximate weights of four marine mammals. How much more does the killer whale weigh than the sea lion?

6 Find the total weight of the manatee, the sea lion, and the walrus. Do these three mammals together weigh more or less than the killer whale?

Use Random Samples

Use with Populations and Samples

Learn It Online
Lab Resources Online

Using a random sample of a population, or simulating a random sample on a graphing calculator, you can make predictions about the population that the random sample represents.

 Use appropriate tools strategically.
CC.7.SP.3 Informally assess the degree of visual overlap of two numerical data distributions with similar variabilities, measuring the difference between the centers by expressing it as a multiple of a measure of variability. *Also CC.7.SP.1, CC.7.SP.2*

Activity 1

Estimate the average shoe size of seventh grade male students by using a random sample of ten male students in your seventh grade class.

① Randomly select ten male seventh grade students and ask their shoe size. Record your results in a table like the one shown here.

② Find the mean, median, and mode shoe size of your data.

③ Make a prediction based on your random sample about the average shoe size for the entire population of male seventh grade students.

Random Sample of Seventh Grade Male Students	
Student	**Shoe Size**

Think and Discuss

1. On what did you base your prediction in Step 3?

2. How do all the predictions in class for Step 3 compare?

3. If you repeated the random sampling with 20 students, do you think the predictions would be different? Explain.

Try This

1. Simulate a random sample of shoes sizes on the graphing calculator. Use the smallest shoe size and the largest shoe size from your actual survey as the numbers between which the calculator will randomly generate.

You can use measures of center and variability from samples of two different populations to compare the populations.

Activity 2

1 Using your seventh grade data from Activity 1, find the mean, median, mode, and lower and upper quartiles.

2 Draw a box-and-whisker plot representing the data.

3 Repeat Activity 1 with male students from the eighth grade.

4 Using your eighth grade data, find the mean, median, mode, and lower and upper quartiles.

5 Draw a box-and-whisker plot.

Compare the box-and-whisker plots of the seventh grade data and eighth grade data.

6 How do the measures of center compare? Explain how you can determine this by comparing the box-and-whisker plots.

7 How do the measures of variation compare? Explain how you can see that by comparing the box plots.

8 Find the mean absolute deviation for each set of data. How do they compare?

Think and Discuss

1. Based on the data collected from random samples, do you think you could predict the shoe size of any seventh or eighth grade male? Explain.

2. How can the measures of center help you predict the shoe sizes of male seventh graders?

3. How can the measures of variation help you predict the shoe sizes of male seventh graders?

Try This

1. A random sample was taken of the number of words in a sentence in a sixth grade English book and an eighth grade English book. Find the mean, median, and mean absolute deviation for each set of data. How do the samples compare?

Sixth Grade Book	6	7	8	11	8	5	8	12	8	7	9	9	9	8	10
Eighth Grade Book	11	14	10	8	9	11	9	9	10	12	10	10	11	12	6

Ready To Go On?

Learn It Online
Resources Online

Quiz for Lessons 1 Through 3

 1 **Mean, Median, Mode, and Range**

The table shows the value of several used trucks.

Mileage (thousands)	Value of Truck ($)
30	20,000
20	18,000
40	14,000
30	24,000
35	10,000

1. Find the mean value of the trucks.

2. Find the mode of the mileage data.

The list shows the life spans in years of vampire bats in captivity.

18 22 5 21 19 21 17 3 19 20 29 18 17

3. Find the mean, median, mode, and range of the data. Round your answers to the nearest tenth of a year.

4. Which measure of central tendency best represents the data? Explain.

 2 **Box-and-Whisker Plots**

5. Make a box-and-whisker plot of the data 14, 8, 13, 20, 15, 17, 1, 12, 18, and 10.

6. On the same number line, make a box-and-whisker plot of the data 3, 8, 5, 12, 6, 18, 14, 8, 15, and 11.

7. Which box-and-whisker plot has a greater interquartile range?

 3 **Populations and Samples**

Determine whether each sample may be biased. Explain.

8. Rickie surveys people at an amusement park to find out the average size of people's immediate family.

9. Theo surveys every fourth person entering a grocery store to find out the average number of pets in people's homes.

10. A biologist estimates that there are 1,800 fish in a quarry. To test this estimate, a student caught 150 fish from the quarry, tagged them, and released them. A few days later, the student caught 50 fish and noted that 4 were tagged. Determine whether the biologist's estimate is likely to be accurate.

The Utah Jazz In 1979, the New Orleans Jazz moved to Salt Lake City, giving the state of Utah its first professional sports team. Since then, the Jazz have appeared frequently in the National Basketball Association's postseason playoffs.

UTAH

Salt Lake City

For 1–5, use the table.

1. Find the mean, median, mode, and range of the data.

2. The mean number of wins for the first two seasons from the table is equal to the number of wins for the 2007–2008 season. How many wins did the Jazz have in the 2007–2008 season?

3. Which season, if any, was an outlier? How does removing this season from the data set affect the mean, median, and mode?

4. Describe possible reasons for the low number of wins in the 2004–2005 season. Explain.

5. Make a box-and-whisker plot of the data.

Wins by the Utah Jazz	
Season	**Wins**
1999–2000	55
2000–2001	53
2001–2002	46
2002–2003	47
2003–2004	42
2004–2005	26
2005–2006	41
2006–2007	51

Real-World Connections

Game Time

Code Breaker

A *cryptogram* is a message written in code. One of the most common types of codes is a substitution code, in which each letter of a text is replaced with a different letter. The table shows one way to replace the letters in a text to make a coded message.

Original Letter	A	B	C	D	E	F	G	H	I	J	K	L	M
Code Letter	J	E	O	H	K	A	U	B	L	Y	V	G	P
Original Letter	N	O	P	Q	R	S	T	U	V	W	X	Y	Z
Code Letter	X	N	S	D	Z	Q	M	W	C	R	F	T	I

With this code, the word MATH is written PJMB. You can also use the table as a key to decode messages. Try decoding the following message.

J EJZ UZJSB OJX EK WQKH MN HLQSGJT HJMJ.

Suppose you want to crack a substitution code but are not given the key. You can use letter frequencies to help you. The bar graph below shows the number of times each letter of the English language is likely to appear in a text of 100 letters.

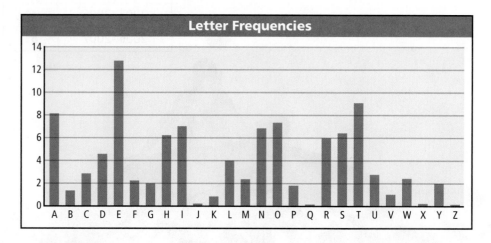

From the graph, you can see that E is the mode. In a coded text, the letter that appears most frequently is likely to represent the letter E. The letter that appears the second most frequently is likely to represent the letter T. Count the number of times each letter appears in the following message. Then use the letter frequencies and a bit of guesswork to decode the message. (*Hint:* In this code, P represents the letter M.)

KSQ PQUR, KSQ PQHGUR, URH KSQ PXHQ KQWW VXE DXPQKSGRT UCXEK U DQK XZ HUKU.

Materials
- card stock
- scissors
- glue
- colored paper
- magnetic strip
- tape
- empty CD case
- graph paper
- stapler

It's in the Bag!

PROJECT **Graph Match**

Use an empty CD case to make a magnetic matching game about different types of graphs.

Directions

1 Trim the card stock to $4\frac{1}{2}$ inches by 5 inches. On the card stock, write "Match the Name and Number" and list the numbers 1 through 5 as shown. Cut small rectangles from the magnetic strip and glue these next to the numbers. **Figure A**

2 Glue colored paper to the rest of the magnetic strip. Write the names of five different types of graphs on the strip. Cut these apart to form magnetic rectangles with the names of the graphs. **Figure B**

3 Put a magnetic name of a graph next to each number on the card stock. Then tape the card stock to the inside back cover of an empty CD case. **Figure C**

4 Cut out five squares of graph paper that are each $4\frac{1}{2}$ inches by $4\frac{1}{2}$ inches. Label the squares 1 through 5. Draw a different type of graph on each square, making sure to match the types that are named on the magnetic rectangles.

5 Staple the graphs together to make a booklet. Insert the booklet into the cover of the CD case.

Putting the Math into Action

Exchange your game with a partner. Can you match each graph with its name?

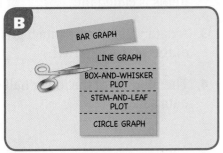

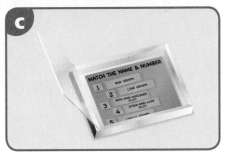

Sam Dudgeon/HMH

Vocabulary

biased sample	mean	random sample
box-and-whisker plot	median	range
convenience sample	mode	sample
interquartile range	outlier	upper quartile
lower quartile	population	

Complete the sentences below with vocabulary words from the list above.

1. When gathering information about a (n) ___?___, researchers often study part of the group, called a (n) ___?___.

2. The sum of the data values divided by the number of data items is called the ___?___ of the data.

3. A data value that is much greater than or less than the other data values of the set is called a (n) ___?___.

4. The median of the lower half of a set of data is called the ___?___ of the data set.

1   Mean, Median, Mode, and Range

■ **Find the mean, median, mode, and range of the data set 3, 7, 10, 2, and 3.**

Mean: $3 + 7 + 10 + 2 + 3 = 25$ $\frac{25}{5} = 5$

Median: 2, 3, **3**, 7, 10

Mode: **3**   Range: $10 - 2 = $ **8**

Find the mean, median, mode, and range of each data set.

5. 324, 233, 324, 399, 233, 299

6. 48, 39, 27, 52, 45, 47, 49, 37

7. When is the median the most useful measure of central tendency?

Use the table for Exercises 8–10.

U.S. Open Winning Scores					
	1995	**1996**	**1997**	**1998**	**1999**
Men	280	278	276	280	279
Women	278	272	274	290	272

8. Find the median and mode winning scores at the U.S. Open for women.

9. Find the mean winning score at the U.S. Open for men.

10. What are the ranges for the winning scores for men and for women?

2   Box-and-Whisker Plots

■ **Use the data to make a box-and-whisker plot: 14, 10, 23, 16, 21, 26, 23, 17, and 25.**

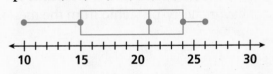

Use the following data for Exercises 11–12: 33, 38, 43, 30, 29, 40, 51, 27, 42, 23, and 31.

11. Make a box-and-whisker plot.

12. What is the interquartile range?

Study Guide: Review

3 Populations and Samples

■ In a random sample of 50 pigeons at a park, 4 are found to have a beak deformation. Is it reasonable to claim that about 20 of the pigeon population of 2,000 have this deformation? Explain.

No; $\frac{4}{50}$ is not closely proportional to $\frac{20}{2,000}$.

13. Fourteen out of 35 people surveyed prefer Brand X detergent. Is it reasonable for the store manager to claim that about 2,500 of the town's 6,000 residents will prefer Brand X detergent?

Determine whether each sample may be biased. Explain.

14. A newspaper reporter randomly chooses 100 different people walking down the street to find out their favorite dessert.

15. The first 25 teenagers exiting a clothing store are surveyed to find out what types of clothes teenagers like to buy.

Determine whether you would survey a sample or the entire population.

16. You are interested in the percentage of seniors in your state that plan on attending college.

17. Members of a table tennis club wants to know if members would play on Sundays.

18. The manager of an ice cream shop wonders if she should discontinue the flavor cherry-pistachio from the menu.

Study Guide: Review

Use the data set 12, 18, 12, 22, 28, 23, 32, 10, 29, and 36 for problems 1–8.

1. Find the mean, median, mode, and range of the data set.

2. How would the outlier 57 affect the measures of central tendency?

3. Make a cumulative frequency table of the data.

4. Make a stem-and-leaf plot of the data.

5. Make a line plot of the data. 6. Make a histogram of the data.

7. Make a box-and-whisker plot of the data. 8. What is the interquartile range?

Use the circle graph for problems 9 and 10. The school has 140 6th graders, 74 7th graders, and 100 8th graders.

9. Ted is in 6th grade, and will survey all of the students in his classes about whether they take the bus to school. Describe how Ted can use his survey results to approximate the number of students at the school that take the bus.

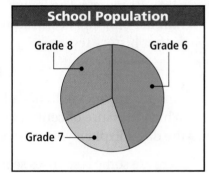

School Population

Grade 8 Grade 6

Grade 7

10. In a survey, 4 out of 5 8th graders participate in after-school activities. Use this information to estimate how many students at the school participate in after-school activities.

Use the table for problems 11 and 12.

11. The table shows passenger car fuel rates in miles per gallon for several years. Find the mean of the data.

12. Suppose the fuel rate in 2005 is equal to the mean fuel rate for 2004 and 2006. Find the fuel rate for 2005.

Year	2000	2002	2004	2006
Rate	21.0	20.7	21.2	21.6

Test Tackler

STANDARDIZED TEST STRATEGIES

Short Response: Write Short Responses

Short-response test items are designed to test your understanding of a math concept. In your response, you usually have to show your work and explain your answer. Scores are based on a 2-point scoring chart called a rubric.

EXAMPLE

Short Response The following data represents the number of hours Leann studied each day after school for her history test.

$$0, 1, 0, 1, 5, 3, 4$$

Find the mean, median, and mode for the data set. Which measure of central tendency best represents the data? Explain your answer.

Here are some responses scored using the 2-point rubric.

2-point response:

$$\frac{0 + 1 + 0 + 1 + 5 + 3 + 4}{7} = 2 \quad \textit{The mean is 2.}$$

0 0 1 ①3 4 5 *The median is 1.*

⓪⓪①① 3 4 5 *The modes are 0 and 1.*

The measure of central tendency that best represents the data is the mean, because it shows the average number of hours that Leann studied before her test.

1-point response:

$$\frac{0 + 1 + 0 + 1 + 5 + 3 + 4}{7} = 2 \quad \textit{The mean is 2.}$$

0 0 1 ①3 4 5 *The median is 1.*

⓪⓪①① 3 4 5 *The modes are 0 and 1.*

0-point response:

The mean is 2, the median is 2, and the mode is 0.

Scoring Rubric

2 points: The student correctly answers the question, shows all work, and provides a complete and correct explanation.

1 point: The student correctly answers the question but does not show all work or does not provide a complete explanation; or the student makes minor errors resulting in an incorrect solution but shows all work and provides a complete explanation.

0 points: The student gives an incorrect answer and shows no work or explanation, or the student gives no response.

Notice that there is no explanation given about the measure of central tendency that best represents the data.

Notice that the answer is incorrect and there is no explanation.

Test Tackler

Underline or highlight what you are being asked to do in each question. Be sure to explain how you get your answer in complete sentences.

Read each test item and use the scoring rubric to answer the questions that follow.

Item A
Short Response The box-and-whisker plot shows the height in inches of seventh-grade students. Describe the spread of the data.

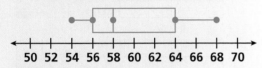

50 52 54 56 58 60 62 64 66 68 70

Student's Answer

> There are more students between 58 and 70 inches tall than there are between 50 and 58 inches tall because the third quartile is farther from the median than the first quartile is.

1. What score should the student's answer receive? Explain your reasoning.

2. What additional information, if any, should the student's answer include in order to receive full credit?

Item B
Short Response Explain the type of graph you would use to represent the number of each type of car sold at a car dealership in May.

Student's Answer

> I would use a bar graph to show how many of each car model was sold during the month.

3. What score should the student's answer receive? Explain your reasoning.

4. What additional information, if any, should the student's answer include in order to receive full credit?

Item C
Short Response The table shows the average daily temperatures of a climate-controlled conference room for a week. Determine the outlier and describe its effect on the mean of the data.

Day of Week	M	T	W	R	F
Temperature (°F)	70	71	83	70	69

Student's Answer

> The mean temperature drops from 72.6 °F to 70 °F.

5. What score should the student's answer receive? Explain your reasoning.

6. What additional information, if any, should the student's answer include in order to receive full credit?

Item D
Short Response A survey was conducted to determine which age group attended the most movies in November. Fifteen people at a movie theater were asked their age, and their responses are as follows: 6, 10, 34, 22, 46, 11, 62, 14, 14, 5, 23, 25, 17, 18, and 55. Make a cumulative frequency table of the data. Then explain which group saw the most movies.

Student's Answer

Age Groups	Frequency	Cumulative Frequency
0-13	4	4
14-26	7	11
27-40	1	12
41-54	1	13
55-68	2	15

7. What score should the student's answer receive? Explain your reasoning.

8. What additional information, if any, should the student's answer include in order to receive full credit?

Test Tackler

Cumulative Assessment
Multiple Choice

1. Which expression is true for the data set? 15, 18, 13, 15, 16, 14

   Ⓐ Mean < mode

   Ⓑ Median > mean

   Ⓒ Median = mean

   Ⓓ Median = mode

2. What is the first step to complete in simplifying this expression?

   $\frac{2}{5} + [3 - 5(2)] \div 6$

   Ⓕ Multiply 5 and 2.

   Ⓖ Divide by 6.

   Ⓗ Subtract 5 from 3.

   Ⓙ Divide 2 by 5.

3. What is the slope of the line shown?

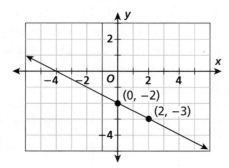

   Ⓐ $\frac{1}{2}$ Ⓒ 2

   Ⓑ $-\frac{2}{1}$ Ⓓ $-\frac{1}{2}$

4. On Monday the temperature was −13 °F. On Tuesday the temperature rose 7 °F. What was the temperature on Tuesday?

   Ⓕ −20 °F   Ⓗ −6 °F

   Ⓖ −8 °F   Ⓙ 7 °F

5. Which model best represents the fraction $\frac{5}{8}$?

   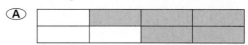

   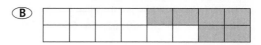

   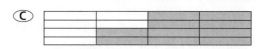

6. Ron eats $\frac{1}{4}$ cup of cereal every day as part of his breakfast. He has had a total of 16 cups of cereal this year. How many days has he eaten cereal?

   Ⓕ 4 days   Ⓗ 32 days

   Ⓖ 16 days   Ⓙ 64 days

7. A store is offering lip gloss at 25% off its original price. The original price of lip gloss is $7.89. Estimate the sale price.

   Ⓐ $6   Ⓒ $4

   Ⓑ $8   Ⓓ $2

8. What is the mode of the data given in the stem-and-leaf plot?

Stems	Leaves
6	1 2 2 5 9
7	0 4 6 7 8
8	3 3 3 5 6

   Key: 7|0 means 70

   Ⓕ 25   Ⓗ 76

   Ⓖ 62   Ⓙ 83

9. Solve $8 + 34x = -60$ for x.

Ⓐ $x = -5$ Ⓒ $x = -2$

Ⓑ $x = -0.97$ Ⓓ $x = 2$

10. Which statement is best supported by the data?

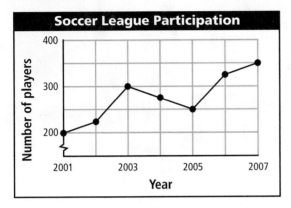

Soccer League Participation

Ⓕ More students played soccer in 2005 than in 2002.

Ⓖ From 2001–2007, soccer participation increased by 100%.

Ⓗ From 2002–2006, soccer participation decreased by 144%.

Ⓙ Participation increased between 2004 and 2005.

Read a graph or diagram as closely as you read the actual test question. These visual aids contain important information.

Gridded Response

11. To the nearest hundredth, what is the difference between the median and the mean of the data set?

14, 11, 14, 11, 13, 12, 9, 15, 16

12. What value represents the upper quartile of the data in the box-and-whisker plot below?

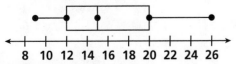

13. The number of free throws changes from 12 to 21. What is the percent of change as a decimal?

Short Response

S1. The graph shows the results of a survey. Aaron read the graph and determined that more than $\frac{1}{5}$ of the students chose drama as their favorite type of movie. Do you agree with Aaron? Why or why not?

S2. A land developer purchases 120 acres of land and plans to divide one part into five 5-acre lots, another part into two 10-acre lots, and the rest into $\frac{1}{2}$-acre lots. Each lot will be sold for a future home site. How many total lots can the developer plan to sell?

Extended Response

E1. Mr. Parker wants to identify the types of activities in which high school students participate after school, so he surveys the twelfth-graders in his science classes. The table shows the results of the survey.

Activity	Boys	Girls
Play sports	36	24
Talk to friends	6	30
Do homework	15	18
Work	5	4

a. What is the mean number of girls per activity? Show your work.

b. What type of sample is used? Is this sample representative of the population? Explain.

c. In all, Mr. Parker surveyed 60 12th-grade boys. If there are 210 boys in 12th grade, estimate the number of boys in 12th grade that play sports.

Geometric Figures

Chapter Focus
- Use facts about distance
and angles to analyze
figures.
- Find unknown measures of
angles.

Why Learn This?

The deck of the Brooklyn Bridge is
suspended by vertical cables. Reinforcement
cables intersect the suspenders and form
geometric shapes such as quadrilaterals.

Learn It Online
Chapter Project Online

Richard Cummins/Corbis

Are You Ready?

✓ Vocabulary

Choose the best term from the list to complete each sentence.

1. An equation showing that two ratios are equal is a(n) __?__.
2. The coordinates of a point on a grid are written as a(n) __?__.
3. A(n) __?__ is a special ratio that compares a number to 100 and uses the symbol %.
4. The number −3 is a(n) __?__.

decimal

integer

percent

proportion

ordered pair

Complete these exercises to review skills you will need for this chapter.

✓ Percents and Decimals

Write each decimal as a percent.

5. 0.77   6. 0.06   7. 0.9   8. 1.04

Write each percent as a decimal.

9. 42%   10. 80%   11. 1%   12. 131%

✓ Find the Percent of a Number

Solve.

13. What is 10% of 40?   14. What is 12% of 100?   15. What is 99% of 60?

16. What is 100% of 81?   17. What is 45% of 360?   18. What is 55% of 1,024?

✓ Inverse Operations

Use the inverse operation to write an equation. Solve.

19. $45 + n = 97$ 20. $n - 18 = 100$ 21. $n - 72 = 91$ 22. $n + 23 = 55$

23. $5 \times t = 105$ 24. $b \div 13 = 8$ 25. $k \times 18 = 90$ 26. $d \div 7 = 8$

✓ Graph Ordered Pairs

Use the coordinate plane at right. Write the ordered pair for each point.

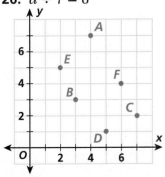

27. point A 28. point B

29. point C 30. point D

31. point E 32. point F

Study Guide: Preview

Where You've Been

Previously, you

- identified angle and line relationships.
- identified similar figures.
- graphed points on a coordinate plane.

In This Chapter

You will study

- classifying pairs of angles as complementary or supplementary.
- identifying parallel and perpendicular lines.
- using congruence to solve problems.

Where You're Going

You can use the skills learned in this chapter

- to solve problems related to architecture and engineering.
- to measure distances indirectly.

Key Vocabulary/Vocabulario

angle	ángulo
congruent	congruente
parallel lines	rectas paralelas
perpendicular lines	rectas perpendiculares
vertex	vértice

Vocabulary Connections

To become familiar with some of the vocabulary terms in the chapter, consider the following. You may refer to the chapter, the glossary, or a dictionary if you like.

1. *Congruent* comes from the Latin word *congruere,* meaning "to agree or correspond." If two figures are **congruent**, do you think they look the same or different?

2. Look at the double l's in the word **parallel**. How can they help you remember the relationship between parallel lines?

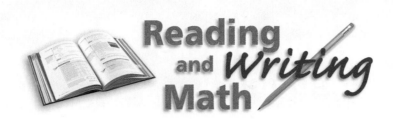 # Reading and Writing Math

Writing Strategy: Keep a Math Journal

Keeping a math journal can help you improve your writing and reasoning skills and help you make sense of math topics that might be confusing.

You can use your journal to reflect on what you have learned in class or to summarize important concepts and vocabulary. Most important, though, your math journal can help you see your progress throughout the year.

> **Journal Entry:** Read the entry Lydia wrote in her math journal about similar figures.

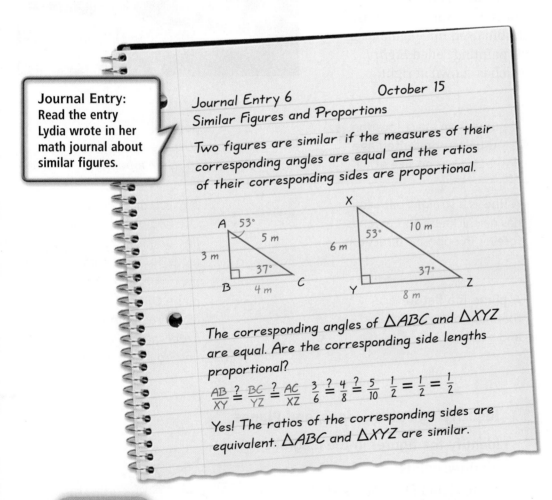

Journal Entry 6   October 15
Similar Figures and Proportions

Two figures are similar if the measures of their corresponding angles are equal <u>and</u> the ratios of their corresponding sides are proportional.

The corresponding angles of $\triangle ABC$ and $\triangle XYZ$ are equal. Are the corresponding side lengths proportional?

$\dfrac{AB}{XY} \overset{?}{=} \dfrac{BC}{YZ} \overset{?}{=} \dfrac{AC}{XZ}$ $\dfrac{3}{6} \overset{?}{=} \dfrac{4}{8} \overset{?}{=} \dfrac{5}{10}$ $\dfrac{1}{2} = \dfrac{1}{2} = \dfrac{1}{2}$

Yes! The ratios of the corresponding sides are equivalent. $\triangle ABC$ and $\triangle XYZ$ are similar.

Try This

Begin a math journal. Make an entry every day for one week. Use the following ideas to begin your entries. Be sure to date each entry.

- What I already know about this lesson is . . .

- The skills I need to be successful in this lesson are . . .

- What challenges did I have? How did I handle these challenges?

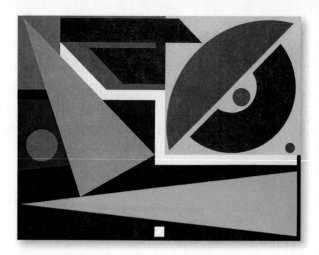

8-1 Building Blocks of Geometry

Points, *lines*, and *planes* are the most basic figures of geometry. Other geometric figures, such as *line segments* and *rays*, are defined in terms of these building blocks.

Artists often use basic geometric figures when creating their works. For example, Auguste Herbin used *line segments* in his painting called *Eight I*, which is shown at right.

Vocabulary

point
line
plane
ray
line segment
congruent

Helpful Hint

A number line is an example of a line, and a coordinate plane is an example of a plane.

A **point** is an exact location. It is usually represented as a dot, but it has no size at all.	• *A*	point *A* *Use a capital letter to name a point.*
A **line** is a straight path that has no thickness and extends forever in opposite directions.	ℓ ←•———•→ *X* *Y*	$\overleftrightarrow{XY}$, $\overleftrightarrow{YX}$, or ℓ *Use two points on the line or a lowercase letter to name a line.*
A **plane** is a flat surface that has no thickness and extends forever.	*Q*• *S*• *R*•	plane *QRS* *Use three points in any order, not on the same line, to name a plane.*

EXAMPLE **1** **Identifying Points, Lines, and Planes**

Identify the figures in the diagram.

A **three points**

A, *E*, and *D*   *Choose any three points.*

B **two lines**

$\overleftrightarrow{BD}$, $\overleftrightarrow{CE}$ *Choose any two points on a line to name a line.*

C **a plane**

plane *ABC*   *Choose any three points not on the same line to name a plane.*

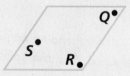

Christie's Images/Corbis

Video   **Lesson Tutorials Online**   my.hrw.com

A **ray** is a part of a line. It has one endpoint and extends forever in one direction.	$\overrightarrow{GH}$ *Name the endpoint first when naming a ray.*
A **line segment** is a part of a line or a ray that extends from one endpoint to another.	$\overline{LM}$ or $\overline{ML}$ *Use the endpoints to name a line segment.*

EXAMPLE 2   Identifying Line Segments and Rays

Identify the figures in the diagram.

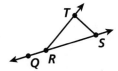

  A three rays
  $\overrightarrow{RQ}$, $\overrightarrow{RT}$, and $\overrightarrow{SQ}$ *Name the endpoint of a ray first.*

  B three line segments
  $\overline{RQ}$, $\overline{QS}$, and $\overline{ST}$ *Use the endpoints in any order to name a line segment.*

Figures are **congruent** if they have the same shape and size. Line segments are congruent if they have the same length.

You can use tick marks to indicate congruent line segments. In the triangle at right, line segments AB and BC are congruent.

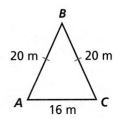

EXAMPLE 3   Identifying Congruent Line Segments

Identify the line segments that are congruent in the figure.

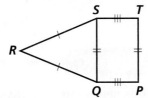

$\overline{QR} \cong \overline{SR}$ *One tick mark*
$\overline{QS} \cong \overline{PT}$ *Two tick marks*
$\overline{QP} \cong \overline{ST}$ *Three tick marks*

MATHEMATICAL PRACTICES

Think and Discuss

1. **Explain** why a line and a plane can be named in more than two ways. How many ways can a line segment be named?

2. **Explain** why it is important to choose three points that are not on the same line when naming a plane.

Learn It Online
Homework Help Online
Exercises 1–12, 21
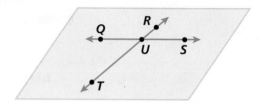

GUIDED PRACTICE

See Example 1 **Identify the figures in the diagram.**

1. three points

2. two lines

3. a plane

See Example 2 4. three rays

5. three line segments

See Example 3 6. Identify the line segments that are congruent in the figure.

INDEPENDENT PRACTICE

See Example 1 **Identify the figures in the diagram.**

7. three points

8. two lines

9. a plane

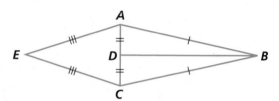

See Example 2 10. three rays

11. three line segments

See Example 3 12. Identify the line segments that are congruent in the figure.

PRACTICE AND PROBLEM SOLVING

Extra Practice
See Extra Practice for more exercises.

13. Identify the points, lines, line segments, and rays that are represented in the illustration, and tell what plane each is in. Some figures may be in more than one plane.

14. **Critical Thinking** How many different line segments can be named in the figure below? Name each segment.

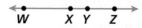

15. Draw a diagram in which a plane, 5 points, 4 rays, and 2 lines can be identified. Then identify these figures.

16. The artwork at right, by Diana Ong, is called *Blocs*.

   a. Copy the line segments in the artwork. Add tick marks to show line segments that appear to be congruent.

   b. Label the endpoints of the segments, including the points of intersection. Then name four pairs of line segments that appear to be congruent.

17. Draw a figure that includes at least three sets of congruent line segments. Label the endpoints and use notation to tell which line segments are congruent.

18. Critical Thinking Can two endpoints be shared by two different line segments? Make a drawing to illustrate your answer.

19. **Write About It** Explain the difference between a line, a line segment, and a ray. Is it possible to estimate the length of any of these figures? If so, tell which ones and why.

20. ⭐ **Challenge** The sandstone sculpture at right, by Georges Vantongerloo, is called *Interrelation of Volumes*. Explain whether two separate faces on the front of the sculpture could be in the same plane.

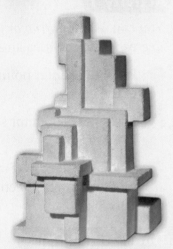

Test Prep

21. Multiple Choice Identify the line segments that are congruent in the figure.

   I $\overline{AB}$, $\overline{BC}$ **II** $\overline{AB}$, $\overline{CD}$

   III $\overline{BC}$, $\overline{CD}$ **IV** $\overline{BC}$, $\overline{AD}$

   Ⓐ I only   Ⓑ I and III   Ⓒ II and IV   Ⓓ II only

22. Short Response Draw a plane that contains each of the following: points *A*, *B*, and *C*; line segment *AB*; ray *BC*; and line *AC*.

Hands-on LAB

Explore Complementary and Supplementary Angles

Use with Classifying Angles

REMEMBER
- An angle is formed by two rays with a common endpoint, called the vertex.

Use appropriate tools strategically.
CC.7.G.5 Use facts about supplementary, complementary, vertical, and adjacent angles... to write and solve simple equations for an unknown angle in a figure

Activity 1

You can use a *protractor* to measure angles in units called *degrees*. Find the measure of ∠AVB.

1. Place the center point of the protractor on the vertex of the angle.

2. Place the protractor so that $\overrightarrow{AV}$ passes through the 0° mark.

3. Using the scale that starts with 0° along $\overrightarrow{AV}$, read the measure where $\overrightarrow{VB}$ crosses the scale. The measure of ∠AVB is 50°.

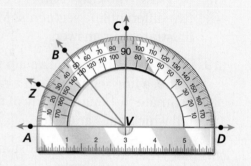

Think and Discuss

1. Explain how to find the measure of ∠BVC without moving the protractor.

Try This

Use the protractor in Activity 1 to find the measure of each angle.

1. ∠AVC   2. ∠AVZ   3. ∠DVC

Activity 2

Copy and measure each pair of angles.

Type of Angle Pair	Examples	Nonexamples
Complementary	1. [angle figure with A, B]	2. [angle figure with C, D]
	3. [angle figure with E, F]	4. [angle figure with G, H]

Type of Angle Pair	Examples		Nonexamples
Supplementary	**5.** *I* *J*	**7.** *M* *N*	**6.** *K* *L* **8.** *O* *P*

Think and Discuss

1. **Make a Conjecture** For each type of angle pair, complementary and supplementary, make a conjecture about how the angle measurements are related.

Try This

Use a protractor to measure each of the angle pairs below. Tell whether the angle pairs are complementary, supplementary, or neither.

1.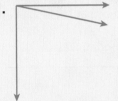

2.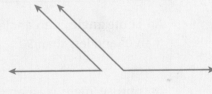

3.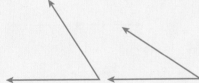

4.

5. **Make a Conjecture** The two angles in Exercise 4 form a straight angle. Make a conjecture about the number of degrees in a straight angle.

6. Use a protractor to find four pairs of complementary angles and four pairs of supplementary angles in the figure at right.

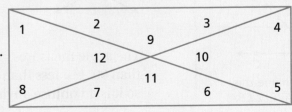

CC.7.G.5 Use facts about supplementary, complementary, vertical, and adjacent angles... to write and solve simple equations for an unknown angle in a figure

Vocabulary

angle

vertex

right angle

acute angle

obtuse angle

straight angle

complementary angles

supplementary angles

Interactivities Online ▶

As an airplane takes off, the path of the airplane forms an *angle* with the ground.

An **angle** is formed by two rays with a common endpoint. The two rays are the sides of the angle. The common endpoint is the **vertex**.

Angles are measured in degrees (°). An angle's measure determines the type of angle it is.

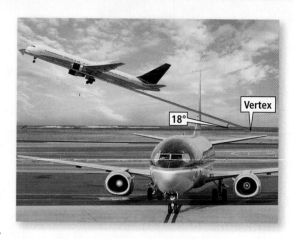

18°   Vertex

A **right angle** is an angle that measures exactly 90°. The symbol ⌐ indicates a right angle.

An **acute angle** is an angle that measures greater than 0° and less than 90°.

An **obtuse angle** is an angle that measures greater than 90° but less than 180°.

A **straight angle** is an angle that measures exactly 180°.

EXAMPLE **1**   **Classifying Angles**

Tell whether each angle is acute, right, obtuse, or straight.

Writing Math

A
1
B
C

You can name this angle ∠*ABC*, ∠*CBA*, ∠*B*, or ∠1.

A

The angle measures greater than 90° but less than 180°, so it is an obtuse angle.

B

The angle measures less than 90°, so it is an acute angle.

If the sum of the measures of two angles is 90°, then the angles are **complementary angles**. If the sum of the measures of two angles is 180°, then the angles are **supplementary angles**.

Video   **Lesson Tutorials Online**   my.hrw.com

Joe Drivas/Photographer's Choice/Getty Images

EXAMPLE 2 Identifying Complementary and Supplementary Angles

Use the diagram to tell whether the angles are complementary, supplementary, or neither.

Helpful Hint

If the angle you are measuring appears obtuse, then its measure is greater than 90°. If the angle is acute, its measure is less than 90°.

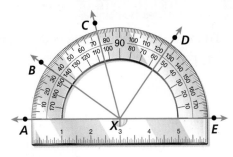

A ∠*DXE* and ∠*AXB*

m∠*DXE* = 55° and m∠*AXB* = 35°

Since 55° + 35° = 90°, ∠*DXE* and ∠*AXB* are complementary.

Reading Math

Read m∠*DXE* as "the measure of angle *DXE*."

B ∠*DXE* and ∠*BXC*

m∠*DXE* = 55°. To find m∠*BXC*, start with the measure that $\overrightarrow{XC}$ crosses, 75°, and subtract the measure that $\overrightarrow{XB}$ crosses, 35°.
m∠*BXC* = 75° − 35° = 40°.

Since 55° + 40° = 95°, ∠*DXE* and ∠*BXC* are neither complementary nor supplementary.

C ∠*AXC* and ∠*CXE*

m∠*AXC* = 75° and m∠*CXE* = 105°

Since 75° + 105° = 180°, ∠*AXC* and ∠*CXE* are supplementary.

EXAMPLE 3 Finding Angle Measures

Angles *R* and *V* are supplementary. If m∠*R* is 67°, what is m∠*V*?

Since ∠*R* and ∠*V* are supplementary, m∠*R* + m∠*V* = 180°.

$$m\angle R + m\angle V = 180°$$
$$67° + m\angle V = 180°$$ *Substitute 67° for m∠R.*
$$\underline{-67° \qquad\qquad -67°}$$ *Subtract 67° from both sides.*
$$m\angle V = 113°$$

The measure of ∠*V* is 113°.

Think and Discuss

1. Describe three different ways to classify an angle.

2. Explain how to find the measure of ∠*P* if ∠*P* and ∠*Q* are complementary angles and m∠*Q* = 25°.

Exercises

Learn It Online
Homework Help Online
Exercises 1–18, 19, 21, 23

GUIDED PRACTICE

See Example **1** Tell whether each angle is acute, right, obtuse, or straight.

1.

2.

3.

See Example **2** Use the diagram to tell whether the angles are complementary, supplementary, or neither.

4. ∠AXB and ∠BXC   **5.** ∠BXC and ∠DXE

6. ∠DXE and ∠AXD   **7.** ∠CXD and ∠AXB

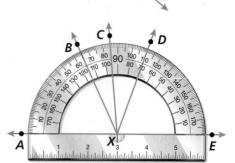

See Example **3** **8.** Angles L and P are complementary. If m∠P is 34°, what is m∠L?

9. Angles B and C are supplementary. If m∠B is 119°, what is m∠C?

INDEPENDENT PRACTICE

See Example **1** Tell whether each angle is acute, right, obtuse, or straight.

10.   **11.**   **12.**

See Example **2** Use the diagram to tell whether the angles are complementary, supplementary, or neither.

13. ∠NZO and ∠MZN **14.** ∠MZN and ∠OZP

15. ∠LZN and ∠NZP **16.** ∠NZO and ∠LZM

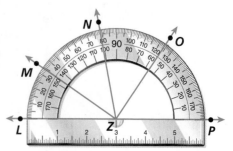

See Example **3** **17.** Angles F and O are supplementary. If m∠F is 85°, what is m∠O?

18. Angles J and K are complementary. If m∠K is 22°, what is m∠J?

PRACTICE AND PROBLEM SOLVING

Extra Practice
See Extra Practice for more exercises.

Classify each pair of angles as complementary or supplementary. Then find the unknown angle measure.

19.

20.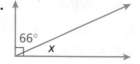

21.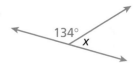

22. **Critical Thinking** The hands of a clock form an acute angle at 1:00. What type of angle is formed at 6:00? at 3:00? at 5:00?

23. **Geography** Imaginary curves around Earth show distances in degrees from the equator and Prime Meridian. On a flat map, these curves are displayed as horizontal lines (latitude) and vertical lines (longitude).

    a. What type of angle is formed where a line of latitude and a line of longitude cross?

    b. Estimate the latitude and longitude of Washington, D.C.

24. **What's the Error?** A student states that when the sum of two angles equals the measure of a straight angle, the two angles are complementary. Explain why the student is incorrect.

25. **Write About It** Explain why two obtuse angles cannot be supplementary to one another.

26. **Challenge** Find m∠*BAC* in the figure.

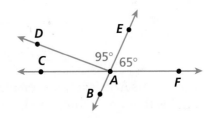

Use the diagram for Exercises 27 and 28.

27. **Multiple Choice** Which statement is NOT true?

    Ⓐ ∠*BAC* is acute.

    Ⓑ ∠*DAE* is a right angle.

    Ⓒ ∠*FAE* and ∠*EAD* are complementary angles.

    Ⓓ ∠*FAD* and ∠*DAC* are supplementary angles.

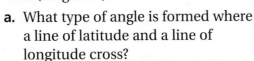

28. **Multiple Choice** What is the measure of ∠*FAD*?

    Ⓕ 30°   Ⓖ 120°   Ⓗ 150°   Ⓙ 180°

Explore Parallel Lines and Transversals

Use with Line and Angle Relationships

REMEMBER
- Two angles are supplementary if the sum of their measures is 180°.
- Angles with measures greater than 0° but less than 90° are acute.
- Angles with measures greater than 90° but less than 180° are obtuse.

Use appropriate tools strategically.

CC.7.G.5 Use facts about supplementary, complementary, vertical, and adjacent angles... to write and solve simple equations for an unknown angle in a figure

Parallel lines are lines in the same plane that never cross. When two parallel lines are intersected by a third line, the angles formed have special relationships. This third line is called a *transversal*.

In San Francisco, California, many streets are parallel such as Lombard St. and Broadway.

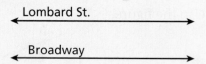

Columbus Ave. is a transversal that runs diagonally across them. The eight angles that are formed are labeled on the diagram below.

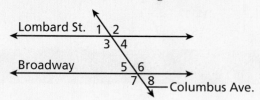

Activity

❶ Copy the table below. Then use a protractor to measure angles 1–8 in the diagram. Write these measures in your table.

Angle Number	Angle Measure
1	
2	
3	
4	
5	
6	
7	
8	

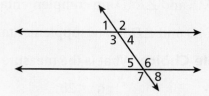

2 Use the table you completed and the corresponding diagram for the following problems.

   a. Angles inside the parallel lines are *interior angles*. Name them.

   b. Angles outside the parallel lines are *exterior angles*. Name them.

   c. Angles 3 and 6 and angles 4 and 5 are *alternate interior angles*. What do you notice about the measures of angles 3 and 6? What do you notice about the measures of angles 4 and 5?

   d. Angles 2 and 7 and angles 1 and 8 are *alternate exterior angles*. How do the measures of each pair of alternate exterior angles compare?

   e. Angles 1 and 5 are *corresponding angles* because they are in the same position relative to the parallel lines. How do the measures of angles 1 and 5 compare? Name another set of corresponding angles.

   f. **Make a Conjecture** What conjectures can you make about the measures of alternate interior angles? alternate exterior angles? corresponding angles?

Think and Discuss

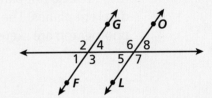

1. $\overleftrightarrow{FG}$ and $\overleftrightarrow{LO}$ are parallel. Tell what you know about the angles that are labeled 1 through 8.

2. Angle 2 measures 125°. What are the measures of angles 1, 3, 4, 5, 6, 7, and 8?

3. A transversal intersects two parallel lines and one of the angles formed measures 90°. Compare the measures of the remaining angles formed by the three lines.

Try This

Use a protractor to measure one angle in each diagram. Then find the measures of all the other angles without using a protractor. Tell how to find each angle measure.

1.

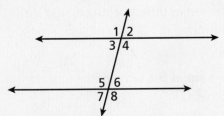

2.

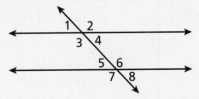

3.

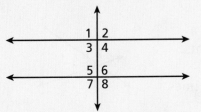

4.

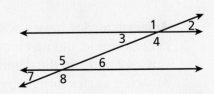

Line and Angle Relationships

COMMON CORE

CC.7.G.5 Use facts about supplementary, complementary, vertical, and adjacent angles in a multi-step problem to write and solve simple equations for an unknown angle in a figure

Vocabulary

perpendicular lines

parallel lines

skew lines

adjacent angles

vertical angles

transversal

When lines, line segments, or rays intersect, they form angles. If the angles formed by two intersecting lines measure 90°, the lines are **perpendicular lines**.

Some lines in the same plane do not intersect at all. These lines are **parallel lines**. Segments and rays that are parts of parallel lines are also parallel. The blue lines in the photograph are parallel.

Skew lines do not intersect, and yet they are also not parallel. They lie in different planes. The yellow lines in the photograph are skew.

EXAMPLE 1

Interactivities Online ▶

Identifying Parallel, Perpendicular, and Skew Lines

Tell whether the lines in the figure appear parallel, perpendicular, or skew.

Reading Math

The symbol ⊥ means "is perpendicular to." The symbol // means "is parallel to."

A $\overleftrightarrow{AB}$ and $\overleftrightarrow{AC}$
$\overleftrightarrow{AB} \perp \overleftrightarrow{AC}$

The lines appear to intersect to form right angles.

B $\overleftrightarrow{CE}$ and $\overleftrightarrow{BD}$
$\overleftrightarrow{CE}$ and $\overleftrightarrow{BD}$ are skew.

The lines are in different planes and do not intersect.

C $\overleftrightarrow{AC}$ and $\overleftrightarrow{BD}$
$\overleftrightarrow{AC}$ // $\overleftrightarrow{BD}$

The lines are in the same plane and do not intersect.

Adjacent angles have a common vertex and a common side, but no common interior points. Angles 2 and 3 in the diagram are adjacent. Adjacent angles formed by two intersecting lines are supplementary.

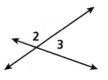

Frank Leather Eye Ubiquitous/Corbis

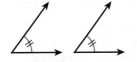

Vertical angles are the opposite angles formed by two intersecting lines. Angles 1 and 3 in the diagram are vertical angles. Vertical angles have the same measure, so they are congruent.

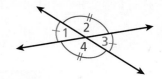

A **transversal** is a line that intersects two or more lines that lie in the same plane. Transversals to parallel lines form special angle pairs.

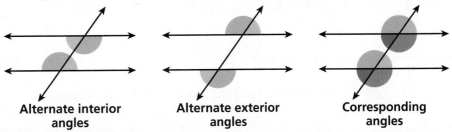

Alternate interior angles	Alternate exterior angles	Corresponding angles

---

PROPERTIES OF TRANSVERSALS TO PARALLEL LINES

If two parallel lines are intersected by a transversal,
- corresponding angles are congruent,
- alternate interior angles are congruent,
- and alternate exterior angles are congruent.

E X A M P L E **2** **Using Angle Relationships to Find Angle Measures**

Line *n* ∥ line *p*. Find the measure of each angle.

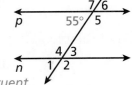

A ∠6

$m\angle 6 = 55°$ *Vertical angles are congruent.*

B ∠1

$m\angle 1 = 55°$ *Corresponding angles are congruent.*

C ∠7

$m\angle 7 + 55° = 180°$ *Adjacent angles formed by two*
$\underline{ -55° \quad -55°}$ *intersecting lines are supplementary.*
$m\angle 7 \qquad = 125°$

D ∠3

$m\angle 3 = 55°$ *Alternate interior angles are congruent.*

MATHEMATICAL PRACTICES

Think and Discuss

1. **Draw** a pair of parallel lines intersected by a transversal. Use tick marks to indicate the congruent angles.

2. **Give** some examples in which parallel, perpendicular, and skew relationships can be seen in the real world.

Learn It Online
Homework Help Online
Exercises 1–12, 13, 15, 17, 19, 21, 23

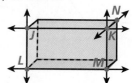

GUIDED PRACTICE

See Example 1 Tell whether the lines appear parallel, perpendicular, or skew.

1. $\overleftrightarrow{JL}$ and $\overleftrightarrow{KM}$

2. $\overleftrightarrow{LM}$ and $\overleftrightarrow{KN}$

3. $\overleftrightarrow{LM}$ and $\overleftrightarrow{KM}$

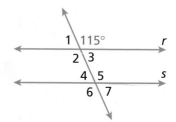

See Example 2 Line $r \parallel$ line s. Find the measure of each angle.

4. $\angle 5$

5. $\angle 2$

6. $\angle 6$

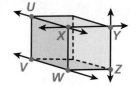

INDEPENDENT PRACTICE

See Example 1 Tell whether the lines appear parallel, perpendicular, or skew.

7. $\overleftrightarrow{UX}$ and $\overleftrightarrow{YZ}$

8. $\overleftrightarrow{YZ}$ and $\overleftrightarrow{XY}$

9. $\overleftrightarrow{UX}$ and $\overleftrightarrow{VW}$

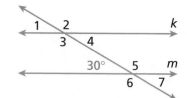

See Example 2 Line $k \parallel$ line m. Find the measure of each angle.

10. $\angle 1$

11. $\angle 4$

12. $\angle 6$

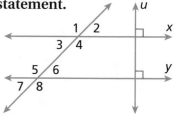

PRACTICE AND PROBLEM SOLVING

Extra Practice
See Extra Practice for more exercises.

For Exercises 13–16, use the figure to complete each statement.

13. Lines x and y are ___?___.

14. Lines u and x are ___?___.

15. $\angle 3$ and $\angle 4$ are ___?___. They are also ___?___.

16. $\angle 2$ and $\angle 7$ are ___?___. They are also ___?___.

17. **Critical Thinking** A pair of complementary angles are congruent. What is the measure of each angle?

18. **Multi-Step** Two lines intersect to form four angles. The measure of one angle is 27°. Draw a diagram to show the measures of the other three angles. Explain your answer.

Tell whether each statement is always, sometimes, or never true.

19. Adjacent angles are congruent.

20. Intersecting lines are skew.

21. Vertical angles are congruent.

22. Parallel lines intersect.

23. **Construction** In the diagram of the partial wall frame shown, the vertical beams are parallel.

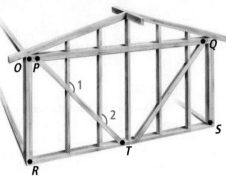

a. Angle *ORT* measures 90°. How are $\overline{OR}$ and $\overline{RS}$ related?

b. $\overline{PT}$ crosses two vertical crossbeams. What word describes $\overline{PT}$?

c. How are ∠1 and ∠2 related?

24. **Critical Thinking** Two lines intersect to form congruent adjacent angles. What can you say about the two lines?

25. **Choose a Strategy** Trace the dots in the figure. Draw all the lines that connect three dots. How many pairs of perpendicular lines have you drawn?

Ⓐ 8   Ⓑ 9   Ⓒ 10   Ⓓ 14

26. **Write About It** Use the definition of a straight angle to explain why adjacent angles formed by two intersecting lines are supplementary.

27. **Challenge** The lines in the parking lot appear to be parallel. How could you check that the lines are parallel?

Test Prep

Use the diagram for Exercises 28 and 29. Line *r* ∥ line *s*.

28. **Multiple Choice** What is the measure of ∠3?

Ⓐ 125°   Ⓑ 75°   Ⓒ 65°   Ⓓ 55°

29. **Multiple Choice** What is the measure of ∠6?

Ⓕ 125°   Ⓖ 75°   Ⓗ 65°   Ⓙ 55°

Hands-on LAB

Construct Bisectors and Congruent Angles

Use with Line and Angle Relationships

REMEMBER
- Congruent angles have the same measure, and congruent segments are the same length.

Learn It Online
Lab Resources Online

 Use appropriate tools strategically.
CC.7.G.5 Use facts about supplementary, complementary, vertical, and adjacent angles...

To bisect a segment or an angle is to divide it into two congruent parts. You can bisect segments and angles, and construct congruent angles without using a protractor or ruler. Instead, you can use a compass and a straightedge.

Activity

1 Construct a perpendicular bisector of a line segment.

a. Draw a line segment $\overline{JS}$ on a piece of paper.

b. Place your compass on endpoint J and, using an opening that is greater than half the length of $\overline{JS}$, draw an arc that intersects $\overline{JS}$.

c. Place your compass on endpoint S and draw an arc using the same opening as you did in Step **b**. The arc should intersect the first arc at both ends.

d. Draw a line to connect the intersections of the arcs. Label the intersection of $\overline{JS}$ and the line point K.

Measure $\overline{JS}$, $\overline{JK}$, and $\overline{KS}$. What do you notice?

The bisector of $\overline{JS}$ is a *perpendicular* bisector because all of the angles it forms with $\overline{JS}$ measure 90°.

2 Bisect an angle.

a. Draw an acute angle GHE on a piece of paper. Label the vertex H.

b. Place the point of your compass on H and draw an arc through both sides of the angle. Label points G and E where the arc crosses each side of the angle.

c. Without changing your compass opening, draw intersecting arcs from point G and point E. Label the point of intersection D.

d. Draw $\overrightarrow{HD}$.

Use your protractor to measure angles GHE, GHD, and DHE. What do you notice?

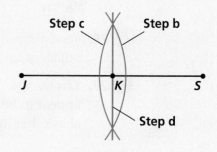

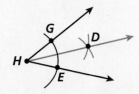

3 Construct congruent angles.

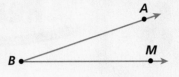

a. Draw ∠ABM on your paper.

b. To construct an angle congruent to ∠ABM, begin by drawing a ray, and label its endpoint C.

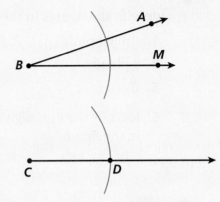

c. With your compass point on B, draw an arc through ∠ABM.

d. With the same compass opening, place the compass point on C and draw an arc through the ray. Label point D where the arc crosses the ray.

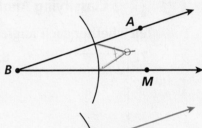

e. With your compass, measure the arc in ∠ABM.

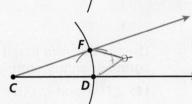

f. With the same opening, place your compass point on D, and draw another arc intersecting the first one. Label the intersection F. Draw $\overrightarrow{CF}$.

Use your protractor to measure ∠ABM and ∠FCD. What do you find?

Think and Discuss

1. How many bisectors would you use to divide an angle into four equal parts?

2. An 88° angle is bisected, and then each of the two angles formed are bisected. What is the measure of each of the smaller angles formed?

Try This

Use a compass and a straightedge to perform each construction.

1. Draw and bisect a line segment.

2. Trace and then bisect ∠GOB.

3. Draw an angle congruent to ∠GOB.

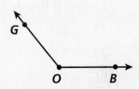

Quiz for Lessons 1 Through 3

 1 | **Building Blocks of Geometry**

Identify the figures in the diagram.

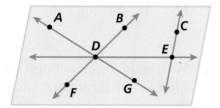

1. three points **2.** three lines

3. a plane **4.** three line segments

5. three rays

6. Identify the line segments that are congruent in the figure.

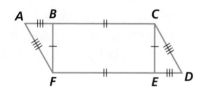

 2 | **Classifying Angles**

Tell whether each angle is acute, right, obtuse, or straight.

7. **8.** **9.** **10.**

Use the diagram to tell whether the angles are complementary, supplementary, or neither.

11. ∠DXE and ∠AXD **12.** ∠AXB and ∠CXD

13. ∠DXE and ∠AXB **14.** ∠BXC and ∠DXE

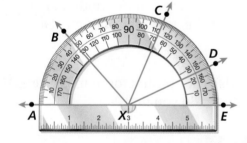

15. Angles *R* and *S* are complementary. If m∠*S* is 17°, what is m∠*R*?

16. Angles *D* and *F* are supplementary. If m∠*D* is 45°, what is m∠*F*?

 3 | **Line and Angle Relationships**

Tell whether the lines appear parallel, perpendicular, or skew.

17. $\overleftrightarrow{KL}$ and $\overleftrightarrow{MN}$ **18.** $\overleftrightarrow{JL}$ and $\overleftrightarrow{MN}$

19. $\overleftrightarrow{KL}$ and $\overleftrightarrow{JL}$ **20.** $\overleftrightarrow{IJ}$ and $\overleftrightarrow{MN}$

Line *a* ∥ line *b*. Find the measure of each angle.

21. ∠3 **22.** ∠4

23. ∠8 **24.** ∠6

25. ∠1 **26.** ∠5

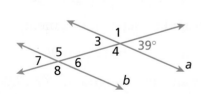

Focus on Problem Solving

Understand the Problem

• **Restate the problem in your own words**

By writing a problem in your own words, you may understand it better. Before writing the problem, you may need to reread it several times, perhaps aloud, so that you can hear yourself saying the words.

Once you have written the problem in your own words, check to make sure you included all of the necessary information to solve it.

 Write each problem in your own words. Check to make sure you have included all of the information needed to solve the problem.

1 The diagram shows a ray of light being reflected off a mirror. The angle of reflection is congruent to the angle of incidence. Use the diagram to find the measure of the obtuse angle formed by the reflected light.

2 At the intersection shown, the turn from northbound Main Street left onto Jefferson Street is dangerous because the turn is too sharp. City planners have decided to change the road to increase the angle of the turn. Explain how the measures of angles 1, 3, and 4 change as the measure of angle 2 increases.

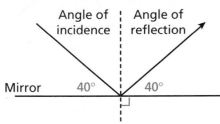

3 Parallel lines *s* and *t* are intersected by a transversal *r*. The obtuse angles formed by lines *s* and *t* measure 134°. Find the measure of the acute angles formed by the intersection of lines *t* and *r*.

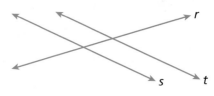

4 Many fashion designers use basic geometric shapes and patterns in their textile designs. In the textile design shown, angles 1 and 2 are formed by two intersecting lines. Find the measures of ∠1 and ∠2 if the angle adjacent to ∠2 measures 88°.

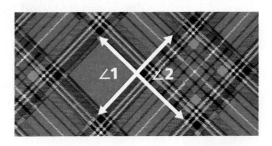

Robert Landau/Corbis

Angles in Polygons

CC.7.G.5 Use facts about supplementary, complementary, vertical, and adjacent angles in a multi-step problem to write and solve simple equations for an unknown angle in a figure *Also CC.7.RP.2c*

Vocabulary

diagonal

If you tear off the corners of a triangle and put them together, you will find that they form a straight angle. This suggests that the sum of the measures of the angles in a triangle is 180°.

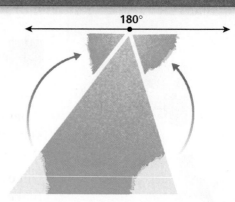

180°

TRIANGLE SUM RULE

The sum of the measures of the angles in a triangle is 180°.

$m\angle 1 + m\angle 2 + m\angle 3 = 180°$

EXAMPLE **1** **Finding an Angle Measure in a Triangle**

Find the unknown angle measure in the triangle.

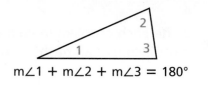

x

$25°$ $37°$

$25° + 37° + x = 180°$ *The sum of the angle measures in a triangle is 180°.*

$ 62° + x = 180°$ *Combine like terms.*

$\underline{-62° -62°}$ *Subtract 62° from both sides.*

$ x = 118°$

The unknown angle measure is 118°.

Interactivities Online ▶ The sum of the angle measures in any four-sided figure can be found by dividing the figure into two triangles. You can divide the figure by drawing a *diagonal*. A **diagonal** is a line segment that connects two non-adjacent vertices of a polygon. Since the sum of the angle measures in each triangle is 180°, the sum of the angle measures in a four-sided figure is 2 · 180°, or 360°.

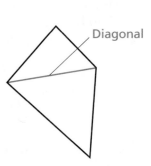

Diagonal

    Video **Lesson Tutorials Online** my.hrw.com

SUM OF THE ANGLES OF A QUADRILATERAL

The sum of the measures of the angles in a quadrilateral is 360°.

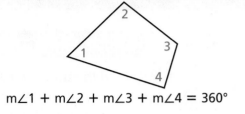

$$m\angle 1 + m\angle 2 + m\angle 3 + m\angle 4 = 360°$$

E X A M P L E **Finding an Angle Measure in a Quadrilateral**

Find the unknown angle measure in the quadrilateral.

$$98° + 137° + 52° + x = 360° \qquad \textit{The sum of the angle measures is 360°.}$$

$$287° + x = 360° \qquad \textit{Combine like terms.}$$

$$\underline{-287° \qquad -287°} \qquad \textit{Subtract 287° from both sides.}$$

$$x = 73°$$

The unknown angle measure is 73°.

In a convex polygon, all diagonals can be drawn within the interior of the figure. By dividing any convex polygon into triangles, you can find the sum of its interior angle measures.

E X A M P L E **3** **Drawing Triangles to Find the Sum of Interior Angles**

Divide the polygon into triangles to find the sum of its angle measures.

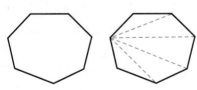

There are 5 triangles.

$$5 \cdot 180° = 900°$$

The sum of the angle measures of a heptagon is 900°.

Think and Discuss

1. Explain how to find the measure of an angle in a triangle when the measures of the two other angles are known.

2. Determine for which polygon the sum of the angle measures is greater, a pentagon or an octagon.

3. Explain how the measure of each angle in a regular polygon changes as the number of sides increases.

Exercises

Learn It Online
Homework Help Online
Exercises 1–18, 19, 21, 23, 25

GUIDED PRACTICE

See Example **1**   Find the unknown angle measure in each triangle.

1.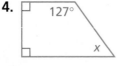

2.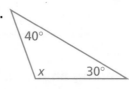

3.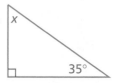

See Example **2**   Find the unknown angle measure in each quadrilateral .

4.

5.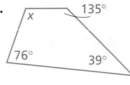

6.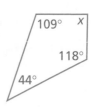

See Example **3**   Divide each polygon into triangles to find the sum of its angle measures.

7.

8.

9.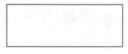

INDEPENDENT PRACTICE

See Example **1**   Find the unknown angle measure in each triangle.

10.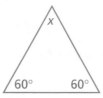

11.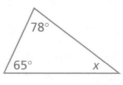

12.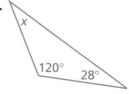

See Example **2**   Find the unknown angle measure in each quadrilateral.

13.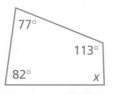

14.

15.

See Example **3**   Divide each polygon into triangles to find the sum of its angle measures.

16.

17.

18.

PRACTICE AND PROBLEM SOLVING

Extra Practice
See Extra Practice for more exercises.

19. Earth Science A sundial consists of a circular base and a right triangle mounted upright on the base. One acute angle in the right triangle is 52°. What is the measure of the other acute angle?

Find the measure of the third angle in each triangle, given two angle measures. Then classify the triangle.

20. 56°, 101°   **21.** 18°, 63°   **22.** 62°, 58°   **23.** 41°, 49°

24. Multi-Step Each outer wall of the Pentagon in Washington, D.C., measures 921 feet. What is the measure of each angle made by the Pentagon's outer walls?

25. Critical Thinking A truss bridge is supported by triangular frames. If every triangular frame in a truss bridge is an isosceles right triangle, what is the measure of each angle in one of the frames? (*Hint:* Two of the angles in each frame are congruent.)

26. Make a Conjecture Use what you have learned to write a formula for finding the sum of interior angle measures in polygons with five or more sides.

27. What's the Error? A student finds the sum of the angle measures in an octagon by multiplying 7 · 180°. What is the student's error?

28. Write About It Explain how to find the sum of the angle measures in a quadrilateral by dividing the quadrilateral into triangles.

29. Challenge The angle between the lines of sight from a lighthouse to a tugboat and to a cargo ship is 27°. The angle between the lines of sight at the cargo ship is twice the angle between the lines of sight at the tugboat. What are the angles at the tugboat and at the cargo ship?

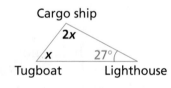

Cargo ship

Tugboat   Lighthouse

Test Prep

30. Multiple Choice A triangle has three congruent angles. What is the measure of each angle?

Ⓐ 50°   Ⓑ 60°   Ⓒ 75°   Ⓓ 100°

31. Gridded Response Two angles of a triangle measure 58° and 42°. What is the measure, in degrees, of the third angle of the triangle?

Construct Triangles with Given Side Lengths

Use before Congruent Figures

Learn It Online
Lab Resources Online

MATHEMATICAL PRACTICES Use appropriate tools strategically.

CC.7.G.2 Draw… geometric shapes with given conditions. Focus on… noticing when the conditions determine a unique triangle, more than one triangle, or no triangle

You can use geometry software to determine if three given side lengths of a triangle determine a unique triangle, several different triangles, or no triangle.

Activity

1. Use geometry software to construct a triangle with given sides of 2 units, 3 units, and 4 units.

    a. Draw three line segments of 2, 3, and 4 units of length.

    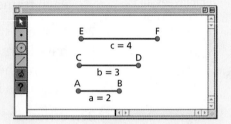

    b. Let $\overline{AB}$ be the base of the triangle. Place end point C on top of endpoint B, and endpoint E on top of endpoint A. These will become two of the vertices of the triangle.

    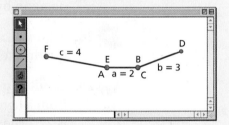

    c. With the endpoints C and E fixed as vertices and lengths EF and CD fixed, rotate points D and F to see if they will meet in a single point.

    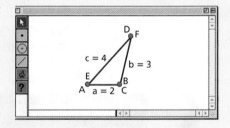

    d. Do the line segments of 2, 3, and 4 units make a triangle?

    e. Repeat steps **b** and **c** two more times, each time starting with a different base length. Do the line segments make the exact same triangle as the original? Explain.

    f. What can you conclude about all triangles with side lengths of 2, 3, and 4, units?

2 Use geometry software to construct a triangle with given sides of 2 units, 3 units, and 6 units.

   a. Draw three line segments of 2, 3, and 6 units of length. Use $\overline{AB}$ as the base.

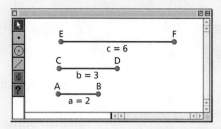

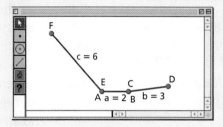

   b. Repeat steps **b** and **c** from part 1.

   c. Do the line segments of 2, 3, and 6 units form a triangle? Explain.

   d. Try using the 6-unit segment as the base length. Can the triangle be constructed with the remaining sides?

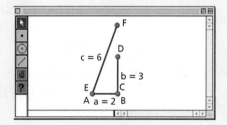

   e. What can you conclude about constructing a triangle with side lengths of 2, 3, and 6 units?

Think and Discuss

  1. Explain how geometry software can help you decide whether three given side lengths determine a unique triangle, more than one triangle, or no triangle.

  2. Can three given side lengths ever determine more than one triangle? Explain.

Try This

Use geometry software to determine if the given side lengths can be used to construct one unique triangle, more than one triangle, or no triangle.

  1. 5 units, 5 units, 10 units

  2. 8 units, 9 units, 10 units

  3. 1 unit, 1 unit, 4 units

  4. 20 units, 20 units, 20 units

8-5 Congruent Figures

COMMON CORE

CC.7.G.2 Focus on... triangles from three measures of angles or sides, noticing when the conditions determine a unique triangle, more than one triangle, or no triangle

Vocabulary

Side-Side-Side Rule

Originally rolled and twisted by hand, pretzels today are primarily manufactured in production lines. After the dough is mixed, automated machines stamp the dough into consistent forms. These forms are the same shape and size. Recall from Lesson 1 that congruent figures are the same shape and size. The automation of the production line process ensures that the pretzels are congruent.

One way to determine whether figures are congruent is to see whether one figure will fit exactly over the other one.

EXAMPLE **1** **Identifying Congruent Figures in the Real World**

Identify any congruent figures.

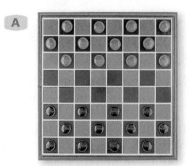

A

The squares on a checkerboard are congruent. The checkers are also congruent.

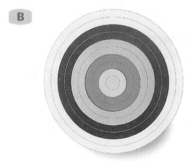

B

The rings on a target are not congruent. Each ring is larger than the one inside of it.

If all of the corresponding sides and angles of two polygons are congruent, then the polygons are congruent. For triangles, if the corresponding sides are congruent, then the corresponding angles will always be congruent. This is called the **Side-Side-Side Rule**. Because of this rule, when determining whether triangles are congruent, you only need to determine whether the sides are congruent.

Video **Lesson Tutorials Online** my.hrw.com

EXAMPLE 2 **Identifying Congruent Triangles**

Determine whether the triangles are congruent.

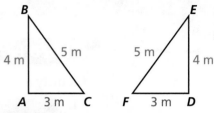

$AC = 3\text{ m}$ $DF = 3\text{ m}$
$AB = 4\text{ m}$ $DE = 4\text{ m}$
$BC = 5\text{ m}$ $EF = 5\text{ m}$

By the Side-Side-Side Rule, $\triangle ABC$ is congruent to $\triangle DEF$, or $\triangle ABC \cong \triangle DEF$. If you flip one triangle, it will fit exactly over the other.

Helpful Hint

The scale factor of congruent figures is 1. Notice that in Example 2 the ratio of corresponding sides is $\frac{3}{3} = \frac{4}{4} = \frac{5}{5} = 1$.

For polygons with more than three sides, it is not enough to compare the measures of their sides. For example, the corresponding sides of the figures below are congruent, but the figures are not congruent.

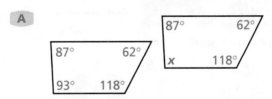

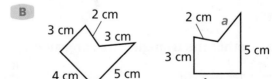

If you know that two figures are congruent, you can find missing measures in the figures.

EXAMPLE 3 **Using Congruence to Find Unknown Measures**

Determine the unknown measure in each set of congruent polygons.

A

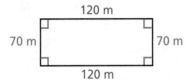

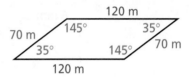

The corresponding angles of congruent polygons are congruent.

The unknown angle measure is 93°.

B

The corresponding sides of congruent polygons are congruent.

The unknown side length is 3 cm.

Think and Discuss

1. Draw an illustration to explain whether an isosceles triangle can be congruent to a right triangle.

2. Explain why congruent figures are always similar figures.

Learn It Online
Homework Help Online
Exercises 1–14, 15, 17, 19

GUIDED PRACTICE

See Example **1** Identify any congruent figures.

1.

2.

3.

See Example **2** Determine whether the triangles are congruent.

4.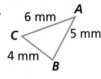

5.

See Example **3** Determine the unknown measure in each set of congruent polygons.

6.

7.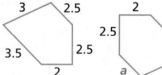
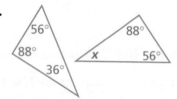

INDEPENDENT PRACTICE

See Example **1** Identify any congruent figures.

8.

9.

10.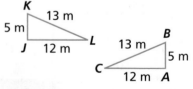

See Example **2** Determine whether the triangles are congruent.

11.

12.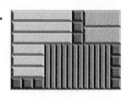

See Example **3** Determine the unknown measures in each set of congruent polygons.

13.

14.
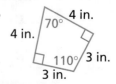

Extra Practice

See Extra Practice for more exercises.

Tell the minimum amount of information needed to determine whether the figures are congruent.

15. two triangles   **16.** two squares   **17.** two rectangles   **18.** two pentagons

19. Surveying In the figure, trees *A* and *B* are on opposite sides of the stream. Jamil wants to string a rope from one tree to the other. Triangles *ABC* and *DEC* are congruent. What is the distance between the trees?

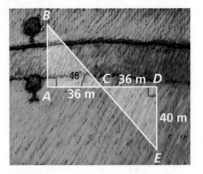

20. Hobbies In the quilt block, which figures appear congruent?

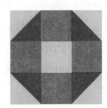

21. Choose a Strategy Anji and her brother Art walked to school along the routes in the figure. They started at 7:40 A.M. and walked at the same rate. Who arrived first?
Ⓐ Anji   Ⓑ Art   Ⓒ They arrived at the same time.

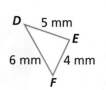

22. Write About It Are similar triangles always congruent? Explain.

23. Challenge If all of the angles in two triangles have the same measure, are the triangles necessarily congruent? Explain.

Test Prep

24. Multiple Choice Which figures are congruent?
Ⓐ   Ⓑ   Ⓒ   Ⓓ

25. Multiple Choice Determine the unknown measure in the set of congruent triangles.

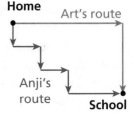

Ⓕ 4 mm   Ⓗ 6 mm
Ⓖ 5 mm   Ⓙ Cannot be determined

Mastering *the* Standards

for Mathematical Practice

The topics described in the Standards for Mathematical Content will vary from year to year. However, the *way* in which you learn, study, and think about mathematics will not. The Standards for Mathematical Practice describe skills that you will use in all of your math courses.

Mathematical Practices

1. *Make sense of problems and persevere in solving them.*
2. *Reason abstractly and quantitatively.*
3. *Construct viable arguments and critique the reasoning of others.*
4. *Model with mathematics.*
5. *Use appropriate tools strategically.*
6. *Attend to precision.*
7. *Look for and make use of structure.*
8. *Look for and express regularity in repeated reasoning.*

---

⑤ Use appropriate tools strategically.

Mathematically proficient students consider the available tools when solving a... problem... [and] are... able to use technological tools to explore and deepen their understanding...

In your book

Hands-on Labs and **Technology Labs** use concrete and technological tools to explore mathematical concepts.

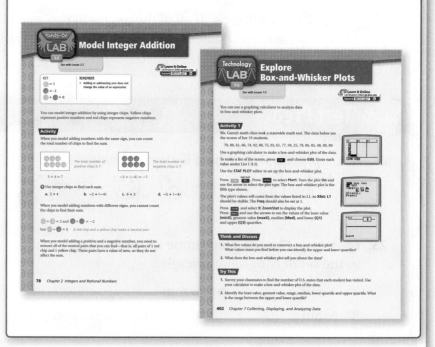

Technology LAB

Explore Transformations

Use with Congruent Figures

 Learn It Online
Lab Resources Online

You can use geometry software to perform transformations of geometric figures.

MATHEMATICAL PRACTICES **Use appropriate tools strategically.**
CC.7.G.2 Draw… geometric shapes with given conditions… noticing when the conditions determine a unique triangle, more than one triangle, or no triangle

Activity

❶ Use your dynamic geometry software to construct a 5-sided polygon like the one below. Label the vertices *A*, *B*, *C*, *D*, and *E*. Use the translation tool to translate the polygon 2 units right and $\frac{1}{2}$ unit up.

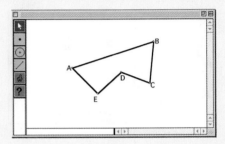 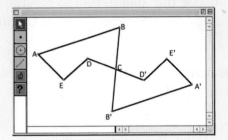

❷ Start with the polygon from ❶. Use the rotation tool to rotate the polygon 30° and then 150°, both about the vertex *C*.

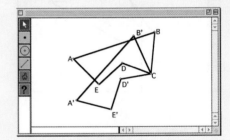 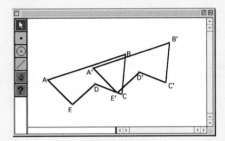

Think and Discuss

1. Rotate a triangle 30° about a point outside the triangle. Can this image be found by combining a vertical translation (slide up or down) and a horizontal translation (slide left or right) of the preimage?

2. After what angle of rotation will the rotated image of a figure have the same orientation as the preimage?

Try This

1. Construct a quadrilateral *ABCD* using the geometry software.

  a. Translate the figure 2 units right and 1 unit up.

  b. Rotate the figure 30°, 45°, and 60°.

Construct Triangles with Given Angle Measures

Use after Congruent Figures

 Learn It Online
Lab Resources Online

You can use geometry software to determine if three given angles of a triangle determine a unique triangle, several different triangles, or no triangle.

MATHEMATICAL PRACTICES **Use appropriate tools strategically.**

CC.7.G.2 Draw… geometric shapes with given conditions… noticing when the conditions determine a unique triangle, more than one triangle, or no triangle

Activity

1. Use geometry software to construct an obtuse triangle with angles that measure 120°, 26°, and 34°.

   a. In a table record the angle measures of the original triangle.

Triangle	Angle 1	Angle 2	Angle 3
Original	120°	26°	34°
Larger			
Smaller			

   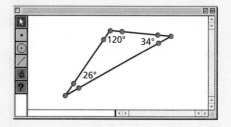

   b. Copy your triangle. Place the triangle on top of the original. Use the "dilate" tool to enlarge the whole triangle so it is bigger than the original.

   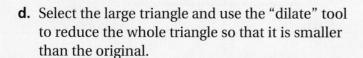

   c. Measure the angles in the new triangle. Record your results in the table.

   d. Select the large triangle and use the "dilate" tool to reduce the whole triangle so that it is smaller than the original.

   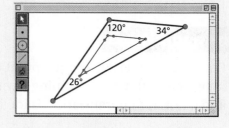

   e. Measure the angles in the new triangle. Record your results in the table.

   f. Are the angle measures always the same?

   g. What can you conclude about constructing triangles with given angles of 120°, 26°, and 34°?

2 Use geometry software to construct an acute triangle.

a. Draw an acute triangle. Use the measuring angles tool and measure each angle in the triangle. Record your results in a table.

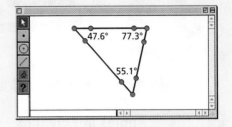

Triangle	Angle 1	Angle 2	Angle 3
Original	47.6°	77.3°	55.1°
Larger			
Smaller			

b. Repeat steps **b–e** from part 1.

Note: Your triangle and angle measures will likely look different from the ones shown here.

Think and Discuss

1. Using your results from parts 1 and 2 what can you conclude about the number of triangles that can be constructed using the same three given angles?

2. Do the shapes of the different triangles with the same angle measures ever change?

3. If you constructed a right triangle with two other given angles, do you think your results would be the same as the results for acute and obtuse triangles?

Try This

1. Using geometry software construct a right triangle with angles 35° and 55°. How many triangles can you construct with these angle measures?

2. Use the measuring tool to measure the sides of your original triangle and large triangle in part 1 of the Activity. Are the ratios of the lengths of the corresponding sides equivalent? Are these triangles similar? Explain.

3. Given the following conditions, tell whether the construction would result in a unique triangle, more than one triangle, or no triangle.

a. three known angles

b. three sides known

c. two angles known

Quiz for Lessons 4 and 5

 4 **Angles in Polygons**

Find the unknown angle measure in each figure.

1. 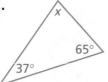 **2.**  **3.** 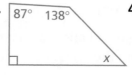 **4.**

5. Find the sum of the angle measures of a square.

6. Find the sum of the angle measures of a 10-sided polygon.

7. How many diagonals does the figure have?

 5 **Congruent Figures**

Determine whether the triangles are congruent.

8. 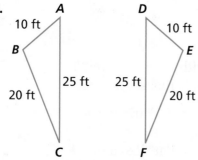   **9.**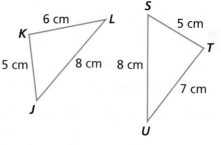

10. Determine the unknown measure in
the pair of congruent polygons.

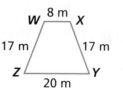 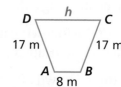

CONNECTIONS

MATHEMATICAL
PRACTICES
Reason
abstractly
and quantitatively.

CHAPTER
8

Piscataqua River Bridge   The first bridge over the
Piscataqua River, built in 1794, was the longest bridge in the
world. The modern bridge, completed in 1971, is not the
world's longest, but it is well known for its elegant symmetric
design. The bridge connects Kittery, Maine with Portsmouth,
New Hampshire.

MAINE

Kittery

1. Does the Piscataqua River Bridge contain any congruent
   figures? If so, make a simple sketch of the bridge and highlight
   any figures that appear to be congruent.

For 2–7, use the diagram.

2. ∠1 and ∠2 are supplementary. Given that m∠1 is 78°, what
   is m∠2?

3. Classify △*AEF* according to its angles. Then measure the sides
   with a ruler, and classify the triangle according to its sides.

4. Quadrilateral *AEFD* is a trapezoid. What can you conclude about
   $\overline{AD}$ and $\overline{EF}$?

5. What can you say about ∠1 and ∠*EAD*? Why?

6. Find m∠*EAD*.

7. Given that m ∠*DFE* is 96°, find m∠3.
   Explain how you found the angle measure.

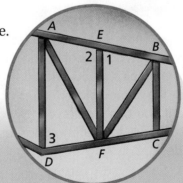

Alexander Svirsky, Massroads.com

Game Time

Networks

A network is a figure that uses vertices and segments to show how objects are connected. You can use a network to show distances between cities. In the network at right, the vertices identify four cities in North Carolina, and the segments show the distances in miles between the cities.

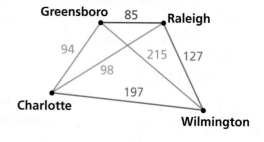

Greensboro 85 Raleigh
94
215 127
98
Charlotte 197
Wilmington

You can use the network to find the shortest route from Charlotte to the other three cities and back to Charlotte. First find all the possible routes. Then find the distance in miles for each route. One route has been identified below.

CGWRC $94 + 215 + 127 + 98 = 534$

Which is the shortest route, and what is the distance?

Color Craze

You can use rhombus-shaped tiles to build a variety of polygons. Each side of a tile is a different color. Build each design by matching the same-colored sides of tiles. Then see if you can create your own designs with the tiles. Try to identify congruent figures in your designs.

A complete set of tiles is available online.

Learn It Online
Game Time Extra

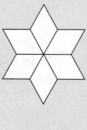

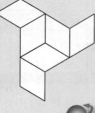
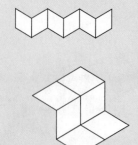

Materials

- sheets of construction paper
- card stock
- scissors
- hole punch
- 4 electrical ties
- white paper
- markers

PROJECT Brochure Book of Geometric Figures

Make an organizer to hold brochures that summarize each lesson of the chapter.

Directions

1 Start with sheets of construction paper that are 12 inches by 18 inches. Fold one sheet in half to make it 12 inches by 9 inches and then in half again to make it 6 inches by 9 inches. **Figure A**

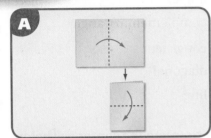

2 Hold the paper with the folds at the bottom and on the right-hand side. Turn the top left-hand corner back and under to form a pocket. **Figure B**

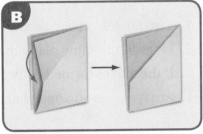

3 Turn the whole thing over and fold the top right-hand corner back and under to form a pocket. Repeat steps 1–3 to make a pocket for each lesson.

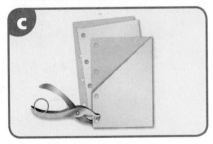

4 Cut out two pieces of card stock that are 6 inches by 9 inches. Punch four equally spaced holes down the length of each piece. Similarly, punch four equally spaced holes on each pocket as shown. **Figure C**

5 Stack the pockets and put the card stock covers on the front and back of the stack. Insert electrical ties into the holes to hold everything together.

Taking Note of the Math

Fold sheets of plain white paper into thirds like a brochure. Use the brochures to take notes on the lessons of the chapter. Store the brochures in the pockets of your organizer.

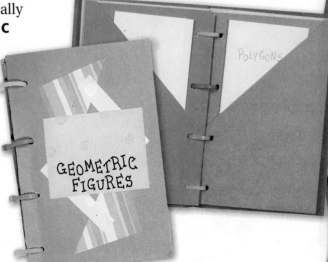

Vocabulary

acute angle	line segment	Side-Side-Side Rule
acute triangle	obtuse angle	skew lines
adjacent angles	parallel lines	straight angle
angle	perpendicular lines	supplementary angles
complementary angles	plane	transversal
congruent	point	vertex
diagonal	ray	vertical angles
line	right angle	

Complete the sentences below with vocabulary words from the list above.

1. Two angles whose measures have a sum of 180° are __?__.

2. Lines in the same plane that do not intersect are __?__.

3. If the angles formed by two intersecting lines are 90°, then the lines are __?__.

4. A(n) __?__ is an angle that measures exactly 180°.

1 Building Blocks of Geometry

Identify the figures in the diagram.

- points: *A, B, C*   ■ lines: $\overleftrightarrow{AB}$
- planes: *ABC*   ■ rays: $\overrightarrow{BA}$; $\overrightarrow{AB}$
- line segments: $\overline{AB}$; $\overline{BC}$

Identify the figures in the diagram.

5. points   6. lines
7. planes   8. rays
9. line segments

2 Classifying Angles

■ Tell whether the angle is acute, right, obtuse, or straight.

The angle is a right angle.

Tell whether each angle is acute, right, obtuse, or straight.

10.   11.

12. Two angles are complementary. If one angle measures 55°, what is the measure of the other angle?

13. Two angles are supplementary. If one angle measures 107°, what is the measure of the other angle?

3 Line and Angle Relationships

■ Tell whether the lines appear parallel, perpendicular, or skew.

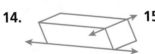

perpendicular

■ Line *a* || line *b*. Find the measure of ∠4. Corresponding angles are congruent.

m∠4 = 74°

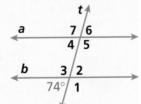

Tell whether the lines appear parallel, perpendicular, or skew.

14.   15.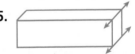

For Exercises 16–19, use the figure at left. Find the measure of each angle.

16. ∠2   17. ∠3
18. ∠5   19. ∠6

Study Guide: Review

4 | Congruent Figures

■ Determine the unknown measure in the set of congruent polygons.

The angle measures 53°.

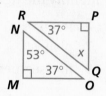

20. Determine the unknown measures in the set of congruent polygons.

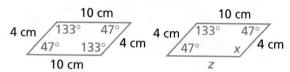

Determine whether the triangles are congruent.

21.

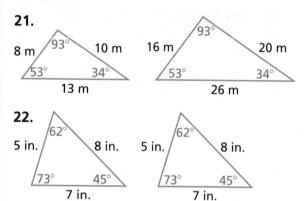

22.

Chapter Test

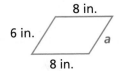

CHAPTER

8

Identify the figures in the diagram.

1. 4 points
2. 3 lines
3. a plane

4. 5 line segments
5. 6 rays

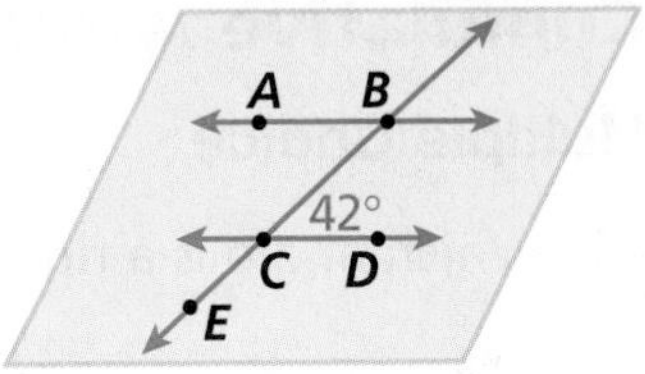

Line AB ∥ line CD in the diagram. Find the measure of each angle and tell whether the angle is acute, right, obtuse, or straight.

6. ∠ABC
7. ∠BCE
8. ∠DCE

Tell whether the lines appear parallel, perpendicular, or skew.

9. $\overleftrightarrow{MN}$ and $\overleftrightarrow{PO}$

10. $\overleftrightarrow{LM}$ and $\overleftrightarrow{PO}$

11. $\overleftrightarrow{NO}$ and $\overleftrightarrow{MN}$

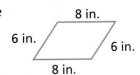

12. Determine the unknown measure in the set of congruent polygons.

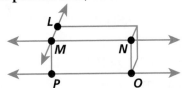

In the diagram, lines k and m are parallel.

13. Find the measure of angle 1.

14. Find the measure of angle 6.

15. What is the measure of the complement of angle 4?

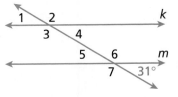

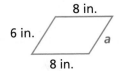

Cumulative Assessment

Multiple Choice

1. Which angle is a right angle?

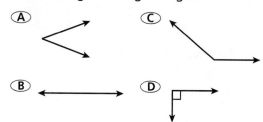

2. What is the number 8,330,000,000 written in scientific notation?

   F 0.83×10^{10}
   H 83.3×10^8
   G 8.33×10^9
   J 833×10^7

3. What are the coordinates of point A?

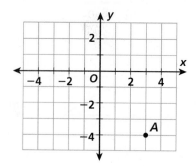

   A $(3, -4)$
   C $(4, -3)$
   B $(-4, 3)$
   D $(0, -4)$

4. Nolan spent $\frac{1}{2}$ hour traveling to his orthodontist appointment, $\frac{3}{5}$ hour at his appointment, and $\frac{3}{4}$ hour traveling home. What is the total amount of time Nolan spent for this appointment?

   F $\frac{7}{11}$ hour
   H $1\frac{17}{20}$ hours
   G $\frac{37}{60}$ hour
   J $\frac{13}{5}$ hours

5. A store sells two dozen rolls of toilet paper for $4.84. What is the unit rate for one roll of toilet paper?

   A $0.13/roll of toilet paper
   B $0.20/roll of toilet paper
   C $0.40/roll of toilet paper
   D $1.21/roll of toilet paper

6. Which statement is true?

   F Skew lines do not intersect.
   G Parallel lines intersect.
   H Vertical angles are not congruent.
   J An obtuse angle has a measure less than 90°.

7. Which expression represents "twice the difference of a number and 8"?

   A $2(x + 8)$
   C $2(x - 8)$
   B $2x - 8$
   D $2x + 8$

8. Find the mode of the data:

   6, 5, 13, 6, 9, 8, 6, 5, 6, 8, 5

   F 5
   G 6
   H 7
   J 13

9. Which ratios form a proportion?

   A $\frac{4}{8}$ and $\frac{3}{6}$
   C $\frac{4}{10}$ and $\frac{6}{16}$
   B $\frac{4}{12}$ and $\frac{6}{15}$
   D $\frac{2}{3}$ and $\frac{5}{8}$

10. The graph shows how Amy spends her earnings each month. Amy earned $100 in May. How much did she spend on transportation and clothing combined?

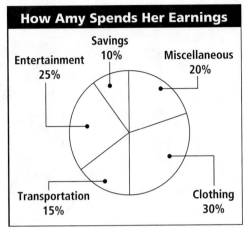

How Amy Spends Her Earnings

Savings 10%
Entertainment 25%
Miscellaneous 20%
Transportation 15%
Clothing 30%

Ⓕ $15 Ⓗ $45

Ⓖ $30 Ⓙ $55

HOT TIP! Once you have answered a short- or extended-response question, check to make sure you have answered all parts of the question.

Gridded Response

11. What is the unknown angle measure in degrees?

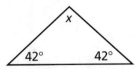

x

42° 42°

12. The number of members of a club increases by 40%. If there were 60 members before the increase, how many members are there now?

13. An antiques dealer bought a chair for $85. The dealer sold the chair at her shop for 45% more than what she paid. To the nearest whole dollar, what was the price of the chair?

14. What is the value of the expression $-4x^2y - y$ for $x = -2$ and $y = -5$?

Short Response

S1. Triangle ABC is similar to triangle DEF. $AB = 10$ and $DE = 16$.

   a. If $CA = 15$, find FD.

   b. The measure of angle E is 66°. What is the measure of angle B?

S2. Taylor's goal is to spend less than 35% of her allowance each month on cell phone bills. Last month, Taylor spent $45 on cell phone bills. If she gets $120 each month as her allowance, did she achieve her goal? Explain your answer.

S3. Seamus can type 375 words in 15 minutes.

   a. Write Seamus's rate as a unit rate in words per minute.

   b. Suppose a page typically has 250 words. Write Seamus's rate in pages per minute.

Extended Response

E1. Four of the angles in a pentagon measure 74°, 111°, 145°, and 95°.

   a. How many sides and how many angles does a pentagon have?

   b. How many diagonals does the pentagon have?

   c. What is the sum of the angle measures of a pentagon? Include a drawing as part of your answer.

   d. Write and solve an equation to determine the missing angle measure of the pentagon.

Chapter Focus

- Solve problems involving area and circumference of circles.
- Investigate cross sections and surface area.

Why Learn This?

The perimeter and area of garden beds can be determined by measuring their dimensions and then using a formula.

Learn It Online
Chapter Project Online

 **Are You Ready?**

 **Vocabulary**

Choose the best term from the list to complete each sentence.

1. A (n) __?__ is a quadrilateral with exactly one pair of parallel sides.

2. A (n) __?__ is a four-sided figure with opposite sides that are congruent and parallel.

3. The __?__ of a circle is one-half the __?__ of the circle.

diameter

parallelogram

radius

right triangle

trapezoid

Complete these exercises to review skills you will need for this chapter.

 **Round Whole Numbers**

Round each number to the nearest ten and nearest hundred.

4. 1,535   5. 294   6. 30,758   7. 497

Round Decimals

Round each number to the nearest whole number and nearest tenth.

8. 6.18   9. 10.50   10. 513.93   11. 29.06

 **Multiply with Decimals**

Multiply.

12. $5.63 \cdot 8$ 13. $9.67 \cdot 4.3$ 14. $8.34 \cdot 16$ 15. $6.08 \cdot 0.56$

16. $0.82 \cdot 21$ 17. $2.74 \cdot 6.6$ 18. $40 \cdot 9.54$ 19. $0.33 \cdot 0.08$

Order of Operations

Simplify each expression.

20. $2 \cdot 9 + 2 \cdot 6$ 21. $2 (15 + 8)$ 22. $4 \cdot 6.8 + 7 \cdot 9.3$

23. $14 (25.9 + 13.6)$ 24. $(27.3 + 0.7) \div 2^2$ 25. $5 \cdot 3^3 - 8.02$

26. $(63 \div 7) \cdot 4^2$ 27. $1.1 + 3 \cdot 4.3$ 28. $66 \cdot [5 + (3 + 3)^2]$

Identify Polygons

Name each figure.

29.   30.   31.

Study Guide: Preview

Where You've Been

Previously, you

- found the perimeter or circumference of geometric figures.

- calculated the area of triangles and parallelograms.

In This Chapter

You will study

- finding the circumference and area of circles.

- finding the area of irregular figures.

- finding the volume and surface area of three-dimensional figures.

Where You're Going

You can use the skills learned in this chapter

- to create an architectural floor plan.

- to design a building access ramp that meets government regulations.

Key Vocabulary/Vocabulario

area	área
circumference	circunferencia
perimeter	perímetro

Vocabulary Connections

To become familiar with some of the vocabulary terms in the chapter, consider the following. You may refer to the chapter, the glossary, or a dictionary if you like.

1. The word *circumference* comes from the Latin word *circumferre*, meaning "to carry around." How does the Latin meaning help you define the **circumference** of a circle?

2. The word *perimeter* comes from the Greek roots *peri*, meaning "all around," and *metron*, meaning "measure." What do the Greek roots tell you about the **perimeter** of a geometric figure?

Study Guide: Preview

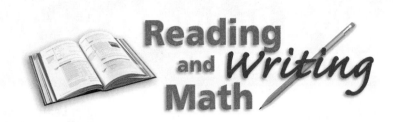

Reading Strategy: Read and Interpret Graphics

Figures, diagrams, tables, and graphs provide important data. Knowing how to read these graphics will help you understand and solve related problems.

Similar Figures

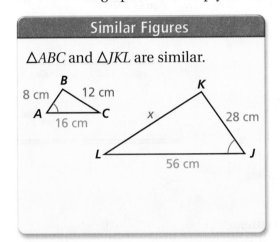

$\triangle ABC$ and $\triangle JKL$ are similar.

How to Read

Read all labels.
$AB = 8$ cm; $AC = 16$ cm; $BC = 12$ cm;
$JK = 28$ cm; $JL = 56$ cm; $KL = x$ cm;
$\angle A$ corresponds to $\angle J$.

Be careful about what you assume.
You may think $\overline{AB}$ corresponds to $\overline{LK}$, but this is not so. Since $\angle A$ corresponds to $\angle J$, you know $\overline{AB}$ corresponds to $\overline{JK}$.

Double-Bar Graph

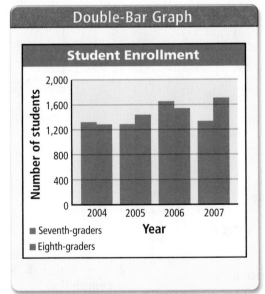

How to Read

Read the title of the graph and any special notes.
Blue indicates seventh-graders.
Purple indicates eighth-graders.

Read each axis label and note the intervals of each scale.
x-**axis**—year increases by 1.
y-**axis**—enrollment increases by 400 students.

Determine what information is presented.
student enrollment for seventh- and eighth-graders per year

 Try This

Use the Student Enrollment graph above to answer the following questions.

1. In which year(s) was the number of eighth graders greater than the number of seventh graders?

2. Which year had the greatest difference between the number of seventh graders and the number of eighth graders?

Hands-on LAB

Explore Perimeter & Circumference

Use with Perimeter and Circumference

Learn It Online
Lab Resources Online

MATHEMATICAL PRACTICES Use appropriate tools strategically.

CC.7.G.4 Know the formulas for the... circumference of a circle...
Also CC.7.EE.2

The distance around a figure is its perimeter. You can use a loop of string to explore the dimensions of a rectangle with a perimeter of 18 inches.

Activity 1

① Cut a piece of string that is slightly longer than 18 inches. Tie the ends together to form an 18-inch loop.

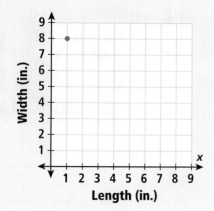

② Make the loop into a rectangle by placing it around four push pins on a corkboard. Both the length and the width of the rectangle should be a whole number of inches.

③ Make different rectangles with whole-number lengths and widths. Record the lengths and widths in a table.

Length (in.)	1	2	3	■	■	■	■	■
Width (in.)	8	■	■	■	■	■	■	■

④ Graph the data in your table by plotting points on a coordinate plane like the one shown.

Think and Discuss

1. What pattern is made by the points on your graph?

2. How is the sum of the length and width of each rectangle related to the rectangle's perimeter of 18 inches?

3. Suppose a rectangle has length ℓ and width w. Write a rule that you can use to find the rectangle's perimeter.

Try This

Use the rule you discovered to find the perimeter of each rectangle.

1.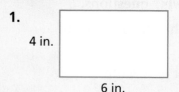
4 in.
6 in.

2. 9 ft
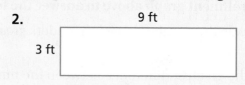
3 ft

3. 5 cm
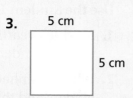
5 cm

The perimeter of a circle is called the *circumference*. You can explore the relationship between a circle's circumference and its diameter by measuring some circles.

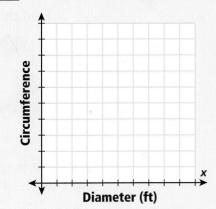

Diameter

Circumference

Activity 2

1 Four students should stand in a circle with their arms outstretched, as shown in the diagram.

2 Another student should find the diameter of the circle by measuring the distance across the middle of the circle with a tape measure.

3 The student should also find the circumference of the circle by measuring the distance around the circle from fingertip to fingertip across the backs of the students.

4 Record the diameter and circumference in a table like the one below.

Diameter					
Circumference					

5 Add one or more students to the circle and repeat the process. Record the diameter and circumference for at least five different circles.

6 Graph the data in your table by plotting points on a coordinate plane like the one shown.

Circumference

Diameter (ft)

Think and Discuss

1. **Make a Conjecture** In general, what do you notice about the points on your graph? What shape or pattern do they seem to form?

2. Calculate the ratio of the circumference to the diameter for each of the data points. Then calculate the mean of these ratios. For any circle, the ratio of the circumference to the diameter is a constant, known as *pi* (π). Give an estimate for π based on your findings.

Try This

1. For a circle with circumference C and diameter d, the ratio of the circumference to the diameter is $\frac{C}{d} = \pi$. Use this to write a formula that you can use to find the circumference of a circle when you know its diameter.

2. Use your estimate for the value of π to find the approximate circumference of the circle at right.

$d = 4$ cm

Perimeter and Circumference

CC.7.G.4 Know the formulas for… circumference of a circle and use them to solve problems… *Also CC.7.RP.3*

Vocabulary

perimeter

circumference

pi

In volleyball, the player serving must hit the ball over the net but keep it within the court's sidelines and end lines. The two sidelines on a volleyball court are each 18 meters long, and the two end lines are each 9 meters long.Together, the four lines form the *perimeter* of the court.

Perimeter is the distance around a geometric figure. To find the perimeter *P* of a rectangular volleyball court, you can add the lengths of its sides. Perimeter is measured in units of length.

EXAMPLE 1 **Finding the Perimeter of a Polygon**

Find the perimeter.

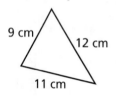

$P = 9 + 12 + 11$ *Use the side lengths.*
$P = 32$ *Add.*

The perimeter of the triangle is 32 cm.

Since opposite sides of a rectangle are equal in length, you can find the perimeter of a rectangle by using a formula.

Interactivities Online ▶

PERIMETER OF A RECTANGLE		
The perimeter *P* of a rectangle is the sum of twice its length ℓ and twice its width *w*.	$P = 2\ell + 2w$	*w* ⬚ ℓ

EXAMPLE 2 **Using Properties of a Rectangle to Find Perimeter**

Find the perimeter.

15 m
32 m

$P = 2\ell + 2w$ *Use the formula.*
$P = (2 \cdot 32) + (2 \cdot 15)$ *Substitute for ℓ and w.*
$P = 64 + 30$ *Multiply.*
$P = 94$ *Add.*

The perimeter of the rectangle is 94 m.

Video   **Lesson Tutorials Online**

The distance around a circle is called **circumference**. For every circle, the ratio of circumference C to diameter d is the same. This ratio, $\frac{C}{d}$, is represented by the Greek letter π, called *pi*. Pi is approximately equal to 3.14 or $\frac{22}{7}$. By solving the equation $\frac{C}{d} = \pi$ for C, you get the formula for circumference.

CIRCUMFERENCE OF A CIRCLE		
The circumference C of a circle is π times the diameter d, or 2π times the radius r.	$C = \pi d$ or $C = 2\pi r$	Radius — Diameter — Circumference

EXAMPLE 3 Finding the Circumference of a Circle

Find the circumference of each circle to the nearest tenth, if necessary. Use 3.14 or $\frac{22}{7}$ for π.

A 8 in.

$C = \pi d$ *You know the diameter.*

$C \approx 3.14 \cdot 8$ *Substitute 3.14 for π and 8 for d.*

$C \approx 25.12$ *Multiply.*

The circumference of the circle is about 25.1 in.

Helpful Hint

If the diameter or radius of a circle is a multiple of 7, use $\frac{22}{7}$ for π.

$C \approx \frac{22}{\underset{1}{7}} \cdot \frac{\overset{3}{21}}{1} \approx 66$

B 14 cm

$C = 2\pi r$ *You know the radius.*

$C \approx 2 \cdot \frac{22}{7} \cdot 14$ *Substitute $\frac{22}{7}$ for π and 14 for r.*

$C \approx 88$ *Multiply.*

The circumference of the circle is about 88 cm.

EXAMPLE 4 *Design Application*

Lily is drawing plans for a circular fountain. The circumference of the fountain is 63 ft. What is its approximate diameter?

$C = \pi d$ *You know the circumference.*

$63 \approx 3.14 \cdot d$ *Substitute 3.14 for π and 63 for C.*

$\frac{63}{3.14} \approx \frac{3.14 \cdot d}{3.14}$ *Divide both sides by 3.14 to isolate the variable.*

$20 \approx d$

The diameter of the fountain is about 20 ft.

MATHEMATICAL PRACTICES

Think and Discuss

1. **Describe** two ways to find the perimeter of a volleyball court.

2. **Explain** how to use the formula $C = \pi d$ to find the circumference of a circle if you know the radius.

Learn It Online
Homework Help Online
Exercises 1–20, 21, 23

GUIDED PRACTICE

Find each perimeter.

See Example **1**

1.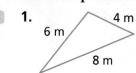
4 m
6 m
8 m

2.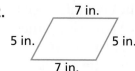
7 in.
5 in.   5 in.
7 in.

3.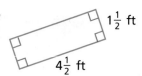
8 ft
8 ft

See Example **2**

4.
6 in.
12 in.

5.
8 m
2 m

6.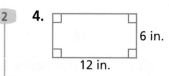
$1\frac{1}{2}$ ft
$4\frac{1}{2}$ ft

See Example **3**

Find the circumference of each circle to the nearest tenth, if necessary.
Use 3.14 or $\frac{22}{7}$ for π.

7.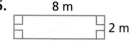
12 m

8.
3 ft

9.
21 in.

See Example **4**

10. A Ferris wheel has a circumference of 440 feet. What is the approximate diameter of the Ferris wheel? Use 3.14 for π.

INDEPENDENT PRACTICE

Find each perimeter.

See Example **1**

11.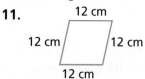
12 cm
12 cm   12 cm
12 cm

12.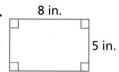
13 ft
7 ft
10 ft

13.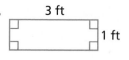
10 m
8 m   10 m
16 m

See Example **2**

14.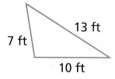
8 in.
5 in.

15.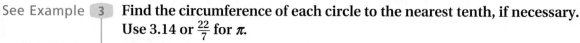
3 ft
1 ft

16.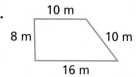
8 cm
10.2 cm

See Example **3**

Find the circumference of each circle to the nearest tenth, if necessary.
Use 3.14 or $\frac{22}{7}$ for π.

17.
35 cm

18.
3 m

19.
5.1 in.

See Example **4**

20. The circumference of Kayla's bicycle wheel is 91 inches. What is the approximate diameter of her bicycle wheel? Use 3.14 for π.

Extra Practice
See Extra Practice for more exercises.

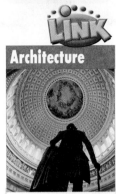

Architecture

The U.S. Capitol Rotunda is 96 ft in diameter and rises 180 ft 3 in. to the canopy. The rotunda contains many historical paintings, including the Frieze of American History and several memorial statues.

Find each missing measurement to the nearest tenth. Use 3.14 for π.

21. $r = $ ▢ ; $d = $ ▢ ; $C = 17.8$ m

22. $r = 6.7$ yd; $d = $ ▢ ; $C = $ ▢

23. $r = $ ▢ ; $d = 10.6$ in.; $C = $ ▢

24. $r = $ ▢ ; $d = $ ▢ ; $C = \pi$

25. **Critical Thinking** Ben is placing rope lights around the edge of a circular patio with a 24.2 ft diameter. The lights are in lengths of 57 inches. How many strands of lights does he need to surround the patio edge?

26. **Geography** The map shows the distances in miles between the airports on the Big Island of Hawaii. A pilot flies from Kailua-Kona to Waimea to Hilo and back to Kailua-Kona. How far does he travel?

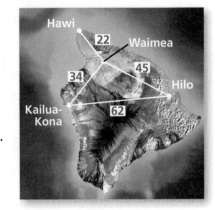

 27. **Architecture** The Capitol Rotunda connects the House and Senate sides of the U.S. Capitol. The rotunda is 180 feet tall and has a circumference of about 301.5 feet. What is its approximate diameter, to the nearest foot?

28. Describe how you could use a piece of string to find the perimeter or circumference of an object.

29. **Write a Problem** Write a problem about finding the perimeter or circumference of an object in your school or classroom.

30. **Write About It** Explain how to find the width of a rectangle if you know its perimeter and length.

31. **Challenge** The perimeter of a regular nonagon is $25\frac{1}{2}$ in. What is the length of one side of the nonagon?

Test Prep

32. **Multiple Choice** Which is the best estimate for the circumference of a circle with a diameter of 15 inches?

　Ⓐ 18.1 inches　　Ⓑ 23.6 inches　　Ⓒ 32.5 inches　　Ⓓ 47.1 inches

33. **Gridded Response** John is building a dog pen that is 6 feet by 8 feet. How many feet of fencing material will he need to go all the way around the pen?

Area of Circles

COMMON CORE

CC.7.G.4 Know the formulas for the area and circumference of a circle and use them to solve problems; give an informal derivation of the relationship between the circumference and area of a circle.

A circle can be cut into equal-sized sectors and arranged to resemble a parallelogram. The height h of the parallelogram is equal to the radius r of the circle, and the base b of the parallelogram is equal to one-half the circumference C of the circle. So the area of the parallelogram can be written as

$A = bh$, or $A = \frac{1}{2}Cr$.

Since $C = 2\pi r$, $A = \frac{1}{2}(2\pi r)r = \pi r^2$.

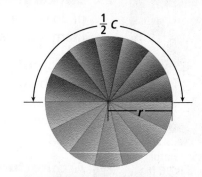

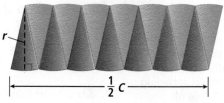

AREA OF A CIRCLE		
The area A of a circle is the product of π and the square of the circle's radius r.	$A = \pi r^2$	

EXAMPLE 1 **Finding the Area of a Circle**

Find the area of each circle to the nearest tenth. Use 3.14 for π.

Remember!

The order of operations calls for evaluating the exponents before multiplying.

A

3 m

$A = \pi r^2$	*Use the formula.*
$A \approx 3.14 \cdot 3^2$	*Substitute. Use 3 for r.*
$A \approx 3.14 \cdot 9$	*Evaluate the power.*
$A \approx 28.26$	*Multiply.*

The area of the circle is about 28.3 m^2.

B

8 in.

$A = \pi r^2$	*Use the formula.*
$A \approx 3.14 \cdot 4^2$	*Substitute. Use 4 for r.*
$A \approx 3.14 \cdot 16$	*Evaluate the power.*
$A \approx 50.24$	*Multiply.*

The area of the circle is about 50.2 in^2.

EXAMPLE 2 **Social Studies Application**

Social Studies LINK

Nomads in Mongolia carried their homes wherever they roamed. These homes, called *yurts*, were made of wood and felt.

A group of historians are building a yurt to display at a local multicultural fair. The yurt has a height of 8 feet 9 inches at its center, and it has a circular floor of radius 7 feet. What is the area of the floor of the yurt? Use $\frac{22}{7}$ for π.

$A = \pi r^2$ *Use the formula for the area of a circle.*

$A \approx \frac{22}{7} \cdot 7^2$ *Substitute. Use 7 for r.*

$A \approx \frac{22}{\cancel{7}_1} \cdot \cancel{49}^{7}$ *Evaluate the power. Then simplify.*

$A \approx 22 \cdot 7$

$A \approx 154$ *Multiply.*

The area of the floor of the yurt is about 154 ft^2.

EXAMPLE 3 **Measurement Application**

Use a centimeter ruler to measure the radius of the circle. Then find the area of the shaded region of the circle. Use 3.14 for π. Round your answer to the nearest tenth.

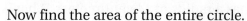

First measure the radius of the circle:
It measures 1.8 cm.

Helpful Hint

To estimate the area of a circle, you can square the radius and multiply by 3.

Now find the area of the entire circle.

$A = \pi r^2$ *Use the formula for the area of a circle.*

$A \approx 3.14 \cdot 1.8^2$ *Substitute. Use 1.8 for r and 3.14 for π.*

$A \approx 3.14 \cdot 3.24$ *Evaluate the power.*

$A \approx 10.1736$ *Multiply.*

Set up a proportion.

$\frac{1}{4} = \frac{x}{10.1736}$ *The shaded area is $\frac{1}{4}$ of the circle.*

$4x = 10.1736$ *The cross products are equal.*

$\frac{4x}{4} = \frac{10.1736}{4}$ *Divide each side by 4 to isolate the variable.*

$x = 2.5434$

The area of the shaded region of the circle is about 2.5 cm^2.

MATHEMATICAL PRACTICES

Think and Discuss

1. **Compare** finding the area of a circle when given the radius with finding the area when given the diameter.

2. **Give an example** of a circular object in your classroom. Tell how you could estimate the area of the object, and then estimate.

GUIDED PRACTICE

See Example 1 **Find the area of each circle to the nearest tenth. Use 3.14 for π.**

1. 5 in.

2. 16 cm

3. 20 yd

4. 1.1 m

See Example 2 **5.** The most popular pizza at Sam's Pizza is the 14-inch pepperoni pizza. What is the area of a pizza with a diameter of 14 inches? Use $\frac{22}{7}$ for π.

See Example 3 **6. Measurement** Use a centimeter ruler to measure the diameter of the circle. Then find the area of the shaded region of the circle. Use 3.14 for π. Round your answer to the nearest tenth.

INDEPENDENT PRACTICE

See Example 1 **Find the area of each circle to the nearest tenth. Use 3.14 for π.**

7. 3 in.

8. 16 ft

9. 6.4 yd

10. 15 cm

See Example 2 **11.** A wheel has a radius of 14 centimeters. What is the area of the wheel? Use $\frac{22}{7}$ for π.

See Example 3 **12. Measurement** Use a centimeter ruler to measure the radius of the circle. Then find the area of the shaded region of the circle. Use 3.14 for π. Round your answer to the nearest tenth.

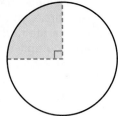

PRACTICE AND PROBLEM SOLVING

Extra Practice
See Extra Practice for more exercises.

13. A radio station broadcasts a signal over an area with a 75-mile radius. What is the area of the region that receives the radio signal?

14. A circular flower bed in Kay's backyard has a diameter of 8 feet. What is the area of the flower bed? Round your answer to the nearest tenth.

15. A company is manufacturing aluminum lids. The radius of each lid is 3 cm. What is the area of one lid? Round your answer to the nearest tenth.

Given the radius or diameter, find the circumference and area of each circle to the nearest tenth. Use 3.14 for π.

16. $r = 7$ m   **17.** $d = 18$ in.   **18.** $d = 24$ ft   **19.** $r = 6.4$ cm

Given the area, find the radius of each circle. Use 3.14 for π.

20. $A = 113.04$ cm^2 **21.** $A = 3.14$ ft^2 **22.** $A = 28.26$ in^2

23. A hiker was last seen near a fire tower in the Catalina Mountains. Searchers are dispatched to the surrounding area to find the missing hiker.

    a. Assume the hiker could walk in any direction at a rate of 3 miles per hour. How large an area would searchers have to cover if the hiker was last seen 2 hours ago? Use 3.14 for π. Round your answer to the nearest square mile.

    b. How much additional area would the searchers have to cover if the hiker was last seen 3 hours ago?

24. Physical Science The tower of a wind turbine is about the height of a 20-story building. Each turbine can produce 24 megawatt-hours of electricity in one day. Find the area covered by the turbine when it is rotating. Use 3.14 for π. Round your answer to the nearest tenth.

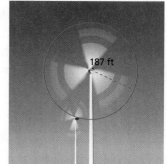

187 ft

25. Critical Thinking Two circles have the same radius. Is the combined area of the two circles the same as the area of a circle with twice the radius?

26. What's the Question? Chang painted half of a free-throw circle that has a diameter of 12 ft. The answer is 56.52 ft². What is the question?

27. Write About It Describe how to find the area of a circle when given only the circumference of the circle.

28. Challenge How does the area of a circle change if you multiply the radius by a factor of *n*, where *n* is a whole number?

Test Prep

29. Multiple Choice The area of a circle is 30 square feet. A second circle has a radius that is 2 feet shorter than that of the first circle. What is the area, to the nearest tenth, of the second circle? Use 3.14 for π.

    Ⓐ 3.7 square feet   Ⓑ 10.0 square feet   Ⓒ 38.0 square feet   Ⓓ 179.2 square feet

30. Short Response A pizza parlor offers a large pizza with a 12-inch diameter. It also offers a "mega" pizza with a 24-inch diameter. The slogan used to advertise the mega pizza is "Twice the pizza of a large, and twice the fun." Is the mega pizza twice as big as the large? If not, how much bigger is it? Explain.

Area of Irregular Figures

COMMON CORE

CC.7.G.6 Solve real-world and mathematical problems involving area, volume and surface area of two- and three-dimensional objects composed of triangles, quadrilaterals, polygons, cubes, and right prisms.

A **composite figure** is made up of simple geometric shapes, such as triangles and rectangles. You can find the area of composite and other irregular figures by separating them into non-overlapping familiar figures. The sum of the areas of these figures is the area of the entire figure. You can also estimate the area of an irregular figure by using graph paper.

EXAMPLE 1 **Estimating the Area of an Irregular Figure**

Vocabulary
composite figure

Estimate the area of the figure. Each square represents 1 ft².

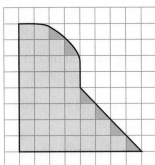

Count the number of filled or almost-filled squares: 35 yellow squares.

Count the number of squares that are about half-filled: 6 blue squares.

Add the number of filled squares plus $\frac{1}{2}$ the number of half-filled squares: $35 + \left(\frac{1}{2} \cdot 6\right) = 35 + 3 = 38$.

The area of the figure is about 38 ft².

EXAMPLE 2 **Finding the Area of a Composite Figure**

Find the area of the figure. Use 3.14 for π.

Step 1: Separate the figure into smaller, familiar figures.

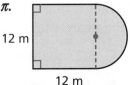

Step 2: Find the area of each smaller figure.

Area of the square:
$A = s^2$
$A = 12^2 = 144$

Area of the semicircle:
$A = \frac{1}{2}\left(\pi r^2\right)$
$A \approx \frac{1}{2}(3.14 \cdot 6^2)$
$A \approx \frac{1}{2}(113.04) \approx 56.52$

Helpful Hint

The area of a semicircle is $\frac{1}{2}$ the area of a circle.
$A = \frac{1}{2}(\pi r^2)$

Step 3: Add the areas to find the total area.
$A \approx 144 + 56.52 = 200.52$

The area of the figure is about 200.52 m².

Video **Lesson Tutorials Online**

EXAMPLE **3** **PROBLEM SOLVING APPLICATION**

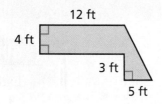

MATHEMATICAL PRACTICES Make sense of problems and persevere in solving them.

Chandra wants to carpet the floor of her closet. A floor plan of the closet is shown at right. How much carpet does she need?

12 ft

4 ft

3 ft

5 ft

1 Understand the Problem

Rewrite the question as a statement:

• Find the amount of carpet needed to cover the floor of the closet.

List the **important information:**

• The floor of the closet is a composite figure.

• The amount of carpet needed is equal to the area of the floor.

2 Make a Plan

Find the area of the floor by separating the figure into familiar figures: a rectangle and a triangle. Then add the areas of the rectangle and triangle to find the total area.

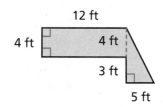

12 ft

4 ft   4 ft

3 ft

5 ft

Helpful Hint

There are often several different ways to separate an irregular figure into familiar figures.

3 Solve

Find the area of each smaller figure.

Area of the rectangle:

$A = \ell w$

$A = 12 \cdot 4$

$A = 48 \text{ ft}^2$

Area of the triangle:

$A = \frac{1}{2}bh$

$A = \frac{1}{2}(5)(3 + 4)$

$A = \frac{1}{2}(35) = 17.5 \text{ ft}^2$

Add the areas to find the total area. $A = 48 + 17.5 = 65.5$

Chandra needs 65.5 ft^2 of carpet.

4 Look Back

The area of the closet floor must be greater than the area of the rectangle (48 ft²), so the answer is reasonable.

MATHEMATICAL PRACTICES

Think and Discuss

1. Describe two different ways to find the area of the irregular figure at right.

2. Explain how dividing the figure into two rectangles with a horizontal line would affect its area and perimeter.

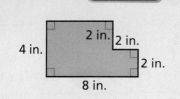

2 in. 2 in.

4 in.

2 in.

8 in.

Learn It Online
Homework Help Online
Exercises 1–12, 13, 15, 17

GUIDED PRACTICE

See Example **1** Estimate the area of each figure. Each square represents 1 ft².

1.

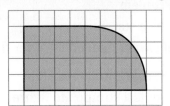

2.

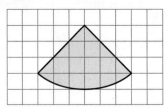

See Example **2** Find the area of each figure. Use 3.14 for π.

3.

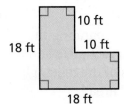

10 ft
18 ft   10 ft
18 ft

4.

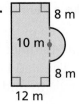

8 m
10 m
8 m
12 m

5.

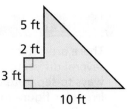

5 ft
2 ft
3 ft
10 ft

See Example **3** **6.** Luis has a model train set. The layout of the track is shown at right. How much artificial grass does Luis need in order to fill the interior of the layout? Use 3.14 for π.

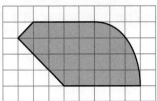

2 ft
4.5 ft

INDEPENDENT PRACTICE

See Example **1** Estimate the area of each figure. Each square represents 1 ft².

7.

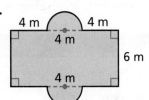

8.

See Example **2** Find the area of each figure. Use 3.14 for π.

9.

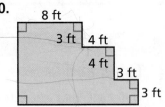

4 m   4 m
4 m
6 m
4 m

10.

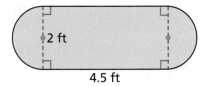

8 ft
3 ft   4 ft
4 ft
3 ft
3 ft

11.

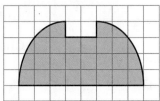

2 cm   5 cm
4 cm
4 cm   4 cm
3 cm   5 cm

See Example **3** **12.** The figure shows the floor plan for a gallery of a museum. The ceiling of the gallery is to be covered with soundproofing material. How much material is needed? Use 3.14 for π.

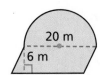

20 m
6 m

Extra Practice

See Extra Practice for more exercises.

Find the area and perimeter of each figure. Use 3.14 for π.

13.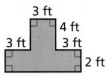
3 ft
4 ft
3 ft 3 ft
2 ft

14.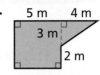
5 m   4 m
3 m
2 m

15.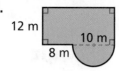
12 m
10 m
8 m

16. Critical Thinking Will the area and perimeter change for the figure in Exercise 14 if the triangle part is reflected to the left side? Explain.

17. Critical Thinking The figure at right is made up of an isosceles triangle and a square. The perimeter of the figure is 44 feet. What is the value of *x*?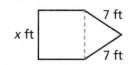

x ft
7 ft
7 ft

18. Multi-Step A figure has vertices $A(-8, 5)$, $B(-4, 5)$, $C(-4, 2)$, $D(3, 2)$, $E(3, -2)$, $F(6, -2)$, $G(6, -4)$, and $H(-8, -4)$. Graph the figure on a coordinate plane. Then find the area and perimeter of the figure.

19. Choose a Strategy A figure is formed by combining a square and a triangle. Its total area is 32.5 m². The area of the triangle is 7.5 m². What is the length of each side of the square?

20. Write About It Describe how to find the area of the composite figure at right.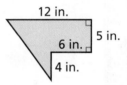

12 in.
5 in.
6 in.
4 in.

21. Challenge Find the area and perimeter of the figure at right. Use 3.14 for π.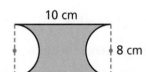

10 cm
8 cm

Test Prep

22. Multiple Choice A rectangle is formed by two congruent right triangles. The area of each triangle is 6 in². Each side of the rectangle is a whole number of inches. Which of these CANNOT be the perimeter of the rectangle?

Ⓐ 26 in.   Ⓑ 24 in.   Ⓒ 16 in.   Ⓓ 14 in.

23. Extended Response The shaded area of the garden represents a patch of carrots. Veronica estimates that she will get about 12 carrots from this patch. Veronica is going to plant the rest of her garden with carrots. Estimate the total number of carrots she can expect to grow. Show your work.

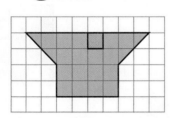

Ready To Go On?

Learn It Online
Resources Online

Quiz for Lessons 1 Through 3

✓ 1 Perimeter and Circumference

1. Find the perimeter of the figure at right.

2. If the circumference of a wheel is 94 cm, what is its approximate diameter?

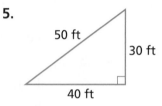

10.2 m
3.0 m

Find each perimeter.

3.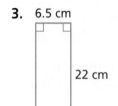
6.5 cm
22 cm

4.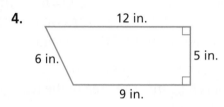
12 in.
6 in.
5 in.
9 in.

5.
50 ft
30 ft
40 ft

✓ 2 Area of Circles

6. Find the area of the circle to the nearest tenth. Use 3.14 or $\frac{22}{7}$ for π.

7. The radius of a clock face is $8\frac{3}{4}$ in. What is its area to the nearest whole number?

28 ft

Given the area, find the radius of each circle. Use 3.14 for π.

8. $A = 28.26 \text{ mm}^2$

9. $A = 153.86 \text{ yd}^2$

10. $A = 50.24 \text{ in}^2$

✓ 3 Area of Irregular Figures

Find the area of each figure to the nearest tenth if necessary. Use 3.14 for π.

11.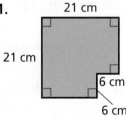
21 cm
21 cm
6 cm
6 cm

12.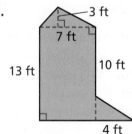
3 ft
7 ft
13 ft
10 ft
4 ft

13.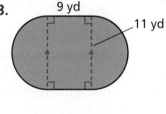
9 yd
11 yd

Focus on Problem Solving

Understand

Understand the Problem

• Identify too much or too little information

Problems involving real-world situations sometimes give too much or too little information. Before solving these types of problems, you must decide what information is necessary and whether you have all the necessary information.

If the problem gives too much information, identify which of the facts are really needed to solve the problem. If the problem gives too little information, determine what additional information is required to solve the problem.

Copy each problem and underline the information you need to solve it. If necessary information is missing, write down what additional information is required.

1 Mrs. Wong wants to put a fence around her garden. One side of her garden measures 8 feet. Another side measures 5 feet. What length of fencing does Mrs. Wong need to enclose her garden?

2 Two sides of a triangle measure 17 inches and 13 inches. The perimeter of the triangle is 45 inches. What is the length in feet of the third side of the triangle? (There are 12 inches in 1 foot.)

3 During swim practice, Peggy swims 2 laps each of freestyle and backstroke. The dimensions of the pool are 25 meters by 50 meters. What is the area of the pool?

4 Each afternoon, Molly walks her dog two times around the park. The park is a rectangle that is 315 yards long. How far does Molly walk her dog each afternoon?

5 A trapezoid has bases that measure 12 meters and 18 meters and one side that measures 9 meters. The trapezoid has no right angles. What is the area of the trapezoid?

Introduction to Three-Dimensional Figures

Three-dimensional figures have three dimensions: length, width, and height. A flat surface of a three-dimensional figure is a **face**. An **edge** is where two faces meet.

A **polyhedron** is a three-dimensional figure whose faces are all polygons. A **vertex** of a polyhedron is a point where three or more edges meet. The face that is used to name a polyhedron is a **base**.

A *prism* has two bases, and a *pyramid* has one base.

Vocabulary

face

edge

polyhedron

vertex

base

prism

pyramid

cylinder

cone

sphere

Prisms	Pyramids
A **prism** is a polyhedron that has two parallel, congruent bases. The bases can be any polygon. The other faces are parallelograms.	A **pyramid** is a polyhedron that has one base. The base can be any polygon. The other faces are triangles.

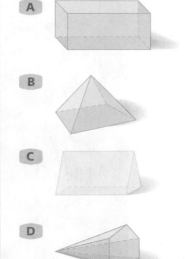

EXAMPLE 1 Naming Prisms and Pyramids

Identify the bases and faces of each figure. Then name the figure.

Interactivities Online ▶

A
There are two rectangular bases.
There are four other rectangular faces.
The figure is a rectangular prism.

B
There is one rectangular base.
There are four triangular faces.
The figure is a rectangular pyramid.

C
There are two triangular bases.
There are three rectangular faces.
The figure is a triangular prism.

Remember!

A polygon with six sides is called a hexagon.

D
There is one hexagonal base.
There are six triangular faces.
The figure is a hexagonal pyramid.

Video **Lesson Tutorials Online**

Other three-dimensional figures include *cylinders*, *cones*, and *spheres*. These figures are not polyhedrons because they are not made of faces that are all polygons.

Cylinders	Cones	Spheres
A **cylinder** has two parallel, congruent bases that are circles. 2 bases 	A **cone** has one base that is a circle and a surface that comes to a point called the vertex. Vertex 1 base 	A **sphere** has a surface made up of all the points that are the same distance from a given point. 

You can use properties to classify three-dimensional figures.

EXAMPLE **2** **Classifying Three-Dimensional Figures**

Classify each figure as a polyhedron or not a polyhedron. Then name the figure.

A

The faces are all polygons, so the figure is a polyhedron.
There is one triangular base.
The figure is a triangular pyramid.

B

The faces are not all polygons, so the figure is not a polyhedron.
There are two circular bases.
The figure is a cylinder.

C

The faces are not all polygons, so the figure is not a polyhedron.
There is one circular base.
The figure is a cone.

MATHEMATICAL PRACTICES

Think and Discuss

1. Explain how to identify a prism or a pyramid.

2. Compare and contrast cylinders and prisms. How are they alike? How are they different?

Exercises

Learn It Online
Homework Help Online
Exercises 1–12, 13, 15, 19, 21

GUIDED PRACTICE

See Example 1 **Identify the bases and faces of each figure. Then name the figure.**

1.

2.

3.

See Example 2 **Classify each figure as a polyhedron or not a polyhedron. Then name the figure.**

4.

5.

6.

INDEPENDENT PRACTICE

See Example 1 **Identify the bases and faces of each figure. Then name the figure.**

7.

8.

9.

See Example 2 **Classify each figure as a polyhedron or not a polyhedron. Then name the figure.**

10.

11.

12.

PRACTICE AND PROBLEM SOLVING

Extra Practice
See Extra Practice for more exercises.

Identify the three-dimensional figure described.

13. two parallel, congruent square bases and four other polygonal faces

14. two parallel, congruent circular bases and one curved surface

15. one triangular base and three other triangular faces

16. all points on the surface are the same distance from a given point

Name two examples of the three-dimensional figure described.

17. two parallel, congruent bases

18. one base

19. The structures in the photo at right are tombs of ancient Egyptian kings. No one knows exactly when the tombs were built, but some archaeologists think the first one might have been built around 2780 B.C.E. Name the shape of the ancient Egyptian structures.

20. The Parthenon was built around 440 B.C.E. by the ancient Greeks. Its purpose was to house a statue of Athena, the Greek goddess of wisdom. Describe the three-dimensional shapes you see in the structure.

21. The Leaning Tower of Pisa began to lean as it was being built. To keep the tower from falling over, the upper sections (floors) were built slightly off center so that the tower would curve away from the way it was leaning. What shape is each section of the tower?

22. ⭐ **Challenge** The stainless steel structure at right, called the Unisphere, became the symbol of the New York World's Fair of 1964–1965. Explain why the structure is not a sphere.

2600 B.C.E.
Ancient Egyptian structures at Giza

440 B.C.E.
Parthenon

1173
Leaning Tower of Pisa

1964
Unisphere

Test Prep

23. Multiple Choice Which figure has six rectangular faces?

   Ⓐ Rectangular prism   Ⓒ Triangular pyramid

   Ⓑ Triangular prism   Ⓓ Rectangular pyramid

24. Multiple Choice Which figure does NOT have two congruent bases?

   Ⓕ Cube   Ⓖ Pyramid   Ⓗ Prism   Ⓙ Cylinder

Cross Sections

CC.7.G.3 Describe the two-dimensional figures that result from slicing three-dimensional figures...

Vocabulary

cross section

When a three-dimensional figure and a plane intersect, the intersection is called a **cross section**. A three-dimensional figure can have many different cross sections. For example, when you cut an orange in half, the cross section that is exposed depends on the direction of the cut.

EXAMPLE **1**   **Identifying Cross Sections**

Identify the cross section that best matches the given figure.

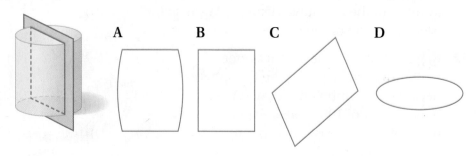

The bases of the cylinder are parallel, so the cross section must contain a pair of parallel lines. The bases of the cylinder meet the lateral surface at right angles, so the cross section must contain right angles. The best choice is **B**.

EXAMPLE **2**   **Sketching and Describing Cross Sections**

Sketch and describe the cross section of a cone that is cut parallel to its base.

The base of a cone is a circle. Any cross section made by cutting the cone parallel to the base will also be a circle.

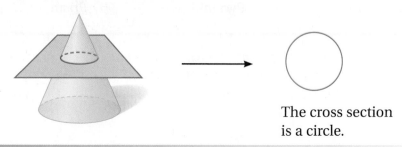

The cross section
is a circle.

Stephanie Friedman/HMH

You can form three-dimensional figures by translating or rotating a cross section through space.

EXAMPLE **Describing Three-Dimensional Figures Formed by Transformations**

Describe the three-dimensional figure formed by rotating an isosceles triangle around its line of symmetry.

Draw an isosceles triangle and its line of symmetry. Visualize rotating the triangle through space around the line. The resulting three-dimensional figure is a cone.

EXTENSION

Exercises

1. Identify the cross section that best matches the given figure.

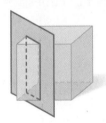

Ⓐ   Ⓑ   Ⓒ   Ⓓ

Sketch and describe each cross section.

2. a cylinder that is cut parallel to its bases

3. a cube that is cut parallel to one of its faces

Describe the three-dimensional figure formed by each transformation.

4. a rectangle that is rotated around a line of symmetry

5. a circle that is translated perpendicularly to the plane in which it lies (*Hint:* Imagine lifting a circle that is lying on a table straight upward.)

6. A sculptor has a block of clay in the shape of a rectangular prism. She uses a piece of wire to cut the clay, and the resulting cross section is a square. Make a sketch showing the prism and how the sculptor may have cut the clay.

Explore the Volume of Prisms and Cylinders

Learn It Online
Lab Resources Online

Use appropriate tools strategically.

CC.7.G.6 Solve real-world and mathematical problems involving… volume… of… three-dimensional objects composed of triangles, quadrilaterals, polygons, cubes, and right prisms.

The volume of a three-dimensional figure is the number of cubes that it can hold. One cube represents one cubic unit of volume.

Activity 1

1. Use centimeter cubes to build the rectangular prism shown. What are the length, width, and height of the prism? How many cubes does the prism hold?

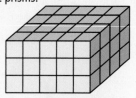

2. You can find out how many cubes the prism holds without counting every cube. First look at the prism from above. How can you find the number of cubes in the top layer without counting every cube?

Top

3. Now look at the prism from the side. How many layers does the prism have? How can you use this to find the total number of cubes in the prism?

Side

Think and Discuss

1. Describe a shortcut for finding the number of cubes in a rectangular prism.

2. **Make a Conjecture** Suppose you know the area of the base of a prism and the height of the prism. How can you find the prism's volume?

3. Let the area of the base of a prism be B and the height of the prism be h. Write a formula for the prism's volume V.

Try This

Use the formula you discovered to find the volume of each prism.

1.

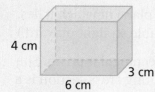

4 cm
3 cm
6 cm

2.

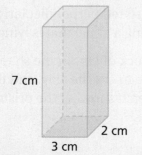

7 cm
2 cm
3 cm

3.

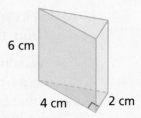

6 cm
4 cm
2 cm

Activity 2

1 You can use a process similar to that in Activity 1 to develop the formula for the volume of a cylinder. You will need an empty soup can or other cylindrical container. Remove one of the bases.

SOUP

2 Arrange centimeter cubes in a single layer at the bottom of the cylinder. Fit as many cubes into the layer as possible. How many cubes are in this layer?

3 To find how many layers of cubes would fit in the cylinder, make a stack of cubes along the inside of the cylinder. How many layers would fit in the cylinder?

4 How can you use what you know to find the approximate number of cubes that would fit in the cylinder?

Think and Discuss

1. Make a Conjecture Suppose you know the area of the base of a cylinder and the height of the cylinder. How can you find the cylinder's volume?

2. Let the area of the base of a cylinder be B and the height of the cylinder be h. Write a formula for the cylinder's volume V.

3. The base of a cylinder is a circle with radius r. How can you find the area of the base? How can you use this in your formula for the volume of a cylinder?

Try This

Use the formula you discovered to find the volume of each cylinder. Use 3.14 for π and round to the nearest tenth.

1.

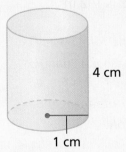

4 cm

1 cm

2.

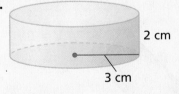

2 cm

3 cm

3.

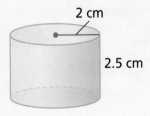

2 cm

2.5 cm

COMMON CORE

CC.7.G.6 Solve real-world and mathematical problems involving area, volume and surface area of two- and three-dimensional objects composed of triangles, quadrilaterals, polygons, cubes, and right prisms.

Vocabulary

volume

Interactivities Online ▶

Any three-dimensional figure can be filled completely with congruent cubes and parts of cubes. The **volume** of a three-dimensional figure is the number of cubes it can hold. Each cube represents a unit of measure called a cubic unit.

To find the volume of a rectangular prism, you can count cubes or multiply the lengths of the edges.

$$4 \text{ cm} \cdot 2 \text{ cm} \cdot 2 \text{ cm} = 16 \text{ cm}^3$$

length · width · height = volume

area of · height = volume
base

The volume of a prism is the area of its base times its height.

VOLUME OF A PRISM		
The volume V of a prism is the area of its base B times its height h.	$V = Bh$	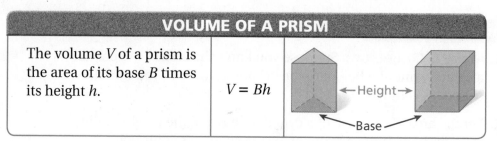

EXAMPLE 1 **Using a Formula to Find the Volume of a Prism**

Find the volume of each figure.

A

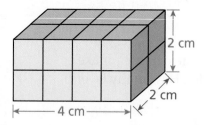

12 in.
8 in.
2 in.

$V = Bh$ Use the formula.
The base is a rectangle: $B = 8 \cdot 2 = 16$.

$V = 16 \cdot 12$ Substitute for B and h.

$V = 192$ Multiply.

The volume of the cereal box is 192 in³.

B

3 in.
4 in.
15 in.

$V = Bh$ Use the formula.
The base is a triangle: $B = \frac{1}{2} \cdot 4 \cdot 3 = 6$.

$V = 6 \cdot 15$ Substitute for B and h.

$V = 90$ Multiply.

The volume of the shipping carton is 90 in³.

Reading Math

Any unit of measurement with an exponent of 3 is a cubic unit. For example, m³ means "cubic meter," and in³ means "cubic inch."

Video **Lesson Tutorials Online**

Finding the volume of a cylinder is similar to finding the volume of a prism.

VOLUME OF A CYLINDER

The volume V of a cylinder is the area of its base B times its height h.	$V = Bh$ or $V = \pi r^2 h$	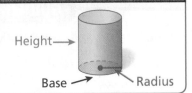

EXAMPLE 2 **Using a Formula to Find the Volume of a Cylinder**

A can of shoe polish is shaped like a cylinder. Find its volume to the nearest tenth. Use 3.14 for π.

$V = Bh$ *Use the formula.*

The base is a circle: $B = \pi \cdot 4^2 \approx 50.24 \text{ cm}^2$.

$V \approx 50.24 \cdot 5$ *Substitute for B and h.*

$V \approx 251.2$ *Multiply.*

The volume of the shoe polish can is about 251.2 cm³.

8 cm

5 cm

A three-dimensional composite figure is made up of two or more simpler three-dimensional figures. To find the volume of a three-dimensional composite figure, add the volumes of the simpler figures.

EXAMPLE 3 **Finding the Volume of a Composite Figure**

Find the volume of the composite figure to the nearest tenth. Use 3.14 for π.

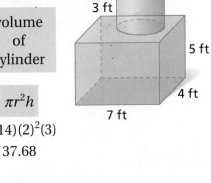

2 ft
3 ft
5 ft
4 ft
7 ft

volume of composite figure	=	volume of prism	+	volume of cylinder
V	=	Bh	+	$\pi r^2 h$
V	$\approx$	$(7)(4)(5)$	+	$(3.14)(2)^2(3)$
V	$\approx$	140	+	37.68
V	$\approx$		177.68	

The volume of the composite figure is about 177.7 ft³.

MATHEMATICAL PRACTICES

Think and Discuss

1. Explain what a cubic unit is. What units would you use for the volume of a figure measured in yards?

2. Compare and contrast the formulas for volume of a prism and volume of a cylinder. How are they alike? How are they different?

Learn It Online
Homework Help Online
Exercises 1–12, 13, 15

GUIDED PRACTICE

See Example ① Find the volume of each figure.

1.

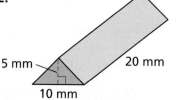

5 in.

6 in.

8 in.

2.

5 mm

20 mm

10 mm

3.

3.5 in.

PLAYING CARDS

2.25 in.   0.5 in.

See Example ② **4.** A can of tomato paste is shaped like a cylinder. It is 4 cm wide and 6 cm tall. Find its volume to the nearest tenth. Use 3.14 for π.

See Example ③ Find the volume of each composite figure to the nearest tenth.
Use 3.14 for π.

5.

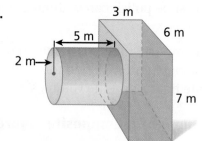

3 m

5 m

6 m

2 m→

7 m

6.

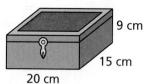

3 ft→

4 ft

5 ft

8 ft

INDEPENDENT PRACTICE

See Example ① Find the volume of each figure.

7.

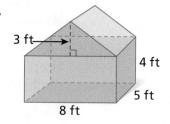

4 ft

12 ft

8 ft

8.

9 cm

15 cm

20 cm

9.

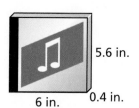

5.6 in.

6 in.   0.4 in.

See Example ② **10.** A paper towel roll is shaped like a cylinder. It is 4 cm wide and 28 cm tall. Find its volume to the nearest tenth. Use 3.14 for π.

See Example ③ Find the volume of each composite figure to the nearest tenth.
Use 3.14 for π.

11.

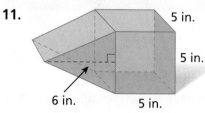

5 in.

5 in.

6 in.   5 in.

12.

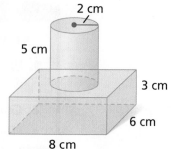

2 cm

5 cm

3 cm

6 cm

8 cm

Extra Practice

See Extra Practice for more exercises.

13. Multi-Step The base of a triangular prism is a right triangle with hypotenuse 10 m long and one leg 6 m long. If the height of the prism is 12 m, what is the volume of the prism?

14. A cylindrical candle has a radius of 1.5 in. and a height of 4 in. What is the volume of the candle in cubic inches? in cubic centimeters? Use 3.14 for π and round your answers to the nearest hundredth. (*Hint:* 1 in^3 ≈ 16.38 cm^3)

15. Recreation The tent shown is in the shape of a triangular prism. How many cubic feet of space are in the tent?

3.5 ft

6 ft   4.5 ft

16. What's the Error? A student said the volume of a cylinder with a 3-inch diameter is two times the volume of a cylinder with the same height and a 1.5-inch radius. What is the error?

17. Write About It Explain the similarities and differences between finding the volume of a cylinder and finding the volume of a triangular prism.

18. Challenge Find the volume, to the nearest tenth, of the material that makes up the pipe shown. Use 3.14 for π.

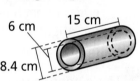

6 cm   15 cm

8.4 cm

Test Prep

19. Multiple Choice What is the volume of a triangular prism that is 10 in. long, 7 in. wide, and 4 in. high?

Ⓐ 110 in^3 Ⓑ 140 in^3 Ⓒ 205 in^3 Ⓓ 280 in^3

20. Multiple Choice Which figures have the same volume?

I

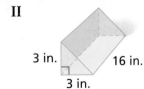

3 in.
8 in.
3 in.

II

3 in.   16 in.
3 in.

III

7 in.   4 in.

Ⓕ I and II   Ⓖ I and III   Ⓗ II and III   Ⓙ I, II, and III

Use Nets to Build Prisms and Cylinders

Use with Surface Area of Prisms and Cylinders

Learn It Online
Lab Resources Online

A net is a pattern of two-dimensional figures that can be folded to make a three-dimensional figure. You can use $\frac{1}{4}$-inch graph paper to help you make nets.

 Use appropriate tools strategically.

CC.7.G.6 Solve... mathematical problems involving... surface area of... three-dimensional objects...

Activity

1 Use a net to construct a rectangular prism.

  a. Draw the net at right on a piece of graph paper. Each rectangle is 10 squares by 4 squares. The two squares are 4 small squares on each side.

  b. Cut out the net. Fold the net along the edges of each rectangle to make a rectangular prism. Tape the edges to hold them in place.

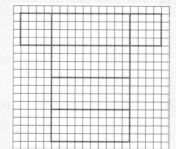

2 Use a net to construct a cylinder.

  a. Draw the net at right on a piece of graph paper. The rectangle is 25 squares by 8 squares. Use a compass to make the circles. Each circle has a radius of 4 squares.

  b. Cut out the net. Fold the net as shown to make a cylinder. Tape the edges to hold them in place.

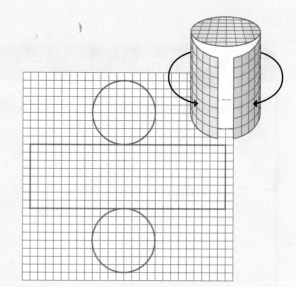

Think and Discuss

1. What are the dimensions, in inches, of the rectangular prism that you built?

2. What is the height, in inches, of the cylinder that you built? What is the cylinder's radius?

Try This

1. Use a net to construct a rectangular prism that is 1 inch by 2 inches by 3 inches.

2. Use a net to construct a cylinder with a height of 1 inch and a radius of $\frac{1}{2}$ in. (*Hint:* The length of the rectangle in the net must match the circumference of the circles, so the length should be $2\pi r = 2\pi\left(\frac{1}{2}\right) \approx 3.14$ inches.)

9-6 Surface Area of Prisms and Cylinders

CC.7.G.6 Solve real-world and mathematical problems involving... surface area of... three-dimensional objects composed of triangles, quadrilaterals, polygons, cubes, and right prisms.

Vocabulary

net

surface area

lateral face

lateral area

Interactivities Online ▶

If you remove the surface from a three-dimensional figure and lay it out flat, the pattern you make is called a **net**.

Nets allow you to see all the surfaces of a solid at one time. You can use nets to help you find the *surface area* of a three-dimensional figure. **Surface area** is the sum of the areas of all of the surfaces of a figure expressed in square units.

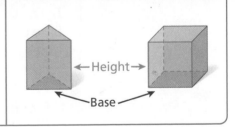

The **lateral faces** of a prism are parallelograms that connect the bases. The **lateral area** of a prism is the sum of the areas of the lateral faces.

The net of a prism can be drawn so that the lateral faces form a rectangle with the same height as the prism. The length of the rectangle is equal to the perimeter of the base of the prism.

$P = a + b + c$

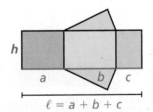

$\ell = a + b + c$

SURFACE AREA OF A PRISM

The surface area S of a prism is twice the base area B plus the lateral area L. The lateral area is the base perimeter P times the height h.	$S = 2B + L$ or $S = 2B + Ph$	

←Height→

Base

EXAMPLE 1 — Finding the Surface Area of a Prism

Find the surface area of the prism.

$S = 2B + Ph$ *Use the formula.*

$S = 2(8)(12) + (40)(6)$ *Substitute.*
$P = 2(8) + 2(12) = 40$

$S = 192 + 240$ *Multiply.*

$S = 432$ *Add.*

The surface area of the prism is 432 in^2.

6 in. 12 in. 8 in.

Find the surface area of the prism.

B $S = 2B + Ph$ *Use the formula.*

     $S = 2\left(\frac{1}{2}bh\right) + Ph$ $B = \frac{1}{2}bh$

     $S = 2\left(\frac{1}{2}\right)(8)(3) + 18(7)$ *Substitute. $P = 8 + 5 + 5 = 18$*

     $S = 24 + 126$ *Multiply.*

     $S = 150$ *Add.*

The area is 150 ft^2.

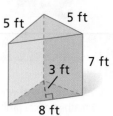

The lateral area of a cylinder is the curved surface that connects the two bases. The net of a cylinder can be drawn so that the lateral area forms a rectangle with the same height as the cylinder. The length of the rectangle is equal to the circumference of the base of the cylinder.

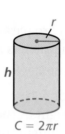

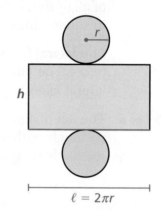

$C = 2\pi r$

$\ell = 2\pi r$

SURFACE AREA OF A CYLINDER

The surface area S of a cylinder is twice the base area B plus the lateral area L. The lateral area is the base circumference $2\pi r$ times the height h.	$S = 2B + L$ or $S = 2\pi r^2 + 2\pi rh$	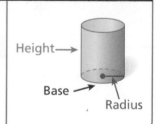

EXAMPLE 2   **Finding the Surface Area of a Cylinder**

Find the surface area of the cylinder to the nearest tenth. Use 3.14 for π.

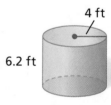

$S = 2\pi r^2 + 2\pi rh$ *Use the formula.*

$S \approx 2(3.14)(4^2) + 2(3.14)(4)(6.2)$ *Substitute.*

$S \approx 100.48 + 155.744$ *Multiply.*

$S \approx 256.224$ *Add.*

$S \approx 256.2$ *Round.*

The surface area of the cylinder is about 256.2 ft^2.

     Video   Lesson Tutorials Online

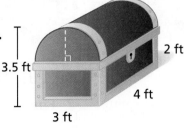

EXAMPLE 3 **PROBLEM SOLVING APPLICATION**

MATHEMATICAL PRACTICES Make sense of problems and persevere in solving them.

The treasure chest is a composite figure. What is the surface area of the chest to the nearest square foot?

3.5 ft

2 ft

4 ft

3 ft

1 Understand the Problem

- The chest is a rectangular prism and one-half of a cylinder.
- The base of the chest is 3 ft by 4 ft and the height is 2 ft.
- The radius of the cylinder is 1.5 ft and the height is 4 ft.

2 Make a Plan

Draw nets of the figures and shade the parts that show the surface area of the chest.

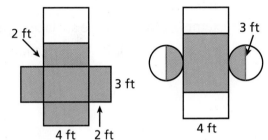

2 ft

3 ft

4 ft 2 ft

3 ft

4 ft

3 Solve

Find the surface area of the shaded part of the prism.

$S = B + Ph$ *Use only one base.*

$= (4)(3) + 14(2)$ *Substitute.*

$= 12 + 28 = 40$

Find the surface area of half of the cylinder.

$S = \frac{1}{2}(2\pi r^2 + 2\pi rh)$ *Use only one-half the cylinder.*

$\approx \frac{1}{2}[2(3.14)(1.5^2) + 2(3.14)(1.5)(4)]$ *Substitute. Use 3.14 for π.*

$\approx \frac{1}{2}(14.13 + 37.68)$

$\approx \frac{1}{2}(51.81) = 25.905$

Add to find the total surface area: $40 + 25.905 = 65.905$.

The surface area of the treasure chest is about 66 ft^2.

4 Look Back

The surface area of the chest should be just less than the surface area of a rectangular prism with the same base and a height of 3.5 ft.

$S = 2B + Ph = 2(12) + 14(3.5) = 73$ ft^2

66 ft^2 is just less than 73 ft^2, so the answer is reasonable.

MATHEMATICAL PRACTICES

Think and Discuss

1. Explain how you would find the surface area of an open-top box that is shaped like a rectangular prism.

GUIDED PRACTICE

See Example **1**   **Find the surface area of each prism.**

1.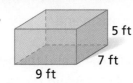
5 ft
7 ft
9 ft

2.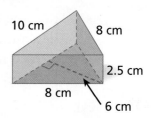
10 cm
8 cm
2.5 cm
8 cm
6 cm

See Example **2**   **Find the surface area of each cylinder to the nearest tenth. Use 3.14 for π.**

3.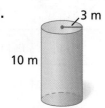
3 m
10 m

4.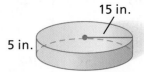
15 in.
5 in.

See Example **3**   **5.** What is the surface area of the breadbox to the nearest square inch? Check your answer for reasonableness.

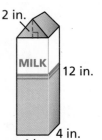
8 in.
16 in.
BREAD
├ 8 in. ┼ 8 in. ┤

INDEPENDENT PRACTICE

See Example **1**   **Find the surface area of each prism.**

6.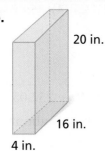
20 in.
16 in.
4 in.

7.
5 yd
5 yd
3 yd
6 yd
8 yd

See Example **2**   **Find the surface area of each cylinder to the nearest tenth. Use 3.14 for π.**

8.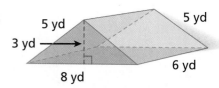
6 in.
15 in.

9.
18.5 cm
1.5 cm

See Example **3**   **10.** What is the surface area of the milk carton to the nearest square inch? Check your answer for reasonableness.

2 in.
MILK
12 in.
4 in.
4 in.

11. A cannery packs tuna into metal cans like the one shown. Round your answers to the nearest tenth, if necessary. Use 3.14 for π.

6.8 cm

4.0 cm

   a. Draw and label a net for the cylinder.

   b. About how many square centimeters of metal are used to make each can?

   c. The label for each can goes all the way around the can. About how many square centimeters of paper are needed for each label?

12. The table shows the dimensions of three boxes that are rectangular prisms.

	Length	Width	Depth
Box 1	3 in.	8 in.	9 in.
Box 2	4 in.	6 in.	9 in.
Box 3	6 in.	6 in.	6 in.

   a. Find the volume of each box.

   b. Which box requires the least material to wrap?

   c. **Make a Conjecture** For rectangular prisms of equal volume, what is true of the edge lengths that give the least surface area?

13. **Choose a Strategy** A cylinder has a circumference of 20π cm and a height that is one-half the radius of the cylinder. What is the surface area of the cylinder? Give your answer in terms of π.

14. **Write About It** Explain how you would find the side lengths of a cube with a surface area of 512 ft^2.

15. **Challenge** Find the surface area of the rectangular prism shown with a rectangular-prism-shaped hole all the way through it.

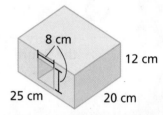

8 cm

12 cm

25 cm

20 cm

Test Prep

16. **Multiple Choice** Find the surface area of the prism.

   Ⓐ 286 in^2 Ⓒ 708 in^2

   Ⓑ 310 in^2 Ⓓ 1,232 in^2

8 in.

11 in.

14 in.

17. **Gridded Response** Find the number of square centimeters in the surface area of a cylinder with a 5 cm radius and a 15 cm height. Use 3.14 for π.

Quiz for Lessons 4 Through 6

4 Surface Area of Prisms and Cylinders

Find the surface area of each figure to the nearest tenth. Use 3.14 for π.

1.
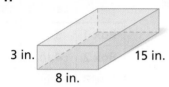

3 in.   15 in.
8 in.

2.
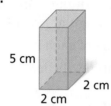

5 cm
2 cm
2 cm

3.

7 in.
15 in.

4. What is the surface area of the composite figure? Use 3.14 for π. Round your answer to the nearest tenth.

3 m

9 m

0.5 m

6 m

5 Introduction to Three-Dimensional Figures

Classify each figure as a polyhedron or not a polyhedron. Then name the figure.

5.

6.

7.

6 Volume of Prisms and Cylinders

8. A box is shaped like a rectangular prism. It is 6 ft long, 2 ft wide, and 3 ft high. Find its volume.

9. A can is shaped like a cylinder. It is 5.2 cm wide and 2.3 cm tall. Find its volume to the nearest tenth. Use 3.14 for π.

Find the volume of each composite figure to the nearest tenth. Use 3.14 for π.

10.
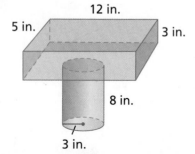

12 in.
5 in.   3 in.

8 in.

3 in.

11.
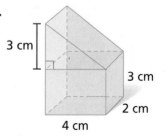

3 cm

3 cm

2 cm

4 cm

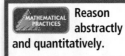

Bluegrass Balloon Festival The annual Bluegrass Balloon Festival in Louisville features more than 90 hot-air balloons. Although most of the balloons have the familiar teardrop shape, it's not unusual to see a balloon in the shape of a cow, a tree, or a teapot.

KENTUCKY

Louisville

1. A balloon manufacturer is making the Birthday Cake balloon shown in the table. How much material is needed to make the balloon? Use 3.14 for π, and round your answer to the nearest square foot.

2. The amount of hot air that a balloon can hold is related to the volume of the balloon. Find the volume of the U.S. Flag balloon.

3. Which of the balloons listed in the table can hold the greatest amount of air? Why?

4. A balloon manufacturer is considering making a larger U.S. Flag balloon by doubling each of the dimensions shown in the table.

Special-Shaped Balloons		
Balloon	**Shape**	**Dimensions**
Birthday Cake	Cylinder	Height: 80 ft Diameter: 71 ft
U.S. Flag	Rectangular Prism	Height: 53 ft Length: 78 ft Width: 29 ft

a. How does the amount of material needed for the larger balloon compare to the amount needed for the balloon in the table?

b. How does the amount of hot air needed to fill the larger balloon compare to the amount needed for the balloon in the table?

Real-World Connections

(cr) altrendo images/Getty Images; (b) Courtesy of Bluegrass Balloon Festival

Game Time

Blooming Minds

Students in the Agriculture Club at Carter Middle School are designing a flower bed for the front of the school. The flower bed will be in the shape of the letter *C*. After considering the two designs shown below, the students decided to build the flower bed that required the least amount of peat moss. Which design did the students choose? (*Hint:* Find the volume of each flower bed.)

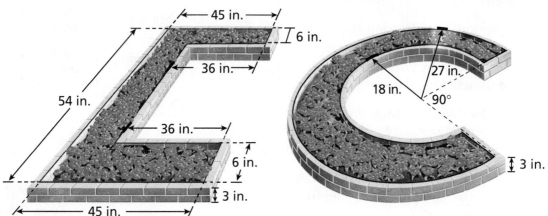

Magic Cubes

Four magic cubes are used in this fun puzzle. A complete set of rules and nets for making the cubes can be found online. Each side of the four cubes has the number 1, 2, 3, or 4 written on it. The object of the game is to stack the cubes so that the numbers along each side of the stack add up to 10. No number can be repeated along any side of the stack.

Learn It Online
Game Time Extra

Materials

- CD envelopes
- hole punch
- chenille stem
- sheets of white paper
- CD
- scissors
- markers

It's in the Bag!

PROJECT **CD 3-D**

Make a set of circular booklets that you can store in CD envelopes.

1 Stack the CD envelopes so that the flap of each envelope is in the back, along the right-hand edge. Punch a hole through the stack in the upper left-hand corner. **Figure A**

2 Insert a chenille stem through the holes, twist to make a loop, and trim the ends. **Figure B**

3 Fold a sheet of white $8\frac{1}{2}$-by-11-inch paper in half to make a sheet that is $8\frac{1}{2}$ inches by $5\frac{1}{2}$ inches. Place the CD on the folded sheet so that it touches the folded edge, and trace around it. **Figure C**

4 Cut out the circular shape that you traced, making sure that the two halves remain hinged together. **Figure D**

5 Repeat the process with the remaining sheets of paper to make a booklet for each lesson.

Taking Note of the Math

Use each booklet to takes notes on one lesson of the chapter. Be sure to record essential vocabulary, formulas, and sample problems.

INTRODUCTION TO THREE-DIMENSIONAL FIGURES

Study Guide: Review

Vocabulary

base	polyhedron
cone	prism
cylinder	pyramid
edge	pyramid
edge	sphere
face	surface area
lateral area	vertex
lateral face	volume
net	

Complete the sentences below with vocabulary words from the list above.

1. A(n) ___?___ has two parallel, congruent circular bases connected by a curved surface.

2. The sum of the areas of the surfaces of a three-dimensional figure is called the ___?___.

3. A(n) ___?___ is a three-dimensional figure whose faces are all polygons.

4. A(n) ___?___ has one circular base and a curved surface.

EXAMPLES

EXERCISES

1 Perimeter and Circumference

■ Find the perimeter of the triangle.

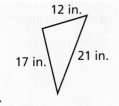
12 in.
17 in.   21 in.

$P = 12 + 17 + 21$
$P = 50$
The perimeter is 50 in.

■ Find the circumference of the circle. Use 3.14 for π.

5 cm

$C = 2\pi r$
$C \approx 2 \cdot 3.14 \cdot 5$
$C \approx 31.4$
The circumference is about 31.4 cm.

Find the perimeter of each polygon.

5.

24 m
12 m   15 m
32 m

6.

24.9 cm
15.8 cm

Find the circumference of each circle to the nearest tenth. Use 3.14 for π.

7.

13 ft

8.
7.8 in.

2 Area of Circles

■ Find the area of the circle to the nearest tenth. Use 3.14 for π.

5 in.

$A = \pi r^2$
$A \approx 3.14 \cdot 5^2$
$A \approx 3.14 \cdot 25$
$A \approx 78.5$
The area of the circle is about 78.5 in^2.

Find the area of each circle to the nearest tenth. Use 3.14 for π.

9.

3.4 m

10.

17 ft

11. The minute hand on a clock is 9 inches long. What is the area of the circle the minute hand covers after one hour? Give your answer in square inches.

3 Area of Irregular Figures

■ Find the area of the irregular figure.

Separate the figure into a rectangle and a triangle.

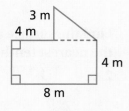
3 m
4 m
4 m
8 m

$A = \ell w$
$\quad = 4 \cdot 8 = 32 \text{ m}^2$
$A = \frac{1}{2}bh$
$\quad = \frac{1}{2}(3 \cdot 4) = 6 \text{ m}^2$
$A = 32 + 6 = 38 \text{ m}^2$

Find the area of each figure. Use 3.14 for π.

12.
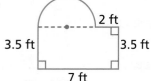
2 ft
3.5 ft   3.5 ft
7 ft

13.
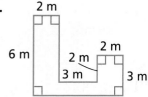
2 m
6 m
2 m   2 m
3 m   3 m

4 | **Introduction to Three-Dimensional Figures**

■ Name the figure.

There are two bases that are hexagons.

The figure is a hexagonal prism.

Name each figure.

14.

15.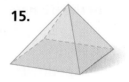

16.

17.

5 | **Volume of Prisms and Cylinders**

■ Find the volume of the cylinder to the nearest tenth. Use 3.14 for π.

$V = \pi r^2 h$
$V \approx 3.14 \cdot 3^2 \cdot 4$
$V \approx 113.04$
The volume is about 113.0 cm^3.

3 cm

4 cm

Find the volume of each figure to the nearest tenth. Use 3.14 for π.

18.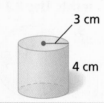
13 cm
7 cm
8 cm

19.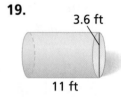
3.6 ft
11 ft

6 | **Surface Area of Prisms and Cylinders**

■ Find the surface area of the rectangular prism.

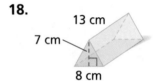
7 mm
12 mm
15 mm

$S = 2B + Ph$
$S = 2(12)(15) + (54)(7)$
$S = 738$
The surface area is 738 mm^2.

Find the surface area of each rectangular prism.

20.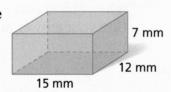
10 m
5 m
5 m

21.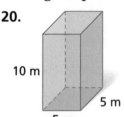
8 cm
1 cm — 1 cm

■ Find the surface area of the cylinder to the nearest tenth. Use 3.14 for π.

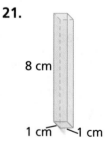
3 m
6.9 m

$S = 2\pi r^2 + 2\pi rh$
$S \approx (2 \cdot 3.14 \cdot 3^2) + (2 \cdot 3.14 \cdot 3 \cdot 6.9)$
$S \approx 186.516$
The surface area is about 186.5 m^2.

Find the surface area of each cylinder to the nearest tenth. Use 3.14 for π.

22.
2.4 cm
15 cm

23.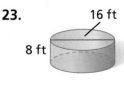
16 ft
8 ft

Study Guide: Review

Classify each figure as a polyhedron or not a polyhedron.
Then name the figure.

1.

2.

3.

Find the volume of each figure to the nearest tenth. Use 3.14 for π.

4.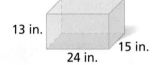

13 in.

15 in.

24 in.

5.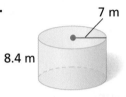

7 m

8.4 m

6.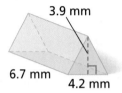

3.9 mm

6.7 mm

4.2 mm

7. Find the perimeter of the trapezoid.

10.5 in.

9.1 in.   6.3 in.

17.2 in.

Find the area of each figure.

8.

8.7 ft

13.6 ft

9.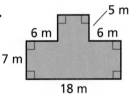

5 m

6 m   6 m

7 m

18 m

10.

$2\frac{1}{2}$ mi

$4\frac{1}{4}$ mi

6 mi

Use the diagram for Items 11 and 12.

11. Find the circumference of the circle to the nearest tenth.

12. Find the area of the circle to the nearest tenth.

$5\frac{1}{2}$ ft

Find the surface area of each figure to the nearest tenth. Use 3.14 for π.

13.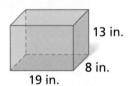

13 in.

8 in.

19 in.

14.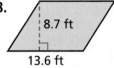

5.5 cm

6.8 cm

15.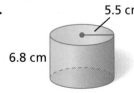

1 ft   1 ft

3 ft

2 ft

7 ft

Cumulative Assessment

Multiple Choice

1. What value represents the median of the data set?

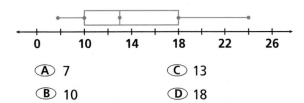

Ⓐ 7   Ⓒ 13

Ⓑ 10   Ⓓ 18

2. Find the simple interest earned on a deposit of $850 for 3 years at an annual simple interest rate of 4.9%.

Ⓕ $41.65   Ⓗ $132.75

Ⓖ $124.95   Ⓙ $974.95

3. A rectangular tank has a height of 9 meters, a width of 5 meters, and a length of 12 meters. What is the volume of the tank?

Ⓐ 540 m³   Ⓒ 45 m²

Ⓑ 180 m³   Ⓓ 26 m²

4. What is 140% of 85?

Ⓕ 11.9   Ⓗ 1,190

Ⓖ 119   Ⓙ 11,900

5. Clay jumps rope at an average rate of 75 jumps per minute. How long does it take him to make 405 jumps if he does not stop?

Ⓐ 5 min   Ⓒ $5\frac{2}{5}$ min

Ⓑ $5\frac{1}{10}$ min   Ⓓ $5\frac{5}{6}$ min

6. A cell-phone company is tracking the sales of a particular model of phone. The sales at one store over six months are shown in the graph. What is the approximate percent of increase in sales of Model B phones from October to November?

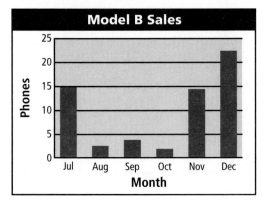

Ⓕ 60%   Ⓗ 6,000%

Ⓖ 600%   Ⓙ 6%

7. What is the decimal equivalent of $4\frac{4}{5}$?

Ⓐ 4.45   Ⓒ 4.8

Ⓑ 4.54   Ⓓ 24.5

8. The circumference of the given cylinder is 6 in. What additional information is needed to find the volume of the cylinder?

Ⓕ diameter   Ⓗ height

Ⓖ area of base   Ⓙ radius

9. The straw has a diameter of 0.6 cm. What is the surface area of the straw to the nearest tenth? Use 3.14 for π.

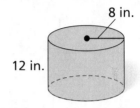

19.5 cm

Ⓐ 11.7 cm²

Ⓑ 5.5 cm²

Ⓒ 37.3 cm²

Ⓓ 36.7 cm²

10. Find the volume of the cylinder to the nearest tenth. Use 3.14 for π.

8 in.

12 in.

Ⓔ 602.9 in³

Ⓙ 1,205.8 in³

Ⓘ 3,215.4 in³

Ⓛ 2,411.5 in³

> **HOT TIP!** Make sure you use the correct units of measure in your responses. Area has square units, and volume has cubic units.

Gridded Response

11. A cube has a volume of 27 cubic meters. Find the surface area of the cube in square meters.

12. A pentagon has angle measures 99°, 105°, 110°, and 95°. Find the remaining angle measure in degrees.

13. The decimal 0.85 is written as a fraction in lowest terms. What is the sum of the numerator and denominator?

14. What is the smallest whole-number value of x that makes the value of the expression $10x - 30$ greater than 0?

15. Angle A and angle B are vertical angles. If angle A measures 62°, what is the degree measure of angle B?

Short Response

S1. The surface area of a cylinder is 64 ft². Cindy estimates that the radius is 3 feet and the height is 6 feet. Do Cindy's estimates make sense? Explain.

S2. A polyhedron has two parallel square bases with edges 9 meters long and a height of 9 meters. Identify the figure and find its volume. Show your work.

S3. A rectangle measures 3 cm by 4 cm. Find its perimeter.

Extended Response

E1. Use the figure for the following problems. Round your answers to the nearest hundredth, if necessary. Use 3.14 for π.

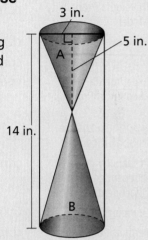

3 in.

5 in.

A

14 in.

B

a. What three-dimensional shapes make up the sculpture?

b. Describe the possible cross-sections if a horizontal or vertical plane intersected figure B.

c. The sculpture fits snugly in the cylindrical case it is shipped in. Find the volume of the case.

Probability

Chapter Focus
- Understand the meaning of theoretical probability.
- Use probability and proportions to make approximate predictions.

Why Learn This?

You can use probability to determine how likely a soccer player is to make a goal.

Learn It Online
Chapter Project Online

Icon Sports Media, Inc./NewsCom

Are You Ready?

Learn It Online
Resources Online

✓ Vocabulary

Choose the best term from the list to complete each sentence.

1. A(n) __?__ is a comparison of two quantities by division.

2. A(n) __?__ is an integer that is divisible by 2.

3. A(n) __?__ is a ratio that compares a number to 100.

4. A(n) __?__ is a number greater than 1 that has more than two whole number factors.

5. A(n) __?__ is an integer that is not divisible by 2.

composite number

even number

odd number

percent

prime number

ratio

Complete these exercises to review skills you will need for this chapter.

✓ Simplify Fractions

Write each fraction in simplest form.

6. $\frac{6}{9}$　　　　**7.** $\frac{12}{15}$　　　　**8.** $\frac{8}{10}$　　　　**9.** $\frac{20}{24}$

10. $\frac{2}{4}$　　　　**11.** $\frac{7}{35}$　　　　**12.** $\frac{12}{22}$　　　　**13.** $\frac{72}{81}$

✓ Write Fractions as Decimals

Write each fraction as a decimal.

14. $\frac{3}{5}$　　　　**15.** $\frac{9}{20}$　　　　**16.** $\frac{57}{100}$　　　　**17.** $\frac{12}{25}$

18. $\frac{3}{25}$　　　　**19.** $\frac{1}{2}$　　　　**20.** $\frac{7}{10}$　　　　**21.** $\frac{9}{5}$

✓ Percents and Decimals

Write each decimal as a percent.

22. 0.14　　　　**23.** 0.08　　　　**24.** 0.75　　　　**25.** 0.38

26. 0.27　　　　**27.** 1.89　　　　**28.** 0.234　　　　**29.** 0.0025

✓ Multiply Fractions

Multiply. Write each answer in simplest form.

30. $\frac{1}{2} \cdot \frac{1}{4}$　　　　**31.** $\frac{2}{3} \cdot \frac{3}{5}$　　　　**32.** $\frac{3}{10} \cdot \frac{1}{2}$　　　　**33.** $\frac{5}{6} \cdot \frac{3}{4}$

34. $\frac{5}{14} \cdot \frac{7}{17}$　　　　**35.** $-\frac{1}{8} \cdot \frac{3}{8}$　　　　**36.** $-\frac{2}{15} \cdot \left(-\frac{2}{3}\right)$　　　　**37.** $\frac{1}{4} \cdot \left(-\frac{1}{6}\right)$

Study Guide: Preview

Where You've Been

Previously, you

- found experimental and theoretical probabilities of compound events.

- used organized lists and tree diagrams to find the sample space of an experiment.

- found the probability that an outcome will not occur.

In This Chapter

You will study

- finding experimental and theoretical probabilities, including those of dependent and independent events.

- using lists and tree diagrams to find combinations and all possible outcomes of an experiment.

- using the Fundamental Counting Principle and factorials to find permutations.

Where You're Going

You can use the skills learned in this chapter

- to determine the effect of chance in games that you play.

- to predict the outcome in situations involving sports and weather.

Key Vocabulary/Vocabulario

combination	combinación
dependent events	sucesos dependientes
event	suceso
experiment	experimento
experimental probability	probabilidad experimental
independent events	sucesos independientes
outcome	resultado
probability	probabilidad
sample space	espacio muestral
theoretical probability	probabilidad teórica

Vocabulary Connections

To become familiar with some of the vocabulary terms in the chapter, consider the following. You may refer to the chapter, the glossary, or a dictionary if you like.

1. An *experiment* is an action done to find out something you do not know. Why can we call flipping a coin, rolling a number cube, or spinning a spinner an **experiment**?

2. Several outcomes, or sometimes just one outcome, make up an *event*. For example, rolling an even number and choosing a challenge card can make up an event in a board game. What is another **event** that can occur when you play board games?

3. The word *depend* comes from the Latin word *dependēre*, meaning "to hang or to be attached." How might the probabilities of **dependent events** be linked?

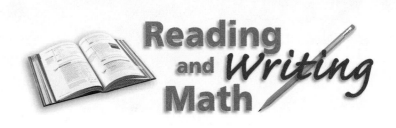 **Reading** and **Writing Math**

Reading Strategy: Read Problems for Understanding

To best understand a word problem, read it once to note what concept is being reviewed. Then read the problem again, slowly and carefully, to identify what the problem is asking. As you read, highlight the key information. When dealing with a multi-step problem, break the problem into parts and then make a plan to solve it.

> **23. Architecture** The steeple on a building is a triangular prism with base area 12 square feet and height 15 feet. How many cubic feet of concrete was used to make the prism?

Step	Question	Answer
Step 1	What concept is being reviewed?	• finding the volume of a prism
Step 2	What are you being asked to do?	• Find the number of cubic feet of concrete used to make the steeple.
Step 3	What is the key information needed to solve the problem?	• The steeple is a triangular prism. • The base area of the prism is 12 square feet. • The height of the prism is 15 feet.
Step 4	What is my plan to solve this multi-part problem?	• Use the formula for finding the volume of a prism: $V = Bh$. • Substitute the values for the base area and the height into the formula. • Solve for V.

Try This

For each problem, complete each step in the four-step method described above.

1. Which has a greater volume: a cylinder with a height of 3 feet and a base with a radius of 3 feet or a cube with a side length of 4 feet?

2. At a party, each child receives the same number of party favors. There are 16 kazoos, 24 snappers, 8 hats, and 32 pieces of gum. What is the greatest number of children that may be at the party?

10-1 Probability

CC.7.SP.5 Understand that the probability of a chance event is a number between 0 and 1 that expresses the likelihood of the event occurring…

Vocabulary

experiment

trial

outcome

event

probability

simple event

compound event

complement

Interactivities Online ▶

An activity involving chance, such as rolling a number cube, is called an **experiment**. Each repetition or observation of an experiment is a **trial**, and each result is an **outcome**. A set of one or more outcomes is an **event**. For example, rolling a 5 (one outcome) can be an event, or rolling an even number (more than one outcome) can be an event.

The **probability** of an event, written P(event), is the measure of how likely the event is to occur. A **simple event** has a single outcome. A **compound event** is two or more simple events. Probability is a measure between 0 and 1, as shown on the number line. You can write probability as a fraction, a decimal, or a percent.

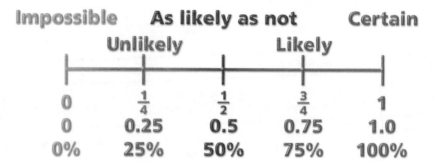

Impossible	Unlikely	As likely as not	Likely	Certain
0	$\frac{1}{4}$	$\frac{1}{2}$	$\frac{3}{4}$	1
0	0.25	0.5	0.75	1.0
0%	25%	50%	75%	100%

EXAMPLE 1 Determining the Likelihood of an Event

Determine whether each event is impossible, unlikely, as likely as not, likely, or certain.

A rolling an even number on a number cube

There are 6 possible outcomes:

Even	*Not* Even
2, 4, 6	1, 3, 5

Half of the outcomes are even.

Rolling an even number is as likely as not.

B rolling a 5 on a number cube

There are 6 possible outcomes:

5	*Not* 5
5	1, 2, 3, 4, 6

Only one outcome is a five.

Rolling a 5 is unlikely.

Video **Lesson Tutorials Online** my.hrw.com

When a number cube is rolled, either a 5 will be rolled or it will not. Rolling a 5 and not rolling a 5 are examples of *complementary events*. The complement of an event is the set of all outcomes that are *not* the event.

Because it is certain that either an event or its complement will occur when an activity is performed, the sum of the probabilities is 1.

$$P(\text{event}) + P(\text{complement}) = 1$$

EXAMPLE 2 **Using Complements**

A bag contains 6 blue marbles, 6 red marbles, 3 green marbles, and 1 yellow marble. The probability of randomly drawing a red marble is $\frac{3}{8}$. What is the probability of not drawing a red marble?

$$P(\text{event}) + P(\text{complement}) = 1$$
$$P(\text{red}) + P(\text{not red}) = 1$$

$$\frac{3}{8} + P(\text{not red}) = 1 \qquad \textit{Substitute } \frac{3}{8} \textit{ for P(red).}$$

$$\underline{-\frac{3}{8} \qquad\qquad\qquad -\frac{3}{8}} \qquad \textit{Subtract } \frac{3}{8} \textit{ from both sides.}$$

$$P(\text{not red}) = \frac{5}{8} \qquad \textit{Simplify.}$$

The probability of not drawing a red marble is $\frac{5}{8}$.

EXAMPLE 3 *School Application*

Eric's math teacher almost always gives a pop quiz if the class did not ask many questions during the lesson on the previous class day. If it is Monday and no one asked questions during class on Friday, should Eric expect a pop quiz? Explain.

Since Eric's teacher often gives quizzes on days after few questions were asked, a quiz on Monday is likely.

Think and Discuss

1. Describe an event that has a probability of 0% and an event that has a probability of 100%.

2. Give an example of a real-world compound event.

3. Give an example of a real-world event and its complement.

GUIDED PRACTICE

See Example **1** **Determine whether each event is impossible, unlikely, as likely as not, likely, or certain.**

1. rolling a number greater than 5 with a number cube

2. drawing a blue marble from a bag of black and white marbles

See Example **2** 3. A bag contains 8 purple beads, 2 blue beads, and 2 pink beads. The probability of randomly drawing a pink bead is $\frac{1}{6}$. What is the probability of not drawing a pink bead?

See Example **3** 4. Natalie almost always sleeps in on Saturday mornings when she does not have to work. If it is Saturday morning and Natalie does not have to work, how likely is it that Natalie will sleep in?

INDEPENDENT PRACTICE

See Example **1** **Determine whether each event is impossible, unlikely, as likely as not, likely, or certain.**

5. randomly drawing a red or pink card from a deck of red and pink cards

6. flipping a coin and getting tails

7. rolling a 6 on a number cube five times in a row

See Example **2** 8. The probability of rolling a 5 or 6 with a number cube is $\frac{1}{3}$. What is the probability of not rolling a 5 or 6?

9. The probability of randomly drawing a green marble from a bag of green, red, and blue marbles is $\frac{3}{5}$. What is the probability of randomly drawing a red or blue marble?

See Example **3** 10. Tim rarely spends more than 30 minutes watching TV in the afternoon. If Tim began watching TV at 4:00 P.M., would you expect that he is still watching TV at 5:00 P.M.? Explain.

PRACTICE AND PROBLEM SOLVING

Extra Practice
See Extra Practice for more exercises.

A bag contains 12 red checkers and 12 black checkers. Determine whether each event is impossible, unlikely, as likely as not, likely, or certain.

11. randomly drawing a red checker

12. randomly drawing a white checker

13. randomly drawing a red or black checker

14. randomly drawing a black checker

15. **Exercise** Luka almost always jogs in the afternoon when the weather is not cold or rainy. The sky is cloudy and the temperature is 41°F. How likely is it that Luka will jog this afternoon?

16. **Life Science** A researcher's garden contains 900 sweet pea plants. More than 700 of the plants have purple flowers and about 200 have white flowers. Would you expect that one plant randomly selected from the garden will have purple or white flowers? Explain.

17. **Life Science** Sharks belong to a class of fishes that have skeletons made of cartilage. Bony fishes, which account for 95% of all species of fish, have skeletons made of bone.

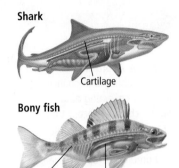

Shark

Cartilage

Bony fish

a. How likely is it that a fish you cannot identify at a pet store is a bony fish? Explain.

b. Only bony fishes have swim bladders, which keep them from sinking. How likely is it that a shark has a swim bladder? Explain.

Bone   Swim bladder

18. **Earth Science** The graph shows the carbon dioxide levels in the atmosphere from 1970 to 2000. How likely is it that the level of carbon dioxide fell from 2000 to 2010? Explain.

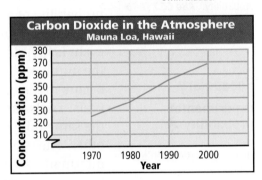

Carbon Dioxide in the Atmosphere
Mauna Loa, Hawaii

19. **Write a Problem** Describe an event that involves rolling a number cube. Determine the likelihood that the event will occur.

20. **Write About It** Explain how to tell whether an event is as likely as not.

21. **Challenge** A bag contains 10 red marbles and 8 blue marbles, all the same size and weight. Keiko randomly draws 2 red marbles from the bag and does not replace them. Will Keiko be more likely to draw a red marble than a blue marble on her next draw? Explain.

Experimental Probability

CC.7.SP.6 Approximate the probability of a chance event by collecting data on the chance process that produces it and observing its long-run relative frequency, and predict the approximate relative frequency given the probability. *Also CC.7.SP.7b*

Vocabulary

experimental probability

Interactivities Online ▶

During field hockey practice, Tanya made saves on 15 out of 25 shots. Based on these numbers, you can estimate the probability that Tanya will make a save on the next shot.

Experimental probability is one way of estimating the probability of an event. The **experimental probability** of an event is found by comparing the number of times the event occurs to the total number of trials. Trials can be conducted at the same time or one after the other. The results give the same information. The more trials you have, the more accurate the estimate is likely to be.

EXPERIMENTAL PROBABILITY
$$\text{probability} \approx \frac{\text{number of times the event occurs}}{\text{total number of trials}}$$

EXAMPLE 1 *Sports Application*

Writing Math

"*P*(event)" represents the probability that an event will occur. For example, the probability of a flipped coin landing heads up could be written as "*P*(heads)."

Tanya made saves on 15 out of 25 shots. What is the experimental probability that she will make a save on the next shot? Write your answer as a fraction, as a decimal, and as a percent.

$$P(\text{event}) \approx \frac{\text{number of times the event occurs}}{\text{total number of trials}}$$

$$P(\text{save}) \approx \frac{\text{number of saves made}}{\text{total number of shots attempted}}$$

$$= \frac{15}{25} \qquad \textit{Substitute data from the experiment.}$$

$$= \frac{3}{5} \qquad \textit{Write in simplest form.}$$

$$= 0.6 = 60\% \qquad \textit{Write as a decimal and as a percent.}$$

The experimental probability that Tanya will make a save on the next shot is $\frac{3}{5}$, or 0.6, or 60%.

Video **Lesson Tutorials Online**   my.hrw.com

REUTERS/Jim Young

EXAMPLE 2

Weather Application

For the past three weeks, Karl has been recording the daily high temperatures for a science project. His results are shown below.

Week 1	Temp (°F)	Week 2	Temp (°F)	Week 3	Temp (°F)
Sun	76	Sun	72	Sun	78
Mon	74	Mon	79	Mon	76
Tue	79	Tue	78	Tue	77
Wed	80	Wed	79	Wed	75
Thu	77	Thu	77	Thu	79
Fri	76	Fri	74	Fri	77
Sat	75	Sat	73	Sat	75

Reading Math

When the frequency of a value is divided by the total number of data values, it is called *relative frequency*.

A **What is the experimental probability that the temperature will be above 75 °F on the next day?**

The number of days the temperature was above 75 °F is 14.

$$P(\text{above 75 °F}) \approx \frac{\text{number of days above 75 °F}}{\text{total number of days}}$$

$$= \frac{14}{21} \qquad \textit{Substitute data.}$$

$$= \frac{2}{3} \qquad \textit{Write in simplest form.}$$

The experimental probability that the temperature will be above 75 °F on the next day is $\frac{2}{3}$.

B **What is the experimental probability that the temperature will not be above 75 °F on the next day?**

$$P(\text{above 75 °F}) + P(\text{not above 75 °F}) = 1 \qquad \textit{Use the complement.}$$

$$\frac{2}{3} + P(\text{not above 75 °F}) = 1 \qquad \textit{Substitute.}$$

$$-\frac{2}{3} \qquad\qquad\qquad\qquad\quad -\frac{2}{3} \qquad \textit{Subtract } \frac{2}{3} \textit{ from both sides.}$$

$$P(\text{not above 75 °F}) = \frac{1}{3} \qquad \textit{Simplify.}$$

The experimental probability that the temperature will not be above 75 °F on the next day is $\frac{1}{3}$.

MATHEMATICAL PRACTICES

Think and Discuss

1. **Describe** a real-world situation in which you could estimate probability using experimental probability.

2. **Explain** how experimental probability could be used for making predictions.

Exercises

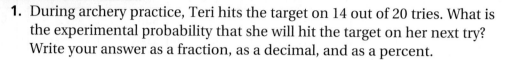
GUIDED PRACTICE

See Example **1**

1. During archery practice, Teri hits the target on 14 out of 20 tries. What is the experimental probability that she will hit the target on her next try? Write your answer as a fraction, as a decimal, and as a percent.

See Example **2**

2. Government A reporter surveys 75 people to determine whether they plan to vote for or against a proposed amendment. Of these people, 65 plan to vote for the amendment.

   a. What is the experimental probability that the next person surveyed would say he or she plans to vote for the amendment?

   b. What is the experimental probability that the next person surveyed would say he or she plans to vote against the amendment?

INDEPENDENT PRACTICE

See Example **1**

3. Sports Jack hit a baseball on 13 out of 30 tries during practice. What is the experimental probability that he will hit the ball on his next try? Write your answer as a fraction, as a decimal, and as a percent.

4. Cam hit the bull's-eye in darts 8 times out of 15 throws. What is the experimental probability that Cam's next throw will hit the bull's-eye?

See Example **2**

5. For the past two weeks, Benita has been recording the number of people at Eastside Park at lunchtime. During that time, there were 50 or more people at the park 9 out of 14 days.

   a. What is the experimental probability that there will be 50 or more people at the park during lunchtime on the fifteenth day?

   b. What is the experimental probability that there will not be 50 or more people at the park during lunchtime on the fifteenth day?

PRACTICE AND PROBLEM SOLVING

Extra Practice
See Extra Practice for more exercises.

6. Recreation While bowling with friends, Alexis rolls a strike in 4 out of the 10 frames. What is the experimental probability that Alexis will roll a strike in the first frame of the next game?

7. Jeremiah is greeting customers at a music store. Of the first 25 people he sees enter the store, 16 are wearing jackets and 9 are not. What is the experimental probability that the next person to enter the store will be wearing a jacket?

8. During the month of June, Carmen kept track of the birds she saw in her garden. She saw a blue jay on 12 days of the month. What is the experimental probability that she will see a blue jay on July 1?

9. Critical Thinking Claudia finds that the experimental probability of her cat waking her between 5:00 A.M. and 6:00 A.M. is $\frac{8}{11}$. About what percent of the time does Claudia's cat not wake her between 5:00 A.M. and 6:00 A.M.?

10. **Multi-Step** The stem-and-leaf plot shows the depth of snow in inches recorded in Buffalo, New York, over a 10-day period.

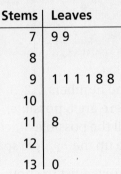

Stems	Leaves
7	9 9
8	
9	1 1 1 1 8 8
10	
11	8
12	
13	0

Key: 7|9 means 7.9

a. What is the median depth of snow for the 10-day period?

b. What is the experimental probability that the snow will be less than 6 in. deep on the eleventh day?

c. What is the experimental probability that the snow will be more than 10 in. deep on the eleventh day?

11. The table shows the high temperatures recorded on July 4 in Orlando, Florida, over an eight-year period.

a. What is the experimental probability that the high temperature on the next July 4 will be below 90 °F?

b. What is the experimental probability that the high temperature on the next July 4 will be above 100 °F?

Year	Temp (°F)	Year	Temp (°F)
1994	86.0	1998	96.8
1995	95.0	1999	89.1
1996	78.8	2000	90.0
1997	98.6	2001	91.0

Source: Old Farmers' Almanac

12. ⭐ **Challenge** A toy company finds that the experimental probability of manufacturing a defective balance ball is $\frac{3}{50}$. About how many defective balls are likely to be in a batch of 1,800 balls?

Test Prep

13. **Multiple Choice** Darian made 26 of the 32 free throws he attempted. Which percent is closest to the experimental probability that he will make his next free throw?

Ⓐ 50% Ⓑ 60% Ⓒ 70% Ⓓ 80%

14. **Multiple Choice** Survey results show that cheese is the favorite pizza topping for 18 out of 24 people. Which percent is closest to the experimental probability that a person's favorite pizza topping will NOT be cheese?

Ⓕ 25% Ⓖ 33% Ⓗ 40% Ⓙ 75%

10-3 Sample Spaces

CC.7.SP.8b Represent sample spaces...

Vocabulary

sample space

Fundamental Counting Principle

Because you can roll the numbers 1, 2, 3, 4, 5, and 6 on a number cube, there are 6 possible outcomes. Together, all the possible outcomes of an experiment make up the **sample space**.

You can make an organized list to show all possible outcomes of an experiment.

EXAMPLE 1

> MATHEMATICAL PRACTICES **Make sense of problems and persevere in solving them.**

PROBLEM SOLVING APPLICATION

Lucia flips two quarters at the same time. What are all the possible outcomes? How many outcomes are in the sample space?

1 Understand the Problem

Rewrite the question as a statement.

- Find all the possible outcomes of flipping two quarters, and determine the size of the sample space.

List the **important information:**

- There are two quarters.
- Each quarter can land heads up or tails up.

2 Make a Plan

You can make an organized list to show all the possible outcomes.

3 Solve

Quarter 1	Quarter 2
H	H
H	T
T	H
T	T

Let H = heads and T = tails.

Record each possible outcome.

The possible outcomes are HH, HT, TH, and TT. There are four possible outcomes in the sample space.

4 Look Back

Each possible outcome that is recorded in the list is different.

When the number of possible outcomes of an experiment increases, it may be easier to track all the possible outcomes on a tree diagram.

Video **Lesson Tutorials Online** my.hrw.com

EXAMPLE **2** **Using a Tree Diagram to Find a Sample Space**

Ren spins spinner A and spinner B. What are all the possible outcomes? How many outcomes are in the sample space?

Make a tree diagram to show the sample space. List each color from spinner A. Then for each color, list each number from spinner B.

Spinner A   Spinner B

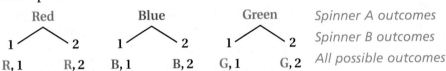

Red   Blue   Green   *Spinner A outcomes*

1 — 2   1 — 2   1 — 2   *Spinner B outcomes*

R, 1   R, 2   B, 1   B, 2   G, 1   G, 2   *All possible outcomes*

There are six possible outcomes in the sample space.

In Example 1, there are two outcomes for each coin, so there are four total outcomes.

2 × 2 = 4
First quarter   Second quarter

In Example 2, there are three outcomes for spinner A and two outcomes for spinner B, so there are six total outcomes.

3 × 2 = 6
Spinner A   Spinner B

The **Fundamental Counting Principle** states that you can find the total number of outcomes for two or more experiments by multiplying the number of outcomes for each separate experiment.

EXAMPLE **3** *Recreation Application*

In a game, each player rolls a number cube and spins a spinner. The spinner is divided into thirds, numbered 1, 2, and 3. How many outcomes are possible during one player's turn?

The number cube has 6 outcomes.   *List the number of outcomes*
The spinner has 3 outcomes.   *for each separate experiment.*

$6 \cdot 3 = 18$ *Use the Fundamental Counting Principle.*

There are 18 possible outcomes during one player's turn.

Think and Discuss

1. Compare using a tree diagram and using the Fundamental Counting Principle to find a sample space.

2. Find the size of the sample space for flipping 5 coins.

Exercises

Learn It Online
Homework Help Online
Exercises 1–8, 9, 11, 13

GUIDED PRACTICE

See Example 1

1. Enrique tosses a coin and spins the spinner at right. What are all the possible outcomes? How many outcomes are in the sample space?

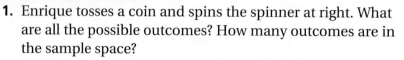

See Example 2

2. An ice cream stand offers cake cones, waffle cones, or cups to hold ice cream. You can get vanilla, chocolate, strawberry, pistachio, or coffee flavored ice cream. If you order a single scoop, what are all the possible options you have? How many outcomes are in the sample space?

See Example 3

3. A game includes a number cube and a spinner divided into 4 equal sectors. Each player rolls the number cube and spins the spinner. How many outcomes are possible?

INDEPENDENT PRACTICE

See Example 1

4. At noon, Aretha can watch a football game, a basketball game, or a documentary about horses on TV. At 3:00, she can watch a different football game, a movie, or a concert. What are all the possible outcomes? How many outcomes are in the sample space?

5. A spinner is divided into fourths and numbered 1 through 4. Jory spins the spinner and tosses a coin. What are all the possible outcomes? How many outcomes are in the sample space?

See Example 2

6. Berto tosses a coin and spins the spinner at right. What are all the possible outcomes? How many outcomes are in the sample space?

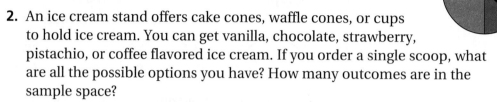

7. For breakfast, Clarissa can choose from oatmeal, cornflakes, or scrambled eggs. She can drink milk, orange juice, apple juice, or hot chocolate. What are all the possible outcomes? How many outcomes are in the sample space?

See Example 3

8. A pizza shop offers thick crust, thin crust, or stuffed crust. The choices of toppings are pepperoni, cheese, hamburger, Italian sausage, Canadian bacon, onions, bell peppers, mushrooms, and pineapple. How many different one-topping pizzas could you order?

PRACTICE AND PROBLEM SOLVING

Extra Practice
See Extra Practice for more exercises.

9. Andie has a blue sweater, a red sweater, and a purple sweater. She has a white shirt and a tan shirt. How many different ways can she wear a sweater and a shirt together?

10. Critical Thinking Suppose you can choose a ball that comes in three colors: blue, red, or green. Make a tree diagram or a list of all the possible ways to choose 2 balls if you are allowed to choose two of the same color.

The American Heart Association recommends that people exercise for 30–60 minutes three or four times a week to maintain healthy hearts.

11. Health For each pair of food groups, give the number of possible outcomes if one item is chosen from each group.

a. group A and group B

b. group B and group D

c. group A and group C

Group A	Group B	Group C	Group D
milk cheese yogurt	beef fish poultry	bread cereal pasta rice	vegetables fruit

12. Health The graph shows the kinds of classes that health club members would like to see offered.

a. If the health club offers the four most popular classes on one day, how many ways could they be arranged?

b. If the health club offers each of the five classes on a different weekday, how many ways could they be arranged?

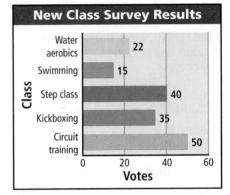

13. Recreation There are 3 trails from the South Canyon trailhead to Lake Solitude. There are 4 trails from Lake Solitude to Hidden Lake. How many possible routes could you take to hike from the South Canyon trailhead to Hidden Lake that pass Lake Solitude?

14. What's the Question? Dan has 4 face cards and 5 number cards. He shuffles the cards separately and places each set in a separate pile. The answer is 20 possible outcomes. What is the question?

15. Write About It Explain how to determine the size of the sample space when you toss three number cubes at the same time.

16. Challenge Suppose you flip a penny, a nickel, and a dime at the same time. What are all the possible outcomes?

Test Prep

17. Multiple Choice Amber rolls two number cubes. How many outcomes are possible?

Ⓐ 6   Ⓑ 12   Ⓒ 24   Ⓓ 36

18. Extended Response A sandwich shop offers 3 choices of breads: white, rye, or garlic; 2 choices of cheese: American or Swiss; and 4 choices of meats: beef, turkey, ham, or pork. List the possible choices for a sandwich with 1 bread, 1 cheese, and 1 meat. How many possible choices are there?

Theoretical Probability

CC.7.SP.8 Find probabilities of compound events using organized lists, tables, tree diagrams, and simulation. **Also CC.7.SP.6**

Vocabulary

theoretical probability

equally likely

fair

In the game of Bingo, balls containing a combination of a letter and a number are randomly selected. Players try to match the combinations on 5 × 5 grid cards. Of the 75 combinations used in Bingo, 15 have the letter *B* on them.

To determine the probability of selecting a *B*, you can randomly select Bingo balls and record your results to find the experimental probability, or you can calculate the *theoretical probability*. **Theoretical probability** is used to find the probability of an event when all outcomes are *equally likely*. **Equally likely** outcomes have the same probability.

Reading Math

You may hear probability described as "odds of winning." For more on odds, see Skills Bank.

> ### THEORETICAL PROBABILITY
>
> $$\text{probability} = \frac{\text{number of ways the event can occur}}{\text{total number of equally likely outcomes}}$$

If each possible outcome of an experiment is equally likely, then the experiment is said to be **fair**. Experiments involving number cubes and coins are usually assumed to be fair.

EXAMPLE 1 **Finding Theoretical Probability**

Find the probability of each event. Write your answer as a fraction, as a decimal, and as a percent.

A selecting one of the 15 *B*s from 75 total Bingo balls

$$P = \frac{\text{number of ways the event can occur}}{\text{total number of equally likely outcomes}}$$

$P(B) = \dfrac{\text{number of } Bs}{\text{total number of Bingo balls}}$ *Write the ratio.*

$ = \dfrac{15}{75}$ *Substitute.*

$ = \dfrac{1}{5}$ *Write in simplest form.*

$ = 0.2 = 20\%$ *Write as a decimal and as a percent.*

The theoretical probability of selecting a *B* is $\frac{1}{5}$, 0.2, or 20%.

Video **Lesson Tutorials Online** my.hrw.com

Find the probability of each event. Write your answer as a fraction, as a decimal, and as a percent.

B **rolling a number greater than 2 on a fair number cube**

There are four ways the event can occur: 3, 4, 5, and 6.
There are six possible outcomes: 1, 2, 3, 4, 5, and 6.

$$P(\text{greater than 2}) = \frac{\text{number of ways the event can occur}}{\text{total number of equally likely outcomes}}$$

$$= \frac{4}{6} \qquad \textit{Write the ratio.}$$

$$= \frac{2}{3} \qquad \textit{Write in simplest form.}$$

$$\approx 0.667 \approx 66.7\% \qquad \textit{Write as a decimal and a percent.}$$

The theoretical probability of rolling a number greater than 2 is $\frac{2}{3}$, or approximately 0.667, or approximately 66.7%.

EXAMPLE **2** *School Application*

There are 11 boys and 16 girls in Mr. Ashley's class. Mr. Ashley has written the name of each student on a craft stick. He randomly chooses one of these sticks to choose a student to answer a question.

A **Find the theoretical probability of choosing a boy's name.**

$$P(\text{boy}) = \frac{\text{number of boys in class}}{\text{total number of students in class}}$$

$$P(\text{boy}) = \frac{11}{27}$$

B **Find the theoretical probability of choosing a girl's name.**

$P(\text{boy}) + P(\text{girl}) =$	1		*Substitute $\frac{11}{27}$ for P(boy).*
$\frac{11}{27} + P(\text{girl}) =$	1		
$-\frac{11}{27}$	$= -\frac{11}{27}$		*Subtract $\frac{11}{27}$ from both sides.*
$P(\text{girl}) =$	$\frac{16}{27}$		*Simplify.*

Remember!

The sum of the probabilities of an event and its complement is 1.

MATHEMATICAL
PRACTICES

Think and Discuss

1. **Give an example** of an experiment in which all of the outcomes are not equally likely. Explain.

2. **Describe** how the probability in Example 2 can be affected if Mr. Ashley does not choose randomly from the craft sticks.

Exercises

Learn It Online
Homework Help Online
Exercises 1–10, 13, 15, 17, 19, 21, 25

GUIDED PRACTICE

See Example **1** Find the probability of each event. Write your answer as a fraction, as a decimal, and as a percent.

1. randomly choosing a red marble from a bag of 15 red, 15 blue, 15 green, 15 yellow, 15 black, and 15 white marbles

2. tossing 2 fair coins and both landing heads up

See Example **2** A set of cards includes 15 yellow cards, 10 green cards, and 10 blue cards. Find the probability of each event when a card is chosen at random.

3. yellow   4. green   5. not yellow or green

INDEPENDENT PRACTICE

See Example **1** Find the probability of each event. Write your answer as a fraction, as a decimal, and as a percent.

6. randomly drawing a heart or a club from a shuffled deck of 52 cards with 13-card suits: diamonds, hearts, clubs, and spades

7. randomly drawing a purple disk from a game with 13 red, 13 purple, 13 orange, and 13 white disks of the same size and shape

8. randomly drawing one of the 30 *G* or *O*s from a bag of 75 Bingo balls

See Example **2** Sifu has 6 girls and 8 boys in his karate class. He randomly selects one student to demonstrate a self-defense technique. Find the probability of each event.

9. selecting a girl   10. selecting a boy

PRACTICE AND PROBLEM SOLVING

Extra Practice
See Extra Practice for more exercises.

Find the probability of each event when two fair number cubes are rolled.

11. P(total of 3)   12. P(total of 7)   13. P(total of 4)

14. P(total of 2)   15. P(total of 9)   16. P(total of 13)

A spinner is divided equally into 10 sectors. The numbers 1 through 5 are each placed in two different sectors. Find the probability of each event.

17. P(less than 3)   18. P(5)   19. P(8)

20. P(less than 6)   21. P(greater than or equal to 4)   22. P(3)

For 23, use the spinner.

23. Is the experiment fair or unfair for the following outcomes? Explain.

     a. landing on a 2   **b.** landing on blue

24. **Recreation** The table shows the approximate number of visitors to five different amusement parks in the United States in one year. Find the probability that a randomly selected visitor to one of the amusement parks visited the parks listed below. Write each answer as a decimal and as a percent.

Amusement Parks	Number of Visitors
Disney World, FL	15,640,000
Disneyland, CA	13,680,000
SeaWorld, FL	4,900,000
Busch Gardens, FL	4,200,000
SeaWorld, CA	3,700,000

a. Disney World

b. a park in California

25. **Gardening** A package of mixed lettuce seeds contains 150 green lettuce seeds and 50 red lettuce seeds. What is the probability that a randomly selected seed will be a red lettuce seed? Write your answer as a percent.

26. **Choose a Strategy** Francis, Amanda, Raymond, and Albert wore different-colored T-shirts. The colors were tan, orange, purple, and aqua. Neither Raymond nor Amanda ever wears orange, and neither Francis nor Raymond ever wears aqua. Albert wore purple. What color was each person's T-shirt?

27. **Write About It** Suppose the probability of an event happening is $\frac{3}{8}$. Explain what each number in the ratio represents.

28. **Challenge** A spinner is divided into three sectors. Half of the spinner is red, $\frac{1}{3}$ is blue, and $\frac{1}{6}$ is green. What is the probability that the spinner will land on either red or green?

Test Prep

29. **Multiple Choice** Renae pulls a marble out of the bag. What is the probability that the marble will be blue?

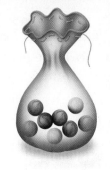

Ⓐ $\frac{1}{8}$ Ⓒ $\frac{1}{3}$

Ⓑ $\frac{1}{2}$ Ⓓ $\frac{1}{4}$

30. **Gridded Response** There are 5 red marbles, 7 green marbles, and 3 yellow marbles in a bag. A marble is drawn at random. What is the probability that the marble will NOT be yellow?

Develop a Probability Model

Use with Theoretical Probability

Learn It Online
Lab Resources Online

Use appropriate tools strategically.
CC.7.SP.7b Develop a probability model by observing frequencies in data generated from a chance process. *Also CC.7.SP.6*

A **probability model** for an event, often displayed in a table, gives all the possible outcomes of the event and the probabilities for that event.

Activity 1

1 Create a probability model using a standard deck of cards. The sample spacewill be the outcomes of drawing a card and noting if it is a heart, diamond, club, or spade.

a. In small groups, draw one card at a time from 52-card deck. Mark which suit the card belongs to in a frequency table.

Card	Tallies	Frequency
Club		
Diamond		
Heart		
Spade		

b. Using the frequency results from part **a** and the sample space of the experiment, create a probability model.

Probability Model				
Card	Club	Diamond	Heart	Spade
Probability				

c. Compare your results with the other groups.

Think and Discuss

1. Is the probability of drawing one suit more likely than drawing any other? Explain.

Try This

1. Create a probability model using a standard deck of cards. The sample space will be the outcomes of drawing a card and noting if it is a king, queen, or jack.

There are times when the outcomes in a sample space do not have equal probabilities of occurring. For example, if a school has more girls than boys, the probability of randomly choosing a girl student is greater than the probability of choosing a boy student.

1 Explore a sample space where the outcomes have different probabilities of occurring. Each group will receive a small bag of 20 different colored balloons.

a. In small groups, count the number of balloons in each color. Complete a frequency table.

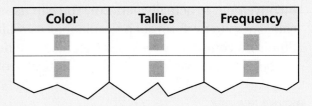

Color	Tallies	Frequency
▦	▦	▦
▦	▦	▦

b. Using the frequency results from part **a** and the sample space, create a probability model.

Probability Model				
Color				
Probability				

c. Compare your results with the other groups.

d. Is the probability of drawing one color more likely than drawing any other colors? Explain.

Think and Discuss

1. Consider probability models for equally likely events, like in Activity 1, and probability models for not equally likely events, like in Activity 2. Discuss how they are alike and how they are different.

Try This

Create frequency tables and probability models to determine the probability of each outcome.

1. Police officers kept record of 75 drivers at a stop sign. They observed 21 people who came to a complete stop, 46 who made a rolling stop, and eight that did not appear to brake at all. What is the probability that a randomly selected driver will come to a complete stop?

2. Fifty seventh graders pick their favorite carnival ride. There were 10 students who chose the roller coaster, 5 who selected the Ferris wheel, 12 who chose the Octopus, and 23 who chose the Bullet. What is the probability that a randomly selected student will choose the Ferris wheel as his or her favorite ride?

Technology LAB — Simulations

Use with Theoretical Probabilty

A *simulation* is a model of an experiment that would be difficult or inconvenient to actually perform. You can use spreadsheets and calculators to perform such simulations as rolling a number cube or flipping a coin. These tools also can help you determine experimental probability and compare it with theoretical probability.

Learn It Online
Lab Resources Online

 Use appropriate tools strategically.
CC.7.SP.7 …Compare probabilities from a model to observed frequencies; if the agreement is not good, explain possible sources of the discrepancy.
Also CC.7.SP.8c

Activity 1

Use a spreadsheet to model rolling a number cube to calculate the experimental probability of rolling a 3.

To simulate rolling a number cube, use a spreadsheet to generate a random integer between 1 and 6. In cell A1, type **=INT(RAND()*6+1)**.

	A	B	C
1	=INT(RAND()*6+1)		
2			

To "roll the cube," press ENTER. You should see an integer between 1 and 6 in cell A1. To model 10 rolls, highlight cells A1 through A10 and choose Fill▶Down from the Edit menu.

	A	B	C
1	1		
2	2		
3	3		

The experimental probability P of rolling a 3 is $P = \frac{\text{number of 3s rolled}}{\text{total number of rolls}}$. The total number of rolls is 10. To count the number of 3s rolled, in cells A1–A10, type the formula **=COUNTIF(A1:A10,3)** in cell C1 and press ENTER.

	A	B	C	D	E
1	1		=COUNTIF(A1:A10,3)		
2	2				
3	3				
4	6				
5	4				
6	4				
7	4				
8	3				
9	2				
10	3				
11					

To calculate the experimental probability of rolling a 3, type the formula **=C1/10** in cell D1 and press ENTER.

Note: Your spreadsheet numbers will likely look different from the ones shown here.

	A	B	C	D	E
1	6		3	0.3	
2	5				
3	3				
4	5				
5	6				
6	3				
7	3				
8	6				
9	4				
10	5				
11					

Think and Discuss

1. How does this simulation compare to theoretical probability? Explain.

2. Explain how you could adapt the spreadsheet to model 100 rolls.

3. Do you think you would get the same experimental probability if you repeat the experiment? Explain.

1. Model 100 rolls, count the number of times each number 1–6 is rolled, and calculate the experimental probability of rolling each number.

2. How does each compare to theoretical probability?

3. **Make a Conjecture** Is the model better with 10 or 100 trials?

Activity 2

A school principal chooses 100 students at random to fill out a survey about cafeteria food. The school has about the same number of boys as girls. Find the experimental probability that any given survey was answered by a girl.

You can model this situation with your calculator's Coin Toss simulation. Press **APPS**, scroll down and select **Prob Sim**, and press any key to get past the title screen.

Then select **1. Toss Coins.** Use the keys below the screen to choose the options shown in the application. Press **WINDOW** to toss a coin once.

Press **GRAPH** and then **Y=** to clear the toss from the screen. Press **TRACE** to flip the coin 50 times. Press **TRACE** again for another 50 flips. Use the ▶ key to see the frequency of heads and tails.

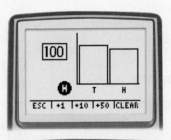

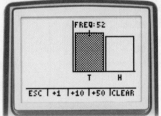

Think and Discuss

1. Explain why tossing a coin is a good model for the situation in Activity 2.

2. Compare the experimental and theoretical probability of a given survey being answered by a girl.

3. Suppose that the ratio of boys to girls was 3:2. How would this affect the outcome?

Try This

1. Suppose that the principal chooses 200 students to fill out the survey. What is the experimental probability of a given survey being answered by a boy?

2. Think of a situation that you could model with a coin toss. Explain the situation, state why a coin toss would be a useful model, conduct the simulation, and find the experimental probability.

10-5 Making Predictions

COMMON CORE

CC.7.SP.8 Find probabilities of compound events using organized lists, tables, tree diagrams, and simulation. *Also CC.7.SP.6, CC.7.SP.7, CC.7.SP.7a, CC.7.SP.7b*

A **prediction** is something you can reasonably expect to happen in the future. Weather forecasters use several different methods of forecasting to make predictions about the weather.

One way to make a prediction is to use probability.

EXAMPLE 1   **Using Experimental Probability to Make Predictions**

Vocabulary

prediction

Caitlyn finds that the experimental probability of her making a three-point shot is 30%. Out of 500 three-point shots, about how many could she predict she would make?

Method 1: Set up an equation.

$\frac{3}{10} \cdot 500 = x$ *Multiply the probability by the total number of 3-point shots.*

$150 = x$ *Solve for x.*

Method 2: Set up a proportion.

$\frac{3}{10} = \frac{x}{500}$ *Think: 3 out of 10 is how many out of 500?*

$3 \cdot 500 = 10 \cdot x$ *The cross products are equal.*

$1{,}500 = 10x$ *Multiply.*

$\frac{1{,}500}{10} = \frac{10x}{10}$ *Divide each side by 10 to isolate the variable.*

$150 = x$

Caitlyn can predict that she will make about 150 of 500 three-point shots.

> **Remember!**
>
> 30% is $\frac{30}{100}$ or $\frac{3}{10}$.

EXAMPLE 2   **Using Theoretical Probability to Make Predictions**

If you roll a number cube 15 times, about how many times do you expect to roll a number less than 6?

$P(\text{less than } 6) = \frac{5}{6}$

$\frac{5}{6} = \frac{x}{15}$ *Think: 5 out of 6 is how many out of 15?*

$5 \cdot 15 = 6 \cdot x$ *The cross products are equal.*

$75 = 6x$ *Multiply.*

$\frac{75}{6} = \frac{6x}{6}$ *Divide each side by 6 to isolate the variable.*

$12.5 = x$

You can expect to roll a number less than 6 about 12 or 13 times.

> **Helpful Hint**
>
> Round to a whole number if it makes sense in the given situation.

Exactostock/SuperStock

Video   **Lesson Tutorials Online**   my.hrw.com

EXAMPLE 3

PROBLEM SOLVING APPLICATION

Make sense of problems and persevere in solving them.

The Wettermark family is planning a 14-day vacation. They would like to go to Pensacola, Florida, sometime in July, August, or September. Pensacola averages 19 rainy days during those 92 days. If the Wettermarks would like no rain on at least 10 days of their vacation, should they go to Pensacola?

1 Understand the Problem

The **answer** will be whether the Wettermarks should go to Pensacola.

List the **important information:**
- Pensacola averages 19 rainy days out of 92 days.
- The Wettermarks want it not to rain 10 out of 14 days.

2 Make a Plan

On average 19 out of 92 days are rainy. After finding out the number of rainy days there should be for 14 days, subtract to find the number of not rainy days.

3 Solve

$$\frac{19}{92} = \frac{x}{14}$$ *Think: 19 out of 92 is how many out of 14?*

$$19 \cdot 14 = 92 \cdot x$$ *The cross products are equal.*

$$266 = 92x$$ *Multiply.*

$$\frac{266}{92} = \frac{92x}{92}$$ *Divide each side by 92 to isolate the variable to find the number of rainy days.*

$$2.89 \approx x$$ *There will be about 3 rainy days in 14 days.*

$$14 - 3 = 11$$ *Subtract the predicted number of rainy days from the total vacation days.*

4 Look Back

Since $11 > 10$, the Wettermarks can reasonably expect at least 10 not rainy days on their vacation and should go to Pensacola.

$$\frac{19 \text{ rainy days}}{92 \text{ total days}} \approx \frac{20}{100} \text{ or } 20\% \qquad \frac{3 \text{ rainy days}}{14 \text{ total days}} \approx \frac{3}{15} \text{ or } 20\%$$

Since both ratios are about 20%, the answer is reasonable.

Think and Discuss

1. **Explain** the difference between a prediction based on experimental probability and one based on theoretical probability.

2. **Explain** whether a prediction based on a probability will always match the actual results.

GUIDED PRACTICE

See Example 1
1. The experimental probability of hearing thunder on any given day in Florida is 25%. Out of 730 days (2 years), about how many days can Floridians predict to hear thunder?

2. A player on the school baseball team reaches first base 40% of the times he is at bat. Out of 50 times at bat, about how many times will the player reach first base?

See Example 2
3. If you flipped a fair coin 18 times, about how many times would you expect heads to appear?

4. A bag contains 6 white marbles and 4 black marbles. You pick out a marble, record its color, and put the marble back in the bag. If you repeat this process 35 times, about how many times do you expect to remove a white marble from the bag?

See Example 3
5. The Escobar family is planning a 7-day vacation. They would like to go to Boulder, Colorado, in December. Based on last December, Boulder had 23 days when it did not snow. If the Escobars would like it to snow on at least 3 days of their vacation, should they go to Boulder?

INDEPENDENT PRACTICE

See Example 1
6. The wettest U.S. city is Mobile, Alabama. The city's chance of rain is 16%. Out of a 30-day period, about how many rainy days would you expect Mobile to have?

7. A student on the basketball team makes 72% of her free-throw attempts. Out of 450 attempts, about how many free throws will this student make?

See Example 2
For 8–9, use the spinner.

8. In 20 spins, about how often can you expect to get a number evenly divisible by 2?

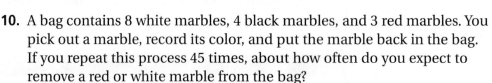

9. In 150 spins, about how often can you expect to get a number less than 6?

10. A bag contains 8 white marbles, 4 black marbles, and 3 red marbles. You pick out a marble, record its color, and put the marble back in the bag. If you repeat this process 45 times, about how often do you expect to remove a red or white marble from the bag?

See Example 3
11. Alexia wants to start taking the light rail train to work. She wants to be late no more than 5% of the time. The light rail train claims to be on time 24 out of 25 times. Should Alexia take the light rail train to work?

Recreation

Snow tubing has become an increasingly popular winter activity. Many ski resorts now offer downhill runs devoted solely for tubing, and tube tows to take tubers back up the hill without having to get off their tube!

12. If 12 out of 15 people recycle aluminum cans, how many people out of 1 million would you expect to recycle?

13. A spinner with equal sections has 7 different dollar amounts. Starting with $1, the amounts increase by being multiplied by 2. How many times in 84 spins are you likely to spin $16 or over?

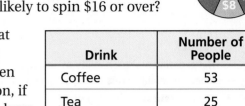

14. **Recreation** A survey of 150 people at a ski resort were asked to name their favorite hot drink. The results are given in the table. Based on this information, if there are 500 people at the ski resort, how many can you predict would name hot chocolate as their favorite hot drink?

Drink	Number of People
Coffee	53
Tea	25
Hot Chocolate	72

15. **Critical Thinking** Roy rolls a fair number cube 18 times. Predict how many times he will roll a number that is odd and greater than 3.

16. **Critical Thinking** People exiting an electronics store were asked whether they own a laptop computer. Out of 10 people, 7 said yes. Based on this information, how many people out of 500 in the general population would you expect to own a laptop computer? Is this a good prediction? Why or why not?

17. **What's the Error?** Ella misses the school bus 1 out of every 60 school days. She sets up the proportion $\frac{1}{60} = \frac{180}{x}$ to predict how many days she will miss the bus in the 180-day school year. What's her error?

 18. **Write About It** Look up the weather predictions for your area for the week. Can you make a prediction for the year based on the information?

19. **Challenge** Two movies open in the same day. Movie A earns 40% of the total box office receipts for the month. Movie B earns $80 million, or 25%, of the month's box office receipts. If Movie A's rate of success continues, how much money will it earn over 3 months?

Test Prep

20. **Gridded Response** If 4 out of 23 toys on an assembly line are defective, about how many toys out of 414 are likely to be defective?

21. **Short Response** A survey reveals that one airline's flights have an 89% probability of being on time. If this airline schedules 5,000 flights in a year, how many flights would you predict to arrive on time? Explain.

Experimental and Theoretical Probability

Use with Making Predicions

Learn It Online
Lab Resources Online

> **REMEMBER**
> • The experimental probability of an event is the ratio of the number of times the event occurs to the total number of trials.
> • The theoretical probability of an event is the ratio of the number of ways the event can occur to the total number of equally likely outcomes.

 Use appropriate tools strategically.

CC.7.SP.7 …Compare probabilities from a model to observed frequencies; if the agreement is not good, explain possible sources of the discrepancy. **Also CC.7.SP.6**

Activity 1

1. Write the letters *A*, *B*, *C*, and *D* on four slips of paper. Fold the slips in half and place them in a bag or other small container.

2. Predict the number of times you expect to choose *A* when you repeat the experiment 12 times.

3. Without looking, choose a slip of paper, note the result, and replace the slip. Repeat this 12 times, mixing the slips between trials. Record your results in a table like the one shown.

4. How many times did you choose *A*? How does this number compare to your prediction?

5. What is the experimental probability of choosing *A*? What is the theoretical probability of choosing *A*?

6. Combine your results with those of your classmates. Find the experimental probability of choosing *A* based on the combined results.

Outcome	Number of Times Chosen
A	//
B	////
C	ЖҐ
D	/

Think and Discuss

1. How is the experimental probability of choosing *A* based on the combined results different from the experimental probability of choosing *A* based on the results of your own experiment?

2. How many times would you expect to choose *A* if you repeat the experiment 500 times?

Try This

1. What is the theoretical probability of choosing *A* from five slips of paper with the letters *A*, *B*, *C*, *D*, and *E*? Predict the number of times you would expect to choose *A* if you repeat the experiment 500 times.

2. **Make a Conjecture** Based on your answers from problem **1**, make a conjecture about experimental and theoretical probability if the number of trials is great.

Activity 2

① Write the letters *A, B, C,* and *D* and the numbers 1, 2, and 3 on slips of paper. Fold the slips in half. Place the slips with the letters in one bag and the slips with the numbers in a different bag.

② In this activity, you will be choosing one slip of paper from each bag without looking. What is the sample space for this experiment? Predict the number of times you expect to choose *A* and 1 (*A*-1) when you repeat the experiment 24 times.

③ Choose a slip of paper from each bag, note the results, and replace the slips. Repeat this 24 times, mixing the slips between trials. Record your results in a table like the one shown.

④ How many times did you choose *A*-1? How does this number compare to your prediction?

⑤ Combine your results with those of your classmates. Find the experimental probability of choosing *A*-1 based on the combined results.

Outcome	Number of Times Chosen
A-1	I
A-2	HHT
A-3	II
B-1	I

Think and Discuss

1. What do you think is the theoretical probability of choosing *A*-1? Why?

2. How many times would you expect to choose *A*-1 if you repeat the experiment 600 times?

3. Explain the difference between the experimental probability of an event and the theoretical probability of the event.

Try This

1. Suppose you toss a penny and a nickel at the same time.

   a. What is the sample space for this experiment?

   b. Predict the number of times you would expect both coins to land heads up if you repeat the experiment 100 times.

   c. Predict the number of times you would expect one coin to land heads up and one coin to land tails up if you repeat the experiment 1,000 times.

2. You spin the spinner at right and roll a number cube at the same time.

   a. What is the sample space for this experiment?

   b. Describe an experiment you could conduct to find the experimental probability of spinning green and rolling a 4 at the same time.

CHAPTER 10 SECTION A

Quiz for Lessons 1 Through 5

 1 **Probability**

Determine whether each event is impossible, unlikely, as likely as not, likely, or certain.

1. rolling 2 number cubes and getting a sum of 2

2. guessing the answer to a true/false question correctly

3. The probability of Ashur's soccer team winning its next game is $\frac{7}{10}$. What is the probability of Ashur's team not winning the next game?

 2 **Experimental Probability**

4. Carl is conducting a survey for the school paper. He finds that 7 students have no pets, 15 have one pet, and 9 have at least two pets. What is the experimental probability that the next student Carl asks will not have a pet?

 3 **Sample Spaces**

5. Shelly and Anthony are playing a game using a number cube and a nickel. Each player rolls the number cube and flips the coin. What are all the possible outcomes during one turn? How many outcomes are in the sample space?

6. A yogurt shop offers 4 different flavors of yogurt and 3 different fruit toppings. How many different desserts are possible if you can choose one flavor of yogurt and one topping?

 4 **Theoretical Probability**

A spinner with 10 equal sectors numbered 1 through 10 is spun. Find the probability of each event. Write your answer as a fraction, as a decimal, and as a percent.

7. $P(5)$ **8.** $P(\text{prime number})$ **9.** $P(20)$

10. Sabina has a list of 8 CDs and 5 DVDs that she would like to buy. Her friends randomly select one of the items from the list to give her as a gift. What is the probability Sabina's friends will select a CD? a DVD?

5 **Making Predictions**

11. Sally finds that the experimental probability of her putting a ball into a hole is 15%. Out of 20 putts, about how many could she predict she would make?

12. If you roll a number cube 25 times, about how many times do you expect to roll a number greater than 3?

Focus on Problem Solving

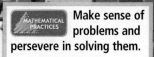

Understand the Problem

• Identify important details

When you are solving word problems, you need to identify information that is important to the problem. Read the problem several times to find all the important details. Sometimes it is helpful to read the problem aloud so that you can hear the words. Highlight the facts that are needed to solve the problem. Then list any other information that is necessary.

 Highlight the important information in each problem, and then list any other important details.

1 A bag of bubble gum has 25 pink pieces, 20 blue pieces, and 15 green pieces. Lauren selects 1 piece of bubble gum without looking. What is the probability that it is not blue?

2 Regina has a bag of marbles that contains 6 red marbles, 3 green marbles, and 4 blue marbles. Regina pulls 1 marble from the bag without looking. What is the probability that the marble is red?

3 Marco is counting the cars he sees on his ride home from school. Of 20 cars, 10 are white, 6 are red, 2 are blue, and 2 are green. What is the experimental probability that the next car Marco sees will be red?

4 Frederica has 8 red socks, 6 blue socks, 10 white socks, and 4 yellow socks in a drawer. What is the probability that she will randomly pull a brown sock from the drawer?

5 During the first 20 minutes of lunch, 5 male students, 7 female students, and 3 teachers went through the lunch line. What is the experimental probability that the next person through the line will be a teacher?

Probability of Independent and Dependent Events

COMMON CORE

CC.7.SP.8 Find probabilities of compound events using organized lists, tables, tree diagrams, and simulation.

Vocabulary

independent events

dependent events

Interactivities Online ▶

Raji and Kara must each choose a solo from a list of music pieces to play for their recital. If Raji's choice has no effect on Kara's choice and vice versa, the events are *independent*. For **independent events**, the occurrence of one event has no effect on the probability that a second event will occur.

If once Raji chooses a solo, Kara must choose from the remaining solos, then the events are *dependent*. For **dependent events**, the occurrence of one event *does* have an effect on the probability that a second event will occur.

EXAMPLE **1** **Determining Whether Events Are Independent or Dependent**

Decide whether each set of events is independent or dependent. Explain your answer.

Reading Math

Sometimes events cannot happen at the same time. These events are called disjoint events. For more on disjoint events, see Skills Bank.

A **Erika rolls a 3 on one number cube and a 2 on another number cube.**

Since the outcome of rolling one number cube does not affect the outcome of rolling the second number cube, the events are independent.

B **Tomoko chooses a seventh-grader for her team from a group of seventh- and eighth-graders, and then Juan chooses a different seventh-grader from the remaining students.**

Since Juan cannot pick the same student that Tomoko picked, and since there are fewer students for Juan to choose from after Tomoko chooses, the events are dependent.

To find the probability that two independent events will happen, multiply the probabilities of the two events.

Probability of Two Independent Events

$$P(A \text{ and } B) = P(A) \cdot P(B)$$

Probability of both events *Probability of first event* *Probability of second event*

Video **Lesson Tutorials Online** my.hrw.com

EXAMPLE 2 **Finding the Probability of Independent Events**

Find the probability of flipping a coin and getting heads and then rolling a 6 on a number cube.

The outcome of flipping the coin does not affect the outcome of rolling the number cube, so the events are independent.

$P(\text{heads and } 6) = P(\text{heads}) \cdot P(6)$

$\qquad = \frac{1}{2} \cdot \frac{1}{6}$ *There are 2 ways a coin can land and 6 ways a number cube can land.*

$\qquad = \frac{1}{12}$ *Multiply.*

The probability of getting heads and a 6 is $\frac{1}{12}$.

To find the probability of two dependent events, you must determine the effect that the first event has on the probability of the second event.

Probability of Two Dependent Events

$$P(A \text{ and } B) = P(A) \cdot P(B \text{ after } A)$$

Probability of both events   *Probability of first event*   *Probability of second event given that A has occurred*

EXAMPLE 3 **Finding the Probability of Dependent Events**

Mica has five $1 bills, three $10 bills, and two $20 bills in her wallet. She picks two bills at random. What is the probability of her picking the two $20 bills?

The first draw changes the number of bills left, and may change the number of $20 bills left, so the events are dependent.

$P(\text{first } \$20) = \frac{2}{10} = \frac{1}{5}$ *There are two $20 bills out of ten bills.*

$P(\text{second } \$20) = \frac{1}{9}$ *There is one $20 bill left out of nine bills.*

$P(\text{first } \$20, \text{ then second } \$20) = P(A) \cdot P(B \text{ after } A)$

$\qquad = \frac{1}{5} \cdot \frac{1}{9}$

$\qquad = \frac{1}{45}$ *Multiply.*

The probability of Mica picking two $20 bills is $\frac{1}{45}$.

MATHEMATICAL PRACTICES

Think and Discuss

1. Compare probabilities of independent and dependent events.

2. Explain whether the probability of two events is greater than or less than the probability of each individual event.

GUIDED PRACTICE

See Example **1** **Decide whether each set of events is independent or dependent. Explain your answer.**

    1. A student flips heads on one coin and tails on a second coin.

    2. A student chooses a red marble from a bag of marbles and then chooses another red marble without replacing the first.

See Example **2** **Find the probability of each set of independent events.**

    3. a flipped coin landing heads up and rolling a 5 or a 6 on a number cube

    4. drawing a 5 from 10 cards numbered 1 through 10 and rolling a 2 on a number cube

See Example **3** **5.** Each day, Mr. Samms randomly chooses 2 students from his class to serve as helpers. There are 15 boys and 10 girls in the class. What is the probability that Mr. Samms will choose 2 girls to be helpers?

INDEPENDENT PRACTICE

See Example **1** **Decide whether each set of events is independent or dependent. Explain your answer.**

    6. A student chooses a fiction book at random from a list of books and then chooses a second fiction book from those remaining.

    7. A woman chooses a lily from one bunch of flowers and then chooses a tulip from a different bunch.

See Example **2** **Find the probability of each set of independent events.**

    8. drawing a red marble from a bag of 6 red and 4 blue marbles, replacing it, and then drawing a blue marble

    9. rolling an even number on a number cube and rolling an odd number on a second roll of the same cube

See Example **3** **10.** Francisco has 7 quarters in his pocket. Of these, 3 depict the state of Delaware, 2 depict Georgia, 1 depicts Connecticut, and 1 depicts Pennsylvania. Francisco removes 1 quarter from his pocket and then removes a second quarter without replacing the first. What is the probability that both will be Delaware quarters?

(all) Sam Dudgeon/HMH

11. An even number is chosen randomly from a set of cards labeled with the numbers 1 through 8. A second even number is chosen without the first card being replaced. Are these independent or dependent events? What is the probability of both events occurring?

12. On a multiple-choice test, each question has five possible answers. A student does not know the answers to two questions, so he guesses. What is the probability that the student will get both answers wrong?

13. The tree diagram shows the probability for choosing 2 fruits from a bag containing 2 red apples and 1 green apple. To find a specific probability, follow the branches of the diagram and multiply the probabilities.

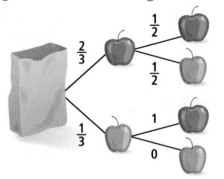

$P(\text{red, then green}) = \frac{2}{3} \cdot \frac{1}{2} = \frac{2}{6} = \frac{1}{3}$

Use the tree diagram to find the following probabilities.

a. $P(\text{green, then red})$ **b.** $P(\text{red, then red})$ **c.** $P(\text{green, then green})$

 14. Write a Problem Describe two events that are either independent or dependent, and make up a probability problem about them.

 15. Write About It At the beginning of a board game, players take turns drawing 7 lettered tiles. Are drawing *A*'s on the first two tiles dependent or independent events? Explain.

 16. Challenge Weather forecasters have accurately predicted rain in one community $\frac{4}{5}$ of the time. What is the probability that they will accurately predict rain two days in a row?

Test Prep

17. Multiple Choice A bag contains 5 red marbles and 5 purple marbles. What is the probability of drawing a red marble and then a purple marble, without replacing the first marble before drawing the second marble?

   Ⓐ $\frac{2}{9}$ Ⓑ $\frac{5}{18}$ Ⓒ $\frac{1}{3}$ Ⓓ $\frac{1}{2}$

18. Short Response José has 8 brown socks and 6 black socks in his drawer. He picked one sock and then another sock. Are the events independent or dependent? Explain. What is the probability that he will pick 2 black socks?

10-7 Combinations

COMMON CORE

CC.7.SP.8 …using organized lists, tables, tree diagrams, and simulation.

Vocabulary
combination

Mrs. Logan's students have to read any two of the following books.

1. *The Adventures of Tom Sawyer,* by Mark Twain

2. *The Call of the Wild,* by Jack London

3. *A Christmas Carol,* by Charles Dickens

4. *Treasure Island,* by Robert Louis Stevenson

5. *Tuck Everlasting,* by Natalie Babbit

How many possible *combinations* of books could the students choose?

A **combination** is a grouping of objects or events in which the order does not matter. For example, a student can choose books 1 and 2 or books 2 and 1. Since the order does not matter, the two arrangements represent the same combination. One way to find all possible combinations is to make a table.

EXAMPLE 1 **Using a Table to Find Combinations**

How many different combinations of two books are possible from Mrs. Logan's list of five books?

Interactivities Online

Begin by making a table showing all of the possible groupings of books taken two at a time.

	1	2	3	4	5
1		1, 2	1, 3	1, 4	1, 5
2	2, 1		2, 3	2, 4	2, 5
3	3, 1	3, 2		3, 4	3, 5
4	4, 1	4, 2	4, 3		4, 5
5	5, 1	5, 2	5, 3	5, 4	

Because order does not matter, you can eliminate repeated pairs. For example, 1, 2 is already listed, so 2, 1 can be eliminated.

	1	2	3	4	5
1		1, 2	1, 3	1, 4	1, 5
2	~~2, 1~~		2, 3	2, 4	2, 5
3	~~3, 1~~	~~3, 2~~		3, 4	3, 5
4	~~4, 1~~	~~4, 2~~	~~4, 3~~		4, 5
5	~~5, 1~~	~~5, 2~~	~~5, 3~~	~~5, 4~~	

There are 10 different combinations of two books on Mrs. Logan's list of five books.

Stone/Getty Images

[Video] **Lesson Tutorials Online** my.hrw.com

You can also use a tree diagram to find possible combinations.

EXAMPLE 2 PROBLEM SOLVING APPLICATION

Make sense of problems and persevere in solving them.

As a caterer, Cuong offers four vegetable choices: broccoli, squash, peas, and carrots. Each person can choose two vegetables. How many different combinations of two vegetables can a person choose?

1 Understand the Problem

Rewrite the question as a statement.
- Find the number of possible combinations of two vegetables a person can choose.

List the **important information:**
- There are four vegetable choices in all.

2 Make a Plan

You can make a tree diagram to show the possible combinations.

3 Solve

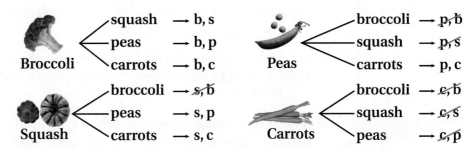

The tree diagram shows 12 possible ways to combine two vegetables, but each combination is listed twice. So there are 12 ÷ 2 = 6 possible combinations.

4 Look Back

You can check by making a table. The broccoli can be paired with three other vegetables, squash with two, and peas with one. The total number of possible pairs is 3 + 2 + 1 = 6.

Think and Discuss

1. **Describe** how to use a tree diagram to find the number of combinations in Example 1.

2. **Describe** how combinations could help you find the probability of an event.

GUIDED PRACTICE

See Example 1

1. If you have an apple, a pear, an orange, and a plum, how many combinations of 2 fruits are possible?

2. How many 3-letter combinations are possible from *A, E, I, O,* and *U*?

See Example 2

3. Robin packs 2 jars of jam in a gift box. She has 5 flavors: blueberry, apricot, grape, peach, and orange marmalade. How many different combinations of 2 jars can she pack in a box?

4. Eduardo has 6 colors of fabric: red, blue, green, yellow, orange, and white. He plans to make flags using 2 colors. How many possible combinations of 2 colors can he choose?

INDEPENDENT PRACTICE

See Example 1

5. A restaurant allows you to "build your own burger" using a choice of any 2 toppings. The available toppings are bacon, grilled onions, sautéed mushrooms, Swiss cheese, and cheddar cheese. How many burgers with 2 different toppings could you build?

6. Jamil has to do reports on 3 cities. He can choose from Paris, New York, Moscow, and London. How many different combinations of cities are possible?

See Example 2

7. A florist can choose from 6 different types of flowers to make a bouquet: carnations, roses, lilies, daisies, irises, and tulips. How many different combinations of 2 types of flowers can he choose?

8. How many different 2-member tennis teams can be made from 7 students?

PRACTICE AND PROBLEM SOLVING

Extra Practice
See Extra Practice for more exercises.

9. At Camp Allen, campers can choose 2 out of 8 free-time activities. Use the chart to find the number of possible combinations of 2 activities.

Free-Time Activities	
hiking	volleyball
mosaics	rafting
tennis	pottery
painting	swimming

10. Rob, Caryn, and Sari are pairing up to play a series of chess matches. In how many different ways can they pair up?

11. Gary has to write biographies about 2 historical figures. He can choose from Winston Churchill, Dr. Martin Luther King, Jr., and Nelson Mandela. How many different combinations of 2 biographies can Gary write?

12. Trina wants to select 3 of Ansel Adams's 5 "surf sequence" photos to hang on her wall. How many possible combinations are there?

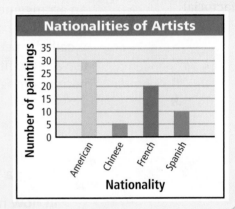

13. Ms. Frennelle is teaching her art history class about famous impressionist painters. She asks her students to choose 2 artists from among Renoir, Monet, Manet, Degas, Pissarro, and Cassatt, and to find information about at least one painting made by each artist. How many possible pairs of artists can be chosen from the six painters?

Boats on the Beach at Etretat, 1883, by Claude Monet

L'Etoile, 1877, by Edgar Degas

14. Multi-Step The graph shows the number of paintings by artists of different nationalities displayed in an art book. In how many ways can you combine 4 paintings by Chinese artists?

15. ⭐ **Challenge** A gallery is preparing a show by a new artist. The gallery has enough space to display 7 pieces of art. The artist has prepared 4 paintings and 5 sculptures. How many distinct combinations of the artist's works are possible?

Nationalities of Artists

Number of paintings vs. Nationality (American, Chinese, French, Spanish)

Test Prep

16. Multiple Choice How many different 2-person teams can be made from 5 people?

Ⓐ 10　　Ⓑ 20　　Ⓒ 24　　Ⓓ 36

17. Gridded Response How many 2-letter combinations are possible from the letters *A, B, C, D, E,* and *F*?

CC.7.SP.8 …using organized lists, tables, tree diagrams, and simulation.

Vocabulary

permutation

factorial

The conductor of a symphony orchestra is planning a concert titled "An Evening with the Killer B's." The concert will feature music by Bach, Beethoven, Brahms, and Bartok. In how many different orders can the conductor arrange the music of the four composers?

An arrangement of objects or events in which the order is important is called a **permutation**. You can use a list to find the number of permutations of a group of objects.

EXAMPLE 1 **Using a List to Find Permutations**

In how many different orders can the conductor arrange the music composed by Bach, Beethoven, Brahms, and Bartok?

Use a list to find the possible permutations.

Let 1 = Bach, 2 = Beethoven, 3 = Brahms, and 4 = Bartok.

Interactivities Online ▶

1-2-3-4	*List all permutations beginning with 1.*	2-1-3-4	*List all permutations beginning with 2.*
1-2-4-3		2-1-4-3	
1-3-2-4		2-3-1-4	
1-3-4-2		2-3-4-1	
1-4-2-3		2-4-1-3	
1-4-3-2		2-4-3-1	
3-1-2-4	*List all permutations beginning with 3.*	4-1-2-3	*List all permutations beginning with 4.*
3-1-4-2		4-1-3-2	
3-2-1-4		4-2-1-3	
3-2-4-1		4-2-3-1	
3-4-1-2		4-3-1-2	
3-4-2-1		4-3-2-1	

There are 24 permutations. Therefore, the conductor can arrange the music by the four composers in 24 different orders.

Video **Lesson Tutorials Online** my.hrw.com

You can use the Fundamental Counting Principle to find the number of permutations.

EXAMPLE 2 **Using the Fundamental Counting Principle to Find the Number of Permutations**

Three students have agreed to serve in leadership positions for the Spanish Club. In how many different ways can the students fill the positions of president, vice-president, and secretary?

Once you fill a position, you have one less choice for the next position.

There are 3 choices for the first position.

    There are 2 remaining choices for the second position.

        There is 1 remaining choice for the third position.

$3 \cdot 2 \cdot 1 = 6$ *Multiply.*

There are 6 different ways that 3 students can fill the 3 positons.

A **factorial** of a whole number is the product of all the whole numbers except zero that are less than or equal to the number.

"3 factorial" is $3! = 3 \cdot 2 \cdot 1 = 6$

"6 factorial" is $6! = 6 \cdot 5 \cdot 4 \cdot 3 \cdot 2 \cdot 1 = 720$

You can use factorials to find the number of permutations.

EXAMPLE 3 **Using Factorials to Find the Number of Permutations**

There are 9 players in a baseball lineup. How many different batting orders are possible for these 9 players?

Number of permutations = $9!$
$$= 9 \cdot 8 \cdot 7 \cdot 6 \cdot 5 \cdot 4 \cdot 3 \cdot 2 \cdot 1$$
$$= 362,880$$

There are 362,880 different batting orders for 9 players.

Think and Discuss

1. Evaluate how the permutations are listed in Example 1. Why is it important to follow a pattern?

2. Explain why 8! gives the number of permutations of 8 objects.

10-8 Exercises

Learn It Online
Homework Help Online
Exercises 1–8, 13, 15, 17, 19, 21

GUIDED PRACTICE

See Example **1**   **1.** In how many ways can you arrange the numbers 1, 2, 3, and 4 to make a 4-digit number?

See Example **2**   **2.** Find the number of permutations of the letters in the word *quiet.*

See Example **3**   **3.** Sam wants to call 6 friends to invite them to a party. In how many different orders can he make the calls?

4. Seven people are waiting to audition for a play. In how many different orders can the auditions be done?

INDEPENDENT PRACTICE

See Example **1**   **5.** In how many ways can Eric, Meera, and Roger stand in line?

See Example **2**   **6.** Find the number of ways you can arrange the letters in the word *art.*

See Example **3**   **7.** How many permutations of the letters *A* through *J* are there?

8. In how many different ways can 8 riders be matched up with 8 horses?

PRACTICE AND PROBLEM SOLVING

Extra Practice
See Extra Practice for more exercises.

Determine whether each problem involves combinations or permutations. Explain your answer.

9. Choose five books to check out from a group of ten.

10. Decide how many ways five people can be assigned to sit in five chairs.

11. Choose a 4-digit PIN using all of the digits 3, 7, 1, and 8.

12. Sports Ten golfers on a team are playing in a tournament. How many different lineups can the golf coach make?

13. Carl, Melba, Sean, and Ricki are going to present individual reports in their Spanish class. Their teacher randomly selects which student will speak first. What is the probability that Melba will present her report first?

14. Using the digits 1 through 7, Pima County is assigning new 7-digit numbers to all households. How many possible numbers can the county assign without repeating any of the digits in a number?

15. How many different 5-digit numbers can be made using the digits 6, 3, 5, 0, and 4 without repetitions?

16. In how many different orders can 12 songs on a CD be played?

17. Multi-Step If you have 5 items, and you can fit 3 of them on a shelf, how many choices do you have for the first item on the shelf? for the second item? for the third item? How many different orders are possible for the 3 items chosen from 5 items?

18. Health A survey was taken to find out how 200 people age 40 and older rate their memory now compared to 10 years ago. In how many different orders could interviews be conducted with people who think their memory is the same?

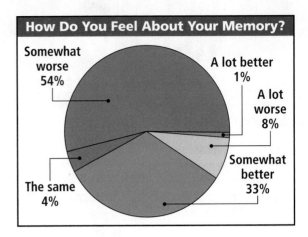

19. Literature The school library has 13 books by Louisa May Alcott. Merina wants to read all 13 of them one after another. Write an expression to show the number of ways she can do that.

Since its initial publication in 1868, *Little Women*, by Louisa May Alcott, has never been out of print. It has been translated into at least 27 languages.

20. Use the letters *A, D, E, R.*

a. How many permutations of the letters are there?

b. How many arrangements form English words?

21. Josie and Luke have 3 sunflowers and 4 bluebonnets. Josie selects a flower at random. Then Luke chooses a flower at random from the remaining flowers. What is the probability that Josie picks a sunflower and Luke chooses a bluebonnet?

22. What's the Error? A student was trying to find 5! and wrote the equation $5 + 4 + 3 + 2 + 1 = 15$. Why is this student incorrect?

23. Write About It Explain the difference between combinations of objects and permutations of objects. Give examples of each.

24. Challenge Evaluate $\dfrac{11!}{3!(11-3)!}$.

Test Prep

25. Multiple Choice Which expression can you use to find the number of 5-digit passwords you can make using the digits 1, 3, 5, 7, and 9, if you do not repeat any of the digits?

Ⓐ $9 + 7 + 5 + 3 + 1$

Ⓑ $9 \cdot 7 \cdot 5 \cdot 3 \cdot 1$

Ⓒ $5 + 4 + 3 + 2 + 1$

Ⓓ $5 \cdot 4 \cdot 3 \cdot 2 \cdot 1$

26. Gridded Response A school play has seven different characters. In how many different ways can seven students be assigned to the roles?

COMMON CORE

CC.7.SP.8 Find probabilities of compound events using organized lists, tables, tree diagrams, and simulation. **Also CC.7.SP.8a**

Jodie checks the online orders for a local pizza parlor. The pizza parlor offers six different pizza toppings: anchovies, mushrooms, olives, onions, pepperoni, and sausage. What is the probability that the next order for a two-topping pizza will be sausage and mushroom?

You can find the probability of compound events using organized lists, tables, and tree diagrams.

Tim Hawley/Foodpix/Getty Images

EXAMPLE 1 **Using an Organized List to Find Probability**

A pizza parlor offers six different pizza toppings: anchovies, mushrooms, olives, onions, pepperoni, and sausage. What is the probability that a random order for a two-topping pizza will be mushroom and sausage?

Let A = anchovies, M = mushrooms, Ol = olives, On = onion, P = pepperoni, and S = sausage. List all possible two-topping pizzas. Because the order of the toppings does not matter, you can eliminate repeated pairs.

Anchovies-M	~~Mushroom-A~~	~~Olives-A~~
Anchovies-Ol	Mushroom-Ol	~~Olives-M~~
Anchovies-On	Mushroom-On	Olives-On
Anchovies-P	Mushroom-P	Olives-P
Anchovies-S	Mushroom-S	Olives-S

~~Onion-A~~	~~Pepperoni-A~~	~~Sausage-A~~
~~Onion-M~~	~~Pepperoni-M~~	~~Sausage-M~~
~~Onion-Ol~~	~~Pepperoni-Ol~~	~~Sausage-Ol~~
Onion-P	~~Pepperoni-On~~	~~Sausage-On~~
Onion-S	Pepperoni-S	~~Sausage-P~~

$$P(\text{M\&S}) = \frac{\text{number of M\&S pizzas}}{\text{total number of equally likely two-topping pizzas}} = \frac{1}{15}$$

The probability that a random two-topping order will be mushroom and sausage is $\frac{1}{15}$.

EXAMPLE 2 Using a Tree Diagram to Find Probability

Bonnie, Corrina, and Deanne line up in random order for softball batting practice. What is the probability that the girls will line up from front to back in alphabetical order?

Make a tree diagram showing possible line-up orders.
Let B = Bonnie, C = Corrina, and D = Deanne.

B
  C — D → $\boxed{BCD}$ *List permutations beginning with*
  D — C → BDC   *Bonnie.*

C
  B — D → CBD   *List permutations beginning with*
  D — B → CDB   *Corrina.*

D
  B — C → DBC   *List permutations beginning with*
  C — B → DCB   *Deanne.*

$P(\text{alpha order}) = \dfrac{\text{number of line-ups in alphabetical order}}{\text{total number of equally likely line-ups}} = \dfrac{1}{6}$

The probability that the girls randomly line up in alphabetical order is $\frac{1}{6}$.

EXAMPLE 3 Finding the Probability of Compound Events

Jen rolls two number cubes. What is the probability that the sum of the two numbers will equal 5?

Make a table of all possible outcomes in the sample space.

	1	2	3	4	5	6
1	1-1	1-2	1-3	(1-4)	1-5	1-6
2	2-1	2-2	(2-3)	2-4	2-5	2-6
3	3-1	(3-2)	3-3	3-4	3-5	3-6
4	(4-1)	4-2	4-3	4-4	4-5	4-6
5	5-1	5-2	5-3	5-4	5-5	5-6
6	6-1	6-2	6-3	6-4	6-5	6-6

Circle all the pairs of numbers that have a sum of 5.

There are 4 out of 36 possible outcomes that have a sum of 5.

The probability of rolling a sum of 5 is $\frac{4}{36} = \frac{1}{9}$, or about 11%.

Think and Discuss

1. Explain how organized lists, tree diagrams, and tables help find the sample space in an experiment.

GUIDED PRACTICE

See Example **1**

1. Kai and Paula are two of the five members of a singing group. Every week, the group picks two names at random to sing a duet. What is the probability that Kai and Paula will be chosen this week?

2. The seven houses on Kent Lane are numbered from 1 to 7. The local newspaper chooses two of the houses at random to receive a free Sunday paper. What is the probability that houses 6 and 7 receive the free paper?

See Example **2**

3. Baby Deegan arranges alphabet blocks for the letters A, B, and T. What is the probability that his arrangement spells a three-letter word?

4. At about 9:00 P.M. every night, flights from Chicago, Miami, and Denver arrive at the local airport in a random order. What is the probability that the Chicago flight will arrive first on any night?

See Example **3**

5. Chaz rolls two number cubes. What is the probability that the sum of the two numbers will be 7?

INDEPENDENT PRACTICE

See Example **1**

6. A cafeteria offers four vegetables: carrots, peas, sweet potatoes, and broccoli. The server prepares ready-to-go meals and puts two vegetables at random on every plate. What is the probability that any randomly-chosen plate has peas and broccoli?

7. For three nights in a row, Jared, Matt, and four other players play chess against each other on the Internet. The computer randomly picks each player's opponent each night. What is the probability that Jared plays against Matt on any night?

See Example **2**

8. Letters A, R, T, and S are arranged in a random order. What is the probability that the arrangement forms the words RATS, TARS, TSAR, or STAR?

9. Four aces are turned face down on a table, and two aces are drawn one after the other. What is the probability that a the Ace of Hearts is drawn second?

See Example **3**

10. Sarah, David, and Ali are friends in science class. The teacher randomly chooses two of the 12 students in the class to work together on a project. What is the probability that two of these three friends will be chosen?

Extra Practice
See Extra Practice for
more exercises.

11. Make a list of the four-letter permutations of the letters A, B, C, and D. What is the probability of randomly choosing one of these permutations?

12. Make a list of the two-letter combinations of the letters A, B, C, D, and E. What is the probability of randomly choosing one of these combinations?

Recreation

13. **Recreation** A deck of cards has 52 cards, four of which are aces. The deck is shuffled, and the first four cards are turned over. What is the probability that each card is an ace?

14. The tree diagram shows the probability for randomly choosing two dinner plates from a cabinet that contains two blue plates and three yellow plates.

Use the tree diagram to find the following probabilities:

a. Choosing two blue plates

b. Choosing a blue and yellow plate in any order

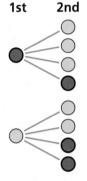

As playing cards became popular, different cultures created their own suits. The four suits that are common today—hearts, diamonds, spades, and clubs—are from a French design from the 15th century.

15. **Write About It** Explain how to create and use tables to help solve a compound probability problem.

16. **Challenge** Cho, Darla, and four others are divided randomly into two teams of three. What is the probability that Cho and Darla are teammates?

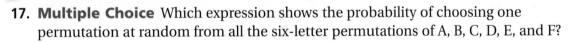

Test Prep

17. **Multiple Choice** Which expression shows the probability of choosing one permutation at random from all the six-letter permutations of A, B, C, D, E, and F?

Ⓐ $\frac{1}{6}$ Ⓑ $\frac{1}{6!}$ Ⓒ $\frac{6}{10!}$ Ⓓ $\frac{1}{10!}$

18. **Gridded Response** For a history assignment, a teacher randomly chooses three presidents from the first 10 presidents. The probability that Washington, Madison, and Monroe are chosen is 1 out of what number?

Quiz for Lessons 6 Through 9

 6 **Probability of Independent and Dependent Events**

Decide whether each set of events is independent or dependent. Explain.

1. Winny rolls two number cubes and gets a 5 on one and a 3 on the other.

2. A card with hearts is drawn from a full deck of cards and not replaced. Then a card with clubs is drawn from the same deck.

A bag contains 8 blue and 7 yellow marbles. Use this information for Exercises 3 and 4.

3. Find the probability of randomly drawing a blue marble and then randomly drawing a yellow marble without replacing the first marble.

4. Find the probability of randomly drawing a blue marble and then randomly drawing another blue marble after replacing the first marble.

 7 **Combinations**

5. Kenny wants the guests to have 2 juice options at his party. There are 8 different juices that he has to choose from. How many different ways can Kenny choose 2 different juices?

6. Find the number of different ways that 2 out of 12 students can volunteer to organize a class party.

7. A restaurant offers entrees with a choice of 2 side dishes. How many combinations of 2 sides are available from a list of 9 side dishes?

 8 **Permutations**

8. Four swimmers are chosen to swim in a relay race. How many orders of the 4 swimmers are possible for the relay race?

9. Employees on the second floor have been given five 1-digit numbers from which to create a 5-digit passcode to unlock a color copier. From how many different passcodes can they choose if the passcode cannot have repeated numbers?

9 **Probability of Compound Events**

10. Tina must choose two tiles in a word game. Of the 21 tiles, 9 are vowels and 12 are consonants. What is the probability that Tina chooses two vowels?

11. A basketball team starts 5 of its 12 available players at random every week. What is the probability that for two consecutive weeks, no player starts twice?

Real-World CONNECTIONS

The Delaware Sports Museum and Hall of Fame

Since 2002, Frawley Stadium in Wilmington has been home to the Delaware Sports Museum and Hall of Fame. The 5000-square-foot hall features artifacts, uniforms, and photos of the outstanding athletes who have been part of Delaware's history.

DELAWARE

Wilmington

For 1–3, use the table.

1. The table shows the 2007 inductees at the hall. Alison is taking pictures of the inductees. She chooses an inductee at random for the first photograph.

   a. What is the probability that the inductee played football?

   b. What is the probability that the inductee did not play football?

2. Alison chooses another inductee at random for the second photograph. What is the probability that the inductees in the first two photos both played football?

3. Alison decides to take a group picture of the inductees who played football.

   a. In how many different ways can these inductees stand in a line?

   b. Alison would like to have two of the football players seated for the photograph. In how many different ways can she choose the two inductees who will be seated?

Delaware Sports Hall of Fame 2007 Inductees	
Name	**Field**
Bernard Briggs	Coaching
Jim Bundren	Football
Bob Immediato	Baseball
Vincent Mayer	Football
Rick McCall	Coaching
Lovett Purnell	Football
Vinnie Scott	Football
David Whitcraft	Soccer
Val Whiting	Basketball

Real-World Connections

Real-World Connections **451**

Game Time

Buffon's Needle

If you drop a needle of a given length onto a wooden floor with evenly spaced cracks, what is the probability that it will land across a crack?

Comte de Buffon (1707–1788) posed this geometric probability problem. To answer his question, Buffon developed a formula using ℓ to represent the length of the needle and d to represent the distance between the cracks.

$$\text{probability} = \frac{2\ell}{\pi d}$$

To re-create this experiment, you need a paper clip and several evenly spaced lines drawn on a piece of paper. Make sure that the distance between the lines is greater than the length of the paper clip. Toss the paper clip onto the piece of paper at least a dozen times. Divide the number of times the paper clip lands across a line by the number of times you toss the paper clip. Compare this quotient to the probability given by the formula.

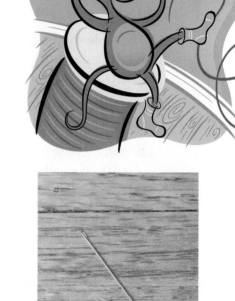

The other interesting result of Buffon's discovery is that you can use the probability of the needle toss to estimate *pi*.

$$\pi = \frac{2\ell}{\text{probability} \cdot d}$$

Toss the paper clip 20 times to find the experimental probability. Use this probability in the formula above, and compare the result to 3.14.

Pattern Match

This game is for two players. Player A arranges four different pattern blocks in a row out of the view of player B. Player B then tries to guess the arrangement. After each guess, player A reveals how many of the blocks are in the correct position without telling which blocks they are. The round ends when player B correctly guesses the arrangement.

A complete set of game pieces are available online.

Learn It Online
Game Time Extra

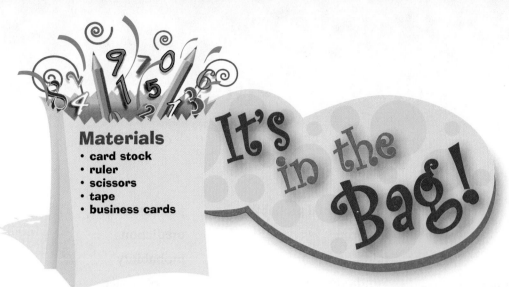

Materials
- card stock
- ruler
- scissors
- tape
- business cards

It's in the Bag!

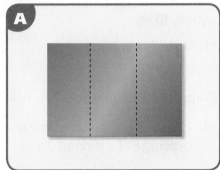

PROJECT The Business of Probability

Make a holder for business cards. Then use the business cards to take notes on probability.

❶ Cut a piece of card stock to $7\frac{1}{2}$ inches by $4\frac{1}{2}$ inches. Fold the card stock in thirds and then unfold it. **Figure A**

❷ Cut out a trapezoid that is about $\frac{1}{2}$-inch tall from one end of the card stock as shown. **Figure B**

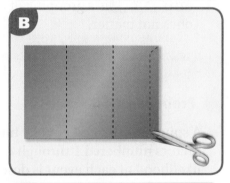

❸ Cut off about $\frac{1}{2}$ inch along the other end of the card stock. Then cut the corners at an angle. **Figure C**

❹ Fold up the bottom section of the card stock and tape the edges closed. **Figure D**

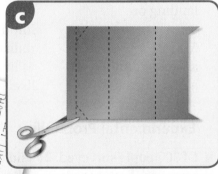

Taking Note of the Math

Use the backs of business cards to take notes on probability. Store the business cards in the holder that you made. Write the name and number of the chapter on the flap of the holder.

It's in the Bag! **453**

Study Guide: Review

Vocabulary

combination	experimental probability	permutation
complement	factorial	prediction
compound event	fair	probability
dependent events	Fundamental Counting Principle	sample space
equally likely		simple event
event	independent events	theoretical probability
experiment	outcome	trial

Complete the sentences below with vocabulary words from the list above.

1. For ___?___, the outcome of one event has no effect on the outcome of a second event.

2. A(n) ___?___ is a grouping of objects or events in which order does not matter.

EXAMPLES

EXERCISES

1 Probability

■ A spinner is divided equally into 8 sectors numbered 1 through 8. The likelihood of each event is described.

landing on:	
0	impossible
5	unlikely
an even number	as likely as not
a number less than 7	likely

Determine whether each event is impossible, unlikely, as likely as not, likely, or certain.

3. rolling a sum of 12 with two number cubes

4. rolling a sum of 24 with two number cubes

2 Experimental Probability

■ Of 50 people surveyed, 21 said they liked mysteries better than comedies. What is the probability that the next person surveyed will prefer mysteries?

$P(\text{mysteries}) = \dfrac{\text{number who like mysteries}}{\text{total number surveyed}}$

$P(\text{mysteries}) = \dfrac{21}{50}$

The probability is $\dfrac{21}{50}$.

Sami has been keeping a record of her math grades. Of her first 15 grades, 10 have been above 82.

5. What is the probability that her next grade will be above 82?

6. What is the probability that her next grade will not be above 82?

3 Sample Spaces

■ **Anita tosses a coin and rolls a number cube. How many outcomes are possible?**

The coin has 2 outcomes. The number cube has 6 outcomes.

List the number of outcomes.

$2 \cdot 6 = 12$

Use the Fundamental Counting Principle.

There are 12 possible outcomes.

Chen spins each of the spinners once.

7. What are all the possible outcomes?

8. How many outcomes are in the sample space?

4 Theoretical Probability

■ **Find the probability of drawing a 4 from a standard deck of 52 playing cards. Write your answer as a fraction, as a decimal, and as a percent.**

$$P(4) = \frac{\text{number of 4's in deck}}{\text{number of cards in deck}}$$

$$= \frac{4}{52} = \frac{1}{13} \approx 0.077 \approx 7.7\%$$

Find each probability. Write your answer as a fraction, as a decimal, and as a percent.

9. There are 9 girls and 12 boys on the student council. What is the probability that a girl will be chosen as president?

10. Anita tosses 3 coins. What is the probability that each coin will land tails up?

5 Making Predictions

■ **Mia's experimental probability of making a free-throw is 21%. Out of 20 free-throw shots, about how many will she make?**

$$\frac{21}{100} \cdot 20 = x$$

$$4.2 = x$$

Mia will make about 4 out of 20 shots.

11. Tim's experimental probability of making a soccer goal is 40%. Out of 50 goal attempts, about how many will he make?

12. If you roll a number cube 12 times, about how many times do you expect to roll an odd number?

6 Probability of Independent and Dependent Events

■ **There are 4 red marbles, 3 green marbles, 6 blue marbles, and 2 black marbles in a bag. What is the probability that Angie will pick a green marble and then a black marble without replacing the first marble?**

$P(\text{green marble}) = \frac{3}{15} = \frac{1}{5}$

$P(\text{black after green}) = \frac{2}{14} = \frac{1}{7}$

$P(\text{green, then black}) = \frac{1}{5} \cdot \frac{1}{7} = \frac{1}{35}$

13. There are 40 tags numbered 1 through 40 in a bag. What is the probability that Glenn will randomly pick a multiple of 5 and then a multiple of 9 without replacing the first tag?

14. Each letter of the word *probability* is written on a card and put in a bag. What is the probability of picking an "i" on the first try and again on the second try if the first card is replaced?

Study Guide: Review

7 | Combinations

■ **Tina, Sam, and Jo are trying out for co-captains. In how many ways can they be chosen as the co-captains?**

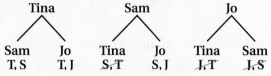

There are 3 possible ways the girls can be chosen as co-captains.

15. How many ways can you select 2 pieces of fruit from a basket of 5 pieces?

16. How many 2-person groups can be chosen from 7 people?

17. How many combinations of 2 balloons can be chosen from 9 balloons?

8 | Permutations

■ **How many different four-digit numbers can you make from the numbers 2, 4, 6, and 8 using each just once?**

There are 4 choices for the first digit, 3 choices for the second, 2 choices for the third, and 1 for the fourth.

$4 \cdot 3 \cdot 2 \cdot 1 = 24$

There are 24 different four-digit numbers.

18. How many different batting orders are possible for 10 players on a league softball team?

19. How many different ways can you arrange the letters in the word *number*?

20. In how many ways can Tanya, Rika, Andy, Evan, and Tanisha line up for lunch?

9 | Probability of Compound Events

■ **A background and border color are randomly chosen as red, blue or green. If the colors cannot be the same, what is the probability that red is used?**

RB	RG	*Write each possible*
BR	BG	*pair of colors. Write*
GR	GB	*the border first.*

The probability red is used is $\frac{2}{3}$.

21. Four friends sit at a square table for lunch each day. If their positions are random, what is the probability Luis sits across from Pam two days in a row?

22. Chase, Ty, Lincoln, and Hector are guards on a basketball team. If the coach starts 2 guards at random for each game, what is the probability Chase and Lincoln start two games in a row?

A box contains 3 orange cubes, 2 white cubes, 3 black cubes, and 4 blue cubes. Determine whether each event is impossible, unlikely, as likely as not, likely, or certain.

1. randomly choosing an orange or black cube

2. randomly choosing a white cube

3. randomly choosing a purple cube

4. Simon tosses a coin 20 times. The coin lands heads up 7 times. Based on these results, how many times can Simon expect the coin to land heads up in the next 100 tosses?

5. Emilio spins a spinner that is divided into 8 equal sectors numbered 1 through 8. In his first three spins, the spinner lands on 8. What is the experimental probability that Emilio will spin a 10 on his fourth spin?

6. A brand of jeans comes in 8 different waist sizes: 28, 30, 32, 34, 36, 38, 40, and 42. The jeans also come in three different colors: blue, black, and tan. How many different combinations of waist sizes and colors are possible?

7. Greg is planning his vacation. He can choose from 3 ways to travel—train, bus, or plane—and four different activities—skiing, skating, snowboarding, or hiking. What are all the possible outcomes? How many different vacations can Greg plan?

Rachel spins a spinner that is divided into 10 equal sectors numbered 1 through 10. Find each probability. Write your answer as a fraction, as a decimal, and as a percent.

8. P(odd number)   9. P(composite number)   10. P(number greater than 10)

For Exercises 11 and 12, find the probability of each event.

11. spinning red on a spinner with equally sized red, blue, yellow, and green sectors, and flipping a coin that lands tails up

12. choosing a card labeled *vanilla* from a group of cards labeled *vanilla, chocolate, strawberry,* and *swirl,* and then choosing a card labeled *chocolate* without replacing the first card

13. If you roll a number cube 12 times, about how many times do you expect to roll a number greater than 1?

14. How many ways can 2 students be chosen from 10 students?

15. Jen has 6 pairs of shoes. She randomly chooses a pair to wear on Monday, and then a different pair on Tuesday. What is the probability that she wore her favorite pair on one of those days?

Test Tackler

All Types: Use a Diagram

Sometimes drawing a diagram helps you solve a problem. When a diagram is given with a test item, use it as a tool. Get as much information from the drawing as possible. Keep in mind that diagrams are not always drawn to scale and can be misleading.

EXAMPLE 1

Multiple Choice What is the probability of flipping a coin and getting tails, and then rolling an even number on a number cube?

Ⓐ $\frac{1}{2}$ Ⓒ $\frac{1}{6}$

Ⓑ $\frac{1}{4}$ Ⓓ $\frac{1}{12}$

You can create a tree diagram to determine the sample space.

Heads   **Tails**

1 2 3 4 5 6   1 2 3 4 5 6

There are 12 possible outcomes but only 3 ways getting tails and an even number can occur. So the probability is $\frac{3}{12}$, or $\frac{1}{4}$, which is answer choice B.

EXAMPLE 2

Short Response Find the volume and surface area of the cylinder, and round your answers to the nearest tenth. Use 3.14 for π.

6 in.
10 in.

In the diagram, it appears that the radius is greater than the height. Remember that the scale of a diagram can be misleading. Rely on the information shown, and substitute the given values into each formula.

$V = \pi r^2 h$ $SA = 2\pi r^2 + 2\pi rh$
$V = \pi(6)^2(10)$ $SA = 2\pi(6)^2 + 2\pi(6)(10)$
$V = 360\pi$ $SA = 226.08 + 376.8$
$V \approx 1{,}130.4 \text{ in}^3$ $SA \approx 602.9 \text{ in}^2$

If you are having trouble understanding a test item, draw a diagram to help you answer the question.

Read each test item, and answer the questions that follow.

Item A
Multiple Choice The volume of a box is 6,336 cm^3. The width of the box is 16 cm, and the height is 18 cm. What is the length of the box?

Ⓐ 396 cm   Ⓒ 220 cm

Ⓑ 22 cm   Ⓓ 11 cm

1. What information about the box is given in the problem statement?

2. Sketch a diagram to help you answer the question. Label each side with the correct dimensions.

3. How does the diagram help you solve the problem?

Item B
Multiple Choice Janet spins two spinners at the same time. One spinner is divided into 3 equal sectors, labeled 1, 2, and 3. The second spinner is divided into 3 equal sectors, labeled A, B, and C. What is the probability that the spinners will land on 1 and A or 1 and C?

Ⓕ $\frac{1}{3}$ Ⓗ $\frac{1}{9}$

Ⓖ $\frac{2}{3}$ Ⓙ $\frac{2}{9}$

4. Make a tree diagram to determine the sample space. Then count the ways getting 1 and either A or C can occur.

5. Explain which answer choice is correct.

6. How does the tree diagram help you solve the problem?

Item C
Short Response Which two vats hold the same amount of liquid? Explain.

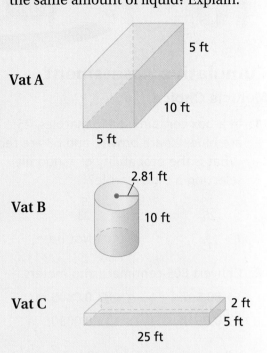

Vat A — 5 ft, 10 ft, 5 ft

Vat B — 2.81 ft, 10 ft

Vat C — 2 ft, 5 ft, 25 ft

7. Explain why you cannot determine the answer by comparing the scale of each diagram.

8. What formulas do you need to find the answer?

9. Explain which two vats hold the same amount of liquid.

Item D
Gridded Response Determine the surface area in square meters of a rectangular prism that has a length of 13 m, a width of 10 m, and a height of 8 m.

10. How do you determine the surface area of a rectangular prism?

11. Create a net for this prism and label it with the correct dimensions.

12. Use the net from problem 11 to find the surface area of the prism.

Standardized Test Prep

Cumulative Assessment

Multiple Choice

1. In a box containing 115 marbles, 25 are blue, 22 are brown, and 68 are red. What is the probability of randomly selecting a blue marble?

   (A) $\frac{115}{25}$

   (B) $\frac{22}{115}$

   (C) $\frac{5}{23}$

   (D) Not here

2. Convert 805 centimeters to meters.

   (F) 80.5 m

   (G) 8.05 m

   (H) 0.0805 m

   (J) 0.00805 m

3. What is the value of $(-8 - 4)^2 + 4^1$?

   (A) -143

   (B) 0

   (C) 145

   (D) 148

4. The graph shows a town's high temperatures over a 5-day period. What was the average high temperature over these 5 days?

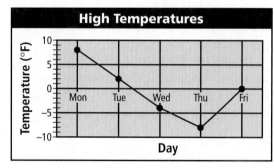

   (F) $-0.4°F$

   (G) $4.4°F$

   (H) $0.4°F$

   (J) $-4.4°F$

5. The fraction $\frac{3}{5}$ is found between which pair of fractions on a number line?

   (A) $\frac{7}{10}$ and $\frac{3}{4}$

   (B) $\frac{2}{7}$ and $\frac{8}{11}$

   (C) $\frac{2}{5}$ and $\frac{1}{2}$

   (D) $\frac{1}{3}$ and $\frac{5}{13}$

6. Stu wants to leave a 15% tip for his dinner that cost $13.40. About how much tip should Stu leave?

   (F) $1.50

   (G) $1.75

   (H) $2.00

   (J) $2.50

7. What is $2\frac{5}{12} \times \frac{12}{7}$?

   (A) $\frac{5}{7}$

   (B) $2\frac{5}{7}$

   (C) $2\frac{17}{19}$

   (D) $4\frac{1}{7}$

8. Find the surface area of the rectangular prism.

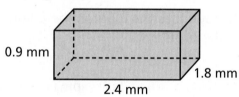

   0.9 mm

   1.8 mm

   2.4 mm

   (F) 8.1 mm^2

   (G) 16.2 mm^2

   (H) 15.84 mm^2

   (J) 3.888 mm^2

9. Horace has test scores of 87, 70, 81, 94, and 81. What is the range of these scores?

   (A) 11

   (B) 14

   (C) 70

   (D) 81

10. An angle has a measure of 100°. Which best classifies this angle?

   (F) acute

   (G) straight

   (H) obtuse

   (J) right

11. Five of the angles in a hexagon measure 155°, 120°, 62°, 65°, and 172°. What is the measure of the sixth angle?

(A) 115°   (C) 180°

(B) 146°   (D) 326°

 HOT TIP! Probability can be expressed as a fraction, decimal, or percent.

Gridded Response

Use the following graph for items 12 and 13.

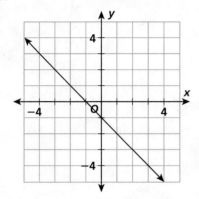

12. Find the *y*-coordinate of the point on the line whose *x*-coordinate is −1.

13. Determine the value of *y* when $x = -6$.

14. Anji bought 4 shirts for $56.80. She later bought a shirt for $19.20. What was the mean cost of all the shirts in dollars?

15. Find 4!.

16. Rosa has a coupon for 60% off the before-tax total of two pairs of shoes. The first pair of shoes is marked $45, and the second pair is marked $32. What is Rosa's total cost, in dollars, after a 5.5% sales tax is added?

17. What is the value of *x*? $12 = x - \frac{3}{4}$

Short Response

S1. The diameter of the larger circle is 36 in., and the radius of the smaller circle is 6 in.

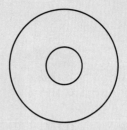

What is the ratio of the smaller circle's area to the larger circle's area written to the nearest whole percent?

S2. Rhonda has 3 different-color T-shirts—red, blue, and green—and a pair of blue jeans and a pair of white jeans. She randomly chooses a T-shirt and a pair of jeans. What is the probability that she will pair the red T-shirt with the white jeans? Show how you found your answer.

S3. Write $\frac{5}{6}$ and $\frac{3}{4}$ as fractions with a common denominator. Then determine whether the fractions are equivalent. Explain your method.

Extended Response

E1. A bag contains 5 blue blocks, 3 red blocks, and 2 yellow blocks.

   a. What is the probability that Tip will draw a red block and then a blue block at random if the first block is replaced before the second is drawn? Show the steps necessary to find your answer.

   b. What is the probability that Tip will draw a red block and then a blue block at random if the first block is not replaced before the second is drawn? Show your work.

   c. Explain how your answers to parts **a** and **b** are affected by whether or not the first block is replaced.

Chapter Focus

- Formulate linear equations in one variable.
- Choose procedures to solve these equations efficiently.

Why Learn This?

Scuba divers can use equations to calculate the depth of their dives or to estimate how much air is remaining in their tanks.

Learn It Online
Chapter Project Online

Plasma/SuperStock

Are You Ready?

✓ Vocabulary

Choose the best term from the list to complete each sentence.

1. __?__ are mathematical operations that undo each other.

2. To solve an equation you need to __?__.

3. A(n) __?__ is a mathematical statement that two expressions are equivalent.

4. A(n) __?__ is a mathematical statement that two ratios are equivalent.

isolate the variable

equation

proportion

inverse operations

expression

Complete these exercises to review skills you will need for this chapter.

✓ Add Whole Numbers, Decimals, Fractions, and Integers

Add.

5. $24 + 16$

6. $-34 + (-47)$

7. $35 + (-61)$

8. $-12 + (-29) + 53$

9. $2.7 + 3.5$

10. $\frac{2}{3} + \frac{1}{2}$

11. $-5.87 + 10.6$

12. $\frac{8}{9} + \left(-\frac{9}{11}\right)$

✓ Evaluate Expressions

Evaluate each expression for $a = 7$ and $b = -2$.

13. $a - b$

14. $b - a$

15. $\frac{b}{a}$

16. $2a + 3b$

17. $\frac{-4a}{b}$

18. $3a - \frac{8}{b}$

19. $1.2a + 2.3b$

20. $-5a - (-6b)$

✓ Solve Multiplication Equations

Solve.

21. $8x = -72$

22. $-12a = -60$

23. $\frac{2}{3}y = 16$

24. $-12b = 9$

25. $12 = -4x$

26. $13 = \frac{1}{2}c$

27. $-2.4 = -0.8p$

28. $\frac{3}{4} = 6x$

✓ Solve Proportions

Solve.

29. $\frac{3}{4} = \frac{x}{24}$

30. $\frac{8}{9} = \frac{4}{a}$

31. $-\frac{12}{5} = \frac{15}{c}$

32. $\frac{y}{50} = \frac{35}{20}$

33. $\frac{2}{3} = \frac{18}{w}$

34. $\frac{35}{21} = \frac{d}{3}$

35. $\frac{7}{13} = \frac{h}{195}$

36. $\frac{9}{-15} = \frac{-27}{p}$

Where You've Been

Previously, you

- solved one-step equations.

- read, wrote, and graphed inequalities on a number line.

- solved one-step inequalities.

In This Chapter

You will study

- solving two-step and multi-step equations and equations with variables on both sides.

- reading, writing, and graphing inequalities on a number line.

- solving one-step and two-step inequalities.

- solving equations for a variable.

Where You're Going

You can use the skills learned in this chapter

- to solve problems in the physical sciences that involve comparing speeds, distances, and weights.

- to make decisions when planning events.

- to evaluate options when distributing budget funds.

Key Vocabulary/Vocabulario

algebraic inequality	desigualdad algebraica
compound inequality	desigualdad compuesta
inequality	desigualdad
solution set	conjunto solución

Vocabulary Connections

To become familiar with some of the vocabulary terms in the chapter, consider the following. You may refer to the chapter, the glossary, or a dictionary if you like.

1. What does the word *inequality* mean? How might an **inequality** describe a mathematical relationship? Give an example using numbers.

2. An example of an algebraic equation is $x + 3 = 8$. How do you think $x + 3 = 8$ would change if you were to write it as an **algebraic inequality** instead of as an equation?

3. A compound sentence is made up of two or more independent clauses joined by the words *and* or *or*. What do you think a **compound inequality** might be?

4. A solution of an equation is a value that makes the equation true. For example, $x = 5$ is a solution of $x + 3 = 8$. A set is a group of "items," such as people or numbers, that have a characteristic in common. What do you think a **solution set** might be?

Study Guide: Preview

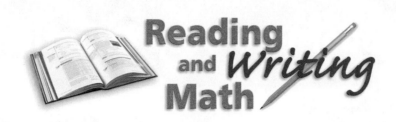

Study Strategy: Prepare for Your Final Exam

Math is a cumulative subject, so your exam will cover all of the material you have learned from the beginning of the course. Being prepared is the key for you to be successful on your exam.

2 weeks before the final exam

- Review lesson notes and vocabulary.
- Look at previous exams and homework. Rework problems that I answered incorrectly or that I did not complete.
- Make a list of all formulas, rules, and important steps.
- Create a practice exam using problems from the book that are similar to problems from the previous tests.

1 week before the final exam

- Take the practice exam and check it. For each problem I miss, find two or three similar problems and work those.
- Look over each chapter's Study Guide: Review.
- Quiz a friend or myself on the formulas and major points from my list.

1 day before the final exam

- Make sure I have pencils and a calculator. (Check the batteries!)
- Review any problem areas one last time.

FINAL

Try This

1. Create a timeline that you will use to study for your final exam.

Model Two-Step Equations

Use with Solving Two-Step Equations

KEY

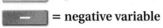 = positive variable

= negative variable

= 1   = −1

REMEMBER

- + − = 0
- + = 0
- In an equation, the expressions on both sides of the equal sign are equivalent.

Use appropriate tools strategically.
CC.7.EE.1 Apply properties of operations as strategies to add, subtract, factor...

You can use algebra tiles to solve two-step equations. When solving a two-step equation, it is easiest to perform addition and subtraction before multiplication and division.

Activity

1 Use algebra tiles to model and solve $2p + 2 = 10$.

$2p + 2 = 10$

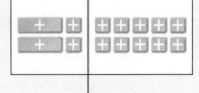

Model the equation.

$$\begin{array}{rr} 2p + 2 &= 10 \\ -2 & -2 \\ \hline 2p &= 8 \end{array}$$

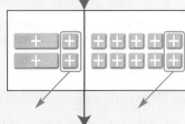

Remove 2 yellow tiles from each side of the mat.

$$\frac{2p}{2} = \frac{8}{2}$$

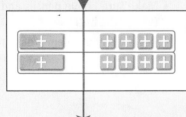

Divide each side into 2 equal groups.

$p = 4$

The solution is p = 4.

2 Use algebra tiles to model and solve $3n + 6 = -15$.

$3n + 6 = -15$

$3n + 6 + (-6) = -15 + (-6)$

$3n = -21$

$\dfrac{3n}{3} = \dfrac{-21}{3}$

$n = -7$

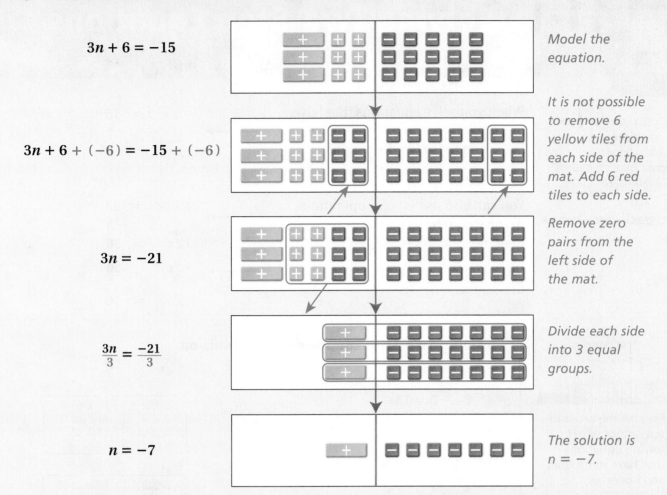

Model the equation.

It is not possible to remove 6 yellow tiles from each side of the mat. Add 6 red tiles to each side.

Remove zero pairs from the left side of the mat.

Divide each side into 3 equal groups.

The solution is $n = -7$.

Think and Discuss

1. When you add a value to one side of an equation, why do you also have to add the same value to the other side?

2. When you solved $3n + 6 = -15$ in the activity, why were you able to remove six yellow unit tiles and six red unit tiles from the left side of the equation?

3. Model and solve $3x - 5 = 10$. Explain each step.

4. How would you check the solution to $3n + 6 = -15$ using algebra tiles?

Try This

Use algebra tiles to model and solve each equation.

1. $4 + 2x = 20$ **2.** $3r + 7 = -8$ **3.** $-4m + 3 = -25$

4. $-2n - 5 = 17$ **5.** $10 = 2j - 4$ **6.** $5 + r = 7$

7. $4h + 2h + 3 = 15$ **8.** $-3g = 9$ **9.** $5k + (-7) = 13$

Solving Two-Step Equations

COMMON CORE

CC.7.EE.1 Apply properties of operations as strategies to add, subtract, factor, and expand linear expressions with rational coefficients.

Interactivities Online ▶

When you solve equations that have one operation, you use an inverse operation to isolate the variable.

$$n + 7 = 15$$
$$\underline{-7 \quad -7}$$
$$n = 8$$

You can also use inverse operations to solve equations that have more than one operation.

$$2x + 3 = 23$$
$$\underline{-3 \quad -3}$$
$$2x = 20$$

Use the inverse of multiplication to isolate x.

$$\frac{2x}{2} = \frac{20}{2}$$
$$x = 10$$

EXAMPLE 1 **Solving Two-Step Equations Using Division**

Solve.

Helpful Hint

Reverse the order of operations when solving equations that have more than one operation.

A $2n + 5 = 13$

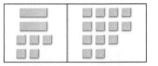

$$2n + 5 = 13$$
$$\underline{-5 \quad -5}$$ *Subtract 5 from both sides.*
$$2n = 8$$

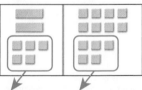

$$\frac{2n}{2} = \frac{8}{2}$$ *Divide both sides by 2.*
$$n = 4$$

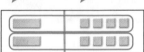

B $19 = -3p - 8$

$$19 = -3p - 8$$
$$\underline{+8 \qquad +8}$$ *Add 8 to both sides.*
$$27 = -3p$$

$$\frac{27}{-3} = \frac{-3p}{-3}$$ *Divide both sides by −3.*
$$-9 = p$$

Check

$$19 = -3p - 8$$
$$19 \overset{?}{=} -3(-9) - 8$$ *Substitute −9 for p.*
$$19 \overset{?}{=} 27 - 8$$
$$19 \overset{?}{=} 19 ✔$$ *−9 is a solution.*

EXAMPLE **2** Solving Two-Step Equations Using Multiplication

Solve.

A $8 + \dfrac{m}{4} = 17$

$$8 + \dfrac{m}{4} = 17$$
$$\underline{-8 \qquad\quad -8} \qquad \text{\textit{Subtract 8 from both sides.}}$$
$$\dfrac{m}{4} = 9$$
$$(4)\dfrac{m}{4} = (4)9 \qquad \text{\textit{Multiply both sides by 4.}}$$
$$m = 36$$

B $3 = \dfrac{u}{6} - 12$

$$3 = \dfrac{u}{6} - 12$$
$$\underline{+12 \qquad\quad +12} \qquad \text{\textit{Add 12 to both sides.}}$$
$$15 = \dfrac{u}{6}$$
$$(6)15 = (6)\dfrac{u}{6} \qquad \text{\textit{Multiply both sides by 6.}}$$
$$90 = u$$

EXAMPLE **3** *Fitness Application*

A new one-year membership at Vista Tennis Center costs $160. A registration fee of $28 is paid up front, and the rest is paid monthly. How much do new members pay each month?

| registration fee | plus | 12 times monthly cost | is | $160 |

Let m represent the monthly cost.

| $28 | + | 12m | = | $160 |

$$28 + 12m = 160$$
$$\underline{-28 \qquad\qquad -28} \qquad \text{\textit{Subtract 28 from both sides.}}$$
$$12m = 132$$
$$\dfrac{12m}{12} = \dfrac{132}{12} \qquad \text{\textit{Divide both sides by 12.}}$$
$$m = 11$$

New members pay $11 per month for a one-year membership.

Fitness

Labeled "the sport for a lifetime," tennis is played by people of all ages. Some tennis matches may take just minutes to complete, while others take hours or even days!

MATHEMATICAL PRACTICES

Think and Discuss

1. Explain how you decide which inverse operation to use first when solving a two-step equation.

2. Tell the steps you would follow to solve $-1 + 2x = 7$.

Image Bank/Getty Images

Exercises

Learn It Online
Homework Help Online
Exercises 1–20, 23, 25, 27, 29, 31, 33, 35

GUIDED PRACTICE

See Example 1 **Solve.**

1. $3n + 8 = 29$

2. $-4m - 7 = 17$

3. $2 = -6x + 4$

See Example 2 **Solve.**

4. $12 + \frac{b}{6} = 16$

5. $\frac{y}{8} - 15 = 2$

6. $10 = -8 + \frac{n}{4}$

See Example 3 **7.** A coffee shop sells a ceramic refill mug for $8.95. Each refill costs $1.50. Last month Rose spent $26.95 on a mug and refills. How many refills did she buy?

INDEPENDENT PRACTICE

See Example 1 **Solve.**

8. $5x + 6 = 41$

9. $-9p - 15 = 93$

10. $-2m + 14 = 10$

11. $-7 = 7d - 8$

12. $-7 = -3c + 14$

13. $12y - 11 = 49$

See Example 2 **Solve.**

14. $24 + \frac{h}{4} = 10$

15. $\frac{k}{5} - 13 = 4$

16. $-17 + \frac{q}{8} = 13$

17. $24 = \frac{m}{10} + 32$

18. $-9 = 15 + \frac{v}{3}$

19. $\frac{m}{-7} - 14 = 2$

See Example 3 **20.** Each Saturday, a gym holds a 45-minute yoga class. The weekday yoga classes last 30 minutes. The number of weekday classes varies. Last week, the yoga classes totaled 165 minutes. How many weekday yoga classes were held?

PRACTICE AND PROBLEM SOLVING

Extra Practice

See Extra Practice for more exercises.

Translate each equation into words, and then solve the equation.

21. $6 + \frac{m}{3} = 18$

22. $3x + 15 = 27$

23. $2 = \frac{n}{5} - 4$

Solve.

24. $18 + \frac{y}{4} = 12$

25. $5x + 30 = 40$

26. $\frac{s}{12} - 7 = 8$

27. $-10 + 6g = 110$

28. $-8 = \frac{z}{7} + 2$

29. $46 = -6w - 8$

30. $15 = -7 + \frac{r}{3}$

31. $-20 = -4p - 12$

32. $\frac{1}{2} + \frac{r}{7} = \frac{5}{14}$

33. Consumer Math A long-distance phone company charges $1.01 for the first 25 minutes of a call, and then $0.09 for each additional minute. A call cost $9.56. How long did it last?

34. The school purchased baseball equipment and uniforms for a total cost of $1,836. The equipment cost $612, and the uniforms were $25.50 each. How many uniforms did the school purchase?

35. If you double the number of calories per day that the U.S. Department of Agriculture recommends for children who are 1 to 3 years old and then subtract 100, you get the number of calories per day recommended for teenage boys. Given that 2,500 calories are recommended for teenage boys, how many calories per day are recommended for children?

36. According to the U.S. Department of Agriculture, children who are 4 to 6 years old need about 1,800 calories per day. This is 700 calories more than half the recommended calories for teenage girls. How many calories per day does a teenage girl need?

37. Hector consumed 2,130 calories from food in one day. Of these, he consumed 350 calories at breakfast and 400 calories having a snack. He also ate 2 portions of one of the items shown in the table for lunch and the same for dinner. What did Hector eat for lunch and dinner?

Calorie Counter		
Food	**Portion**	**Calories**
Stir-fry	1 cup	250
Enchilada	1 whole	310
Pizza	1 slice	345
Tomato soup	1 cup	160

38. ⭐ **Challenge** There are 30 mg of cholesterol in a box of macaroni and cheese. This is 77 mg minus $\frac{1}{10}$ the number of milligrams of sodium it contains. How many milligrams of sodium are in a box of macaroni and cheese?

Test Prep

39. Multiple Choice For which equation is $x = -2$ a solution?

Ⓐ $2x + 5 = 9$ Ⓑ $8 = 10 - x$ Ⓒ $\frac{x}{2} + 3 = 2$ Ⓓ $-16 = -4x - 8$

40. Short Response A taxi cab costs $1.25 for the first mile and $0.25 for each additional mile. Write an equation for the total cost of a taxi ride, where x is the number of miles. How many miles can be traveled in the taxi for $8.00?

Solving Multi-Step Equations

COMMON CORE

CC.7.EE.4 Use variables to represent quantities in a real-world or mathematical problem, and construct simple equations and inequalities to solve problems by reasoning about the quantities. **Also CC.7.EE.1, CC.7.EE.4a**

Jamal owns twice as many graphic novels as Levi owns. If you add 6 to the number of graphic novels Jamal owns and then divide by 7, you get the number of graphic novels Brooke owns. Brooke owns 30 graphic novels. How many graphic novels does Levi own? To answer this question, you need to set up an equation that requires more than two steps to solve.

EXAMPLE 1 **Combining Like Terms to Solve Equations**

Solve $7n - 1 - 2n = 14$.

$$7n - 1 - 2n = 14$$
$$5n - 1 = 14 \qquad \text{Combine like terms.}$$
$$\underline{+ 1 \qquad + 1} \qquad \text{Add 1 to both sides.}$$
$$5n = 15$$

$$\frac{5n}{5} = \frac{15}{5} \qquad \text{Divide both sides by 5.}$$
$$n = 3$$

You may need to use the Distributive Property to solve an equation that has parentheses. Multiply each term inside the parentheses by the factor that is outside the parentheses. Then combine like terms.

EXAMPLE 2 **Using the Distributive Property to Solve Equations**

Solve $3(z - 1) + 8 = 14$.

> **Remember!**
>
> The Distributive Property states that $a(b + c) = ab + ac$. For instance, $2(3 + 5) = 2(3) + 2(5)$.

$$3(z - 1) + 8 = 14$$
$$3(z) - 3(1) + 8 = 14 \qquad \text{Distribute 3 on the left side.}$$
$$3z - 3 + 8 = 14 \qquad \text{Simplify.}$$
$$3z + 5 = 14 \qquad \text{Combine like terms.}$$
$$\underline{- 5 \qquad - 5} \qquad \text{Add } -5 \text{ to both sides.}$$
$$3z = 9$$
$$\frac{3z}{3} = \frac{9}{3} \qquad \text{Divide both sides by 3.}$$
$$z = 3$$

Video **Lesson Tutorials Online**

EXAMPLE **3** **PROBLEM SOLVING APPLICATION**

Make sense of problems and persevere in solving them.

Jamal owns twice as many graphic novels as Levi owns. Adding 6 to the number of graphic novels Jamal owns and then dividing by 7 gives the number Brooke owns. Brooke owns 30 graphic novels. How many does Levi own?

READY TO TAKE 'EM?

I WAS BORN READY!

1 **Understand the Problem**

Rewrite the question as a statement.

• Find the number of graphic novels that Levi owns.

List the **important information:**

• Jamal owns 2 times as many graphic novels as Levi owns.

• The number of graphic novels Jamal owns added to 6 and then divided by 7 equals the number Brooke owns.

• Brooke owns 30 graphic novels.

2 **Make a Plan**

Let g represent the number of graphic novels Levi owns. Then $2g$ represents the number Jamal owns, and $\frac{2g+6}{7}$ represents the number Brooke owns, which equals 30. Solve the equation $\frac{2g+6}{7} = 30$ for g.

3 **Solve**

$$\frac{2g+6}{7} = 30$$

$$(7)\frac{2g+6}{7} = (7)30 \qquad \textit{Multiply both sides by 7 to eliminate fractions.}$$

$$2g + 6 = 210$$

$$2g + 6 - 6 = 210 - 6 \qquad \textit{Subtract 6 from both sides.}$$

$$2g = 204$$

$$\frac{2g}{2} = \frac{204}{2} \qquad \textit{Divide both sides by 2.}$$

$$g = 102$$

Levi owns 102 graphic novels.

4 **Look Back**

Make sure that your answer makes sense in the original problem. Levi has 102 graphic novels. Jamal has $2\,(102) = 204$. Brooke has $\frac{204+6}{7} = 30$.

MATHEMATICAL PRACTICES

Think and Discuss

1. List the steps required to solve $-n + 5n + 3 = 27$.

2. Describe how to solve the equations $\frac{2}{3}x + 7 = 4$ and $\frac{2x+7}{3} = 4$. Are the solutions the same or different? Explain.

Exercises

Learn It Online
Homework Help Online
Exercises 1–20, 21, 23, 25, 29, 31, 33, 35

GUIDED PRACTICE

Solve.

See Example **1**
1. $14n + 2 - 7n = 37$
2. $10x - 11 - 4x = 43$
3. $1 = -3 + 4p - 2p$

See Example **2**
4. $12 - (x + 3) = 10$
5. $15 = 2(q + 4) + 3$
6. $5(m - 2) + 36 = -4$

See Example **3**
7. Keisha read twice as many books this year as Ben read. Subtracting 4 from the number of books Keisha read and dividing by 2 gives the number of books Sheldon read. Sheldon read 10 books. How many books did Ben read?

INDEPENDENT PRACTICE

Solve.

See Example **1**
8. $b + 18 + 3b = 74$
9. $10x - 3 - 2x = 4$
10. $18w - 10 - 6w = 50$
11. $19 = 5n + 7 - 3n$
12. $-27 = -3p + 15 - 3p$
13. $-x - 8 + 14x = -34$

See Example **2**
14. $2(x + 4) + 6 = 22$
15. $1 - 3(n + 5) = -8$
16. $4.3 - 1.4(p + 7) = -9.7$
17. $3(0.6 + 2n) - 3.2 = 7.6$
18. $0 = 9\left(k - \frac{2}{3}\right) + 33$
19. $6(t - 2) - 76 = -142$

See Example **3**
20. Abby ran 3 times as many laps as Karen. Adding 4 to the number of laps Abby ran and then dividing by 7 gives the number of laps Jill ran. Jill ran 1 lap. How many laps did Karen run?

PRACTICE AND PROBLEM SOLVING

Extra Practice
See Extra Practice for more exercises.

Solve.

21. $\frac{0.5x + 7}{8} = 5$
22. $4(t - 8) + 20 = 5$
23. $63 = 8w + 2.6 - 3.6$
24. $17 = -5(3 + w) + 7$
25. $\frac{\frac{1}{4}a - 12}{8} = 4$
26. $9 = -(r - 5) + 11$
27. $\frac{2b - 3.4}{0.6} = -29$
28. $8.44 = \frac{34.6 + 4h}{5}$
29. $5.7 = -2.5x + 18 - 1.6x$

30. **Consumer Math** Three friends ate dinner at a restaurant. The friends decided to add a 15% tip and then split the bill evenly. Each friend paid $10.35. What was the total bill for dinner before tip?

31. Ann earns 1.5 times her normal hourly pay for each hour that she works over 40 hours in a week. Last week she worked 51 hours and earned $378.55. What is her normal hourly pay?

32. **Geometry** The base angles of an isosceles triangle are congruent. The measure of each of the base angles is twice the measure of the third angle. Find the measures of all three angles.

33. Consumer Math Patrice used a $15 gift certificate when she purchased a pair of sandals. After 8% sales tax was applied to the price of the sandals, the $15 was deducted. Patrice had to pay a total of $12 for the sandals. How much did the sandals cost before tax?

34. Physical Science To convert temperatures between degrees Celsius and degrees Fahrenheit, you can use the formula $F = \frac{9}{5}C + 32$. The table shows the melting points of various elements. Round to the nearest degree.

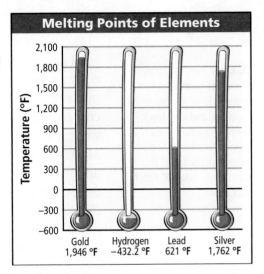

Melting Points of Elements

Gold	Hydrogen	Lead	Silver
1,946 °F	−432.2 °F	621 °F	1,762 °F

a. What is the melting point in degrees Celsius of gold?

b. What is the melting point in degrees Celsius of hydrogen?

35. On his first two social studies tests, Billy made an 86 and a 93. What grade must Billy make on the third test to have an average of 90 for all three tests?

36. What's the Question? Three friends shared a taxi ride from the airport to their hotel. After adding a $7.00 tip, the friends divided the cost of the ride evenly. If solving the equation $\frac{c + \$7.00}{3} = \$11.25$ gives the answer, what is the question?

37. Write About It Explain why multiplying first in the equation $\frac{2x - 6}{5} = 2$ makes finding the solution easier than adding first does.

38. Challenge Are the solutions to the following equations the same? Explain.

$$\frac{3y}{4} + 2 = 4 \text{ and } 3y + 8 = 16$$

Test Prep

39. Multiple Choice Solve $\frac{2x - 2}{4} = 7$.

 Ⓐ $x = 15$ Ⓑ $x = 18$ Ⓒ $x = 20$ Ⓓ $x = 21$

40. Multiple Choice For which equation(s) is $x = 3$ a solution?

 I $2x - 5 + 3x = 10$ II $\frac{-x + 7}{2} = 2$ III $\frac{-4x}{6} = 2$ IV $6.3x - 2.4 = 16.5$

 Ⓕ I only Ⓖ I and II Ⓗ I, II, and III Ⓙ I, II, and IV

11-3 Solving Equations with Variables on Both Sides

COMMON CORE

CC.7.EE.4 Use variables to represent quantities in a real-world or mathematical problem, and construct simple equations and inequalities to solve problems by reasoning about the quantities. *Also CC.7.EE.1, CC.7.EE.4a*

Mari can rent a video game console for $14.49 per week or buy a rebuilt one for $72.45. The cost of renting a game is $7.95 per week. How many weeks would Mari have to rent both the game and the console to pay as much as she would if she had bought the used console and rented the game instead?

Problems such as this require you to solve equations that have the same variable on both sides of the equal sign. To solve this kind of problem, you need to get the terms with variables on one side of the equal sign.

EXAMPLE 1 **Using Inverse Operations to Group Terms with Variables**

Group the terms with variables on one side of the equal sign, and simplify.

A $6m = 4m + 12$

$$6m = 4m + 12$$
$$6m - 4m = 4m - 4m + 12 \qquad \textit{Subtract 4m from both sides.}$$
$$2m = 12 \qquad \textit{Simplify.}$$

B $-7x - 198 = 5x$

$$-7x - 198 = 5x$$
$$-7x + 7x - 198 = 5x + 7x \qquad \textit{Add 7x to both sides.}$$
$$-198 = 12x \qquad \textit{Simplify.}$$

EXAMPLE 2 **Solving Equations with Variables on Both Sides**

Interactivities Online ▶

Solve.

A $5n = 3n + 26$

$$5n = 3n + 26$$
$$5n - 3n = 3n - 3n + 26 \qquad \textit{Subtract 3n from both sides.}$$
$$2n = 26 \qquad \textit{Simplify.}$$
$$\frac{2n}{2} = \frac{26}{2} \qquad \textit{Divide both sides by 2.}$$
$$n = 13$$

Video **Lesson Tutorials Online**

Corbis/Photolibrary

Solve.

B $19 + 7n = -2n + 37$

$$19 + 7n = -2n + 37$$
$19 + 7n + 2n = -2n + 2n + 37$ *Add 2n to both sides.*
$19 + 9n = 37$ *Simplify.*
$19 + 9n - 19 = 37 - 19$ *Subtract 19 from both sides.*
$9n = 18$ *Simplify.*
$\dfrac{9n}{9} = \dfrac{18}{9}$ *Divide both sides by 9.*
$n = 2$

C $\dfrac{5}{9}x = \dfrac{4}{9}x + 9$

$$\dfrac{5}{9}x = \dfrac{4}{9}x + 9$$
$\dfrac{5}{9}x - \dfrac{4}{9}x = \dfrac{4}{9}x - \dfrac{4}{9}x + 9$ *Subtract $\dfrac{4}{9}x$ from both sides.*
$\dfrac{1}{9}x = 9$ *Simplify.*
$(9)\dfrac{1}{9}x = (9)9$ *Multiply both sides by 9.*
$x = 81$

EXAMPLE 3   *Consumer Math Application*

Mari can buy a video game console for $72.45 and rent a game for $7.95 per week, or she can rent a console and the same game for a total of $22.44 per week. How many weeks would Mari need to rent both the video game and the console to pay as much as she would if she had bought the console and rented the game instead?

Let w represent the number of weeks.

$$22.44w = 72.45 + 7.95w$$
$22.44w - 7.95w = 72.45 + 7.95w - 7.95w$ *Subtract 7.95w from both sides.*
$14.49w = 72.45$ *Simplify.*
$\dfrac{14.49w}{14.49} = \dfrac{72.45}{14.49}$ *Divide both sides by 14.49.*
$w = 5$

Mari would need to rent the video game and the console for 5 weeks to pay as much as she would have if she had bought the console.

Think and Discuss

1. **Explain** how you would solve $\dfrac{1}{2}x + 7 = \dfrac{2}{3}x - 2$.

2. **Describe** how you would decide which variable term to add or subtract on both sides of the equation $-3x + 7 = 4x - 9$.

GUIDED PRACTICE

See Example 1   **Group the terms with variables on one side of the equal sign, and simplify.**

1. $5n = 4n + 32$ **2.** $-6x - 28 = 4x$ **3.** $8w = 32 - 4w$

See Example 2   **Solve.**

4. $4y = 2y + 40$ **5.** $8 + 6a = -2a + 24$ **6.** $\frac{3}{4}d + 4 = \frac{1}{4}d + 18$

See Example 3   **7. Consumer Math** Members at the Star Theater pay $30.00 per month plus $1.95 for each movie. Nonmembers pay the regular $7.95 admission fee. How many movies would both a member and a nonmember have to see in a month to pay the same amount?

INDEPENDENT PRACTICE

See Example 1   **Group the terms with variables on one side of the equal sign, and simplify.**

8. $12h = 9h + 84$ **9.** $-10p - 8 = 2p$ **10.** $6q = 18 - 2q$

11. $-4c - 6 = -2c$ **12.** $-7s + 12 = -9s$ **13.** $6 + \frac{4}{5}a = \frac{9}{10}a$

See Example 2   **Solve.**

14. $9t = 4t + 120$ **15.** $42 + 3b = -4b - 14$ **16.** $\frac{6}{11}x + 4 = \frac{2}{11}x + 16$

17. $1.5a + 6 = 9a + 12$ **18.** $32 - \frac{3}{8}y = \frac{3}{4}y + 5$ **19.** $-6 - 8c = 3c + 16$

See Example 3   **20. Consumer Math** Members at a swim club pay $5 per lesson plus a one-time fee of $60. Nonmembers pay $11 per lesson. How many lessons would both a member and a nonmember have to take to pay the same amount?

PRACTICE AND PROBLEM SOLVING

Extra Practice

See Extra Practice for more exercises.

Solve. Check each answer.

21. $3y + 7 = -6y - 56$ **22.** $-\frac{7}{8}x - 6 = -\frac{3}{8}x - 14$

23. $5r + 6 - 2r = 7r - 10$ **24.** $-10p + 8 = 7p + 12$

25. $9 + 5r = -17 - 8r$ **26.** $0.8k + 7 = -0.7k + 1$

27. A choir is singing at a festival. On the first night, 12 choir members were absent, so the choir stood in 5 equal rows. On the second night, only 1 member was absent, so the choir stood in 6 equal rows. The same number of people stood in each row each night. How many members are in the choir?

28. Consumer Math Jaline can purchase tile at a store for $0.99 per tile and rent a tile saw for $24. At another store, she can borrow the tile saw for free if she buys tile there for $1.49 per tile. How many tiles must she buy for the cost to be the same at both stores?

The figures in each pair have the same perimeter. Find the value of each variable.

29.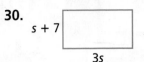

x $x + 4$ x $x + 9$ $x + 5$

30.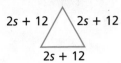

$s + 7$ $3s$ $2s + 12$ $2s + 12$ $2s + 12$

31. Recreation A rock-climbing gym charges nonmembers $18 per day to use the wall plus $7 per day for equipment rental. Members pay an annual fee of $400 plus $5 per day for equipment rental. How many days must both a member and a nonmember use the wall in one year so that both pay the same amount?

32. Multi-Step Two families drove from Denver to Cincinnati. After driving 582 miles the first day, the Smiths spread the rest of the trip equally over the next 3 days. The Chows spread their trip equally over 6 days. The distance the Chows drove each day was equal to the distance the Smiths drove each of the three days.

  a. How many miles did the Chows drive each day?

  b. How far is it from Denver to Cincinnati?

33. What's the Error? To combine terms in the equation $-8a - 4 = 2a + 34$, a student wrote $-6a = 38$. What is the error?

34. Write About It If the same variable is on both sides of an equation, must it have the same value on each side? Explain your answer.

35. Challenge Combine terms before solving the equation $12x - 4 - 12 = 4x + 8 + 8x - 24$. Do you think there is just one solution to the equation? Why or why not?

Test Prep

36. Multiple Choice For which equation is $x = 0$ NOT a solution?

  Ⓐ $3x + 2 = 2 - x$ Ⓑ $2.5x + 3 = x$ Ⓒ $-x + 4 = 3x + 4$ Ⓓ $6x + 2 = x + 2$

37. Extended Response One calling plan offers long-distance calls for $0.03 per minute. Another plan costs $2.00 per month but offers long-distance service for $0.01 per minute. Write and solve an equation to find the number of long-distance minutes for which the two plans would cost the same. Write your answer in a complete sentence.

Examine Solution Methods

COMMON CORE

CC.7.EE.4 Use variables to represent quantities in a real-world or mathematical problem, and construct simple equations and inequalities to solve problems by reasoning about the quantities. *Also CC.7.EE.4a*

Bella loves to ride long distances with her friends. She rides a three-part route that is a total of 30 miles. One part of that route is 4.5 miles, and another part is 5.2 times that distance.

How can you find the third distance that Bella rode? There are two possible methods:

- numeric solution method
- algebraic solution method

Either method requires that you organize the information before you can solve the problem.

moodboard/Alamy

EXAMPLE 1 **Comparing Solution Methods**

Bella rides from her house to her friend Kate's house. Bella and Kate ride 4.5 miles to their friend Mason's house. From there, the three ride a bike loop that starts and ends at his house. The bike loop is 5.2 times the distance from Kate's house to Mason's house. The total distance that Bella has ridden when they get back to Mason's house is 30 miles. Show a numeric and an algebraic method for finding the distance Bella rides to Kate's.

First, organize the information.

Total Distance: 30 miles

Part of Bike Ride	Description	Distance (mi)
Part A	From Bella's to Kate's	x
Part B	From Kate's to Mason's	4.5
Part C	Bike Loop	$5.2 \cdot 4.5$

Method 1 Numeric: Work backward

Begin with the 30-mile total, and work backward.

Find the distance of the bike loop and subtract it from the total distance of 30 miles.

$5.2 \cdot 4.5 \text{ mi} = 23.4 \text{ mi}$ *Multiply to find the distance of the loop.*
$30 \text{ mi} - 23.4 \text{ mi} = 6.6 \text{ mi}$ *Subtract.*

Then subtract the distance Bella rode from Kate's to Mason's.

$6.6 \text{ mi} - 4.5 \text{ mi} = 2.1 \text{ mi}$ *Subtract.*

The distance from Bella's to Kate's is 2.1 miles.

Helpful Hint

When solving an equation, always check your solution. Substitute the solution back into the equation.

Method 2 Algebraic: Write and solve an equation.

All three parts of Bella's bike ride total a sum of 30 miles.

Part A + Part B + Part C = 30

Part A + 4.5 + 5.2 · 4.5 = 30   *Substitute known distances.*

Part A + 4.5 + 23.4 = 30   *Multiply to find Part C.*

Part A + 27.9 = 30   *Combine like terms.*

−27.9 = −27.9   *Subtract 27.9 from both sides.*

Part A = 2.1

Part A, the distance from Bella's to Kate's, is 2.1 miles.

EXTENSION

Exercises

1. Give some advantages and disadvantages of using a numeric solution method.

2. Give some advantages and disadvantages of using an algebraic solution method.

Use both numeric and algebraic solution methods to solve each problem. Then tell which one you prefer and why.

3. A chef decides to add two more teaspoons of pepper to the amount listed in a recipe. After another taste, she triples the total amount of pepper to 12 teaspoons. What was the original amount of pepper listed in the recipe?

4. Ten milliliters (mL) of water were added to a solution. The solution was then tripled to a volume of 45 mL. What was the volume of the original solution?

5. After three weeks, a killer whale is fed 50 more pounds of fish per day. In the fourth week, sickness reduces this amount by half to 220 pounds. How many pounds of fish per day was the killer whale eating at the beginning of the four weeks?

6. After doubling the weight being pulled by a dog sled, the sled driver added 20 more pounds. The final weight of the dog sled was 180 pounds. What was the initial weight of the sled?

7. The number of people at a concert decreased by 120. Shortly after that, the number of people decreased by 50% to 450. How many people were initially at the concert?

8. After rolling down a hill, a boulder's elevation decreased by half. It then rolls another 20 feet down in elevation to 137 feet. At what elevation did the boulder start?

9. Twelve is added to a number. This value is then tripled to 51. What is the number?

10. Five less than three times a number is 25. What is the number?

11. Twenty more than four times a number is 200. What is the number?

12. Six less than the square of a positive number is 10. What is the number?

13. Five more than a positive number squared is 30. What is the number?

14. Twice a number plus 16 is 50. What is the number?

Ready To Go On?

Quiz for Lessons 1 Through 3

1 Solving Two-Step Equations

Solve.

1. $-4x + 6 = 54$

2. $15 + \dfrac{y}{3} = 6$

3. $\dfrac{z}{8} - 5 = -3$

4. $-33 = -7a - 5$

5. $-27 = \dfrac{r}{12} - 19$

6. $-13 = 11 - 2n$

7. $3x + 13 = 37$

8. $\dfrac{p}{-8} - 7 = 12$

9. $\dfrac{u}{7} + 45 = -60$

10. A taxi service charges an initial fee of $1.50 plus $1.50 for every mile traveled. A taxi ride costs $21.00. How many miles did the taxi travel?

2 Solving Multi-Step Equations

Solve.

11. $\dfrac{3x - 4}{5} = 7$

12. $3(3b + 2) = -30$

13. $-12 = \dfrac{15c + 3}{6}$

14. $\dfrac{24.6 + 3a}{4} = 9.54$

15. $\dfrac{2b + 9}{11} = 18$

16. $13 = 2c + 3 + 5c$

17. $\dfrac{1}{2}(8w - 6) = 17$

18. $\dfrac{1.2s + 3.69}{0.3} = 47.9$

19. $\dfrac{1}{2} = \dfrac{5p - 8}{12}$

20. Peter used a $5.00 gift certificate to help pay for his lunch. After adding a 15% tip to the cost of his meal, Peter still had to pay $2.36 in cash. How much did Peter's meal cost?

21. A group of 10 friends had lunch together at a restaurant. The meal cost a total of $99.50, including a 15% tip. How much was the total bill for lunch before tip?

3 Solving Equations with Variables on Both Sides

Solve.

22. $12m = 3m + 108$

23. $\dfrac{7}{8}n - 3 = \dfrac{5}{8}n + 12$

24. $1.2x + 3.7 = 2.2x - 4.5$

25. $-7 - 7p = 3p + 23$

26. $-2.3q + 16 = -5q - 38$

27. $\dfrac{3}{5}k + \dfrac{7}{10} = \dfrac{11}{15}k - \dfrac{2}{5}$

28. $-19m + 12 = -14m - 8$

29. $\dfrac{2}{3}v + \dfrac{1}{6} = \dfrac{7}{9}v - \dfrac{5}{6}$

30. $8.9 - 3.3j = -2.2j + 2.3$

31. $4a - 7 = -6a + 12$

32. One shuttle service charges $10 for pickup and $0.10 per mile. Another shuttle service has no pickup fee but charges $0.35 per mile. Find the number of miles for which the cost of the two shuttle services is the same.

Focus on Problem Solving

Solve

- **Write an equation**

When you are asked to solve a problem, be sure to read the entire problem before you begin solving it. Sometimes you will need to perform several steps to solve the problem, and you will need to know all of the information in the problem before you decide which steps to take.

Read each problem and determine what steps are needed to solve it. Then write an equation that can be used to solve the problem.

1 Martin can buy a pair of inline skates and safety equipment for $49.50. At a roller rink, Martin can rent a pair of inline skates for $2.50 per day, but he still needs to buy safety equipment for $19.50. How many days would Martin have to skate in order to pay as much to rent skates and buy safety equipment as he would have to pay to buy both?

2 Christopher sells paintings at the local outdoor mall. He charges $5 for a small painting and $15 for a larger painting. In one day, Christopher earned $175. He sold 20 small paintings that day. How many larger paintings did he sell?

3 Book-club members are required to buy a minimum number of books each year. Leslee bought 3 times the minimum. Denise bought 7 more than the minimum. Together, they bought 23 books. What is the minimum number of books?

4 Coach Willis has won 150 games during his career. This is 10 more than $\frac{1}{2}$ as many games as Coach Gentry has won. How many games has Coach Gentry won?

5 The perimeter of an isosceles triangle is 4 times the length of the shortest side. The longer sides are 4.5 ft longer than the shortest side. What is the length of each side of the triangle?

6 Miss Rankin's class has raised $100.00 for a class trip. The class needs to collect a total of $225.00. How many $0.50 carnations must the class sell to reach its goal?

An **inequality** states that two quantities either are not equal or may not be equal. An inequality uses one of the following symbols:

Symbol	Meaning	Word Phrases
<	Is less than	Fewer than, below
>	Is greater than	More than, above
≤	Is less than or equal to	At most, no more than
≥	Is greater than or equal to	At least, no less than

EXAMPLE 1 **Writing Inequalities**

Vocabulary

inequality

algebraic inequality

solution set

compound inequality

Write an inequality for each situation.

A **There are at least 25 students in the auditorium.**

number of students ≥ 25   *"At least" means greater than or equal to.*

B **No more than 150 people can occupy the room.**

room capacity ≤ 150   *"No more than" means less than or equal to.*

An inequality that contains a variable is an **algebraic inequality**. A value of the variable that makes the inequality true is a solution of the inequality.

An inequality may have more than one solution. Together, all of the solutions are called the **solution set**.

Interactivities Online ▶ You can graph the solutions of an inequality on a number line. If the variable is "greater than" or "less than" a number, then that number is indicated with an open circle.

This open circle shows that 5 is not a solution.

$a > 5$

If the variable is "greater than or equal to" or "less than or equal to" a number, that number is indicated with a closed circle.

This closed circle shows that 3 is a solution.

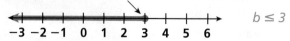

$b \leq 3$

Video **Lesson Tutorials Online**

EXAMPLE 2 **Graphing Simple Inequalities**

Graph each inequality.

A $x > -2$

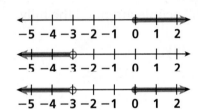

Draw an open circle at −2. The solutions are values of x greater than −2, so shade to the right of −2.

B $-1 \geq y$

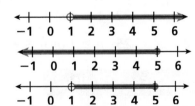

Draw a closed circle at −1. The solutions are −1 and values of y less than −1, so shade to the left of −1.

Writing Math

The compound inequality $-2 < y$ and $y < 4$ can be written as $-2 < y < 4$.

A **compound inequality** is the result of combining two inequalities. The words *and* and *or* are used to describe how the two parts are related.

$x > 3$ or $x < -1$

x is either greater than 3 or less than −1.

$-2 < y$ and $y < 4$

y is both greater than −2 and less than 4. y is between −2 and 4.

EXAMPLE 3 **Graphing Compound Inequalities**

Graph each compound inequality.

A $s \geq 0$ or $s < -3$

Graph $s \geq 0$.

Graph $s < -3$.

Combine the graphs.

Reading Math

$1 < p$ is the same as $p > 1$.

B $1 < p \leq 5$

Graph $1 < p$.

Graph $p \leq 5$.

Graph the common solutions.

MATHEMATICAL PRACTICES

Think and Discuss

1. Compare the graphs of the inequalities $y > 2$ and $y \geq 2$.

2. Explain how to graph each type of compound inequality.

Exercises

Learn It Online
Homework Help Online
Exercises 1–26, 27, 29, 31, 35, 37

GUIDED PRACTICE

See Example 1 **Write an inequality for each situation.**

1. No more than 18 people are allowed in the gallery at one time.

2. There are fewer than 8 fish in the aquarium.

3. The water level is above 45 inches.

See Example 2 **Graph each inequality.**

4. $x < 3$ **5.** $\frac{1}{2} \geq r$ **6.** $2.8 < w$ **7.** $y \geq -4$

See Example 3 **Graph each compound inequality.**

8. $a > 2$ or $a \leq -1$ **9.** $-4 < p \leq 6$ **10.** $-2 \leq n < 0$

INDEPENDENT PRACTICE

See Example 1 **Write an inequality for each situation.**

11. The temperature is below 40 °F.

12. There are at least 24 pictures on the roll of film.

13. No more than 35 tables are in the cafeteria.

14. Fewer than 250 people attended the rally.

See Example 2 **Graph each inequality.**

15. $s \geq -1$ **16.** $y < 0$ **17.** $n \leq -3$

18. $2 < x$ **19.** $-6 \leq b$ **20.** $m < -4$

See Example 3 **Graph each compound inequality.**

21. $p > 3$ or $p < 0$ **22.** $1 \leq x \leq 4$ **23.** $-3 < y < -1$

24. $k > 0$ or $k \leq -2$ **25.** $n \geq 1$ or $n \leq -1$ **26.** $-2 < w \leq 2$

PRACTICE AND PROBLEM SOLVING

Extra Practice
See Extra Practice for more exercises.

Graph each inequality or compound inequality.

27. $z \leq -5$ **28.** $3 > f$ **29.** $m \geq -2$

30. $3 > y$ or $y \geq 6$ **31.** $-9 < p \leq -3$ **32.** $q > 2$ or $-1 > q$

33. Write About It Explain how to graph the inequality $13 \geq x$.

34. Critical Thinking The *Reflexive Property* states that $x = x$. For which inequality symbols would the Reflexive Property apply? Give examples and explain your answer.

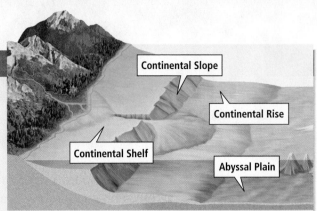

Continental Slope

Continental Rise

Continental Shelf

Abyssal Plain

The portion of the earth's surface that lies beneath the ocean and consists of continental crust is the continental margin. The continental margin is divided into the continental shelf, the continental slope, and the continental rise.

35. The continental shelf begins at the shoreline and slopes toward the open ocean. The depth of the continental shelf can reach 200 meters. Write a compound inequality for the depth of the continental shelf.

36. The continental slope begins at the edge of the continental shelf and continues down to the flattest part of the ocean floor. The depth of the continental slope ranges from about 200 meters to about 4,000 meters. Write a compound inequality for the depth of the continental slope.

37. The bar graph shows the depth of the ocean in various locations as measured by different research vessels. Write a compound inequality that shows the ranges of depth measured by each vessel.

38. ⭐ **Challenge** Water freezes at 32 °F and boils at 212 °F. Write three inequalities to show the ranges of temperatures for which water is a solid, a liquid, and a gas.

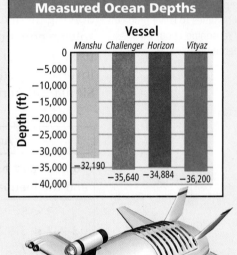

Measured Ocean Depths

Vessel

Manshu Challenger Horizon Vityaz

Depth (ft)

0, −5,000, −10,000, −15,000, −20,000, −25,000, −30,000, −35,000, −40,000

−32,190   −35,640   −34,884   −36,200

Test Prep

39. Multiple Choice Which inequality represents *a number that is greater than −4 and less than 3?*

Ⓐ $-4 \geq n \geq 3$ Ⓑ $-4 < n < 3$ Ⓒ $-4 > n > 3$ Ⓓ $-4 \leq n \leq 3$

40. Multiple Choice Which inequality is shown by the graph?

$$\longleftarrow \begin{array}{ccccccccccc} -5 & -4 & -3 & -2 & -1 & 0 & 1 & 2 & 3 & 4 & 5 \end{array} \longrightarrow$$

Ⓕ $x < -1$ or $x \leq 2$ Ⓖ $x < -1$ or $x \geq 2$ Ⓗ $x \leq -1$ or $x < 2$ Ⓙ $x \leq -1$ or $x > 2$

11-5 Solving Inequalities by Adding or Subtracting

COMMON CORE

CC.7.EE.4 Use variables to represent quantities in a real-world or mathematical problem, and construct simple equations and inequalities to solve problems by reasoning about the quantities.

A high temperature of 74 °F means that the temperature that day is always less than or equal to 74 °F. You can solve problems involving temperatures by using inequalities.

Solving inequalities is very similar to solving equations. Recall that you use the properties of equality and inverse operations to solve equations. Similar properties apply to inequalities.

Addition and Subtraction Properties of Inequality			
You can add or subtract the same number on both sides of an inequality, and the inequality will still be true.			
$3 < 5$	$6 > 2$	$4 \leq 7$	$0 \geq -3$
$3 + 2 < 5 + 2$	$6 - 1 > 2 - 1$	$4 + 3 \leq 7 + 3$	$0 - 4 \geq -3 - 4$
$5 < 7$	$5 > 1$	$7 \leq 10$	$-4 \geq -7$

<u>Interactivities Online</u> ▶ You can use the Addition and Subtraction Properties of Inequality and inverse operations to solve inequalities.

EXAMPLE **1** **Using the Addition Property of Inequality**

Solve. Then graph each solution set on a number line.

Remember!

Draw a closed circle when the inequality includes the point and an open circle when it does not include the point.

A $x - 12 > 32$

$$x - 12 > \quad 32$$
$$\underline{+ 12 \quad + 12} \qquad \textit{Add 12 to both sides.}$$
$$x \qquad > \quad 44$$

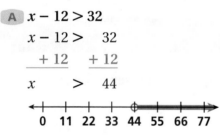

Draw an open circle at 44. Solutions are values of x greater than 44, so shade to the right of 44.

B $y - 8 \leq -14$

$$y - 8 \leq -14$$
$$\underline{+ 8 \quad + 8} \qquad \textit{Add 8 to both sides.}$$
$$y \leq \quad -6$$

Draw a closed circle at −6. Solutions are −6 and values of y less than −6, so shade to the left of −6.

National Geographic

488 *Chapter 11 Multi-Step Equations and Inequalities*

Video **Lesson Tutorials Online**

You can check the solution to an inequality by choosing any number in the solution set and substituting it into the original inequality.

EXAMPLE 2 **Using the Subtraction Property of Inequality**

Solve. Check each answer.

A $c + 9 \geq 20$

$$
\begin{array}{rl}
c + 9 \geq & 20 \\
-9 \quad & -9 \\
\hline
c \quad \geq & 11
\end{array}
$$

Subtract 9 from both sides.

Check

$$
c + 9 \geq 20
$$
$$
20 + 9 \overset{?}{\geq} 20
$$
$$
29 \overset{?}{\geq} 20 \ ✔
$$

20 is greater than 11. Substitute 20 for c.

Helpful Hint

When checking your solution, choose a number in the solution set that is easy to work with.

B $-2 < x + 16$

$$
\begin{array}{rl}
-2 < & x + 16 \\
-16 \quad & -16 \\
\hline
-18 < & x
\end{array}
$$

Subtract 16 from both sides.

Check

$$
-2 < x + 16
$$
$$
-2 \overset{?}{<} 0 + 16
$$
$$
-2 \overset{?}{<} 16 \ ✔
$$

0 is greater than −18. Substitute 0 for x.

EXAMPLE 3 *Weather Application*

Sunday's high temperature of 72 °F was at least 40 °F higher than Monday's high temperature. What was Monday's high temperature?

Sunday's high	was at least	40 °F higher than		Monday's high.
72	$\geq$	40	+	t

$$
\begin{array}{rl}
72 \geq & 40 + t \\
-40 \quad & -40 \\
\hline
32 \geq & t \\
t \leq & 32
\end{array}
$$

Subtract 40 from both sides.
Rewrite the inequality.

Monday's high temperature was at most 32 °F.

Think and Discuss

1. **Compare** solving addition and subtraction equations with solving addition and subtraction inequalities.

2. **Describe** how to check whether −36 is a solution of $s - 5 > 1$.

Learn It Online
Homework Help Online
Exercises 1–21, 23, 25, 27, 29, 31, 35, 39

GUIDED PRACTICE

See Example 1   **Solve. Then graph each solution set on a number line.**

1. $x - 9 < 18$ **2.** $y - 11 \geq -7$ **3.** $4 \geq p - 3$

See Example 2   **Solve. Check each answer.**

4. $n + 5 > 26$ **5.** $b + 21 \leq -3$ **6.** $9 \leq 12 + k$

See Example 3   **7. Weather** Yesterday's high temperature was 30 °F. Tomorrow's weather forecast includes a high temperature that is no more than 12 °F warmer than yesterday's. What high temperatures are forecast for tomorrow?

INDEPENDENT PRACTICE

See Example 1   **Solve. Then graph each solution set on a number line.**

8. $s - 2 > 14$ **9.** $m - 14 < -3$ **10.** $b - 25 > -30$

11. $c - 17 \leq -6$ **12.** $-25 > y - 53$ **13.** $71 \leq x - 9$

See Example 2   **Solve. Check each answer.**

14. $w + 16 < 4$ **15.** $z + 9 > -3$ **16.** $p + 21 \leq -4$

17. $26 < f + 32$ **18.** $65 > k + 54$ **19.** $n + 29 \geq 25$

See Example 3   **20.** Clark scored at least 12 points more than Josh scored. Josh scored 15 points. How many points did Clark score?

21. Life Science Adriana is helping track bird populations. She counted 8 fewer birds on Tuesday than on Thursday. She counted at most 32 birds on Thursday. How many birds did Adriana count on Tuesday?

PRACTICE AND PROBLEM SOLVING

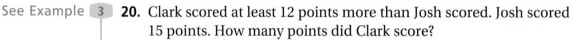

Extra Practice
See Extra Practice for more exercises.

Solve.

22. $k + 3.2 \geq 8$ **23.** $a - 1.3 > -1$ **24.** $c - 6\frac{1}{2} < -1\frac{1}{4}$

25. $-20 \geq 18 + m$ **26.** $4 < x + 7.02$ **27.** $g + 3\frac{2}{3} < 10$

28. $-109 > r - 58$ **29.** $5.9 + w \leq 21.6$ **30.** $n - 21.6 > 26$

31. $-150 \leq t + 92$ **32.** $y + 4\frac{3}{4} \geq 1\frac{1}{8}$ **33.** $v - 0.9 \leq -1.5$

34. Consumer Math To get a group discount for baseball tickets, Marco's group must have at least 20 people. The group needs at least 7 more people to sign up. How many have signed up so far?

35. Mila wants to spend at least $20 on a classified ad in the newspaper. She has $12. How much more does she need?

Animals

Dogs can be trained to accompany people with hearing impairments. The dogs can alert them to fire alarms, telephones, doorbells, and other noises.

36. Transportation The *shinkansen*, or bullet train, of Japan travels at an average speed of 162.3 miles per hour. It has a top speed of 186 miles per hour. At most, how many more miles per hour can the train travel beyond its average speed before it reaches its maximum speed?

37. Life Science The giant spider crab, the world's largest crab, lives off the southeastern coast of Japan. Giant spider crabs can grow as much as 3.6 meters across. A scientist finds one that could still grow another 0.5 m across. How wide is the giant spider crab that he found?

38. The line graph shows the number of miles Amelia rode her bike in each of the last four months. She wants to ride at least 5 miles more in May than she did in April. At least how many miles does Amelia want to ride in May?

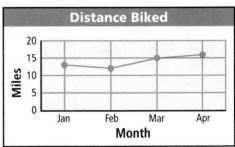

39. Physical Science The average human ear can detect sounds that have frequencies between 20 hertz and 20,000 hertz. The average dog ear can detect sounds with frequencies of up to 30,000 hertz greater than those a human ear can detect. Up to how many hertz can a dog hear?

? 40. Choose a Strategy If five days ago was the day after Saturday, what was the day before yesterday?

41. Write About It Explain how to solve and check the inequality $n - 9 < -15$.

42. Challenge Solve the inequality $x + \left(4^2 - 2^3\right)^2 > -1$.

Test Prep

43. Multiple Choice Which inequality has the following graphed solution?

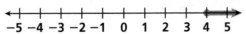

Ⓐ $x - 2 \geq -2$ Ⓑ $x + 3 \geq 7$ Ⓒ $x - 3 \leq 1$ Ⓓ $x + 5 < 9$

44. Short Response The highest-paid employee at the movie theater is the manager, who earns \$10.25 per hour. The lowest-paid employees earn \$3.90 less per hour than the manager. Write and graph a compound inequality to show all the other hourly wages earned at the movie theater.

Solving Inequalities by Multiplying or Dividing

COMMON CORE

CC.7.EE.4 Use variables to represent quantities in a real-world or mathematical problem, and construct simple equations and inequalities to solve problems by reasoning about the quantities.

Some problems will require you to multiply or divide to solve an inequality. There are special rules for multiplying and dividing to solve an inequality.

Multiplication and Division Properties of Inequality	
Positive	**Negative**
You can multiply or divide both sides of an inequality by the same **positive number**, and the statement will still be true.	You can multiply or divide both sides of an inequality by the same **negative number**, but you must reverse the direction of the inequality symbol for the statement to be true.
$8 > 6$ $\quad$ $8 \cdot 2 > 6 \cdot 2$ $\quad$ $16 > 12$ $\qquad$ $-10 \le 14$ $\quad$ $\dfrac{-10}{2} \le \dfrac{14}{2}$ $\quad$ $-5 \le 7$	$3 \ge -2$ $\quad$ $3(-3) \le -2(-3)$ $\quad$ $-9 \le 6$ $\qquad$ $-9 < 18$ $\quad$ $\dfrac{-9}{-9} > \dfrac{18}{-9}$ $\quad$ $1 > -2$

Notice that you reverse the direction of the inequality symbol when you multiply or divide both sides of an inequality by a negative number. If you do not, the resulting inequality will not be correct.

$$4 < 5$$
$$4(-1) \overset{?}{<} 5(-1)$$
$$-4 \overset{?}{<} -5$$
$$-4 > -5$$

EXAMPLE 1   Using the Multiplication Property of Inequality

Interactivities Online ▶

Solve.

A $\dfrac{x}{11} < 3$

$$\dfrac{x}{11} < 3$$

$$(11)\dfrac{x}{11} < (11)3 \qquad \textit{Multiply both sides by 11.}$$

$$x < 33$$

B $4.8 \le \dfrac{r}{-6}$

$$4.8 \le \dfrac{r}{-6}$$

$$(-6)4.8 \ge (-6)\dfrac{r}{-6} \qquad \textit{Multiply both sides by } -6, \text{ and}$$
$$\textit{reverse the inequality symbol.}$$

$$-28.8 \ge r$$

EXAMPLE 2 **Using the Division Property of Inequality**

Solve. Check each answer.

A $4x > 9$

$4x > 9$

$\dfrac{4x}{4} > \dfrac{9}{4}$ *Divide both sides by 4.*

$x > \dfrac{9}{4}$, or $2\dfrac{1}{4}$

Check

$4x > 9$

$4(3) \overset{?}{>} 9$ *3 is greater than $2\frac{1}{4}$. Substitute 3 for x.*

$12 \overset{?}{>} 9$ ✔

B $-60 \ge -12y$

$-60 \ge -12y$

$\dfrac{-60}{-12} \le \dfrac{-12y}{-12}$ *Divide both sides by -12, and reverse the inequality symbol.*

$5 \le y$

Check

$-60 \ge -12y$

$-60 \overset{?}{\ge} -12(10)$ *10 is greater than 5. Substitute 10 for y.*

$-60 \overset{?}{\ge}$

EXAMPLE 3 *Agriculture Application*

It cost the Schmidts $517 to raise watermelons. How many watermelons must they sell at $5 apiece to make a profit?

To make a profit, the Schmidts need to earn more than $517. Let w represent the number of watermelons they must sell.

$5w > 517$ *Write an inequality.*

$\dfrac{5w}{5} > \dfrac{517}{5}$ *Divide both sides by 5.*

$w > 103.4$

The Schmidts cannot sell 0.4 watermelon, so they need to sell at least 104 watermelons to earn a profit.

Agriculture LINK

In Japan, some watermelons are grown in glass boxes, making them cube-shaped. These watermelons are easier to store and ship, but are also more expensive.

MATHEMATICAL PRACTICES

Think and Discuss

1. **Compare** solving multiplication and division equations with solving multiplication and division inequalities.

2. **Explain** how you would solve the inequality $0.5y > 4.5$.

GUIDED PRACTICE

See Example 1 Solve.

1. $\frac{w}{8} < -4$

2. $\frac{z}{-6} \geq 7$

3. $-4 < \frac{p}{-12}$

See Example 2 Solve. Check each answer.

4. $3m > -15$

5. $11 > -8y$

6. $25c \leq 200$

See Example 3 7. It cost Deirdre \$212 to make candles. How many candles must she sell at \$8 apiece to make a profit?

INDEPENDENT PRACTICE

See Example 1 Solve.

8. $\frac{s}{5} > 1.4$

9. $\frac{m}{-4} < -13$

10. $\frac{b}{6} > -30$

11. $\frac{c}{-10} \leq 12$

12. $\frac{y}{9} < 2.5$

13. $\frac{x}{1.1} \geq -1$

See Example 2 Solve. Check each answer.

14. $6w < 4$

15. $-5z > -3$

16. $15p \leq -45$

17. $-9f > 27$

18. $20k < 30$

19. $-18n \geq 180$

See Example 3 20. Attendance at a museum more than tripled from Monday to Saturday. On Monday, 186 people went to the museum. How many people went to the museum on Saturday?

21. It cost George \$678 to make wreaths. How many wreaths must he sell at \$15 apiece to make a profit?

PRACTICE AND PROBLEM SOLVING

Extra Practice
See Extra Practice for more exercises.

Solve.

22. $\frac{a}{65} \leq -10$

23. $0.4p > 1.6$

24. $-\frac{m}{5} < -20$

25. $\frac{2}{3}y \geq 12$

26. $\frac{x}{-9} \leq \frac{3}{5}$

27. $\frac{g}{2.1} > 0.3$

28. $\frac{r}{6} \geq \frac{2}{3}$

29. $4w \leq 1\frac{1}{2}$

30. $-10n < 10^2$

31. $-1\frac{3}{5}t > -4$

32. $-\frac{y}{12} < 3\frac{1}{2}$

33. $5.6v \geq -14$

34. A community theater group produced 8 plays over the last two years. The group's goal for the next two years is to produce at least $1\frac{1}{2}$ times as many plays as they did in the two previous years. How many plays does the group want to produce in the next two years?

35. Tammy is going to a family reunion 350 miles away. She plans to travel no faster than 70 miles per hour. What is the least amount of time it will take her to get there?

36. Social Studies Of the total U.S. population, about 874,000 people are Pacific Islanders. The graph shows where most of these Americans live.

a. How many Pacific Islanders live in the Midwest?

b. How many Pacific Islanders live in the South?

c. Critical Thinking How many Pacific Islanders live in the Midwest and Northeast combined?

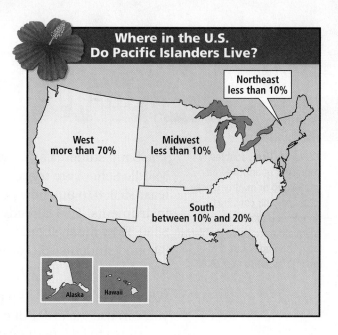

Where in the U.S. Do Pacific Islanders Live?

Northeast less than 10%

West more than 70%

Midwest less than 10%

South between 10% and 20%

Alaska   Hawaii

37. Seventh-graders at Mountain Middle School have sold 360 subscriptions to magazines. This is $\frac{3}{4}$ of the number of subscriptions that they need to sell to reach their goal and to beat the eighth grade's sales. How many total subscriptions must they sell to reach their goal?

38. Recreation Malcolm has saved $362 to spend on his vacation. He wants to have at least $35 a day available to spend. How many days of vacation does Malcolm have enough money for?

39. Write a Problem Write a word problem that can be solved using the inequality $\frac{x}{2} \geq 7$. Solve the inequality.

40. Write About It Explain how to solve the inequality $\frac{n}{-8} < -40$.

41. Challenge Use what you have learned about solving multi-step equations to solve the inequality $4x - 5 \leq 7x + 4$.

Test Prep

42. Multiple Choice Solve $\frac{x}{4} > -2$.

Ⓐ $x > -8$　　　　Ⓑ $x < -8$　　　　Ⓒ $x < 8$　　　　Ⓓ $x > 8$

43. Gridded Response It cost John and Jamie $150 to grow tomatoes. They sell each tomato for $0.50. How many tomatoes must they sell to make a profit?

Solving Multi-Step Inequalities

CC.7.EE.4 Use variables to represent quantities in a real-world or mathematical problem, and construct simple equations and inequalities to solve problems by reasoning about the quantities. *Also CC.7.EE.4b*

The band students at Newman Middle School are trying to raise at least $5,000 to buy new percussion instruments. They already have raised $850. How much should each of the 83 band students still raise, on average, to meet the goal?

When you solve two-step equations, you can use the order of operations in reverse to isolate the variable. You can use the same process when solving two-step inequalities.

EXAMPLE 1 Solving Two-Step Inequalities

Solve. Then graph each solution set on a number line.

A $\dfrac{x}{5} - 15 < 10$

$$\dfrac{x}{5} - 15 < 10$$

$$\underline{+15 \qquad +15}$$ *Add 15 to both sides.*

$$\dfrac{x}{5} < 25$$

$$(5)\dfrac{x}{5} < (5)25$$ *Multiply both sides by 5.*

$$x < 125$$

<--+---+---+---+---+---+---⊖---+---+-->
−25 0 25 50 75 100 125 150 175

B $42 \le \dfrac{y}{-9} + 30$

$$42 \le \dfrac{y}{-9} + 30$$

$$\underline{-30 -30}$$ *Subtract 30 from both sides.*

$$12 \le \dfrac{y}{-9}$$

$$-9(12) \ge (-9)\dfrac{y}{-9}$$ *Multiply both sides by −9, and reverse the inequality symbol.*

$$-108 \ge y$$

<--+---+---+---+---●---+---+-->
−124 −120 −116 −112 −108 −104 −100

Video   **Lesson Tutorials Online**

EXAMPLE 2 Solving Multi-Step Inequalities

Solve. Then graph each solution set on a number line.

A $3x - 12 - x > -18$

$$2x - 12 > -18 \qquad \text{Combine like terms.}$$
$$\underline{+12 \qquad +12} \qquad \text{Add 12 to both sides.}$$
$$2x > -6 \qquad \text{Divide both sides by 2.}$$
$$\frac{2x}{2} > \frac{-6}{2}$$
$$x > -3$$

$-12\ -11\ -10\ -9\ -8\ -7\ -6$

B $-5(x + 2) - 7 \leq 38$

$$-5(x) - 5(2) - 7 \leq 38 \qquad \text{Distribute the } -5 \text{ on the left side.}$$
$$-5x - 10 - 7 \leq 38 \qquad \text{Simplify.}$$
$$-5x - 17 \leq 38 \qquad \text{Combine like terms.}$$
$$\underline{+17 \qquad +17} \qquad \text{Add 17 to both sides.}$$
$$-5x \leq 55 \qquad \text{Divide both sides by } -5 \text{, and reverse}$$
$$\frac{-5x}{-5} \geq \frac{55}{-5} \qquad \text{the inequality symbol.}$$
$$x \geq -11$$

$-12\ -11\ -10\ -9\ -8\ -7\ -6$

EXAMPLE 3 *School Application*

The 83 members of the Newman Middle School Band are trying to raise at least $5,000 to buy new percussion instruments. They have already raised $850. How much should each student still raise, on average, to meet the goal?

Let d represent the average amount each student should still raise.

$$83d + 850 \geq 5{,}000 \qquad \text{Write an inequality.}$$
$$\underline{- 850 \qquad - 850} \qquad \text{Subtract 850 from both sides.}$$
$$83d \geq 4{,}150$$
$$\frac{83d}{83} \geq \frac{4{,}150}{83} \qquad \text{Divide both sides by 83.}$$
$$d \geq 50$$

On average, each band member should raise at least $50.

MATHEMATICAL PRACTICES

Think and Discuss

1. Tell how you would solve the inequality $8x + 5 < 20$.

2. Explain why the *greater than or equal to* symbol was used in the inequality in Example 3.

GUIDED PRACTICE

Solve. Then graph each solution set on a number line.

See Example 1
1. $5x + 3 < 18$
2. $-19 \geq \frac{z}{7} + 23$
3. $3y - 4 \geq 14$

See Example 2
4. $5m - 1 + 2m < 20$
5. $28 \leq 6(x + 4)$
6. $5t > 3t - 10$

See Example 3
7. Three students collected more than $93 washing cars. They used $15 to reimburse their parents for cleaning supplies. Then they divided the remaining money equally. How much did each student earn?

INDEPENDENT PRACTICE

Solve. Then graph each solution set on a number line.

See Example 1
8. $5s - 7 > -42$
9. $\frac{b}{2} + 3 < 9$
10. $19 \leq -2q + 5$

11. $-8c - 11 \leq 13$
12. $\frac{y}{-4} + 6 > 10$
13. $\frac{x}{9} - 5 \leq -8$

See Example 2
14. $4(4 - r) + 1 > 13$
15. $3j - 8 - 5j \geq -16$
16. $4d - 12 + 2d < 6$

See Example 3
17. Rico has $5.00. Bagels cost $0.65 each, and a small container of cream cheese costs $1.00. What is the greatest number of bagels Rico can buy if he also buys one small container of cream cheese?

18. The 35 members of a drill team are trying to raise at least $1,200 to cover travel costs to a training camp. They have already raised $500. How much should each member still raise, on average, to meet the goal?

PRACTICE AND PROBLEM SOLVING

Extra Practice
See Extra Practice for more exercises.

Solve.

19. $32 \geq -4x + 8$
20. $0.5 + \frac{n}{5} > -0.5$
21. $1.4 + \frac{c}{3} < 2$

22. $-1 < -\frac{3}{4}b - 2.2$
23. $12 + 2w - 8 \leq 20$
24. $5k + 6 - k \geq -14$

25. $\frac{s}{2} + 9 > 12 - 15$
26. $2(4t - 6) - 10t < -6$
27. $\frac{d}{2} + 1 + \frac{d}{2} \leq 5$

28. Mr. Monroe keeps a bag of small prizes to distribute to his students. He likes to keep at least twice as many prizes in the bag as he has students. The bag currently has 79 prizes in it. Mr. Monroe has 117 students. How many more prizes does he need to buy?

29. Manny needs to buy 5 work shirts that are each the same price. After he uses a $20 gift certificate, he can spend no more than $50. What is the maximum amount that each shirt can cost?

30. **Business** Darcy earns a salary of $1,400 per month, plus a commission of 4% of her sales. She wants to earn a total of at least $1,600 this month. What is the least amount of sales she needs?

31. **Multi-Step** The bar graph shows how many students from Warren Middle School participated in a reading challenge each of the past four years. This year, the goal is for at least 10 more students to participate than the average number of participants from the past four years. What is the goal for this year?

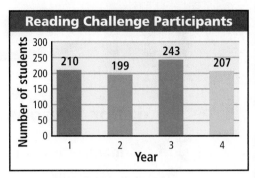

Reading Challenge Participants

32. **Consumer Math** Michael wants to buy a belt that costs $18. He also wants to buy some shirts that are on sale for $14 each. He has $70. At most, how many shirts can Michael buy together with the belt?

33. **Earth Science** A granite rock contains the minerals feldspar, quartz, and biotite mica. The rock has $\frac{1}{3}$ as much biotite mica as quartz. The rock is at least 30% quartz. What percent of the rock is feldspar?

Feldspar   Quartz

Biotite mica   Granite

34. **What's the Error?** A student's solution to the inequality $\frac{x}{-9} - 5 > 2$ was $x > 63$. What error did the student make in the solution?

35. **Write About It** Explain how to solve the inequality $4y + 6 < -2$.

36. **Challenge** A student scored 92, 87, and 85 on three tests. She wants her average score for five tests to be at least 90. What is the lowest score the student can get, on average, on her fourth and fifth tests?

Test Prep

37. **Multiple Choice** Which inequality has the following graphed solution?

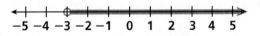

-5 -4 -3 -2 -1 0 1 2 3 4 5

Ⓐ $2x - 5 > 1$ Ⓑ $-x + 3 < 6$ Ⓒ $3x - 12 < -3$ Ⓓ $-5x - 2 > -13$

38. **Gridded Response** Gretta earns $450 per week plus a 10% commission on book sales. How many dollars of books must she sell to earn at least $650 per week?

Quiz for Lessons 4 Through 7

 **4** **Inequalities**

Write an inequality for each situation.

1. Gray has at least 25 blue T-shirts.

2. The room can hold no more than 50 people.

Graph each inequality.

3. $b > -1$ **4.** $5 \leq t$ **5.** $-3 \geq x$

Graph each compound inequality.

6. $5 \geq p$ and $p > -1$ **7.** $-8 > g$ or $g \geq -1$ **8.** $-4 \leq x < 0$

5 **Solving Inequalities by Adding or Subtracting**

Solve. Then graph each solution set on a number line.

9. $28 > m - 4$ **10.** $8 + c \geq -13$ **11.** $-1 + v < 1$

12. $5 \leq p - 3$ **13.** $-8 > f + 1$ **14.** $-7 - w < 10$

15. A group of climbers are at an altitude of at most 17,500 feet. They are on their way to the top of Mount Everest, which is at an altitude of 29,035 feet. How many more feet do they have left to climb?

6 **Solving Inequalities by Multiplying or Dividing**

Solve. Check each answer.

16. $-8s > 16$ **17.** $\frac{x}{-2} \leq 9$ **18.** $-7 \leq \frac{b}{3}$

19. $\frac{c}{-3} \geq -4$ **20.** $28 > 7h$ **21.** $6y < -2$

7 **Solving Multi-Step Inequalities**

Solve. Then graph each solution set on a number line.

22. $2x - 3 > 5$ **23.** $3 \geq -2d + 4$ **24.** $3g - 2 - 10g > 5$

25. $14 < -2a + 6 - 2a$ **26.** $3.6(1 + 2k) + 2 < 27.2$ **27.** $5z - 2 - 2z \leq 13$

28. A concert is being held in a gymnasium that can hold no more than 450 people. The bleachers seat 60 people. There will also be 26 rows of chairs set up. At most, how many people can sit in each row?

29. The 23 members of the Westview Journalism Club are trying to raise at least $2,100 to buy new publishing design software. The members have already raised $1,180. How much should each student still raise, on average, to meet the goal?

MATHEMATICAL PRACTICES Reason abstractly and quantitatively.

CHAPTER
11

Rock Climbing New Hampshire is nicknamed the Granite State, so it's not surprising that it offers some of the best rock climbing in the country. For those who want to practice or take lessons, the state has more than a dozen indoor climbing gyms.

NEW HAMPSHIRE

1. Ethan is planning to learn rock climbing at an indoor climbing gym. The table shows the day-use fees and cost of lessons at Indoor Ascent.

   a. Look for a pattern in the table. Let x represent the number of days. Write an expression for the fees.

   b. The total cost is the price of the two lessons plus the day-use fees. Write an expression that gives the total cost for x days.

2. A different gym has a day-use fee of $25, but the two lessons are included for free. Write and solve an inequality to find out when it is less expensive to go to Indoor Ascent.

3. Ethan's budget for lessons and fees at Indoor Ascent is $185. Write and solve an equation to find out how many days he can go to that gym.

4. Ethan saves $45 per month. For how many months must he save to have at least enough money to pay for the lessons and fees? Show how to solve this problem using an inequality.

INDOOR ASCENT CLIMBING GYM

Day-Use Fees		Lessons
Days	Fees	Introductory Lesson $35
1	$12	
2	$24	Technique Lesson $30
3	$36	
4	$48	

Real-World Connections

Jose Azel/Aurora/Getty Images

Game Time

Flapjacks

Five pancakes of different sizes are stacked in a random order. How can you get the pancakes in order from largest to smallest by flipping portions of the stack?

To find the answer, stack five disks of different sizes in no particular order. Arrange the disks from largest to smallest in the fewest number of moves possible. Move disks by choosing a disk and flipping over the whole stack from that disk up.

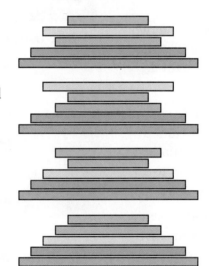

Start with a stack of five.

Flip the stack from the second disk up.

Now flip the stack from the third disk up.

Finally, flip the stack from the second disk up.

At most, it should take $3n - 2$ turns, where n is the number of disks, to arrange the disks from largest to smallest. The five disks above were arranged in three turns, which is less than $3(5) - 2 = 13$. Try it on your own.

Leaping Counters

Remove all but one of the counters from the board by jumping over each counter with another and removing the jumped counter. The game is over when you can no longer jump a counter. A perfect game would result in one counter being left in the center of the board.

A complete copy of the rules and a game board are available online.

Learn It Online
Game Time Extra

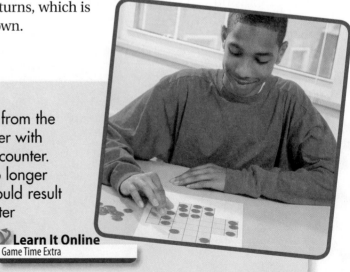

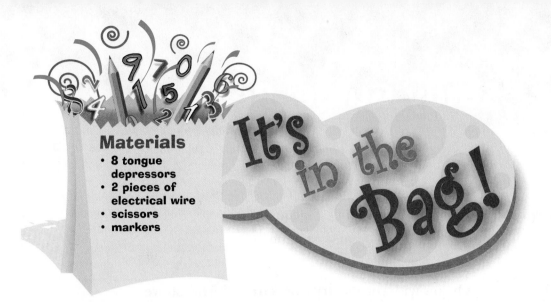

Materials
- 8 tongue depressors
- 2 pieces of electrical wire
- scissors
- markers

It's in the Bag!

PROJECT | **Wired for Multi-Step Equations**

These "study sticks" will help you sort out the steps in solving equations.

Directions

❶ Twist a piece of electrical wire around each end of a tongue depressor. Twist the wire tightly so that it holds the tongue depressor securely. **Figure A**

❷ Slide another tongue depressor between the ends of the wires. Slide it down as far as possible and then twist the wires together to hold this tongue depressor securely. **Figure B**

❸ Continue in the same way with the remaining tongue depressors.

❹ Twist the wires together at the top to make a handle. Trim the wires as needed.

Taking Note of the Math

Write the title of the chapter on the top tongue depressor. On each of the remaining tongue depressors, write the steps for solving a sample multi-step equation.

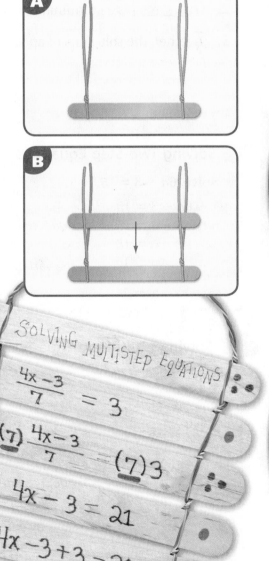

SOLVING MULTISTEP EQUATIONS

$$\frac{4x-3}{7} = 3$$

$$(7)\frac{4x-3}{7} = (7)3$$

$$4x - 3 = 21$$

$$4x - 3 + 3 = 21 + 3$$

$$4x = 24$$

$$\frac{4x}{}$$

Study Guide: Review

Vocabulary

algebraic inequality

inequality

compound inequality

solution set

Complete the sentences below with vocabulary words from the list above.

1. A(n) __?__ states that two quantities either are not equal or may not be equal.

2. A(n) __?__ is a combination of more than one inequality.

3. Together, the solutions of an inequality are called the __?__.

EXAMPLES

EXERCISES

1 Solving Two-Step Equations

■ Solve $6a - 3 = 15$.

$$6a - 3 = 15$$
$$6a - 3 + 3 = 15 + 3 \quad \textit{Add 3 to both sides.}$$
$$6a = 18 \qquad \textit{Divide to isolate}$$
$$\frac{6a}{6} = \frac{18}{6} \qquad \textit{the variable.}$$
$$a = 3$$

Solve.

4. $-5y + 6 = -34$

5. $9 + \frac{z}{6} = 14$

6. $-8 = \frac{w}{-7} + 13$

2 Solving Multi-Step Equations

■ Solve $\frac{4x - 3}{7} = 3$.

$$\frac{4x - 3}{7} = 3$$
$$(7)\frac{4x - 3}{7} = (7)3 \quad \textit{Multiply.}$$
$$4x - 3 = 21$$
$$4x - 3 + 3 = 21 + 3 \quad \textit{Add 3 to both sides.}$$
$$4x = 24$$
$$\frac{4x}{4} = \frac{24}{4} \qquad \textit{Divide both}$$
$$\textit{sides by 4.}$$
$$x = 6$$

Solve.

7. $7a + 4 - 13a = 46$ 8. $9 = \frac{6j - 18}{4}$

9. $\frac{8b - 5}{3} = 9$ 10. $52 = -9 + 16y - 19$

11. Noelle biked twice as many miles as Leila. Adding 2 to the number of miles Noelle biked and dividing by 3 gives the number of miles Dani biked. Dani biked 18 miles. How many miles did Leila bike?

3 Solving Equations with Variables on Both Sides

Solve $8a = 3a + 25$.

$$8a = 3a + 25$$
$$8a - 3a = 3a - 3a + 25 \quad \textit{Subtract.}$$
$$5a = 25$$
$$\frac{5a}{5} = \frac{25}{5} \quad \textit{Divide.}$$
$$a = 5$$

Solve.

12. $-6b + 9 = 12b$

13. $5 - 7c = -3c - 19$

14. $18m - 14 = 12m + 2$

15. $4 - \frac{2}{5}x = \frac{1}{5}x - 8$

16. Mercedes saves $50 each month. Ken saves $40 each month, and he started with $100. After how many months will they have the same amount saved?

4 Inequalities

Write an inequality for each situation.

- You have to be at least 16 years old to drive a car in New Jersey.
  age of driver ≥ 16

- Graph $x < -1$.

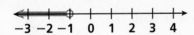

Write an inequality for each situation.

17. A bridge's load limit is at most 9 tons.

18. The large tree in the park is more than 200 years old.

Graph each inequality.

19. $y \geq 3$

20. $-2 \leq k < -1$

5 Solving Inequalities by Adding or Subtracting

Solve. Graph each solution set.

- $b + 6 > -10$

$$b + 6 > -10$$
$$b + 6 - 6 > -10 - 6$$
$$b > -16$$

- $p - 17 \leq 25$

$$p - 17 \leq 25$$
$$p - 17 + 17 \leq 25 + 17$$
$$p \leq 42$$

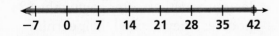

Solve. Graph each solution set.

21. $r - 16 > 9$

22. $-14 \geq 12 + x$

23. $\frac{3}{4} + g < 8\frac{3}{4}$

24. $\frac{5}{6} > \frac{2}{3} + t$

25. $7.46 > r - 1.54$

26. $u - 57.7 \geq -123.7$

27. The Wildcats scored at least 13 more points than the Stingrays scored. The Stingrays scored 25 points. How many points did the Wildcats score?

28. Gabe saved $113. This amount was at least $19 more than his brother saved. How much money did Gabe's brother save?

6 Solving Inequalities by Multiplying or Dividing

Solve.

■ $\frac{m}{-4} \geq 3.8$

$\frac{m}{-4} \geq 3.8$

$(-4)\frac{m}{-4} \leq (-4)3.8$ *Multiply and reverse the inequality symbol.*

$m \leq -15.2$

■ $8b < -48$

$8b < -48$

$\frac{8b}{8} < -\frac{48}{8}$ *Divide both sides by 8.*

$b < -6$

Solve.

29. $\frac{n}{-8} > 6.9$

30. $-18 \leq -3p$

31. $\frac{k}{13} < -10$

32. $-5p > -25$

33. $2.3 \leq \frac{v}{1.2}$

34. $\frac{c}{-11} < -3$

35. It cost Carlita $204 to make beaded purses. How many purses must Carlita sell at $13 apiece to make a profit?

7 Solving Multi-Step Inequalities

Solve. Graph each solution set.

■ $\frac{k}{3} - 18 > 24$

$\frac{k}{3} - 18 > 24$

$\frac{k}{3} - 18 + 18 > 24 + 18$

$\frac{k}{3} > 42$

$(3)\frac{k}{3} > (3)42$

$k > 126$

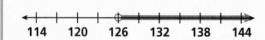

■ $-10b + 11 + 5b \leq -4$

$-10b + 11 + 5b \leq -4$

$-5b + 11 \leq -4$

$-5b + 11 - 11 \leq -4 - 11$

$-5b \leq -15$

$\frac{-5b}{-5} \geq \frac{-15}{-5}$

$b \geq 3$

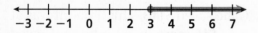

Solve. Graph each solution set.

36. $-7b - 16 > -2$

37. $3.8 + \frac{d}{5} < 2.6$

38. $15 - 4n + 9 \leq 40$

39. $\frac{y}{-3} + 18 \geq 12$

40. $\frac{c}{3} + 7 > -11$

41. $32 \geq 4x - 8$

42. $18 + \frac{h}{6} \geq -8$

43. $14 > -2t - 6$

44. $-3 < \frac{w}{-2} + 10 + \frac{w}{4}$

45. $3\left(\frac{y}{21} + 1.3\right) \leq 8.9$

46. Luis has $53.55. T-shirts cost $8.95 each, and a belt costs $16.75. How many T-shirts can Luis buy if he also buys a new belt?

47. Clay, Alberto, and Ciana earned more than $475 by teaching swimming lessons together. After paying the $34 pool fee, they divided their earnings equally. How much money did each teacher earn?

Study Guide: Review

Chapter Test

Solve.

1. $3y - 8 = 16$

2. $\frac{x}{3} + 12 = -4$

3. $\frac{a}{6} - 7 = -4$

4. $-7b + 5 = -51$

5. $\frac{5y - 4}{3} = 7$

6. $8r + 7 - 13 = 58$

7. $6 = \frac{12s - 6}{5}$

8. $8.7 = \frac{19.8 - 4t}{3}$

9. $-14q = 4q - 126$

10. $\frac{5}{6}p + 4 = \frac{1}{6}p - 16$

11. $9 - 6k = 3k - 54$

12. $-3.6d = -7d + 34$

13. The bill for the repair of a computer was $179. The cost of the parts was $44, and the labor charge was $45 per hour. How many hours did it take to repair the computer?

14. Members of the choir are baking cookies for a fund-raiser. It costs $2.25 to make a dozen cookies, and the choir's initial expenses were $15.75. They sell the cookies for $4.50 a dozen. How many dozen do they have to sell to cover their costs?

Write an inequality for each situation.

15. You must be more than 4 ft tall to go on the ride.

16. You cannot go more than 65 miles per hour on Route 18.

Graph each inequality.

17. $a < -2$

18. $-5 < d$ and $d \leq 2$

19. $c > -1$ or $c < -5$

20. $b \geq 3$

Solve. Then graph each solution set on a number line.

21. $n + 8 < -9$

22. $n - 124 > -59$

23. $-40 > \frac{x}{32}$

24. $-\frac{3}{4}y \leq -12$

25. Rosa wants to save at least $125 to buy a new skateboard. She has already saved $46. How much more does Rosa need to save?

26. Gasoline costs $2.75 a gallon. At most, how many gallons can be bought for $22.00?

Solve. Then graph each solution set on a number line.

27. $m - 7.8 \leq 23.7$

28. $6z > -2\frac{2}{3}$

29. $\frac{w}{-4.9} \leq 3.4$

30. $-15 < 4a + 9$

31. $2.8 - \frac{c}{4} \geq 7.4$

32. $2\left(\frac{d}{10} - 4\right) > -4$

33. The seventh-grade students at Fulmore Middle School are trying to raise at least $7,500 for the local public library. So far, each of the 198 students has raised an average of $20. How much more money must each seventh-grader collect, on average, to reach the goal?

Chapter Test

Cumulative Assessment

Multiple Choice

1. Nolan has 7 red socks, 3 black socks, 10 white socks, and 5 blue socks in a drawer. If Nolan chooses one sock at a time and puts the sock immediately on his foot, what is the probability that he will choose 2 white socks?

   (A) $\frac{3}{20}$ (C) $\frac{2}{5}$

   (B) $\frac{4}{25}$ (D) $\frac{19}{25}$

2. Of the 10,500 books in the school library, $\frac{2}{5}$ of the books are fiction. Given that 30% of the remaining books are biographies, how many books are biographies?

   (F) 4,200   (H) 1,260

   (G) 2,940   (J) 1,890

3. There are 126 girls and 104 boys attending a luncheon. Each person at the luncheon writes his or her name on a piece of paper and puts the paper in a barrel. One name is randomly selected from the barrel to win a new MP3 player. What is the probability the person selected is male?

   (A) 45.2%   (C) 82.5%

   (B) 54.8%   (D) Not here

4. A trapezoid has two bases, b_1 and b_2, and height h. For which values of b_1, b_2, and h is the area of the trapezoid equal to 16 in²?

   (F) $b_1 = 8$ in., $b_2 = 4$ in., $h = 2$ in.

   (G) $b_1 = 5$ in., $b_2 = 3$ in., $h = 4$ in.

   (H) $b_1 = 2$ in., $b_2 = 8$ in., $h = 6$ in.

   (J) $b_1 = 2$ in., $b_2 = 4$ in., $h = 4$ in.

5. Between which two integers does $-\sqrt{32}$ lie?

   (A) -2 and -3 (C) 0 and -1

   (B) -5 and -6 (D) -7 and -8

6. Three friends divide $2\frac{1}{2}$ pounds of grapes evenly. How many pounds of grapes does each friend receive?

   (F) $\frac{5}{6}$ pound   (H) $1\frac{1}{5}$ pounds

   (G) $\frac{2}{3}$ pound   (J) $7\frac{1}{2}$ pounds

7. Martha buys a surfboard that costs $405 for 40% off. How much money does she save?

   (A) $243   (C) $24

   (B) $162   (D) $17

8. The total number of students in seventh grade at Madison Middle School is expected to increase by 15% from year three to year four. What will enrollment be in year four?

   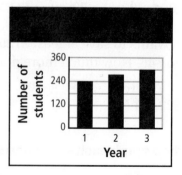

   (F) 42   (H) 345

   (G) 295   (J) 238

9. Calculate 16.0 ft − 9.03 ft.
   - Ⓐ 7.03 ft
   - Ⓑ 7 ft
   - Ⓒ 6.97 ft
   - Ⓓ 6 ft

10. Which rational number is greater than $-3\frac{1}{3}$ but less than $-\frac{4}{5}$?
    - Ⓕ −0.4
    - Ⓖ $-\frac{22}{5}$
    - Ⓗ −0.19
    - Ⓙ $-\frac{9}{7}$

11. Becky tutors third-graders two days after school each week. She saves $\frac{3}{5}$ of her earnings. What percent of her earnings does Becky save?
    - Ⓐ 35%
    - Ⓑ 45%
    - Ⓒ 60%
    - Ⓓ 70%

 HOT TIP! Create and use a number line to help you order rational numbers quickly.

Gridded Response

12. Solve: $25 - 3x = 4$

13. Fiona has 18 coins, consisting of quarters and dimes, in her pocket. She has 6 more dimes than quarters. How many quarters does she have?

14. Freddy counted the number of bats he saw each night for one week. What is the median of the data set?

    Number of Bats Spotted
    42, 21, 36, 28, 40, 21, 31

15. Solve for y. $3y + 17 = -2y + 25$

16. What is the probability of flipping a coin and getting tails and then rolling a number greater than or equal to 4 on a 6-sided number cube? Write your answer as a decimal.

Short Response

S1. Solve the inequality $-7y \geq 126$ and then graph the solution set on a number line. Is zero part of the solution set? Explain.

S2. Nine less than four times a number is the same as twice the number increased by 11. What is the number?
    - a. Write the above statement as an equation.
    - b. Solve the equation.

S3. Hallie is baking 5 batches of brownies for the bake sale. Each batch requires $1\frac{2}{3}$ cups of flour. Hallie has $8\frac{1}{4}$ cups of flour. Does she have enough flour to make five batches? Explain your answer.

Extended Response

E1. Tim and his crew trim trees. They charge a service fee of $40 for each job, plus an hourly rate.

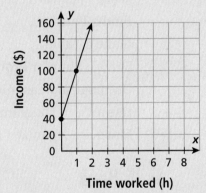

Time worked (h)

   - a. Use the graph to determine the crew's hourly rate. Explain how you found your answer.
   - b. Write an equation to find y, the crew's income for x hours of work.
   - c. How many hours did Tim's crew work if they earned $490? Show your work.

 Student Handbook

Extra Practice ... Chapter 1

LESSON 1

Simplify each expression. Use the order of operations to justify your answer.

1. $9 \div 3 + 6 \cdot 5$

2. $16 + (20 \div 5) - 3^2$

3. $(6 - 3)^3 \div 9 + 7$

4. $(4 \cdot 9) - (9 - 3)^2$

5. $5 + 9 \cdot 2^2 \div 6$

6. $6{,}842 - (5^3 \cdot 5 \cdot 10)$

7. Charlotte bought 4 shirts and 3 pairs of pants. She got the pants at a discount. Simplify the expression $4 \cdot 32 + 3 \cdot 25 - (3 \cdot 25) \div 5$ to find out how much she paid for the clothes.

LESSON 2

Tell which property is represented.

8. $9 \cdot 2 = 2 \cdot 9$

9. $9 + 0 = 9$

10. $12 \cdot 1 = 1 \cdot 12$

11. $1 \cdot (2 \cdot 3) = (1 \cdot 2) \cdot 3$

12. $xy = yx$

13. $(x + y) + z = x + (y + z)$

Simplify each expression. Justify each step.

14. $5 + 6 + 19$

15. $5 \cdot 10 \cdot 2$

16. $3 \cdot (5 \cdot 9)$

17. $(25 \cdot 8) \cdot 4$

18. $30 + (121 + 39)$

19. $125 \cdot (2 \cdot 3)$

Use the Distributive Property to find each product.

20. $8 \cdot (2 + 10)$

21. $3 \cdot (19 + 4)$

22. $(10 - 2) \cdot 7$

23. $15 \cdot (13 - 8)$

24. $(47 + 88) \cdot 4$

25. $5 \cdot (157 - 45)$

LESSON 3

Evaluate each expression for the given value of the variable.

26. $8k - 7$ for $k = 4$

27. $9n + 12$ for $n = 6$

28. $12t - 15$ for $t = 4$

29. $v \div 5 + v$ for $v = 20$

30. $3r - 20 \div r$ for $r = 5$

31. $5x^2 + 3x$ for $x = 3$

Evaluate each expression for the given value of the variables.

32. $x + \frac{15}{y} - 2$ for $x = 10$ $y = 5$

33. $3j + 4k - 20$ for $j = 12$ and $k = 2$

34. $17 + 5a - \frac{4b}{2}$ for $a = 3$ and $b = 6$

35. $s^2 - 3r + 50$ for $s = 8$ and $r = 7$

36. $\frac{m}{9} + n^2 + 5$ for $m = 36$ and $n = 6$

37. $21 + 9e - 10f$ for $e = 5$ and $f = 1$

Extra Practice ... Chapter 1

LESSON 4

Write each phrase as an algebraic expression.

38. 12 less than a number

39. the quotient of a number and 8

40. add 7 to 8 times a number

41. 6 times the sum of 13 and a number

42. A music store sells packages of guitar strings. David bought s strings for $24. Write an algebraic expression for the cost of one string.

LESSON 5

Identify like terms in each list.

43. $2d$ $5d^2$ x $4x^2$ d^2 $6x$

44. 9 $5y$ $\frac{y}{2}$ $4g^2$ y^2 y

Simplify. Justify your steps using the Commutative, Associative, and Distributive Properties when necessary.

45. $5b + 3t + b$

46. $t + 3b + 3t + 3b + x$

47. $8g + 3g + 12$

48. $3u + 6 + 5k + u$

49. $11 + 5t^2 + t + 6t$

50. $y^3 + 3y + 6y^3$

51. Write an expression for the perimeter of the given figure. Then simplify the expression.

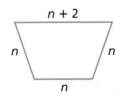

Extra Practice ... Chapter 2

LESSON 1

Use a number line to order the integers from least to greatest.

1. $5, -3, -1, 2, 0$ **2.** $-4, -1, 3, 1, 4$ **3.** $-5, 0, -3, 2, 4$

Use a number line to find each absolute value.

4. $|-22|$ **5.** $|9|$ **6.** $|-13|$ **7.** $|21|$

LESSON 2

Find each sum.

8. $8 + (-4)$ **9.** $-3 + (-6)$ **10.** $-5 + 9$ **11.** $-7 + (-2)$

Evaluate $c + d$ for the given values.

12. $c = 5, d = -9$ **13.** $c = 12, d = 9$ **14.** $c = -7, d = -2$ **15.** $c = -16, d = 8$

16. The temperature in Pierre at 8:00 A.M. was $-33\,°F$. It rose $20\,°F$ in 9 hours. What was the temperature at 5:00 P.M.?

LESSON 3

Find each difference.

17. $6 - (-3)$ **18.** $-4 - (-8)$ **19.** $2 - 7$ **20.** $3 - (-4)$

Evaluate $a - b$ for each set of values.

21. $a = 5, b = -8$ **22.** $a = -12, b = -6$ **23.** $a = 6, b = 13$ **24.** $a = 9, b = -17$

25. The highest point in the United States is Mount McKinley at about 20,320 feet. Death Valley, California, is the lowest point at about 282 feet below sea level. What is the difference in elevation between the highest and lowest points in the United States?

LESSON 4

Find each product or quotient.

26. $-9 \div 3$ **27.** $8 \cdot (-3)$ **28.** $16 \div 4$ **29.** $-7 \cdot 3$

30. $-2 \cdot 9$ **31.** $15 \div (-5)$ **32.** $6 \cdot 7$ **33.** $-72 \div (-12)$

Evaluate xy for each set of values.

34. $x = 2, y = -3$ **35.** $x = -4, y = 5$ **36.** $x = -2, y = -8$ **37.** $x = -1, y = -9$

38. A submarine descends below the ocean's surface at a rate of 75 feet per minute. How many feet below the ocean's surface will the submarine be in 12 minutes?

Extra Practice ... Chapter 2

LESSON

Solve each equation. Check your answer.

39. $n - 25 = -18$ **40.** $y + (-13) = 61$ **41.** $21 = \frac{s}{4}$ **42.** $15y = -45$

43. $\frac{k}{-18} = 2$ **44.** $h - (-7) = -42$ **45.** $6 = \frac{z}{9}$ **46.** $68 = 4 + p$

47. On Monday, Martin deposited $76 into his bank account. On Tuesday, he withdrew $100. He then had $202 in his account. How much money did he start with on Monday?

LESSON 6

Write each fraction as a decimal. Round to the nearest hundredth, if necessary.

48. $\frac{4}{5}$ **49.** $\frac{6}{8}$ **50.** $\frac{57}{15}$ **51.** $-\frac{75}{10}$

Write each decimal as a fraction in simplest form.

52. 0.85 **53.** -0.04 **54.** 0.875 **55.** 2.6

56. Brianna brought 96 CDs to sell at her concert. At the concert, she sold 84 CDs. What portion of the CDs did she sell? Write your answer as a decimal.

57. Jacob used 44 of the 60 pages in his journal. What portion of the pages did he use? Write your answer as a decimal rounded to the nearest hundredth.

LESSON 7

Compare the fractions or decimals. Write < or >.

58. $\frac{8}{13}$ $\frac{5}{13}$ **59.** 0.82 ▓ 0.88 **60.** $-\frac{8}{9}$ ▓ $-\frac{11}{12}$ **61.** -1.024 ▓ 1.007

Order the numbers from least to greatest.

62. 0.5, 0.58, $\frac{6}{13}$ **63.** 2.7, 2.59, $2\frac{7}{12}$ **64.** $-0.61, -0.55, -\frac{9}{15}$

65. Brian operates an ice cream stand in a large city. He spends 0.4 of his budget on supplies, $\frac{1}{12}$ on advertising, and 0.08 on taxes and fees. Does Brian spend more on advertising or more on taxes and fees?

Extra Practice ... Chapter 3

LESSON 1

Add or subtract. Estimate to check whether each answer is reasonable.

1. $8.79 + 45.63$

2. $-7.85 - (-34.7)$

3. $43.67 - 14.81$

4. $-18 + (-7.32)$

5. $34.43 + (-62.57)$

6. $-8.26 + 7.4$

7. $-8.75 - 5.43$

8. $-35.4 - (-24.08)$

9. Zoe gets to work in 25.5 minutes and gets home from work in 37.5 minutes. How much time does she spend commuting each day?

LESSON 2

Multiply. Estimate to check whether each answer is reasonable.

10. $4.3 \cdot 2.8$

11. $-3.38 \cdot 0.8$

12. $-8 \cdot (-0.07)$

13. $7.59 \cdot (-36)$

14. $-67.4 \cdot (-8.7)$

15. $5.66 \cdot (-16.34)$

16. $-43.9 \cdot (-4.7)$

17. $73.3 \cdot 6.85$

18. Griffin works after school and on weekends. He worked 18.5 hours last week and gets paid $7.90 per hour. How much did he earn last week?

LESSON 3

Divide. Estimate to check whether each answer is reasonable.

19. $16.9 \div (-1.3)$

20. $74.25 \div 6.6$

21. $-4.8 \div 0.12$

22. $-0.63 \div (-0.7)$

23. $-36.04 \div 4.24$

24. $34.672 \div (-4.4)$

25. $-128.685 \div 37.3$

26. $-231.28 \div (-41.3)$

27. $15 \div 2.4$

28. $70 \div -3.5$

29. $-66 \div 13.2$

30. $43 \div -8.6$

31. $-17 \div -1.7$

32. $-87 \div 5.8$

33. $-99 \div -3.3$

34. $22 \div -2.5$

35. Miley is training to run a 10K race. Miley ran 10 kilometers in 62 minutes. If she runs each kilometer at the same pace, how long did it take Miley to run one kilometer?

36. The diameter of a northern red oak tree grows an average of 0.4 inches per year. At this rate, how long will it take the tree's diameter to grow to 24.8 inches?

LESSON 4

Solve. Justify your steps.

37. $4.7 + s = 9$

38. $t - 1.35 = -22$

39. $-4.8 = -6x$

40. $9.6 = \frac{v}{8}$

41. $-6.5 + n = 5.9$

42. $x - 1.07 = -8.5$

43. $-6.2y = -21.08$

44. $\frac{r}{13} = 3.25$

45. Billy worked 7.5 hours and earned $56.70. What is Billy's hourly wage?

46. A single movie ticket costs $7.25. The Brown family consists of Mr. and Mrs. Brown, Amy, and her two brothers. What does it cost the Brown family to go to the movies together?

47. The same cereal costs $3.99 per box at one store, $3.25 per box at another store, and $3.59 per box at a third store. What is the average price per box of the cereal?

LESSON 5

Add or subtract. Write each answer in simplest form.

48. $\frac{1}{4} + \frac{1}{3}$ **49.** $\frac{3}{11} - \frac{3}{22}$ **50.** $-\frac{3}{6} + \frac{2}{3}$ **51.** $-\frac{1}{4} - \frac{7}{10}$

52. $\frac{3}{7} + \frac{5}{9}$ **53.** $\frac{7}{8} - \frac{2}{3}$ **54.** $\frac{7}{12} + \frac{5}{6}$ **55.** $\frac{4}{5} - \frac{9}{10}$

56. Jacob and Julius spent $\frac{1}{4}$ hour swimming, $\frac{1}{10}$ hour eating a snack, and then $\frac{1}{2}$ hour hiking. How long did these activities take Jacob and Julius?

LESSON 6

Multiply. Write each answer in simplest form.

57. $\frac{2}{3} \cdot 12\frac{3}{4}$ **58.** $3\frac{2}{9} \cdot \frac{1}{2}$ **59.** $\frac{5}{7} \cdot 4\frac{3}{8}$ **60.** $5\frac{2}{3} \cdot \frac{7}{12}$

61. $4\frac{3}{5} \cdot 3\frac{2}{3}$ **62.** $3\frac{1}{3} \cdot 2\frac{5}{6}$ **63.** $2\frac{1}{4} \cdot 3\frac{3}{4}$ **64.** $4\frac{1}{5} \cdot 5\frac{1}{12}$

65. $-3\frac{1}{5} \cdot -6\frac{3}{8}$ **66.** $-5 \cdot \frac{1}{3}$ **67.** $\frac{3}{7} \cdot -1\frac{1}{2}$ **68.** $-2 \cdot -3\frac{1}{10}$

69. Mary is $2\frac{1}{2}$ times as old as Victor. If Victor is $7\frac{1}{2}$ years old, how old is Mary?

70. Admission to a museum in 2008 was $22.50. In 1998, the admission price was $\frac{3}{5}$ of the admission price in 2008. What was the admission price in 1998?

LESSON 7

Divide. Write each answer in simplest form.

71. $\frac{7}{8} \div \frac{5}{6}$ **72.** $\frac{7}{12} \div \frac{7}{8}$ **73.** $\frac{2}{3} \div \frac{2}{5}$ **74.** $2\frac{1}{4} \div \frac{1}{2}$

75. $5\frac{7}{8} \div \frac{5}{6}$ **76.** $3\frac{3}{4} \div 1\frac{1}{4}$ **77.** $2\frac{5}{6} \div 4\frac{1}{3}$ **78.** $5\frac{2}{3} \div 2\frac{1}{2}$

79. $\frac{4}{5} \div 3$ **80.** $1\frac{1}{8} \div \frac{2}{9}$ **81.** $2\frac{1}{4} \div 3\frac{1}{2}$ **82.** $5 \div \frac{1}{5}$

83. Each serving of chicken weighs $\frac{1}{3}$ pound. Melanie bought 12 pounds of chicken for a party. How many servings does she have?

84. Jessika, Alfred, and Judith are driving round-trip to a football game that is 190 miles from their town. If each of them drives the same distance, how far will each person drive?

Extra Practice ... Chapter 3

LESSON 8

Solve. Write each answer in simplest form.

85. $\frac{1}{3} + s = \frac{2}{5}$ **86.** $t - \frac{3}{8} = -\frac{5}{6}$ **87.** $-\frac{5}{6} = -\frac{1}{3}x$ **88.** $\frac{2}{3}w = 240$

89. $-\frac{5}{8} + n = \frac{5}{6}$ **90.** $x - \frac{5}{8} = -\frac{5}{8}$ **91.** $-\frac{2}{3}y = -\frac{3}{4}$ **92.** $\frac{r}{6} = \frac{1}{8}$

93. $j + \frac{4}{5} = -\frac{1}{10}$ **94.** $\frac{3}{4} + e = \frac{11}{12}$ **95.** $-\frac{1}{2}s = \frac{5}{8}$ **96.** $\frac{i}{7} = \frac{2}{3}$

97. Jorge owns $1\frac{3}{4}$ acres of land. Juanita, his neighbor, owns $2\frac{2}{3}$ acres. How many acres do they own in all?

98. Kyra uses $2\frac{1}{4}$ feet of ribbon to wrap each of the identical fruit baskets that she sells. How many baskets can she wrap with a 144-foot roll of ribbon?

99. Matilda uses $1\frac{2}{3}$ cup milk for a muffin recipe. If she wants to make 3 times the amount of muffins, how much milk will she use?

Extra Practice ... Chapter 4

LESSON 1

1. Danielle skipped a rope 248 times in 4 minutes. On average, how many times did Danielle skip rope per minute?

2. A serving of 8 crackers contains 128 calories. What is the number of calories per cracker?

3. Jamie's family drives 350 miles to her grandparents' house in 7 hours. What is their average speed in miles per hour?

4. A store sells milk in three different sizes. The 128 fl oz container costs $4.59, the 64 fl oz container costs $3.29, and the 32 fl oz container costs $1.99. Which size has the lowest price per fluid ounce?

LESSON 2

Determine whether the ratios are proportional.

5. $\frac{25}{40}, \frac{30}{48}$

6. $\frac{32}{36}, \frac{24}{28}$

7. $\frac{5}{6}, \frac{15}{18}$

8. $\frac{21}{49}, \frac{18}{42}$

Find a ratio equivalent to each ratio. Then use the ratios to write a proportion.

9. $\frac{72}{81}$

10. $\frac{15}{40}$

11. $\frac{24}{32}$

12. $\frac{5}{13}$

LESSON 3

Use cross products to solve each proportion.

13. $\frac{8}{n} = \frac{12}{18}$

14. $\frac{4}{7} = \frac{p}{28}$

15. $\frac{u}{14} = -\frac{21}{28}$

16. $\frac{3}{21} = \frac{t}{49}$

17. $\frac{y}{35} = \frac{63}{45}$

18. $-\frac{6}{n} = -\frac{48}{12}$

19. $\frac{32}{x} = \frac{52}{117}$

20. $\frac{56}{80} = \frac{105}{m}$

21. The ratio of a person's weight on Earth to his weight on the Moon is 6 to 1. Rafael weighs 90 pounds on Earth. How much would he weigh on the Moon?

22. In 2 weeks, a taxi traveled 2,460 miles. At this rate, how many miles will the taxi travel in one year (52 weeks)?

Extra Practice ... Chapter 4

LESSON 4

Tell whether the figures are similar.

23.

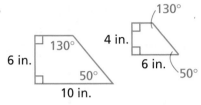

24.

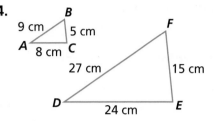

LESSON 5

Find the unknown measures.

25. $\triangle XYZ \sim \triangle RQS$

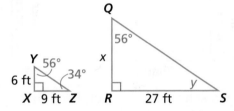

26. A 5-foot-tall girl casts a 7-foot-long shadow. At the same time, a nearby telephone pole casts a 35-foot-long shadow. What is the height of the telephone pole?

27. A 24-foot-tall tree casts a 30-foot-long shadow. A 4-foot-tall child is standing nearby. How long is the child's shadow?

28. A flagpole casts a shadow that is 26 ft long. At the same time, a yardstick casts a shadow that is 4 ft long. How tall is the flagpole?

29. An amoeba is 0.8 millimeter in length. At the science museum, there is a scale model of the amoeba that is 160 millimeters in length. What is the scale factor?

LESSON 6

30. A scale model of the Empire State Building is 3.125 feet tall with a scale factor of $\frac{1}{400}$. Find the actual height of the Empire State Building.

31. Kira is drawing a map of her state with a scale of 1 inch:30 miles. The actual distance between Park City and Gatesville is 80 miles. How far from Gatesville should Kira place Park City on her map?

32. On a map, the distance between the cities of Brachburg and Trunktown is 4.3 cm. The map scale is 1 cm:25 km. What is the actual distance between the cities?

Extra Practice

LESSON 1

Plot each point on a coordinate plane. Identify the quadrant that contains each point.

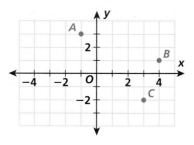

1. $M(-1, 1)$ **2.** $N(4, 4)$ **3.** $Q(3, -1)$

Give the coordinates of each point.

4. A **5.** B **6.** C

LESSON 2

7. Abby rode her bike to the park. She had a picnic there with friends before biking home. Which graph best shows the situation?

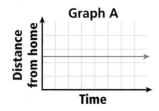
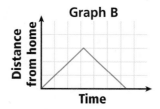
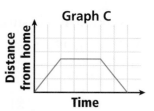

8. Jose is selling tins of popcorn for a school fund-raiser. Each tin of popcorn sells for $12. Draw a graph to show his possible income from sales.

LESSON 3

Tell whether the slope is positive or negative. Then find the slope.

9.

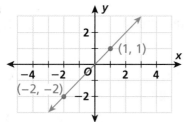

10.

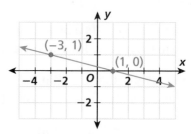

Use the given slope and point to graph each line.

11. $\frac{1}{2}$; $(2, 1)$ **12.** $-\frac{2}{3}$; $(4, 1)$ **13.** $-\frac{4}{5}$; $(-2, -3)$ **14.** 3; $(1, -3)$

LESSON 4

Tell whether each equation represents a direct variation. If so, identify the constant of variation.

15. $3x = 5y$ **16.** $y = x^2$ **17.** $y = 0.9x$ **18.** $y = 2x + 12$

19. Peter has decided to save $30 each week to buy a new stereo system.
     a. Write a direct variation equation for the amount of money d that Peter has saved in w weeks.
     b. Graph the data.
     c. How many weeks will it take Peter to save $270?

Extra Practice ... Chapter 6

LESSON 1

Write each decimal as a percent.

1. 0.06   **2.** 0.54   **3.** 1.69   **4.** 42.0   **5.** 0.898

Write each fraction as a percent.

6. $\frac{15}{34}$ **7.** $\frac{29}{86}$ **8.** $\frac{33}{44}$ **9.** $\frac{61}{91}$ **10.** $1\frac{2}{5}$

Decide whether using pencil and paper, mental math, or a calculator is most useful when solving the following problem. Then solve.

11. Tyler wants to donate 49% of his 50 stuffed animals to the children's hospital. About how many stuffed animals will he donate?

LESSON 2

Use a fraction to estimate the percent of each number.

12. 48% of 200   **13.** 27% of 76   **14.** 65% of 300   **15.** 15% of 15

16. Kel has $25 to spend on a pair of jeans. One pair is on sale for 30% off the regular price of $29.99. Does she have enough money to buy the jeans? Explain.

Use 1% or 10% to estimate the percent of each number.

17. 21% of 88   **18.** 19% of 109   **19.** 2% of 56   **20.** 48% of 200

21. Last year, Maria's retirement fund lost 19%. If the fund was worth $18,000 at the beginning of the year, how much money did she lose?

22. Every year, about 300 movies are made. Only 13% are considered to be hits. About how many movies are considered hits in a year?

LESSON 3

Use the Distributive Property to write equivalent expressions showing two ways to calculate each problem.

23. Greg has 40 coins. Half of them are quarters, and the rest are nickels. What is the value of the coins?

24. A rectangular frame is 12 inches by 13 inches. What is the perimeter of the frame?

Write an equivalent equation that does not contain fractions. Then solve the equation.

25. $\frac{2}{3}x - 1 = \frac{1}{2}$ **26.** $3x + \frac{4}{5} = 8$ **27.** $\frac{3}{4} = 2 - \frac{1}{2}x$

Extra Practice ... Chapter 6

LESSON 4

Find each percent of change. Round answers to the nearest tenth of a percent, if necessary.

28. 54 is increased to 68.   **29.** 90 is decreased to 82.   **30.** 60 is increased to 80.

31. 76 is decreased to 55.   **32.** 75 is increased to 120.   **33.** 50 is decreased to 33.

34. Abby's Appliances sells DVD players at 7% above the wholesale cost of $89. How much does the store charge for a DVD player?

35. A market's old parking lot held 48 cars. The new lot holds 37.5% more cars. How many parking spaces are on the new lot?

36. A regular bag of potato chips contains 12 ounces. A jumbo bag of chips contains $166\frac{2}{3}$% more chips. How many ounces does the jumbo bag contain?

LESSON 5

37. An electronics salesperson sold $15,486 worth of computers last month. She makes 3% commission on all sales and earns a monthly salary of $1200. What was her total pay last month?

38. Jon bought a printer for $189 and a set of printer cartridges for $129. Sales tax on these items was 6.5%. What is Jon's total bill for these items?

39. Last year, Wendy earned $36,825. From this amount, $3830.50 was spent on food. What percent of her income went to food, to the nearest tenth of a percent?

40. In her shop, Stephanie earns 16% on all the clothes she sells. This month she earned $3920. What were her total sales of clothes?

41. Eli works in a clothes shop where he earns a commission of 8% and no weekly salary. What will Eli's weekly sales have to be for him to earn $425?

LESSON 6

Use the simple interest formula $I = P \cdot r \cdot t$.

42. Fatin borrowed $6500 to make home repairs and to put in a new skylight. The bank charges $7\frac{1}{2}$% simple interest over 5 years. What is the total Fatin will repay the bank?

43. Rebekah invested $15,000 in a mutual fund at a yearly rate of 8%. She earned $7200 in simple interest. How long was the money invested?

44. Shu earned $1000, which he used to buy a 10-year certificate of deposit (CD). The CD paid simple interest at 8%. What will the CD be worth at the end of 10 years?

45. Rich borrowed $16,000 for 12 years at simple interest to help pay for his schooling. If he repaid a total of $31,360, at what interest rate did he borrow the money?

Extra Practice ... Chapter 7

LESSON 1

Find the mean, median, mode, and range of each data set.

1. 13, 8, 40, 19, 5, 8

2. 21, 19, 23, 26, 15, 25, 25

Identify the outlier in each data set. Then determine how the outlier affects the mean, median, and mode of the data. Then tell which measure of central tendency best describes the data with and without the outlier.

3. 23, 27, 31, 19, 56, 22, 25, 21

4. 66, 78, 57, 87, 66, 59, 239, 84

LESSON 2

5. Use the data to make a box-and-whisker plot. 22, 41, 39, 27, 29, 30, 40, 61, 25, 28, 32

The box-and-whisker plots show the ages of members at a health club. Use the plots for Exercises 6–8.

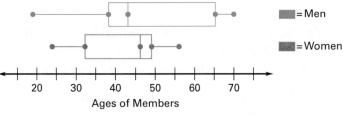

6. Which group of members has a greater median?

7. Which group of members has a greater interquartile range?

8. Does either group have an outlier? Explain.

LESSON 3

Determine whether each sample may be biased. Explain.

9. A bank asks the first 10 customers that enter in the morning if they are satisfied with the bank's late afternoon lobby hours.

10. Members of a polling organization survey 1,000 residents by randomly choosing names from a list of all residents.

Extra Practice ... Chapter 8

LESSON 1

Identify the figures in the diagram.

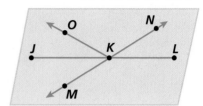

1. three points   **2.** a line   **3.** a plane

4. three rays   **5.** three line segments

6. Identify the line segments that are congruent in the figure.

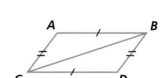

LESSON 2

Tell whether each angle is acute, right, obtuse, or straight.

7.   **8.**   **9.**   **10.**

Use the diagram to tell whether the angles are complementary, supplementary, or neither.

11. ∠GMH and ∠HMJ

12. ∠HMJ and ∠JMK

13. ∠LMK and ∠GMK

14. ∠JMK and ∠KML

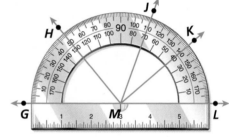

15. Angles Q and S are complementary. If m∠Q is 77°, what is m∠S?

16. Angles M and N are supplementary. If m∠M is 17°, what is m∠N?

LESSON 3

Tell whether the lines in the figure appear parallel, perpendicular, or skew.

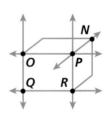

17. $\overleftrightarrow{PN}$ and $\overleftrightarrow{QR}$ **18.** $\overleftrightarrow{OQ}$ and $\overleftrightarrow{QR}$

19. $\overleftrightarrow{OP}$ and $\overleftrightarrow{QR}$ **20.** $\overleftrightarrow{PN}$ and $\overleftrightarrow{OQ}$

Line j ∥ line k. Find the measure of each angle.

21. ∠1

22. ∠3

23. ∠8

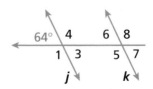

Extra Practice ... Chapter 8

LESSON 4

Find the unknown angle measure in each triangle.

24.
64°
60°   x

25.
x   57°

26.
49°
33°   x

27.
104°
38°   x

Divide each polygon into triangles to find the sum of its angle measures.

28.

29.

30.

31.

LESSON 5

Determine whether the triangles are congruent.

32.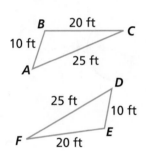
B   20 ft   C
10 ft
A   25 ft
D
25 ft   10 ft
F   20 ft   E

33.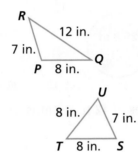
R   12 in.
7 in.
P   8 in.   Q
U
8 in.   7 in.
T   8 in.   S

34.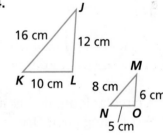
J
16 cm   12 cm
K   10 cm   L
M
8 cm   6 cm
N   O
5 cm

Extra Practice

LESSON 1

Find each perimeter.

1.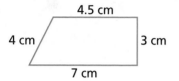
4.5 cm
4 cm
3 cm
7 cm

2.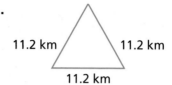
11.2 km
11.2 km
11.2 km

3.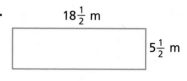
$18\frac{1}{2}$ m
$5\frac{1}{2}$ m

Find the circumference of each circle to the nearest tenth. Use 3.14 or $\frac{22}{7}$ for π.

4.
7 yd

5.
16.5 in.

6.
23.7 mm

LESSON 2

Find the area of each circle to the nearest tenth. Use 3.14 for π.

7.
17 in.

8.
29.8 m

9.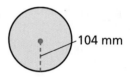
104 mm

10. A circular fountain has a diameter of 42 ft. What is the area of the wading pool? Use $\frac{22}{7}$ for π.

LESSON 3

Estimate the area of each figure. Each square represents 1 ft².

11.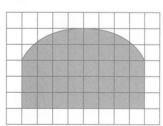

12.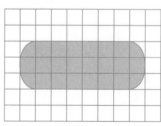

Find the area of each figure. Use 3.14 for π.

13.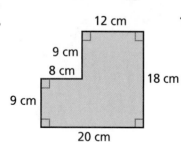
12 cm
9 cm
8 cm
18 cm
9 cm
20 cm

14.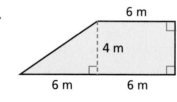
6 m
4 m
6 m
6 m

15.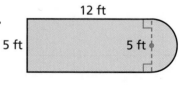
12 ft
5 ft
5 ft

LESSON 4

Identify the bases and faces of each figure. Then name the figure.

16.

17.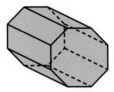

18.

LESSON 5

19. The back of a moving van is shaped like a rectangular prism. It is 24 ft long, 7 ft wide, and 8 ft high. Find the volume of the moving van.

20. A drum is shaped like a cylinder. It is 12.5 in. wide and 8 in. tall. Find its volume. Use 3.14 for π.

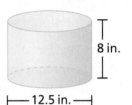

Find the volume of the composite figure to the nearest tenth. Use 3.14 for π.

21.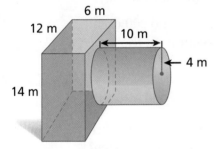

22.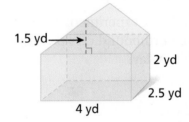

LESSON 6

Find the surface area of each prism.

23.

24.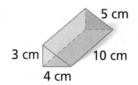

25.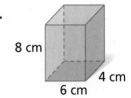

Extra Practice ... Chapter 10

LESSON

Determine whether each event is impossible, unlikely, as likely as not, likely, or certain.

1. flipping a coin and getting heads twelve times in a row

2. drawing a green bead from a bag of white and red beads

3. The probability of rolling a 2 on a number cube is $\frac{1}{6}$. What is the probability of not rolling a 2?

LESSON

4. Bess bowls a strike on 6 out of 15 tries. What is the experimental probability that she will bowl a strike on her next try? Write your answer as a fraction, as a decimal, and as a percent.

5. For the past 10 days, a city planner has counted the number of northbound cars that pass through a particular intersection. During that time, 200 or more cars were counted 9 out of 10 days.

   a. What is the experimental probability that there will be 200 or more northbound cars passing through the intersection on the eleventh day?

   b. What is the experimental probability that there will not be 200 or more northbound cars passing through the intersection on the eleventh day?

LESSON

6. Ronald flips a coin and rolls a number cube at the same time. What are all the possible outcomes? How many outcomes are in the sample space?

7. For lunch, Amy can choose from a salad, a taco, a hamburger, or a fish fillet. She can drink lemonade, milk, juice, or water. What are all the possible outcomes? How many outcomes are in the sample space?

8. A café makes 23 flavors of ice cream. You can get each flavor in a waffle cone, a sugar cone, a cake cone, or a cup. How many outcomes are possible?

LESSON 4

Find the probability of each event. Write your answer as a fraction, as a decimal, and as a percent.

9. rolling a number less than 5 on a fair number cube

10. randomly drawing a pink sock out of a drawer of 6 pink, 4 black, 8 white, and 2 blue socks all of the same size

LESSON **5**

11. The experimental probability that it will rain on any given day in Sacramento, California, is about 15%. Out of 365 days (a year), about how many days can residents of Sacramento predict rain?

12. If you roll a number cube 22 times, about how many times do you expect to roll a number less than 4?

13. A family is planning a 7-day vacation during July at a city where there is a water park and an amusement park. The city experiences an average of 8 rainy days in July. When it rains, both parks are closed. If the family would like to spend at least 2 days at each park, should they go?

LESSON **6**

Decide whether each set of events is independent or dependent. Explain your answer.

14. Mr. Fernandez's class contains 14 boys and 16 girls. Mr. Fernandez randomly picks a boy and a girl to represent the class at the school spelling bee.

15. There are 52 playing cards in a standard card deck. Alex draws a card and holds onto it while Suzi draws a card.

Find the probability of each set of independent events.

16. flipping 2 coins at the same time and getting heads on both coins

17. drawing a 3 from 5 cards numbered 1 through 5 and rolling an even number on a number cube

LESSON **7**

18. Philip has 5 different coins. How many combinations of 3 coins can he make from the 5 coins?

19. A juice bar offers 8 different juices. You and a friend want to each try a different blend. How many different combinations of 2 juices are possible?

LESSON **8**

20. In how many different ways can Ralph, Randy, and Robert stand in line at the movie theater?

21. In how many different ways can 5 students be matched up with 5 mentors?

LESSON **9**

22. A bag has tiles with the numbers 1–5 on them. Two tiles are removed one at a time, and laid out in the order they were drawn.
   a. What is the probability that the 1 is removed first?
   b. What is the probability that the 1 is removed?

LESSON 1

Solve. Check each answer.

1. $4c - 13 = 15$
2. $3h + 14 = 23$
3. $-5j - 13 = 22$
4. $\frac{e}{7} + 2 = 5$
5. $\frac{m}{6} - 3 = 1$
6. $\frac{x}{3} + 5 = -13$

7. If you multiply the number of DVDs Sarah has by 6 and then add 5, you get 41. How many DVDs does Sarah have?

LESSON 2

Solve.

8. $2w - 11 + 4w = 7$
9. $7v + 5 - v = 11$
10. $-7z + 4 - z = -12$
11. $\frac{5x - 7}{3} = 15$
12. $2t - 7 - 5t = 11$
13. $3(t + 2) + 1 = 8$
14. $12a - 3 - 8a = -1$
15. $\frac{2.9h - 5.1}{2} = 4.7$
16. $4(8 - s) + 6 = -2$
17. $\frac{10 - 4t}{8} = -12$

18. Erika has received scores of 82, 87, 93, 95, 88, and 90 on math quizzes. What score must Erika get on her next quiz to have an average of 90?

LESSON 3

Group the terms with variables on one side of the equal sign, and simplify.

19. $6a = 4a - 8$
20. $3d - 5 = 7d - 9$
21. $-2j + 6 = j - 3$
22. $7 + 5m = 2 - m$

Solve.

23. $7y - 9 = -2y$
24. $2c - 13 = 5c + 11$
25. $\frac{2}{5}g + 9 = -6 - \frac{6}{10}g$
26. $7d + 4 = 8 - d$
27. $-3p + 8 = -7p - 12$
28. $1.2k + 2.3 = -0.5k + 7.4$

29. Roberta and Stanley are collecting signatures for a petition. So far, Roberta has twice as many signatures as Stanley. If she collects 30 more signatures, she will have 4 times as many signatures as Stanley currently has. How many signatures has Stanley collected?

30. Gym members pay $3 per workout with a one time membership fee of $98. Nonmembers pay $10 per workout. How many workouts would both a member and a nonmember have to do to pay the same amount?

Extra Practice ... Chapter 11

LESSON 4

Write an inequality for each situation.

31. The cafeteria could hold no more than 50 people.

32. There were fewer than 20 boats in the marina.

Graph each inequality.

33. $y < -2$ **34.** $f \geq 3$ **35.** $n \leq -1.5$ **36.** $x > 4$

Graph each compound inequality.

37. $1 < s < 4$ **38.** $-1 \leq v < 2$ **39.** $w < 0$ or $w \geq 5$ **40.** $-3.5 \leq y < -2$

LESSON 5

Solve. Then graph each solution set on a number line.

41. $c - 6 > -5$ **42.** $v - 3 \geq 1$ **43.** $w - 6 \leq -7$ **44.** $a - 2 \leq 5$

Solve. Check each answer.

45. $q + 3 \leq 5$ **46.** $m + 1 > 0$ **47.** $p + 7 \leq 4$ **48.** $z + 2 \geq -3$

49. By Saturday night, 3 inches of rain had fallen in Happy Valley. The weekend forecast predicted at least 8 inches of rain. How much more rain must fall on Sunday for this forecast to be correct?

LESSON 6

Solve. Check each answer.

50. $\frac{a}{5} \leq 4.5$ **51.** $-\frac{v}{2} > 2$ **52.** $\frac{x}{3.9} \geq -2$ **53.** $-\frac{c}{4} < 2.3$

54. $13y < 39$ **55.** $2t \leq 5$ **56.** $-7r > 56$ **57.** $3s \geq -4.5$

58. The local candy store buys candy in bulk and then sells it by the pound. If the store owner spends \$135 on peppermints and then sells them for \$3.50 per pound, how many pounds must he sell to make a profit?

LESSON 7

Solve. Then graph each solution set on a number line.

59. $\frac{m}{3} - 1 \leq 2$ **60.** $7.2x - 4.8 > 24$ **61.** $-5.5h + 2 < 13$

62. $-1 - \frac{s}{3.5} \geq 1$ **63.** $-\frac{w}{1.5} - 8 \leq -10$ **64.** $4j - 6 > 16$

65. $5 - 2u < 15$ **66.** $\frac{r}{7} - 1 \geq 0$ **67.** $5 - \frac{m}{9} \leq 17$

68. Jill, Serena, and Erin are trying to earn enough money to rent a beach house for a week. They estimate that it will cost at least \$1,650. If Jill has already earned \$600, how much must each of the others earn?

Draw a Diagram

When problems involve objects, distances, or places, you can **draw a diagram** to make the problem easier to understand. You can use the diagram to look for relationships among the given data and to solve the problem.

Problem Solving Strategies

Draw a Diagram	Make a Table
Make a Model	Solve a Simpler Problem
Guess and Test	Use Logical Reasoning
Work Backward	Use a Venn Diagram
Find a Pattern	Make an Organized List

A bald eagle has built a nest 18 feet below the top of a 105-foot-tall oak tree. The eagle sits on a limb 72 feet above the ground. What is the vertical distance between the eagle and its nest?

Corbis

Understand the Problem

Identify the important information.

- The height of the tree is 105 feet.
- The eagle's nest is 18 feet from the top of the tree.
- The eagle is perched 72 feet above the ground.

The answer will be the vertical distance between the eagle and its nest.

Make a Plan

Use the information in the problem to **draw a diagram** showing the height of the tree and the locations of the eagle and its nest.

Solve

To find the height of the nest's location, subtract the distance of the nest from the top of the tree from the height of the tree.

105 feet − 18 feet = 87 feet

To find the vertical distance from the eagle to its nest, subtract the height of the eagle's location from the height of the nest's location.

87 feet − 72 feet = 15 feet

The vertical distance between the eagle and its nest is 15 feet.

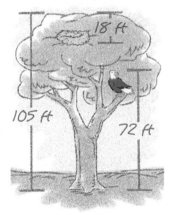

Look Back

Be sure that you have drawn your diagram correctly. Does it match the information given in the problem?

PRACTICE

1. A truck driver travels 17 miles south to drop off his first delivery. Then he drives 19 miles west to drop off a second delivery, and then he drives 17 miles north to drop off another delivery. Finally, he drives 5 miles east for his last delivery. How far is he from his starting point?

2. A table that is standing lengthwise against a wall is 10 feet long and 4 feet wide. Sarah puts balloons 1 foot apart along the three exposed sides, with one balloon at each corner. How many balloons does she use?

Problem Solving Handbook

Make a Model

When problems involve objects, you can **make a model** using those objects or similar objects. This can help you understand the problem and find the solution.

Problem Solving Strategies

Draw a Diagram   Make a Table
Make a Model   Solve a Simpler Problem
Guess and Test   Use Logical Reasoning
Work Backward   Use a Venn Diagram
Find a Pattern   Make an Organized List

A company packages 6 minipuzzles in a decorated 4 in. cube. They are shipped to the toy store in cartons shaped like rectangular prisms. Twenty cubes fit in each carton. If the height of each carton is 8 in., what are the possible dimensions of the carton?

 **Understand the Problem**

Identify the important information.

- Each cube is 4 inches on a side.
- Twenty cubes fit in one carton.
- The height of the carton is 8 inches.

The answer is the dimensions of the carton.

 **Make a Plan**

You can use 20 cubes to **make a model** of cubes packed in a carton. Record possible values for length and width, given a height of 8 in.

 Solve

Begin with a carton that is 8 in., or 2 cubes, high. Use all 20 cubes to make a rectangular prism.

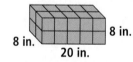

8 in.   8 in.
20 in.

The possible dimensions of the carton are 20 in. × 8 in. × 8 in.

Look Back

The volume of each carton should equal the volume of the 20 cubes.

Volume of cartons: 8 in. × 20 in. × 8 in. = 1,280 in^3

Volume of 1 cube: 4 in. × 4 in. × 4 in. = 64 in^3

Volume of 20 cubes: 20 × 64 = 1,280 in^3

1,280 in^3 = 1,280 in^3 ✔

PRACTICE

1. Give two sets of possible dimensions of a rectangular prism made up of twenty 1-inch cubes.

2. John uses exactly eight 1-inch cubes to form a rectangular prism. Find the length, width, and height of the prism.

Guess and Test

If you do not know how to solve a problem, you can always make a **guess.** Then **test** your guess using the information in the problem. Use what you find out to make a second guess. Continue to **guess and test** until you find the correct answer.

 Problem Solving Strategies

Draw a Diagram	Make a Table
Make a Model	Solve a Simpler Problem
Guess and Test	Use Logical Reasoning
Work Backward	Use a Venn Diagram
Find a Pattern	Make an Organized List

Shannon used equal numbers of quarters and nickels to buy an embossing template that cost $1.50. How many of each coin did she use?

Understand the Problem

Identify the important information.

- Shannon used equal numbers of quarters and nickels.
- The coins she used total $1.50.

The answer will be the number of quarters and the number of nickels Shannon used.

Make a Plan

Start with an educated **guess** in which the numbers of quarters and nickels are the same. Then **test** to see whether the coins total $1.50.

Solve

Make a first guess of 4 quarters and 4 nickels, and find the total value of the coins.

Guess: 4 quarters and 4 nickels
Test: $(4 \times \$0.25) + (4 \times \$0.05) = \$1.00 + \$0.20 = \$1.20$

$1.20 is too low. Increase the number of coins.

Guess: 6 quarters and 6 nickels
Test: $(6 \times \$0.25) + (6 \times \$0.05) = \$1.50 + \$0.30 = \$1.80$

$1.80 is too high. The number of each coin must be between 4 and 6. So Shannon must have used 5 quarters and 5 nickels.

Look Back

Test the answer to see whether the coins add up to $1.50.
$(5 \times \$0.25) + (5 \times \$0.05) = \$1.25 + \$0.25 = \$1.50$ ✔

PRACTICE

1. The sum of Richard's age and his older brother's age is 63. The difference between their ages is 13. How old are Richard and his brother?

2. In the final game of the basketball season, Trinka scored a total of 25 points on 2-point shots and 3-point shots. She made 5 more 2-point shots than 3-point shots. How many of each did she make?

Work Backward

Some problems give you a sequence of information and ask you to find something that happened at the beginning. To solve a problem like this, you may want to start at the end of the problem and **work backward**.

Problem Solving Strategies

Draw a Diagram	Make a Table
Make a Model	Solve a Simpler Problem
Guess and Test	Use Logical Reasoning
Work Backward	Use a Venn Diagram
Find a Pattern	Make an Organized List

Tony is selling dried fruit snacks to help raise money for a new school computer. Half of the fruit snacks in the bag are apricots. Of the rest of the fruit snacks, half of them are bananas, and the other 8 are cranberries. How many fruit snacks are in the bag?

Understand the Problem

Identify the important information.

- Half of the fruit snacks are apricots.
- Half of the remaining fruit snacks are bananas.
- The final 8 fruit snacks are cranberries.

The answer will be the total number of fruit snacks in the bag.

Make a Plan

Start with the 8 cranberries, and **work backward** through the information in the problem to find the total number of fruit snacks in the bag.

Solve

There are 8 cranberries.   8

The other half of the remaining fruit snacks are bananas, so there must be 8 bananas. $8 + 8 = 16$

The other half of the fruit snacks are apricots, so there must be 16 apricots. $16 + 16 = 32$

There are 32 fruit snacks in the bag.

Look Back

Using the starting amount of 32 fruit snacks, work from the beginning of the problem following the steps.

Start: 32
Half of 32: $32 \div 2 = 16$
Half of 16: $16 \div 2 = 8$
Minus 8: $8 - 8 = 0$ ✓

PRACTICE

1. In a trivia competition, each finalist must answer 4 questions correctly. Each question is worth twice as much as the question before it. The fourth question is worth $1,000. How much is the first question worth?

2. The Ramirez family has 5 children. Sara is 5 years younger than her brother Kenny. Felix is half as old as his sister Sara. Kaitlen, who is 10, is 3 years older than Felix. Kenny and Celia are twins. How old is Celia?

Find a Pattern

Problem Solving Strategies

In some problems, there is a relationship between different pieces of information. Examine this relationship and try to **find a pattern.** You can then use this pattern to find more information and the solution to the problem.

Draw a Diagram   Make a Table
Make a Model   Solve a Simpler Problem
Guess and Test   Use Logical Reasoning
Work Backward   Use a Venn Diagram
Find a Pattern   Make an Organized List

John made a design using hexagons and triangles. The side lengths of each hexagon and triangle are 1 inch. What is the perimeter of the next figure in his design?

Understand the Problem

Identify the important information.

- The first 5 figures in the design are given.
- The side lengths of each hexagon and triangle are 1 inch.

The answer will be the perimeter of the sixth figure in the design.

Make a Plan

Try to **find a pattern** in the perimeters of the first 5 figures. Use the pattern to find the perimeter of the sixth figure.

Solve

Find the perimeter of the first 5 figures.

Figure	Perimeter (in.)	Pattern
1	6	
2	7	6 + 1 = 7
3	11	7 + 4 = 11
4	12	11 + 1 = 12
5	16	12 + 4 = 16

The pattern appears to be add 1, add 4, add 1, add 4, and so on. So the perimeter of the sixth figure will be 16 + 1, or 17.

Look Back

Use another strategy. **Draw a diagram** of the sixth figure. Then find the perimeter.

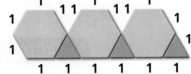

PRACTICE

Describe the pattern, and then find the next number.

1. 1, 5, 9, 13, 17, …

2. 1, 4, 16, 64, 256, …

Make a Table

When you are given a lot of information in a problem, it may be helpful to organize that information. One way to organize information is to **make a table.**

Problem Solving Strategies

Draw a Diagram	**Make a Table**
Make a Model	Solve a Simpler Problem
Guess and Test	Use Logical Reasoning
Work Backward	Use a Venn Diagram
Find a Pattern	Make an Organized List

On November 1, Wendy watered the Gribbles' yard and the Milams' yard. If she waters the Gribbles' yard every 4 days and the Milams' yard every 5 days, when is the next date that Wendy will water both yards?

 **Understand the Problem**

Identify the important information.

- Wendy waters the Gribbles' yard every 4 days and the Milams' yard every 5 days. She watered both yards on November 1.

The answer will be the next date that she waters both yards again.

 **Make a Plan**

Make a table using X's to show the days that Wendy waters each yard. Make one row for the Gribbles and one row for the Milams.

 Solve

Start with an X in both rows for November 1. For the Gribbles, add an X on every fourth day after November 1. For the Milams, add an X every fifth day after November 1.

Date	1	2	3	4	5	6	7	8	9	10	11	12	13	14	15	16	17	18	19	20	21
Gribble	X				X				X				X				X				X
Milam	X					X					X					X					X

November 21 is the next date that Wendy will water both yards.

 **Look Back**

The sum of 1 and five 4's should equal the sum of 1 and four 5's.
$1 + 4 + 4 + 4 + 4 + 4 = 21$ $1 + 5 + 5 + 5 + 5 = 21$ ✔

PRACTICE

1. Jess, Kathy, and Linda work on the math club's newspaper. One is the editor, one is the reporter, and one is the writer. Linda does not participate in sports. Jess and the editor play tennis together. Linda and the reporter are cousins. Find each person's job.

2. A toll booth accepts any combination of coins that total exactly $0.75, but it does not accept pennies or half dollars. In how many different ways can a driver pay the toll?

Solve a Simpler Problem

Problem Solving Strategies

Sometimes a problem may contain large numbers or require many steps to solve. It may appear complicated to solve. Try to **solve a simpler problem** that is similar to the original problem.

Draw a Diagram	Make a Table
Make a Model	**Solve a Simpler Problem**
Guess and Test	Use Logical Reasoning
Work Backward	Use a Venn Diagram
Find a Pattern	Make an Organized List

Lawrence is making touch pools for a project about sea creatures. The pools are squares that will be arranged side by side. The side of each pool is a 1-meter-long piece of wood. How many meters of wood does Lawrence need to complete 20 square sections of touch pools?

 **Understand the Problem**

Identify the important information.

- Each square side is a 1-meter-long piece of wood.
- There are 20 square sections set side by side.

The answer will be the total meters of wood needed.

 **Make a Plan**

You could sketch all 20 pools and then count the number of meters of wood. However, it would be easier to first **solve a simpler problem**. Start with 1 square pool, and then move on to 2 and then 3. Then look for a way to solve the problem for 20 pools.

 Solve

The first pool requires 4 sides to complete. After that, only 3 sides are needed for each pool.

Notice that 1 pool requires 4 meters of wood, and the 19 other pools require 3 meters of wood each. So 4 + (19 × 3) = 61. The pools require 61 meters of wood.

1 square:

2 squares:

3 squares:

Number of Squares	Number of Meters
1	4(1) = 4
2	4 + (1 × 3) = 7
3	4 + (2 × 3) = 10
4	4 + (3 × 3) = 13

 Look Back

If the pattern is correct, Lawrence would need 16 meters of wood for 5 pools. Complete the next row of the table to check this answer.

PRACTICE

1. The numbers 11; 444; and 8,888 all contain repeated single digits. How many numbers between 10 and 1,000,000 contain repeated single digits?

2. How many diagonals are there in a dodecagon (a 12-sided polygon)?

(all) Richard Herrmann

Use Logical Reasoning

Sometimes a problem may provide clues and facts that you must use to find a solution. You can use **logical reasoning** to solve this kind of problem.

Problem Solving Strategies

Draw a Diagram	Make a Table
Make a Model	Solve a Simpler Problem
Guess and Test	**Use Logical Reasoning**
Work Backward	Use a Venn Diagram
Find a Pattern	Make an Organized List

Problem Solving Handbook

Jennie, Rachel, and Mia play the oboe, the violin, and the drums. Mia does not like the drums, and she is the sister of the oboe player. Rachel has soccer practice with the person who plays the drums. Which instrument does each person play?

 **Understand the Problem**

Identify the important information.

- There are three people, and each person plays a different instrument.

 **Make a Plan**

Start with clues given in the problem, and **use logical reasoning** to determine which instrument each person plays.

Solve

Make a table. Make a column for each instrument and a row for each person. Work with the clues one at a time. Write "Yes" in a box if the clue reveals that a person plays an instrument. Write "No" in a box if the clue reveals that a person does not play an instrument.

a. Mia does not like the drums, so she does not play the drums.

b. Mia is the sister of the person who plays the oboe, so she does not play the oboe.

	Oboe	Violin	Drums
Jennie			
Rachel			No
Mia	No		No

c. Rachel has soccer practice with the person who plays the drums, so she does not play the drums.

Jennie must play the drums, and Mia must play the violin. So Rachel must play the oboe.

Look Back

Compare your answer to the clues in the problem. Make sure none of your conclusions conflict with the clues.

PRACTICE

1. Kent, Jason, and Newman have a dog, a fish, and a hamster, though not in that order. Kent's pet does not have fur. The owner of the hamster has class with Jason. Match the owners with their pets.

2. Seth, Vess, and Benica are in the sixth, seventh, and eighth grades, though not in that order. Seth is not in seventh grade. The sixth-grader has band with Benica and the same lunchtime as Seth. Match the students with their grades.

(tr) Victoria Smith/HMH

Use a Venn Diagram

You can use a **Venn diagram** to display relationships among sets in a problem. Use ovals, circles, or other shapes to represent individual sets.

Problem Solving Strategies

Draw a Diagram
Make a Model
Guess and Test
Work Backward
Find a Pattern

Make a Table
Solve a Simpler Problem
Use Logical Reasoning
Use a Venn Diagram
Make an Organized List

At Landry Middle School, 127 students take French, 145 take Spanish, and 31 take both. How many students take only French? How many students take only Spanish?

Understand the Problem

Identify the important information.

- There are 127 students who take French, 145 who take Spanish, and 31 who take both.

Make a Plan

Use a Venn diagram to show the sets of students who take French and Spanish.

Solve

Draw and label two overlapping circles. Write "31" in the area where the circles overlap. This represents the number of students who take French and Spanish.

To find the number of students who take only French, subtract the number of students who take both French and Spanish from those who take French. To find the number of students who take only Spanish, subtract the number of students who take both French and Spanish from those who take Spanish.

So 96 students take only French, and 114 students take only Spanish.

Look Back

Check your Venn diagram carefully against the information in the problem. Make sure your diagram agrees with the facts given.

PRACTICE

Responding to a survey, there were 60 people who said they like pasta, 45 who like chicken, and 70 who like hot dogs. There were 15 people who said they like both pasta and chicken, 22 who like both hot dogs and chicken, and 17 who like both hot dogs and pasta. Only 8 people said they like all 3.

1. How many people like only pasta?

2. How many people like only hot dogs?

Make an Organized List

Problem Solving Strategies

In some problems, you will need to find out exactly how many different ways an event can happen. When solving this kind of problem, it is often helpful to **make an organized list**. This will help you count all the possible outcomes.

Draw a Diagram
Make a Model
Guess and Test
Work Backward
Find a Pattern

Make a Table
Solve a Simpler Problem
Use Logical Reasoning
Use a Venn Diagram
Make an Organized List

A spinner has 4 different colors: red, blue, yellow, and white. If you spin the spinner 2 times, how many different color combinations could you get?

Understand the Problem

Identify the important information.

- You spin the spinner 2 times.
- The spinner is divided into 4 different colors.

The answer will be the total number of different color combinations the spinner can land on.

Make a Plan

Make an organized list to determine all the possible different color outcomes. List all the different combinations for each color.

Solve

First consider the color red. List all the different outcomes for the color red. Then consider blue, adding all the different outcomes, then yellow, and finally white.

Red	Blue	Yellow	White
RR	BB	YY	WW
RB	BY	YW	
RY	BW		
RW			

So there are 10 possible different color combinations.

Look Back

Make sure that all the possible combinations of color are listed and that each set of colors is different.

PRACTICE

1. The Pizza Planet has 5 different choices of pizza toppings: ham, pineapple, pepperoni, olive, and mushroom. You want to order a pizza with 2 different toppings. How many different combinations of toppings can you order?

2. How many ways can you make change for a fifty-cent piece by using a combination of dimes, nickels, and pennies?

Problem Solving Handbook

Skills Bank . . .

Read and Write Decimals

When reading and writing a decimal, you need to know the place value of the digit in the last decimal place. Also, remember the following:

- "and" goes in place of the decimal point for numbers greater than one.
- a hyphen is used in two-digit numbers, such as twenty-five.
- a hyphen is used in two-word place values, such as ten-thousandths.

EXAMPLE

Write 728.34 in words.

The 4 is in the hundredths place, so 728.34 is written as
"seven hundred twenty-eight and thirty-four hundredths."

PRACTICE

Write each decimal in words.

1. 17.238 **2.** 9.0023 **3.** 534.01972 **4.** 33.00084 **5.** 4,356.67

Rules for Rounding

To round a number to a certain place value, locate the digit with that place value, and look at the digit to the right of it.

- If the digit to the right is 5 or greater, increase the number in the rounding place by 1.
- If the digit to the right is 4 or less, leave the number in the rounding place as is.

EXAMPLE

A **Round 765.48201 to the nearest hundredth.**

765.48201 *Locate the hundredths place.*

The digit to the right is less than 5, so the digit in the rounding place stays the same.

765.48

B **Round 765.48201 to the nearest tenth.**

765.48201 *Locate the tenths place.*

The digit to the right is greater than 5, so the digit in the rounding place increases by 1.

765.5

PRACTICE

Round 203.94587 to the place indicated.

1. hundreds **2.** hundredths **3.** thousandths **4.** tens **5.** ones

Properties

Addition and multiplication follow certain rules. The tables show basic properties of addition and multiplication.

ADDITION PROPERTIES	
Commutative:	$a + b = b + a$
Associative:	$(a + b) + c = a + (b + c)$
Identity Property of Zero:	$a + 0 = a$
Inverse Property:	$a + (-a) = 0$
Closure Property:	The sum of two real numbers is a real number.

MULTIPLICATION PROPERTIES	
Commutative:	$a \times b = b \times a$
Associative:	$(a \times b) \times c = a \times (b \times c)$
Identity Property of One:	$a \times 1 = a$
Inverse Property:	$a \times \frac{1}{a} = 1$ if $a \neq 0$
Property of Zero:	$a \times 0 = 0$
Closure Property:	The product of two real numbers is a real number.
Distributive:	$a(b + c) = a \times b + a \times c$

The following properties are true when a, b, and c are real numbers.

Substitution Property: If $a = b$, then a can be substituted for b in any expression.

Transitive Property: If $a = b$ and $b = c$, then $a = c$.

PRACTICE

Name the property represented by each equation.

1. $8 + 0 = 8$

2. $(9 \times 3) \times 7 = 9 \times (3 \times 7)$

3. 3×5 is a real number.

4. $n \times m = m \times n$

5. $2(3 + 5) = 2 \times 3 + 2 \times 5$

6. $15 \times \frac{1}{15} = 1$

7. $3.6 + 4.4 = 4.4 + 3.6$

8. $\frac{3}{4} \times \frac{4}{4} = \frac{3}{4}$

9. $d + (-d) = 0$

10. $(5 + 17) + 23 = 5 + (17 + 23)$

11. $f \times 1 = f$

12. $p \times 0 = 0$

Overestimates and Underestimates

An **overestimate** is an estimate that is greater than the actual value. An **underestimate** is an estimate that is less than the actual value.

EXAMPLE

A Pauline has $30 to spend on school supplies. She wants to buy a set of pens for $12.58, paper for $8.49, and scissors for $6.38. Does Pauline have enough money to buy her supplies? Explain whether an overestimate or underestimate is appropriate. Then find the estimate and determine whether it is sufficient to answer the question.

Pauline should use an overestimate for her total cost, so her actual cost is less. If she has enough for the overestimate, then she has enough for the actual cost.

$12.58 + $8.49 + $6.38

$13 + $9 + $7 = $29   *To overestimate, round each number up.*

Since the estimate is less than $30, she can buy her supplies. If the overestimate was greater than $30, then the estimate would not be sufficient to answer the question.

B Lee's friend lives 245 miles away. Can Lee get to his friend's house in 5.5 hours if he drives at an average speed of 52 miles per hour? Explain whether an overestimate or underestimate is appropriate. Then find the estimate and determine whether it is sufficient to answer the question.

Lee should use an underestimate for the distance he travels in 5.5 hours. If the underestimate of the distance is greater than 245 miles, then his actual time is less than 5.5 hours.

52 · 5.5   *To underestimate, round each number down.*

50 · 5 = 250

Since the estimate is greater than 245, Lee can get to his friend's house in 5.5 hours. If the underestimate was less than 245, then the estimate would not be sufficient to answer the question.

PRACTICE

Explain whether an overestimate or underestimate is appropriate for each situation. Then find the estimate and determine whether it is sufficient.

1. Raul has $55 to buy art supplies. He wants to buy a watercolor set for $28.45, a brush for $12.95, and a sketch pad for $15.75. Does Raul have enough money to buy the items?

2. Fiona's car has 8.5 gallons of gas in its tank. Her car can travel about 21 miles per gallon. Does she have enough gas to drive 158 miles?

Compatible Numbers

Compatible numbers are close to the actual numbers used in a computation. Using compatible numbers allows you to use mental math to estimate easily.

EXAMPLE 1

Use compatible numbers to estimte each answer.

A 236 + 132

240 + 130   *Round to the nearest ten.*
370   *Add.*

B 16 ÷ 3.3

15 ÷ 3   *Choose numbers close to 16 and 3.3 that are easy to divide.*
5   *Divide.*

C. 613 × 28

600 × 30   *Choose numbers close to 613 and 28 that are easy to multiply.*
18,000   *Multiply.*

You can also use *compensation* to make addition easier. **Compensation** is when you adjust one number up or down to make it easier to add, and then adjust the other number in the opposite way to keep the sum the same.

EXAMPLE 2

Use compensation to find the sum.

43 + 19

(43 − 3) + (19 + 3)   *Take away 3 from 43 to get 40. Then add 3 to 19 to compensate.*
40 + 22   *It is easier to add 40 to 22.*
62   *Add.*

PRACTICE

Use compatible numbers to estimate each answer.

1. 48 + 24   **2.** 204 − 63   **3.** 58 × 73

4. 6.3 × 9.8   **5.** 34 ÷ 7.2   **6.** 324 ÷ 76

Use compensation to find the sum.

7. 38 + 14   **8.** 19 + 24   **9.** 56 + 78

10. Charlie's car has 11 gallons of gas in its tank. His car can travel approximately 28 miles per gallon. Estimate how far Charlie can drive before he runs out of gas.

11. Sue drives to her friend's house at an average speed of 52 miles per hour. Her friend lives 247 miles away. Estimate how long it takes Sue to reach her friend's house.

Divisibility Rules

A number is divisible by another number if the quotient is a whole number with no remainder.

A number is divisible by . . .	Divisible	Not Divisible
2 if the last digit is an even number.	13,776	4,221
3 if the sum of the digits is divisible by 3.	327	97
4 if the last two digits form a number divisible by 4.	3,128	526
5 if the last digit is 0 or 5.	9,415	50,501
6 if the number is divisible by 2 and 3.	762	62
9 if the sum of the digits is divisible by 9.	21,222	96
10 if the last digit is 0.	1,680	8,255

PRACTICE

Determine whether each number is divisible by 2, 3, 4, 5, 6, 9, or 10.

1. 324　　　　**2.** 501　　　　**3.** 200　　　　**4.** 812　　　　**5.** 60

Significant Digits

In a measurement, all the digits that are known with certainty are called **significant digits**. The table shows some rules for identifying significant digits.

Rule	Example	Number of Significant Digits
All nonzero digits	15.32	All 4
Zeros between significant digits	43,001	All 5
Zeros after the last nonzero digit that are to the right of the decimal point.	0.0070	2; 0.00**70**

Zeros at the end of a whole number are assumed to be nonsignificant.

EXAMPLE

Determine the number of significant digits in each measurement.

A **120.1 mi**

120.1　　*1, 2, 0, and 1 are significant.*
All 4 digits are significant.

B **0.0350 kg**

0.0350　　*3, 5, and 0 are significant.*
There are 3 significant digits.

PRACTICE

Determine the number of significant digits in each measurement.

1. 2.703 g　　　　**2.** 0.02 km　　　　**3.** 28,000 lb　　　　**4.** 4.003 L

5. 0.650 cm　　　　**6.** 2,800.0 mi　　　　**7.** 30.05 kg　　　　**8.** 100 yd

Factors

A **factor** of a number is any whole number that divides into it without leaving a remainder.

EXAMPLE

List all the factors of 28.

The possible factors are whole numbers from 1 to 28.

$1 \cdot 28 = 28$ *1 and 28 are factors of 28.* $4 \cdot 7 = 28$ *4 and 7 are factors of 28.*

$2 \cdot 14 = 28$ *2 and 14 are factors of 28.* $5 \cdot \,? = 28$ *No whole number multiplied by 5 equals 28, so 5 is not a factor of 28.*

$3 \cdot \,? = 28$ *No whole number multiplied by 3 equals 28, so 3 is not a factor of 28.*

$6 \cdot \,? = 28$ *No whole number multiplied by 6 equals 28, so 6 is not a factor of 28.*

The factors of 28 are 1, 2, 4, 7, 14, and 28.

PRACTICE

List all the factors of each number.

1. 10   **2.** 8   **3.** 18   **4.** 54   **5.** 27   **6.** 36

Roman Numerals

In the Roman numeral system, numbers do not have place values to show what they represent. Instead, numbers are represented by letters.

$I = 1$ $V = 5$ $X = 10$ $L = 50$ $C = 100$ $D = 500$ $M = 1,000$

The values of the letters do not change based on their place in a number.

If a numeral is to the right of an equal or greater numeral, add the two numerals' values. If a numeral is immediately to the left of a greater numeral, subtract the numeral's value from the greater numeral.

EXAMPLE

A   **Write CLIV as a decimal number.**

$$CLIV = C + L + (V - I)$$
$$= 100 + 50 + (5 - 1)$$
$$= 154$$

B   **Write 1,109 as a Roman numeral.**

$$1,109 = 1,000 + 100 + 9$$
$$= M + C + (X - I)$$
$$= MCIX$$

PRACTICE

Write each decimal number as a Roman numeral and each Roman numeral as a decimal number.

1. XXVI   **2.** 29   **3.** MCMLII   **4.** 224   **5.** DCCCVI

Relate Metric Units of Length, Mass, and Capacity

A cube that has a volume of 1 cm³ has a capacity of 1 mL. If the cube were filled with water, the mass of the water would be 1 g.

EXAMPLE

Find the capacity of a 50 cm × 60 cm × 30 cm rectangular box. Then find the mass of the water that would fill the box.

Volume: 50 cm × 60 cm × 30 cm = 90,000 cm³

Capacity: 1 cm³ = 1 mL, so 90,000 cm³ = 90,000 mL, or 90 L.

Mass: 1 mL of water has a mass of 1 g, so 90,000 mL of water has a mass of 90,000 g, or 90 kg.

PRACTICE

Find the capacity of each box. Then find the mass of the water that would fill the box.

1. 2 cm × 5 cm × 8 cm   **2.** 10 cm × 18 cm × 4 cm   **3.** 8 cm × 8 cm × 8 cm

4. 10 cm × 10 cm × 10 cm   **5.** 15 cm × 18 cm × 16 cm   **6.** 23 cm × 19 cm × 11 cm

Basic Geometric Figures

You can use a straightedge to draw geometric figures made up of segments.

EXAMPLE

Draw and label a rectangle with a length of 3.5 cm and a width of 2 cm.

Draw a horizontal segment 3.5 cm long. Next draw two vertical segments each 2 cm long to represent the vertical sides of the rectangle. Finally, draw a second horizontal segment 3.5 cm long.

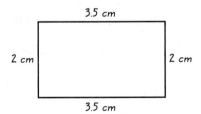

PRACTICE

Draw and label each figure that is described.

1. A square with sides of 4 cm
2. A rectangle with a length of 1.5 in. and a width of 1 in.
3. A square with sides of 2 in.
4. A rectangle with a length of 5 cm and a width of 3 cm

Elapsed Time

The amount of time between a starting time and an ending time is called
elapsed time .

EXAMPLE

A Jody drove 1 hour and 25 minutes from Lima to Trenton. Jody
arrived in Trenton at 2:30 P.M. At what time did Jody leave Lima?

Time Jody arrived: 2:30 P.M.   *Think: 1 hour before 2:30 P.M. is 1:30 P.M.*

Time Jody left: 1:05 P.M.   *25 minutes before 1:30 P.M. is 1:05 P.M.*

Jody left Lima at 1:05 P.M.

B Rael ran his first lap in 2 minutes and 36 seconds. He ran his
second lap in 2 minutes and 45 seconds. How much time elapsed
during the two laps?

2 min 36 s + 2 min 45 s   *Find the sum of the two times.*

(2 min + 2 min) + (36 s + 45 s)   *Regroup minutes and seconds.*

(4 min) + (81 s)   *Add minutes, and then add seconds.*

(4 min) + (1 min 21 s)   *Change 81 seconds to 1 minute 21 seconds.*

5 min 21 s *Add minutes.*

The total time elapsed during the two laps is 5 minutes and
21 seconds.

PRACTICE

1. Larry was scheduled to arrive at his grandfather's house at 10:45 A.M.
   He was 1 hour and 20 minutes late. When did Larry arrive?

2. A train arrived at its destination at 12:15 P.M. If the trip took 2 hours
   and 50 minutes, at what time did the bus depart?

3. Will ran for 22 minutes and 30 seconds and then ran for 34 minutes
   and 54 seconds. How much time elapsed during his run?

4. Sheila completed a race in 6 hours and 6 minutes. She completed
   the first half of the race in 2 hours and 58 minutes. How much time
   elapsed during the second half of the race?

5. A movie starts at 7:20 P.M. The movie ends at 9:17 P.M. How long was
   the movie?

Polynomials

A **monomial** is a number or a product of numbers and variables with exponents that are whole numbers. The expressions $2n$, x^3, $4a^4b^3$, and 7 are all examples of monomials. The expressions $x^{1.5}$, $2\sqrt{y}$, and $\frac{3}{m}$ are not monomials.

A **polynomial** is one monomial or the sum or difference of monomials. Polynomials can be classified by the number of terms. A monomial has one term, a **bionomial** has two terms, and a **trinomial** has three terms.

EXAMPLE

Classify each expression as a monomial, a binomial, a trinomial, or not a polynomial.

A $43h + 14b$

   binomial   *The expression is a polynomial with 2 terms.*

B $3x^2 - 4xy + \frac{3}{x}$

   not a polynomial   *There is a variable in a denominator.*

PRACTICE

Classify each expression as a monomial, a binomial, a trinomial, or not a polynomial.

1. $5a^3 + 6a^2 - 3$ **2.** $4xy^2$ **3.** $7b + \frac{1}{b^2}$ **4.** $6c^2d - 4$

Odds

Similar to probability, odds are a way to express the likelihood that an event will occur. The **odds** of an event are the ratio of the number of favorable outcomes to the number of unfavorable outcomes. Odds are usually written as $a{:}b$, but can also be written as a to b or $\frac{a}{b}$.

EXAMPLE

In a school raffle, 500 tickets were sold, and there were 10 winners. What are the odds of winning the raffle?

odds of winning $= \dfrac{\text{number of favorable outcomes}}{\text{number of unfavorable outcomes}}$

$\qquad\qquad = \dfrac{10}{490}$ *The number of unfavorable outcomes is 500 − 10, or 490.*

The odds of winning the raffle are 10:490, or 1:49.

PRACTICE

A bag of 20 marbles contains 9 yellow marbles and 11 purple marbles.

1. Find the odds of choosing a yellow marble.

2. Find the odds of choosing a purple marble.

Probability of Two Mutually Exclusive Events

In probability, two events are considered to be **mutually exclusive**, or disjoint, if they cannot happen at the same time. For example, rolling a 5 and rolling a 6 on a 1–6 number cube are mutually exclusive events because they cannot both happen on a single roll.

Suppose A and B are mutually exclusive events.

- $P(\text{both } A \text{ and } B \text{ will occur}) = 0$

- $P(\text{either } A \text{ or } B \text{ will occur}) = P(A) + P(B)$

To find the probability of event A or event B, add the probabilities of each event.

EXAMPLE

Find the probability of each set of mutually exclusive events.

A **rolling either a 5 or a 6 on a 1–6 number cube**

$$P(5 \text{ or } 6) = P(5) + P(6)$$
$$= \frac{1}{6} + \frac{1}{6}$$
$$= \frac{2}{6}$$

The probability of rolling a 5 or a 6 is $\frac{2}{6}$, or $\frac{1}{3}$.

B **choosing either an A or an E from the letters in the word** *mathematics*

$$P(A \text{ or } E) = P(A) + P(E)$$
$$= \frac{2}{11} + \frac{1}{11}$$
$$= \frac{3}{11}$$

The probability of choosing an A or an E is $\frac{3}{11}$.

PRACTICE

Find the probability of each set of mutually exclusive events.

1. tossing a coin and getting heads or tails

2. spinning red or green on a spinner that has four equal sectors colored red, green, blue, and yellow

3. drawing a black marble or a red marble from a bag that contains 4 white marbles, 3 black marbles, and 2 red marbles

4. choosing either a boy or a girl from a class of 13 boys and 17 girls

5. choosing either A or E from a list of the five vowels

6. choosing either a number less than 3 or a number greater than 12 from a set of 20 cards numbered 1–20

Inductive and Deductive Reasoning

You use **inductive reasoning** when you look for a pattern in individual cases to draw conclusions. Conclusions drawn using inductive reasoning are sometimes like predictions. They may be proven false.

You use **deductive reasoning** when you use given facts to draw conclusions. A conclusion based on facts must be true.

EXAMPLE

Identify the type of reasoning used. Explain your answers.

A *Statement:* **A number pattern begins with 2, 5, 8, 11, . . .**
   Conclusion: **The next number in the pattern will be 14.**

   This is inductive reasoning. The conclusion is based on the pattern established by the first four terms in the sequence.

B *Statement:* **It has rained for the past three days.**
   Conclusion: **It will rain tomorrow.**

   This is inductive reasoning. The conclusion is based on the weather pattern over the past three days.

C *Statement:* **The measures of two angles of a triangle are 30° and 70°.**
   Conclusion: **The measure of the third angle is 80°.**

   This is deductive reasoning. Since you know that the measures of the angles of a triangle have a sum of 180°, the third angle of this triangle must measure 80° (30° + 70° + 80° = 180°).

PRACTICE

Identify the type of reasoning used. Explain your answers.

1. *Statement:* Shawna has received a score of 100 on the last five math tests.
   Conclusion: Shawna will receive a score of 100 on the next math test.

2. *Statement:* The mail has arrived late every Monday for the past 4 weeks.
   Conclusion: The mail will arrive late next Monday.

3. *Statement:* Three angles of a quadrilateral measure 100°, 90°, and 70°.
   Conclusion: The measure of the fourth angle is 100°.

4. *Statement:* Perpendicular lines *AB* and *CD* intersect at point *E*.
   Conclusion: Angle *AED* is a right angle.

5. *Statement:* A pattern of numbers begins 1, 2, 4, . . .
   Conclusion: The next number in the pattern is 8.

6. *Statement:* Ten of the first ten seventh-grade students surveyed listed soccer as their favorite sport.
   Conclusion: Soccer is the favorite sport of all seventh-graders.

Make Conjectures

Conjecture is another word for conclusion. Conjectures in math are based on observations and in some cases have not yet been proven to be true. To prove that a conjecture is false, you need to find just one case, or *counterexample*, for which the conclusion does not hold true.

EXAMPLE 1

Test each conjecture to decide whether it is true or false. If the conjecture is false, give a counterexample.

A The sum of two even numbers is always an even number.

An even number is divisible by 2. The sum of two even numbers can be written as $2m + 2n = 2(m + n)$, which is divisible by 2, so it is even. The conjecture is true.

B Three points on a plane always form a triangle.

Three points can lie on the same line. The conjecture is false.

EXAMPLE 2

Formulate a conjecture based on the given information. Then test your conjecture.

$$1 \cdot 3 = 3 \qquad 3 \cdot 5 = 15 \qquad 5 \cdot 7 = 35 \qquad 7 \cdot 9 = 63$$

Conjecture: The product of two odd numbers is always an odd number.

An odd number does not have 2 as a factor, so the product of two odd numbers also does not have 2 as a factor. The conjecture is true.

PRACTICE

Test each conjecture to decide whether it is true or false. If the conjecture is false, give a counterexample.

1. The sum of two odd numbers is always an odd number.

2. The product of two even numbers is always an even number.

3. The sum of twice a whole number and 1 is always an odd number.

4. Every pair of supplementary angles includes one obtuse angle.

5. If you multiply two fractions, the product will always be greater than either fraction.

Formulate a conjecture based on the given information. Then test your conjecture.

6. $12 + 21 = 33 \qquad 13 + 31 = 44 \qquad 23 + 32 = 55 \qquad 17 + 71 = 88$

7. $15 \times 15 = 225 \qquad 25 \times 25 = 625 \qquad 35 \times 35 = 1{,}225$

Trigonometric Ratios

You can use ratios to find information about the sides and angles of a right triangle. These ratios are called *trigonometric ratios*, and they have names, such as sine (abbreviated *sin*), cosine (abbreviated *cos*), and tangent (abbreviated *tan*).

The **sine** of $\angle 1 = \sin \angle 1 = \dfrac{\text{length of side opposite } \angle 1}{\text{length of hypotenuse}} = \dfrac{a}{c}$.

The **cosine** of $\angle 1 = \cos \angle 1 = \dfrac{\text{length of side adjacent to } \angle 1}{\text{length of hypotenuse}} = \dfrac{b}{c}$.

The **tangent** of $\angle 1 = \tan \angle 1 = \dfrac{\text{length of side opposite } \angle 1}{\text{length of side adjacent to } \angle 1} = \dfrac{a}{b}$.

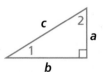

EXAMPLE 1

Find the sine, cosine, and tangent of $\angle J$.

$\sin \angle J = \dfrac{LK}{JK} = \dfrac{3}{5}$

$\cos \angle J = \dfrac{JL}{JK} = \dfrac{4}{5}$

$\tan \angle J = \dfrac{LK}{JL} = \dfrac{3}{4}$

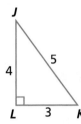

EXAMPLE 2

Use your calculator to find the length of $\overline{MN}$ to the nearest tenth.

$\overline{MN}$ is adjacent to the 58° angle. The length of the hypotenuse is given. The ratio that uses the lengths of the adjacent side and the hypotenuse is cosine.

$\cos(58°) = \dfrac{MN}{9}$ *Write the ratio that is equal to the cosine of 58°.*

$9 \cdot \cos(58°) = MN$ *Multiply both sides by 9.*

9 [×] [COS] 58 [ENTER]   *Use your calculator.*

$MN \approx 4.8$

PRACTICE

Find the sine, cosine, and tangent of each angle.

1. $\angle D$ 2. $\angle F$

Use your calculator to find the length of each side, to the nearest tenth.

3. $\overline{QR}$ 4. $\overline{PR}$

Skills Bank

Cubes and Cube Roots

The volume of the cube at right is $5 \cdot 5 \cdot 5$, or 125 cubic units. Because 5 is a factor 3 times, you can use an exponent to write the expression as 5^3, which is read "5 cubed."

EXAMPLE 1

Evaluate 8^3.

$8^3 = 8 \cdot 8 \cdot 8$ *Use 8 as a factor 3 times.*

    $= 512$ *Multiply.*

Finding a cube root is the inverse of cubing a number. The symbol $\sqrt[3]{}$ means "cube root." For example, $\sqrt[3]{125} = 5$.

EXAMPLE 2

Evaluate $\sqrt[3]{64}$.

$\sqrt[3]{64} = 4$ *$4^3 = 4 \cdot 4 \cdot 4 = 64$, so $\sqrt[3]{64} = 4$.*

You can use a calculator to estimate cube roots.

EXAMPLE 3

Use your calculator to evaluate $\sqrt[3]{43}$ to the nearest tenth.

Press **MATH** and select 4: $\sqrt[3]{}$ (from the menu.) Then enter 43 **)** **ENTER** .

$$\sqrt[3]{43} \approx 3.5$$

PRACTICE

Evaluate each expression.

1. 2^3 **2.** 1^3 **3.** 7^3 **4.** 10^3

5. 6^3 **6.** 30^3 **7.** 0^3 **8.** 4^3

9. $\sqrt[3]{8}$ **10.** $\sqrt[3]{27}$ **11.** $\sqrt[3]{1,000}$ **12.** $\sqrt[3]{1}$

Use your calculator to evaluate each cube root to the nearest tenth.

13. $\sqrt[3]{30}$ **14.** $\sqrt[3]{68}$ **15.** $\sqrt[3]{100}$ **16.** $\sqrt[3]{3}$

17. $\sqrt[3]{260}$ **18.** $\sqrt[3]{1,255}$ **19.** $\sqrt[3]{17}$ **20.** $\sqrt[3]{89}$

21. $\sqrt[3]{54}$ **22.** $\sqrt[3]{1,728}$ **23.** $\sqrt[3]{25}$ **24.** $\sqrt[3]{3,375}$

Properties of Exponents

To multiply powers with the same base, keep the base and add the exponents.

$$x^3 \cdot x^2 = (x \cdot x \cdot x) \cdot (x \cdot x) = x^{3+2} = x^5$$

This is the *Product of Powers Property*.

To divide powers with the same base, keep the base and subtract the exponents.

$$\frac{y^5}{y^2} = \frac{y \cdot y \cdot y \cdot y \cdot y}{y \cdot y} = y^{5-2} = y^3$$

This is the *Quotient of Powers Property*.

To raise a power to a power, keep the base and multiply the exponents.

$$(5^3)^2 = 5^3 \cdot 5^3 = (5 \cdot 5 \cdot 5) \cdot (5 \cdot 5 \cdot 5) = 5^{3 \cdot 2} = 5^6$$

This is the *Power of a Power Property*.

EXAMPLE 2

Rewrite each expression as a single power of the base.

A $7^9 \cdot 7^{11}$

$\quad 7^9 \cdot 7^{11} = 7^{9+11}$ *Use the Product of Powers Property.*

$\qquad\qquad = 7^{20}$ *Add the exponents.*

B $\dfrac{x^{22}}{x^{15}}$

$\quad \dfrac{x^{22}}{x^{15}} = x^{22-15}$ *Use the Quotient of Powers Property.*

$\qquad\quad = x^7$ *Subtract the exponents.*

C $(b^6)^9$

$\quad (b^6)^9 = b^{6 \cdot 9}$ *Use the Power of a Power Property.*

$\qquad\quad = b^{54}$ *Multiply the exponents.*

PRACTICE

Rewrite each expression as a single power of the base.

1. $c^{12} \cdot c^5$ **2.** $5^6 \cdot 5^{22}$ **3.** $\dfrac{y^{50}}{y^{28}}$

4. $\dfrac{6^{14}}{6^8}$ **5.** $(a^{11})^{12}$ **6.** $(8^9)^7$

7. $3^4 \cdot 3^4$ **8.** $\dfrac{5^7}{5^4}$ **9.** $(2^4)^2$

10. $x^3 \cdot x^9$ **11.** $\dfrac{s^7}{s}$ **12.** $(n^2)^5$

Absolute Value and Distance

The absolute value of a number is its distance from 0 on the number line. Since distance can never be negative, absolute values are never negative. The symbol for absolute value is $| \ |$.

EXAMPLE 1

Find the absolute value of each real number.

A 2.7

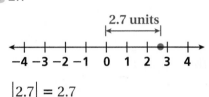

$|2.7| = 2.7$

B $-\pi$

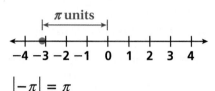

$|-\pi| = \pi$

Suppose that A and B are points on a number line that have coordinates a and b. Since distance can never be negative, the distance between A and B can be calculated as the absolute value of the difference of the two numbers. This distance can be written as $|b - a|$ or $|a - b|$.

EXAMPLE 2

Find the distance between each set of points on the number line.

A

$|-5 - 3| = |-8| = 8$
The distance is 8 units.

B

$|-7 - (-6)| = |-1| = 1$
The distance is 1 unit.

PRACTICE

Find the absolute value of each real number.

1. $-\frac{3}{4}$
2. 5.8
3. $-\sqrt{10}$
4. $3\frac{5}{8}$
5. $\sqrt{3}$
6. -0.16
7. $-1\frac{1}{10}$
8. $\frac{15}{12}$

Find the distance between each set of points on the number line.

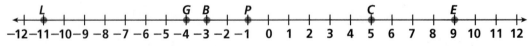

9. B and C
10. E and G
11. L and B
12. P and E
13. L and E
14. G and P
15. P and C
16. C and G

Networks and Paths

A **network** is a set of points and line segments or arcs that connect the points. The points of a network are called **vertices**. The segments or arcs are called **edges**.

A **path** is a way to travel around a network by moving along the edges from one vertex to another. In a simple path, no point is visited more than once.

EXAMPLE

The network represents the major roads connecting five cities. Each vertex represents a city. Each edge represents a road. The numbers along each edge give the distance in miles between cities.

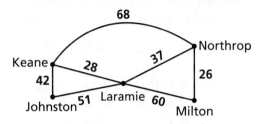

A Determine the number of simple paths from Johnston to Northrop.

 1. Johnston-Keane-Laramie-Milton-Northrop
 2. Johnston-Keane-Laramie-Northrop
 3. Johnston-Keane-Northrop
 4. Johnston-Laramie-Keane-Northrop
 5. Johnston-Laramie-Milton-Northrop
 6. Johnston-Laramie-Northrop

Make an organized list of the simple paths.

There are 6 simple paths.

B Determine the shortest simple path from Johnston to Northrop.

 1. $42 + 28 + 60 + 26 = 156$
 2. $42 + 28 + 37 = 107$
 3. $42 + 68 = 110$
 4. $51 + 28 + 68 = 147$
 5. $51 + 60 + 26 = 137$
 6. $51 + 37 = 88$

For each simple path above, add the distances between the cities.

The shortest simple path is Johnston to Laramie to Northrop.

PRACTICE

The network represents the direct nonstop train routes connecting six cities. The numbers along each edge give the time it takes in minutes to travel each direct nonstop train route one way.

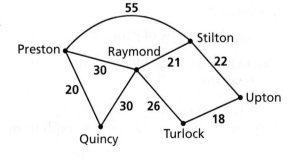

 1. Determine the number of simple paths from Preston to Upton. Then determine the shortest simple path in time between the two cities.

 2. Determine the number of simple paths from Quincy to Turlock. Then determine the shortest simple path in time between the two cities.

Quadratic Relationships

Quadratic relationships involve one squared value related to another value. An example of a quadratic relationship is shown in the equation $a = x^2 + 5$. If you know the value of one variable, you can substitute for it in the equation and then solve to find the second variable.

EXAMPLE

The distance d in feet that an object falls is related to the amount of time t in seconds that it falls. This relationship is given by the equation $d = 16t^2$.

What distance will an object fall in 3 seconds?

$$d = 16t^2 \qquad \textit{Write the equation.}$$
$$d = 16 \cdot (3)^2 \quad \textit{Substitute 3 for t.}$$
$$= 144 \qquad \textit{Simplify.}$$

The object will fall 144 feet in 3 seconds.

PRACTICE

A small rocket is shot vertically upward from the ground. The distance d in feet between the rocket and the ground as the rocket goes up can be found by using the equation $d = 128t - 16t^2$, where t is the amount of time in seconds that the rocket has been flying upward.

1. How far above the ground is the rocket at 1 second and at 2 seconds?

2. Did the rocket's distance change by the same amount in each of the first 2 seconds? Explain.

3. When the rocket is returning to the ground, the distance that the rocket falls is given by the equation $d = 16t^2$. If the rocket hits the ground 4 seconds after it starts to return, how far up did it go?

4. As the rocket falls to the ground, does it fall the same distance each second? Explain.

The graph for $y = x^2$ is shown at right. Use the graph for problems 5–7.

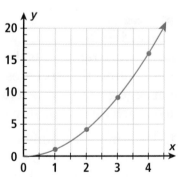

5. Find the value of y for $x = 1, 2, 3, 4,$ and 5.

6. Does y increase by the same amount for each value of x? Explain.

7. How would the part of the graph from $x = 5$ to $x = 6$ compare to the part of the graph from $x = 4$ to $x = 5$?

Exponential Relationships

An **exponential relationship** can be described by a function of the form $y = ab^x$, where a is a constant not equal to 0 and b is a positive number not equal to 1.

EXAMPLE

Create a table of values for each function, and then graph the function.

A $y = 2 \cdot 3^x$

Choose several values of x and generate ordered pairs.

x	y
−2	$\frac{2}{9}$
−1	$\frac{2}{3}$
0	2
1	6
2	18

Plot the points $(-2, \frac{2}{9})$, $(-1, \frac{2}{3})$ $(0, 2)$, and $(1, 6)$, and connect them with a smooth curve.

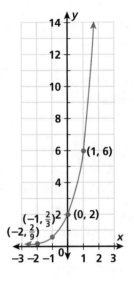

B $y = 3 \cdot \left(\frac{1}{2}\right)^x$

Choose several values of x and generate ordered pairs.

x	y
−2	12
−1	6
0	3
1	$\frac{3}{2}$
2	$\frac{3}{4}$

Plot the points $(-2, 12)$, $(-1, 6)$ $(0, 3)$, $(1, \frac{3}{2})$, and $(2, \frac{3}{4})$ and connect them with a smooth curve.

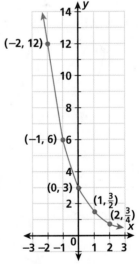

PRACTICE

Create a table of values for each function, and then graph the function.

1. $y = \frac{1}{2} \cdot 3^x$

2. $y = 4 \cdot \left(\frac{1}{3}\right)^x$

3. $y = 5 \cdot \left(\frac{2}{5}\right)^x$

4. An exponential relationship is described by the function $y = ab^x$ where $a > 0$. For what positive values of b would the graph of the function be increasing? For what positive values of b would the graph of the function be decreasing?

AAA, SAS, SSS Similarity

Two figures are similar if their corresponding angle measures are equal *and* if the ratios of the lengths of their corresponding sides are proportional. To prove that two triangles are similar, it is not necessary to show that both of these conditions are always true. They are also considered to be similar if they meet any of the following conditions:

Angle-Angle-Angle (AAA) Similarity	Two triangles are similar if all corresponding angles are congruent.
Side-Angle-Side (SAS) Similarity	Two triangles are similar if the ratios of two pairs of corresponding sides are equal and the corresponding included angles are congruent.
Side-Side-Side (SSS) Similarity	Two triangles are similar if the ratios of all pairs of corresponding sides are equal.

EXAMPLES

Explain why the pairs of triangles are similar.

A

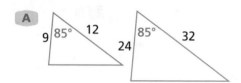

The ratios of two pairs of corresponding sides are equal: $\frac{9}{24} = \frac{12}{32}$. The corresponding included angles are congruent since they both measure 85°.

The triangles are similar because of SAS.

B

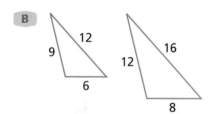

The ratios of all pairs of corresponding sides are equal: $\frac{12}{9} = \frac{8}{6} = \frac{16}{12}$.

The triangles are similar because of SSS.

C

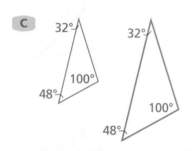

All corresponding angles are congruent since corresponding angle measures are equal: 32° = 32°, 48° = 48°, and 100° = 100°.

The triangles are similar because of AAA.

PRACTICE

Explain why the pairs of triangles are similar.

1.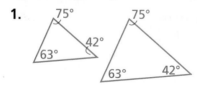

2.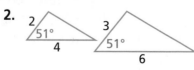

3.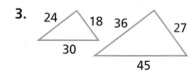

Graph Linear Inequalities on a Coordinate Plane

A **linear inequality** is a mathematical sentence of the form $y < mx + b$, $y > mx + b$, $y \le mx + b$, or $y \ge mx + b$, where m and b are constants. The graph of a linear inequality is a shaded region with a straight-line boundary. Any ordered pair that makes the inequality true is a solution.

To graph a linear inequality, first graph the related line $y = mx + b$. If the inequality is $\ge$ or $\le$, make the line solid. If the inequality is $>$ or $<$, make the line dashed. Then test a point not on the line to see which side of the line to shade. If the point is a solution of the inequality, then shade the side that includes the point. If the point is not a solution, then shade the side that does not include the point.

EXAMPLE

Graph each linear inequality.

A $y > 3x + 2$

Graph $y = 3x + 2$. Use a dashed line for $>$.

$y > 3x + 2$

$0 \overset{?}{>} 3(0) + 2$ *Test the point (0, 0).*

$0 \overset{?}{>} 2$

Since $0 \not> 2$, (0, 0) is not a solution of $y > 3x + 2$.
Shade the side of the line that does not include (0, 0).

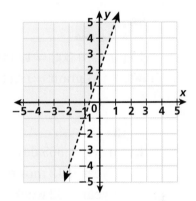

B $y \le 2x + 3$

Graph $y = 2x + 3$. Use a solid line for $\le$.

$y \le 2x + 3$

$0 \overset{?}{\le} 2(0) + 3$ *Test the point (0, 0).*

$0 \overset{?}{\le} 3$

Since $0 \le 3$, (0, 0) is a solution of $y \le 2x + 3$.
Shade the side that includes (0, 0).

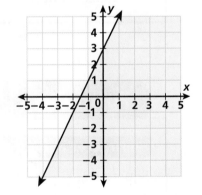

PRACTICE

Graph each linear inequality.

1. $y \le 4x - 1$ **2.** $y > -2x + 3$ **3.** $y \ge \frac{1}{3}x - 2$

4. Julia earns $10 per hour at her job. Each day, she receives a bonus of at least $20. The inequality $y \ge 10x + 20$ represents how much she earns in dollars for x hours of work. Graph the inequality.

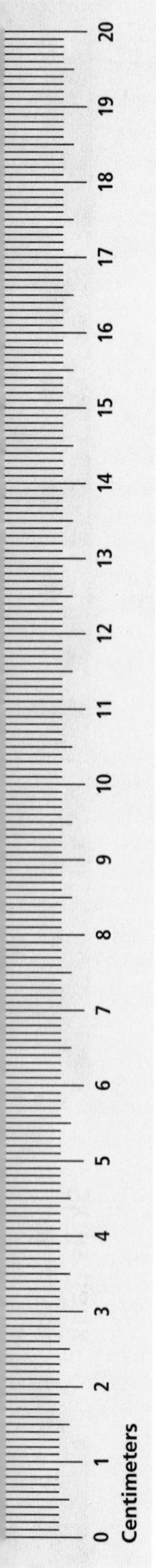

Table of Measures

METRIC	CUSTOMARY

Length

Length	**Length**

1 kilometer (km) = 1,000 meters (m)
1 meter = 100 centimeters (cm)
1 centimeter = 10 millimeters (mm)

1 mile (mi) = 5,280 feet (ft)
1 yard (yd) = 3 feet
1 foot = 12 inches (in.)

Capacity

1 liter (L) = 1,000 milliliters (mL)

Capacity

1 gallon (gal) = 4 quarts (qt)
1 quart = 2 pints (pt)
1 pint = 2 cups (c)
1 cup = 8 fluid ounces (fl oz)

Mass

1 kilogram (kg) = 1,000 grams (g)
1 gram = 1,000 milligrams (mg)

Weight

1 ton (T) = 2,000 pounds (lb)
1 pound = 16 ounces (oz)

TIME

1 year (yr) = 365 days
1 year = 12 months (mo)
1 year = 52 weeks (wk)
1 week = 7 days

1 day = 24 hours (h)
1 hour = 60 minutes (min)
1 minute = 60 seconds (s)

Formulas

Perimeter and Circumference

Square	$P = 4s$
Rectangle	$P = 2\ell + 2w$ or $P = 2(\ell + w)$
Polygon	$P =$ sum of the lengths of the sides
Circle	$C = 2\pi r$ or $C = \pi d$

Area

Square	$A = s^2$
Rectangle	$A = \ell w$ or $A = bh$
Parallelogram	$A = bh$
Triangle	$A = \frac{1}{2}bh$ or $A = \frac{bh}{2}$
Trapezoid	$A = \frac{1}{2}(b_1 + b_2)h$ or $A = \frac{(b_1 + b_2)h}{2}$
Circle	$A = \pi r^2$

Centimeters

Formulas

Volume*

Prism	$V = Bh$
Rectangular Prism	$V = Bh$ or $V = \ell wh$
Cylinder	$V = Bh$ or $V = \pi r^2 h$
Pyramid	$V = \dfrac{1}{3} Bh$
Cone	$V = \dfrac{1}{3} Bh$ or $V = \dfrac{1}{3} \pi r^2 h$

Surface Area*

Prism	$S = 2B + L$ or $S = 2B + Ph$
Cylinder	$S = 2B + L$ or $S = 2\pi r^2 + 2\pi rh$
Regular Pyramid	$S = B + L$ or $S = B + \dfrac{1}{2} P\ell$
Cone	$S = B + L$ or $S = \pi r^2 + \pi r\ell$

*B represents the area of the base of a solid figure.

Temperature

Celsius (°C)	$C = \dfrac{5}{9}(F - 32)$
Fahrenheit (°F)	$F = \dfrac{9}{5} C + 32$

Other

Diameter	$d = 2r$
Simple Interest	$I = Prt$
Pythagorean Theorem	$a^2 + b^2 = c^2$

Symbols

$<$	is less than
$>$	is greater than
$\leq$	is less than or equal to
$\geq$	is greater than or equal to
$=$	is equal to
$\neq$	is not equal to
$\approx$	is approximately equal to
10^2	ten squared
10^3	ten cubed
2^6	two to the sixth power
2^{-5}	two to the negative fifth power
$2.\overline{6}$	repeating decimal 2.66666...
$|-4|$	the absolute value of negative 4
$\sqrt{}$	square root
$5/h	the rate $5 per hour
$1:2$	ratio of 1 to 2
$\%$	percent

(x, y)	ordered pair
$P(\text{event})$	the probability of an event
$n!$	n factorial
$\cong$	is congruent to
$\sim$	is similar to
$\perp$	is perpendicular to
$\parallel$	is parallel to
$\overleftrightarrow{AB}$	line AB
$\overrightarrow{AB}$	ray AB
$\overline{AB}$	line segment AB
$\angle ABC$	angle ABC
$m\angle A$	measure of $\angle A$
$\triangle ABC$	triangle ABC
$\circ$	degree
π	pi; $\pi \approx 3.14$ or $\pi \approx \dfrac{22}{7}$
A'	A prime

Inches
0
1
2
3
4
5
6
7
8

1 Exercises

1. 47 **3.** 23 **5.** 4 **7.** $280 **9.** 42
11. 15 **13.** 73 **15.** 588 **17.** $139
19. 18 **21.** 20 **23.** 1 **25.** > **27.** >
29. = **31.** $4 \cdot (8 - 3) = 20$
33. $(12 - 2)^2 \div 5 = 20$
35. $(4 + 6 - 3) \div 7 = 1$ **37.** $82
39a. $4 \cdot 15$ **39b.** $2 \cdot 30$
39c. $4 \cdot 15 + 2 \cdot 30 + 6$
43. C **45.** D

2 Exercises

1. Assoc. Prop. **3.** Comm. Prop.
5. Assoc. Prop. **7.** 33 **9.** 1,100
11. 47 **13.** 38 **15.** 44 **17.** 208
19. Ident. Prop. **21.** Assoc. Prop.
23. Ident. Prop. **25.** 1,600 **27.** 900
29. 163 **31.** 135 **33.** 174 **35.** 92
41. 220 ft^2 **43.** 9,000 **45.** 17,500
47. 15 **49.** 0 **51.** 8 **53.** 2 **59.** H

3 Exercises

1. 12 **3.** 20 **5.** 8 **7.** 19 **9.** 22
11. 5 **13.** 11 **15.** 24 **17.** 12
19. 41 **21.** 300 **23.** 10 **25.** 22
27. 24 **29.** 13 **31.** 31 **33.** $4.50
35. 86 °F **41.** H

4 Exercises

1. $7p$ **3.** $\frac{n}{12}$ **5.** $5 \div n$, or $\frac{5}{n}$
7. $5 + x$ **9.** $n \div 8$ **11.** $3y - 10$
13. $5 + 2t$ **15.** $\frac{23}{u} - t$ **17.** $2(y + 5)$
19. $35(r - 5)$ **21.** $65,000 + 2b$
23. 90 divided by y
25. 16 multiplied by t
27. the difference between
4 times p and 10
29. the quotient of m and 15 plus 3
31. $15y + 12$
37. $(104 + 19 \cdot 2)x$; $426

5 Exercises

1. $6b$ and $\frac{b}{2}$ **3.** $8x$ **5.** There are
no like terms. **7.** b^6 and $3b^6$
9. m and $2m$ **11.** $8a + 2b$
13. $3a + 3b + 2c$ **15.** $3q^2 + 2q$
17. $2n + 3a + 3a + 2n + 5$
19. $27y$ **21.** $2d^2 + d$
23. no like terms
25. no like terms
27. $4n + 5n + 6n = 15n$
29a. $21.5d + 23d + 15.5d + 19d$
b. $750.50 **c.** the amount Brad
earned in June **31.** $23x^2$ **35.** D

Chapter Study Guide: Review

1. numerical expression
2. Identity Property
3. algebraic expression
4. coefficient
5. evaluate **6.** 3 **7.** 103
8. 5 **9.** 67 **10.** $55
11. Comm. Prop. of Add.
12. Identity Prop. of Add.
13. Distributive Property
14. 65 **15.** 2,300 **16.** 280
17. 168 **18.** 4; Commut. Prop.
19. 32; Ident. Prop.
20. 15; Assoc. Prop. **21.** 19
22. 524 **23.** 10
24. 220; 220 miles
25. $\frac{n}{9}$ **26.** $2n - 6$
27. $4 \div (n + 12)$ **28.** $2(t - 11)$
29. $32 \div s$
30. p^3 and $2p^3$, 18 and 5
31. $3a^4$ and $2a^4$, $6b$ and $\frac{1}{3}b$
32. $10b^2 + 8$ **33.** $15a^2 + 2$
34. $x^4 + x^3 + 6x^2$
35. $n + n + n + n + 2$; $4n + 2$

Selected Answers ... Chapter 2

1 Exercises

5. > **7.** < **9.** −5, −3, −1, 4, 6
11. −6, −4, 0, 1, 3 **13.** 8 **15.** 10
21. > **23.** < **25.** −9, −7, −5, −2, 0
27. 16 **29.** 20 **31.** < **33.** = **35.** =
37. = **39.** Aug, Jul, Sep, May, Jun,
Apr, Mar, Oct **41.** −29
45. decreased by about 9% **51.** G

2 Exercises

1. 12 **3.** −2 **5.** 15 **7.** −15 **9.** −12
11. −20 **13.** −9 **15.** 13 **17.** 7
19. −17 **21.** −19 **23.** −16
25. −88 **27.** −55 **29.** −14
31. −13 **33.** −13 **35.** −26 **37.** 14
39. > **41.** > **43.** > **45.** 45 + 18 +
27 + (−21) + (−93); −24;
Cody's account is reduced by $24.
47. −16 **49.** 3 **51.** 4,150 ft **57.** F

2 Extension

1. 32 **3.** 32 **5.** −50; the number
of floors to descend to the ground
floor **7.** −11 **9.** 32 km

3 Exercises

1. −3 **3.** 6 **5.** −4 **7.** −10 **9.** 7
11. −14 **13.** −5 **15.** 8 **17.** 12
19. 16 **21.** −17 **23.** 8 **25.** 50
27. 18 **29.** 16 **31.** −5 **33.** −20
35. 83 °F **37.** −14 **39.** −2 **41.** 2
43. 16 **45.** −27 **47.** −17 **49.** −13,
−17, −21 **51.** 1,234 °F **53.** 265 °F
57. $m + n$ has the least absolute
value.

4 Exercises

1. −15 **3.** −15 **5.** 15 **7.** −15
9. −8 **11.** 4 **13.** 7 **15.** undefined
17. 450 feet **19.** −10 **21.** −12
23. 48 **25.** 35 **27.** 7 **29.** −8
31. −9 **33.** −9 **35.** −40 **37.** −3
39. 50 **41.** −3 **43.** 30 **45.** −42
47. −60 ft **49.** 1 **51.** −12
53. 1,400 **55.** 11 **57.** less; −$72
59. more; $12 **63.** C

5 Exercises

1. $w = 4$ **3.** $k = -7$ **5.** $y = -30$
7. $57 million **9.** $k = -3$
11. $v = -4$ **13.** $a = 20$
15. $t = -32$ **17.** $n = 150$
19. $\ell = -144$ **21.** $y = 100$
23. $j = -63$ **25.** $c = 17$
27. $y = -11$ **29.** $w = -41$
31. $x = -58$ **33.** $x = 4$ **35.** $t = 9$
37. 3 mi **39.** $-13 + p = 8$
41. $t - 9 = -22$ **43.** oceans or
beaches **49.** H

6 Exercises

1. 0.57 **3.** 1.83 **5.** 0.12 **7.** 0.05
9. $\frac{1}{125}$ **11.** $-2\frac{1}{20}$ **13.** 0.720
15. 6.4 **17.** 0.88 **19.** 1 **21.** 1.92
23. 0.8 **25.** 0.55 **27.** $\frac{1}{100}$ **29.** $-\frac{2}{25}$
31. $\frac{61}{4}$ **33.** $8\frac{3}{8}$ **35.** 8.75 **37.** $5\frac{5}{100}$
39. $\frac{307}{20}$ **41.** 4.003 **43.** yes **45.** no
47. yes **49.** no **51.** $18\frac{1}{20}$, $18\frac{1}{25}$,
$18\frac{11}{20}$ **55.** D

7 Exercises

1. < **3.** < **5.** < **7.** < **9.** $-\frac{13}{5}$,
2.05, 2.5 **11.** < **13.** > **15.** >
17. > **19.** > **21.** < **23.** < **25.** $\frac{5}{8}$,
0.7, 0.755 **27.** −2.25, 2.05, $\frac{21}{10}$
29. −2.98, $-2\frac{9}{10}$, 2.88 **31.** $\frac{3}{4}$
33. $\frac{7}{8}$ **35.** 0.32 **37.** $-\frac{7}{8}$
41. sloths **47.** J

Chapter Study Guide: Review

1. rational number; integer;
terminating decimal
2. integers; opposite **3.** > **4.** <
5. −6, −2, 0, 4, 5, **6.** −8, −3, 1, 2,
8 **7.** 0 **8.** 17 **9.** 6 **10.** −3 **11.** 1
12. −56 **13.** 9 **14.** 10 **15.** −5
16. 11 °F **17.** 6 **18.** −9 **19.** −1
20. −9 **21.** 3 **22.** 14 **23.** −10
24. −50 **25.** 3 **26.** 16 **27.** −2
28. −12 **29.** −3 **30.** $120
31. $y = 10$ **32.** $d = 14$
33. $j = -26$ **34.** $n = 72$
35. $c = 13$ **36.** $m = -4$ **37.** 18 ft
38. $\frac{1}{4}$ **39.** $-\frac{1}{250}$ **40.** $\frac{1}{20}$ **41.** 3.5
42. 0.6 **43.** $0.\overline{6}$ **44.** $\frac{1}{4}$ **45.** <
46. > **47.** > **48.** <
49. −0.55, $\frac{6}{13}$, $\frac{1}{2}$, 0.58

Selected Answers ... Chapter 3

1 Exercises

1. 21.82 **3.** 12.826 **5.** 1.98 **7.** 1.77
9. $37.2 billion **11.** 18.97
13. -25.52 **15.** 10.132 **17.** -15.89
19. 9.01 **21.** 16.05 **23.** 5.1
25. 22.77 **27.** 77.13 g **29.** -4.883
31. 14.33 **33.** 1.92 **35.** 30.12
37. -1.26 **39.** -3.457 **41.** You must keep the place value units together. **43.** 1915 **49.** G

2 Exercises

1. -3.6 **3.** 0.18 **5.** 2.04 **7.** -0.315
9. 334.7379 miles **11.** 0.35 **13.** 3.2
15. -20.4 **17.** 9.1 **19.** 4.48
21. 2.814 **23.** -9.256 **25.** 6.161
27. 5.445 mi **29.** 0.0021 **31.** 0.432
33. -2.88 **35.** 1.911 **37.** 0.351
39. 0.00864 **41.** 28.95 in. of mercury **43.** -8.904 **45.** -0.027
47. 1,224.1152 **53.** 11.3 mi

3 Exercises

1. 0.9 **3.** 4.6 **5.** -3.2 **7.** 2.5
9. -16 **11.** -4.8 **13.** 28 mi/gal
15. -0.12 **17.** -14 **19.** 4.2
21. 47.5 **23.** 4 **25.** -48.75
27. 2.4 min **29.** 22.5 **31.** -0.4
33. 25 **35.** 18 **37.** 6.4
39. 2,500 years **41.** 18.47 million visits **45.** C **47.** 9.93

4 Exercises

1. $w = 7$ **3.** $k = 24.09$ **5.** $b = 5.04$
7. $t = 9$ **9.** $4.25 **11.** $c = 44.56$

13. $a = 5.08$ **15.** $p = -53.21$
17. $z = 16$ **19.** $w = 11.76$
21. $a = -74.305$ **23.** $7.50
25. $n = -4.92$ **27.** $r = 0.72$
29. $m = -0.15$ **31.** $k = 0.9$
33. $t = 0.936$ **35.** $v = -2$
37. $n = 12.254$ **39.** $j = 11.107$
41. $g = 0.5$ **43.** $171
45a. 148.1 million **b.** between English and Italian **49.** C

5 Exercises

1. $\frac{1}{3}$ **3.** $\frac{3}{7}$ **5.** $\frac{1}{2}$ **7.** $\frac{19}{24}$ **9.** $\frac{1}{12}$ **11.** $\frac{1}{2}$
13. $\frac{3}{5}$ **15.** $\frac{2}{3}$ **17.** $\frac{1}{5}$ **19.** $\frac{1}{4}$ **21.** $\frac{3}{4}$
23. $-\frac{1}{6}$ **25.** $\frac{8}{15}$ **27.** $\frac{1}{6}$ mi **29.** $\frac{13}{18}$
31. $\frac{4}{5}$ **33.** $-\frac{1}{12}$ **35.** $\frac{1}{2}$ **37.** $-\frac{1}{20}$
39. $\frac{14}{15}$ **41.** $\frac{41}{63}$ **43.** $\frac{41}{45}$ **45.** 0
47. $\frac{91}{121}$ **49.** $\frac{5}{6}$ hour **51.** $\frac{13}{24}$ mi
53. Cai **55.** $\frac{3}{8}$ lb of cashews
61. 0.1

6 Exercises

1. 18 **3.** $\frac{3}{32}$ **5.** $\frac{1}{4}$ **7.** 2 **9.** 3 capes
11. 18 **13.** $4\frac{3}{8}$ **15.** $\frac{1}{27}$ **17.** -40
19. $\frac{5}{14}$ **21.** -14 **23.** $\frac{88}{7}$ **25.** $9\frac{3}{5}$
27. 6 pieces **29.** -2 **31.** $-\frac{16}{25}$
33. $\frac{21}{2}$ **35.** $\frac{1}{3}$ **37.** -1
43. 87 hamburger patties
47. 11 in. **51.** G

7 Exercises

1. $a = \frac{3}{4}$ **3.** $p = \frac{3}{2}$ **5.** $r = \frac{9}{10}$
7. $1\frac{1}{8}$ c **9.** $t = \frac{5}{8}$ **11.** $x = \frac{53}{24}$

13. $y = \frac{7}{60}$ **15.** $w = \frac{1}{2}$ **17.** $z = \frac{1}{12}$
19. $n = 1\frac{23}{25}$ **21.** $t = \frac{1}{4}$ **23.** $w = 6$
25. $x = \frac{3}{5}$ **27.** $n = \frac{12}{5}$ **29.** $y = \frac{1}{2}$
31. $r = \frac{1}{77}$ **33.** $h = -\frac{1}{12}$ **35.** $v = \frac{3}{4}$
37. $d = 14\frac{17}{40}$ **39.** $11\frac{3}{16}$ lb
41. 15 million species
43. 48 stories **49.** G

Chapter Study Guide: Review

1. reciprocals **2.** 27.88 **3.** -51.2
4. 6.22 **5.** 52.902 **6.** 14.095
7. 35.88 **8.** 29.2 cm **9.** 3.5
10. -38.7 **11.** 40.495 **12.** 60.282
13. 77.348 **14.** -18.81 **15.** $38.08
16. 5 **17.** -40 **18.** 800 **19.** -5
20. -6.24 **21.** 340 **22.** 4.5
23. -1.09 **24.** -15.4 **25.** -500
26. 2 **27.** 4 **28.** 193.0175 mi/h
29. $x = -10.44$ **30.** $s = 107$
31. $n = 0.007$ **32.** $k = 8.64$
33. $e = -5.05$ **34.** $w = -3.08$
35. 56 hours **36.** $\frac{5}{12}$ **37.** $\frac{17}{20}$
38. $\frac{5}{11}$ **39.** $\frac{1}{9}$ **40.** $7\frac{1}{2}$ **41.** $1\frac{21}{25}$
42. $17\frac{17}{63}$ **43.** $6\frac{1}{4}$ **44.** $\frac{4}{75}$ **45.** $\frac{2}{15}$
46. 1 **47.** $1\frac{11}{12}$ **48.** 28 slices
49. $1\frac{2}{3}$ **50.** $\frac{1}{15}$ **51.** $1\frac{5}{7}$ **52.** $\frac{13}{28}$
53. $1\frac{3}{4}$ cups

Selected Answers ... Chapter 4

1 Exercises

1. 83.5 mL per min **3.** 458 mi/h
5. $7.75 per h **7.** about 74.63 mi/h
9. 3 runs per game **11.** $335
per mo **13.** 18.83 mi per gal
15. $5.75 per h **17.** 122 mi per trip
19. 0.04 mi per min
21. $\frac{1,026 \text{ students}}{38 \text{ classes}}$; 27 students
per class **23.** $0.06, $0.07; $\frac{\$2.52}{42 \text{ oz}}$ is
the better buy. **27.** 289, 328, 609
(France, Poland, Germany) **31.** D

2 Exercises

1. yes **3.** yes **5.** yes **7.** no **13.** no
15. no **17.** no **19.** no **29.** 3, 24, 15
39a. $\frac{1 \text{ can}}{4 \text{ hours}}$ **b.** No, 1:4 = x:2,080;
the class recycled 520 cans.
43a. 8:5 **b.** Mill Pond and Clear
Pond **49.** H

3 Exercises

1. $x = 60$ **3.** $m = 16.4$ **5.** 3 lb
7. $h = 144$ **9.** $v = 336$ **11.** $t = 36$
13. $n = 22\frac{2}{5}$ **15.** 227 grams

29. about 23 dimes
31. 22 counselors **33.** $\frac{4}{10} = \frac{6}{15}$
35. $\frac{3}{75} = \frac{4}{100}$ **37.** $\frac{5}{6} = \frac{90}{108}$
39. 105 oxygen atoms **45.** $\frac{4}{6}$

4 Exercises

1. similar **3.** similar **5.** not similar
7. similar **9.** no **11.** similar
13. yes **15.** yes **17.** no
19. no **23.** C

5 Exercises

1. $a = 22.5$ cm; $b = 89°$
3. 28 ft **5.** $x = 13.5$ in.;
$n = 40°$ **7.** 249.18 in. **9.** 21 m
15. B

6 Exercises

1. $\frac{1}{14}$ **3.** 67.2 cm tall, 40 cm wide
5. $\frac{1}{15}$ **7.** 135 in. **9.** 16 in.
11. 75 cm; 141 cm; 240 cm
13. 2 in. **15.** about 25 mi
17. 1 mi:0.25 ft or 1 ft:4 mi
19. B

Chapter Study Guide: Review

1. similar **2.** ratio **3.** scale factor
4. 6 ft/s **5.** 109 mi/h **6.** $2.24,
about $2.14; $\frac{\$32.05}{15 \text{ gal}}$ **7.** $32/g,
$35/g; $\frac{\$160}{5 \text{ g}}$ **8.** $7.90/h **9.** no
10. no **11.** yes **12.** Possible
answer: $\frac{10}{12} = \frac{30}{36}$ **13.** Possible
answer: $\frac{45}{50} = \frac{90}{100}$ **14.** Possible
answer: $\frac{9}{15} = \frac{27}{45}$ **15.** $n = 2$
16. $a = 6$ **17.** $b = 4$ **18.** $x = 66$
19. $y = 10$ **20.** $w = 20$ **21.** not
similar **22.** similar **23.** $x = 100$ ft;
$a = 84°$ **24.** 8 cm **25.** about 8 ft
26. 12.1 in. **27.** 163.4 mi

Selected Answers ... Chapter 5

1 Exercises

1. II **3.** III

5, 7.

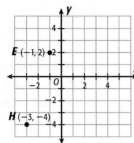

9. (6, −3) **11.** (−4, 0) **13.** I **15.** IV

17, 19.

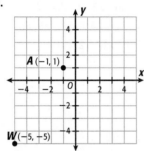

21. (−4, 4) **23.** (−5, −4) **25.** (5, 6)

27. triangle; Quadrants I and II

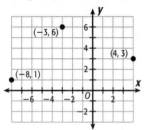

29. III

31. IV **33.** (12, 7) **39.** B **41.** −6

2 Exercises

1. A **3.** B

7.

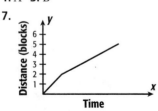

9. One of the mothers is the daughter of the other mother.

3 Exercises

1. positive; 1

3.

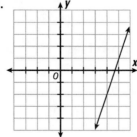

5.

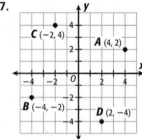

7. constant **9.** constant

11. negative; −3

13.

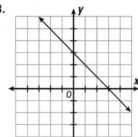

15.

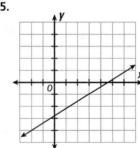

17. constant **19.** variable

21. −7 **23.** −3 **25.** $\frac{3}{2}$

29. The y-values decrease.

33. B

4 Exercises

1. no **3.** yes; $k = \frac{1}{4}$ **5.** no **7.** no

9a. $y = 4x$ **c.** 80 gal **11.** yes; $k = \frac{2}{3}$ **13.** no **15.** yes, $k = 2$, $y = 2x$ **17.** no **19.** $y = \frac{2}{7}x$

21. $y = 2x$ **23.** $y = 40$ **25.** yes; the ratio of total pay y to number of hours worked x, is always constant, so $y = kx$ where k is the rate of pay per hour **27.** 1,800 m

33. $y = 0.65x$; $13.65

Chapter Study Guide: Review

1. quadrant **2.** constant of variation **3.** y-axis

4–7.

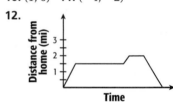

8. (2, −1), IV **9.** (−2, 3), II

10. (1, 0) **11.** (−4, −2)

12.

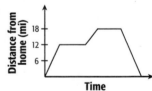

13.

14. variable **15.** constant

16. yes; $k = 18$; $k = 18x$ **17.** no

Selected Answers ... Chapter 6

1 Exercises

1. 60% **3.** 54.4% **5.** 8.7%
7. 12% **9.** 17.5% **11.** 50%, $\frac{11}{20}$, $0.\overline{5}$
13. $-\frac{1}{10}$, 1%, 10% **15.** $\frac{35}{54}$, $0.\overline{6}$, 72%
17. mental math; 40% **19.** 83%
21. 8.1% **23.** 75% **25.** 37.5%
27. 28% **29.** -0.7, $-\frac{2}{3}$, 7%
31. $-\frac{1}{9}$, -0.1, 1% **33.** $-\frac{1}{6}$, -0.01,
2% **35.** pencil and paper; 20%
37. > **39.** < **41.** 1%
45. ≈33.3% **49.** D

2 Exercises

1. 30 **3.** 5 **5.** Yes; 35% of $43.99
is close to $\frac{1}{3}$ of $45, which is
$15. Since $45 − $15 = $30,
Darden will have enough money.
7. 8 **9.** 7.7 **11.** 26 **13.** 70 **15.** 216
17. 13 **19.** Fancy Feet **21.** 24
23. 12 **25.** 12 **27.** 24 **29.** 60
31. 3 **33.** 72 **35.** 15 **37.** about
26 oz **39.** about 2% more

3 Exercises

1. $26.00 **3.** $14\frac{5}{8}$ **5.** $-6\frac{17}{24}$ **7.** $17\frac{1}{5}$
9. 8 weeks **11.** 10.5 hours
13. $11\frac{1}{4}$ **15.** 6 **17.** $-10\frac{3}{4}$ **19.** $-33\frac{5}{6}$
21. 8 markers **23.** 89 miles
25. $-10\frac{1}{2}$ **27.** $11\frac{1}{10}$ **29.** 38.4 **35.** B

4 Exercises

1. 28% **3.** 16.1% **5.** $34.39
7. 37.5% **9.** 22.2% **11.** $55.25
13. 100% **15.** 43.6% **17.** 30
19. 56.25 gal **21.** $48.25
23a. $41,500 **b.** $17,845 **c.** 80.7%
25. about 8,506 trillion Btu **27.** A

5 Exercises

1. 48% increase **3.** 100% increase
5. $9773.60 **7.** 22% increase
9. ≈8.6% **11.** 33% decrease
13. 39% decrease **15.** 24%
decrease **17.** $500 **19.** 120 **21.** 50
23a. $78 **b.** $117 **c.** $39 **d.** 80%
25. 24,900% **27.** percent
decrease; 13% **33.** $7.49; $31.76
35. 50% **37.** 311.75

6 Exercises

1. $574 **3.** 11.6% **5.** $603.50
7. 3.1% **9.** $15.23 **11.** $38.07
13. $81,200 **17a.** $64,208
b. $12,717 **c.** ≈17.8% **d.** ≈19.8%
19. $695 **21.** yes **23.** yes
25. 50% decrease

Chapter Study Guide: Review

1. interest; simple interest;
principal; rate of interest
2. percent of increase **3.** percent
of decrease **4.** commission
5. 60% **6.** 16.7% **7.** 9% **8.** 80%
9. 66.7% **10.** 0.56% **11.** -2.6, 30%,
$0.\overline{33}$, $2\frac{3}{5}$ **12.** Possible answer: 8
13. Possible answer: 90
14. Possible answer: 24
15. Possible answer: 32
16. Possible answer: 40
17. Possible answer: 3
18. Possible answer: $3 **19.** 5%
20. $-13\frac{1}{2}$ **21.** $3\frac{1}{2}$ **22.** $5\frac{5}{6}$ **23.** $-3\frac{1}{9}$
24. $2\frac{1}{2}$ **25.** $11\frac{3}{5}$ **26.** 50% **27.** 14.3%
28. 30% **29.** 83.1% **30.** 23.1%
31. 75% **32.** $16,830 **33.** $3.55
34. $3171.88 **35.** $400 **36.** 7%
37. 0.5 yr **38.** $1000 at 3.75% for 3
years; $7.50 **39.** 14,750

1 Exercises

1. 20; 20; 5 and 20; 30 **3.** median
5. 83.3; 88; 88; 28 **7.** 4.3; 4.4; 4.4
and 6.2; 4.2 **9.** mean and median
11. 151 **13.** 9; 8; 12 **15.** 22.5, 23.5,
14 **21.** J

2 Exercises

1. The range is 16, the interquartile
range is 11, the lower quartile is
35 and the upper quartile is 36.
3. airplane B **5.** The range is 16,
the interquartile is 12, the lower
quartile is 73, and the upper
quartile is 85. **7.** city A **11.** the
range **19.** 15

3 Exercises

1. Daria's method **3.** biased
5. Vonneta's method **7.** not biased
9. entire population **11.** entire
population **13.** yes **17.** B

Chapter Study Guide: Review

1. population; sample **2.** mean
3. outlier **4.** lower quartile
5. 302; 311.5; 233 and 324; 166
6. 43; 46; none; 25 **7.** when the
data set has an outlier
8. 274; 272 **9.** 278.6 **10.** 4; 18
11.

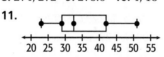

12. 13
13. 2,500 is a reasonable estimate
based on the data. **14.** not biased;
random sample **15.** biased; it
is likely that not all teenagers
like the same type of clothing
16. sample **17.** population
18. sample

Selected Answers ... Chapter 8

1 Exercises

1. *Q, R, S* **3.** plane *QRS* **5.** $\overline{QU}$, $\overline{RU}$, $\overline{SU}$ **7.** *D, E, F* **9.** plane *DEF* **11.** $\overline{DE}$, $\overline{EF}$, $\overline{DF}$ **21.** C

2 Exercises

1. right **3.** straight
5. complementary
7. complementary **9.** 61° **11.** right
13. complementary
15. supplementary **17.** 95°
19. supplementary; 152°
21. supplementary; 46° **23a.** right
angle **b.** about 39° N, 77° W **27.** C

3 Exercises

1. parallel **3.** perpendicular
5. 115° **7.** skew **9.** parallel
11. 30° **13.** parallel

Chapter 8

15. supplementary; adjacent
17. 45° **19.** sometimes **21.** always
23a. They are perpendicular.
b. transversal **c.** They are
corresponding angles. **29.** F

4 Exercises

1. 77° **3.** 55° **5.** 110° **7.** 720°
9. 360° **11.** 37° **13.** 88° **15.** 101°
17. 1,080° **19.** 38° **21.** 99°; obtuse
23. 90°; right **25.** 45°, 45°, 90°
31. 80°

5 Exercises

1. the triangles on the game
board and the holes on the game
board **3.** 2 triangles; 2 rectangles;
2 green pentagons **5.** no **7.** 2.5
9. the triangles in the kite's design

11. no **13.** 112°; 8 cm **15.** the
lengths of all the sides **17.** the
lengths of adjacent sides in each
rectangle **19.** 40 m **25.** G

Chapter Study Guide: Review

1. supplementary **2.** parallel lines
3. perpendicular **4.** straight
5. *D, E, F* **6.** $\overleftrightarrow{DF}$ **7.** plane *DEF*
8. $\overrightarrow{ED}$, $\overrightarrow{FD}$, $\overline{DF}$ **9.** $\overline{DE}$, $\overline{DF}$, $\overline{EF}$
10. acute **11.** straight **12.** 35°
13. 73° **14.** skew **15.** parallel
16. 74° **17.** 106° **18.** 106°
19. 74° **20.** no **21.** yes
22. $x = 133°$; $z = 10$ cm

Selected Answers

1 Exercises

1. 18 m **3.** 32 ft **5.** 20 m **7.** 37.7 m
9. 132 in. **11.** 48 cm **13.** 44 m
15. 8 ft **17.** 110 cm **19.** 32.0 in.
21. 2.8 m; 5.7 m **23.** 5.3 in.; 33.3 in.
25. 16 strands **27.** 96 ft **33.** 28 ft

2 Exercises

1. 78.5 in^2 **3.** 314 yd^2 **5.** 154 in^2
7. 28.3 in **9.** 32.2 yd^2 **11.** 616 cm^2
13. 17,662.5 mi^2 **15.** 28.3 cm^2
17. 56.5 in.; 254.3 in^2 **19.** 40.2 cm;
128.6 cm^2 **21.** $r = 1$ ft
23a. 113 mi^2 **b.** 141 mi^2 **29.** A

3 Exercises

1. 29 ft^2 **3.** 224 ft^2 **5.** 38 ft^2
7. 25 ft^2 **9.** 84.56 m^2 **11.** 46 cm^2
13. 30 ft^2; 30 ft **15.** 255.25 m^2;
65.7 m **17.** 10 **23.** 240

4 Exercises

1. pentagon; triangles; pentagonal
pyramid **3.** triangles; rectangles;
triangular prism **5.** polyhedron;
hexagonal pyramid **7.** triangle;
triangles; triangular pyramid
9. hexagon; triangles; hexagonal
pyramid **11.** not polyhedron;
cylinder **13.** square prism
15. triangular pyramid
19. rectangular pyramid
21. cylinder **23.** A

4 Extension

1. D **5.** cylinder

5 Exercises

1. 240 in^3 **3.** 3.9375 in^3
5. 188.8 m^3 **7.** 192 ft^3
9. 13.44 in^3 **11.** 200 in^3
13. 288 m^3 **15.** 47.25 ft^3

6 Exercises

1. 286 ft^2 **3.** 244.9 cm^2 **5.** 941 in^2
7. 132 yd^2 **9.** 188.4 cm^2
11b. 158.0 cm^2 **c.** 85.4 cm^2
17. 628

Chapter Study Guide: Review

1. cylinder **2.** surface area
3. polyhedron **4.** cone
5. 83 m **6.** 81.4 cm **7.** 40.8 ft
8. 49.0 in. **9.** 36.3 m^2
10. 226.9 ft^2 **11.** 254.34 in^2
12. 34.31 ft^2 **13.** 21 m^2
14. cylinder **15.** rectangular
prism **16.** triangular pyramid
17. cone **18.** 364 cm^3
19. 111.9 ft^3 **20.** 250 m^2
21. 34 cm^2 **22.** 262.3 cm^2
23. 803.8 ft^2

Selected Answers ... Chapter 10

1 Exercises

1. unlikely   **3.** $\frac{5}{6}$ **5.** certain
7. unlikely   **9.** $\frac{2}{5}$ **11.** as likely as not
13. certain   **15.** not likely
17a. It is very likely.   **b.** It is
impossible.   **23.** $\frac{1}{2}$

2 Exercises

1. 70%   **3.** ≈43%   **5a.** $\frac{9}{14}$ **5b.** $\frac{5}{14}$
7. $\frac{16}{25}$ **9.** ≈27%   **11a.** $\frac{3}{8}$ **13.** D

3 Exercises

1. H1, H2, T1, T2; 4   **3.** 24   **5.** 1H,
1T, 2H, 2T, 3H, 3T, 4H, 4T; 8
7. 12   **9.** 6   **11a.** 9 outcomes
b. 6 outcomes   **c.** 12 outcomes
13. 12   **17.** D

4 Exercises

1. ≈17%   **3.** $\frac{3}{7}$ **5.** $\frac{2}{7}$ **7.** 25%   **9.** $\frac{3}{7}$
11. $\frac{1}{18}$ **13.** $\frac{1}{12}$ **15.** $\frac{1}{9}$ **17.** $\frac{2}{5}$ **19.** 0
21. $\frac{2}{5}$ **23a.** unfair   **25.** 25%   **29.** D

5 Exercises

1. 183 days   **3.** 9   **5.** No; it
will only snow 2 days on their
vacation.   **7.** 324   **9.** 94   **11.** Yes; it
is late only 4% of the time.   **13.** 36
15. 3   **21.** about 4,450 flights

6 Exercises

1. independent   **3.** $\frac{1}{6}$ **5.** $\frac{3}{20}$
7. independent   **9.** $\frac{1}{4}$
11. dependent   **13a.** $\frac{1}{3}$ **17.** B

7 Exercises

1. 6   **3.** 10   **5.** 10   **7.** 15   **9.** 28
11. 3   **13.** 15   **17.** 15

8 Exercises

1. 24   **3.** 720   **5.** 6   **7.** 3,628,000
9. combinations   **11.** permutations
13. $\frac{1}{4}$ **15.** 120   **17.** 5 × 4 × 3 = 60
19. 13!   **21.** $\frac{2}{7}$ **25.** D

9 Exercises

1. $\frac{1}{100}$ **3.** $\frac{2}{9}$ **5.** $\frac{1}{19}$, 600   **7.** $\frac{16}{125}$
9. $\frac{1}{36}$ **11.** $\frac{1}{24}$ **13.** $\frac{1}{270,725}$
17. B

Chapter Study Guide: Review

1. independent events
2. combination   **3.** unlikely
4. impossible   **5.** $\frac{2}{3}$ **6.** $\frac{1}{3}$ **7.** R1,
R2, R3, R4, W1, W2, W3, W4,
B1, B2, B3, B4   **8.** 12 possible
outcomes   **9.** ≈43%
10. 12.5%   **11.** about 20 goals
12. about 6 times   **13.** $\frac{4}{195}$ **14.** $\frac{4}{121}$
15. 10 ways   **16.** 21 committees
17. 36 combinations
18. 3,628,800 ways   **19.** 720 ways
20. 120 ways   **21.** $\frac{1}{9}$ **22.** $\frac{1}{36}$

1 Exercises

1. $n = 7$ **3.** $x = \frac{1}{3}$ **5.** $y = 136$
7. 12 refills **9.** $p = -12$ **11.** $d = \frac{1}{7}$
13. $y = 5$ **15.** $k = 85$ **17.** $m = -80$
19. $m = -112$ **21.** 6 more than a number divided by 3 equals 18; $m = 36$. **23.** 2 equals 4 less than a number divided by 5; $n = 30$.
25. $x = 2$ **27.** $g = 20$ **29.** $w = -9$
31. $p = 2$ **33.** 120 min **35.** 1,300 calories **37.** 2 slices of pizza for lunch and again for dinner
39. C

2 Exercises

1. $n = 5$ **3.** $p = 2$ **5.** $q = 2$
7. 12 books **9.** $x = \frac{7}{8}$ **11.** $n = 6$
13. $x = -2$ **15.** $n = -2$
17. $n = 1.5$ **19.** $t = -9$ **21.** $x = 66$
23. $w = 8$ **25.** $a = 176$ **27.** $b = -7$
29. $x = 3$ **31.** $6.70 **33.** $25 **35.** 91
39. A

3 Exercises

1. $n = 32$ **3.** $12w = 32$ **5.** $a = 2$
7. 5 movies **9.** $-8 = 12p$
11. $-6 = 2c$ **13.** $6 = \frac{1}{10}a$
15. $b = -8$ **17.** $a = -0.8$
19. $c = -2$ **21.** $y = -7$ **23.** $r = 4$
25. $r = -2$ **27.** 67 members
29. $x = 6$ **31.** 20 days
37. $0.03m = 2 + 0.01m$; $m = 100$; 100 minutes makes the cost for long distance from both plans equal.

3 Extension

3. 2 tsp **5.** 390 lb
7. 1,020 people **9.** 5
11. 45 **13.** 5

4 Exercises

1. number of people ≤ 18
3. water level > 45
5.

7.

9.

11. temperature < 40
13. number of tables ≤ 35
15.

17.

19.

21.

23.

25.

27.

29.

31.

35. $-200 \leq$ depth ≤ 0 **37.** $0 \geq$ *Manshu* depth measurement $\geq$ $-32,190$ ft; $0 \geq$ *Challenger* depth measurement $\geq -35,640$ ft; $0 \geq$ *Horizon* depth measurement $\geq$ $-34,884$ ft; $0 \geq$ *Vityaz* depth measurement $\geq -36,200$ ft **39.** B

5 Exercises

1. $x < 27$ **3.** $p \leq 7$ **5.** $b \leq -24$
7. no more than 42 °F **9.** $m < 11$
11. $c \leq 11$ **13.** $x \geq 80$ **15.** $z > -12$
17. $f > -6$ **19.** $n \geq -4$ **21.** at most 24 birds **23.** $a > 0.3$ **25.** $m \leq -38$
27. $g < 6\frac{1}{3}$ **29.** $w \leq 15.7$
31. $t \geq -242$ **33.** $v \leq -0.6$
35. at least $8 **39.** up to 50,000 hertz **43.** B

6 Exercises

1. $w < -32$ **3.** $p < 48$ **5.** $y > -\frac{11}{8}$ or $-1\frac{3}{8}$ **7.** at least 27 candles
9. $m > 52$ **11.** $c \geq -120$
13. $x \geq -1.1$ **15.** $z < \frac{3}{5}$

17. $f < -3$ **19.** $n \leq -10$
21. at least 46 wreaths **23.** $p > 4$
25. $y \geq 18$ **27.** $g > 0.63$ **29.** $w \leq \frac{3}{8}$
31. $t < \frac{5}{2}$ **33.** $v \geq -2.5$ **35.** 5 hours
37. at least 480 subscriptions
43. 301

7 Exercises

1. $x < 3$ **3.** $y \geq 6$ **5.** $x \geq \frac{2}{3}$
7. more than $26 each **9.** $b < 12$
11. $c \geq -3$ **13.** $x \leq -27$ **15.** $j \leq 2$
17. at most 6 bagels **19.** $x \geq -6$
21. $c < 1.8$ **23.** $w \leq 8$ **25.** $s > -24$
27. $d \leq 4$ **29.** $14 **31.** at least 225 students **33.** at most 60% **37.** B

Chapter Study Guide: Review

1. inequality **2.** compound inequality **3.** solution set
4. $y = 8$ **5.** $z = 30$ **6.** $w = 147$
7. $a = -7$ **8.** $j = 9$ **9.** $b = 4$
10. $y = 5$ **11.** 26 mi **12.** $b = \frac{1}{2}$
13. $c = 6$ **14.** $m = \frac{8}{3}$ or $2\frac{2}{3}$
15. $x = 20$ **16.** 10 months
17. weight limit ≤ 9 tons
18. age > 200
19.

20.

21. $r > 25$ **22.** $x \leq -26$ **23.** $g < 8$
24. $t \leq \frac{1}{6}$ **25.** $9 > r$ **26.** $u \geq -66$
27. at least 38 points **28.** at most $94 **29.** $n < -55.2$ **30.** $p \leq 6$
31. $k < -130$ **32.** $p < 5$
33. $v \geq 2.76$ **34.** $c > 33$
35. at least 16 purses **36.** $b < -2$
37. $d < -6$ **38.** $n \geq -4$
39. $y \leq 18$ **40.** $c > -54$
41. $x \leq 10$ **42.** $h \geq -156$
43. $-10 < t$ **44.** $52 > w$
45. $y \leq 35$ **46.** at most 4 T-shirts
47. more than $147

Glossary/Glosario ...

A

ENGLISH	SPANISH	EXAMPLES
absolute value The distance of a number from zero on a number line; shown by | |.	**valor absoluto** Distancia a la que está un número de 0 en una recta numérica. El símbolo del valor absoluto es | |.	$\|5\| = 5$ $\|-5\| = 5$
accuracy The closeness of a given measurement or value to the actual measurement or value.	**exactitud** Cercanía de una medida o un valor a la medida o el valor real.	
acute angle An angle that measures greater than 0° and less than 90°.	**ángulo agudo** Ángulo que mide más de 0° y menos de 90°.	
acute triangle A triangle with all angles measuring less than 90°.	**triángulo acutángulo** Triángulo en el que todos los ángulos miden menos de 90°.	
addend A number added to one or more other numbers to form a sum.	**sumando** Número que se suma a uno o más números para formar una suma.	In the expression 4 + 6 + 7, the numbers 4, 6, and 7 are addends.
Addition Property of Equality The property that states that if you add the same number to both sides of an equation, the new equation will have the same solution.	**Propiedad de igualdad de la suma** Propiedad que establece que puedes sumar el mismo número a ambos lados de una ecuación y la nueva ecuación tendrá la misma solución.	$\begin{aligned} x - 6 &= 8 \\ +6 & \quad +6 \\ x &= 14 \end{aligned}$
Addition Property of Opposites The property that states that the sum of a number and its opposite equals zero.	**Propiedad de la suma de los opuestos** Propiedad que establece que la suma de un número y su opuesto es cero.	$12 + (-12) = 0$
additive inverse The opposite of a number.	**inverso aditivo** El opuesto de un número.	The additive inverse of 5 is −5.
adjacent angles Angles in the same plane that have a common vertex and a common side.	**ángulos adyacentes** Angulos en el mismo plano que comparten un vértice y un lado.	∠1 and ∠2 are adjacent angles.
algebraic expression An expression that contains at least one variable.	**expresión algebraica** Expresión que contiene al menos una variable.	$x + 8$ $4(m - b)$

|---|---|---|

algebraic inequality An inequality that contains at least one variable.

desigualdad algebraica Desigualdad que contiene al menos una variable.

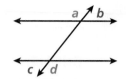

$x + 3 > 10$
$5a > b + 3$

---

alternate exterior angles A pair of angles on the outer side of two lines cut by a transversal that are on opposite sides of the transversal.

ángulos alternos externos Par de ángulos en los lados externos de dos líneas intersecadas por una transversal, que están en lados opuestos de la transversal.

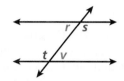

∠a and ∠d are alternate exterior angles.

---

alternate interior angles A pair of angles on the inner sides of two lines cut by a transversal that are on opposite sides of the transversal.

ángulos alternos externos Par de ángulos en los lados internos de dos líneas intersecadas por una transversal, que están en lados opuestos de la transversal.

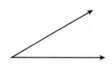

∠r and ∠v are alternate interior angles.

---

angle A figure formed by two rays with a common endpoint called the vertex.

ángulo Figura formada por dos rayos con un extremo común llamado vértice.

---

arc A part of a circle named by its endpoints.

arco Parte de un círculo que se nombra por sus extremos.

---

area The number of square units needed to cover a given surface.

área El número de unidades cuadradas que se necesitan para cubrir una superficie dada.

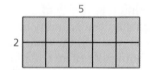

The area is 10 square units.

---

arithmetic sequence A sequence in which the terms change by the same amount each time.

sucesión aritmética Una sucesión en la que los términos cambian la misma cantidad cada vez.

The sequence 2, 5, 8, 11, 14 … is an arithmetic sequence.

Associative Property of Addition The property that states that for all real numbers a, b, and c, the sum is always the same, regardless of their grouping.

Propiedad asociativa de la suma Propiedad que establece que para todos los números reales a, b y c, la suma siempre es la misma sin importar cómo se agrupen.

$2 + 3 + 8 = (2 + 3) + 8 = 2 + (3 + 8)$

Associative Property of Multiplication The property that states that for all real numbers a, b, and c, their product is always the same, regardless of their grouping.

Propiedad asociativa de la multiplicación Propiedad que para todos los números reales a, b y c, el producto siempre es el mismo sin importar cómo se agrupen.

$2 \cdot 3 \cdot 8 = (2 \cdot 3) \cdot 8 = 2 \cdot (3 \cdot 8)$

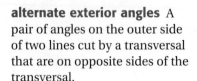

asymmetry Not identical on either side of a central line; not symmetrical.

asimetría Ocurre cuando dos lados separados por una línea central no son idénticos; falta de simetría.

The quadrilateral has asymmetry.

axes The two perpendicular lines of a coordinate plane that intersect at the origin.

ejes Las dos rectas numéricas perpendiculares del plano cartesiano que se intersecan en el origen.

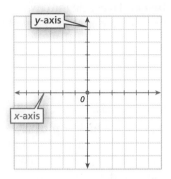

B

bar graph A graph that uses vertical or horizontal bars to display data.

gráfica de barras Gráfica en la que se usan barras verticales u horizontales para presentar datos.

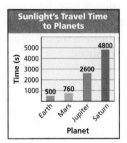

base-10 number system A number system in which all numbers are expressed using the digits 0–9.

sistema de base 10 Sistema de numeración en el que todos los números se expresan con los dígitos 0–9.

base (in numeration) When a number is raised to a power, the number that is used as a factor is the base.

base (en numeración) Cuando un número es elevado a una potencia, el número que se usa como factor es la base.

$3^5 = 3 \cdot 3 \cdot 3 \cdot 3 \cdot 3$; 3 is the base.

base (of a polygon) A side of a polygon.

base (de un polígono) Lado de un polígono.

base (of a three-dimensional figure) A face of a three-dimensional figure by which the figure is measured or classified.

base (de una figura tridimensional) Cara de una figura tridimensional a partir de la cual se mide o se clasifica la figura.

Bases of a cylinder   Bases of a prism

Base of a cone   Base of a pyramid

ENGLISH	SPANISH	EXAMPLES

biased sample A sample that does not fairly represent the population.

muestra no representativa Muestra que no representa adecuadamente la población.

---

bisect To divide into two congruent parts.

trazar una bisectriz Dividir en dos partes congruentes.

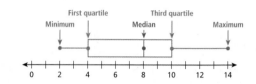

$\overrightarrow{JK}$ bisects ∠*LJM*.

---

box-and-whisker plot A graph shows how data are distributed by using the median, quartiles, least value, and greatest value; also called a box plot.

gráfica de mediana y rango Gráfica que muestra los valores máximo y mínimo, los cuartiles superior e inferior, así como la mediana de los datos.

---

break (graph) A zigzag on a horizontal or vertical scale of a graph that indicates that some of the numbers on the scale have been omitted.

discontinuidad (gráfica) Zig-zag en la escala horizontal o vertical de una gráfica que indica la omisión de algunos de los números de la escala.

C

---

capacity The amount a container can hold when filled.

capacidad Cantidad que cabe en un recipiente cuando se llena.

A large milk container has a capacity of 1 gallon.

Celsius A metric scale for measuring temperature in which 0 °C is the freezing point of water and 100 °C is the boiling point of water; also called *centigrade*.

Celsius Escala métrica para medir la temperatura, en la que 0° C es el punto de congelación del agua y 100° C es el punto de ebullición. También se llama *centígrado*.

---

center (of a circle) The point inside a circle that is the same distance from all the points on the circle.

centro (de un círculo) Punto interior de un círculo que se encuentra a la misma distancia de todos los puntos de la circunferencia.

---

center (of rotation) The point about which a figure is rotated.

centro (de una rotación) Punto alrededor del cual se hace girar una figura.

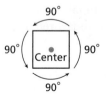

ENGLISH	SPANISH	EXAMPLES
central angle of a circle An angle with its vertex at the center of a circle.	**ángulo central de un círculo** Ángulo cuyo vértice se encuentra en el centro de un círculo.	
certain (probability) Sure to happen; having a probability of 1.	**seguro (probabilidad)** Que con seguridad sucederá. Representa una probabilidad de 1.	
chord A line segment with endpoints on a circle.	**cuerda** Segmento de recta cuyos extremos forman parte de un círculo.	
circle The set of all points in a plane that are the same distance from a given point called the center.	**círculo** Conjunto de todos los puntos en un plano que se encuentran a la misma distancia de un punto dado llamado centro.	
circumference The distance around a circle.	**circunferencia** Distancia alrededor de un círculo.	
clockwise A circular movement to the right in the direction shown.	**en el sentido de las manecillas del reloj** Movimiento circular en la dirección que se indica.	
coefficient The number that is multiplied by the variable in an algebraic expression.	**coeficiente** Número que se multiplica por la variable en una expresión algebraica.	5 is the coefficient in 5*b*.
combination An arrangement of items or events in which order does not matter.	**combinación** Agrupación de objetos o sucesos en la cual el orden no es importante.	For objects *A, B, C, and D*, there are 6 different combinations of 2 objects: *AB, AC, AD, BC, BD, CD.*
commission A fee paid to a person for making a sale.	**comisión** Page que recibe una persona por realizar una venta.	
commission rate The fee paid to a person who makes a sale expressed as a percent of the selling price.	**tasa de comisión** Page que recibe una persona por hacer una venta, expresado como un porcentaje del precio de venta.	A commission rate of 5% and a sale of $10,000 results in a commission of $500.
common denominator A denominator that is the same in two or more fractions.	**común denominador** Denominador que es común a dos o más fracciones.	The common denominator of $\frac{5}{8}$ and $\frac{2}{8}$ is 8.

ENGLISH	SPANISH	EXAMPLES
common difference In an arithmetic sequence, the nonzero constant difference of any term and the previous term.	**diferencia común** En una sucesión aritmética, diferencia constante distinta de cero entre cualquier término y el término anterior.	In the arithmetic sequence 3, 5, 7, 9, 11, ..., the common difference is 2.
common factor A number that is a factor of two or more numbers.	**factor común** Número que es factor de dos o más números.	8 is a common factor of 16 and 40.
common multiple A number that is a multiple of each of two or more numbers.	**común múltiplo** Número que es múltiplo de dos o más números.	15 is a common multiple of 3 and 5.
Commutative Property of Addition The property that states that two or more numbers can be added in any order without changing the sum.	**Propiedad conmutativa de la suma** Propiedad que establece que sumar dos o más números en cualquier orden no altera la suma.	$8 + 20 = 20 + 8$
Commutative Property of Multiplication The property that states that two or more numbers can be multiplied in any order without changing the product.	**Propiedad conmutativa de la multiplicación** Propiedad que establece que multiplicar dos o más números en cualquier orden no altera el producto.	$6 \cdot 12 = 12 \cdot 6$
compatible numbers Numbers that are close to the given numbers that make estimation or mental calculation easier.	**números compatibles** Números que están cerca de los números dados y hacen más fácil la estimación o el cálculo mental.	To estimate 7,957 + 5,009, use the compatible numbers 8,000 and 5,000: 8,000 + 5,000 = 13,000.
complement The set of all outcomes that are not the event.	**complemento** La serie de resultados que no están en el suceso.	When rolling a number cube, the complement of rolling a 3 is rolling a 1, 2, 4, 5, or 6.
complementary angles Two angles whose measures add to 90°.	**ángulos complementarios** Dos ángulos cuyas medidas suman 90°.	
composite figure A figure made up of simple geometric shapes.	**figura compuesta** Figura formada por figuras geométricas simples.	
composite number A number greater than 1 that has more than two whole-number factors.	**número compuesto** Número mayor que 1 que tiene más de dos factores que son números cabales.	4, 6, 8, and 9 are composite numbers.
compound event An event made up of two or more simple events.	**suceso compuesto** Suceso que consista de dos o más sucesos simples.	Rolling a 3 on a number cube and spinning a 2 on a spinner is a compound event.

ENGLISH	SPANISH	EXAMPLES
compound inequality A combination of more than one inequality.	**desigualdad compuesta** Combinación de dos o más desigualdades.	$-2 \leq x < 10$
cone A three-dimensional figure with one vertex and one circular base.	**cono** Figura tridimensional con un vértice y una base circular.	
congruent Having the same size and shape, the symbol for congurent is ≅.	**congruentes** Que tiene el mismo tamaño y la misma forma, expresado por ≅.	$\triangle ABC \cong \triangle DEF$
congruent angles Angles that have the same measure.	**ángulos congruentes** Ángulos que tienen la misma medida.	$\angle ABC \cong \angle DEF$
conjecture A statement believed to be true.	**conjetura** Enunciado que se supone verdadero.	
constant A value that does not change.	**constante** Valor que no cambia.	$3, 0, \pi$
constant of variation The constant k in direct and inverse variation equations.	**constante de variación** La constante k en ecuaciones de variación directa e inversa.	$y = 5x$ ↑ constant of variation
convenience sample A sample based on members of the population that are readily available.	**muestra de conveniencia** Una muestra basada en miembros de la población que están fácilmente disponibles.	
coordinate One of the numbers of an ordered pair that locate a point on a coordinate graph.	**coordenada** Uno de los números de un par ordenado que ubica un punto en una gráfica de coordenadas.	
coordinate plane A plane formed by the intersection of a horizontal number line called the x-axis and a vertical number line called the y-axis.	**plano cartesiano** Plano formado por la intersección de una recta numérica horizontal llamada eje x y otra vertical llamada eje y.	y-axis O x-axis
correlation The description of the relationship between two data sets.	**correlación** Descripción de la relación entre dos conjuntos de datos.	

ENGLISH	SPANISH	EXAMPLES
corresponding angles (for lines) Angles in the same position formed when a third line intersects two lines.	**ángulos correspondientes (en líneas)** Ángulos en la misma posición formaron cuando una tercera línea interseca dos líneas.	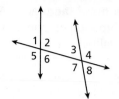 $\angle 1$ and $\angle 3$ are corresponding angles.
corresponding angles (of polygons) Angles in the same relative position in polygons with an equal number of sides.	**ángulos correspondientes (en polígonos)** Ángulos que se ubican en la misma posición relativa en dos o más polígonos.	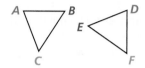 $\angle A$ and $\angle D$ are corresponding angles.
corresponding sides Matching sides of two or more polygons.	**lados correspondientes** Lados que se ubican en la misma posición relativa en dos o más polígonos.	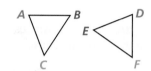 $\overline{AB}$ and $\overline{DE}$ are corresponding sides.
counterclockwise A circular movement to the left in the direction shown.	**en sentido contrario a las manecillas del reloj** Movimiento circular en la dirección que se indica.	
counterexample An example that shows that a statement is false.	**contraejemplo** Ejemplo que demuestra que un enunciado es falso.	
cross product The product of numbers on the diagonal when comparing two ratios.	**producto cruzado** El producto de los números multiplicados en diagonal cuando se comparan dos razones.	For the proportion $\frac{2}{3} = \frac{4}{6}$, the cross products are $2 \cdot 6 = 12$ and $3 \cdot 4 = 12$.
cube (geometric figure) A rectangular prism with six congruent square faces.	**cubo (figura geométrica)** Prisma rectangular con seis caras cuadradas congruentes.	
cube (in numeration) A number raised to the third power.	**cubo (en numeración)** Número elevado a la tercera potencia.	$5^3 = 5 \cdot 5 \cdot 5 = 125$
cumulative frequency The frequency of all data values that are less than or equal to a given value.	**frecuencia acumulativa** La frecuencia de todos los datos que son menores que o iguales a un valor dado.	

ENGLISH	SPANISH	EXAMPLES
customary system of measurement The measurement system often used in the United States.	**sistema usual de medidas** El sistema de medidas que se usa comúnmente en Estados Unidos.	inches, feet, miles, ounces, pounds, tons, cups, quarts, gallons
cylinder A three-dimensional figure with two parallel, congruent circular bases connected by a curved lateral surface.	**cilindro** Figura tridimensional con dos bases circulares paralelas y congruentes, unidas por una superficie lateral curva.	

decagon A polygon with ten sides.	**decágono** Polígono de 10 lados.	
decimal system A base-10 place value system.	**sistema decimal** Sistema de valor posicional de base 10.	
deductive reasoning Using logic to show that a statement is true.	**razonamiento deductivo** Uso de la lógica para demostrar que un enunciado es verdadero.	
degree The unit of measure for angles or temperature.	**grado** Unidad de medida para ángulos y temperaturas.	
denominator The bottom number of a fraction that tells how many equal parts are in the whole.	**denominador** Número de abajo de una fracción que indica en cuántas partes iguales se divide el entero.	$\frac{3}{4}$ ⟵ denominator
dependent events Events for which the outcome of one event affects the probability of the second event.	**sucesos dependientes** Dos sucesos son dependientes si el resultado de uno afecta la probabilidad del otro.	A bag contains 3 red marbles and 2 blue marbles. Drawing a red marble and then drawing a blue marble without replacing the first marble is an example of dependent events.
diagonal A line segment that conects two non-adjacent vertices of a polygon.	**diagonal** Segmento de recta que une dos vértices no adyacentes de un polígono.	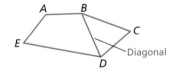
diameter A line segment that passes through the center of a circle and has endpoints on the circle, or the length of that segment.	**diámetro** Segmento de recta que pasa por el centro de un círculo y tiene sus extremos en la circunferencia, o bien la longitud de ese segmento.	
difference The result when one number is subtracted from another.	**diferencia** El resultado de restar un número de otro.	In 16 − 5 = 11, 11 is the difference.

ENGLISH	SPANISH	EXAMPLES
dimension The length, width, or height of a figure.	**dimensión** Longitud, ancho o altura de una figura.	
direct variation A linear relationship between two variables, x and y, that can be written in the form $y = kx$, where k is a nonzero constant.	**variacion directa** Relación lineal entre dos variables, x e y, que puede expresarse en la forma $y = kx$, donde k es una constante distinta de cero.	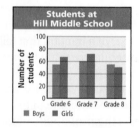 $y = 2x$
Distributive Property For all real numbers, a, b, and c, $a(b + c) = ab + ac$ and $a(b - c) = ab - ac$.	**Propiedad distributiva** Dado números reales a, b, y c, $a(b + c) = ab + ac$ y $a(b - c) = ab - ac$.	$5(20 + 1) = 5 \cdot 20 + 5 \cdot 1$
dividend The number to be divided in a division problem.	**dividendo** Número que se divide en un problema de división.	In $8 \div 4 = 2$, 8 is the dividend.
divisible Can be divided by a number without leaving a remainder.	**divisible** Que se puede dividir entre un número sin dejar residuo.	18 is divisible by 3.
Division Property of Equality The property that states that if you divide both sides of an equation by the same nonzero number, the new equation will have the same solution.	**Propiedad de igualdad de la división** Propiedad que establece que puedes dividir ambos lados de una ecuación entre el mismo número distinto de cero, y la nueva ecuación tendrá la misma solución.	$4x = 12$ $\dfrac{4x}{4} = \dfrac{12}{4}$ $x = 3$
divisor The number you are dividing by in a division problem.	**divisor** El número entre el que se divide en un problema de división.	In $8 \div 4 = 2$, 4 is the divisor.
double-bar graph A bar graph that compares two related sets of data.	**gráfica de doble barra** Gráfica de barras que compara dos conjuntos de datos relacionados.	
double-line graph A line graph that shows how two related sets of data change over time.	**gráfica de doble línea** Gráfica lineal que muestra cómo cambian con el tiempo dos conjuntos de datos relacionados.	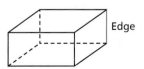

edge The line segment along which two faces of a polyhedron intersect.

arista Segmento de recta donde se intersecan dos caras de un poliedro.

Edge

Glossary/Glosario

ENGLISH	SPANISH	EXAMPLES
endpoint A point at the end of a line segment or ray.	**extremo** Un punto ubicado al final de un segmento de recta o rayo.	
equally likely Outcomes that have the same probability.	**resultados igualmente probables** Resultados que tienen la misma probabilidad de ocurrir.	
equation A mathematical sentence that shows that two expressions are equivalent.	**ecuación** Enunciado matemático que indica que dos expresiones son equivalentes.	$x + 4 = 7$ $6 + 1 = 10 - 3$
equilateral triangle A triangle with three congruent sides.	**triángulo equilátero** Triángulo con tres lados congruentes.	
equivalent Having the same value.	**equivalentes** Que tienen el mismo valor.	
equivalent fractions Fractions that name the same amount or part.	**fracciones equivalentes** Fracciones que representan la misma cantidad o parte.	$\frac{1}{2}$ and $\frac{2}{4}$ are equivalent fractions.
equivalent ratios Ratios that name the same comparison.	**razones equivalentes** Razones que representan la misma comparación.	$\frac{1}{2}$ and $\frac{2}{4}$ are equivalent ratios.
estimate (n) An answer that is close to the exact answer and is found by rounding, or other methods.	**estimación (s)** Una solución aproximada a la respuesta exacta que se halla mediante el redondeo u otros métodos.	
estimate (v) To find an answer close to the exact answer by rounding or other methods.	**estimar (v)** Hallar una solución aproximada a la respuesta exacta mediante el redondeo u otros métodos.	
evaluate To find the value of a numerical or algebraic expression.	**evaluar** Hallar el valor de una expresión numérica o algebraica.	Evaluate $2x + 7$ for $x = 3$. $2x + 7$ $2(3) + 7$ $6 + 7$ 13
even number An integer that is divisible by two.	**número par** Número entero divisible entre 2.	2, 4, 6
event An outcome or set of outcomes of an experiment or situation.	**suceso** Un resultado o una serie de resultados de un experimento o una situación.	When rolling a number cube, the event "an odd number" consists of the outcomes 1, 3, and 5.

Glossary/Glosario

ENGLISH	SPANISH	EXAMPLES
expanded form A number written as the sum of the values of its digits.	**forma desarrollada** Número escrito como suma de los valores de sus dígitos.	236,536 written in expanded form is 200,000 + 30,000 + 6,000 + 500 + 30 + 6.
experiment In probability, any activity based on chance, such as tossing a coin.	**experimento** En probabilidad, cualquier actividad basada en la posibilidad, como lanzar una moneda.	Tossing a coin 10 times and noting the number of "heads"
experimental probability The ratio of the number of times an event occurs to the total number of trials, or times that the activity is performed.	**probabilidad experimental** Razón del número de veces que ocurre un suceso al número total de pruebas o al número de veces que se realiza el experimento.	Kendra attempted 27 free throws and made 16 of them. Her experimental probability of making a free throw is $\frac{\text{number made}}{\text{number attempted}} = \frac{16}{27} \approx 0.59$.
exponent The number that indicates how many times the base is used as a factor.	**exponente** Número que indica cuántas veces se usa la base como factor.	$2^3 = 2 \cdot 2 \cdot 2 = 8$; 3 is the exponent.
exponential form A number is in exponential form when it is written with a base and an exponent.	**forma exponencial** Se dice que un número está en forma exponencial cuando se escribe con una base y un exponente.	4^2 is the exponential form for $4 \cdot 4$.
expression A mathematical phrase that contains operations, numbers, and/or variables.	**expresión** Enunciado matemático que contiene operaciones, números y/o variables.	$6x + 1$

F

face A flat surface of a polyhedron.	**cara** Superficie plana de un poliedro.	Face
factor A number that is multiplied by another number to get a product.	**factor** Número que se multiplica por otro para hallar un producto.	7 is a factor of 21 since $7 \cdot 3 = 21$.
factor tree A diagram showing how a whole number breaks down into its prime factors.	**árbol de factores** Diagrama que muestra cómo se descompone un número cabal en sus factores primos.	12 3 · 4 2 · 2 $12 = 3 \cdot 2 \cdot 2$
factorial The product of all whole numbers except zero that are less than or equal to a number.	**factorial** El producto de todos los números cabales, excepto cero que son menores que o iguales a un número.	4 factorial = $4! = 4 \cdot 3 \cdot 2 \cdot 1$

ENGLISH	SPANISH	EXAMPLES
Fahrenheit A temperature scale in which 32 °F is the freezing point of water and 212 °F is the boiling point of water.	**Fahrenheit** Escala de temperatura en la que 32° F es el punto de congelación del agua y 212° F es el punto de ebullición.	
fair When all outcomes of an experiment are equally likely, the experiment is said to be fair.	**justo** Se dice de un experimento donde todos los resultados posibles son igualmente probables.	
first quartile The median of the lower half of a set of data; also called *lower quartile*.	**primer cuartil** La mediana de la mitad inferior de un conjunto de datos. También se llama *cuartil inferior*.	
formula A rule showing relationships among quantities.	**fórmula** Regla que muestra relaciones entre cantidades.	$A = \ell w$ is the formula for the area of a rectangle.
fraction A number in the form $\frac{a}{b}$, where $b \neq 0$.	**fracción** Número escrito en la forma $\frac{a}{b}$, donde $b \neq 0$.	
frequency The number of times the value appears in the data set.	**frecuencia** Cantidad de veces que aparece el valor en un conjunto de datos.	In the data set 5, 6, 6, 7, 8, 9, the data value 6 has a frequency of 2.

frequency table A table that lists items together according to the number of times, or frequency, that the items occur.

tabla de frecuencia Una tabla en la que se organizan los datos de acuerdo con el número de veces que aparece cada valor (o la frecuencia).

Data set: 1, 1, 2, 2, 3, 4, 5, 5, 5, 6, 6, 6, 6

Frequency table:

Data	1	2	3	4	5	6
Frequency	2	2	1	1	3	4

function An input-output relationship that has exactly one output for each input.

función Relación de entrada-salida en la que a cada valor de entrada corresponde exactamente un valor de salida.

function table A table of ordered pairs that represent solutions of a function.

tabla de función Tabla de pares ordenados que representan soluciones de una función.

x	3	4	5	6
y	7	9	11	13

Fundamental Counting Principle If one event has m possible outcomes and a second event has n possible outcomes after the first event has occurred, then there are $m \cdot n$ total possible outcomes for the two events.

Principio fundamental de conteo Si un suceso tiene m resultados posibles y otro suceso tiene n resultados posibles después de ocurrido el primer suceso, entonces hay $m \cdot n$ resultados posibles en total para los dos sucesos.

There are 4 colors of shirts and 3 colors of pants. There are $4 \cdot 3 = 12$ possible outfits.

geometric sequence A sequence in which each term is multiplied by the same value to get the next term.

sucesión geométrica Una sucesión en la que cada término se multiplica por el mismo valor para obtener el siguiente término.

The sequence 2, 4, 8, 16 … is a geometric sequence.

graph of an equation A graph of the set of ordered pairs that are solutions of the equation.

gráfica de una ecuación Gráfica del conjunto de pares ordenados que son soluciones de la ecuación.

greatest common factor (GCF) The largest common factor of two or more given numbers.

máximo común divisor (MCD) El mayor de los factores comunes compartidos por dos o más números dados.

The GCF of 27 and 45 is 9.

height In a pyramid or cone, the perpendicular distance from the base to the opposite vertex.

altura En una pirámide o cono, la distancia perpendicular desde la base al vértice opuesto.

In a triangle or quadrilateral, the perpendicular distance from the base to the opposite vertex or side.

En un triángulo o cuadrilátero, la distancia perpendicular desde la base de la figura al vértice o lado opuesto.

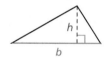

In a prism or cylinder, the perpendicular distance between the bases.

En un prisma o cilindro, la distancia perpendicular entre las bases.

heptagon A seven-sided polygon.

heptágono Polígono de siete lados.

hexagon A six-sided polygon.

hexágono Polígono de seis lados.

histogram A bar graph that shows the frequency of data within equal intervals.

histograma Gráfica de barras que muestra la frecuencia de los datos en intervalos iguales.

Glossary/Glosario

ENGLISH	SPANISH	EXAMPLES
hypotenuse In a right triangle, the side opposite the right angle.	**hipotenusa** En un triángulo rectángulo, el lado opuesto al ángulo recto.	

I

Identity Property of One The property that states that the product of 1 and any number is that number.	**Propiedad de identidad del uno** Propiedad que establece que el producto de 1 y cualquier número es ese número.	$3 \cdot 1 = 3$ $-9 \cdot 1 = -9$
Identity Property of Zero The property that states that the sum of zero and any number is that number.	**Propiedad de identidad del cero** Propiedad que establece que la suma de cero y cualquier número es ese número.	$5 + 0 = 5$ $-4 + 0 = -4$
image A figure resulting from a transformation.	**imagen** Figura que resulta de una transformación.	

impossible (probability) Can never happen; having a probability of 0.	**imposible (en probabilidad)** Que no puede ocurrir. Suceso cuya probabilidad de ocurrir es 0.
improper fraction A fraction in which the numerator is greater than or equal to the denominator.	**fracción impropia** Fracción en la que el numerador es mayor que o igual al denominador. $\frac{5}{5}$ $\frac{7}{4}$
independent events Events for which the outcome of one event does not affect the probability of the other.	**sucesos independientes** Dos sucesos son independientes si el resultado de uno no afecta la probabilidad del otro. A bag contains 3 red marbles and 2 blue marbles. Drawing a red marble, replacing it, and then drawing a blue marble is an example of independent events.
indirect measurement The technique of using similar figures and proportions to find a measure.	**medición indirecta** La técnica de usar figuras semejantes y proporciones para hallar una medida.
inductive reasoning Using a pattern to make a conclusion.	**razonamiento inductivo** Uso de un patrón para sacar una conclusión.
inequality A mathematical sentence that shows the relationship between quantities that are not equivalent.	**desigualdad** Enunciado matemático que muestra una relación entre cantidades que no son equivalentes. $5 < 8$ $5x + 2 \geq 12$

ENGLISH	SPANISH	EXAMPLES
input The value substituted into an expression or function.	**valor de entrada** Valor que se usa para sustituir una variable en una expresión o función.	For the function $y = 6x$, the input 4 produces an output of 24.
integers The set of whole numbers and their opposites.	**enteros** Conjunto de todos los números cabales y sus opuestos.	$\dots -3, -2, -1, 0, 1, 2, 3, \dots$
interest The amount of money charged for borrowing or using money, or the amount of money earned by saving money.	**interés** Cantidad de dinero que se cobra por el préstamo o uso del dinero, o la cantidad que se gana al ahorrar dinero.	
interquartile range The difference between the upper and lower quartiles in a box-and-whisker plot.	**rango entre cuartiles** La diferencia entre los cuartiles superior e inferior en una gráfica de mediana y rango.	Lower half Upper half 18, (23,) 28, 29, (36,) 42 ↑ Lower quartile ↑ Upper quartile Interquartile range: $36 - 23 = 13$
intersecting lines Lines that cross at exactly one point.	**líneas secantes** Líneas que se cruzan en un solo punto.	
interval The space between marked values on a number line or the scale of a graph.	**intervalo** El espacio entre los valores marcados en una recta numérica o en la escala de una gráfica.	
inverse operations Operations that undo each other: addition and subtraction, or multiplication and division.	**operaciones inversas** Operaciones que se cancelan mutuamente: suma y resta, o multiplicación y división.	Addition and subtraction are inverse operations: $5 + 3 = 8; 8 - 3 = 5$ Multiplication and division are inverse operations: $2 \cdot 3 = 6; 6 \div 3 = 2$
Inverse Property of Addition The sum of a number and its opposite, or additive inverse, is 0.	**propiedad inversa de la suma** La suma de un número y su opuesto, o inverso aditivo, es cero.	$3 + (-3) = 0; a + (-a) = 0$
irrational number A number that cannot be expressed as a ratio of two integers or as a repeating or terminating decimal.	**número irracional** Número que no puede expresarse como una razón de dos enteros ni como un decimal periódico o finito.	$\sqrt{2}, \pi$
isolate the variable To get a variable alone on one side of an equation or inequality in order to solve the equation or inequality.	**despejar la variable** Dejar sola la variable en un lado de una ecuación o desigualdad para resolverla.	$\begin{array}{rl} x + 7 = & 22 \\ -7 & -7 \\ \hline x = & 15 \end{array}$
isosceles triangle A triangle with at least two congruent sides.	**triángulo isósceles** Triángulo que tiene al menos dos lados congruentes.	

L

lateral area The sum of the areas of the lateral faces of a prism or pyramid, or the area of the lateral surface of a cylinder or cone.

área lateral Suma de las áreas de las caras laterales de un prisma o pirámide, o área de la superficie lateral de un cilindro o cono.

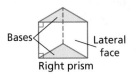

Lateral area = (28) (12) = 336 cm²

lateral face A face of a prism or a pyramid that is not a base.

Cara lateral Cara de un prisma o pirámide que no es una base.

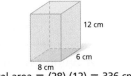

Bases — Lateral face
Right prism

least common denominator (LCD) The least common multiple of two or more denominators.

mínimo común denominador (mcd) El mínimo común múltiplo de dos o más denominadores.

The LCD of $\frac{3}{4}$ and $\frac{5}{6}$ is 12.

least common multiple (LCM) The least number, other than zero, that is a multiple of two or more given numbers.

mínimo común múltiplo (mcm) El menor de los números, distinto de cero, que es múltiplo de dos o más números.

The LCM of 10 and 18 is 90.

legs In a right triangle, the sides that include the right angle; in an isosceles triangle, the pair of congruent sides.

catetos En un triángulo rectángulo, los lados adyacentes al ángulo recto. En un triángulo isósceles, el par de lados congruentes.

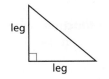

like terms Terms with the same variables raised to the same exponents.

términos semejantes Términos que contienen las mismas variables elevada a las mismas exponentes.

In the expression $3a^2 + 5b + 12a^2$, $3a^2$ and $12a^2$ are like terms.

line A straight path that has no thickness and extends forever.

línea Trayectoria recta que no tiene ningún grueso y que se extiende por siempre.

line graph A graph that uses line segments to show how data changes.

gráfica lineal Gráfica que muestra cómo cambian los datos mediante segmentos de recta.

line of best fit A straight line that comes closest to the points on a scatter plot.

línea de mejor ajuste la línea recta que más se aproxima a los puntos de un diagrama de dispersión.

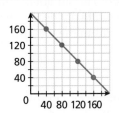

line of reflection A line that a figure is flipped across to create a mirror image of the original figure.

línea de reflexión Línea sobre la cual se invierte una figura para crear una imagen reflejada de la figura original.

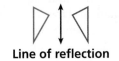

Line of reflection

ENGLISH	SPANISH	EXAMPLES

line of symmetry The imaginary "mirror" in line symmetry.

eje de simetría El "espejo" imaginario en la simetría axial.

---

line plot A number line with marks or dots that show frequency.

diagrama de acumulación Recta numérica con marcas o puntos que indican la frecuencia.

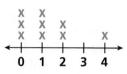

Number of pets

---

line segment A part of a line made of two endpoints and all points between them.

segmento de recta Parte de una línea con dos extremos.

A   B

---

line symmetry A figure has line symmetry if one-half is a mirror-image of the other half.

simetría axial Una figura tiene simetría axial si una de sus mitades es la imagen reflejada de la otra.

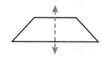

---

linear equation An equation whose solutions form a straight line on a coordinate plane.

ecuación lineal Ecuación cuyas soluciones forman una línea recta en un plano cartesiano.

$y = 2x + 1$

---

linear function A function whose graph is a straight line.

función lineal Función cuya gráfica es una línea recta.

$y = x - 1$

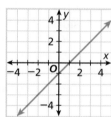

---

lower quartile The median of the lower half of a set of data.

cuartil inferior La mediana de la mitad inferior de un conjunto de datos.

Lower half   Upper half

18, (23), 28, 29, 36, 42

↑
Lower quartile

 M

---

mean The sum of the items in a set of data divided by the number of items in the set; also called *average*.

media La suma de todos loselementos de un conjunto de datos dividida entre el número de elementos del conjunto. También se llama *promedio*.

Data set: 4, 6, 7, 8, 10
Mean:
$$\frac{4 + 6 + 7 + 8 + 10}{5} = \frac{35}{5} = 7$$

---

measure of central tendency A measure used to describe the middle of a data set; the mean, median, and mode are measures of central tendency.

medida de tendencia dominante Medida que describe la parte media de un conjunto de datos; la media, la mediana y la moda son medidas de tendencia dominante.

ENGLISH	SPANISH	EXAMPLES
median The middle number, or the mean (average) of the two middle numbers, in an ordered set of data.	**mediana** El número intermedio, o la media (el promedio), de los dos números intermedios en un conjunto ordenado de datos.	Data set: 4, 6, 7, 8, 10 Median: 7
metric system of measurement A decimal system of weights and measures that is used universally in science and commonly throughout the world.	**sistema métrico de medición** Sistema decimal de pesos y medidas empleado universalmente en las ciencias y comúnmente en todo el mundo.	centimeters, meters, kilometers, grams, kilograms, milliliters, liters
midpoint The point that divides a line segment into two congruent line segments.	**punto medio** El punto que divide un segmento de recta en dos segmentos de recta congruentes.	A B C *B* is the midpoint of $\overline{AC}$.
mixed number A number made up of a whole number that is not zero and a fraction.	**número mixto** Número compuesto por un número cabal distinto de cero y una fracción.	$5\frac{1}{8}$
mode The number or numbers that occur most frequently in a set of data; when all numbers occur with the same frequency, we say there is no mode.	**moda** Número o números más frecuentes en un conjunto de datos; si todos los números aparecen con la misma frecuencia, no hay moda.	Data set: 3, 5, 8, 8, 10 Mode: 8
multiple The product of any number and any nonzero whole number is a multiple of that number.	**múltiplo** El producto de un número y cualquier número cabal distinto de cero es un múltiplo de ese número.	30, 40, and 90 are all multiples of 10.
Multiplication Property of Equality The property that states that if you multiply both sides of an equation by the same number, the new equation will have the same solution.	**Propiedad de igualdad de la multiplicación** Propiedad que establece que puedes multiplicar ambos lados de una ecuación por el mismo número y la nueva ecuación tendrá la misma solución.	$\frac{1}{3}x = 7$ $(3)(\frac{1}{3}x) = (3)(7)$ $x = 21$
Multiplication Property of Zero The property that states that for all real numbers a, $a \times 0 = 0$ and $0 \times a = 0$.	**Propiedad de multiplicación del cero** Propiedad que establece que para todos los números reales a, $a \times 0 = 0$ y $0 \times a = 0$.	$6 \cdot 0 = 0$ $-5 \cdot 0 = 0$
Multiplicative Inverse Property The product of a nonzero number and its reciprocal, or multiplicative inverse, is one.	**Propiedad inversa de la multiplicación** El producto de un número distinto a cero y su recíproco, o inverso multiplicativo, es uno.	$\frac{2}{3} \cdot \frac{3}{2} = 1$; $\frac{a}{b} \cdot \frac{b}{a} = 1$
mutually exclusive Two events are mutually exclusive if they cannot occur in the same trial of an experiment.	**mutuamente excluyentes** Dos sucesos son mutuamente excluyentes cuando no pueden ocurrir en la misma prueba de un experimento.	

N

negative correlation Two data sets have a negative correlation, or relationship, if one set of data values increases while the other decreases.

correlación negativa Dos conjuntos de datos tienen correlación, o relación, negativa, si los valores de un conjunto aumentan a medida que los valores del otro conjunto disminuyen.

negative integer An integer less than zero.

entero negativo Entero menor que cero.

−2 is a negative integer.

net An arrangement of two-dimensional figures that can be folded to form a polyhedron.

plantilla Arreglo de figuras bidimensionales que se doblan para formar un poliedro.

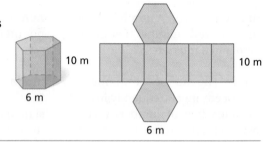

no correlation Two data sets have no correlation when there is no relationship between their data values.

sin correlación Caso en que los valores de dos conjuntos de datos no muestran ninguna relación.

nonlinear function A function whose graph is not a straight line.

función no lineal Función cuya gráfica no es una línea recta.

nonterminating decimal A decimal that never ends.

decimal infinito Decimal que nunca termina.

numerator The top number of a fraction that tells how many parts of a whole are being considered.

numerador El número de arriba de una fracción; indica cuántas partes de un entero se consideran.

$\frac{4}{5}$ ← numerator

numerical expression An expression that contains only numbers and operations.

expresión numérica Expresión que incluye sólo números y operaciones.

$(2 \cdot 3) + 1$

O

obtuse angle An angle whose measure is greater than 90° but less than 180°.

ángulo obtuso Ángulo que mide más de 90° y menos de 180°.

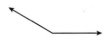

ENGLISH	SPANISH	EXAMPLES
obtuse triangle A triangle containing one obtuse angle.	**triángulo obtusángulo** Triángulo que tiene un ángulo obtuso.	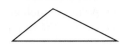
octagon An eight-sided polygon.	**octágono** Polígono de ocho lados.	
odd number An integer that is not divisible by two.	**número impar** Entero que no es divisible entre 2.	
odds A comparison of the number of ways an event can occur and the number of ways an event can NOT occur.	**posibilidades** Comparación del numero de las maneras que puede ocurrir un suceso y el numero de maneras que no puede ocurrir el suceso.	
opposites Two numbers that are an equal distance from zero on a number line; also called *additive inverse.*	**opuestos** Dos números que están a la misma distancia de cero en una recta numérica. También se llaman *inversos aditivos.*	5 and −5 are opposites. 
order of operations A rule for evaluating expressions: first perform the operations in parentheses, then compute powers and roots, then perform all multiplication and division from left to right, and then perform all addition and subtraction from left to right.	**orden de las operaciones** Regla para evaluar expresiones: primero se hacen las operaciones entre paréntesis, luego se hallan las potencias y raíces, después todas las multiplicaciones y divisiones de izquierda a derecha y, por último, todas las sumas y restas de izquierda a derecha.	$3^2 - 12 \div 4$ $9 - 12 \div 4$ Evaluate the power. $9 - 3$ Divide. 6 Subtract.
ordered pair A pair of numbers that can be used to locate a point on a coordinate plane.	**par ordenado** Par de números que sirven para ubicar un punto en un plano cartesiano.	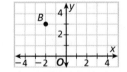 The coordinates of *B* are (−2, 3).
origin The point where the *x*-axis and *y*-axis intersect on the coordinate plane; (0, 0).	**origen** Punto de intersección entre el eje *x* y el eje *y* en un plano cartesiano: (0, 0).	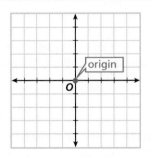
outcome A possible result of a probability experiment.	**resultado** Posible resultado de un experimento de probabilidad.	When rolling a number cube, the possible outcomes are 1, 2, 3, 4, 5, and 6.

ENGLISH	SPANISH	EXAMPLES
outlier A value much greater or much less than the others in a data set.	**valor extremo** Un valor mucho mayor o menor que los demás de un conjunto de datos.	Most of data · Mean · Outlier
output The value that results from the substitution of a given input into an expression or function.	**valor de salida** Valor que resulta después de sustituir un valor de entrada determinado en una expresión o función.	For the function $y = 6x$, the input 4 produces an output of 24.
overestimate An estimate that is greater than the exact answer.	**estimación alta** Estimación mayor que la respuesta exacta.	100 is an overestimate for the sum $23 + 24 + 21 + 22$.

P

ENGLISH	SPANISH	EXAMPLES
parallel lines Lines in a plane that do not intersect.	**líneas paralelas** Líneas que se encuentran en el mismo plano pero que nunca se intersecan.	
parallelogram A quadrilateral with two pairs of parallel sides.	**paralelogramo** Cuadrilátero con dos pares de lados paralelos.	
pentagon A five-sided polygon.	**pentágono** Polígono de cinco lados.	
percent A ratio comparing a number to 100.	**porcentaje** Razón que compara un número con el número 100.	$45\% = \frac{45}{100}$
percent of change The amount stated as a percent that a number increases or decreases.	**porcentaje de cambio** Cantidad en que un número aumenta o disminuye, expresada como un porcentaje.	
percent of decrease A percent change describing a decrease in a quantity.	**porcentaje de disminución** Porcentaje de cambio en que una cantidad disminuye.	An item that costs $8 is marked down to $6. The amount of the decrease is $2 and the percent of decrease is $\frac{2}{8} = 0.25 = 25\%$.
percent of increase A percent change describing an increase in a quantity.	**porcentaje de incremento** Porcentaje de cambio en que una cantidad aumenta.	The price of an item increases from $8 to $12. The amount of the increase is $4 and the percent of increase is $\frac{4}{8} = 0.5 = 50\%$.
perfect square A square of a whole number.	**cuadrado perfecto** El cuadrado de un número cabal.	$5^2 = 25$, so 25 is a perfect square.

Glossary/Glosario

ENGLISH	SPANISH	EXAMPLES
perimeter The distance around a polygon.	**perímetro** Distancia alrededor de un polígono.	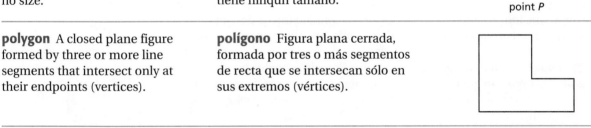 18 ft, 6 ft perimeter = 18 + 6 + 18 + 6 = 48 ft
permutation An arrangement of items or events in which order is important.	**permutación** Arreglo de objetos o sucesos en el que el orden es importante.	For objects *A*, *B*, and *C*, there are 6 different permutations, *ABC*, *ACB*, *BAC*, *BCA*, *CAB*, *CBA*.
perpendicular bisector A line that intersects a segment at its midpoint and is perpendicular to the segment.	**mediatriz** Línea que cruza un segmento en su punto medio y es perpendicular al segmento.	ℓ *A* *B*
perpendicular lines Lines that intersect to form right angles.	**líneas perpendiculares** Líneas que al intersecarse forman ángulos rectos.	*n* *m*
pi (π) The ratio of the circumference of a circle to the length of its diameter; $\pi \approx 3.14$ or $\frac{22}{7}$.	**pi (π)** Razón de la circunferencia de un círculo a la longitud de su diámetro; $\pi \approx 3.14$ ó $\frac{22}{7}$.	
plane A flat surface that has no thickness and extends forever.	**plano** Superficie plana que no tiene ningún grueso y que se extiende por siempre.	*A* *C* $\mathcal{R}$ *B* plane *ABC*
point An exact location that has no size.	**punto** Ubicación exacta que no tiene ninqún tamaño.	*P* point *P*
polygon A closed plane figure formed by three or more line segments that intersect only at their endpoints (vertices).	**polígono** Figura plana cerrada, formada por tres o más segmentos de recta que se intersecan sólo en sus extremos (vértices).	
polyhedron A three-dimensional figure in which all the surfaces or faces are polygons.	**poliedro** Figura tridimensional cuyas superficies o caras tienen forma de polígonos.	
population The entire group of objects or individuals considered for a survey.	**población** Grupo completo de objetos o individuos que se desea estudiar.	In a survey about the study habits of middle school students, the population is all middle school students.

positive correlation Two data sets have a positive correlation, or relationship, when their data values increase or decrease together.

correlación positiva Dos conjuntos de datos tienen una correlación, o relación, positiva cuando los valores de ambos conjuntos aumentan o disminuyen al mismo tiempo.

---

positive integer An integer greater than zero.

entero positivo Entero mayor que cero.

---

power A number produced by raising a base to an exponent.

potencia Número que resulta al elevar una base a un exponente.

$2^3 = 8$, so 2 to the 3rd power is 8.

---

precision The level of detail of a measurement, determined by the unit of measure.

precisión Detalle de una medición, determinado por la unidad de medida.

A ruler marked in millimeters has a greater level of precision than a ruler marked in centimeters.

---

prediction Something you can reasonably expect to happen in the future.

predicción Algo que se puede razonablemente esperar suceder en el futuro.

---

preimage The original figure in a transformation.

imagen original Figura original en una transformación.

Preimage

---

prime factorization A number written as the product of its prime factors.

factorización prima Un número escrito como el producto de sus factores primos.

$10 = 2 \cdot 5$
$24 = 2^3 \cdot 3$

---

prime number A whole number greater than 1 that has exactly two factors, itself and 1.

número primo Número cabal mayor que 1 que sólo es divisible entre 1 y él mismo.

5 is prime because its only factors are 5 and 1.

---

principal The initial amount of money borrowed or saved.

capital Cantidad inicial de dinero depositada o recibida en préstamo.

---

prism A polyhedron that has two congruent polygon-shaped bases and other faces that are all parallelograms.

prisma Poliedro con dos bases congruentes con forma de polígono y caras con forma de paralelogramo.

---

probability A number from 0 to 1 (or 0% to 100%) that describes how likely an event is to occur.

probabilidad Un número entre 0 y 1 (ó 0% y 100%) que describe qué tan probable es un suceso.

A bag contains 3 red marbles and 4 blue marbles. The probability of randomly choosing a red marble is $\frac{3}{7}$.

---

product The result when two or more numbers are multiplied.

producto Resultado de multiplicar dos o más números.

The product of 4 and 8 is 32.

ENGLISH	SPANISH	EXAMPLES
proper fraction A fraction in which the numerator is less than the denominator.	**fracción propia** Fracción en la que el numerador es menor que el denominador.	$\frac{3}{4}, \frac{1}{12}, \frac{7}{8}$
proportion An equation that states that two ratios are equivalent.	**proporción** Ecuación que establece que dos razones son equivalentes.	$\frac{2}{3} = \frac{4}{6}$
protractor A tool for measuring angles.	**transportador** Instrumento para medir ángulos.	
pyramid A polyhedron with a polygon base and triangular sides that all meet at a common vertex.	**pirámide** Poliedro cuya base es un polígono; tiene caras triangulares que se juntan en un vértice común.	
Pythagorean Theorem In a right triangle, the square of the length of the hypotenuse is equal to the sum of the squares of the lengths of the legs.	**Teorema de Pitágoras** En un triángulo rectángulo, la suma de los cuadrados de los catetos es igual al cuadrado de la hipotenusa.	13 cm 5 cm 12 cm $5^2 + 12^2 = 13^2$ $25 + 144 = 169$

Q

quadrant The x- and y-axes divide the coordinate plane into four regions. Each region is called a quadrant.	**cuadrante** El eje x y el eje y dividen el plano cartesiano en cuatro regiones. Cada región recibe el nombre de cuadrante.	Quadrant II │ Quadrant I ——0—— Quadrant III │ Quadrant IV
quadratic function A function of the form $y = ax^2 + bx + c$, where $a \neq 0$.	**función cuadrática** Función del tipo $y = ax^2 + bx + c$, donde $a \neq 0$.	$y = 2x^2 - 12x + 10$, $y = 3x^2$
quadrilateral A four-sided polygon.	**cuadrilátero** Polígono de cuatro lados.	
quartile Three values, one of which is the median, that divide a data set into fourths. See also *first quartile, third quartile*.	**cuartiles** Cada uno de tres valores, uno de los cuales es la mediana, que dividen en cuartos un conjunto de datos. Ver también *primer cuartil, tercer cuartil*.	
quotient The result when one number is divided by another.	**cociente** Resultado de dividir un número entre otro.	In $8 \div 4 = 2$, 2 is the quotient.

radical sign The symbol $\sqrt{}$ used to represent the nonnegative square root of a number.	**símbolo de radical** El símbolo $\sqrt{}$ con que se representa la raíz cuadrada no negativa de un número.	$\sqrt{36} = 6$
radius A line segment with one endpoint at the center of a circle and the other endpoint on the circle, or the length of that segment.	**radio** Segmento de recta con un extremo en el centro de un círculo y el otro en la circunferencia; o bien la longitud de ese segmento.	Radius
random sample A sample in which each individual or object in the entire population has an equal chance of being selected.	**muestra aleatoria** Muestra en la que cada individuo u objeto de la población tiene la misma oportunidad de ser elegido.	Mr. Henson chose a random sample of the class by writing each student's name on a slip of paper, mixing up the slips, and drawing five slips without looking.
range (in statistics) The difference between the greatest and least values in a data set.	**rango (en estadística)** Diferencia entre los valores máximo y mínimo de un conjunto de datos.	Data set: 3, 5, 7, 7, 12 Range: $12 - 3 = 9$
rate A ratio that compares two quantities measured in different units.	**tasa** Una razón que compara dos cantidades medidas en diferentes unidades.	The speed limit is 55 miles per hour, or 55 mi/h.
rate of change A ratio that compares the amount of change in a dependent variable to the amount of change in an independent variable.	**tasa de cambio** Razón que compara la cantidad de cambio de la variable dependiente con la cantidad de combio de la variable independiente.	The cost of mailing a letter increased from 22 cents in 1985 to 25 cents in 1988. During this period, the rate of change was $\dfrac{\text{change in cost}}{\text{change in year}} = \dfrac{25-22}{1988-1985} = \dfrac{3}{3}$
rate of interest The percent charged or earned on an amount of money; see *simple interest*.	**tasa de interés** Porcentaje que se cobra por una cantidad de dinero prestada o que se gana por una cantidad de dinero ahorrada; ver *interés simple*.	
ratio A comparison of two quantities by division.	**razón** Comparación de dos cantidades mediante una división.	12 to 25, 12:25, $\frac{12}{25}$
rational number Any number that can be expressed as a ratio of two integers.	**número racional** Número que se puede escribir como una razón de dos enteros.	6 can be expressed as $\frac{6}{1}$. 0.5 can be expressed as $\frac{1}{2}$.
ray A part of a line that starts at one endpoint and extends forever in one direction.	**rayo** Parte de una recta que comienza en un extremo y se extiende infinitamente en una dirección.	$\bullet \longrightarrow$ D
real number A rational or irrational number.	**número real** Número racional o irracional.	

Glossary/Glosario

ENGLISH	SPANISH	EXAMPLES
reciprocal One of two numbers whose product is 1; also called *multiplicative inverse*.	**recíproco** Uno de dos números cuyo producto es igual a 1. También se llama *inverso multiplicativo*.	The reciprocal of $\frac{2}{3}$ is $\frac{3}{2}$.
rectangle A parallelogram with four right angles.	**rectángulo** Paralelogramo con cuatro ángulos rectos.	
rectangular prism A polyhedron whose bases are rectangles and whose other faces are parallelograms.	**prisma rectangular** Poliedro cuyas bases son rectángulos y cuyas caras tienen forma de paralelogramo.	
reflection A transformation of a figure that flips the figure across a line.	**reflexión** Transformación que ocurre cuando se invierte una figura sobre una línea.	
regular polygon A polygon with congruent sides and angles.	**polígono regular** Polígono con lados y ángulos congruentes.	
regular pyramid A pyramid whose base is a regular polygon and whose lateral faces are all congruent.	**pirámide regular** Pirámide que tiene un polígono regular como base y caras laterales congruentes.	
relative frequency The frequency of a data value or range of data values divided by the total number of data values in the set.	**frecuencia relativa** La frecuencia de un valor o un rango de valores dividido por el número total de los valores en el conjunto.	
relatively prime Two numbers are relatively prime if their greatest common factor (GCF) is 1.	**primo relatívo** Dos números son primos relativos si su máximo común divisor (MCD) es 1.	8 and 15 are relatively prime.
repeating decimal A decimal in which one or more digits repeat infinitely.	**decimal periódico** Decimal en el que uno o más dígitos se repiten infinitamente.	$0.757575\ldots = 0.\overline{75}$
rhombus A parallelogram with all sides congruent.	**rombo** Paralelogramo en el que todos los lados son congruentes.	
right angle An angle that measures 90°.	**ángulo recto** Ángulo que mide exactamente 90°.	

ENGLISH	**SPANISH**	**EXAMPLES**
right triangle A triangle containing a right angle.	**triángulo rectángulo** Triángulo que tiene un ángulo recto.	
rise The vertical change when the slope of a line is expressed as the ratio $\frac{rise}{run}$, or "rise over run."	**distancia vertical** El cambio vertical cuando la pendiente de una línea se expresa como la razón $\frac{\text{distancia vertical}}{\text{distancia horizontal}}$, o "distancia vertical sobre distancia horizontal".	For the points (3, −1) and (6, 5), the rise is 5 − (−1) = 6.
rotation A transformation in which a figure is turned around a point.	**rotación** Transformación que ocurre cuando una figura gira alrededor de un punto.	
rotational symmetry A figure has rotational symmetry if it can be rotated less than 360° around a central point and coincide with the original figure.	**simetría de rotación** Ocurre cuando una figura gira menos de 360° alrededor de un punto central sin dejar de ser congruente con la figura original.	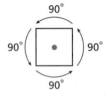
rounding Replacing a number with an estimate of that number to a given place value.	**redondear** Sustituir un número por una estimación de ese número hasta cierto valor posicional.	2,354 rounded to the nearest thousand is 2,000, and 2,354 rounded to the nearest 100 is 2,400.
run The horizontal change when the slope of a line is expressed as the ratio $\frac{rise}{run}$, or "rise over run."	**distancia horizontal** El cambio horizontal cuando la pendiente de una línea se expresa como la razón $\frac{\text{distancia vertical}}{\text{distancia horizontal}}$, o "distancia vertical sobre distancia horizontal".	For the points (3, −1) and (6, 5), the run is 6 − 3 = 3.

sales tax A percent of the cost of an item, which is charged by governments to raise money.	**impuesto sobre la venta** Porcentaje del costo de un artículo que los gobiernos cobran para recaudar fondos.	
sample A part of the population.	**muestra** Una parte de la población.	In a survey about the study habits of middle school students, a sample is a survey of 100 randomly-chosen students.
sample space All possible outcomes of an experiment.	**espacio muestral** Conjunto de todos los resultados posibles de un experimento.	When rolling a number cube, the sample space is 1, 2, 3, 4, 5, 6.
scale The ratio between two sets of measurements.	**escala** La razón entre dos conjuntos de medidas.	1 cm:5 mi

ENGLISH	SPANISH	EXAMPLES

scale drawing A drawing that uses a scale to make an object smaller than or larger than the real object.

dibujo a escala Dibujo en el que se usa una escala para que un objeto se vea mayor o menor que el objeto real al que representa.

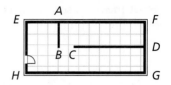

A blueprint is an example of a scale drawing.

scale factor The ratio used to enlarge or reduce similar figures.

factor de escala Razón que se usa para agrandar o reducir figuras semejantes.

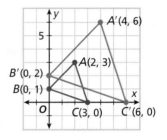

Scale factor: 2

scale model A proportional model of a three-dimensional object.

modelo a escala Modelo proporcional de un objeto tridimensional.

scalene triangle A triangle with no congruent sides.

triángulo escaleno Triángulo que no tiene lados congruentes.

scatter plot A graph with points plotted to show a possible relationship between two sets of data.

diagrama de dispersión Gráfica de puntos que se usa para mostrar una posible relación entre dos conjuntos de datos.

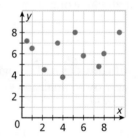

scientific notation A method of writing very large or very small numbers by using powers of 10.

notación científica Método que se usa para escribir números muy grandes o muy pequeños mediante potencias de 10.

$12{,}560{,}000{,}000{,}000 = 1.256 \times 10^{13}$

sector A region enclosed by two radii and the arc joining their endpoints.

sector Región encerrada por dos radios y el arco que une sus extremos.

ENGLISH	**SPANISH**	**EXAMPLES**

sector (data) A section of a circle graph representing part of the data set.

sector (datos) Sección de una gráfica circular que representa una parte del conjunto de datos.

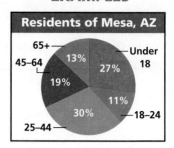

Residents of Mesa, AZ

65+ 13%
45–64
19%
25–44 30%
27% — Under 18
11%
18–24

The circle graph has 5 sectors.

---

segment A part of a line between two endpoints.

segmento Parte de una línea entre dos extremos.

---

sequence An ordered list of numbers.

sucesión Lista ordenada de números.

2, 4, 6, 8, 10, ...

---

side A line bounding a geometric figure; one of the faces forming the outside of an object.

lado Línea que delimita las figuras geométricas; una de las caras que forman la parte exterior de un objeto.

A *B*
Side —
E
D

Side-Side-Side (SSS) A rule stating that if three sides of one triangle are congruent to three sides of another triangle, then the triangles are congruent.

Lado-Lado-Lado (LLL) Regla que establece que dos triángulos son congruentes cuando sus tres lados correspondientes son congruentes.

B
4 m 5 m
A 3 m *C*
E
5 m 4 m
F 3 m *D*

$\triangle ABC \cong \triangle DEF$

---

significant digits The digits used to express the precision of a measurement.

dígitos significativos Dígitos usados para expresar la precisión de una medida.

0.048 has 2 significant digits.
5.003 has 4 significant digits.

---

similar Figures with the same shape but not necessarily the same size are similar.

semejantes Figuras que tienen la misma forma, pero no necesariamente el mismo tamaño.

---

simulation A model of an experiment, often one that would be too difficult or too time-consuming to actually perform.

simulación Representación de un experimento, por lo regular de uno cuya realización sería demasiado difícil o llevaría mucho tiempo.

---

simple event An event consisting of only one outcome.

suceso simple Suceso que tiene sólo un resultado.

In the experiment of rolling a number cube, the event consisting of the outcome 3 is a simple event.

Glossary/Glosario

ENGLISH	SPANISH	EXAMPLES
simple interest A fixed percent of the principal. It is found using the formula $I = Prt$, where P represents the principal, r the rate of interest, and t the time.	**interés simple** Un porcentaje fijo del capital. Se calcula con la fórmula $I = Cit$, donde C representa el capital, i, la tasa de interés y t, el tiempo.	$100 is put into an account with a simple interest rate of 5%. After 2 years, the account will have earned $I = 100 \cdot 0.05 \cdot 2 = \$10$.
simplest form A fraction is in simplest form when the numerator and denominator have no common factors other than 1.	**mínima expresión** Una fracción está en su mínima expresión cuando el numerador y el denominador no tienen más factor común que 1.	Fraction: $\frac{8}{12}$ Simplest form: $\frac{2}{3}$
simplify To write a fraction or expression in simplest form.	**simplificar** Escribir una fracción o expresión numérica en su mínima expresión.	
skew lines Lines that lie in different planes that are neither parallel nor intersecting.	**líneas oblicuas** Líneas que se encuentran en planos distintos, por eso no se intersecan ni son paralelas.	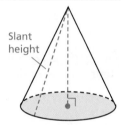 $\overleftrightarrow{AB}$ and $\overleftrightarrow{CG}$ are skew lines.
slant height of a cone The distance from the vertex of a cone to a point on the edge of the base.	**altura inclinada de un cono** Distancia desde el vértice de un cono hasta un punto en el borde de la base.	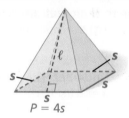 Slant height
slant height of a pyramid The distance from the vertex of a pyramid to the midpoint of an edge of the base.	**altura inclinada de una pirámide** Distancia desde el vértice de una pirámide hasta el punto medio de una arista de la base.	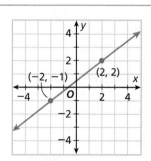 $P = 4s$
slope A measure of the steepness of a line on a graph; the rise divided by the run.	**pendiente** Medida de la inclinación de una línea en una gráfica. Razón de la distancia vertical a la distancia horizontal.	(-2, -1), (2, 2) Slope $= \frac{\text{Rise}}{\text{Sun}} = \frac{3}{4}$
slope-intercept form A linear equation written in form $y = mx + b$, where m represents slope and b represents the y-intercept.	**forma de pendiente-intersecciíon** Ecuación lineal escrita en la forma $y = mx + b$, donde m es la pendiente y b es la intersección con el eje y.	$y = 6x - 3$

ENGLISH	SPANISH	EXAMPLES
solid figure A three-dimensional figure.	**cuerpo geométrico** Figura tridimensional.	
solution of an equation A value or values that make an equation true.	**solución de una ecuación** Valor o valores que hacen verdadera una ecuación.	Equation: $x + 2 = 6$ Solution: $x = 4$
solution of an inequality A value or values that make an inequality true.	**solución de una desigualdad** Valor o valores que hacen verdadera una desigualdad.	Inequality: $x + 3 \geq 10$ Solution: $x \geq 7$
solution set The set of values that make a statement true.	**conjunto solución** Conjunto de valores que hacen verdadero un enunciado.	Inequality: $x + 3 \geq 5$ Solution set: $x \geq 2$ $-4\ -3\ -2\ -1\ \ 0\ \ 1\ \ 2\ \ 3\ \ 4\ \ 5\ \ 6$
solve To find an answer or a solution.	**resolver** Hallar una respuesta o solución.	
sphere A three-dimensional figure with all points the same distance from the center.	**esfera** Figura tridimensional en la que todos los puntos están a la misma distancia del centro.	
square (geometry) A rectangle with four congruent sides.	**cuadrado (en geometría)** Rectángulo con cuatro lados congruentes.	
square (numeration) A number raised to the second power.	**cuadrado (en numeración)** Número elevado a la segunda potencia.	In 5^2, the number 5 is squared.
square number The product of a number and itself.	**cuadrado de un número** El producto de un número y sí mismo.	25 is a square number. $5 \cdot 5 = 25$.
square root A number that is multiplied by itself to form a product is called a square root of that product.	**raíz cuadrada** El número que se multiplica por sí mismo para formar un producto se denomina la raíz cuadrada de ese producto.	$\sqrt{16} = 4$, because $4^2 = 4 \cdot 4 = 16$
standard form (in numeration) A way to write numbers by using digits.	**forma estándar (en numeración)** Una manera de escribir números por medio de dígitos.	Five thousand, two hundred ten in standard form is 5,210.
stem-and-leaf plot A graph used to organize and display data so that the frequencies can be compared.	**diagrama de tallo y hojas** Gráfica que muestra y ordena los datos, y que sirve para comparar las frecuencias.	Stem | Leaves 3 | 2 3 4 4 7 9 4 | 0 1 5 7 7 7 8 5 | 1 2 2 3 *Key: 3|2 means 3.2*

ENGLISH	SPANISH	EXAMPLES

straight angle An angle that measures 180°.

ángulo llano Ángulo que mide exactamente 180°.

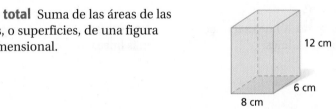

---

substitute To replace a variable with a number or another expression in an algebraic expression.

sustituir Reemplazar una variable por un número u otra expresión en una expresión algebraica.

Subtraction Property of Equality The property that states that if you subtract the same number from both sides of an equation, the new equation will have the same solution.

Propiedad de igualdad de la resta Propiedad que establece que puedes restar el mismo número de ambos lados de una ecuación y la nueva ecuación tendrá la misma solución.

$$\begin{aligned} x + 6 &= 8 \\ -6 \quad &\ -6 \\ x &= 2 \end{aligned}$$

---

sum The result when two or more numbers are added.

suma Resultado de sumar dos o más números.

The sum of 6 + 7 + 1 is 14.

---

supplementary angles Two angles whose measures have a sum of 180°.

ángulos suplementarios Dos ángulos cuyas medidas suman 180°.

30° 150°

---

surface area The sum of the areas of the faces, or surfaces, of a three-dimensional figure.

área total Suma de las áreas de las caras, o superficies, de una figura tridimensional.

12 cm
6 cm
8 cm

Surface area = 2(8)(12) + 2(8)(6) + 2(12)(6) = 432 cm²

T

term (in an expression) The parts of an expression that are added or subtracted.

término (en una expresión) Las partes de una expresión que se suman o se restan.

$3x^2 \quad + \quad 6x \quad - \quad 8$
↑   ↑   ↑
Term   Term   Term

---

term (in a sequence) An element or number in a sequence.

término (en una sucesión) Elemento o número de una sucesión.

5 is the third term in the sequence 1, 3, 5, 7, 9, . . .

---

terminating decimal A decimal number that ends, or terminates.

decimal finito Decimal con un número determinado de posiciones decimales.

6.75

---

tessellation A repeating pattern of plane figures that completely covers a plane with no gaps or overlaps.

teselado Patrón repetido de figuras planas que cubren totalmente un plano sin superponerse ni dejar huecos.

Glossary/Glosario **G33**

ENGLISH	SPANISH	EXAMPLES
theoretical probability The ratio of the number of ways an event can occur to the total number of equally likely outcomes.	**probabilidad teórica** Razón del numero de las maneras que puede ocurrir un suceso al numero total de resultados igualmente probables.	When rolling a number cube, the theoretical probability of rolling a 4 is $\frac{1}{6}$.
third quartile The median of the upper half of a set of data; also called *upper quartile*.	**tercer cuartil** La mediana de la mitad superior de un conjunto de datos. También se llama *cuartil superior*.	
transformation A change in the position or orientation of a figure.	**transformación** Cambio en la posición u orientación de una figura.	
translation A movement (slide) of a figure along a straight line.	**traslación** Desplazamiento de una figura a lo largo de una línea recta.	
transversal A line that intersects two or more lines.	**transversal** Línea que cruza dos o más líneas.	
trapezoid A quadrilateral with exactly one pair of parallel sides.	**trapecio** Cuadrilátero con un par de lados paralelos.	
tree diagram A branching diagram that shows all possible combinations or outcomes of an event.	**diagrama de árbol** Diagrama ramificado que muestra todas las posibles combinaciones o resultados de un suceso.	
trial Each repetition or observation of an experiment.	**prueba** Una sola repetición u observación de un experimento.	When rolling a number cube, each roll is one trial.
triangle A three-sided polygon.	**triángulo** Polígono de tres lados.	
Triangle Sum Theorem The theorem that states that the measures of the angles in a triangle add to 180°.	**Teorema de la suma del triángulo** Teorema que establece que las medidas de los ángulos de un triángulo suman 180°.	

triangular prism A polyhedron whose bases are triangles and whose other faces are parallelograms.

prisma triangular Poliedro cuyas bases son triángulos y cuyas demás caras tienen forma de paralelogramo.

underestimate An estimate that is less than the exact answer.

estimación baja Estimación menor que la respuesta exacta.

unit conversion The process of changing one unit of measure to another.

conversión de unidades Proceso que consiste en cambiar una unidad de medida por otra.

unit conversion factor A fraction used in unit conversion in which the numerator and denominator represent the same amount but are in different units.

factor de conversión de unidades Fracción que se usa para la conversión de unidades, donde el numerador y el denominador representan la misma cantidad pero están en unidades distintas.

$\frac{60 \text{ min}}{1\text{h}}$ or $\frac{1\text{h}}{60 \text{ min}}$

unit price A unit rate used to compare prices.

precio unitario Tasa unitaria que sirve para comparar precios.

unit rate A rate in which the second quantity in the comparison is one unit.

tasa unitaria Una tasa en la que la segunda cantidad de la comparación es la unidad.

10 cm per minute

upper quartile The median of the upper half of a set of data.

cuartil superior La mediana de la mitad superior de un conjunto de datos.

Lower half   Upper half

18, 23, 28, 29, (36,) 42

↑

Upper quartile

variable A symbol used to represent a quantity that can change.

variable Símbolo que representa una cantidad que puede cambiar.

In the expression $2x + 3$, x is the variable.

Venn diagram A diagram that is used to show relationships between sets.

diagrama de Venn Diagrama que muestra las relaciones entre conjuntos.

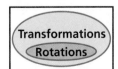

verbal expression A word or phrase.

expresión verbal Palabra o frase.

Glossary/Glosario

vertex On an angle or polygon, the point where two sides intersect.

vértice En un ángulo o polígono, el punto de intersección de dos lados.

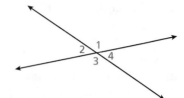

A is the vertex of ∠*CAB*.

---

vertical angles A pair of opposite congruent angles formed by intersecting lines.

ángulos opuestos por el vértice Par de ángulos opuestos congruentes formados por líneas secantes.

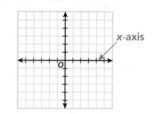

∠1 and ∠3 are vertical angles.
∠2 and ∠4 are vertical angles.

X

---

volume The number of cubic units needed to fill a given space.

volumen Número de unidades cúbicas que se necesitan para llenar un espacio.

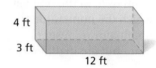

4 ft

3 ft

12 ft

Volume = 3 · 4 · 12 = 144 ft³

---

x-axis The horizontal axis on a coordinate plane.

eje x El eje horizontal del plano cartesiano.

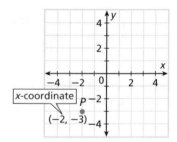

x-axis

---

x-coordinate The first number in an ordered pair; it tells the distance to move right or left from the origin, (0, 0).

coordenada x El primer número en un par ordenado; indica la distancia que debes avanzar hacia la izquierda o hacia la derecha desde el origen, (0, 0).

x-coordinate

P

(−2, −3)

***x*-intercept** The *x*-coordinate of the point where the graph of a line crosses the *x*-axis.

intersección con el eje *x*
Coordenada *x* del punto donde la gráfica de una línea cruza el eje *x*.

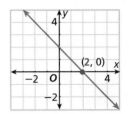

The *x*-intercept is 2.

***y*-axis** The vertical axis on a coordinate plane.

eje *y* El eje vertical del plano cartesiano.

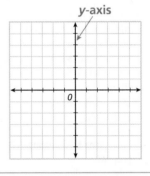

***y*-coordinate** The second number in an ordered pair; it tells the distance to move up or down from the origin, (0, 0).

coordenada *y* El segundo número de un par ordenado; indica la distancia que debes avanzar hacia arriba o hacia abajo desde el origen, (0, 0).

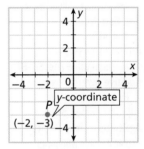

***y*-intercept** The *y*-coordinate of the point where the graph of a line crosses the *y*-axis.

intersección con el eje *y*
Coordenada *y* del punto donde la gráfica de una línea cruza el eje *y*.

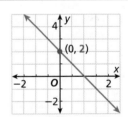

The *y*-intercept is 2.

Glossary/Glosario

Glossary/Glosario

Index . . .

Index

Index

underestimate, SB3
unit rates, 150–151, 204
upper quartile, 280
Uranus, 84
U.S. Department of Agriculture, 471

Vantongerloo, Georges, 313
variable rate of change, 207
variables, 18
    on both sides, solving equations with,
      476–477
variation, direct, 211–213
Venus, 84, 118
vertex
    of angles, 314, 316
    of polyhedron, 374
vertical angles, 323
Vocabulary Connections, 4, 44, 98, 148,
    192, 230, 272, 308, 356, 404, 464
volleyball, 360
volume
    of composite figure, 383
    of cylinders, 380–383
    of prisms, 380–383
Vostok, Antarctica, 48

Waimea, 363
wakeboarding, 49
water
    changes of state, 21
    density of eggs and, 103
    household use, 85
watermelons, 493
weather, 103, 106, 132, 197, 411,
    426–427, 489
Weather Link, 197
What's the Error?, 15, 21, 49, 57, 69,
    85, 115, 133, 157, 197, 210, 215, 235,
    283, 319, 333, 385, 429, 445, 479,
    499
What's the Question?, 25, 29, 55, 161,
    257, 279, 367, 417, 475
wind turbines, 367
words, translating into algebraic
    expressions, 22–23
Write About It
    Write About It exercises are found in
      every lesson. Some examples: 10,
      15, 243, 257
Write a Problem, 111, 121, 153, 169,
    239, 409, 437, 495
Writing Math, 316, 407, 410, 485
Writing Strategies. *See also* Reading and
    Writing Math
    Keep a Math Journal, 309
    Translate Between Words and Math, 45
    Use Your Own Words, 149
    Write a Convincing Argument, 193

x-axis, 194

y-axis, 194
Yellowstone National Park, 2
Yurts, 365

zero, division and, 67

Index

Southern Lehigh Middle School
3715 Preston Lane
Center Valley, PA 18034